The Documentary Heritage of Ohio

Ohio Bicentennial Series

Editor: Clarence E. Wunderlin, Jr.

H. Roger Grant, *Ohio on the Move: Transportation in the Buckeye State*
Phillip R. Shriver and Clarence E. Wunderlin, Jr., eds., *The Documentary Heritage of Ohio*

The Documentary Heritage of Ohio

Edited by Phillip R. Shriver and
Clarence E. Wunderlin, Jr.

Ohio University Press
Athens, Ohio

Ohio University Press, Athens, Ohio 45701
© 2000 by Phillip R. Shriver and Clarence E. Wunderlin, Jr.
Printed in the United States of America
All rights reserved

Ohio University Press books are printed on acid-free paper ⊖™

09 08 07 06 05 04 03 02 01 00   5 4 3 2 1

The publication of this book was made possible in part
by the generous support of the Ohio Bicentennial Commission.

Library of Congress Cataloging-in-Publication Data

The documentary heritage of Ohio / edited by Phillip R. Shriver and Clarence
    E. Wunderlin, Jr.
                          p. cm. — (Ohio bicentennial series)
    Includes bibliographical references and index.
    ISBN 0-8214-1334-1 (cloth : alk. paper)
    1. Ohio—History—Sources. I. Shriver, Phillip R. (Phillip Raymond),
    1922- II. Wunderlin, Clarence E. III. Series.

F491 .D64 2000
977.1—dc21
                                                        00-022207

Pages 425–26 constitute a continuation of the copyright page.

Contents

Part Two: The Gilded Age to the Present
Edited by Clarence E. Wunderlin, Jr.

Preface

THE EXPLORERS, MISSIONARIES, AND MERCHANTS of the fur trade who traveled to the "Ohio Country"—the territory stretching from the Allegheny River to the Maumee River—from the early seventeenth to the late eighteenth centuries quickly grasped the importance of the lands they visited. The Ohio Country possessed a wealth of natural resources, a diverse and skilled Native American population, and a strategic location important to any European empire desiring to conquer the New World. In the great era of industrialization that extended from the early nineteenth to the twentieth centuries, the State of Ohio retained its prominence among the states of the union because of that location and natural bounty, and a new, but equally diverse and skilled, population. Over the last four centuries the peoples of the Ohio Country and the state that Congress created from it made a most remarkable history.

It is the record of Ohio's remarkable past, a view of its history from the age of exploration to the postindustrial era, that is the subject of this collection of documents. This volume is the second in the Ohio Bicentennial Series published by Ohio University Press. It represents the efforts of the editors, Ohio University Press, and the Ohio Bicentennial Commission to make the state's documentary heritage more accessible to students at the college level and to lay readers with an interest in the region. Phillip R. Shriver edited the first nine chapters; Clarence E. Wunderlin, Jr., prepared the final eight chapters.

In the selection of documents for publication, the editors have attempted to adhere to, but were not strictly bound by, the following set of criteria. First, they included documents that offer readers a glimpse of Ohio and the "Ohio Country," its landscape, and the everyday life of its peoples at various points in history. Second, they added documents that record the most significant political, economic, and social events, trends, tendencies, or conflicts over time.

Avid readers of Ohio history will no doubt recognize that the structure of this volume somewhat parallels that of George W. Knepper's excellent *Ohio and Its Peoples*. That is no accident. The editors have organized the volume to suit the needs of instructors of college courses and will supplement the narrative of Knepper's text. Therefore, the editors have attempted to keep the annotation to a minimum, offering only what information is necessary to place a document in context.

In an effort to remain faithful to the texts, we have retained the typographic and stylistic elements of the original documents wherever possible.

The editors would like to thank several people who assisted in the preparation of this volume. Elizabeth Smith of the Department of History at Miami University typed the documents and annotation for Part I. Bette Sawicki of the Department of History at Kent State University keyed large sections of Part II. The editors also wish to acknowledge the contributions of two others whose understanding patience and tireless devotion made the completion of this project possible. Martha Shriver postponed knee replacement surgery until the draft of Part I was finished in February 1999. Mary Ann Heiss read the entire manuscript, vastly improved the editorial notes in Part II, and offered numerous suggestions for paring it down for publication. Last, but certainly not least, the editors wish to thank everyone at Ohio University Press who has assisted them on this project. David Sanders, director of the press, persuaded them to undertake the project and remained supportive throughout the entire editorial process. The success of the Ohio Bicentennial Series is due entirely to his vision.

Part One

From the Dawn of History to Reconstruction

Edited by Phillip R. Shriver

I.   Native Americans and the First Europeans

The Dawn of History of the Peoples between
Lake Erie and the Ohio River

A BOOK ON THE HISTORY OF OHIO should begin with acknowledgment that for 15,000 years or more the land between Lake Erie and the Ohio River was occupied by a succession of human cultures, descendants of those who had migrated during the last ice age from Asia to America perhaps twenty thousand years ago. Their artifacts of bone and stone, metal and shell, petroglyphs and earthworks (including some of the most impressive mounds in North America) are still all about us. But a book on *documentary* heritage must, of necessity, be based on *written* records. And the documentary heritage of Ohio begins in the seventeenth century with the coming of the French, as explorers, missionaries, trappers, and traders, who have left us written records in the form of letters, diaries, maps, and journals, as well as an invaluable collection of reports of Jesuit missionaries to their superiors in Quebec and France, reports known as the *Jesuit Relations.*

Other Europeans followed the French in the eighteenth century—English, Scots, Irish, and Germans principal among them. They, too, would leave a host of written records, many, like those of the French, dealing with the land and its native peoples whose place-names still "smolder on the map," as Walter Havighurst has observed, "like embers of old campfires."

Most of Ohio is bordered by water—a great lake to the north and a great river to the south and east. Formed at the close of the last ice age, they and their tributaries are among the Ohio country's greatest natural resources. Indeed, the very word *Ohio* is from the Iroquoian word *O-y-o,* or *O-he-yo,* meaning "great river," this because the Iroquois believed that the Allegheny-Ohio constituted the headwaters of the principal river of North America, the one we call the Mississippi. It is generally believed that the French explorer René Robert Cavalier Sieur de La Salle was the first European to travel along the Ohio. Impressed by the river's scenic beauty, he called it *la belle rivière,* the beautiful river. It is not by accident that the state song is "Beautiful Ohio" to this day. The year that LaSalle first explored the Ohio is uncertain, though French maps have ascribed its "discovery" to him as early as 1673 and 1674. It was the same La Salle who in 1679 built and sailed the first sailing vessel on Lake Erie and the Great Lakes, the forty-five-ton *Griffin*.

The last of the Great Lakes to be "discovered," Lake Erie had been explored and formally claimed for Louis XIV, the king of France, a decade earlier in 1669 when two French expeditions crossed its waters. The first was led by Adrien Joliet and Jean Peré, who entered Lake Erie from the west while returning to Quebec from Lake Superior via Lake Huron, Lake St. Clair, and the Detroit River. Continuing on to the Niagara portage, Lake Ontario, and the St. Lawrence River, they were the first to open an alternate to the Lake Huron-Georgian Bay-Ottawa River route long followed by the French in order to bypass the English and their Iroquois allies in New York. Later that same year, two Sulpician missionaries, François Dollier de Casson and René de Bréhan de Galinée, reinforced French claims by entering Lake Erie from the east.

Though not officially claimed by France until 1669, Lake Erie and the people called "Erie," who lived on its southeastern shore and from whom the lake got its name, were known to the French at least as early as 1640. On a map believed to have been prepared by the Jesuit missionary Paul Ragueneau and described in the *Jesuit Relations* of that year, Lake Erie appears with the name Lac du Chat, or "Lake of the Cat." South of the lake appear the words *Erie—Nation du Chat,* or "Erie—Nation of the Cat," in reference to the raccoon, or "wild cat," the meat and fur of which fed and clothed the Erie people, whose villages extended from the vicinity of present Erie, Pennsylvania, eastward to the Niagara frontier. To the east of Lake Erie appears the name *Iroquois,* while to the east of Lake Huron and Georgian Bay appears the name *Hurons.*[1]

Nearly the entire history of the Eries and much of the history of the Hurons relates to their defeat and dispersal in the late 1640s and 1650s in the course of what have been called the Wars of the Iroquois, or Beaver Wars. Stimulated by the insatiable demand of the garment trades in Europe for the soft underfur of the beaver used in making high-style hats and coats, the Indian peoples of eastern North America, particularly the Iroquois, became the economic allies of European fur traders, primarily English and Dutch, who found it expedient to trade European guns for the beaver furs they coveted. In contrast, the French, whose principal Indian allies were the Hurons, usually withheld such weapons, preferring instead to trade in non-military goods and to emphasize the saving of souls through their missions rather than to encourage the waging of war against real or potential rivals in the fur trade. Erie and Huron arrows proved no match for the new guns of the Iroquois as the old intertribal balance of power was quickly shattered. It took but a single week of war in 1649 to break the Hurons. However, it took two years of war (1654–56) for the Iroquois to destroy the Erie nation, highlighted by the storming of the palisaded stronghold of the Eries at the site of Erie, Pennsylvania, by attacking Iroquois warriors of the Onondaga nation. Carrying their long war canoes above their heads as shields against the volleys of Erie arrows, the attackers used those same canoes to scale the walls and with their guns finished off the defenders inside the Erie fort, not sparing even women and children.

The Beaver Wars of the Iroquois to monopolize the fur trade of North America carried them inevitably into the Ohio country. As reported by the Jesuit missionary

Paul Le Jeune on December 1, 1657, "[the] Iroquois have discovered, beyond the Cat Nation, other and numerous Nations who speak the Algonquin language. There are more than thirty villages whose inhabitants have never had any knowledge of Europeans; they still use only stone hatchets and knives, . . . the Iroquois carry fire and war thither."[2]

Even as the Hurons and Eries had been vanquished and dispersed, so too were the tribes of the Ohio country, believed to have been Kickapoo in northeastern Ohio, the Mascouten in northwestern Ohio, and the Shawnee in southern Ohio. By the 1660s, Iroquois strength prevailed all the way to the Mississippi. Except for occasional hunting parties, Ohio's streams and forests were largely devoid of human contact until the turn of the century.

About 1701 the long silence in the Ohio wilderness finally was broken as bands of Hurons who had taken refuge in northern Michigan on the west side of the lake that bears their name began to drift southward into the valleys of the Detroit, the Maumee, and the Sandusky. The French had called them Hurons, or "bristle tops," because the men wore their hair short on the side and high, stiff, and bristly on top, resembling in the eyes of the French the spinal hair of the boar hog, or *huré*. The Hurons, however, referred to themselves as Wendats, later transliterated by the English to "Wyandots," the name by which they would be known in the Ohio country, where they would remain until their removal to the west in 1843.

In the early and mid-eighteenth century other Native American tribes joined in the occupation of the Ohio country. From the north came the Ottawas, moving into the general area occupied by the Wyandots, with whom they maintained close relations. From upper New York into northeastern Ohio came bands of Iroquois, primarily Senecas and Mingoes, or mixed-blood Iroquois, reflecting the adoption practices of the Iroquois nations whose ranks had been depleted during the Beaver Wars of the preceding century. From the Delaware Valley in the east came the Lenape, or Delawares, to occupy the valleys of the Muskingum, the Walhonding, the Kokosing, and the Tuscarawas. From the south, returning to their ancestral Scioto Valley homeland, came the Shawnee, or "people of the south wind," while from the west came the Miamis, or "people of the peninsula," so named from their earlier homeland on the Door Peninsula on Green Bay in east central Wisconsin. Soon three rivers of western Ohio would bear their name—the Miami of the Lake (later changed to Maumee), which emptied into the Erie Lake, and the Great and Little Miami Rivers, tributaries of the Ohio.

Save for the Shawnees, the historic tribes of the Ohio country of the eighteenth century, like the Europeans who were also coming into the land between the river and the lake, were themselves relative newcomers. Two different but highly informative accounts by Europeans of Indian life are here presented. The first is by the French Jesuit missionary, Paul Le Jeune, who wrote primarily about the Hurons (or Wyandots) of New France in 1657 in a report contrasting the marked differences in customs, clothing, food, and daily habits between the French and Indians. The second, written more than a century later in 1779–80 by a German-speaking missionary, David Zeisberger, while serving the Lenape (or Delawares) in the Moravian missions in the Muskingum and Tuscarawas valleys, is a record of the Ohio wilderness and its Native American peoples already well along in the process of transformation through the introduction of European trade goods and Western ways in a time of struggle within the British Empire.

1. See Phillip R. Shriver, "Who Discovered the Lake of the Eries?" *Timeline* 1, no. 2 (December 1984-January 1985): 37.

2. See Reuben Gold Thwaites, ed., *The Jesuit Relations and Allied Documents,* vol. 44, *1656-1658* (Cleveland: Burrows, 1899), 49.

I.1.   Differences between Native Americans and Europeans: The Report of the French Jesuit Paul Le Jeune

In the aftermath of the destruction of the Erie Nation and the defeat and dispersal of the Huron/Wyandot people and the tribes of the Ohio country by the Iroquois, Paul Le Jeune, for many years one of the principal leaders of the French Jesuits (the famous "black robes") in North America, was moved to write a compelling essay—"Of the Difference between the Manners and Customs of the French, or the Europeans, and Those of the Savages"—which was included as chapter 7 of the Jesuit Relations *for 1657-58. (See the translation from the French in Reuben Gold Thwaites, ed.,* The Jesuit Relations and Allied Documents *[Cleveland: Burrows, 1899], 44:277-309.)*

Born in 1591 of French Huguenot parents, Le Jeune converted to Catholicism on reaching his majority and joined the Jesuit Order, or Society of Jesus. After teaching in a number of Jesuit academies and colleges, he was appointed superior of all the missions of the Society of Jesus in New France and left France for Quebec in 1632. He served as superior from 1632 to 1639, during which time he lived for a while among the Montagnais Indians, composed a dictionary, established a mission at Three Rivers, preached the sermon at the funeral of Samuel de Champlain (the founder of Quebec and the "Father of New France"), was empowered for a time to act as governor, opened a school for Indian children, and founded a college in Quebec. In 1639 he asked to be relieved of his responsibilities as superior in order to devote the next decade to more active missionary work out among the Indians, during which time he founded the mission at Tadoussac in 1641 and made innumerable visits to other missions throughout New France. He also found time to send reports and letters to Jesuit officials in Paris, many of these reports becoming embodied in the official documents known as the Jesuit Relations. *He returned to France in 1649 and died there in 1664, maintaining an interest in the Indians of North America until his death.*

Because of his preeminent role in Jesuit affairs in New France for so many years, he was singularly well qualified to report on his personal observations as well as those of his missionary colleagues respecting the habits and customs of the Native Americans (in the vernacular of that time he referred to those not yet baptized as "Savages") who lived throughout the length and breadth of New France. His report provides rare insight into their lives in the mid-seventeenth century.

*T*he temperament of our senses—whencesoever it comes, whether from our birth or from our habits—gives . . . inclination or aversion, love or hate, for the objects presented to them. From this source, as I believe, arises the great difference that exists between the senses of the Savages and those of the French, or of the Europeans; for you would say, in many instances, that what is sugar to the one people is wormwood to the other. Let us begin with the sense of smell.

There are found, in these regions of America, animals to which the French have given the name of musk-Rats, because in truth they resemble the rats of France — except that they are much larger — and smell of musk in the Spring. The French are very fond of this odor; the Savages dislike it as if it were a stench. They anoint themselves, and smear their heads and faces with oils and grease that smell to us like carrion. It is their musk, their orangeade, and their benzoin. The rose, the pink, the clove, the nutmeg, and similar odors, which are agreeable to us, are insipid to them; and tobacco, which causes nausea to those unaccustomed to smell it, constitutes one of their chief delights.

Concerning the sense of hearing, although the Savages take much pleasure in singing, a concert of music sounds to them like a confusion of voices, . . . their own songs, which are so heavy and dismal as to give us ideas of night, seem to them as beautiful as the blush of dawn. They sing amid dangers, in torments, and at the approach of death; while the French usually preserve a deep silence on all such occasions.

Salt, which seasons all viands eaten in Europe, renders them bitter to the Savage taste. Their smoked meat, which to us is almost soot, is very savory to them. . . . I have never seen a Savage that did not abhor Dutch cheese, radishes, spices, mustard, and similar condiments. I remember in this connection the following incident. A Savage chanced to be at table with some French people when mustard was served, and his curiosity to taste of every dish, without knowing its nature, made him dip his spoon into this condiment. Taking a tolerably good dose, he thrust it into his mouth before any one had told him how it was usually eaten. God knows whether he furnished merriment for all the company. It is a Savage's glory to be a hearty eater, as it is that of many a European to be a lusty drinker; and this good fellow, wishing to show the strength of his courage, strove to keep his countenance. His tears, however, betrayed him, although he set his teeth and compressed his lips to the utmost; until at last the little maintenance of appearances and facial control that he possessed escaped him, and he was left highly astonished at the strength of that "yellow porridge," as he called it. Finally, he was instructed how mustard was eaten; but he never put the lesson into practice, being content with that first experience for the rest of his days. Sauces, condiments, dressings, which are the delight of epicures, would here make a little hell for the Savage's gullet. . . .

In France, to make a face more beautiful, it is cleansed of oil and washed as carefully as possible. The Savages, on the contrary, anoint and grease it as much as they can, thinking it more pleasing the more shiny it is with their grease or oil. To make oneself hideous in Europe, one daubs himself with black, yellow, and blue; and that is the very thing that makes a Savage handsome and of very pleasing appearance. When one of them wishes to pay a visit or attend some feast or dance, he has his face painted in various colors by some woman or girl; . . . . After he has been well bedaubed, he is looked upon as a handsome man, whereas in Europe he would be taken for a demon. . . .

In France, hair that is a little blond, well washed with soap and cleansed of oil, carefully arranged and curled, is the most beautiful. Negroes like it short, black, and very crisp. The Savages wish it long, stiff, black, and all lustrous with grease. A curly head is as ugly to them as it is beautiful in France. There is nothing so grotesque as a Savage's headdress. . . . They sprinkle their well-greased hair with down, or the tiny feathers of birds, and with this fine adornment think themselves as comely as those who wear ribbons. Indeed, this down is as delicate as the web of the silkworm.

The hair is not dressed according to fashion in that country. Their fancy is their fashion. Some wear it erect on the head, pointing upward. . . . Others have shaved the middle of the head, wearing hair only on the two sides, like great mustaches. Some lay bare all one side, leaving the other wholly covered. . . .

In [the] new world, a beard is the greatest disfigurement that a face can have. The peoples of those countries call the Europeans "bearded," as a gross insult. . . . They have such dread of this disfigurement that, if some hair is inclined to grow on their chins, they pluck it out immediately, to rid themselves of what is beautiful to us, but ugly to them. . . .

In France, men and women have their clothes made rather tight-fitting, in order to impart a lighter appearance, the girls especially priding themselves on their slenderness. In Canadas, every one dresses so as to look large. . . .

In France, pattens and raised shoes are considered the most beautiful; but among those peoples the ugliest, because the most uncomfortable. The Savages' shoes are as flat as tennis-shoes, but much wider, especially in winter, when they stuff and line them amply to keep away the cold. . . .

Politeness and propriety have taught us to carry handkerchiefs. In this matter the Savages charge us with filthiness—because, they say, we place what is unclean in our pockets as something very precious, while they throw it upon the ground. . . .

When the Savages are not hunting or on a journey, their usual posture is to recline or sit on the ground. They cannot remain standing, maintaining that their legs become swollen immediately. Seats higher than the ground they dislike; the French, on the contrary, use chairs, benches, or stools, leaving the ground and litter to animals.

A good dancer in France does not move his arms much, and holds his body erect, moving his feet so nimbly that, you would say, he spurns the ground and wishes to stay in the air. The Savages, on the contrary, bend over in their dances, thrusting out their arms and moving them violently as if they were kneading bread, while they strike the ground with their feet so vigorously that one would say they are determined to make it tremble, or to bury themselves in it up to the neck. . . .

In France, when a father gives his daughter in marriage, he allows her a dowry. Here, it is given to the girl's father.

In Europe, the children inherit from their parents; among the Hurons the nephews, sons of the father's sister, are their uncle's heirs; and the Savage's small belongings will be given to the friends of the deceased, rather than to his children. . . .

In France, the man usually takes to his house the woman whom he marries; here, the man goes to the woman's house to dwell. . . .

In Europe, we unclothe the dead as much as we can, leaving them only what is necessary to veil them and hide them from our eyes. The Savages, however, give them all that they can, anointing and attiring them as if for their wedding, and burying them with all their favorite belongings. . . .

I.2. The Native Americans from the Perspective of the Moravian Missionary David Zeisberger

Though short-lived Jesuit missions were established by the French among the Miamis in the Maumee Valley and the Hurons/Wyandots at Sandusky, more enduring missions were subsequently achieved by Moravians among the Lenape or Delaware Indians of the Tuscarawas and Muskingum Valleys. Tragically caught up in the frontier warfare of the American Revolution, however, the neutral Moravian missions also faltered, then were in part reoccupied, with new ones added in the postwar years. (See the next chapter for more on the missions of Schoenbrunn and Gnadenhutten.)

As their name suggests, the Moravian Brethren originated in Moravia in the Austrian Empire. A pietistic Protestant sect of simple, Quakerlike beliefs, they believed in the salvation of souls by winning converts to Christianity among the Indians of North America. Foremost among their missionaries was David Zeisberger. Born in Moravia in 1721 and educated in German Saxony, he and his parents had migrated to the British North American colony of Georgia while he was still a teenager. They then moved to Bethlehem, Pennsylvania, the headquarters of the Moravian Church in America, where young David became interested in service as a "black coat," a Moravian missionary to the Native Americans. From 1745 until his death in 1808 he lived and worked among the Indians, primarily the Iroquois and the Delawares, though he also spent time among the Wyandots and Shawnees and could speak all four Indian languages.

Based on his years of nearly uninterrupted life among the Indians, Zeisberger's History of the North American Indians *was written in 1779–80. Consisting of a series of notes written in German, the original is now in the Moravian Archives at Bethlehem, Pennsylvania. Translated into English and edited by Archer B. Hulbert and William N. Schwarze, Zeisberger's* History *appeared in the* Ohio Archaeological and Historical Publications *19 (1910): 12–132, from which the following excerpts have been taken.*

*T*he North American Indians are of middle size, well built, straight, light-footed, well adapted for travel through the forest, much of which is due to the fact that they do no heavy work, but support themselves by the chase. Their color is brown, but of different shades. . . . Their hair is jet-black and coarse, almost like the hair of a horse's mane. Their heads become gray or even white in old age, otherwise they are without exception, black. The men rarely let the hair grow long. . . . It is very common that they wear a plume of feathers on the middle of the head, rising straight up or hanging downward. They frequently cut the helix of the ear, leaving the upper and lower ends intact and then hang bits of lead to it so that it is stretched. Then this curved border of the auricle is bound with brass wire, distending it considerably, and decorated with silver ornaments. Among Indians who have come in contact with whites this is less often done. They, also, pierce the nose and adorn it with silver. The beard is rooted out as soon as it begins to grow. The men tattoo their bodies in arm, leg or face with all manner of figures, serpents, birds or other animals, which are marked out by pricking the skin with a needle, powder or soot being afterward rubbed into the punctures. Occasionally, the women mark their bodies thus. The women let the hair grow long, so that it sometimes reaches to the knees; they do not braid it but tie a cloth around it. The Mingoes [mixed-blood Iroquois, primarily Seneca], Shawano [Shawnee] and Wiondatoo [Wyandot] women have a long braid reaching the hips, bound in cloth and red ribbon, in the case of the rich, being further adorned with silver clasps of considerable weight from top to bottom. The Delawares, also, do this, though not so generally. The women wear earrings of wampum, coral or silver.

The men hunt, secure meat for the household, clothing for their wives and children, getting it in exchange for hides, build houses or huts, and also help their wives clear the land for cultivation and build fences around it. The duties of the women are cooking, finding fire-wood, planting and reaping. They plant corn, principally, making of this their bread, which is baked in the ashes, and preparing with it various dishes. Besides, they raise pumpkins of various kinds, potatoes, beans and other vegetables, which they have learned to know through the whites, such as cabbage, turnips, etc. . . .

Their dress is light; they do not hang much clothing upon themselves. If an Indian has a Match-coat, that is a blanket of the smaller sort, a shirt and brich clout and a pair of leggins he thinks himself well dressed. . . . Their shoes are made of deer skin, which they prepare themselves, the women being particularly skilled in doing this and in working all manner of designs; Mingoe women excel all others in this particular. Some wear hats or caps secured in trading with the whites; others do not cover themselves but go bare-headed. . . .

Men as well as women wear silver bracelets, and the latter also arrange silver clasps in their hair or wear a band about the head with as many silver ornaments on it as it will hold. All these things they secure from the whites, principally from traders who in times of peace bring their wares to the Indian towns to exchange for skins and pelts. In course of such occupation many traders have, in the event of Indian wars, lost all their goods and even their lives. . . .

Houses of the Indians were formerly only huts and for the most part remain such humble structures, particularly in regions far removed from the habitation of whites. These huts are built either of bast (tree-bark peeled off in the summer) or the walls are made of boards covered with bast. They are low structures. Fire is made in the middle of the hut under an opening whence the smoke escapes. Among the Mingoes and the Six Nations [Iroquois] one rarely sees houses other than such huts built entirely of bast, which, however, are frequently very long, having at least from two to four fire-places; as many families inhabiting such a house as there are fire-places, the families being related. Among the Delawares each family prefers to have its own house, hence they are small. The Mingoes make a rounded arched roof, the Delawares on the contrary, a high pitched, peaked roof. The latter, coming much in contact with the whites, as they do not live more than a hundred miles from Pittsburgh, have learned to build block houses or have hired whites to build them. Christian Indians generally build proper and comfortable houses and the savages who seek to follow their example in work and household arrangement learn much from them. . . .

Dances take place every night, all young people, men and women, attending. The dancing takes place either in a large house or in the open about the fire. The men lead in the dance, the women closing the circle. Such is the exultant shouting on these occasions that it can be heard two or three miles away. The dance usually lasts until midnight, though there are intervals of rest. The drum which keeps the time is a thin deer-skin stretched across a barrel, or, in lieu of this, a kettle. . . .

The Indians have both capacity and skill for work, if they only had the inclination. Such is their mental constitution that they readily grasp and understand. Some who have been much with whites have begun to work in iron, have fashioned hatchets, axes, etc., right well, have given up the chase because they have found regular work much more profitable and less hard on clothing and shoes than wandering through the forest in pursuit of game. It is, however, true that in the forest they are a wonderful people. They can go on a journey of many days in the forest where there is neither path nor trail, without getting lost. It is as if Nature had fixed the compass in their heads. No European is equal to them in this respect. If they would go anywhere and have determined on the journey, nothing prevents the carrying out of their purpose. Though creeks and rivers are often swollen and progress is difficult, they know what to do when white men would be at their wit's end. In company of Indians one may be sure not to be lost nor to suffer starvation.

On their journeys they are never in haste, for they are everywhere at home and whithersoever they wander they find sustenance in the forest. Therefore, if a white man travels with them it is wisest that he be content not to hasten but accommodate himself to their movements. In the morning they do not break camp early, not until they have eaten heartily, by which time the sun has usually been above the horizon two or three hours. Thereafter, they proceed very steadily until near sundown, when they go into camp. In rainy weather they peel bast from the trees and speedily build a hut, that is, a roof supported by four posts, under which they remain comfortably dry. This they do not only in summer but also in winter, at which time they know what trees to peel. In more northerly regions, as near . . . the Mingoe country, where the snow is apt to be deep in winter, they go on snowshoes over the deepest snow. Here along the Muskingum, however, where the snow is never deep, this is not necessary; hence, in this means of locomotion the Delawares are not as skilled as the Mingoes. . . .

Indians are not less, rather more, subject to disease than Europeans, their rough manner of life and the hardships of travel and the chase being contributing causes. On journeys they mind neither water nor snow nor ice, even though creeks and rivers be ever so full of running ice they go through and nothing holds them up. On the chase they not only steal through the woods to get, unnoticed, near the game, but also pursue it should it run before them, until they get within range, thus often tiring the deer they may have chased from morn till eve and then at the end of the day shooting one after another, sometimes eight or ten miles away from their hunting lodge no food having been tasted the entire day. So long as they are young and strong, they suffer no ill effects, but with advancing years, the inevitable results are felt. Rheumatism is common among them, often leading to lameness, deafness or blindness. The women who carry everything by means of a carrying girth fixed to the forehead, whence the whole burden — and a hundred weight is not considered heavy — is suspended down the back, suffer in back and neck as they grow older. The men carry everything hung to a carrying girth fixed across the chest. A deer weighing from a hundred to a hundred and thirty pounds they will carry the entire way home before allowing themselves to rest. . . .

It is a custom of the Indians, even when they are tired or have caught cold, to go into a sweating oven several times a week. For this purpose every town has on its outskirts a sweating oven. It is built of timber and boards, covered completely with earth. They crawl in through a small opening, the latter being closed as soon as they have gone in. A fire is usually built in front of the opening before they go in and hot stones placed in the middle of the inclosed area. Not long after they have entered, they are covered with perspiration, then they crawl out and cool off, returning to repeat the same thing three or four times. Women have their own sweating ovens though they do not use them as commonly as do the men. . . .

Bow and arrow have fallen into disuse among those Indians that trade with whites; are, indeed, only used for small game, such as the pigeon, fox and raccoon, in order to save powder. There are, however, whole tribes to the west and northwest that use nothing but bow and arrow in the chase and that have no European weapons, that are not even anxious to obtain them; for, say they, if we discard bow and arrow, who will then make for us enough of powder and shot. They prefer, therefore, to hold to their old custom and usage. . . .

Rarely does an Indian have two or more wives, being fearful of strife in the house. Blood relations do not marry; in this particular they are even more strict than the whites. They claim that division of the race into tribes came about in order to make it more readily certain that a man in taking a wife was not marrying a near relative. . . .

Families have from four to six children. More than this number is unusual. Birth of twins is rarely heard of. . . .

In the management of household affairs the husband leaves everything to his wife and never interferes in things committed to her. She cooks victuals regularly twice a day. If she neglects to do it in proper time, or even altogether, the husband never says a word but goes to a friend, being assured that he will find something to eat, for when a stranger comes into the house the first attention shown is to put food before him, if there is anything in the house. The husband never offers to put wood on the fire, except it be that he has guests or some other extraordinary call to do it, for the woman cuts the wood and brings it to the house and is, therefore, the proper person to take care of the fire.

If his wife longs for meat, and gives him a hint of it, the husband goes out early in the morning without victuals and seldom returns without some game, should he even be obliged to stay out till late in the evening. When he returns with a deer, he throws it down before the door of the hut and walks in, saying nothing. But his wife, who had heard him lay down his burden, gives him something to eat, dries his clothes and then goes out to bring in the game. She may then do what she pleases with it. He says nothing, if she even gives the greatest part of it to her friends, which is a very common custom. A woman generally remembers her friends when meat has been secured, or when her husband has brought flour from the whites.

If the husband intends to take a journey or go hunting, he gives his wife notice, and then she knows that it is her business to furnish him with proper provisions. If any dissatisfaction arises between them, the husband commonly takes his gun and walks off into the woods, without telling his wife whither he is going. Sometimes he does not return for some days, when both parties have generally forgotten their quarrels and live again in peace. . . .

Cursing and swearing are never heard among the Indians; they have no words of this character in their language. If women or men would berate one another—rarely the case among men, except in case of the younger, more frequent among women—they direct words and speeches at one another which would not be considered terrible by other people but are very seriously taken by the Indians. If they would revile one another in extremest fashion, they use some obscene expressions. . . .

The Indians are lovers of finery and dress, the women more than the men; the latter take care that the women adorn themselves in proper manner. The men clothe themselves rather meanly, regarding it as a disgrace to be better appareled than their wives. . . .

Their towns are generally laid out near a lake, river or brook, yet sufficiently elevated to escape the danger of inundations, which are very common in spring. In building towns no regular plan is observed but every one builds according to his fancy. The houses are not built close together. . . .

Of inheritances they know nothing. Every Indian knows that whatever he leaves at his death is divided among his friends. . . .

Though the Indians are a free people and not subject to the rule of any one, each nation, considering itself a unit, has a kind of government of its own choosing, imperfect as it may be. . . . A chief may not presume to rule over the people, as in that case he would immediately be forsaken by the whole tribe, and his counselors would refuse to assist him. He must ingratiate himself with the people and stand by his counselors. Hence, it is that the chiefs are generally friendly, gracious, hospitable, communicative, affable and their house is open to every Indian. Even strangers who come on business put up in the chief's house and are accommodated with the best it affords. The ambassadors of other nations generally lodge with the chief and they are well cared for. If their number is too great, and it has happened in connection with weighty affairs concerning several nations that ten or twenty men of other nations have arrived at the principal chief's house, they are put into a separate house and provided with everything at the public expense, the counselors taking care that they are entertained most hospitably in order that the nation may be in good repute amongst other nations.

In externals a chief has no advantages above others. He must provide for his own maintenance, for no one is under any obligation to supply his wants. His wife, whose duty it is to provide sufficient corn for the year, is usually assisted by other women in her plantations, for much corn is required in such a house. If the chief is young and able to hunt he will, his official duties permitting, occasionally join the chase. He will even secure his own firewood as far as possible. In case he is old his friends, of whom there are usually many, and other Indians will furnish him with game, especially if he be popular.

The council house is either the house of the chief, which is commonly large and roomy, or a building erected for that purpose. Here public councils are held, that is, such where messages which have arrived from whites or other Indians are published. Every one may listen and the messages are also discussed. In case there is something of particular importance to consider, only the chief and the counselors assemble and determine upon the matter. The old chief Netawatwes [a Delaware chief also known as "Newcomer," whose village was and still is called Newcomerstown, Ohio] used to lay all affairs of state before his council for consideration. When they gave him their opinion, he either approved of it or indicated what was missing or not correct in the speech, upon which they would make the necessary amendments. Thus he kept them active and was held in great esteem.

The wampum which Europeans make and barter to the Indians is made of sea-mussel shells. One variety is quite white, the other dark violet, a quarter of an inch in length, and eighth of an inch in thickness and round. A hole is bored lengthwise through each shell, large enough to admit a heavy cord. They are strung like beads. Wampum constitutes the money of the Indians. Two hundred shells cost a buck hide, or a Spanish dollar. Before the white people came they had no such wampum for want of proper instruments to make it. The white are a little less in value than the dark.

The French seem to possess a greater share of the goodwill of the Indians than the English, being regarded by the Indians as being more akin to themselves, probably because they enter more easily into the Indian manner of living and appear always good-humored. Indians have more faith in the French than in other Europeans. . . . All the Americans . . . are known as Big Knives . . . because, from the beginning, the Indians saw them . . . on all occasions of negotiations with the Indians wearing long swords. . . .

Judged by the mere appearance of the Indians one is surprised how modest and careful they are in relation to each other and imagines that the whites, if they were as free a people and had neither government nor punishment to fear, would not be as united and peaceable as the Indians appear to be. The towns and villages of the latter are not indeed governed by force or law. Each individual is at liberty to live where he pleases. . . .

Few houses are locked when the people go out. A stick is placed against the door on the outside and the passerby sees that no one is at home and does not enter. Each one is free to do as he pleases without let or hindrance, yet he will rarely do another injury.

Their old people, even though they are only able to crawl about and are a source of trouble and have nothing to bequeath to anyone, are faithfully cared for by their friends who seem to wish that their lives should be prolonged. That they are unmerciful and insensible towards the poor and needy may not be said of them. Even strangers who have no friends are given assistance. A poor widow, even though she have children, finds it possible to make a living if she is willing to work. They pay her above the worth of her services in food and clothing; if it is summer she may work on the plantations; in winter she may prepare wood for fire. They are willing to help the poor but always expect them to render some service in return. It has been known that good has been done to prisoners condemned to death, even to whites, though this had to be done secretly.

A few negroes are found among the Indians having been either bought from the whites or secured as prisoners. These are looked upon as of their own kind and allowed full liberty. Indians and negroes intermarry and their mulatto children are as much loved as children of pure Indian blood.

That the Indians have some sort of religion and mode of worship whereby they endeavor to please the Deity, cannot be denied. . . .

They believe and have from time immemorial believed that there is an Almighty Being who has created heaven and earth and man and all things else. This they have learned from their ancestors, but where the dwelling place of the Deity is they know not. They have always heard that whoever lives a virtuous life, refrains from stealing, murder and immorality, would at death go to some good place where conditions would be better than here, where there would be a superfluity of everything and a happy life of joy and dancing. On the contrary, whoever lived an evil life would arrive at no good place but have to wander about sad and unhappy. Hence nothing is so terrible and awful to them as death, because they do not know how it will be after this life nor whither they shall go. Whenever they think of death they are filled with anxiety, but rather than consider how they ought to live they seek to rid themselves of thoughts of death. They fear the thunderbolt, because it occasionally strikes and shatters the trees, but they seek to disguise their fear. Yet they believe that the Deity is graciously and mercifully disposed towards men, because he imparts power to the plants to grow, causes the rain to fall and the sun to shine and gives game to man for his support. Indeed, as to fish and deer they imagine them given particularly to the Indians and not so much to the whites for the Indians were created to sustain themselves by the chase and the whites by the work of their hands. . . .

They believe in numerous spirits or subordinate deities. Almost all animals and the elements are looked upon as spirits, one exceeding the other in dignity and power. There is scarcely an Indian who does not believe that one or more of these spirits has not been particularly given him to assist him and make him prosper. This, they claim, has been made known to them in a dream, even as their religious belief and witchcraft is alleged to have been made known to them in a dream. One has, in a dream, received a serpent or a buffalo, another the sun or the moon, another an owl or some other bird, another a fish, some even ridiculously insignificant creatures such as ants. These are considered their spirits or *Manittos*. If an Indian has no *Manitto* to be his friend he considers himself forsaken, has nothing upon which he may lean, has no hope of any assistance and is small in his own eyes. On the other hand those who have been thus favored possess a high and proud spirit.

Of writing they know nothing, except the painting of hieroglyphics, . . . which they know very well how to interpret. These drawings in red by the warriors may be legible for fifty years. After a hero has died, his deeds may, therefore, be kept in mind for many years by these markings. A letter, especially, if it is sealed, is considered a very important thing. If any treaties, contracts or deeds are required to be delivered to the Europeans, signed by their chiefs, captains, or counselors, they make their mark and get others to subscribe their names. The mark may be a hook, or the foot of a turkey or a turtle or represent something else. They are very generally ashamed of their Indian names and prefer the names given them by the whites. Some have learned to write the initial letters of their new names.

In reckoning time they do not count the days but the nights. An Indian says, "I have traveled so many nights." Only if the entire journey has been accomplished in one day, will he speak of a day's journey. Most of them determine a number of years by so many winters, springs, summers or autumns. They say, "In spring when we boil sugar," that is March, or "when we plant," that is May, so and so will be of such an age. Few know their age when they get to be over thirty. . . .

Of the spherical form of the earth they have no conception. Some declare that the earth floats upon the sea and that an enormous tortoise bears it on its back. The sky, they say, rests upon the water probably because it appears so to do when they look out upon the sea. . . . Thunder is a mighty spirit dwelling in the mountains and sometimes issuing from their fastnesses suffers himself to be heard. . . .

II. Rival Claims and Successive Wars
The Struggle for Control of the Ohio Country

IT HAS BEEN SAID THAT WHERE THE LINES of empire of two rival nations cross, a noose will be formed for one of them. It was in the mid-eighteenth century that the lines of imperial advance of the French and the English met and crossed in the Ohio country, resulting in what American history has called the French and Indian War and the near total dissolution of the French empire in North America.

French claims to Canada had begun with the voyages of Verrazano in 1524 and Jacques Cartier in 1534, 1535, and 1541. It was on Cartier's first voyage that he discovered the Gulf of the St. Lawrence and the Gaspé Peninsula. There he took possession of the surrounding country in the name of Francis I of France. On his second voyage Cartier sailed up the St. Lawrence as far as an Indian village called Hochelaga on an island next to a towering hill that he named Mount Royal, or Montreal. On his third voyage, he tried unsuccessfully to found the first French colony in the New World near the site of the present city of Quebec.

What Cartier failed to do in 1541, Samuel de Champlain accomplished in 1608 when he established a permanent settlement at Quebec. Through the explorations of such men as Louis Hennepin and Father Jean Nicolet, New France was extended in the mid-seventeenth century westward to the Great Lakes. Then, in 1673, it expanded southward along the Mississippi to the Arkansas River with the expedition of Father Jacques Marquette and Louis Joliet. Finally, in 1682, the French explorer La Salle reached the mouth of the Mississippi River, claiming the vast watershed of the river and its tributaries for France and naming it Louisiana in honor of Louis XIV, the king of France.

Thus, by the end of the seventeenth century New France described an enormous crescent-shaped empire extending from Fortress Louisburg on Cape Breton Island at the mouth of the St. Lawrence, through the Great Lakes and south to New Orleans at the mouth of the Mississippi. With the numbers of French settlers in this huge colony never very large (no more than sixty thousand by mid-eighteenth century), travel and communication between the extremes of this empire for those challenged with its defense was both laborious and time consuming. Inevitably a shortcut between these extremes was mandated, and the shortest distance between these two points lay in the Ohio country, via the Ohio River and Lake Erie.

While the line of empire of the French extended from the North Atlantic to the Gulf of Mexico, the main line of the British empire in the New World—once the first permanent settlement at Jamestown had been established in 1607—moved steadily from east to west, from New England and the Atlantic coast to the Alleghenies and the Appalachian range, and then beyond, toward the Ohio Valley and the Mississippi. In contrast to the French, who sought to hold an enormous colony with a thin line of set-tlers, the English moved westward much more deliberately, clearing the forests and set-tling the land compactly with many more inhabitants, an estimated three million by the 1760s, or roughly fifty times the number of French in New France.

While the French claims in North America were based on a continuum of explora-tion over a century and a half by such explorers as Cartier, Champlain, and La Salle, Eng-lish claims were based on an initial exploration by John Cabot in 1497, which predated those of the French, followed by charters granted by the Crown to colonies established by commercial companies and individual proprietors in the seventeenth and eighteenth cen-turies. Of the thirteen colonies that emerged from these charters, four had claims on the Ohio country. Of these, Virginia, Massachusetts, and Connecticut had sea-to-sea grants that included parts of Ohio, while New York based its claim on areas conquered and later occupied by the Iroquois as a consequence of the Beaver Wars.

As early as 1685 an English expedition led by a Dutch settler from the Hudson Valley, Johannes Rooseboom, was sent out by the royal governor of New York, Thomas Dongan, to challenge French control of the Great Lakes fur trade with the Indians. Crossing Lake Erie and Lake Huron, he brought back to Albany eleven canoe loads of furs from the area about Michilimackinac. A second expedition the following year was intercepted and captured by the French, who recognized the very real threat to their monopoly of the lucrative fur trade posed by the English and their subjects.

Reflecting French-English rivalry for colonial and commercial supremacy, not only in North America but around the world, in 1689 the first of a succession of wars erupted between the two Europeans powers, wars that would not finally be concluded until 1815. Collectively referred to as the Second Hundred Years' War by later historians, these sepa-rate though related conflicts were known by different names to the peoples of Europe and America, a reflection of differing perceptions of why they were fought.

Europe	*America*
War of the League of Augsburg, 1689–97	King William's War, 1689–97
War of the Spanish Succession, 1701–13	Queen Anne's War, 1702–13
War of the Austrian Succession, 1740–48	King George's War, 1744–48
Seven Years' War, 1756–63	French and Indian War, 1754–63
War of the American Revolution, 1775–83	Revolutionary War, 1775–83
War of the French Revolution, 1792–1802	
Napoleonic Wars, 1803–15	War of 1812, 1812–15

Though a fort was built by LaMothe Cadillac at Detroit in 1701 to guard the straits between Lakes Erie and Huron, the Ohio country was remote from most of the fighting until the French and Indian War, which, as earlier noted, had its inception in the Ohio Valley. By 1748 and the end of King George's War, the buildup of Indian population and the riches of the concomitant fur trade made the Ohio country one of the continent's principal economic prizes as well as one of its most strategic locations. By that year literally dozens of fur buyers and their packhorses from the English colonies on the eastern seaboard were actively engaged in trade with Indian villages scattered along the Ohio and its tributaries. Offering higher prices for furs and lower prices for trade goods such as rum and blankets, hatchets and beads, often of better quality than those of their French competitors, it was not long before the English traders, most from the nearby colonies of Pennsylvania and Virginia, had broken the long-standing French monopoly of the fur trade in the Ohio country.

Of particular importance among the new British tradesmen was George Croghan, an Irishman who migrated to Pennsylvania and then came west to establish fur-trading posts on the Tuscarawas, Sandusky, and Cuyahoga Rivers, as well as at Logstown, near the Forks of the Ohio. Sometimes called Ohio's first successful entrepreneur, Croghan earned a widespread reputation for honesty and fair dealing. Soon the furs he was purchasing were being sold in markets around the world.

Inevitably, the attention of prospective investors was drawn to the large profits to be made in the fur trade of the Ohio Valley. At the suggestion of Thomas Lee, a member of the Governor's Council, an Ohio Company was formed at Williamsburg, Virginia, in 1748 by Thomas Cresap, George Mason, Augustus and Lawrence Washington, and others who petitioned King George II for a grant of five hundred thousand acres of land on either or both sides of the Ohio River between the Kanawha and Monongahela Rivers. It was proposed that two hundred thousand acres be selected at once, to be free of any royal taxes if the company should colonize a hundred families on the land within seven years. For the protection of these settlers a fort was also to be built by the company. Approval was given the plan in 1749. The beginning of British settlement in the Ohio Valley was now in prospect.

Alarmed by mounting reports of British presence on lands they believed to be theirs, the French were quick to respond. Captain Pierre-Joseph de Céloron de Blainville was commissioned in the summer of 1749 by the Marquis de La Galissonière, governor-general of New France, to lead an expeditionary force of some 250 French and Indians to the Ohio Valley to order all British subjects to get out of the land claimed by France and to warn the Ohio tribes from further trade with any who were not loyal subjects of Louis XV of France. Six tablets of lead proclaiming the land as French were buried at the confluence of key tributaries and the Ohio River. Particular target of the expedition was La Demoiselle (as he was called by the French), or Old Britain (as he was known to the British), the Miami chief headquartered at Pickawillany, the largest of the Indian towns of Ohio at that time, in the upper valley of the Great Miami River. Two years earlier he had purposely moved his people away from the French Fort Miamis at the headwaters of the Maumee in order to be closer to British traders from Virginia and Pennsylvania.

In the following year, 1750, Christopher Gist, a surveyor, trader, and woodsman, was sent by the Ohio Company of Virginia to make a survey of desirable land for the company's initial settlement and also to ascertain the mood of the Ohio tribes in the wake of Céloron's expedition of the previous summer. Meeting George Croghan at his post at Coshocton, the two men made their way to Pickawillany, where Old Britain, despite the earlier warning of the French, assured them that he was and intended to continue to be a friend of the British.

When the news of his seeming duplicity reached their ears, the French determined to make an object lesson of the one they called La Demoiselle, literally meaning "the young lady," so named by them because they regarded him as being as fickle as a young woman. In June 1752, a party of 240 French, Ottawas, and Chippewas under the command of Charles Langlade came down from Detroit to attack and destroy Pickawillany, capture British traders, and kill the Miami chief and many of his warriors in what some historians have called the first battle of the French and Indian War.

Convinced that military might alone would keep the British out of the Ohio Valley, a new French governor-general, the Marquis de Duquesne, in 1753 ordered an army of fifteen hundred men to commence the construction of a chain of forts linking the Erie Lake at Presqu'Isle with the Ohio and Allegheny Rivers. To counter this move, Governor Robert Dinwiddie of Virginia, one of the colonies with claims on the Ohio country, sent a twenty-one-year-old militia major, George Washington, whose brothers were stockholders in the Ohio Company, to carry a message to Philippe Joincaré, the commander of French forces in the Upper Ohio Valley, advising him that the land was Virginia's and to take his army and leave. Together with Christopher Gist, Washington made his way to Fort LeBoeuf in the late fall and winter of 1753–54, only to be spurned by Joincaré, whose reply to Washington (to be carried back to Dinwiddie) was that the land was French and the British were the trespassers.

The response of Dinwiddie was the dispatch of Captain William Trent with an army of three hundred Virginians to commence the hasty construction of a British fort at the Forks of the Ohio. An attack by the French quickly forced the surrender of Trent and his men, whose fort was then completed by the French and named by them Duquesne in honor of the governor-general. A second British fort nearby, named Necessity by its builder, George Washington, was also soon surrendered by the young Virginia major on 4 July 1754, the only time in his long military career that Washington was forced to surrender.

The subsequent dispatch of General Edward Braddock and an army of fifteen hundred soldiers to drive the French out of the Ohio Valley ended disastrously just a few miles south of Fort Duquesne on 9 July 1755, with the death of Braddock and the destruction of a significant part of his army in an ambush directed by the Ohio Shawnee Chief Black Hoof.

The French and Indian War, which began in the Ohio Valley, soon spread to other parts of the world—Europe, India, and South Africa, as well as other areas of North America. For a time Ohio Indians (notably the Shawnees of the Scioto Valley and the Delawares of the Muskingum), as allies of the French, raided English settlements in western Virginia and western Pennsylvania. But in July 1758, Christian Frederick Post, a lone black-coated Moravian missionary from a place called Bethlehem in Pennsylvania, ventured into the villages of these tribes and persuaded them to lay down their arms, to follow the path of neutrality. With their Indian allies no longer at their side, the French found the retention of the forts in the Upper Ohio Valley no longer tenable and withdrew. In November 1758, British forces under General John Forbes and George Washington recaptured Fort Duquesne and promptly renamed it Fort Pitt in honor of the British prime minister, William Pitt.

With the fall of Quebec in 1759 and Montreal in 1760, the dissolution of the French empire in North America was assured. Though fighting continued on other continents for several more years, peace finally came with the Treaty of Paris of 1763. To England went French possessions east of the Mississippi River, including the Ohio country. To Spain, an old friend and ally, France ceded its claims to the Louisiana territory to the west of the Mississippi. All that remained of New France were two small islands off the coast of Newfoundland, suitable for the drying of cod, and two others in the Caribbean, useful in the sugar, molasses, and rum trade.

In May 1763, while white men in powdered wigs in Paris were signing a treaty of peace that would end French control over much of North America, Indians in war paint in the Ohio Valley, who were not represented at Paris, were dancing around council fires far into the night in protest. Influenced by the persuasive eloquence of the great Ottawa chief, Pontiac, they came together, as Ottawas, Wyandots, Delawares, Shawnees, Miamis, and Mingoes, in confederation, to protest the passing of their lands to Britain. It made a difference to them that the French, who had been comparatively few and far between and had been a forest people much like themselves, were now to be displaced by the English, who were fifty times as numerous and who cut down the forests and turned the land into farms.

What followed has been called Pontiac's Conspiracy or Pontiac's Rebellion. Before 1763 was over, more than two thousand settlers and their families had been killed or made captive in Indian attacks that spilled out of the Ohio country into western Virginia and western Pennsylvania. Nine British forts, including those at Le Boeuf, Sandusky, and Presqu'Isle, were captured. Only two west of the Allegheny Mountains, Fort Pitt and Fort Detroit, survived lengthy sieges. To bring an end to the uprising, two expeditions were sent from the east in the spring and fall of 1764. The first, under Colonel John Bradstreet, failed to achieve a lasting peace. The second, under a Swiss soldier of fortune, Colonel Henri Bouquet, marched fifteen hundred men strong to the Delaware town of Coshocton and, threatening its destruction, persuaded the Delawares and then the other tribes to come to peace and to return all their white prisoners as evidence of their sincerity. In all, 206 captives, including 126 women and children, many by now more Indian than white, were brought to Coshocton. With the conclusion of a formal treaty of peace in the spring of 1765 at Fort Pitt, the Pontiac Rebellion was over.

Out of the contest between Indians and the British for control of the Ohio Valley came a Royal Proclamation in 1763 that affirmed a new imperial policy for Britain. Seeking the segregation of the races as means to the securing and maintaining of peace, it directed that colonists thereafter stay to the east of the Alleghenies and Indians to the west, with a ten-thousand-man patrol force to keep them apart. Since it was expected that the colonists whose lives were being protected by the new policy should pay the bill for the maintenance of the patrol force, the Proclamation gave rise to a succession of new taxes, beginning with a Sugar Act in 1764, a Stamp Act in 1765, and the Townshend Acts of 1767. To colonists who had been rejoicing over the end of French dominance in the Ohio Valley, it seemed that the British government was now slapping them down with closure of the frontier and a host of hated taxes to keep it closed. Particularly upset were the shareholders of the Ohio Company of Virginia, including the Washington family, who since 1748 had been anticipating the opening of the Ohio country for settlement.

Because of organized colonial opposition to the new taxes, in the levying of which the colonists had no representation, the ten-thousand-man patrol force never materialized. As a result, it did not take long for colonists to appreciate that the new imperial policy was unenforceable. Among those soon crossing the Allegheny Mountains and coming into the Ohio Valley despite the provisions of the Proclamation of 1763 was George Washington, who, in October and November 1770, journeyed to the Ohio country to find and claim some ten thousand acres for his family as their share of the investment they had made in the Ohio Company of Virginia.

Crossing the Allegheny divide as well were Moravian missionaries, who felt their calling to bring Christianity to the Ohio Indians transcended the man-made impediment of the Royal Proclamation. With the encouragement of the Delaware Chief Netawatwes, in the spring of 1772 David Zeisberger commenced the first successful Moravian mission in Ohio in the Tuscarawas Valley at the place he called Schoenbrunn, or "Beautiful Spring." With the help of John Heckewelder, who served as the mission's pastor, Schoenbrunn by 1776 had a church membership of 417, with more than 100 Indian children attending the mission school, the very first school in Ohio. In the fall of 1772, ten miles from Schoenbrunn, a second mission was also established at a place called Gnadenhutten, or "Tents of Grace."

The presence of growing numbers of whites west of the mountains, many of them trappers and traders, proved troublesome to many Indians, who saw their rights to the land increasingly threatened. It took but a spark to touch off another clash between the Ohio tribes and colonial frontiersmen, this coming on 3 May 1774, at a place called Baker's Cabin on an island in the Ohio River some fifteen miles north of the site of present-day Steubenville. There a party of whites, led by Captain Daniel Greathouse, fired on a group of Mingoes with whom they had come to trade. Numbered among those killed were the members of the family of Tahgajute, better known as Logan, a Mingo chief long regarded as a friend of white men. Included among the dead were his wife, his mother, his brothers, a sister, and two cousins.

Seeking revenge, Logan went on the warpath, personally taking more than fifty scalps. Soon both Wyandots and Shawnees joined the Mingoes as the frontier again became aflame. Led by the Shawnee Cornstalk, what followed has been called Lord Dunmore's War, because it was John Murray, the Earl of Dunmore, in his position as governor of Virginia, who called out the Virginia militia to quell the uprising in the Ohio Valley. Following a decisive battle on 10 October 1774, at Point Pleasant near the mouth of the Kanawha River, where the Indians under Cornstalk were defeated, Lord Dunmore called on the tribal leaders to meet him at his headquarters at Camp Charlotte in the Pickaway Plains to discuss terms of peace, terms demanding recognition of the Ohio River as boundary between white men and red instead of the Allegheny Mountains. Cornstalk and the other chiefs agreed—all, that is, save Logan, who refused to come to Camp Charlotte, stopping instead under a great elm tree a few miles away. There he was met by Colonel John Gibson, who had been dispatched by Lord Dunmore to try to persuade the Mingo chief to join the others in bringing an end to the war. It was believed if anyone could persuade Logan to do this it was Gibson, for Gibson was the brother-in-law of the Mingo chief. His wife, Logan's sister, had been one of those killed at Baker's Cabin, so Gibson shared in Logan's grief. Despite the pleas of Gibson, however, Logan still refused to come to Camp Charlotte and uttered a lament that has echoed through the centuries, as countless American school children can attest.

Notwithstanding the absence of Logan, peace returned to the Ohio Valley in October 1774, and some two thousand Virginia militiamen began their journey home. At Fort Gower at the mouth of the Hocking River, on 4 November 1774, on learning of the denunciation by the First Continental Congress of England's "Intolerable Acts" in the wake of the Boston Tea Party, the officers of the only colonial army in the field at that time declared their allegiance to the "just rights of America" in what became known as the "Fort Gower Resolves." Five months later, in April 1775, the American Revolution began in Massachusetts, and on 4 July 1776, the goal of that revolt became complete separation from the mother country, England, and independence for the former thirteen colonies as a new nation, the United States of America.

Lord Dunmore's War usually rates only a footnote on the pages of our nation's history; but it was significant beyond such casual mention, for it furnished valuable military experience for a number of officers who would play leading roles in the fight for independence that followed, such as Andrew Lewis, who had led Dunmore's militiamen to victory at Point Pleasant, as well as Daniel Morgan and George Rogers Clark, who also had served with distinction in that same battle. It was important as well because it strengthened Virginia's claim to the Ohio country, for it was its quarrel alone with the Ohio Indians, the other colonies remaining aloof from the fray. Its principal significance, however, was the fact that it kept the Ohio Indians at peace during the crucial early years of the American Revolution. Having had their fingers burned under Pontiac in 1763-64 and under Cornstalk and Logan in 1774, they were inclined to "sit this one out," despite the blandishments of Lord Dunmore, who as the *royal* governor of Virginia now urged them to attack the same settlers who only a year earlier he had punished them for attacking. Not until after the tragic death of Cornstalk, the great Shawnee leader, at Fort Randolph at the hands of American troops on 10 October 1777, did the Ohio tribes enter the conflict on the side of the British, whom they now regarded as the lesser of two evils. Had they supported the British when the Revolution first began, the outcome might have been dramatically different. As it was, when they entered the war late in 1777, their involvement was soon countered by the entry of France on the side of the Americans against France's enemies, the British.

The role of Ohio in the American Revolution was primarily the role played by Ohio's tribes in attacks on American forts and settlements in Pennsylvania, Virginia, and Kentucky, and on the only Revolutionary War fort in Ohio, Fort Laurens, in the Tuscarawas Valley. It was also marked by retaliatory attacks by George Rogers Clark and his

Kentucky riflemen against the Shawnees in the Battle of Piqua, four miles west of present-day Springfield, on 8 August 1780, and by Daniel Broadhead and the Pennsylvania militia against the Delawares in the Battle of Coshocton, 14 April 1781. Frustrated by the defeat of the Delawares at Coshocton, and the refusal of the neutral mission Indians (primarily Delawares) to fight with them, Wyandot warriors came down from the Sandusky Valley and made prisoners of the mission Indians, removing them to what was called Captives' Town on the Sandusky River. The winter of 1781–82 proved a starving time for the captives, who finally persuaded their captors to permit some of their number to return to Schoenbrunn and Gnadenhutten to harvest the corn that had been left standing in the fields. While they were there, an Indian raid in western Pennsylvania in which one of the raiding party was purported to have spoken to another in German, led to an erroneous conclusion that the mission Indians had finally entered the war on the side of the British. This in turn precipitated a punitive attack on the missions by a band of some ninety Pennsylvania militiamen under the command of Captain David Williamson. Ninety-six Christian Indians (fifty-seven adults and thirty-nine children), none of whom offered any resistance, were taken prisoner at Gnadenhutten and, after a final night of prayer and hymns, were taken out by twos and bludgeoned to death in what has rightfully been called "one of the most atrocious massacres in the annals of warfare." Two young boys who were left for dead managed to make their way through the snow to warn the other mission Indians at Schoenbrunn in time for them to flee back to Captives' Town. The wrath of the militia on finding Schoenbrunn deserted was vented against the town, which was destroyed, not to be reconstructed until 1923, where today it is maintained as a historic property by the Ohio Historical Society. At Gnadenhutten, a memorial marker still stands on the site where the massacre took place.

That cruelty was not the monopoly of one side to the exclusion of the other was manifest in the fate of Colonel William Crawford, who, in the course of an expedition against the Wyandots and remnant Delawares, was captured after separation from most of the rest of his army of 480 Pennsylvanians in the battles of the Sandusky and the Olentangy, 5–6 June 1782. In retaliation for the massacre at Gnadenhutten, in which he had had no part, he was burned at the stake while, ironically, his subordinate, David Williamson, managed to lead most of the rest of the army back to Pennsylvania unscathed.

Long months after Cornwallis surrendered his army in October 1781 at Yorktown to bring fighting in the east to a close, campaigning in the Ohio country continued, highlighted by a final expedition of George Rogers Clark against Shawnee and Miami towns in the Miami valleys in November 1782.

Because the thirteen colonies, now the United States, as a condition of the alliance of 1778, had committed themselves to remaining in the war as long as France was in the conflict, and because France, as a condition of a separate secret alliance with Spain, had committed itself to fighting as long as necessary to assure the return of Gibraltar to Spain, it became painfully evident to the United States that though fighting in America had ended by 1782, American independence had become "chained to the Rock of Gibraltar." The threat of a separate peace between Britain and its former colonies finally brought all parties to the peace table, and on 3 September 1783, the Treaty of Paris was signed. The new nation was formally recognized as free and independent, with a western boundary set at the Mississippi River. Though the battles in the Ohio country had been relatively minor in contrast with those fought in the east, the consequence of their having been fought at all was major, for the new nation now found itself with an empire of its own—the vast expanse of land between the mountains and the Mississippi, of which the Ohio country was an integral part.

II.1. The French Encounter with La Demoiselle at Pickawillany in 1749: The Journal of Céloron de Blainville

One of the principal objectives of the expedition of Céloron de Blainville to the Ohio country in 1749 was to win back the support and allegiance of the Ohio tribes to the French. Not alone had the Shawnees become disaffected with their monopolistic trading practices—but so, too, had the Miamis. It was the chief of the Piankeshaw band of the Miami nation, La Demoiselle, who led a rebellion against French dominance of trade at Kekionga (also called Kiskakon) on the headwaters of the Maumee, at the fort the French called Miamis. In 1747 he moved his village from Kekionga eastward to a site near the junction of Loramie Creek and the Great Miami River, which he named Pickawillany. There a flourishing trade was built up with English tradesmen from Pennsylvania and Virginia, who paid more for Miami furs and sold European goods for less than their French competitors. Soon Pickawillany was the largest of all the Miami towns, and its chief, La Demoiselle, had gained a new name, "Old Britain."

The journal Céloron kept during his trip down the Ohio contains a detailed account of his unsuccessful and immensely frustrating experience in trying to persuade La Demoiselle to leave Pickawillany and the English traders and return with his people to Kekionga (or Kiskakon) and the French traders at Fort Miamis.[1]

*T*he 26th [of August, 1749]. I set out at ten in the morning from St. Yotoc [Sinhioto, or lower Shawnee Town on the Scioto River]; all the Indians were under arms and fired a salute when I passed before the village. The 27th of August I arrived at the White River [the Little Miami] about six in the evening. I knew that at a distance of three leagues in the country there were cabins of my friends, and that influenced me to pass the night in this place. The 28th, I sent M. Devillier and my son to these cabins in order to tell those Indians to come and speak with me. They brought them back with them, and I induced them to come with me to the village of the Demoiselle, whither I was going to bring the word of their father Onontio [the governor-general of New France]. They gave their consent and asked [to be permitted] to remain till the next day in order to have time to prepare for the journey. There are in this village two cabins of Sonontouans [Senecas]. It is the policy of these nations to have always along with them some [other Indians] who serve as a hostage. I induced one of these Sonontouans who spake Miami very well, to come with me to the Demoiselle, for I had need of him, having no interpreter, though I had to treat with these people on matters of importance.

The 29th. I wrote to M. Raimond [Charles D. Raymond], captain and commander among the Miamis [at Fort Miamis], and besought him to send me the so-called royal interpreter with as many horses as he possibly could, to transport our baggage over a portage of fifty leagues.

The 30th the Indians of the White River [or Little Miami River, who were led by Le Baril, a Miami chief], having arrived, I embarked to gain the Rock River [the Great Miami], and at the entrance I had a leaden plate buried, and the arms of the King attached to a tree, of which I drew up an official statement.

Official statement of the sixth leaden plate buried at the entrance of the Rock River, the 31st day of August, 1749:

> The year 1749, we, Céloron, Knight of the Royal and Military Order of St. Louis, Captain, commanding a detachment sent by the orders of M. the Marquis de la Galissoniere, Governor-General of Canada, upon the Beautiful River, otherwise called the Ohio, accompanied by the principal officers of our detachment, have buried at the point formed by the right bank of the Ohio and the left bank of Rock River, a leaden plate, and have attached to a tree the arms of the King. In testimony whereof, we have drawn up and signed with Messrs. the officers, the present official statement.

The inscription is always the same [reaffirming possession, in the name of King Louis XV, "of this river and of all those which fall into it"].

7th September. This done, I embarked; owing to the scarcity of water in this river, it took thirteen days in ascending it. . . .

The 13th. I arrived at the village of the Demoiselle. I pitched my camp, placed my sentinels, and awaited the arrival of the interpreter I had asked of M. de Raimond. During this interval, I sounded their minds in order to learn if they were disposed to return to Kiskakon, for that is the name of their ancient village. It seemed to me that they had not much objection. They had two English soldiers in their village whom I obliged to go away before speaking to these people. Those who had spent the summer there trading, had already departed overland with their effects; they had ways of communication from one village to another.

The 17th. Wearied at the fact of the interpreter not arriving, and because my provisions were being consumed while thus waiting, I determined to speak to the Demoiselle by means of an Iroquois who knew Miami well. I showed them magnificent presents on the part of M. the General to induce them to return to their villages, and I explained to them his invitations in these terms:

Speech of M. the General to the Miamis of the band of the Demoiselle, established at Rock River, and at the Baril located at the White River, brought by M. de Céloron, 17th of September, 1749, with eight belts of wampum for the two villages:

> "My children: The manner in which I behave toward you, despite all you have done to the French whom I sent you to maintain your wives and your children, ought to be a sufficient proof of the attachment which I have for you and the sincerity of my feelings. I forget what you have done to me, and I bury it in the depth of the earth in order to never more remember it, convinced that you have

acted only at the instigation of a people [the English] whose policy is to trouble the land and destroy the good disposition of those with whom they have relations, and who avail themselves of the unhappy ascendency which you have let them get over you. They make you commit faults and they incite you to an evil course without their seeming to have any part in it, in order to ruin you in my estimation.

"It is then to enlighten you that I send you my message; listen carefully to it, and pay attention to it, my children; it is the word of a father that loves you, and in whose eyes your interests are dear. I extinguish by these two belts of wampum the two fires which you lighted during the last two years, both at the Rock River and at White River. I extinguish them in such a way that not a single spark can escape."

[Belts are given to the Demoiselle and to the Baril.]

"My children: I have just told you that these are belts of wampum with which I extinguish the fires that you lighted, both at Rock River and at White River. By these belts I lift you from your mats and I lead you by the hand in order to bring you to Quiskakon, where I light your fire and make it more enduring than ever. It is in this country, my children, that you will enjoy a perfect peace, and where I will be ever at hand to give you marks of my friendship; it is in this country, my children, that you will enjoy the pleasures of life, it being the place where repose the bones of your ancestors, and those of M. de Vincennes [Jean Baptiste Bissot, Sieur de Vincennes, who had been burned at the stake by Chickasaws in 1736], whom you loved so much and who always governed you in such a way that your affairs were ever in good order. If you have forgotten the counsels which he gave you, these ashes shall recall to you the memory of them; the bones of your fathers suffer from your estrangement. Have pity on the dead who call you back to your village.

"Follow, along with your wives and your children, the chief [Céloron] whom I will send to bring you my message, and who will again light your fire at Quiskakon in such a manner that it shall no more be extinguished. I will afford you all the assistance which you have a right to expect from my friendship, and remember, my children, that I am doing for you what I have never done for any other nation. . . .'"

The council over, every one retired. They carried away the presents to their village where they assembled to deliberate on their answer.

The 18th. About nine A.M., they came to give their answer.

Answers of the Demoiselle, chief of Miamis, established at the Rock River, and of the Baril, established at White River, the 18th of September, 1749, with pipes of peace:

"It is an ancient custom among us when one speaks of agreeable affairs to present, first of all, pipes. We earnestly entreat you to listen to us. We are going to answer what you have asked of us. This pipe is a token of the pleasure which we have in smoking with you, and we hope to smoke the very same pipe with our father next year.

[A belt is given to Céloron.]

"My father: Yesterday, we listened with pleasure to your speech. We have seen clearly that you are come only on a good mission. We have none other but good answers to give you. You have made us recall to memory the bones of our forefathers, who mourn to see us in this place, and who remind us continually of it. You have made us a good road to return to our ancient home, and we thank you for it, my father, and we promise you to return thither immediately after the coming spring. We thank you for the kind words which you have addressed us. We see clearly that you have not forgotten us. Be convinced that we will labor to deal fairly with the Chauanones [Shawnees]. We still remember the good advice which M. de Vincennes gave us. My father, you have to treat with people without spirit, and who are, perhaps, unable to answer you as well as you hoped; but they will tell you the truth, for it is not from the lips that they speak to you, but from the bottom of their heart. You have bid us reflect seriously upon what you told us. We have done so, and we shall continue to do so during the whole winter. We hope to have the pleasure of making you a good speech this spring if the hunting is abundant. We will correct our faults, and we assure you, my father, that we will not listen to evil counsel, and that we will pay no attention to the rumors we hear at present."

Answer to the Demoiselle and the Baril in the same council, by M. de Céloron:

"I have listened to you, my children, and I have weighed well your words. Whether you may not have understood me, or that you feign not to have done so, you do not answer to what I asked of you. I proposed to you on the part of your father Onontio, to come with me to Kiskakon to light there your fire and to build up your wigwam, but you put off doing so till next spring. I would have been delighted to be able to say to your father Onontio that I had brought you back. That would have caused him great pleasure on account of the interest he takes in all that concerns you. You give me your word that you will return there at the end of the winter. Be faithful then to your promise. You have assured him of this, because he is much stronger than you, and if you be wanting to it, fear the resentment of a father, who has only too much reason to be angry with you, and who has offered you the means of regaining his favor."

Answer to Céloron's speech by the Demoiselle and the Baril:

"My father, we shall be faithful in carrying out the promise that we have made you, and at the end of the winter we shall betake ourselves to our ancient habitation, and if the Master of Life favors our hunting, we hope to be able to repair our past faults; so be convinced that we do not speak from the end of our lips but from the bottom of the heart. We could not at present return whither you would have us go, for the season is too far advanced."

The council ended, I detained some of the old men for the purpose of finding out if what they had just said was sincere, so I spoke with these Indians who assured me that both the villages would return in the spring to Quiskakon, and all that kept them back was the fact of having no cabins built where I would conduct them, and that whilst hunting through the winter they were approaching their villages, and that they would return there absolutely. Rois [the interpreter], whom I had asked of M. de Raimond, arrived.

The 19th. I remained to endeavor by the agency of Rois, to induce the Demoiselle, along with some other chiefs, to come with me to light their fires and make their wigwams at Quiskakon, but I could not succeed in this. They kept always saying and assuring me that they would return thither next spring. . . .

1. The Céloron Journal was first published in English translation in 1886 by the Reverend A. A. Lambing in the *Catholic Historical Researches* in Pittsburgh, Pennsylvania. The account cited here is taken from the *Ohio Archaeological and Historical Quarterly* 29, no. 3 (1920): 335–96.

II.2. Counterdiplomacy: The Visit of Christopher Gist and George Croghan to the Ohio Tribes, 1750–1751, as Recorded in Gist's Journal

As in a game of chess, the French expedition to the Ohio Valley under Céloron de Blainville in 1749 was soon countered by the visit of two British agents, Christopher Gist, a veteran woodsman and surveyor in the employ of the Ohio Company of Virginia, and George Croghan, the fur trader who was the representative of the governor of Pennsylvania. The two men met quite by accident in mid-December 1750, at the Wyandot town on the present site of Coshocton, where Croghan had one of his storehouses. Discovering their mutual interest in assuring British dominance in the area, they agreed to journey together on a trip that would take them across southern and central Ohio to a number of Indian villages, including both Lower Shawnee Town and Pickawillany, earlier visited by Céloron.

Accompanied by Andrew Montour, a Canadian half-Indian interpreter, they reached Lower Shawnee Town (site of present Portsmouth) on 29 January 1751 and remained there until 11 February, holding meetings with Shawnee leaders including Chief Big Hannaona. They then proceeded on horseback across the snow-covered Ohio wilderness to Pickawillany, the Miami (or Twightwee) town of Old Britain, arriving there on 17 February and remaining until 1 March, during which time they helped to persuade the Miami chief to refuse the gifts of a delegation of pro-French Ottawas from Detroit and instead to reaffirm his friendship for the British, a decision that later cost Old Britain his life and led to the subsequent French and Indian War.

In his instructions from the Ohio Company, Gist had been asked to "find a large quantity of good, level land, such as you think will suit the Company," and also "to observe what Nations of Indians inhabit there, their Strength & Numbers, who they trade with, & in what Comodities they deal." With these mandates, the following entries from his journal reflect the scrutiny of a man on a mission to find the best location for a Virginia settlement and trading post in the Ohio country and to assure the strengthening of British relations with the Indian tribes. Though terse, his observations concerning the beauty and fertility of the land provide an excellent portrait of the Ohio country in the mid-eighteenth century.[1]

*F*rom Thursday Jan 31 to Monday Feby 11.—Stayed in the Shannoah [Lower Shawnee] Town, while I was here the Indians had a very extraordinary Kind of a Festival, at which I was present and which I have exactly described at the End of my Journal—As I had particular Instructions from the President of Virginia to discover the Strength & Numbers of some Indian Nations to the Westward of Ohio who had lately revolted from the French, and had some Messages to deliver them from him, I resolved to set out for the Twigtwee Town. . . .

Sunday [February] 17.—Crossed the little Miamee River, and altering our Course We went SW 25 M, to the big Miamee River, opposite the Twigtwee Town. All the Way from the Shannoah Town to this Place (except the first 20 M which is broken) is fine, rich level Land, well timbered with large Walnut, Ash, Sugar Trees, Cherry Trees &c, it is well watered with a great Number of little Streams or Rivulets, and full of beautiful natural Meadows, covered with wild Rye, blue Grass and Clover, and abounds with Turkeys, Deer, Elks and most Sorts of Game particularly Buffaloes, thirty or forty of which are frequently seen feeding in one Meadow: In short it wants Nothing but Cultivation to make it a most delightful Country—The Ohio and all the large Branches are said to be full of fine Fish of several Kinds, particularly a Sort of Cat Fish of a prodigious Size; but as I was not there at the proper Season, I had not an opportunity of seeing any of them—The Traders had always reckoned it 200 M, from the Shannoah Town to the Twigtwee Town, but by my Computation I could make it no more than 150—The Miamee River being high, We were obliged to make a Raft of old Loggs to transport our Goods and Saddles and swim our Horses over—After firing a few Guns and Pistols, & smoaking in the Warriours Pipe, who came to invite Us to the Town (according to their Custom of inviting and welcoming Strangers and Great Men) We entered the Town with English Colours before Us, and were kindly received by their King, who invited Us into his own House, & set our Colours upon the Top of it—The Firing of Guns held about a Quarter of an Hour, and then all the white Men and Traders that were there, came and welcomed us to the Twigtwee Town—This Town is situate on the NW Side of the Big Miamee River about 150M from the Mouth thereof; it consists of about 400 Families, & daily encreasing, it is accounted one of the strongest Indian Towns upon this Part of the Continent—The Twigtwees are a very numerous People consisting of many different Tribes under the same Form of Government. Each tribe has a particular Chief or King, one of which is chosen indifferently out of any Tribe to rule the whole Nation, and is vested with greater Authorities than any of the others—They are accounted the most powerful People to the Westward of the English Settlements, & much superior to the six Nations with whom they are now in Amity: their Strength and Numbers are not thoroughly known, as they have but lately traded with the English, and indeed have very little Trade among them: they deal in much the same Commodities with the Northern Indians. There are other Nations or Tribes still further to the Westward daily coming in to them, & 'tis thought their Power and Interest reaches to the Westward of the Mississippi, if not across the Continent; they are at present very well affected to the English, and seem fond of an Alliance with them—they formerly lived on the farther Side of the Obache [Wabash], and were in the French Interest, who supplied them with some few Trifles at a most exorbitant Price—they were called by the French Miamees; but they have now revolted from them, and left their former Habitations for the Sake of trading with the English; and notwithstanding all the Artifices the French have used, they have not been able to recall them. . . .

Friday March 1.—We received the following Speech from the Twigtwees the Speaker stood up and addressing himself as to the Governor of Pensylvania with two Strings of Wampum in his Hand, He said—"Brothers our Hearts are glad that you have taken Notice of Us, and surely Brothers We hope that You will order a Smith to settle here to mend our Guns and Hatchets, Your kindness makes Us so bold to ask this Request. You told Us our Friendship should last as long, and be as the greatest Mountain, We have considered well, and all our great Kings & Warriors are come to a Resolution never to give Heed to what the French say to Us, but always to hear & believe what You our Brothers say to Us—Brothers We are obliged to You for your kind Invitation to receive a Present at the Loggs Town, but as our foreign Tribes are not yet come, We must wait for them, but You may depend We will come as soon as our Women have planted Corn to hear what our Brothers will say to Us—Brothers We present You with this Bundle of Skins, as We are but poor to be for Shoes for You on the Road, and We return You our hearty Thanks for the Clothes which You have put upon our Wives and Children."—We then took our Leave of the Kings and Chiefs, and they ordered that a small Party of Indians shoud go with Us as far as Hockhockin; but as I had left my Boy and Horses at the lower Shannoah Town, I was obliged to go by myself or to go sixty or seventy Miles out of my Way, which I did not care to do; so we all came over the Miamee river together this Evening, but Mr Croghan & Mr Montour went over again & lodged in the Town, but I stayed on this Side at one Robert Smith's (a Trader) where We had left our Horses—Before the French Indians had come into Town, We had drawn Articles of Peace and Alliance between the English and the Wawaughtanneys [Wea band of the Miamis] and Pyankeshees [Piankeshaw band of the Miamis]; the Indentures were signed sealed and delivered on both Sides, and as I drew them I took a Copy—The Land upon the great Miamee River is very rich level and well timbered, some of the finest Meadows that can be: the Indians and Traders assure Me that the Land holds as good and if possible better, to the Westward as far as the Obache [Wabash] which is accounted 100 Miles, and quite up to the Head of the Miamee River, which is 60 Miles above the Twigtwee Town, and down the said River quite to the Ohio which is reckoned 150 Miles—The Grass here grows to a great Height in the clear Fields, of which there are a great Number, & the Bottoms are full of white Clover, wild Rye, and blue Grass. . . .

1. See William M. Darlington, ed., *Christopher Gist's Journals* (Pittsburgh: J. R. Weldin, 1893), 31-53.

II.3.   The Destruction of Pickawillany: "The First Battle of the French and Indian War"

The contest between France and Great Britain for control of the Ohio country and trade with its Indian peoples ultimately exploded into war. The flash point came on 21 June 1752 at the Miami (or Twightwee) village of Pickawillany, near the mouth of Loramie Creek where it empties into the Great Miami River. Exasperated by the news that La Demoiselle (or Old Britain) had spurned his gifts and had welcomed the British agents Gist and Croghan, Céloron de Blainville, now the French commandant at Fort Detroit, with the backing of the governor-general, determined on a punitive course of action. Led by a French-Canadian half-blood, Charles Langlade, an army of 240 (primarily Indians) left Detroit for a raid on Pickawillany, the town that by this time had become the key to the western fur trade.

At an early morning hour, with most of the Miami warriors off on the summer hunt and the town reduced largely to old men, women, and children, as well as some eight English traders, the French force suddenly attacked. Though five of the traders and twenty of the Miamis managed to get into the fort the English had built to protect the village and its trading post, most of the rest fled into the forest. Others who were unable to escape because of old age or infirmity were made prisoner. After a six-hour siege, during which fourteen of the defending Miamis were killed, including the chief, the fort fell to the attackers and was burned along with the rest of the town. Then before the horrified eyes of the five captured English traders and the captive Miamis, Old Britain—chief of the Piankeshaw sept or band of the Miamis—was quartered, boiled, and eaten by the victors as an example of what could happen to Indian leaders who befriended the English as he had done.

Of the three English traders who had not gotten into the fort, one was killed during the melee, while the other two managed to escape with surviving villagers into the forest. Weeks later, one of these traders, Thomas Burney, reached Carlisle, Pennsylvania, to give to officials an account of the destruction of Pickawillany and its chief. He brought with him a message of support to the governor of Pennsylvania, James Hamilton, from the surviving Miamis (or Twightwees, as they were called by the English). His account and the Twightwee message foreshadowed the French and Indian War that followed, with Indians fighting on both sides, principal actions coming at the Forks of the Ohio, Niagara, Quebec, and Montreal, and with the Ohio country one of the principal stakes.[1]

*T*hen was read the following Letter and Paper enclosed in it, sent by Express from Carlisle to the Governor:

"CARLISLE, AUG. 30TH, 1752

"May it Please Your Honour:

"Last night Thomas Burney who lately resided at the Twightwee's Town in Allegheny, came here and gives the following account of the unhappy Affair that was lately transacted there: On the twenty-first Day of June last, early in the Morning, two Frenchmen and about two hundred and forty Indians came to the Twightwee's Town, and in a Hostile Manner attacked the People there residing. In the Skirmish there was one White man and fourteen Indians killed, and five white men taken Prisoners.

"The Party who came to the Twightwee's Town reported that they had received as a Commission two Belts of Wampum from the Governor of Canada to kill all such Indians as are in Amity with the English, and to take the Persons and Effects of all such English Traders as they could meet with, but not to kill any of them if they could avoid it, which Instructions were in some measure obeyed.

"Mr. Burney is now here, and is willing to be qualified not only to this but to sundry other matters which he can discover concerning this Affair; if your Honour thinks it proper for him to come to Philadelphia to give you the Satisfaction of Examining more particularly in relation to it he will readily attend your Honour upon that occasion, or make an affidavit of the particulars here. Such orders as your Honour pleases to send on this occasion shall certainly be obeyed by,

"May it please your Honour,

"Your Honour's most obedient Servant,

"ROBᵗ CELLENDER.

1. Thomas Burney's account of the destruction of Pickawillany and the message from the Twightwees to Governor James Hamilton are to be found in the *Minutes of the Provincial Council of Pennsylvania* (Harrisburg, 1851), 5:599–600.

II.4.   George Washington Warns the French to Get Out of the Ohio Valley

Lead tablets buried along the Ohio River and royal coats-of-arms of France nailed on forest trees had failed to keep the British out of the Ohio country. In the wake of the destruction of Pickawillany, Governor Duquesne of New France devised another strategy to keep them out. A line of forts beginning with Presqu'Isle on Lake Erie and extending southward to the Upper Ohio Valley would be built by a French army of fifteen hundred men. Even as a second fort, LeBoeuf, was nearing completion at the headwaters of French Creek, Governor Robert Dinwiddie of Virginia determined to counter Duquesne's strategy with one of his own. On 31 October 1753, he dispatched a twenty-one-year-old militia major, George Washington, whose family had invested heavily in the Ohio Company of Virginia, to warn the French to get out of the Ohio Valley and to regain support for Virginia's trading interests from Ohio's tribes. With Christopher Gist as his guide and Jacob Vanbraam as his French interpreter, and with the help of Half-King, a Seneca chief and principal representative of the Iroquois among the Ohio Indians, Washington made his way to Venango, at the mouth of the French Creek, where an English trader, John Frazier, had maintained a trading post until driven out by the French. There Washington encountered Philippe Joincaré, who had command of all French forces in the Ohio country but who directed Washington to proceed to Fort LeBoeuf to confer with its commandant, Legardeur de St. Pierre, for an official answer to the Virginia governor's ultimatum.

In informal discussions with Joincaré and formal talks with St. Pierre, Washington was told bluntly and forcibly that he and Gist were the trespassers on French soil, not the other way around, and that Dinwiddie's ultimatum was unacceptable. On their return trip to Williamsburg, Washington and Gist passed a pack train of supplies bound for the Forks of the Ohio, where an English fort was being constructed hastily by William Trent and a force of three hundred militia directly in the path of the chain of French forts coming down from Lake Erie. After delivering the French reply to Dinwiddie's ultimatum, Washington was ordered by the governor to return to the Upper Ohio to assist Trent at the fort at the Forks; but before he could do so, news came that the French under Joincaré had already seized it. Completed by the French it was named Fort Duquesne in honor of the governor-general. A year later, in July 1755, it would be the scene of a disastrous defeat inflicted by French and Indians on the army of General Edward Braddock, sent from England in an effort to reestablish British control of the Ohio Valley. With this action the French and Indian War was fully engaged.

George Washington's journal of his trip to the Upper Ohio Valley in the fall and winter of 1753–54, was first printed in Williamsburg in 1754 by William Hunter. A London edition was subsequently printed that same year due to widespread interest in the developing contest for control of the Ohio country between England and France. The excerpts reproduced here are drawn from a facsimile of the Hunter edition, a copy of which is on display in the reconstructed colonial Capitol at Williamsburg, Virginia, and from The Heritage of America, *edited by Henry Steele Commager and Allan Nevins and published in Boston in 1945.*

... we arrived [at Venango] the 4th of December [1753] without anything remarkable happening but a continued series of bad weather.

This is an old Indian town, situated at the mouth of French Creek on Ohio, and lies near N. about 60 miles from the Loggs-Town [Logstown, an English trading post on the Ohio River] but more than 70 the way we were obliged to go.

We found the French colors hoisted at a house from which they had driven Mr. John Frazier, an English subject. I immediately repaired to it to know where the commander resided. There were three officers, one of whom, Captain Joncaire, informed me that he had the command of the Ohio, but that there was a General Officer at the near fort [LeBoeuf] where he advised me to apply for an answer [to the Virginia governor's ultimatum]. He invited us to sup with them, and treated us with the greatest complaisance. . . .

13th. — The chief officers retired to hold a council of war, which gave me an opportunity of taking the dimensions of the fort and making what observations I could. . . .

I could get no certain account of the number of men here, but, according to the best judgment I could form, there are an hundred exclusive of officers, of which there are many. I also gave orders to the people who were with me to take an exact account of the canoes which were hauled up to convey their forces down in the spring. This they did, and told fifty of birchbark and one hundred and seventy of pine, besides many others which were blocked out in readiness to make. . . .

14th. — As I found many plots concerted to retard the Indians' business and prevent their returning with me, I endeavored all that lay in my power to frustrate their schemes and hurry them on to execute their intended design. They accordingly pressed for admittance this evening, which at length was granted them, privately, with the commander and one or two other officers. The Half-King told me that he offered the wampum to the commander, who evaded taking it, and made many fair promises of love and friendship; said he wanted to live in peace and trade amicably with them, as a proof of which he would send some goods immediately down to the Loggs Town for them. But I rather think the design of that is to bring away all our straggling traders they meet with, as I privately understood they intended to carry an officer etc., with them. And what rather confirms this opinion—I was inquiring of the commander by what authority he had made prisoners of several of our English subjects. He told me that the country belonged to them; that no Englishman had a right to trade upon those waters; and that he had orders to make every person prisoner who attempted it on the Ohio, or the waters of it. . . .

II.5.   The Royal Proclamation of 1763: A New Imperial Policy for Great Britain

Though not formally declared until 1756, the French and Indian War (or Seven Years' War, as it was known in Europe) had its inception in the Ohio country with the destruction of Pickawillany in 1752 and the defeat of General Edward Braddock near Fort Duquesne in 1755. Though it did not end until 1763, by 1760, following the fall of Quebec and Montreal, the triumph of the British over the French in North America was assured. By the Treaty of Paris of 1763, France surrendered its claims to Canada and the area east of the Mississippi, including the Ohio country, to Great Britain.

Despite the fact that many Indians had long chafed under the monopolistic restrictions imposed by the French on the fur trade, most had fought with the French during the war. With the emergence of Great Britain as the dominant power in North America, they foresaw the end of their way of life as a forest people. The French had been relatively few and far between, had preserved the forests, and had intermarried extensively with the Native Americans. The British, in contrast, came in far greater numbers, leveled a large part of the forests, and, with few exceptions, did not intermarry with the Indians. Led by the Ohio-born Ottawa chief, Pontiac, the tribes banded together in 1763 to resist the further encroachment of British subjects on their hunting lands west of the mountains.

With the outbreak of what was soon called Pontiac's Conspiracy, or Pontiac's Rebellion, the British government in far-off London determined to invoke a new imperial policy to restore and preserve peace in North America. The Royal Proclamation of 1763 sought to accomplish this by segregating the races on opposite sides of the mountains, whites and blacks to the east, reds to the west, with a British patrol force stationed along the divide to keep them apart.[1] To colonists who had anticipated the opening of the western lands to settlement in the wake of the defeat of France, the new proclamation and resultant taxes to support the maintenance of a patrol force were anathema. The stage would soon be set for an ultimate conflict between colonists and the British government, the conflict known as the American Revolution.

By the KING. A PROCLAMATION. GEORGE, R.

Whereas we have taken into our royal consideration the extensive and valuable acquisitions in America, secured to our crown by the late definitive treaty of peace concluded at Paris the 10th day of February last [1763]; and being desirous that all our loving subjects, as well of our kingdoms as of our colonies in America, may avail themselves, with all convenient speed, of the great benefits and advantages which must accrue therefrom to their commerce, manufactures, and navigation; we have thought fit, with the advice of our privy council, to issue this our royal proclamation, . . .

And whereas it is just and reasonable, and essential to our interest, and the security of our colonies, that the several nations or tribes of Indians, with whom we are connected, and who live under our protection, should not be molested or disturbed in the possession of such parts of our dominions and territories as, not having been ceded to, or purchased by us, are reserved to them, or any of them, as their hunting grounds; we do therefore, with the advice of our privy council, declare it to be our royal will and pleasure, that no governor or commander in chief of our . . . colonies or plantations in

America, do presume for the present, and until our further pleasure be known, to grant warrant of survey, or pass patents for any lands beyond the heads or sources of any of the rivers which fall into the Atlantic Ocean from the west or north-west; or upon any lands whatever, which not having been ceded to, or purchased by us, as aforesaid, are reserved to the said Indians, or any of them.

And we do further declare it to be our royal will and pleasure, for the present, as aforesaid, to reserve under our sovereignty, protection and dominion, for the use of the said Indians, all the land and territories not included within the limits of our said three new governments [Quebec, East Florida, and West Florida], or within the limits of the territory granted to the Hudson's Bay company; as also all the land and territories lying to the westward of the sources of the rivers which fall into the sea from the west and north-west as aforesaid; and we do hereby strictly forbid, on pain of our displeasure, all our loving subjects from making any purchase or settlements whatever, or taking possession of any of the lands above reserved, without our especial leave and license for that purpose first obtained.

And we do further strictly enjoin and require all persons whatever, who have either wilfully or inadvertently seated themselves upon any lands within the countries above described, or upon any other lands which, not having been ceded to or purchased by us, are still reserved to the said Indians as aforesaid, forthwith to remove themselves from such settlements. . . .

And we do further expressly enjoin and require all officers whatever, as well military as those employed in the management and direction of Indian affairs within the territories reserved as aforesaid, for the use of the said Indians, to seize and apprehend all persons whatever who, standing charged with treasons, misprisions of treason, murders, or other felonies or misdemeanors, shall fly from justice and take refuge in the said territory, and to send them under a proper guard to the colony where the crime was committed of which they shall stand accused, in order to take their trial for the same.

Given at our Court at St. James's, the 7th day of October 1763, in the third year of our reign. GOD save the KING.

1. For the full text of the Royal Proclamation of 1763, see *The Annual Register for the Year 1763* (London, 1763), 208–13.

II.6.   Bouquet's Expedition Forces the Repatriation of Captives and Brings an End to the Pontiac Rebellion, 1764

With the outbreak of Pontiac's Rebellion in 1763, nine British forts and a host of isolated frontier settlements soon fell to attacking Indians. Only Forts Detroit and Pitt (as the former Fort Duquesne was now called) still remained in British hands west of the Alleghenies. The contest for control of the Ohio country now pitted red men against white and led directly to the Royal Proclamation of 1763 that sought to end the crisis through forced segregation of the races on opposite sides of the Allegheny divide. But as the rebellion threatened to spread even farther westward, British military leaders on the eastern seaboard determined to crush it at its source. In 1764 two expeditions were dispatched by General Thomas Gage to subdue the Ohio tribes. The first, under Colonel John Bradstreet, was directed at the tribes along the Lake Erie shore, most notably the Wyandots and Ottawas, but did little more than engage the Indians in fruitless discussions that failed to bring peace. The second, under a Swiss soldier of fortune, Colonel Henry Bouquet, proved far more effective in dealing with the tribes of southern and eastern Ohio. Marching his army of fifteen hundred men into the heartland of the Delawares in the Tuscarawas and Muskingum valleys, Bouquet made his camp outside the principal Delaware town of Goshgoshgunk, or Coshocton. There Bouquet demanded that the Delawares, Shawnees, and Mingoes bring all their captives, both white and black, to him within thirteen days as a condition of peace and threatened to destroy their villages one by one, beginning with Goshgoshgunk, if they refused to do so. Awed by Bouquet's decisive presence and show of strength, the tribes agreed. Though some Shawnee captives from distant towns would not be repatriated until the following spring at Fort Pitt, 206 captives were brought to Coshocton from Delaware, Mingo, and nearby Shawnee villages. Of these, 126 were women and children. The captivities of some, both men and women, had extended over many years. In speech, dress, and way of life, many of these were to all intents and purposes Indians and were loath to be repatriated. For most, however, the return to family and friends was cause for rejoicing.

The return of the captives in November 1764 marked the beginning of the end of Pontiac's Rebellion, for in its wake Bouquet successfully mandated that the Ohio tribes send representatives to Fort Pitt in the spring of 1765 to agree on a treaty of peace. Abandoned by his Indian allies, Pontiac left the Ohio country for the Mississippi Valley, where a few months later he was killed by a Kaskaskian warrior who envisioned his own immortality by taking the life of the great Ottawa chief.

One of the truly dramatic and significant moments in Ohio's early history, the return of the captives at Coshocton has been described by Dr. William Smith, provost of the College of Philadelphia (later called the University of Pennsylvania), in a book that he published in 1765 based on papers "which an officer of long experience made available to him."[1]

The scene . . . was the arrival of the prisoners in the camp; where were to be seen fathers and mothers recognizing and clasping their once-lost babes; husbands hanging round the necks of their newly-recovered wives; sisters and brothers unexpectedly meeting together after long separation, scarce able to speak the same language, or, for some time, to be sure that they were children of the same parents! In all these interviews, joy and rapture inexpressible were seen, while feelings of a very different nature were painted in the looks of others; — flying from place to place in eager enquiries after relatives not found! trembling to receive an answer to their questions! distracted with doubts, hopes and fears, on obtaining no account of those they fought for! or stiffened into living monuments of horror and woe, on learning their unhappy fate!

The Indians too, as if wholly forgetting their usual savageness, bore a capital part in heightning this most affecting scene. They delivered up their beloved captives with the utmost reluctance; shed torrents of tears over them, recommending them to the care and protection of the commanding officer. Their regard to them continued all the time they remained in camp. They visited them from day to day; and brought them what

corn, skins, horses and other matters, they had bestowed on them, while in their families; accompanied with other presents, and all the marks of the most sincere and tender
affection. Nay, they did not stop here, but, when the army marched, some of the Indians
sollicited and obtained leave to accompany their former captives all the way to Fort-Pitt,
and employed themselves in hunting and bringing provisions for them on the road. A
young Mingo carried this still further, and gave an instance of love which would make
a figure even in romance. A young woman of Virginia was among the captives, to whom
he had form'd so strong an attachment, as to call her his wife. Against all remonstrances
of the imminent danger to which he exposed himself by approaching to the frontiers,
he persisted in following her, at the risk of being killed by the surviving relations of
many unfortunate persons, who had been captivated or scalped by those of his nation.

Those qualities in savages challenge our just esteem. They should make us chari-
tably consider their barbarities as the effects of wrong education, and false notions of
bravery and heroism; while we should look on their virtues as sure marks that nature has
made them fit subjects of cultivation as well as us; and that we are called by our superior
advantages to yield them all the helps we can in this way. Cruel and unmerciful as they
are, by habit and long example, in war, yet whenever they come to give way to the native
dictates of humanity, they exercise virtues which Christians needs not blush to imitate.
When they once determine to give life, they give every thing with it, which in their apprehension, belongs to it. From every enquiry that has been made, it appears — that no
woman thus saved is preserved from base motives, or need fear the violation of her
honor. No child is otherwise treated by the persons adopting it than the children of their
own body. The perpetual slavery of those captivated in war, is a notion which even their
barbarity has not yet suggested to them. Every captive whom their affection, their ca-
price, or whatever else, leads them to save, is soon incorporated with them, and fares
alike with themselves. . . .

Among the children who had been carried off young, and had long lived with the
Indians, it is not to be expected that any marks of joy would appear on being restored
to their parents or relatives. Having been accustomed to look upon the Indians as the
only connexions they had, having been tenderly treated by them, and speaking their
language, it is no wonder that they considered their new state in the light of a captivity,
and parted from the savages with tears.

But it must not be denied that there were even some grown persons who showed
an unwillingness to return. The Shawnese were obliged to bind several of their prisoners and force them along to the camp; and some women, who had been delivered up,
afterwards found means to escape and run back to the Indian towns. Some, who could
not make their escape, clung to their savage acquaintance at parting, and continued
many days in bitter lamentations, even refusing sustenance.

For the honor of humanity, we would suppose those persons to have been of the
lowest rank, either bred up in ignorance and distressing penury, or who had lived so long
with the Indians as to forget all their former connexions. For, easy and unconstrained as
the savage life is, certainly it could never be put in competition with the blessings of
improved life and the light of religion, by any persons who have had the happiness of
enjoying, and the capacity of discerning, them. . . .

1. William Smith, *An Historical Account of the Expedition against the Ohio Indians, in the Year 1764, under the Command of Henry Bouquet* (Philadelphia, 1765), 26–29. Reproduced by University Microfilms of Ann Arbor, Michigan. See also Francis Parkman, *Historical Account of Bouquet's Expedition against the Ohio Indians in 1764* (Cincinnati: R. Clarke, 1868), xi–xvi; and J. C. Reeve, "Henry Bouquet, His Indian Campaigns," *Ohio Archaeological and Historical Quarterly* 26 (October 1917): 489–505.

II.7. Dunmore's War and Logan's Lament, 1774

Although the Royal Proclamation of 1763 sought to protect Indian tribal interests west of the Alleghenies at least temporarily from land-hungry settlers, and Bouquet's expedition the following year helped pacify the Ohio tribes, it was an uneasy peace that prevailed in the Ohio country in the decade that followed. The ten-thousand-man peacekeeping force that was to have been stationed in the mountains to keep the races apart failed to materialize, the consequence of colonial boycotts and protests that effectively nulled the taxes levied in London to pay for it. Without the means of enforcement, the restrictions imposed by the proclamation soon proved meaningless, except as an irritating reminder of the subordinate role of the colonies and colonists in the British Empire. Among those from the East who soon crossed the mountains into the Ohio country were land speculators eager to see the western lands opened to settlement. George Washington journeyed to the Ohio Valley in 1770 hoping to stake out ten thousand acres of some of the richest bottomland as his family's share in the Ohio Company of Virginia. Others who came included Moravian missionaries seeking to save souls among the Indians of the Muskingum and Tuscarawas valleys. There the mission settlements of Schoenbrunn and Gnadenhutten were established in 1772. Far more numerous were the squatters for whom the prospect on the Ohio frontier of a better life than they had realized in the settled areas of the East seemed particularly alluring.

With mounting numbers of whites crossing the mountains, it was only a question of time before a spark would touch off a new conflict in the ongoing struggle for control of the Ohio country. It came on 3 May 1774 at a place called Baker's Cabin on the Ohio River near the mouth of Yellow Creek. There the family of the Mingo Chief Logan, or Tahgajute, was murdered by a party of white traders following a drunken brawl. Almost alone among Ohio's Indian chiefs, Logan had refused to follow Pontiac in the rebellion of 1763 and had been stigmatized as the friend of white men as a consequence. Logan and the Mingo warriors of his village were off on a hunt at the time of the massacre. When they returned to find Logan's family murdered, they went on the warpath, seeking vengeance, and were soon joined by Chief Cornstalk and the Shawnees.

What followed has been called Dunmore's War because it was John Murray, the Earl of Dunmore, serving as royal governor of Virginia, who called out that colony's militia to put down the uprising. Though Logan personally took fifty scalps in seeking revenge, the Indian forces under Cornstalk were defeated in the only major battle of the war, fought at Point Pleasant at the mouth of the Kanawha River on 10 October 1774. In the peace conference that followed at Camp Charlotte on the Pickaway Plains, all the tribal leaders save Logan were on hand. Hearing that Logan had come as far as a great elm tree a half-dozen miles away, Dunmore sent one of his aides, Colonel John Gibson, to attempt to persuade the Mingo leader to come to the peace table. If anyone could convince Logan to come, it was Gibson. He had been one of the Indian captives repatriated by Bouquet at Coshocton in 1764. He was also Logan's brother-in-law, and Logan's sister, Gibson's wife, had been one of those murdered at Baker's Cabin. He shared Logan's grief.

Logan poured out his emotions to Gibson in explaining why he refused to come to Camp Charlotte in a lament that has echoed through the years, as attested by generations of school children around the world who memorized it. As an oration, Thomas Jefferson invited its comparison with anything from Cicero or Demosthenes.[1]

I appeal to any white man to say if ever he entered Logan's cabin hungry, and he gave him not meat; if ever he came cold and naked, and he clothed him not. During the last long and bloody war, Logan remained idle in his cabin, an advocate for peace. Such was my love for the whites, that my countrymen pointed as they passed by, and said, "Logan is the friend of white men." I had even thought to have lived with you, had it not been for the injuries of one man. Colonel Cresap,[2] the last spring, in cold blood, and unprovoked murdered all the relations of Logan, not even sparing my women and children. There was not a drop of my blood in the veins of any living creature. This called on me for revenge. I have sought it; I have killed many; I have fully glutted my vengeance. For my country I rejoice at the beams of peace; but do not harbour a thought that mine is the joy of fear. Logan never felt fear. He will not turn upon his heel to save his life. Who is there to mourn for Logan? Not one.

1. Thomas Jefferson, *The Speech of Logan* (New York, 1803), 4. See also Thomas Jefferson, *Notes on the State of Virginia* (Philadelphia, 1801), appendix; Reuben Gold Thwaites and Louise Phelps Kellogg, eds., *Documentary History of Dunmore's War, 1774* (Madison: Wisconsin Historical Society, 1905), 9-17; 246-47; 302-7; Howard Jones, "Logan and the Logan Elm," *Ohio Archaeological and Historical Publications* 32 (1923): 315-27.

2. Logan was mistaken. It was not Colonel Michael Cresap but rather Captain Daniel Greathouse who had been in charge of the party of whites involved in the murder of Logan's family.

II.8.   The Fort Gower Resolves, 1774

Even as the Virginia governor and Indian tribal leaders were meeting at Camp Charlotte on the Pickaway Plains to bring an end to Lord Dunmore's War, colonists on the eastern seaboard were protesting Britain's "Intolerable Acts" (directed primarily against Massachusetts as punishment for the Boston Tea Party) and also the Quebec Act. The latter, ending the restrictions imposed by the Royal Proclamation of 1763, antagonized many in Virginia, New York, Connecticut, and Massachusetts (all with claims on the Ohio country) by attaching the region between the Ohio River and the Great Lakes to the predominantly French province of Quebec (formerly New France). The First Continental Congress, organized to coordinate opposition to these unpopular and coercive British laws, began meeting in Phila-

delphia on 5 September 1774 and affirmed the right of the residents of the thirteen American seaboard colonies to "life, liberty, and property."

While returning to Virginia by way of Fort Gower, a frontier outpost at the mouth of the Hocking River, the militia forces of Lord Dunmore learned there of the actions taken by the Continental Congress. On 4 November 1774, the officers of the army "declared their allegiance to the just rights of America" in a series of resolves, or resolutions. "By signing the Fort Gower Resolves, the only colonial army in the field, although isolated on the Ohio frontier, declared itself to the protection of American liberty."[1]

RESOLVED, That we will bear the most faithful allegiance to His Majesty, King George the Third, whilst His Majesty delights to reign over a brave and free people; that we will, at the expense of life, and everything dear and valuable, exert ourselves in support of his crown, and the dignity of the British Empire. But as lovers of liberty, and attachment to the real interests and just rights of America outweigh every other consideration, we resolve that we will exert every power within us for the defense of American liberty, and for the support of her just rights and privileges; not in any precipitate, riotous or tumultuous manner, but when regularly called forth by the unanimous voice of our countrymen.

RESOLVED, That we entertain the greatest respect for His Excellency, the Right Honorable Lord Dunmore, who commanded the expedition against the Shawnees; and who, we are confident, underwent the great fatigue of this singular campaign from no other motive than the true interest of this country.

Signed by order and in behalf of the whole corps.

Benjamin Ashby Clerk.

1. Ohio American Revolution Bicentennial Commission, *Third Annual Report, July 1, 1974-June 30, 1975* (Columbus, 1975), appendix A. See also, "Unveiling of Tablet at Fort Gower," *Ohio Archaeological and Historical Publications* 33 (1924): 87-94.

II.9.   The Gnadenhutten Massacre, 1782

The role of the Ohio country in the American Revolution, while not major, was nonetheless important. Essentially pitting British, empire loyalists, and Indians against frontier settlers and patriot militia, the fighting was sporadic and waged over a large expanse of wilderness. Highlighted by the campaigns of George Rogers Clark, the sieges of Fort Laurens, and the battles of Piqua, Coshocton, and the Sandusky and Olentangy, it was also marked by one of the most tragic events in the history of Indian-white relations, the Gnadenhutten Massacre of 7-8 March 1782. Ninety-six mission Indians, neutrals in the fight between Britain and its colonies and schooled in the Moravian principle of nonviolence, were killed by Pennsylvania militiamen under the command of Captain David Williamson in the mistaken belief that some among them had taken up arms in support of the British.

Two weeks after the massacre the account of it reached the Moravian missionaries, John Heckewelder[1] *and David Zeisberger,*[2] *who with their families were on their way to Fort*

Detroit from Captives' Town on the Sandusky, having been summoned by the British commandant Major Arent Schuyler De Peyster. The grief of the two missionaries has echoed through the years.

Comments of John Heckewelder

Many of the Brethren and Sisters who were murdered were born of Christian Indian parents who were members of the church in Pennsylvania in 1763 and 1764. Here they were now murdered together with their children. The loving children! who had so harmoniously raised their voices in the Chapel, at their schools and in their parents' houses in singing praises to the Lord. Their tender years, innocent countenances and tears made no impression on these pretended white Christians. These children were all butchered with the rest!

Comments of David Zeisberger

The militia, some 200 in number, as we hear, came first to Gnadenhutten. A mile from town they met young Schebosh in the bush, whom they at once killed and scalped, and near by the houses, two friendly Indians, not belonging to us, but who had gone there with our people from Sandusky, among whom there were several other friends who perished likewise. Our Indians were mostly on the plantations and saw the militia come, but no one thought of fleeing, for they suspected no ill. The militia came to them and bade them come into the town, telling them no harm should befall them. They trusted and went, but were all bound, the men being put into one house, the women into another. . . . Then they began to sing hymns and spoke words of encouragement and consolation one to another until they were all slain, and Abraham was the first to be led out, but the others were killed in the house. The sisters also afterwards met the same fate, who also sang hymns together. Christina, the Mohican, who well understood German and English, fell upon her knees before the captain, begging for life, but got for answer that he could not help her. Two well-grown boys, who saw the whole thing and escaped, gave this information. One of these lay under the heaps of slain and was scalped, but finally came to himself and found opportunity to escape. The same did Jacob, Rachel's son, who was wonderfully rescued. For they came close upon him suddenly outside the town, so that he thought they must have seen him, but he crept into a thicket and escaped their hands. He went a long way about, and observed what went on. . . . The boy who was scalped and got away, said the blood flowed in streams in the house. They burned the dead bodies, together with the houses, which they set on fire. . . .

The militia separated the next day, one part going to Salem, the other to Schoenbrunn, where however, they found no one, although our Indians saw them in the town; . . .

1. William H. Rice, "The Rev. John Heckewelder," *Ohio Archaeological and Historical Publications* 7 (1899): 331–32.

2. Eugene F. Bliss, ed., *Diary of David Zeisberger, A Missionary among the Indians of Ohio* (Cincinnati: R. Clarke, 1885), 1:78–81. See also Earl P. Olmstead, *Blackcoats among the Delaware: David Zeisberger on the Ohio Frontier* (Kent: Kent State University Press, 1991), 54–56.

II.10. The Treaty of Paris, 1783

Independence of the thirteen colonies and the creation of a new nation, the United States of America, first set as a goal on 4 July 1776, became a reality on 3 September 1783 with the conclusion of a definitive treaty of peace at Paris. In large measure because of the battles and campaigns waged west of the Alleghenies during the American Revolution, it was agreed that the western boundary of the new nation should be the Mississippi River. The contest for control of the Ohio country was over.[1]

*I*t having pleased the Divine Providence to dispose the hearts of the most serene and most potent Prince George the Third, . . . and of the United States of America, to forget all past misunderstandings and differences that have unhappily interrupted the good correspondence and friendship which they mutually wish to restore; and to establish such a beneficial and satisfactory intercourse between the two countries, upon the ground of reciprocal advantages and mutual convenience, as may promote and secure to both perpetual peace and harmony: . . . have agreed upon and confirmed the following articles:

ARTICLE I.

His Britannic Majesty acknowledges the said United States, viz. New Hampshire, Massachusetts Bay, Rhode Island, and Providence Plantations, Connecticut, New York, New Jersey, Pennsylvania, Delaware, Maryland, Virginia, North Carolina, South Carolina, and Georgia, to be free, sovereign and independent States; that he treats with them as such, and for himself, his heirs and successors, relinquishes all claims to the Government, proprietary and territorial rights of the same, and every part thereof.

ARTICLE II.

[That] all disputes which might arise in future, on the subject of the boundaries of the said United States may be prevented, it is hereby agreed and declared, that the following are, and shall be their boundaries, viz.: From the northwest angle of Nova Scotia, viz.: that angle which is formed by a line drawn due north from the source of Saint Croix River to the Highlands; along the said Highlands which divide those rivers that empty themselves into the river St. Lawrence, from those which fall into the Atlantic Ocean, to the northwesternmost head of Connecticut River; thence down along the middle of that river, to the forty-fifth degree of north latitude; from thence, by a line due west on said latitude, until it strikes the river Iroquois or Cataraquy; thence along the middle of said river into Lake Ontario, through the middle of said lake until it strikes the communication by water between that lake and Lake Erie; thence along the middle of said communication into Lake Erie, through the middle of said lake until it arrives at the water communication between that lake and Lake Huron; thence along the middle of said water communication into the Lake Huron; thence through the middle of said lake to the water communication between that lake and Lake Superior; thence through Lake Superior northward of the Isles Royal and Phelipeaux, to the Long Lake; thence through the middle of said Long Lake, and the water communication between it and the Lake of the Woods, to the said Lake of the Woods; thence through the said lake to the most northwestern point thereof, and from thence on a due west course to the river Mississippi; thence by a line to be drawn along the middle of the said river Mississippi until it shall intersect the northernmost part of the thirty-first degree of north latitude. South, by a line to be drawn due east from the determination of the line last mentioned, in the latitude of thirty-one degrees north of the Equator, to the middle of the river Apalachicola or Catahouche; thence along the middle thereof to its junction with the Flint River; thence straight to the head of St. Mary's River; and thence down along the middle of St. Mary's River to the Atlantic Ocean. East, by a line to be drawn along the middle of the river St. Croix, from its mouth in the Bay of Fundy to its source, and from its source directly north to the aforesaid Highlands, which divide the rivers that fall into the Atlantic Ocean from those which fall into the river St. Lawrence; comprehending all islands within twenty leagues of any part of the shores of the United States, and lying between lines to be drawn due east from the points where the aforesaid boundaries between Nova Scotia on the one part, and East Florida on the other, shall respectively touch the Bay of Fundy and the Atlantic Ocean; excepting such islands as now are, or heretofore have been, within the limits of the said province of Nova Scotia. . . .

ARTICLE VII.

There shall be a firm and perpetual peace between His Britannic Majesty and the said States, and between the subjects of the one and the citizens of the other, wherefore all hostilities, both by sea and land, shall from henceforth cease; All prisoners on both sides shall be set at liberty, and His Britannic Majesty shall, with all convenient speed, and without causing any destruction, or carrying away any negroes or other property of the American inhabitants, withdraw all his armies, garrisons and fleets from the said United States, and from every port, place, and harbour within the same; leaving in all fortifications the American artillery that may be therein; And shall also order and cause all archives, records, deeds, and papers, belonging to any of the said States, or their citizens, which, in the course of the war, may have fallen into the hands of his officers, to be forthwith restored and deliver'd to the proper States and persons to whom they belong.

ARTICLE VIII.

The navigation of the river Mississippi, from its source to the ocean, shall forever remain free and open to the subjects of Great Britain, and the citizens of the United States. . . .

Done at Paris, this third day of September, in the year of our Lord one thousand seven hundred and eighty-three.

> D. HARTLEY.
> JOHN ADAMS.
> B. FRANKLIN.
> JOHN JAY.

1. U.S. Sen. Doc. no. 36, *Treaties and Conventions Concluded between the United States of America and Other Powers, Since July 4, 1776* (Washington, 1871), 314–18.

III. An "Empire of Liberty"
Planning the Growth of a New Nation

EVEN BEFORE THE AMERICAN REVOLUTION had ended, it was evident that many questions had to be addressed concerning the future of the lands west of the Allegheny Mountains. Would these western lands "belong" to the new nation and be subject to the control of Congress, or would they "belong" to individual states in accord with their colonial charters? That this was a thorny issue was evident in the lengthy delay experienced in the ratification of the Articles of Confederation. The states without western land claims — Maryland, Delaware, Rhode Island, New Jersey, Pennsylvania, and New Hampshire — insisted that a condition of ratification ought to be the surrender of state claims on western lands to the proposed new central government, with proceeds from their eventual sale accruing to the benefit of all thirteen states and not just to the seven holding those claims — Massachusetts, Connecticut, New York, Virginia, North and South Carolina, and Georgia. Only when the seven with claims promised to eventually surrender them to the central authority pending the final outcome of the war were the Articles of Confederation finally ratified in 1781, more than four years after their formulation. Even then, two states — Virginia and Connecticut — held out for special concessions after the war and were permitted to retain a Military District and a Western Reserve in southern and northeastern Ohio respectively.

Once state claims had been resolved, plans for the survey, sale, and settlement of the western lands and a policy for their subsequent relationship to the states already in the union had to be developed. Proposing an "Empire of Liberty" for the area between the Alleghenies and the Mississippi, Thomas Jefferson devised a plan for the creation of sixteen new states, ten of which were to be located north of the Ohio and named Metropotamia, Sylvania, Illinoia, Michigania, Assenisipia, Polypotamia, Cherronesus, Pelisipia, Washington, and Saratoga. Jefferson's proposal also called for a rectangular grid to define the contiguous boundaries of the new states without regard to natural physiographic features such as lakes and rivers, this in an effort to get land sales under way as quickly as possible in order to provide financial support for the infant nation. A modified version of Jefferson's plan was adopted by the Congress in April 1784 as the

Report of Government for the Western Territory, more familiarly known as the Ordinance of 1784.

Drawing on Jefferson's plan for a rectangular survey of the western lands but with due recognition of the importance of natural boundaries, a land ordinance was approved by Congress in 1785 that superseded the survey provisions of the Ordinance of 1784. It called for a rectangular survey of the lands north and west of the Ohio River into ranges, townships, and sections, beginning at the point of intersection of that river with the western boundary of the state of Pennsylvania. Each range was to be six miles wide, each township six miles square, and each section one mile square. Ranges were to be numbered consecutively westward, beginning at the Pennsylvania border; townships were to be numbered consecutively northward, beginning at the Ohio River. Land was to be sold at auction, but not for less than one dollar per acre and in amounts not less than one full section, or 640 acres.

Soon evident after the adoption of the Land Ordinance of 1785 by the Congress was the inability of most individual settlers to come up with the minimum necessary ($640) to buy land directly from the federal government. It was not long before joint-stock companies emerged to raise capital through the sale of shares of stock, capital that could then be used to buy western lands from the federal government in large blocks of a million or more acres, at discounted prices, which could then be sold in small tracts at inflated prices but at a total price within reach of most prospective settlers.

A further question also demanded an answer. What would be the status of those who might buy land and move across the mountains to the area north and west of the Ohio River? Would they enjoy the same rights and privileges of citizenship as those remaining behind in the East, or would they occupy a subordinate status comparable to that which the colonists had known in the British Empire? The answer to that question came in 1787 with passage by the Congress of the Northwest Ordinance, which, with its six articles of compact, assured guarantees of individual rights and freedoms for those coming into the area north and west of the Ohio River (to be called the Northwest Territory) that were not yet assured even to most of the inhabitants of the settled eastern coast.

With the passage of the Land Ordinance of 1785 and the Northwest Ordinance of 1787, and with the encouragement of land companies such as the Ohio Company of Associates (of Massachusetts) and the Symmes Purchase Group (of New Jersey), it was not long before settlers in steadily increasing numbers were crossing the mountains and the river with permanent communities such as Marietta and Cincinnati emerging in the Ohio Valley.

III.1. The Congressional Resolution on the Public Lands in the West, 1780

After years of bickering over the question of federal versus state control over the lands west of the Alleghenies, the Continental Congress on 10 October 1780, on a motion made by the delegates of Virginia, adopted a policy that it proposed to follow respecting any western lands ceded to it by the states.[1] *This marked a breakthrough in the impasse between those states with western land claims and those without. When Maryland, the thirteenth and final state to ratify the Articles of Confederation, did so on 1 March 1781, a long step toward a truly United States of America was taken.*

Resolved, That the unappropriated lands that may be ceded or relinquished to the United States, by any particular states, pursuant to the recommendation of Congress of the 6 day of September last, shall be disposed of for the common benefit of the United States and be settled and formed into distinct republican states, which shall become members of the federal union, and have the same rights of sovereignty, freedom and independence, as the other states: that each state which shall be so formed shall contain a suitable extent of territory, not less than one hundred nor more than one hundred and fifty miles square, or as near thereto as circumstances will admit;

That the necessary and reasonable expences which any particular state shall have incurred since the commencement of the present war, in subduing any of the British posts, or in maintaining forts or garrisons within and for the defence, or in acquiring any part of the territory that may be ceded or relinquished to the United States, shall be reimbursed;

That the said lands shall be granted and settled at such times and under regulations as shall hereafter be agreed on by the United States in Congress assembled, or any nine or more of them.

1. Gaillard Hunt, ed., *Journals of the Continental Congress, 1774–1789* (Washington, 1910), 18:915.

III.2. Virginia Cedes Its Western Lands but Retains a Military District or "Bounty Lands," 1783

Four states—Virginia, Massachusetts, Connecticut, and New York—had claims on the Ohio country arising from their colonial charters granted in the seventeenth century by the British Crown. The first three were sea-to-sea in nature, while the fourth, that of New York, included the lands conquered and occupied by the Iroquois during and after the Beaver Wars. The most tenuous of all, New York's claims were ceded to the Congress in 1785 following resolution of a boundary dispute between that state and its neighbor, Massachusetts, in the western Berkshires. The claims of Connecticut (to northern Ohio) and Virginia (to southern Ohio), however, were more substantial, had greater economic potential, and were thus more consequential in their resolution.

Of all the states with interest in the Ohio country, Virginia had claims that were the oldest (dating back to the charter of 1609) and the most extensive (arising from the Ohio Company's contract of 1748, the colony's unilateral involvement in Lord Dunmore's War, as well as the several campaigns of George Rogers Clark during the American Revolution). Led by such consummate nationalists as George Washington, Thomas Jefferson, James Madison, and James Monroe, Virginia's decision to surrender its western land claims to the new national government, albeit with the stipulation that the area between the Scioto and Little Miami Rivers be retained under its control as a Military District, or "Bounty Lands," was of enormous significance to the future of the nation.

On 20 December 1783, the legislature of Virginia passed an act authorizing the delegates of that state to the Continental Congress (Thomas Jefferson, Samuel Hardy, Arthur Lee, and James Monroe) to convey to the United States all the rights of that commonwealth to the territory north and west of the Ohio River, but with the stipulation of the set-aside of a Military District.[1] *On 1 March 1784, the agreement was consummated in the Congress.*

Virginia Act of Cession—20 December 1783

Section 1. Whereas the Congress of the United States did, by their act of the 6th day of September, in the year 1780, recommend to the several States in the Union, having claims to waste and unappropriated lands in the western country, a liberal cession to the United States of a portion of their respective claims for the common benefit of the Union:

Section 2. And whereas this commonwealth did, on the 2d day of January, in the year 1781, yield to the Congress of the United States, for the benefit of the said States, all right, title, and claim which the said commonwealth had to the territory northwest of the river Ohio, subject to the conditions annexed to the said act of cession:

Section 3. And whereas the United States in Congress assembled have, by their act of the 13th of September last, stipulated the terms on which they agree to accept the cession of this State, should the legislature approve thereof, which terms, although they do not come fully up to the propositions of this commonwealth, are conceived, on the whole, to approach so nearly to them as to induce this State to accept thereof, in full confidence that Congress will, in justice to this State for the liberal cession she hath made, earnestly press upon the other States claiming large tracts of waste and uncultivated territory the propriety of making cessions equally liberal for the common benefit and support of the Union:

Be it enacted by the general assembly, That it shall and may be lawful for the delegates of this State to the Congress of the United States, or such of them as shall be assembled in Congress, and the said delegates, or such of them so assembled, are hereby fully authorized and empowered, for and on behalf of this State, by proper deeds or instrument in writing, under their hands and seals, to convey, transfer, assign, and make over unto the United States, in Congress assembled, for the benefit of the said States, all right, title, and claim, as well of soil as jurisdiction, which this commonwealth hath to the territory or tract of country within the limits of the Virginia charter, situate, lying, and being to the northwest of the river Ohio, subject to the terms and conditions contained in the before-recited act of Congress of the 13th day of September last, that is to say: Upon condition that the territory so ceded shall be laid out and formed into States, containing a suitable extent of territory, not less than one hundred nor more than one hundred and fifty miles square, or as near thereto as circumstances will admit; and that the States so formed shall be distinct republican States, and admitted members of the Federal Union, having the same rights of sovereignty, freedom, and independence as the other States; that the necessary and reasonable expenses incurred by this State in subduing any British posts, or in maintaining forts or garrisons within and for the defence, or in acquiring any part of the territory so ceded or relinquished, shall be fully reimbursed by the United States; and that one commissioner shall be appointed by Congress, one by this commonwealth, and another by those two commissioners, who, or a majority of them, shall be authorized and empowered to adjust and liquidate the account of the necessary and reasonable expenses incurred by this State, which they shall judge to be comprised within the intent and meaning of the act of Congress of the 10th of October, 1780, respecting such expenses. That the French and Canadian inhabitants, and other settlers of the Kaskaskies, Saint Vincents, and the neighboring villages, who have professed themselves citizens of Virginia, shall have their possessions and titles confirmed to them, and be protected in the enjoyment of their rights and liberties. That a quantity, not exceeding one hundred and fifty thousand acres, of land, promised by this State, shall be allowed and granted to the then Colonel, now General, George Rogers Clarke, and to the officers and soldiers of his regiment who marched with him when the posts of Kaskaskies and Saint Vincents were reduced, and to the officers and soldiers that have been since incorporated into the said regiment, to be laid off in one tract, the length of which not to exceed double the breadth, in such place on the northwest side of the Ohio as a majority of the officers shall choose, and to be afterwards divided among the said officers and soldiers in due proportion according to the laws of Virginia. That in case the quantity of good lands on the southeast side of the Ohio, upon the waters of Cumberland River, and between the Green River and Tennessee River, which have been reserved by law for the Virginia troops upon continental establishment, should, from the North Carolina line bearing in further upon the Cumberland lands than was expected, prove insufficient for their legal bounties, the deficiency should be made up to the said troops in good lands, to be laid off between the rivers Scioto and Little Miami, on the northwest side of the river Ohio, in such proportions as have been engaged to them by the laws of Virginia. That all the lands within the territory so ceded to the United States, and not reserved for or appropriated to any of the before-mentioned purposes, or disposed of in bounties to the officers and soldiers of the American Army, shall be considered as a common fund for the use and benefit of such of the United States as have become, or shall become members of the confederation or federal alliance of the said States, Virginia inclusive, according to their usual respective proportions in the general charge and expenditure, and shall be faithfully and bona fide disposed of for that purpose, and for no other use or purpose whatsoever: Provided, That the trust hereby reposed in the delegates of this State shall not be executed unless three of them, at least, are present in Congress.

1. Francis N. Thorpe, ed., *The Federal and State Constitutions, Colonial Charters, and Other Organic Laws* (Washington, 1909), 2:955-56.

III.3. Connecticut Retains a Western Reserve and Creates the "Firelands"

While southern Ohio between the Scioto and Little Miami Rivers bears the unmistakable stamp of the "Bounty Lands" or Military District of Virginia, northeastern Ohio to this day reflects the heritage of New England and most particularly Connecticut. Evidenced in the white spires of Congregational churches, village greens, and the names of many communities, much of the area has often been called "more Connecticut than Connecticut itself." This is not by accident, for when Congress agreed to a cession of Connecticut's western lands in 1786, it recognized the right of that state to reserve for itself a 120-mile-wide parcel of land westward from the Pennsylvania border, bounded by Lake Erie to the north and the forty-first parallel to the south. Called variously "New Connecticut" and the "Connecticut Western Reserve," it would come to be known in Ohio as simply the "Western Reserve."

Of the more than three million acres of the Reserve, the westernmost five hundred thousand acres was set aside by Connecticut in 1792 as the "Firelands" for the relief of those residents of seaboard towns whose homes had been burned and other property destroyed in British raids during the American Revolution. The rest of the Western Reserve was then sold by the state for $1.2 million on 2 September 1795 to the Connecticut Land Company, a group of thirty-five speculators headed by Oliver Phelps with Moses Cleaveland as general agent, the proceeds from the sale going into a permanent fund to support the public schools of Connecticut. Surveyed into five-mile ranges and townships rather than the six-mile pattern that characterized most of the rest of Ohio, Connecticut's Western Reserve was virtually an independent state until 1800, when legal jurisdiction was finally relinquished by Connecticut to the Congress of the United States.

Retaining a Western Reserve

By a deed of cession, September 14, 1786, Connecticut gave up to the Congress . . . all the right, title, interest, jurisdiction, and claim of the State of Connecticut to certain western lands beginning at the completion of the forty-first degree of north latitude one hundred and twenty miles west of the western boundary line of Pennsylvania as now claimed by said Commonwealth; and from thence by a line drawn parallel to and one hundred and twenty miles west of said west line of Pennsylvania, and to continue north until it comes to forty-two degrees and two minutes north latitude.[1]

Creating the Firelands

The Connecticut General Assembly on May 10, 1792, took action in the form of the following grant:

Upon the memorial of the inhabitants of the towns of Fairfield and Norwalk, showing to this assembly that many of the inhabitants of said towns suffered great losses by the devastations of the enemy during the late war, praying a compensation therefor, and a report of a committee appointed by this assembly at this session held at Hartford, in May, 1791, to ascertain . . . the amount of the losses of said memorialists, and others under similar circumstances . . . and also to ascertain the advancements which have been made for sufferers by abatement of taxes or otherwise, and to report the same, with their opinion relative to the ways and means of affording . . . relief. . . .

Resolved, By this assembly, that there be and hereby are released and quit-claimed to the sufferers hereafter named . . . five hundred thousand acres of land belonging to this State, lying west of the State of Pennsylvania, and bounding northerly on the shore of Lake Erie, beginning at the West Line of said lands and extending eastward to a line running northerly and southerly parallel to the east line of said tract . . . and extending the whole width of such lands, and easterly so far as to make said quantity of five hundred thousand acres . . . to be divided to and among the said sufferers, and their legal representatives where they are dead, in proportion to the several sums annexed to their names, as follows in the annexed list. . . .[2]

1. See Harlan Hatcher, *The Western Reserve: The Story of New Connecticut in Ohio* (Kent: Kent State University Press, Ohio, 1991), 10.

2. See Clarence D. Laylin, "The Firelands Grant," *Ohio Archaeological and Historical Publications* 10 (1902): 439–40.

III.4. Thomas Jefferson and the Ordinance of 1784

With independence from Great Britain in 1783 came realization that the new United States of America constituted a foreign nation in the eyes of the former mother country, and that British mercantilistic policies that had formerly assured the thirteen colonies guaranteed markets for their raw materials now operated against them. In the meantime, the infant nation had the costs of self-government to bear, including the maintenance of an army and navy, the establishment of a postal system, and the construction of a network of roads. The most immediate prospect of raising necessary funds was not through taxation (anathema for most after their experience in the British Empire in the 1760s and 1770s). Rather, it was through land sales, particularly the lands west of the Alleghenies, that there appeared the best prospect of both early and sufficient income for the support of government and its services.

Since the adoption by the Continental Congress on 10 October 1780 of the Resolution on Public Lands proposed by Thomas Jefferson and the other Virginia delegates, the western land policy of the new nation had been based on three premises: that the western lands deeded over by the states should be disposed of for the common benefit of all of the United States; that they in turn should be settled and formed into distinct republican states with membership in the Federal Union; and that they should have the same rights of sovereignty, freedom, and independence as each of the other states, including the original thirteen. Continuing these themes for what he called an "Empire of Liberty" in the West, Jefferson proposed in 1784 a new ordinance to flesh out the details of how the evolution from territories to states might be accomplished. All of the land west of the Alleghenies to the Mississippi was to be divided into sixteen prospective states, ten of them north and west of the Ohio River, with names such as Assenisipia and Metropotamia. Because quick income was an immediate need, Jefferson also proposed to simply drop a grid over the entire area and, in checkerboard fashion, without regard for natural boundaries, accomplish the survey of the western lands in readiness for sale. Within each of the prospective states a temporary government would be established by Congress until a population of twenty thousand inhabitants had been achieved. Once that population was reached, an assembly could be elected and a nonvoting delegate sent to Congress. Then when a prospective state had a free population equal to that of the smallest of the thirteen original states, it was to be admitted to the Union as an equal with each of the other states.

Significantly, Jefferson's proposed ordinance included a provision, "That after the year 1800 there shall be neither slavery nor involuntary servitude in any of the sd. [said] states," a provision that was subsequently defeated in the Congress by a vote of seven states to six. Eliminated as well was his proposal for the creation of ten states north and west of the Ohio River, together with the names he would have given them. The result was a stripped-down version of Jefferson's proposed Ordinance of 1784 that finally did gain the approval of the Congress on 23 April 1784, and even that version was altered by the Land Ordinance of 1785 and then repealed by the Northwest Ordinance of 1787. Yet, as links in the continuing quest to assure self-government for the inhabitants of the territories of the United States and ultimate statehood for those territories, Jefferson's proposal and the subsequent Ordinance of 1784[1] were of major importance.

The Ordinance as Finally Adopted on 23 April 1784

Resolved, That so much of the territory ceded or to be ceded by individual states to the United States, as is already purchased or shall be purchased of the Indian inhabitants, and offered for sale by Congress, shall be divided into distinct states, in the following manner, as nearly as such cessions will admit; that is to say, by parallels of latitude, so that each State shall comprehend from north to south two degrees of latitude, beginning to count from the completion of forty-five degrees north of the equator; and by meridians of longitude, one of which shall pass through the lowest point of the rapids of Ohio, and the other through the western cape of the mouth of the Great Kanhaway: but the territory eastward of this last meridian, between the Ohio, Lake Erie and Pensylvania, shall be one State whatsoever may be its comprehension of latitude. That which may lie beyond the completion of the 45th degree between the said meridians, shall make part of the State adjoining it on the south: and that part of the Ohio, which is between the same meridians coinciding nearly with the parallel of 39° shall be substituted so far in lieu of that parallel as a boundary line.

That the settlers on any territory so purchased, and offered for sale, shall, either on their own petition or on the order of Congress, receive authority from them, with appointments of time and place, for their free males of full age within the limits of their State to meet together, for the purpose of establishing a temporary government, to adopt the constitution and laws of any one of the original States; so that such laws nevertheless shall be subject to alteration by their ordinary legislature; and to erect, subject to a like alteration, counties, townships, or other divisions, for the election of members for their legislature.

That when any such State shall have acquired twenty thousand free inhabitants, on giving due proof thereof to Congress, they shall receive from them authority with appointments of time and place, to call a convention of representatives to establish a permanent constitution and government for themselves. Provided that both the temporary and permanent governments be established on these principles as their basis:

First. That they shall for ever remain a part of this confederacy of the United States of America.

Second. That they shall be subject to the Articles of Confederation in all those cases in which the original states shall be so subject, and to all the acts and ordinances of the United States in Congress assembled, conformable thereto.

Third. That they in no case shall interfere with the primary disposal of the soil by the United States in Congress assembled, nor with the ordinances and regulations which Congress may find necessary, for securing the title in such soil to the bona fide purchasers.

Fourth. That they shall be subject to pay a part of the federal debts contracted or to be contracted, to be apportioned on them by Congress, according to the same common rule and measure by which apportionments thereof shall be made on the other states.

Fifth. That no tax shall be imposed on lands, the property of the United States.

Sixth. That their respective governments shall be republican.

Seventh. That the lands of non-resident proprietors shall, in no case, be taxed higher than those of residents within any new State, before the admission thereof to a vote by its delegates in Congress.

That whensoever any of the said states shall have, of free inhabitants, as many as shall then be in any one of the least numerous of the thirteen Original states, such State shall be admitted by its delegates into the Congress of the United States, on an equal footing with the said original states; provided the consent of so many states in Congress is first obtained as may at the time be competent to such admission. And in order to adapt the said Articles of Confederation to the state of Congress when its numbers shall be thus increased, it shall be proposed to the legislatures of the states, originally parties thereto, to require the assent of two-thirds of the United States in Congress assembled, in all those cases wherein, by the said articles, the assent of nine states is now required, which being agreed to by them, shall be binding on the new states. Until such admission by their delegates into Congress, any of the said states, after the establishment of their temporary government, shall have authority to keep a member in Congress, with a right of debating but not of voting. . . .

1. See Gaillard Hunt, ed., *Journals of the Continental Congress, 1774–1789* (Washington, 1784), 26:275–79; also, John Porter Bloom, ed., *The American Territorial System* (Athens: Ohio University Press, 1973), 5:23–33, and Henry Steele Commager, ed., *Documents of American History,* 7th ed. (New York: Appleton-Century-Crofts, 1963), 121–22.

III.5. The Land Ordinance of 1785

Jefferson's plan of 1784 for the rectangular survey of the western lands, including the ultimate creation of a number of rectangular states without regard for natural boundaries, while flawed, still possessed considerable merit. In striking contrast to what would take place in the Virginia Military District, where that state's revolutionary war veterans could establish land claims of every conceivable configuration (usually but not always following the twists and turns of creeks and rivers along whose banks could be found the most fertile bottomlands), Jefferson envisioned for the rest of the west an orderly and easily understood survey of the land along straight north-south and east-west lines. Once surveyed the land would be opened for sale, the proceeds to help finance the new nation, which in turn would grow with new states emerging from the influx of settlers onto the land.

Combining Jefferson's plan for a rectangular survey with realistic appreciation of the need to recognize the importance of natural boundaries such as major rivers and lakes, the Congress on 20 May 1785 adopted a land ordinance that would lay the foundation for the public land system not only for Ohio but ultimately for most of the rest of the west. Beginning at the intersection of the western border of Pennsylvania with the Ohio River, it called for a survey of the land into ranges six miles wide, townships within each range six miles square, and sections within each township one mile square (or 640 acres), each range, township, and section to be numbered in orderly sequence. The ordinance has left as its legacy the checkerboard appearance of our landscape to this day.

Significantly, the Ordinance of 1785 set aside Section 16 of each township for the support of public schools and four other sections (8, 11, 26, and 29) for future sale, when their value would be enhanced by the development of the property around them. Clearly, in foresight and enduring impact the Land Ordinance of 1785[1] constituted one of the most significant legislative enactments of the Congress operating under the Articles of Confederation.

An Ordinance for ascertaining the mode of disposing of Lands in the Western Territory.

*B*e it ordained by the United States in Congress assembled, that the territory ceded by individual States to the United States, which has been purchased of the Indian inhabitants, shall be disposed of in the following manner:

A surveyor from each state shall be appointed by Congress, or a committee of the States, who shall take an Oath for the faithful discharge of his duty, before the Geographer of the United States, who is hereby empowered and directed to administer the same; and the like oath shall be administered to each carrier, by the surveyor under whom he acts. . . .

The Surveyors, as they are respectively qualified, shall proceed to divide the said territory into townships of six miles square, by lines running due north and south, and others crossing these at right angles, as near as may be, unless where the boundaries of the late Indian purchases may render the same impracticable, and then they shall depart from this rule no farther than such particular circumstances may require; and each surveyor shall be allowed and paid at the rate of two dollars for every mile, in length, he shall run, including the wages of chain carriers, markers, and every other expense attending the same.

The first line, running north and south as aforesaid, shall begin on the river Ohio, at a point that shall be found to be due north from the western termination of a line, which has been run as the southern boundary of the state of Pennsylvania; and the first line, running east and west, shall begin at the same point, and shall extend throughout the whole territory. Provided, that nothing herein shall be construed, as fixing the western boundary of the state of Pennsylvania. The geographer shall designate the townships, or fractional parts of townships, by numbers progressively from south to north; always beginning each range with number one; and the ranges shall be distinguished by their progressive numbers to the westward. The first range, extending from the Ohio to the lake Erie, being marked number one. The Geographer shall personally attend to the running of the first east and west line; and shall take the latitude of the extremes of the first north and south line, and of the mouths of the principal rivers.

The lines shall be measured with a chain; shall be plainly marked by chaps on the trees, and exactly described on a plat; whereon shall be noted by the surveyor, at their proper distances, all mines, salt springs, salt licks and mill seats, that shall come to his knowledge, and all water courses, mountains and other remarkable and permanent things, over and near which such lines shall pass, and also the quality of the lands.

The plats of the townships respectively, shall be marked by subdivisions into lots of one mile square, or 640 acres, in the same direction as the external lines, and numbered from 1 to 36; always beginning the succeeding range of the lots with the number next to that with which the preceding one concluded. And where, from the causes before mentioned, only a fractional part of a township shall be surveyed, the lots, protracted thereon, shall bear the same numbers as if the township had been entire. . . .

As soon as seven ranges of townships, and fractional parts of townships, in the direction from south to north, shall have been surveyed, the geographer shall transmit plats thereof to the board of treasury, who shall record the same, with the report, in well bound books to be kept for that purpose. And the geographer shall make similar returns, from time to time, of every seven ranges as they may be surveyed. The Secretary at War shall have recourse thereto, and shall take by lot therefrom, a number of townships, and fractional parts of townships, as well from those to be sold entire as from those to be sold in lots, as will be equal to one seventh part of the whole of such seven ranges, as nearly as may be, for the use of the late continental army; . . .

There shall be reserved for the United States out of every township, the four lots, being numbered 8, 11, 26, 29, and out of every fractional part of a township, so many lots of the same numbers as shall be found thereon, for future sale. There shall be reserved the lot No. 16, of every township, for the maintenance of public schools, within the said township; also one third part of all gold, silver, lead and copper mines, to be sold, or otherwise disposed of as Congress shall hereafter direct. . . .

And whereas Congress, by their resolutions of September 16 and 18 in the year 1776, and the 12th of August, 1780, stipulated grants of land to certain officers and soldiers of the late continental army, . . . for complying therefore with such engagements,

Be it ordained, That the secretary at war, from the returns in his office, or such other sufficient evidence as the nature of the case may admit, determine who are the objects of the above resolutions and engagements, and the quantity of land to which such persons or their representatives are respectively entitled, and cause the townships, or fractional parts of townships, hereinbefore reserved for the use of the late continental army, to be drawn for in such manner as he shall deem expedient, to answer the purpose of an impartial distribution. . . .

And be it further Ordained, That the towns of Gnadenhutten, Schoenbrun and Salem, on the Muskingum, and so much of the lands adjoining to the said towns, with the buildings and improvements thereon, shall be reserved for the sole use of the Christian Indians, who were formerly settled there, or the remains of that society, as may, in the judgment of the Geographer, be sufficient for them to cultivate.

Saving and reserving always, to all officers and soldiers entitled to lands on the northwest side of the Ohio, by donation or bounty from the commonwealth of Virginia, and to all persons claiming under them, all rights to which they are so entitled, under the deed of cession executed by the delegates for the state of Virginia, on the first day of March, 1784, and the act of Congress accepting the same: and to the end, that the said rights may be fully and effectually secured, according to the true intent and meaning of the said deed of cession and act aforesaid, Be it Ordained, that no part of the land included between the rivers called little Miami and Sciota, on the northwest side of the river Ohio, be sold, or in any manner alienated, until there shall first have been laid off and appropriated for the said Officers and Soldiers, and persons claiming under them, the lands they are entitled to, agreeably to the said deed of cession and act of Congress accepting the same. . . .

1. See John C. Fitzpatrick, ed., *Journals of the Continental Congress, 1774–1789* (Washington, 1933), 28 (1785): 375–81.

III.6. The Northwest Ordinance of 1787

Of the hundreds of documents in America's long history that are significant, only a handful can be called truly fundamental. The three most fundamental in the formation of the American nation were the Declaration of Independence, the United States Constitution, and the Northwest Ordinance. Adopted by the Continental Congress on 13 July 1787, the Northwest Ordinance[1] provided the plan by which the new nation could grow, from a small cluster of thirteen eastern seaboard states to a world power of fifty. Though specifically written for the territory north and west of the Ohio River, from which no fewer than three nor more than five states were to emerge, it established the pattern by which subsequent states could be added from other territories of the nation, across the continent and beyond, a pattern or plan that still lives.

Drawing on the principles enunciated in the Resolution on Public Lands adopted by the Congress on 10 October 1780 and reaffirmed and extended in the Ordinance of 1784, the Northwest Ordinance constituted what some historians have called the most magnani-

mous colonial policy the world had ever seen. After more than a century and a half of dependent status in the British Empire, the new nation was determined not to hold its colonies in perpetual subservience to the mother country of thirteen original states. Indeed, it would not even use the detested words colonies and colonists, but rather would call its western lands territories and those who would occupy them settlers, and instead of a second-class status it would call for equality of the new states that would emerge from the territories with those states already in the Federal Union.

In six articles of compact, the Northwest Ordinance guaranteed rights and freedoms for those who would cross the mountains and the Ohio River into what was to be called the Northwest Territory, rights and freedoms that were not yet guaranteed even to all the residents of the original thirteen states. A mother country could not be more liberal than that! These articles — in effect the New World's very first Bill of Rights — included freedom of worship, trial by jury, proportionate representation of the people in an elected legislature, the right of daughters as well as sons to inherit the property of parents dying intestate, no cruel or unusual punishments, freedom from arbitrary arrest, sanctity of contracts, support of education, the right to travel on waterways (anticipating later roads and highways), and freedom from slavery or indentured servitude. By this ordinance, the Northwest Territory became the first land made free by the Congress of the United States. Under its provisions, five states, Ohio (1803), Indiana (1816), Illinois (1818), Michigan (1837), and Wisconsin (1848), as well as part of a sixth, Minnesota (1858), were brought into the Union. The symbolism of the Northwest Ordinance can be seen in the present American flag of fifty stars, each equal to each of the others, rather than a flag of thirteen large stars (representing the original mother country) surrounded by a galaxy of smaller, subordinate stars (representing the states subsequently added to the Union).

An Ordinance for the government of the territory of the United States northwest of the river Ohio.

Be it ordained by the United States in Congress assembled, That the said territory, for the purposes of temporary government, be one district, subject, however, to be divided into two districts, as future circumstances may, in the opinion of Congress, make it expedient.

Be it ordained by the authority aforesaid, That the estates, both of resident and nonresident proprietors in the said territory, dying intestate, shall descend to, and be distributed among their children, and the descendants of a deceased child, in equal parts; the descendants of a deceased child or grandchild to take the share of their deceased parent in equal parts among them: And where there shall be no children or descendants, then in equal parts to the next of kin in equal degree; and among collaterals, the children of a deceased brother or sister of the intestate shall have, in equal parts among them, their deceased parents' share; and there shall in no case be a distinction between kindred of the whole and half-blood; saving, in all cases, to the widow of the intestate her third part of the real estate for life, and one-third part of the personal estate; and this law relative to descents and dower, shall remain in full force until altered by the legislature of the district. And until the governor and judges shall adopt laws as herein-after mentioned, estates in the said territory may be devised or bequeathed by wills in writing, signed and sealed by him or her in whom the estate may be (being of full age), and attested by three witnesses; and real estates may be conveyed by lease and release, or bargain and sale, signed, sealed, and delivered by the person, being of full age, in whom the estate may be, and attested by two witnesses, provided such wills be duly proved, and such conveyances be acknowledged, or the execution thereof duly proved, and be recorded within one year after proper magistrates, courts, and registers shall be appointed for that purpose; and personal property may be transferred by delivery; saving, however to the French and Canadian inhabitants, and other settlers of the Kaskaskies, St. Vincents and the neighboring villages who have heretofore professed themselves citizens of Virginia, their laws and customs now in force among them, relative to the descent and conveyance, of property.

Be it ordained by the authority aforesaid, That there shall be appointed from time to time by Congress, a governor, whose commission shall continue in force for the term of three years, unless sooner revoked by Congress; he shall reside in the district, and have a freehold estate therein in 1,000 acres of land, while in the exercise of his office.

There shall be appointed from time to time by Congress, a secretary, whose commission shall continue in force for four years unless sooner revoked; he shall reside in the district, and have a freehold estate therein in 500 acres of land, while in the exercise of his office. It shall be his duty to keep and preserve the acts and laws passed by the legislature, and the public records of the district, and the proceedings of the governor in his executive department, and transmit authentic copies of such acts and proceedings, every six months, to the Secretary of Congress: There shall also be appointed a court to consist of three judges, any two of whom to form a court, who shall have a common law jurisdiction, and reside in the district, and have each therein a freehold estate in 500 acres of land while in the exercise of their offices; and their commissions shall continue in force during good behavior.

The governor and judges, or a majority of them, shall adopt and publish in the district such laws of the original States, criminal and civil, as may be necessary and best suited to the circumstances of the district, and report them to Congress from time to time: which laws shall be in force in the district until the organization of the General Assembly therein, unless disapproved of by Congress; but afterwards the Legislature shall have authority to alter them as they shall think fit.

The governor, for the time being, shall be commander-in-chief of the militia, appoint and commission all officers in the same below the rank of general officers; all general officers shall be appointed and commissioned by Congress.

Previous to the organization of the general assembly, the governor shall appoint such magistrates and other civil officers in each county or township, as he shall find necessary for the preservation of the peace and good order in the same: After the general assembly shall be organized, the powers and duties of the magistrates and other civil officers shall be regulated and defined by the said assembly; but all magistrates and other civil officers not herein otherwise directed, shall, during the continuance of this temporary government, be appointed by the governor.

For the prevention of crimes and injuries, the laws to be adopted or made shall have force in all parts of the district, and for the execution of process, criminal and civil, the governor shall make proper divisions thereof; and he shall proceed from time to time as circumstances may require, to lay out the parts of the district in which the Indian titles shall have been extinguished, into counties and townships, subject however to such alterations as may thereafter be made by the legislature.

So soon as there shall be five thousand free male inhabitants of full age in the district, upon giving proof thereof to the governor, they shall receive authority, with time and place, to elect representatives from their counties or townships to represent them in the general assembly: *Provided*, That, for every five hundred free male inhabitants, there shall be one representative, and so on progressively with the number of free male inhabitants shall the right of representation increase, until the number of representatives shall amount to twenty-five; after which, the number and proportion of representatives shall be regulated by the legislature: *Provided*, That no person be eligible or qualified to act as a representative unless he shall have been a citizen of one of the United States three years, and be a resident in the district, or unless he shall have resided in the district three years; and, in either case, shall likewise hold in his own right, in fee simple, two hundred acres of land within the same: *Provided, also,* That a freehold in fifty acres of land in the district, having been a citizen of one of the states, and being resident in the district, or the like freehold and two years residence in the district, shall be necessary to qualify a man as an elector of a representative.

The representatives thus elected, shall serve for the term of two years; and, in case of the death of a representative, or removal from office, the governor shall issue a writ to the county or township for which he was a member, to elect another in his stead, to serve for the residue of the term.

The general assembly, or legislature, shall consist of the governor, legislative council, and a house of representatives. The legislative council shall consist of five members, to continue in office five years, unless sooner removed by Congress; and three of whom to be a quorum: and the members of the council shall be nominated and appointed in the following manner, to wit: As soon as representatives shall be elected, the governor shall appoint a time and place for them to meet together; and, when met, they shall nominate ten persons, residents in the district, and each possessed of a freehold in five hundred acres of land, and return their names to Congress; five of whom Congress shall appoint and commission to serve as aforesaid; and, whenever a vacancy shall happen in the council, by death or removal from office, the house of representatives shall nominate two persons, qualified as aforesaid, for each vacancy, and return their names to Congress; one of whom Congress shall appoint and commission for the residue of the term. And every five years, four months at least before the expiration of the time of service of the members of the council, the said house shall nominate ten persons, qualified as aforesaid, and return their names to Congress; five of whom Congress shall appoint and commission to serve as members of the council five years, unless sooner removed. And the governor, legislative council, and house of representatives, shall have authority to make laws in all cases, for the good government of the district, not repugnant to the principles and articles in this ordinance established and declared. And all bills, having passed by a majority in the house, and by a majority in the council, shall be referred to the governor for his assent; but no bill, or legislative act whatever, shall be of any force without his assent. The governor shall have power to convene, prorogue, and dissolve the general assembly, when, in his opinion, it shall be expedient.

The governor, judges, legislative council, secretary, and such other officers as Congress shall appoint in the district, shall take an oath or affirmation of fidelity and of office; the governor before the president of congress, and all other officers before the governor. As soon as a legislature shall be formed in the district, the council and house assembled, in one room, shall have authority, by joint ballot, to elect a delegate to Congress, who shall have a seat in Congress, with a right of debating but not of voting during this temporary government.

And, for extending the fundamental principles of civil and religious liberty, which form the basis whereon these republics, their laws and constitutions are erected; to fix and establish those principles as the basis of all laws, constitutions, and governments, which forever hereafter shall be formed in the said territory; to provide, also, for the establishment of States, and permanent government therein, and for their admission to a share in the Federal councils on an equal footing with the original States, at as early periods as may be consistent with the general interest:

It is hereby ordained and declared, . . . That the following articles shall be considered as articles of compact between the original States and the people and States in the said territory and forever remain unalterable, unless by common consent, to wit:

ARTICLE I

No person, demeaning himself in a peaceable and orderly manner, shall ever be molested on account of his mode of worship or religious sentiments, in the said territory.

ARTICLE II

The inhabitants of the said territory shall always be entitled to the benefits of the writ of *habeas corpus,* and of the trial by jury; of a proportionate representation of the people in the legislature; and of judicial proceedings according to the course of the common law. All persons shall be bailable, unless for capital offences, where the proof shall be evident or the presumption great. All fines shall be moderate; and no cruel or unusual punishments shall be inflicted. No man shall be deprived of his liberty or property, but by the judgment of his peers or the law of the land; and, should the public exigencies make it necessary, for the common preservation, to take any person's property, or to demand his particular services, full compensation shall be made for the same. And, in the just preservation of rights and property, it is understood and declared, that no law ought ever to be made, or have force in the said territory, that shall, in any manner whatever, interfere with or affect private contracts or engagements, *bona fide,* and without fraud, previously formed.

ARTICLE III

Religion, morality, and knowledge, being necessary to good government and the happiness of mankind, schools and the means of education shall forever be encouraged. The utmost good faith shall always be observed towards the Indians; their lands and property shall never be taken from them without their consent; and, in their property, rights, and liberty, they shall never be invaded or disturbed, unless in just and lawful wars authorized by Congress; but laws founded in justice and humanity, shall from time to time be made for preventing wrongs being done to them, and for preserving peace and friendship with them.

ARTICLE IV

The said territory, and the States which may be formed therein, shall forever remain a part of this Confederacy of the United States of America, subject to the Articles of Confederation, and to such alterations therein as shall be constitutionally made; and to all the acts and ordinances of the United States in Congress assembled, conformable thereto. The inhabitants and settlers in the said territory shall be subject to pay a part of the federal debts contracted or to be contracted, and a proportional part of the expenses of government, to be apportioned on them by Congress according to the same common rule and measure by which apportionments thereof shall be made on the other States; and the taxes for paying their proportion shall be laid and levied by the authority and direction of the legislatures of the district or districts, or new States, as in the original States, within the time agreed upon by the United States in Congress assembled. The legislatures of those districts or new States, shall never interfere with the primary disposal of the soil by the United States in Congress assembled, nor with any regulations Congress may find necessary for securing the title in such soil to the *bona fide* purchasers. No tax shall be imposed on lands the property of the United States; and, in no case, shall non-resident proprietors be taxed higher than residents. The navigable waters leading into the Mississippi and St. Lawrence, and the carrying places between the same, shall be common highways and forever free, as well to the inhabitants of the said territory as to the citizens of the United States, and those of any other States that may be admitted into the confederacy, without any tax, impost, or duty therefor.

ARTICLE V

There shall be formed in the said territory, not less than three nor more than five States; and the boundaries of the States, as soon as Virginia shall alter her act of cession, and consent to the same, shall become fixed and established as follows, to wit: The western State in the said territory, shall be bounded by the Mississippi, the Ohio, and Wabash Rivers; a direct line drawn from the Wabash and Post Vincents, due North, to the territorial line between the United States and Canada; and, by the said territorial line, to the Lake of the Woods and Mississippi. The middle State shall be bounded by the said direct line, the Wabash from Post Vincents to the Ohio, by the Ohio, by a direct line, drawn due north from the mouth of the Great Miami, to the said territorial line, and by the said territorial line. The eastern State shall be bounded by the last mentioned direct line, the Ohio, Pennsylvania, and the said territorial line: *Provided, however,* and it is further understood and declared, that the boundaries of these three States shall be subject so far to be altered, that if Congress shall hereafter find it expedient, they shall have authority to form one or two States in that part of the said territory which lies north of an east and west line drawn through the southerly bend or extreme of lake

Michigan. And, whenever any of the said States shall have sixty thousand free inhabitants therein, such State shall be admitted, by its delegates, into the Congress of the United States, on an equal footing with the original States in all respects whatever, and shall be at liberty to form a permanent constitution and State government: *Provided*, the constitution and government so to be formed, shall be republican, and in conformity to the principles contained in these articles; and, so far as it can be consistent with the general interest of the confederacy, such admission shall be allowed at an earlier period, and when there may be a less number of free inhabitants in the State than sixty thousand.

ARTICLE VI

There shall be neither slavery nor involuntary servitude in the said territory, otherwise than in the punishment of crimes whereof the party shall have been duly convicted: *Provided, always,* That any person escaping into the same, from whom labor or service is lawfully claimed in any one of the original States, such fugitive may be lawfully reclaimed and conveyed to the person claiming his or her labor or service as aforesaid.

Be it ordained by the authority aforesaid, That the resolutions of the 23rd of April 1784, relative to the subject of this ordinance, be, and the same are hereby repealed and declared null and void.

Done by the United States, in Congress assembled, the 13th day of July, in the year of our Lord one thousand seven hundred and eighty-seven, and of their sovereignty and independence the twelfth.

1. Francis N. Thorpe, ed., *The Federal and State Constitutions, Colonial Charters, and Other Organic Laws* (Washington, 1909), 2:957-62. See also Phillip R. Shriver, "Freedom's Proving Ground: The Heritage of the Northwest Ordinance," in Sherrod Brown, Secretary of State, *Manual of Ohio Government, 1989-1990* (Columbus, 1990), 35-44; and Robert F. Berkhofer Jr., "The Northwest Ordinance and the Principle of Territorial Evolution," in John Porter Bloom, ed., *The American Territorial System* (Athens: Ohio University Press, 1973), 5:45-52. Also, Henry Steele Commager, ed., *Documents of American History,* 7th ed. (New York: Appleton-Century-Crofts, 1963), 128-32.

III.7. Marietta, 1788: The Organized Settlement of the Northwest Territory Begins

Though several thousand squatters had already crossed the Ohio River, posing challenges to federal officers who had to try to remove them, it was with the passage of the Land Ordinance of 1785 and the Northwest Ordinance of 1787 that organized settlement of the Northwest Territory finally began. Because the Land Ordinance mandated the minimum sale of full sections of 640 acres at a price no lower than $1 per acre, and because most prospective settlers not only envisioned farms only a fraction that size but had little or no capacity to come up with a bid of at least $640 in federal auctions, the situation was made to order for the emergence of joint-stock companies capable of contracting with Congress for huge tracts of land of a million or more acres at discounted prices well below $1 per acre. As an example, if a settler *was only interested in a farm of 40 acres, a purchase price of $2 an acre set by a land company meant a cash outlay of only $80, far below the $640 required of an individual bidder to purchase land directly from the federal government. The settler benefited, the company was able to realize a profit, and the federal treasury was enhanced from sizable sales of land in a short period of time.*

First to appear among the speculative land companies was the Ohio Company of Associates. Organized by eleven men in a meeting at the Bunch of Grapes Tavern in Boston, Massachusetts, on 1 March 1786, it proposed to raise $1 million in Continental certificates through the sale of 1,000 shares of stock at $1,000 per share. Within a year 250 shares had been sold. A skillful lobbyist, the Reverend Manasseh Cutler then succeeded in prevailing on Congress to pass the Northwest Ordinance of 1787 with provisions particularly attractive to prospective settlers. By assuring the company's support of Arthur St. Clair, the presiding officer of the Congress, for the governorship of the Northwest Territory, and by combining forces with another speculative group, the Scioto Company, Cutler and the Ohio Company were able to obtain a much larger purchase of Ohio land than would otherwise have been possible. They bargained for 1.5 million acres for a purchase price of $1 million. When finally surveyed, their grant actually amounted to 1,781,760 acres, on both sides of the Muskingum River, between the seventh and seventeenth ranges. The first Seven Ranges, so named and earlier surveyed, were being sold in federal auction. On 7 April 1788, an advance party of forty-eight men led by General Rufus Putnam arrived at the mouth of the Muskingum, on the west bank of which was the small federal outpost named Fort Harmar. On the east bank they established the first organized settlement of the Northwest Territory, which they named "Marietta" in honor of the French queen, Marie Antoinette, whose country had aided the thirteen colonies to achieve their independence from England.

One of the early settlers in Marietta was Joseph Barker, who arrived with his family in the new frontier village on 1 November 1789 from New Hampshire. In 162 handwritten pages of reminiscences, now in the Marietta College Library, he has left an invaluable account of the formative years of the Ohio Company and Ohio's first organized settlement.[1]

. . . a meeting was held in Boston, March ye 1st, 1786 [by those officers and soldiers] who formed an association by the Name of the Ohio Company, who appointed five directors, a Treasurer, & Secretary. Another meeting was held the 29th of August which adjourned to the 21st of November, at which time they met at Bracketts Tavern in Boston.

At this meeting the directors & Agents of the Company Resolved that they would send out to the Muskingum four surveyors & twenty two Men: six Boat Builders, four House Carpenters, One Blacksmith, & nine common workman. That the Boat builders & men, with the Surveyors, be proprietors of the Company; that their tools, one ax & one hoe to each Man, & thirty pounds weight of Baggage, be carried in the Companies Waggons; & their subsistance on their Journey be furnished by the Company.

That each Man furnish himself with a good small arm, bayonet, 6 flints, a powder horn & pouch, priming wire & brush, half a pound of powder, one pound of balls, & one pound of Buckshot—be subject to the orders of the superintendent, & in case of interuption from an enemy, [be subject] to Military command, on forfit of their wages.

[That] Col° Ebenezer Sprat [Sproat] from Road Island, Anselm Tupper & John Mathews from Massachusetts, Col° R. J. Meigs from Connecticut [be] Surveyors.

That Gen¹ Rufus Putnam be the superintendent of all the business afforesaid, & he is to be Obeyed & respected accordingly.

That the Boat Builders shall proceed next Monday, & the surveyers rendezvous at Hartford, the first day of January, 1788 — on their way to the Muskingum.

Resolved that this meeting of Directors & Agents of the Ohio C° be hereby adjourned to the first monday of March, 1788, to be holden at Rices Tavern in the Town of Providence, State of Roade Island.

When the Men & meterial were collected Gen¹ Putnam moved on for the Muskingum. When near the Mountains he sent Major Haffield White forward to Sumrills Ferry, thirty miles above Pittsburg on the Yohiogany, with some Boat builders to procure Timber & Commence building a Boat. The Company arrived about three weeks after, but found nothing in forwardness for the Boat.

Gen¹ Putnam imployed Capᵗ Jonathan Devol, who had been engaged in Ship building in Rhoade Island, to take the charge of constructing a Boat forty five feet long, twelve feet wide; the bow was curved, strongly knee'd at the corners & otherwise substatially built, & covered with a roof like a House.

On the 7ᵗʰ of April, 1788, As the Boat was floating down along side of Kerrs Island, in the Morning, Capᵗ Devol said to Gen¹ Putnam, I think it time to take an observation. We must be not far from the mouth of the Muskingum — & directly they came in sight of Fort Harmer, but as the banks were thickley covered with trees, the mouth of the River was but dimly seen. They were too far advanced to make the upper point, so they floated on & Landed a little below Fort Harmer, towed the Boat back & across the River, and raised their Markee & tents on the upper point.

The surveyers immediately commenced work. Col° R. J. Meigs took the meanders of the Muskingum, the others surveying the small Lots; parties were sent out in the imploy of the Compʸ to examine & Report the best situations for settlements along the streams. They went in a Canoo, took provisions, cooking utentials — one [man] to keep Camp & Cook, & probably [a] hunter. These parties were composed promiscously of those belonging to the Compʸ & those Imigrants who subsequently arrived. On their report, settlements were platted which afterwards were surveyed into hundred Acre Lots & given to Actual setlers, agreeable to the Compʸˢ Resolution of Decemʳ, 1788, which express'd the conditions of the donation. . . .

On the first of November, 1789, the day I arrived, Ninety families had landed & associations amounting to 250 setlers had been formed, & improvements had commenced in many of them; & by May, 1790, there were very few Lots in Belprie & Newberry without a setler.

On a Return of all the Men enroled for Militia duty in the County, made to the secretary of War in March, 1791, their N° amounted to 195 — but often that I think the N° increased, & the hundred thousand acres Granted by Congress for Donation purposes induced many to remain, & many more to come in to avail themselves of the terms of the Donation. . . ."[2]

1. See George J. Blazier, ed., *Joseph Barker: Recollections of the First Settlement of Ohio* (Marietta: Richardson, 1958), 2–5.

2. The Donation Tract of 100,000 acres was set aside in the northeastern corner of the Ohio Company lands and was to be parceled out in grants of 100 acres to males eighteen years of age or older who were not stockholders in the company and who intended to be actual settlers. Designed to stimulate an immediate flow of 1,000 settlers onto Ohio Company lands, the lands were to be given without charge, but with a number of conditions attached before title could be received: a house at least twenty-four by eighteen feet had to be built; fifty apple or pear trees and twenty peach trees had to be planted within three years; fifteen acres had to be cleared for mowing or pasture; and another five acres had to be prepared for corn and other grains. If all these conditions were met within a time frame of five years, the settler would then receive title to the land. Understandably, with that much work invested in the property, few among those moving into the Donation Tract would be inclined to sell and move out very soon. Instead, many would encourage friends and relatives back home to come out to the Ohio Company lands in the Muskingum Valley.

III.8.   John Cleves Symmes and the Miami Purchase, 1788

Notable among the several land companies that bargained successfully with the Congress for the acquisition of major parcels of Ohio land in the Northwest Territory was one headed by John Cleves Symmes of New Jersey. Symmes, a Revolutionary War veteran, then an associate justice on the New Jersey Supreme Court, and later a member of the Continental Congress, received a charter from the latter body (at a time when conflict of interest was not an issue) on 15 October 1788, to develop a tract of land between the Little Miami and Great Miami Rivers known as the Miami Purchase. Appointed a judge for the Northwest Territory, also by the Congress, he proposed to develop a million acres in the Miami valleys for which he and his associates were to pay 66⅔ cents per acre. In his haste to get the Miami Purchase settled and his obligation to Congress paid off, he sold some of the land before legal titles had been cleared, a situation ultimately leading to nearly endless litigation. Notwithstanding, a second area of permanent, organized Ohio settlement soon appeared in the Miami valleys and along the Ohio River between them, with three distinct communities emerging in 1788 and 1789.

First among these was the village of Columbia, a mile west of the mouth of the Little Miami River near the present site of the Lunken airport. Part of a tract of twenty thousand acres purchased from Symmes by Benjamin Stites on 7 December 1787, as Miami Land Warrant No. 1, even before Symmes had received his charter from Congress, Columbia was settled by Stites and a party of twenty-six settlers from New Jersey and Pennsylvania on 18 November 1788.

The second settlement was organized by another New Jerseyan, Mathias Denman, and his partner, John Filson, a surveyor and Latin scholar, who, along with Robert Patterson, the founder of Lexington, Kentucky, selected a site of 747 acres directly across the Ohio River from the mouth of the Licking River of Kentucky. It was Filson who proposed its

name—*Losantiville*—*in Latin, the* ville *(city)* anti *(across from or before) the* os *(mouth)
of the L (or Licking River). On 28 December 1788, Patterson led the initial settlers, some
eleven families and twenty-four men, to Losantiville, a name that, after the disappearance
of John Filson (apparently the victim of an Indian attack), soon gave way to "Cincinnati,"
so named by Governor Arthur St. Clair, a proud member of the patriotic Society of Cincin-
natus, when he transferred his territorial capital from Marietta to Cincinnati in 1790.*

*The third settlement to appear in the Miami Purchase was one organized by Symmes
himself at the last northerly bend of the Ohio, west of Losantiville, or Cincinnati, before the
great river heads south and west toward its rendezvous with the Mississippi. Just east of the
mouth of the Great Miami River, North Bend (as Symmes named it) was settled by Symmes
and his family in early February 1789. Convinced that North Bend would become the hub
of the Northwest Territory, Symmes likened it and the rich farmland around it as "Egypt on
the Miami." Unfortunately, his dream would soon be complicated by strife between the
Indian peoples of the Miami valleys, who wanted to keep the land forever Indian, and the
land-hungry settlers streaming westward along the Ohio and its tributaries. Instead of "Egypt
on the Miami," the area would soon be dubbed the "Miami Slaughterhouse."*

*Conscious of both the promise and the problems of his Miami Purchase, Symmes sent
what was in effect a progress report in May 1789 to one of his New Jersey associates and principal investors in the Purchase, Congressman Jonathan Dayton. The youngest delegate to the
Constitutional Convention of 1787 at the age of twenty-six, Dayton would soon find his own
name associated with yet another key settlement at the junction of the Mad and Miami Rivers in the Miami Purchase. Symmes's report is revealing in the detail of the challenges and
opportunities in the developing Miami country on the eve of frontier war.*[1]

> The Honble Jonathan Dayton Esqr.
>   delegate in Congress, New York
>   Northbend, May the 18th 19th & 20th 1789.

Dear Sir,

I am sure that you begin to be impatient to hear from Miami. I shall therefore give
you a short history of my efforts to carry into effect what I had premised before I left
New Jersey, in the settleing of this purchase. In doing this I have not succeeded fully to
my expectation; but I am very far from despairing. . . .

This season was remarkable for the amazing high fresh [water level] which was in
the Ohio, being several feet higher than had been known since the white people had introduced themselves into Kentucky. I embarked with the bough of my boat even with
the high bank on which my house at that place is built. When we arrived at Columbia
I found the place deluged in water; but one house on a higher spot of ground escaped.
The soldiers had been drove from the ground floor of their blockhouse into the loft, and
from the loft into a boat which they had wisely preserved from the destruction of the
previous ice, and the then raging torrent of the Ohio.

We tarried but one night & proceeded to Losantiville. Here the water began to
ebb, tho the town had suffered nothing from the fresh. On the second of February I fell
down to this place whence I now write. From the time of my first arrival in September
last, I had remained in a great degree ignorant of the plot of ground at the old fort [Fort

Finney]. I had been but once on the spot; and then expecting so soon to return to Miami [Fort Washington], did not inform myself fully of the ground proposed for the City. Through the winter I had been frequently told that the point overflowed. Finding Columbia under water, I did not think it proper to go as far down as the old fort, before I had informed myself, whether the ground was eligible for a town or not. This together with two other considerations (viz) first, that of being more in the way of the surveyors who could not have access to me but at the trouble of walking ten miles farther in going down into the neck of land on which the old fort stands, and returning to the body of their work, than they otherwise would have occasion to do if I landed here. The other which in reality was the principal was this: From the river elevated as I was in my boat by the height of the water: I could observe that the riverhills appeared to fall away in such a manner that no considerable rise appeared between the Ohio and the great Miami. I knew the distance across the neck did not much, if any, exceed a mile to the great Miami, and flattered myself with the prospect of finding a good tract of ground extending from River to river, on which the City might be built, with more propriety than it would be to crowd it so far down in the point from the body of the country round it; I was for these reasons determined to make my first lodgement in the most northerly bend of the river where the distance is the least, and the lands the lowest over to the Miami; When I arrived at the place, the banks were inviting from their secure appearance from the then fresh in the Ohio. . . .

The extent of country spreading for many miles on both sides of the G. Miami, is beyond all dispute equal, I believe superior in point of soil, water & timber, to any tract of equal contents to be found in the United States. From this Egypt on Miami, in a very few years will be poured down its stream to the Ohio, the products of the country, from two hundred miles above the mouth of G. Miami; . . .

Amazing has been the pains which many in Kentucky have taken to prejudice strangers against the Miami settlements. The cause has principally been owing to the piques of disappointment. Last September many land-jobbers from Kentucky came into the purchase, and applied for lands; and actually pointed out on paper where they wished to take them. I gave them time to the first of November to make payment for one half; and to the present month of May for the other half. The surveying and registering fees was to be paid at the time of the first half.

Some of them agreed to give an advanced price in consideration that I would wait till May come twelve-months for the purchase money. this I was content to do on their paying the surveying fees by the first of November, and allowing interest on the principal sum until paid. After this the greater part of them deserted me when about forty miles up the Miami where I had ventured on their promise to escort me down that river, meandering its courses; which so disobliged me that I have been very indifferent ever since whether one of them came into the purchase or not; as I found them very ungovernable and seditious; not to be awed or persuaded. To the disobedience of these men I impute the death of poor Filson, who had no rest afterwards while with me for fear of the Indians. And at length attempting to escape to the body of men I had left on the Ohio, he was destroyed by the savages.

These pretending purchasers neglecting to pay me one farthing until January, and the surveying business suffering greatly by the want of the fees: I was induced to publish an advertisement in the Lexington gazette; requiring of all those purchasers payment of the surveying fees, by the first of february and of one half of the purchase money by the first of March. and the residue by the first of May ensuing, or I should consider all negotiations for land void wherein they did not comply herewith; or give the advanced price on a longer credit. Very few indeed have complied: the others have endeavoured to assperse my character, & throw the reasons of their noncompliance on me. But let the world judge whether it is even probable that they had either intention or ability to accomplish the payment for seventeen townships, the contents of what they had dextriously located as they called it in the space of a very few days. . . .

As to the quality of soil throughout the purchase, it is generally good, with a very few exceptions. The military range is held to be equal, if not better land than any range in the tract. There are very few hills after one leaves those of the Ohio: but large bodies of meadow land of excellent quality in many places. It is generally very well watered, as you will perceive by the map; not a stream being laid down therein but what the surveyors noted under oath in their field books as they ran the lines. A variety of stone is met with in the purchase: such as mill-stonerock, lime-stone, and a gray stone, flat & well formed for building. The timber is in many parts excellent; in some others but indifferent, owing to the soils being too rich. This may seem a paradox to you; but in this country on the richest soil grows the least useful timber. But what I call the beauty of the country is, the many pararies which lie in the neighbourhood of Mad river: these are at once without labour, proper for ploughing or mowing. Mad river itself is a natural curiosity, about six poles wide on an average and very deep, gliding along with the utmost rapidity: its waters are beautifully clear and deep, but confined for the most part within its banks. What can give its current such velocity in the midst of so level a country, is a matter of astonishment to all who beholds it. Some of the surveyors & others who went out about three weeks ago, returned lately to this, and reported to me, that they had explored the country as high as the tenth range; that it was a most agreeable country and tract of land, from one Miami to the other, interspersed with the plats of old Indian Towns, and fine streams of water proper for mill-building. That the head branches of the little Miami were nearly run down by them; being nothing larger than good mill-streams. As to the latitude & climate, I find that we are situate half a degree more northerly than I had imagined, being in 38°-30′ North; I am fully of opinion that the climate is an healthy one; there has been no complaint of agues or fevers since the first lodgement was made in November last; very little stagnant water is to be met with; and where the land is a little wet, it may be drained without difficulty.

I now Sir beg leave to ask why it is that we are so neglected on the score of troops at the settlements on the Miami purchase? Is it a matter of no moment to the United States whether we are saved or destroyed by the savages? Tis true the Indians have hitherto been unexpectedly pacific; but who can vouch for a continuance of peace. They are a subtil enemy, & all their boasted friendship may be only to learn our numbers, and what state of defence we are in. The Shawanose nation (and they are nearest to us) would not treat with Governor St. Clair at Muskingum; and why shou'd they refuse him peace, and observe it with us? There are several companies of troops in Muskingum, even so many that all the surveyors of the Ohio company have always been escorted with a guard: What guards have the Miami Surveyors had? nothing more than their own vigilance and courage to carry them into the very focus of danger. . . .

1. John Cleves Symmes to Jonathan Dayton, 18, 19, and 20 May 1789, in Beverly W. Bond, ed., *The Correspondence of John Cleves Symmes* (New York: Macmillan, 1926), 53–95. See also, Thomas H. Smith, ed., *An Ohio Reader: 1750 to the Civil War* (Grand Rapids, Mich.: Eerdmans, 1975), 1:52–58; Daniel Hurley, *Cincinnati, The Queen City,* (Cincinnati: Cincinnati Historical Society, 1982), 8–15.

IV. Territorial Government, the Indian Wars, and the Quest for Statehood

THE NORTHWEST ORDINANCE OF 1787 PROVIDED a three-stage evolution for a territory to become a state: (1) at the outset, Congress would appoint a governor, a secretary, and three judges to administer the affairs of the territory and its people; (2) once a population of five thousand free adult males over the age of twenty-one had been achieved, a representative assembly was to be elected by those who owned at least fifty acres in the territory; (3) when a total population of sixty thousand free inhabitants had been reached in any one of the states proposed to emerge from the territory, Congress could admit the new state into the union "on an equal footing with the original States in all respects whatever." As that part of the Northwest Territory closest to the populous eastern seaboard, Ohio was destined to become the first state to be admitted under the provisions of the great ordinance.

The first stage began with the appointment by Congress of Arthur St. Clair, a British-born general who had served the patriot forces in the American Revolution, as governor of the Northwest Territory. He had been serving as the presiding officer of the Congress when the Northwest Ordinance was passed and had been supported strongly for the governorship by the Ohio Company of Associates. Consequently, it was no surprise when he came out to the company's first organized settlement, Marietta, and made it his territorial capital. On 15 July 1788, shortly after his arrival, he addressed the people of the tiny settlement in projecting his views of the future of the area while formally inaugurating government in the Northwest Territory.

As settlement advanced westward along the course of the Ohio River, St. Clair moved his headquarters in January 1790 to Losantiville, which he soon renamed Cincinnati since he felt the former name unbecoming a territorial capital. Growing resentment of the encroachment of white settlers from the East upon their hunting grounds provoked a succession of Indian attacks on settlers in the Miami valleys, which in turn prompted the new national government under President George Washington to order retaliation against the Native Americans. The Indian Wars that followed found the federal forces headquartered at Fort Washington near Cincinnati and the Indian forces, loosely united under the leadership of the Miami chief, Little Turtle, in what would be called the Miami Confederacy, primarily concentrated at Kekionga at the headwaters of the Miami River of the Lake, later renamed the Maumee.

The Indian Wars were marked by three principal campaigns. The first, directed by General Josiah Harmar, found the U.S. Army repulsed at Kekionga in October 1790. The second, led by Governor Arthur St. Clair himself, ended near the headwaters of the Wabash River in early November 1791 in the worst defeat ever inflicted on a United States army by a force of Indians. The third, commanded by General Anthony Wayne, resulted in the defeat of the Indians, then led by the Shawnee Blue Jacket, at Fallen Timbers near the Maumee on 20 August 1794.

The following year, on 3 August 1795, peace was restored in the Ohio country with the signing of the Treaty of Greenville, which through the voiding of Indian claims opened the southern and eastern two-thirds of the future state of Ohio to the prospect of immediate settlement. Preceded by the Jay Treaty with England in 1794, by which the British agreed to evacuate the forts and posts they had been holding in the Northwest despite the provisions of the Treaty of Paris of 1783, the Greenville Treaty assured that the Ohio country would soon be inundated by a tidal wave of immigration so considerable that statehood for Ohio would be realized by 1803, with settlements such as Cleveland, Dayton, Franklinton (Columbus), and Youngstown springing into being.

This is not to say that the quest for statehood was without challenge. Indeed, the eight years following Greenville found proponents, led by such newcomers to the territory as Edward Tiffin, Thomas Worthington, and William Henry Harrison, and opponents, led by Governor Arthur St. Clair, engaged in a succession of maneuvers calculated to enhance or impede the move toward statehood. Finally, the supporters of statehood succeeded in enlisting the aid of President Thomas Jefferson and a sympathetic Congress in getting an Enabling Act passed on 30 April 1802 to authorize the residents of the proposed new state of Ohio to move forward with the election of delegates to a constitutional convention, this despite the fact that the population was then well below the sixty thousand mandated by the Northwest Ordinance. Drafted at Chillicothe in November 1802, the new constitution was received by Congress, which, in turn, authorized elections to be held under it for the selection of the governor and other state officials. On 1 March 1803, government in the new state of Ohio began to function in the first state capital at Chillicothe. The seventeenth state had taken its place in the federal union.

IV.1. Territorial Government Begins: The Inaugural Address of Governor Arthur St. Clair to the People of Marietta, 1788

Construction of a land office, a home for General Rufus Putnam, and the fortified area enclosing these and other buildings, known as Campus Martius, absorbed the energies of the forty-eight men in the employ of the Ohio Company of Associates as Marietta, the first organized settlement in the Northwest Territory, slowly took form on the eastern bank of the

Muskingum River in the spring of 1788. Scarcely three months after their arrival, those pioneer settlers and the soldiers from Fort Harmar across the Muskingum were joined on 9 July by "His Excellency, Major General Arthur St. Clair, Governeur and Commander in Chief of the Territory North West of the River Ohio," who came to establish territorial government with the new settlement as its capital.

On Tuesday, 15 July 1788, Governor St. Clair met the people of Marietta in a public gathering. The provisions of the Northwest Ordinance were read, the officers appointed by the Congress to administer the territory in accord with the provisions of the ordinance were introduced,[1] and the governor in solemn dignity befitting the occasion delivered his inaugural address,[2] thus formally establishing government in the Northwest Territory. The first step in the preparation of Ohio for eventual statehood had been taken.

The Executive Part of the Administration of this Government has been entrusted to me, & I am truly Sensible of the Importance of the Trust, & how much depends upon the due Execution of it—to you Gentlemen, over whom it is to be immediately exercised—to your Posterity! perhaps to the whole Community of America! Would to God I were more equal to the Discharge of it! but my best Endeavours shall not be wanting to fulfil the Desire & the Expectations of Congress, that you may find yourselves happy under it; which is the surest way for me, at once, to meet their Approbation, & to render it honourable to myself; nor, when I reflect upon the Characters of the Men under whose immediate Influence & Example this particular Settlement, which will probably give a tone to all that may succeed it, will be formed, have I much Reason to fear a Disappointment—Men who duly weigh the Importance to Society of a strict Attention to the Duties of Religion & Morality;—in whose Bosoms the Love of Liberty & of Order is a masterly Passion;—who respect the Rights of Mankind, & have sacrificed much to support them,—& who are no Strangers to the Decencies & to the Elegancies of Life. I esteem it also a singular Happiness, to you & to me that the Gentlemen appointed to the judicial Department of such Distinguished Characters & so well known to you—On one Side the Respect which is due to their Stations is secured; whilst on the other it will be yielded with the most perfect good Will.—

You will observe Gentlemen, that the System which has been formed for this Country, & is now to take Effect, is temporary only—suited to your infant Situation, & to continue no longer than that State of Infancy shall last: During that Period the Judges, with my Assistance are to select from the Codes of the Mother States such Laws as may be thought proper for you.—This is a very important Part of our Duty, & will be attended to with the greatest Care—But Congress have not intrusted this great Business wholly to our Prudence or Discretion; & here again you have a fresh Proof of their paternal Attention,—We are bound to report to them all Laws that shall be introduced, & they have reserved to themselves the Power of annulling them—so that if any Law not proper in itself, or not suited to your Circumstances, either From our not seeing the whole Extent of its Operation, or any other Circumstance should be imposed it will be immediately repealed. But with all the Care & Attention to your Interest & Happiness that can be taken, you have many Difficulties to struggle with—The subduing a new Country, notwithstanding its natural Advantages, is alone an arduous Task:—a Task however that Patience & Perseverance will Surmount, & these Virtues so necessary in every Situation, but peculiarly so in yours you must resolve to exercise—neither is the reducing a Country from a State of Nature to a State of Civilization so irksome as it may appear from a slight or superficial View—Even every sensible Pleasures attend it;—the gradual Progress of Improvement fills the Mind with delectable Ideas—Vast Forests converted into arable Fields, & Cities rising in Places which were lately the Habitation of wild Beasts give a Pleasure something like that attendant on Creation, if we can form an Idea of it—the Imagination is ravished, & a Taste communicated of even the "Joy of God to see a happy World."—. . .

The present Situation of the Territory calls for Attention in various Places, & will necessarily induce frequent Absence both of the Judges & myself from this delightful Spot; but at all Times & Places as it is my indispensable Duty, so it is very much my Desire to do every thing within the Compass of my Power for the Peace, good Order & perfect Establishment of the Settlement—& as I look for, not only a cheerful Acquiescence in, & Submission to, necessary measures, but a cordial Cooperation; so I flatter myself my well meant Endeavours will be accepted in the Spirit in which they are rendered, & our Satisfaction will be mutual and complete.

1. In addition to Arthur St. Clair as governor, the other officers included Samuel Holden Parsons and James Mitchell Varnum as judges and Winthrop Sargent as secretary.

2. See Clarence E. Carter, ed., *The Territorial Papers of the United States* (Washington, 1934), 3:263-66; also, William H. Smith, ed., *The St. Clair Papers* (Cincinnati: R. Clarke, 1882), 2:53-56.

IV.2. The United Indian Nations Address the Congress, 1786

Though state claims to Ohio and the rest of the Northwest Territory had been surrendered by 1786, with all lands turned over to the control of Congress save for Connecticut's Western Reserve and Virginia's Military District, there remained the thorny question of Indian claims to the entire region. To the new republic, whether governed under the Articles of Confederation or the subsequent Constitution, the western lands belonged to the United States by right of diplomacy and conquest, as affirmed by the Treaty of Paris of 1783. To the several Indian nations, the lands were still rightfully theirs, since, unlike Cornwallis's dramatic surrender in 1781, they had never been conclusively defeated during the American Revolution. Instead, though allied with the defeated British, they had continued to resist the patriot forces in the West, as attested by the Battles of the Sandusky and the Olentangy and Clark's campaign in the Miami Valleys.

The whole question of Indian claims to the Ohio country was complicated by the continued presence of the British in border forts on American soil, including those at Michilimackinac and Detroit. Insisting that they would not leave them until the United States complied with provisions of the Treaty of Paris respecting payment of prewar debts, the British were using these posts to continue to siphon the fur trade of the Great Lakes into Canada while simultaneously supporting Indian claims to the land, looking to the day that an Indian buffer nation might be established to protect Canada from possible future American expansion, or even to aid in the return of the lost colonies of the eastern seaboard to the British Empire. Particularly useful in keeping British ties to the tribes strong were loyalist agents of the war years such as Simon Girty, Alexander McKee, and Matthew Elliott, who persuasively articulated the theme that unless treaties were negotiated with all the tribes they were binding on none.

At meetings on 28 November and 18 December 1786 at the Huron village at the mouth of the Detroit River, not far from the British-held Fort Detroit, key Indian leaders of an intertribal confederacy known as the United Indian Nations petitioned Congress to recognize Indian rights to the land north and west of the Ohio River and to accept the principle that in order to be binding, Indian treaties had to be made with all of the tribes and not with just one or several of them, "holding all partial treaties as void and of no effect."[1]

Speech of the United Indian Nations, at their Confederate Council, held near the mouth of the Detroit river, 28 November and 18 December, 1786.

PRESENT—The five Nations [Mohawks, Onondagas, Oneidas, Cayugas, Senecas], the Hurons, Delawares, Shawanese, Ottawas, Chippewas, Powtewattimies, Twichtwees [Miamis], Cherokees, and the Wabash confederates [Weas, Piankeshaws].

To the Congress of the United States of America:

BROTHERS: We still are of the same opinion as to the means which may tend to reconcile us to each other, but we are sorry to find, although we had the best thoughts in our minds, during the before mentioned period, mistake has, nevertheless, happened between you and us. We are still anxious of putting our plan of accommodation into execution, and we shall briefly inform you of the means that seem most probable to us of effecting a firm and lasting peace and reconciliation: the first step towards which should, in our opinion, be, that all treaties carried on with the United States, on our parts, should be with the general voice of the whole confederacy, and carried on in the most open manner, without any restraint on either side; and especially as landed matters are often the subject of our councils with you, a matter of the greatest importance and of general concern to us, in this case we hold it indispensably necessary that any cession of our lands should be made in the most public manner, and by the united voice of our confederacy; holding all partial treaties as void and of no effect.

BROTHERS: We think it is owing to you that the tranquility which, since the peace between us, has not lasted, and that that essential good has been followed by mischief and confusion, having managed every thing respecting us your own way. You kindled your council fires where you thought proper, without consulting us, at which you held separate treaties, and have entirely neglected our plan of having a general conference with the different nations of the confederacy. Had this happened, we have reason to believe every thing would now have been settled between us in a most friendly manner. We did every thing in our power, at the treaty of fort Stanwix, to induce you to follow this plan, as our real intentions were, at that very time, to promote peace and concord between us, and that we might look upon each other as friends, having given you no cause or provocation to be otherwise.

BROTHERS: Notwithstanding the mischief that has happened, we are still sincere in our wishes to have peace and tranquillity established between us, earnestly hoping to find the same inclination in you. We wish, therefore, you would take it into serious consideration, and let us speak to you in the manner we proposed. Let us have a treaty with you early in the spring; let us pursue reasonable steps; let us meet half ways, for our mutual convenience; we shall then bring in oblivion the misfortunes that have happened, and meet each other on a footing of friendship. . . .

BROTHERS: We again request of you, in the most earnest manner, to order your surveyors and others, that mark out lands, to cease from crossing the Ohio, until we shall have spoken to you, because the mischief that has recently happened has originated in that quarter; we shall likewise prevent our people from going over until that time.

BROTHERS: It shall not be our faults if the plans which we have suggested to you should not be carried into execution; in that case the event will be very precarious, and if fresh ruptures ensue, we hope to be able to exculpate ourselves, and shall most assuredly, with our united force, be obliged to defend those rights and privileges which have been transmitted to us by our ancestors; and if we should be thereby reduced to misfortunes, the world will pity us when they think of the amicable proposals we now make to prevent the unnecessary effusion of blood. These are our thoughts and firm resolves, and we earnestly desire that you will transmit to us, as soon as possible, your answer, be it what it may.

Done at our Confederated Council Fire, at the Huron village, near the mouth of the Detroit river, December 18th, 1786.

> The Five Nations,
> Hurons, Ottawas, Twichtwees, Shawanese,
> Chippewas, Cherokees, Delawares,
> Powtewatimies, The Wabash Confederates.

1. Walter Lowrie and Matthew St. Clair Clarke, eds., *American State Papers: Indian Affairs,* vol. 1, no. 1, (1st Congress, 1st session), (Washington, 1832), 8–9.

IV.3. "President Washington's Indian War": Little Turtle and St. Clair's Defeat, 1791

As settlers continued to cross the Ohio River to take up lands under the Ordinances of 1785 and 1787, Indian attacks, encouraged by the British-induced argument that treaties that had not involved all the tribes were binding on none, spread across the Ohio country but with particular intensity in the Miami Valleys, the so-called Slaughterhouse. Mindful of the seriousness of these challenges to its authority, Congress in 1790 authorized President George

Washington to order troops to assemble at Fort Washington in Cincinnati in preparation for possible war. Under the command of General Josiah Harmar, an army of more than 1,400 men was gathered, including 320 regulars and some 1,100 militia from Virginia, Kentucky, and western Pennsylvania.

Determined to make a show of force calculated to demoralize the Indians and assure peace in the territory, Governor Arthur St. Clair, with the approval of the secretary of war, Henry Knox, and the president, ordered Harmar to lead his army from Fort Washington northward 170 miles to Kekionga (present Fort Wayne) at the headwaters of the Maumee, the site of the principal Miami town and headquarters of what was now being referred to as the "Miami Confederacy." Though Harmar's ill-trained and poorly equipped army succeeded in burning Kekionga and other nearby villages, a counterattack on 17 October 1790, led by the Miami war chief, Little Turtle (or Mishikinakwa), caught by surprise a militia detachment under the command of Colonel John Hardin. Two days later, Little Turtle attacked another militia company with such intensity that what was left of Harmar's army was sent reeling in disarray back to Fort Washington, leaving behind 183 men dead or missing. What some have called "President Washington's Indian War" was now fully engaged.[1]

After Harmar's disastrous defeat, the Indians grew emboldened. In January 1791, a group of Shawnees and Delawares raided a settlement known as Big Bottom north and west of Marietta on the Muskingum River, killing nearly half of the settlers. With this news, President Washington and the Congress authorized Governor St. Clair to raise an army and to lead it himself against the Indian confederacy.

On 4 October 1791, St. Clair set out from Fort Washington at the head of a force of twenty-nine hundred, including some twenty-three hundred regulars and six hundred militia, the largest army to fight in the Ohio country to this time. Strategy dictated the need for construction of a line of forts directed toward Kekionga, now rebuilt by Little Turtle and the Miamis, so that in the event of a surprise attack St. Clair and his men would have bases to which they could fall back. Though Secretary Knox had authorized their construction even before Harmar's expedition had been launched the preceding fall, they could no longer be delayed, as Harmar's disastrous defeat and flight had shown. In September 1791, Fort Hamilton had been built. More were added in October as St. Clair's army moved northward: Fort St. Clair, built by General James Wilkinson at the site of present-day Eaton, and Fort Jefferson, on the site still known by that name.

As the army marched toward Kekionga, its numbers steadily diminished, a circumstance only partially explained by the need to man the new outposts. Rather, it was the specter of desertion on the part of undisciplined soldiers that brought anguish to St. Clair, who soon found that sending other troops out to catch and return the deserters often led to the desertion of those troops as well. Observing the gradual meltdown of the American army were scouts of the Indian forces, among them a young Shawnee, Tecumseh. By the time St. Clair made camp on the banks of the Wabash near present-day Fort Recovery, Ohio, on the night of 3 November 1791, the army numbered only about fourteen hundred, less than half the number that had left Fort Washington the month before. With this report from his scouts, Little Turtle determined that the time had come for action.

Just before dawn the next morning, the Indian forces, numbering some fifteen hundred warriors, attacked, catching some of St. Clair's men still in their bedrolls and others preparing for breakfast. Before the battle had ended, 630 of St. Clair's army had been killed (593 sol-diers and 37 officers, including General Richard Butler) and more than 300 others had been wounded. Had it not been for the time consumed in scalping, the annihilation might have been complete. As it was, the worst defeat ever suffered by a U.S. army at the hands of a force of Indians had been inflicted by Little Turtle and his warriors. President Washington's Indian War had taken an unexpected turn! The future of the nation was now clearly on the line.

General St. Clair to the Secretary of War Henry Knox

Fort Washington, 9th November, 1791.[2]

Sir:—Yesterday afternoon the remains of the army under my command got back to this place, and I have now the painful task to give you an account of as warm and as unfortunate an action as almost any that has been fought, in which every corps was engaged and worsted, except the First regiment, that had been detached upon a service I had the honor to inform you of in my last dispatch, and had not joined me.

On the 3d instant, the army had reached a creek about twelve yards wide, running to the southward, which I believe to have been the river St. Mary, that empties into the Miami of the lake [the Maumee River]; arrived at the village about four o'clock in the afternoon, having marched near nine miles, and were immediately encamped upon a commanding piece of ground in two lines, having the above-mentioned creek in front. The right wing composed of Butler's, Clarke's, and Patterson's battalions, commanded by Major-General Butler, formed the first line; and the left wing, consisting of Bedinger's and Gaither's battalions, and the Second regiment, commanded by Colonel Darke, formed the second line, with an interval between them of about seventy yards, which was all the ground would allow.

The right flank was pretty well secured by the creek, a steep bank, and Faulkener's corps; some of the cavalry and their pickets covered the left flank; the militia were thrown over the creek, and advanced about one quarter of a mile, and advanced in the same order; there were a few Indians who appeared on the opposite side of the creek, but fled with the utmost precipitation on the advance of the militia; at this place, which I judged to be about fifteen miles from the Miami village, I had determined to throw up a slight work, the plan of which was concerted that evening with Major Ferguson, wherein to have deposited the men's knapsacks, and every thing else that was not absolutely necessary, and to have moved on to attack the enemy as soon as the First regiment was come up; but they did not permit me to execute either, for on the 4th, about half an hour before sunrise, and when the men had just been dismissed from the parade (for it was a constant practice to have them all under arms a considerable time before daylight), an attack was made upon the militia. Those gave way in a very little time, and rushed into camp, through Major Butler's battalion, which, together with part of Clarke's, they threw into considerable disorder, and which, notwithstanding the exertions of both those officers, was never altogether remedied, the Indians following close at their heels; the fire, however, of the front line checked them, but almost instantly a heavy attack began upon that line, and in a few minutes it was extended to the second likewise; the great weight of it was directed against the center of each, where the artillery was placed, and from which the men were repeatedly driven with great slaughter; finding no great effect from our fire, and confusion beginning to spread from the great number of men who were falling in all quarters, it became necessary to try what could be done with the bayonet.

Lieutenant-Colonel Darke was accordingly ordered to make a charge with part of the second line, and to turn the left flank of the enemy. This was executed with great spirit. The Indians instantly gave way, and were driven back three or four hundred yards; but, for the want of a sufficient number of riflemen to pursue this advantage, they soon returned, and the troops were obliged to give back in their turn. At this moment they had entered our camp by the left flank, having pursued back the troops that were posted there.

Another charge was made here by the Second regiment, Butler's and Clarke's battalions, with equal effect, and it was repeated several times, and always with success; but in all of them many men were lost, and particularly the officers, which, with some raw troops was a loss altogether irredeemable. In that I just spoke of, made by the Second regiment and Butler's battalion, Major Butler was dangerously wounded, and every officer of the Second regiment fell except three, one of whom, Mr. Greaton, was shot through the body.

Our artillery being now silenced, and all the officers killed except Captain Ford, who was badly wounded, more than half of the army fallen, being cut off from the road, it became necessary to attempt the regaining it, and to make a retreat if possible. To this purpose, the remains of the army were formed, as well as circumstances would admit, towards the right of the encampment; from which, by the way of the second line, another charge was made upon the enemy, as if with the design to turn their right flank, but, in fact, to gain the road; this was effected, and as soon as it was open, the militia took along it, followed by the troops, Major Clarke, with his battalion, covering the rear.

The retreat in those circumstances was, you may be sure, a very precipitate one; it was, in fact, a flight. The camp and the artillery were abandoned, but that was unavoidable; for not a horse was left alive to have drawn them off had it otherwise been practicable. But the most disgraceful part of the business is that the greatest part of the men threw away their arms and accouterments, even after the pursuit, which continued about four miles, had ceased. I found the road strewed with them for many miles, but was not able to remedy it; for, having had all my horses killed, and being mounted upon one that could not be pricked out of a walk, I could not get forward myself, and the orders I sent forward, either to halt the front, or to prevent the men parting with their arms, were unattended to. The rout continued quite to Fort Jefferson, twenty-nine miles, which was reached a little after sun-setting. The action began about half an hour before sunrise, and the retreat was attempted at half an hour after nine o'clock.

I have not yet been able to get returns of the killed and wounded; but Major-General Butler, Lieutenant-Colonel Oldham, of the militia, Major Ferguson, Major Hart, and Major Clarke are among the former. Colonel Sargent, my adjutant-general, Lieutenant-Colonel Drake, Lieutenant-Colonel Gibson, Major Butler, and the Viscount Malartie, who served me as an aid-de-camp, are among the latter; and a great number of captains and subalterns in both.

I have now, sir, finished my melancholy tale—a tale that will be felt sensibly by every one that has sympathy for private distress, or for public misfortune. I have nothing, sir, to lay to the charge of the troops but their want of discipline, which, from the short time they had been in service, it was impossible they should have acquired, and which rendered it very difficult, when they were thrown into confusion, to reduce them again to order, which is one reason why the loss has fallen so heavy upon the officers, who did every thing in their power to effect it. Neither were my own exertions wanting; but, worn down with illness, and suffering under a painful disease, unable either to mount or dismount a horse without assistance, they were not so great as they otherwise would, and, perhaps, ought to have been. We were overpowered by numbers; but it is no more than justice to observe that, though composed of so many different species of troops, the utmost harmony prevailed through the whole army during the campaign. . . .

I have said, sir, . . . , that we were overpowered by numbers. Of that, however, I have no evidence; but the weight of the fire, which was always a most deadly one, and generally delivered from the ground, few of the enemy showing themselves afoot except when they were charged, and that, in a few minutes, our whole camp, which extended above three hundred and fifty yards in length, was entirely surrounded and attacked on all quarters.

The loss, sir, the public has sustained, by the fall of so many officers, particularly General Butler and Major Ferguson, can not be too much regretted; but it is a circumstance that will alleviate the misfortune, in some measure, that all of them fell most gallantly doing their duty. . . .

1. See Wiley Sword, *President Washington's Indian War: The Struggle for the Old Northwest, 1790-1795* (Norman: University of Oklahoma Press, 1985).
2. William Henry Smith, ed., *The St. Clair Papers* (Cincinnati: R. Clarke, 1882), 2:262-67.

IV.4. The First Newspaper of Ohio: Cincinnati's *Centinel of the North-Western Territory,* 1793

Even as the Indian War was being fought, the Ohio country had its first newspaper, a weekly appropriately named The Centinel of the North-Western Territory, *which began publishing in Cincinnati, then the territorial capital with a population of some two hundred settlers, on 9 November 1793. Edited and published by William Maxwell, a Revolutionary War veteran who came to Ohio from Lexington, Kentucky, the paper provided a digest of local, national, and world news as well as scientific and literary articles, including poetry and short stories. Its initial issue carried news items from London, New York, and Philadelphia, dated as early as mid-July, as well as a detailed account of particular local interest concerning an Indian attack in early September on a U.S. army supply train between Fort Jefferson and Fort St. Clair, which had killed fifteen officers and men, with seventy horses also killed or stolen.*

Determined that his paper would serve as a "centinel" for the common defense as well as provide his readers with an impartial presentation of the news and editorial comment, Maxwell carried in the masthead the promise that the paper would be "Open to all parties—

but influenced by none." Readers were encouraged to express their opinions, whether in defense or in criticism of territorial or national government or on any other subject of interest to them. The importance of an unfettered press, serving the people of a new territory, was underscored by editor Maxwell in the lead article on the first page of his first issue.[1]

The *Printer* of the CENTINEL of the North-Western TERRITORY, to the *Public.*

Having arrived at *Cincinnati,* he has applied himself to that which has been the principal object of his removal to this country, the Publication of a *News-Paper.*

This country is in its infancy, and the inhabitants are daily exposed to an enemy who, not content with taking away the lives of men in the field, have swept away whole families, and burnt their habitations. We are well aware that the want of a regular and certain trade down the Mississippi, deprives this country in a great measure, of money at the present time. There are discouragements, nevertheless I am led to believe the people of this country are disposed to promote science, and have the fullest assurance that the *Press* from its known utility will receive proper encouragement. And on my part am content with small gains, at the present, flattering myself that from attention to business, I shall preserve the good wishes of those who have already countenanced me in this undertaking, and secure the friendship of subsequent population.

It is to be hoped that the CENTINEL will prove of great utility to the people of this Country, not only to inform them of what is going on on the east of the Atlantic in arms, and in arts of peace—but what more particularly concerns us, the different transactions of the states in the union, and especially of our own Territory, at so great a distance from the seat of general government—it is a particular grievance, that the people have not been acquainted with the proceedings of the legislature of the union, in which they are as much interested, as any part of the United States.—It is expected the CENTINEL, will in a great measure remedy this misfortune.

These are substantial advantages, which will result from the publication of this paper; but it must be an agreeable amusement to know a thousand particulars which make up the intelligence, though not so immediately interesting to the property & persons of men, whether they be of a philosophical, political, historical or moral nature.

The EDITOR therefore rests his success on the merits of the publication, but as an inducement to the people of this country, to make exertions to support the *Press,* he must observe that they will have an opportunity, by means of this *paper* to make themselves and their situations known abroad; if they have valuable lands to dispose of, it can be made known; if they have grievances to lay before the public, it can now be done. I hope therefore, all men of public spirit will consider the undertaking as a proper object of attention, and not consult only their own personal interest, but the interest of the public and the coming time.

1. See the Ohio Historical Society, *Fundamental Documents of Early Ohio* (Columbus, n.d.); Robert C. Wheeler, ed., *Ohio Newspapers: A Living Record* (Columbus: Ohio History Press, 1950), 68–72; and Charles B. Galbreath, "The First Newspaper of the Northwest Territory," in *Ohio Archaeological and Historical Publications* (Columbus, 1904), 13:332–49.

IV.5.   Anthony Wayne and the Battle of Fallen Timbers, 1794

Little Turtle's victory over St. Clair and the American army on the banks of the Wabash on 4 November 1791 brought migration to the Ohio country to a virtual standstill and emboldened the British governor in Canada, Lord Dorchester, to make inflammatory speeches encouraging the confederated tribes to drive American settlers from the territory north and west of the Ohio. With two expeditionary forces under Harmar and then St. Clair having failed to bring peace in the territory, President Washington determined to send a third, this one under the leadership of General Anthony Wayne, nicknamed "Mad Anthony" because of his boldness in action in the recent American Revolution. Now nearly fifty, more cautious and conservative, and in poor health, Wayne was still one of the country's top fighting men when he began to gather what he would call the Legion of the West at Pittsburgh in the summer of 1792.

After months of training in the art of frontier warfare, Wayne's force of twenty-five hundred men moved by boat down the Ohio to Cincinnati in April 1793, where six months more were spent before Wayne felt his legion was ready for the move northward, which began in October. Slowly, cautiously, he made his way from Fort Washington to Fort Hamilton, then on to Forts St. Clair and Jefferson before pausing in December 1793 to build his winter headquarters, a fifty-acre fort he named Greene Ville (later spelled Greenville) in honor of his old friend and Revolutionary War comrade General Nathanael Greene. There he spent the winter months drilling his legion, adding a company of horsemen from Kentucky, and cutting a number of roads in radial fashion outward from the fort in order to keep the Indians guessing what his next move would be in the spring. While at Fort Greene Ville he dispatched a part of his army to the site of St. Clair's defeat, where yet another fort was constructed, named by him Recovery.

Alarmed by Wayne's moves northward and concerned that he might be bound eventually for Detroit, the lieutenant governor of Canada, John Graves Simcoe, directed the construction of a British fort below the rapids of the Maumee in April 1794, forty miles inside the United States. Named Fort Miami, it was calculated not only to protect Detroit (still in British hands) but also to stiffen the resolve of the tribes to keep fighting. With its construction, many of the Indians came down the Maumee from Kekionga to cluster their summer camps near it.

On 28 July 1794, Wayne and his legion left Fort Greene Ville and struck northward toward Fort Miami and the Indian forces gathered near it. From 2 to 5 August he paused to construct Fort Adams, named for Vice President John Adams, on the St. Marys River. While there Wayne nearly lost his life when a tree being felled by axmen knocked him from his horse, severely injuring him. Though at the time it was thought to be an accident, a journal account divulged a century later revealed that the mishap was intentional, that some of Wayne's men, disgruntled by his stern discipline, particularly toward deserters, had sought to remove him from his command before the coming engagement with the Indians. Too tough to die, Wayne bound his wounds and continued his campaign.

On 8 August, reaching the junction of the Auglaize and the Maumee Rivers, the site of the birthplace of the great Indian leader Pontiac, Wayne built one of his strongest forts and called it Defiance. Said he, "I defy the British, the Indians, or all the devils of hell to take it." Defiance it has been ever since.

While at the Glaize, as the area was called, Wayne sent a final ultimatum to the Indians for peace on his terms. The chiefs of the several tribes gathered to consider it on a great rock called the "Roche de Boeuf" in the middle of the Maumee near the rapids. There Little Turtle counseled peace, arguing that unlike Harmar and St. Clair, Wayne was a general "who never sleeps" and thus could not be surprised by ambush or sudden attack. Vowing to continue the fight to the finish, the Shawnee Chief Blue Jacket succeeded to leadership of the confederacy.

On 20 August 1794, the two armies met in combat as Wayne's legion approached the rapids of the Maumee in an area where a tornado had leveled acres of tall trees. There the Indian army of more than a thousand braves lay concealed. The Battle of Fallen Timbers, as it has been called, lasted about an hour, the turning point coming when the Kentucky cavalrymen, riding between the fallen trees, forced the Indians from their protective cover.

Retreating from the battlefield, the Indians sought protection from the British in Fort Miami, only a mile away. But the fort's commander, Major William Campbell, refused to open the gates to admit them, knowing that to do so could well provoke an attack by Wayne and his legion, quite possibly precipitating a war between Britain and the United States.

After pounding on the fort's gates in vain, the Indians finally realized that in this, their hour of greatest need, their British friends had deserted them. Their pleas soon turned to curses, and then they vanished northward along the Maumee into the forest.

For his part, Wayne refused to pursue them and instead made camp at the edge of the clearing outside Fort Miami, content in the knowledge that the Indians, having been defeated, were no longer his principal threat. Rather, he decided to humiliate Campbell and the British soldiers in the fort by burning the adjoining house of the British Indian agent, Alexander McKee, and then setting fire to nearby Indian villages and their fields of corn, more than a thousand acres in all. This done, his army finally left Fort Miami to proceed up the Maumee to the site of the original objective of all three American armies, Kekionga. There his men built one final fort and called it Wayne in his honor.

On 28 August 1794, Wayne detailed the Battle of Fallen Timbers in a report to Henry Knox, the secretary of war. President Washington's Indian War was all but over.[1]

General Anthony Wayne to Secretary of War Henry Knox

No. 83   Head Quarters
                                                 Grand Glaize 28th Augt. 1794

Sir

It's with infinite pleasure that I now announce to you the brilliant success of the Federal army under my Command in a General action with the combined force of the Hostile Indians & a considerable number of the Volunteers & Militia of Detroit on the 20th Instant, on the banks of the Miamis, in the vicinity of the British post & Garrison at the foot of the rapids.

The army advanced from this place on the 15th & arrived at Roche de Bout, on the 18th. The 19th we were employed in making a temporary post for the reception of

our stores & baggage, & in reconnoitring the position of the enemy who were encamped behind a thick brushy wood and the British Fort. [The "temporary post" was
named Fort Deposit.]

At 8. OClock on the morning of the 20th the army again advanced in Columns
agreeably to the standing order of March—the Legion on the right, its right flank
cover'd by the Miamis, One Brigade of Mounted Volunteers on the left, under Brigr
General Todd, & the other in the rear under Brigr Genl Barbee, a select Battalion of
Mounted Volunteers moved in front of the Legion commanded by Major Price, who
was directed to keep sufficiently advanced, so as to give timely notice for the troops to
form in case of Action.

It being yet undetermined whether the Indians wou'd decide on peace or war:

After advancing about Five miles, Major Price's corps received so severe a fire from
the enemy, who were secreted in the woods & high grass, as to compel them to retreat.

The Legion was immediately formed in two lines principally in a close thick wood
which extended for miles on our left & for very considerable distance in front, the
ground being cover'd with old fallen timber probably occasioned by a tornado, which
render'd it impracticable for the Cavalry to act with effect, & afforded the enemy the
most favorable covert for their mode of warfare these savages were formed in three lines
within supporting distance of each other & extending near two miles at right angles
with the River. I soon discover'd from the weight of the fire, & extent of their Lines that
the enemy were in full force in front in possession of their favorite ground & endeavoring to turn our left flank, I therefore gave orders for the second line to advance to support the first, & directed Major Genl Scott to gain & turn the right flank of the savages
with the whole of the Mounted Volunteers by a circuitous route, at the same time I ordered the front line to advance & charge with trailed arms & rouse the Indians from
their coverts at the point of the bayonet, & when up to deliver a close & well directed
fire on their backs followed by a br[i]sk charge, so as not to give time to load again I also
order'd Capt. Mis Campbell who commanded the Legionary Cavalry to turn the left
flank of the Enemy next the river & which afforded a favorable field for that Corps to
act in,

All those orders were obeyed with spirit & promptitude, but such was the impetuosity of the charge by the first line of Infantry—that the Indians & Canadian Militia &
Volunteers were drove from all their Coverts in so short a time, that altho every possible
exertion was used by the Officers of the second line of the Legion & by Generals Scottl,
Todd & Barbee of the Mounted Volunteers, to gain their proper position's but part of
each cou'd get up in season to participate in the Action, the enemy being drove in the
course of One hour more than two miles thro' the thick woods already mentioned by
less than one half their Numbers, from Every account the Enemy amounted to two
thousand combatants, the troops actually engaged against them were short of nine hundred; [illegible] Savages with their allies abandoned themselves to flight & dispersed
with terror & dismay, leaving our victorious army in full & quiet possession of the field
of battle, which terminated under the influence of the Guns of the British Garrison, as
you will observe by the enclosed correspondence between Major Campbell, the Commandant & myself upon the Occasion.

The bravery & Conduct of every Officer belonging to the Army from the Generals down to the Ensigns merits my highest approbation; there were however some whose rank & situation placed their Conduct in a very conspicuous point of view, and which I observed with pleasure & the most lively gratitude, among whom I must beg leave to mention Brigr Genl Wilkinson & Colo Hamtramck the Commandants of the right & left wings of the Legion whose brave example inspired the troops, to them I must add the names of my faithful & Gallant Aids de Camp Captains DeButts & T Lewis & Lieut [William Henry] Harrison who with the Adjt General Major Mills, rendered the most essential services by communicating my orders in every direction & by their Conduct & bravery exciting the troops to press for Victory; Lieut. Covington upon whom the Command of the Cavalry now devolved cut down two savages with his own hand & Lieut Webb one in turn & [illegible] the Enemies left flank.

The wounds received by Captains Slough & Prior & Lieut Campbell Smith (an extra aid de Camp to Genl Wilkinson) of the Legionary Infantry & Capt Van Renselaer of the Dragoons, Captain Rawlins Lieut McKenny & Ensign Duncan of the Mounted Volunteers, bear honorable testimony of their bravery & Conduct.

Captains H Lewis & Brock with their Companies of light Infantry had to sustain an unequal combat for some time which they supported with fortitude, in fact every Officer & soldier who had an Opportunity to come into action displayed that true bravery which will always insure success: & here permit me to declare that I never discover'd more true spirit & anxiety for Action than appeared to pervade the whole of the Mounted Volunteers, & I am well persuaded that had the Enemy maintained their favorite ground but for one half hour longer they wou'd have most severely felt the prowess of that Corps.

But whilst I pay this just tribute to the living I must not forget the Gallant dead, among whom we have to lament the early death of those worthy & brave Officers Capt Mis Campbell of the Dragoons & Lieut Towles of the Light Infantry of the Legion who fell in the first Charge.

enclosed is a particular return of the killed & Wounded — the loss of the Enemy was more that [than] double to that of the Federal Army — the woods were strewed for a considerable distance with the dead bodies of Indians & their white Auxiliaries, the latter armed with British Muskets & bayonets:

After remaining three days & nights on the banks of the Miamis in front of the Field of battle during which time all the Houses & Corn fields were consumed & destroyed for a considerable distance both above & below Fort Miamis as well as within pistol shot of the Garrison who were compeled to remain tacit spectators to this general devestation & Conflagration; among which were the Houses stores & property of Colo McKee the British Indian Agent & principal stimulator of the War now existing between the United States & the savages.

The army returned to this place on the 27th by easy marches laying waste the Villages & Corn fields for about Fifty miles on each side of the Miamis — there remains yet a number of Villages & a great Quantity of Corn to be consumed or destroyed upon Au Glaize & the Miamis above this place which will be effected in the course of a few days.

In the interim we shall improve Fort Defiance & as soon as the Escort return[s] with the necessary supplies from Greeneville & Fort Recovery—the Army will proceed to the Miami Villages in order to accomplish the Object of the Campaign.

It is however not improbable that the Enemy may make one more desperate effort against the Army—as it is said that a Reinforcement was hourly expected at Fort Miamis from Niagara, as well as Numerous tribes of Indians living on the Margins & Islands of the Lakes: This is a business rathar to be wished for than dreaded whilst the army remain in force—their Numbers will only tend to confuse the Savages—& the victory will be the more complete & decisive—& which may eventually ensure a permanent and happy peace.

Under those Impressions I have the honor to be Your Most Obt & very Huml Sert

Anty Wayne

The Honble
Major Genl H Knox
Secretary of War

1. Richard C. Knopf, ed., *Anthony Wayne: A Name in Arms* (Pittsburgh: University of Pittsburgh Press, 1960), 351-55. See also Wiley Sword, *President Washington's Indian War: The Struggle for the Old Northwest, 1790-1795* (Norman: University of Oklahoma Press 1985).

IV.6.   The Jay Treaty, 1794: The British Agree to Evacuate the Border Posts

War between Great Britain and the United States had come perilously close to realization on 20 August 1794, when General Anthony Wayne and his Legion of the West confronted Major William Campbell and the British troops garrisoned at Fort Miami on the Maumee River, forty miles inside the United States, following Wayne's victory over the confederated Indian tribes in the Battle of Fallen Timbers. Fortunately, neither Wayne nor Campbell had "pulled the trigger," but would the two nations be as fortunate whenever and wherever the next crisis might occur?

Britain's retention of the northwest border posts at Michilimackinac and Detroit, followed by construction of Fort Miami on the Maumee, all in contravention to the provisions of the Treaty of Paris of 1783, together with the intrigues of its agents with America's Indians and interference with our neutral trade, had created a climate of mistrust between the two nations that required only a spark to touch off a major conflagration. Yet neither side wanted a war in 1794. Britain had all it could handle in the developing French Revolution. The infant United States had all it could do to stay afloat in a sea of troubles, not the least of which involved its own native peoples.

To attempt to resolve some of the major differences with Britain and avert war, President George Washington in 1794 appointed Chief Justice John Jay as envoy extraordinary to conclude a treaty of peace. The resultant Treaty of Amity, Commerce, and Navigation, better

known simply as the Jay Treaty, was signed at London on 19 November 1794 and was sub-
mitted to the U.S. Senate for approval the following 8 June 1795. Eventually ratified after
lengthy and often acrimonious debate, which revealed the sense of many Americans that Jay
had given away too much in his effort to achieve accord with the British, the Jay Treaty was
nonetheless significant in that it ended, at least for the time being, a drift toward war with
the former mother country that might have had disastrous consequences for the young nation
had it been fought in 1794-95 instead of 1812.[1]

Article 1.

There shall be a firm inviolable and universal Peace, and a true and sincere Friendship between His Britannick Majesty, His Heirs and Successors, and the United States
of America; and between their respective Countries, Territories, Cities, Towns and People of every Degree, without Exception of Persons or Places.

Article 2.

His Majesty will withdraw all His Troops and Garrisons from all Posts and Places
within the Boundary Lines assigned by the Treaty of Peace [of 1783] to the United
States. This Evacuation shall take place on or before the first Day of June One Thousand seven hundred and ninety six, and all the proper Measures shall in the interval be
taken by concert between the Government of the United States, and His Majesty's
Governor General in America, for settling the previous arrangements which may be
necessary respecting the delivery of the said Posts: The United States in the mean Time
at Their discretion extending their settlements to any part within the said boundary
line, except within the precincts or Jurisdiction of any of the said Posts. All Settlers and
Traders, within the Precincts or Jurisdiction of the said Posts, shall continue to enjoy,
unmolested, all their property of every kind, and shall be protected therein. They shall
be at full liberty to remain there, or to remove with all or any part of their Effects; and
it shall also be free to them to sell their Lands, Houses, or Effects, or to retain the property thereof, at their discretion; such of them as shall continue to reside within the said
Boundary Lines shall not be compelled to become Citizens of the United States, or take
any Oath of allegiance to the Government thereof, but they shall be a full liberty so to
do, if they think proper, and they shall make and declare their Election within one year
after the Evacuation aforesaid. And all persons who shall continue there after the expiration of the said year, without having declared their intention of remaining Subjects of
His Britannick Majesty, shall be considered as having elected to become Citizens of the
United States.

Article 3.

It is agreed that it shall at all Times be free to His Majesty's Subjects, and to the
Citizens of the United States, and also to the Indians dwelling on either side of the said
Boundary Line freely to pass and repass by Land, or Inland Navigation, into the respec-
tive Territories and Countries of the Two Parties on the Continent of America (the
Country within the Limits of the Hudson's Bay Company only excepted) and to navi-

gate all the Lakes, Rivers, and waters thereof, and freely to carry on trade and commerce with each other. But it is understood, that this Article does not extend to the admission of Vessels of the United States into the Sea Ports, Harbours, Bays, or Creeks of His Majesty's said Territories; nor into such parts of the Rivers in His Majesty's said Territories as are between the mouth thereof, and the highest Port of Entry from the Sea, except in small vessels trading bona fide between Montreal and Quebec, under such regulations as shall be established to prevent the possibility of any Frauds in this respect. Nor to the admission of British vessels from the Sea into the Rivers of the United States, beyond the highest Ports of Entry for Foreign Vessels from the Sea. The River Mississippi, shall however, according to the Treaty of Peace be entirely open to both Parties; And it is further agreed, That all the ports and places on its Eastern side, to whichsoever of the parties belonging, may freely be resorted to, and used by both parties, in as ample a manner as any of the Atlantic Ports or Places of the United States, or any of the Ports or Places of His Majesty in Great Britain.

All Goods and Merchandize whose Importation into His Majesty's said Territories in America, shall not be entirely prohibited, may freely, for the purposes of Commerce, be carried into the same in the manner aforesaid, by the Citizens of the United States, and such Goods and Merchandize shall be subject to no higher or other Duties than would be payable by His Majesty's Subjects on the Importation of the same from Europe into the said Territories. And in like manner, all Goods and Merchandize whose Importation into the United States shall not be wholly prohibited, may freely, for the purposes of Commerce, be carried into the same, in the manner aforesaid, by His Majesty's Subjects, and such Goods and Merchandize shall be subject to no higher or other Duties than would be payable by the Citizens of the United States on the Importation of the same in American Vessels into the Atlantic Ports of the said States. And all Goods not prohibited to be exported from the said Territories respectively, may in like manner be carried out of the same by the Two Parties respectively, paying Duty as aforesaid.

No Duty of Entry shall ever be levied by either Party on Peltries brought by Land, or Inland Navigation into the said Territories respectively, nor shall the Indians passing or repassing with their own proper Goods and Effects of whatever nature, pay for the same any Impost or Duty whatever. But Goods in Bales, or other large Packages unusual among Indians shall not be considered as Goods belonging bona fide to Indians.

No higher or other Tolls or Rates of Ferriage than what are, or shall be payable by Natives, shall be demanded on either side; And no Duties shall be payable on any Goods which shall merely be carried over any of the Portages, or carrying Places on either side, for the purpose of being immediately reimbarked, and carried to some other Place or Places. But as by this Stipulation it is only meant to secure to each Party a free passage across the Portages on both sides, it is agreed, that this Exemption from Duty shall extend only to such Goods as are carried in the usual and direct Road across the Portage, and are not attempted to be in any manner sold or exchanged during their passage across the same, and proper Regulations may be established to prevent the possibility of any Frauds in this respect.

As this Article is intended to render in a great Degree the local advantages of each Party common to both, and thereby to promote a disposition favourable to Friendship and good neighbourhood, It is agreed, that the respective Governments will mutually promote this amicable Intercourse, by causing speedy and impartial Justice to be done, and necessary protection to be extended, to all who may be concerned therein.

Article 4.

Whereas it is uncertain whether the River Mississippi extends so far to the Northward as to be intersected by a Line to be drawn due West from the Lake of the woods in the manner mentioned in the Treaty of Peace between His Majesty and the United States, it is agreed, that measures shall be taken in Concert between His Majesty's Government in America, and the Government of the United States, for making a joint Survey of the said River, from one Degree of Latitude below the falls of St Anthony to the principal Source or Sources of the said River, and also of the parts adjacent thereto, And that if on the result of such Survey it should appear that the said River would not be intersected by such a Line as is above mentioned; The two Parties will thereupon proceed by amicable negotiation to regulate the Boundary Line in that quarter as well as all other Points to be adjusted between the said Parties, according to Justice and mutual Convenience, and in Conformity, to the Intent of the said Treaty. . . .

1. Hunter Miller, ed., *Treaties and Other International Acts of the United States of America*, vol. 2, 1776-1818 (Washington, 1931), 245-78.

IV.7.   The Treaty of Greene Ville, 1795: Peace with the Indians

For long years at the very summit of the rotunda of the capitol building in Columbus and still prominently displayed in that seat of government of the State of Ohio is a painting by Howard Chandler Christy titled "Signing the Treaty of Greene Ville." Of the many near life-sized figures depicted on it, two stand out from the rest: Anthony Wayne, commissioned by President George Washington and his new secretary of war, Timothy Pickering, to represent the United States; and Mishikinakwa, the Little Turtle of the Miamis, principal leader of the Indian confederacy in the ill-fated struggle to keep the Ohio country forever Indian. Of all the treaties negotiated on Ohio soil over the years, none was of greater significance than the one signed at Fort Greene Ville (now Greenville, Ohio) on 3 August 1795, for it was the treaty that brought peace between the new nation and the tribes of the Northwest Territory in the wake of the Battle of Fallen Timbers.[1] In so doing, it opened the southern and eastern two-thirds of the future state of Ohio to the prospect of immediate settlement with the concurrence of all of the tribes, a condition of unanimity long argued by the tribes (particularly the Shawnees and the Miamis) and the British as necessary for an Indian treaty to be binding. Preceded by the Jay Treaty of 19 November 1794, which provided for the evacuation of all British posts on American soil, including Fort Miami on the Maumee, by 1 June 1796, the way was now open for statehood to be realized by Ohio in less than a decade.

A Treaty of Peace between the United States of America and the Tribes of Indians called the Wyandots, Delawares, Shawnoes, Ottawas, Chipewas, Putawatimes, Miamis, Eel River, Weea's, Kickapoos, Piankashaws and Kaskaskias.

To put an end to a destructive War to settle all controversies and to restore harmony & friendly intercourse between the said United States and Indian Tribes; Anthony Wayne Major General, commanding the Army of the United States, & sole Commissioner for the good purposes above mentioned, and the said tribes of Indians, by their Sachems Chiefs, and Warriors met together at Greene Ville the Head Quarters of the said Army, have agreed on the following Articles; which, when ratified by the President with the advice and consent of the Senate of the United States, shall be binding on them and the said Indian tribes.

ARTICLE 1ST Henceforth all hostilities shall cease; peace is hereby established, & shall be perpetual, and a friendly intercourse shall take place, between the said United States and Indian tribes.

ARTICLE 2nd All prisoners shall on both sides be restored. The Indians, prisoners to the United States shall be immediately set at liberty. The people of the United States still remaining prisoners among the Indians shall be delivered up in Ninety days from the date hereof to the General or Commanding Officer at Greene Ville, Fort Wayne, or Fort Defiance, and ten Chiefs of the said tribes shall remain at Greene Ville as hostages, until the delivery of the prisoners shall be effected.

ARTICLE 3rd The General boundary line between the lands of the United States, and the lands of the said Indian tribes, shall begin at the Mouth of Cayahoga River & run thence up the same to the portage between that and the Tuscarawas branch of the Muskingum, thence down that branch to the crossing place above Fort Lawrence [Fort Laurens], thence Westerly to a fork of that branch of the Great Miami River running into the Ohio, at or near which fork stood Loromies store, and where commences the portage between the Miami of the Ohio, & St Marys River, which is a branch of the Miami, which runs into Lake Erie, thence a westerly course to Fort Recovery, which stands on a branch of the Wabash, then South Westerly in a direct line to the Ohio, so as to intersect that river Opposite the Mouth of Kentucke or Cuttawa River. . . .

And the said Indian tribes will allow to the people of the United States a free passage by land and by Water, as one and the other shall be found Convenient, thro' their Country, along the chain of Posts herein before mentioned; that is to say, from the commencement of the portage aforesaid at or near Loromies store, thence along said portage to the St Mary's and down the same to Fort Wayne, and then down the Miami [the Maumee] to Lake Erie. — again from the commencement of the portage at or near Loromies store along the portage from thence to the river Au-Glaize, and down the same to its junction with the Miami at Fort Defiance. — again from the commencement of the portage aforesaid, to Sandusky River and down the same to Sandusky bay & Lake Erie, & from Sandusky to the post which shall be taken at or near the foot of the rapids of the Miami of the Lake; and from thence to Detroit. Again from the mouth of Chikago, to the Commencement of the portage, between that River & the Illinoi's, & down the Illinois River to the Mississippi — also from Fort Wayne along the portage aforesaid which leads to the Wabash, and then down the Wabash to the Ohio. And the said Indian tribes will also allow to the people of the United States the free use of the harbours and mouths of Rivers along the Lakes adjoining the Indian lands, for sheltering Vessells and boats, & liberty to land their cargoes where necessary for their safety. . . .

ARTICLE 7th The said tribes of Indians, parties to this Treaty shall be at liberty to hunt within the territory and lands which they have now ceded to the United States without hindrance or molestation so long as they demean themselves peaceably, and offer no injury to the people of the United States.

ARTICLE 8th Trade shall be opened with the said Indian tribes; and they do hereby respectively engage to afford protection to such persons with their property as shall be duly licensed to reside among them for the purpose of trade & to their Agents & Servants; but no person shall be permitted to reside at any of their towns or hunting Camps as a trader, who is not furnished with a license for that purpose under the hand and seal of the superintendent of the Department Northwest of the Ohio, or such other person as the President of the United States shall authorise to grant such licences; to the end that the said Indians may not be imposed on in their trade. and if any licensed trader shall abuse his privilege by unfair dealing, upon complaint and proof thereof his licence Shall be taken from him; and he shall be further punished according to the laws of the United States. And if any person shall intrude himself as a trader without such license the said Indians shall take and bring him before the Superintendent or his Deputy to be dealt with according to law. And to prevent impositions by forged licences, the said Indians shall at least once a year give information to the Superintendent or his deputies of the names of the traders residing among them.

ARTICLE 9th Lest the firm peace and friendship now established should be interrupted by the misconduct of individuals, the United States, and the said Indian tribes agree, that for injuries done by individuals on either side, no private revenge or retaliation shall take place; but instead thereof, complaint shall be made by the party injured to the other; by the said Indian tribes or any of them to the President of the United States or the Superintendent by him Appointed; and by the Superintendent or other person appointed by the President to the principal chiefs of the said Indian tribes, or of the tribe to which the Offender belongs; and such prudent Measures shall then be pursued as shall be necessary to preserve the said peace & friendship unbroken, until the legislature (or Great Council) of the United States shall make Other equitable provision in the Case, to the Satisfaction of both parties. Should any Indian tribes meditate a War against the United States or either of them, and the same shall come to the knowledge of the before mentioned tribes or either of them, they do hereby engage to give immediate notice thereof to the General or Officer Commanding the troops of the United States at the nearest post. And should any tribe with hostile intentions against the United States or either of them attempt to pass thro' their Country, they will endeavour to prevent the same, and in like manner give information of such attempt, to the General or Officer Commanding, as soon as possible, that all causes of Mistrust and Suspicion may be avoided between them and the United States: in like manner the United States shall give notice to the said Indian tribes of any harm that may be meditated against them, or either of them, that shall come to their knowledge: and do all in their power to hinder and prevent the same; that the Friendship between them may be Uninterrupted.

ARTICLE 10th All other Treaties heretofore made between the United States and the said Indian tribes, or any of them since the treaty of 1783 between the United States, and Great Britain, that come within the Purview of this treaty, shall henceforth cease and become Void. . . .

1. See Clarence E. Carter, ed., *The Territorial Papers of the United States,* vol. 2, *The Territory Northwest of the River Ohio, 1787-1803* (Washington, 1934), 525-31. The Eel River, Wea, and Piankashaw tribes enumerated in the treaty had all at one time been septs or bands of the Miamis.

IV.8.   Moses Cleaveland and the Settlement of the Western Reserve

The Treaty of Greene Ville and peace with the Indians, coupled with the Jay Treaty and the withdrawal of the British from their American posts, prompted an unprecedented surge of settlement in the Ohio country. In a few short years, Chillicothe, Dayton, Zanesville, Athens, and Franklinton (Columbus) were founded in southern Ohio, while Conneaut, Hudson, Warren, Youngstown, and Cleveland emerged in the northeast, in the area known as the Connecticut Western Reserve. Not all of the Reserve was immediately opened for settlement, however, only the area east of the Cuyahoga River, the headwaters of the Tuscarawas, and the Portage Path between. Not until the Treaty of Fort Industry (1805) was the land west of the Cuyahoga opened for settlement, but by that time Ohio had already entered the Union as the seventeenth state.

Headed by Oliver Phelps, the thirty-five associates of the Connecticut Land Company who had purchased the three-million-acre Reserve (exclusive of the Fire Lands) for $1.2 million from the state of Connecticut in May 1795 were determined after Greene Ville to get the tract surveyed (into five-mile-wide ranges and five-square-mile townships in contrast to the six-mile pattern of survey mandated for the Congress lands) and opened for sale as quickly as possible. Appointing one of their number, General Moses Cleaveland, to head a party of nearly fifty, including six surveyors, a commissary, and a physician, the directors charged Cleaveland to superintend "the agents and men, sent on to survey and make locations on said land, to make, and enter into friendly negotiations with the natives who are on said land, or contiguous thereto, and may have any pretended claim to the same, and secure such friendly intercourse among them as will establish peace, quiet, and safety to the survey and settlement of such lands, not ceded by the natives under the authority of the United States."[1]

Gathered in Schenectady in early June 1796, with some proceeding overland from there and others by boat along the Mohawk and eventually the Lake Erie shore, the entire party reached the Western Reserve on the Fourth of July, in honor of which they named their first settlement Port Independence, now Conneaut. Though much of the journal kept by Cleaveland is no longer extant, a portion of it that does exist contains some interesting commentary respecting the party's observance of the Fourth of July and their subsequent interactions with a nearby village of "Massasagoes" or Eastern Ojibwas, also called Chippewas.[2]

From Port Independence, or Conneaut, Moses Cleaveland and his party proceeded westward by boat along the Lake Erie shore, searching for the mouth of the Cuyahoga (or Crooked) River, which was as far west as they could go in accord with the boundary line established by the Treaty of Greene Ville. They reached the mouth of the Cuyahoga on 22 July and found it an ideal location for a town. The constitution or charter of the Connecticut Land Company had provided for a "Capital town . . . to be surveyed into small lots." In his travels through other parts of the Reserve in the next two months, no other site had quite the appeal to Cleaveland as the place where the Cuyahoga entered the lake.

Back in Conneaut, or Port Independence, on 5 August Cleaveland sent his first report to Oliver Phelps and the other associates in Connecticut about his observations of what he had seen in the Reserve thus far. Respecting the area about the Cuyahoga, he was particularly enthusiastic.[3]

Samuel P. Orth has noted that "in consonance with this report, he [Cleaveland] returned to the Cuyahoga and determined that it was the most available 'place for the capital.' The survey of the town lots was completed by the 17th of October and a name for the capital had been found. It was originally proposed to call it Cuyahoga but its Indian accents were evidently not pleasing to the surveyors, and they urged upon the general the propriety of giving his name to the town. On his return home he speaks of this: 'I laid out a town on the banks of Lake Erie which was called by my name.'"[4]

Cleaveland it was, but Cleveland it later became when, in 1832, a newspaper, the Cleaveland Herald, changed the typeface in its masthead and one letter had to go. However, the "a" was hardly missed, for many gazetteers and maps had already dropped the letter well before the newspaper administered the final coup de grace.

Extract from the Journal of Moses Cleaveland, 4–7 July 1786[5]

On this creek ("Conneaught") in New Connecticut, July 4th, 1796, under General Moses Cleaveland, the surveyors, and men sent by the Connecticut Land Company to survey and settle the Connecticut Reserve, and were the first English people who took possession of it. The day, memorable as the birthday of American Independence, and freedom from British tyranny, and commemorated by all good freeborn sons of America, and memorable as the day on which the settlement of this new country was commenced, and in time may raise her head amongst the most enlightened and improved States. And after many difficulties perplexities and hardships were surmounted, and we were on the good and promised land, felt that a just tribute of respect to the day ought to be paid. There were in all, including men, women and children, fifty in number. The men, under Captain Tinker ranged themselves on the beach, and fired a Federal salute of fifteen rounds, and then the sixteenth in honor of New Connecticut. . . .

First Report of Moses Cleaveland to the Connecticut Land Company, August 5, 1796[6]

*T*he Cuyahoga is navigable for sloops about eight miles as the river runs, and for boats to the portage, if the immense quantity of trees drove down and lodged are cleared out. The land excellent, the water clear and lively current, and streams and springs falling into all three rivers [the Cuyahoga, the Grand, and the Ashtabula]. We went in a Schenectady boat, the 'Cuyahoga,' about twenty-five miles to the old Moravian Indian town, and I imagine, on a meridian line, not more than twelve or fifteen miles. Here the bottoms widened and as I am informed, increase in width and if possible in quality. I believe we could have proceeded further up the river but found the time allotted and the provision inadequate to perform the whole route. At this place we found a stream that empties into the river which will make a good mill seat [Tinker's creek]. The lands on the lake shore in some places low, here and there a small cranberry pond, not of any great extent, nor discovered low drowned lands of any bigness for twenty or thirty miles on the lake shore. On the east of the Cuyahoga are clay banks from twenty to forty feet high, on the top of the land level covered with chestnut, oak, walnut, ash and some sugar maple. There are but few hemlocks and those only on a swamp, pond or lake, and in the immense quantity of flood wood lodged on the lakes and rivers, I rarely found any of that wood. The shore west of the mouth of the Cuyahoga is a steep bank for ten miles, the quality of the soil I know not, but from the growth and kind of timber, these present no unfavorable aspect. I should, with great pleasure, readily comply with what I suppose you have heretofore expected, that I should leave this country about this time. I have not as yet been interrupted in a constant attention to business, more than I could have imagined or would have voluntarily entered into, and I see no prospect of its lessening at present. Those who are meanly envying the compensation and sitting at their ease and see their prosperity increasing at the loss of health, ease and comfort of others, I wish might experience the hardships for one month; if not then satisfied, their grumbling would give me no pain. I apprehend the stagnant waters in Lake Erie (except to the westward) must be of small dimensions. The interior lakes and ponds, though not included in Livingston's computation, are, I expect, few and small, unless the land bears more to the northwest after it passes the Cuyahoga than it does this side, the surplus will not be consequential. It is impossible at present to determine on the place for the capital. More information of the extent of the ceded lands and ye traverse of the lakes and rivers are wanted. This will cause delay and require examination. I believe it will be on the Cuyahoga, it must command the greatest communication, either by land or water, of any other place on the purchase or any ceded lands west of the head of the Mohawk. I expect soon to leave this for the westward and shall make my residence there until I am ready to return to Connecticut. The men are remarkably healthy, though without sauce or vegetables, and in good spirits.

1. Charles Whittlesey, *Early History of Cleveland, Ohio* (Cleveland, 1867), 187.
2. Ibid., 181–83.

3. Samuel P. Orth, *A History of Cleveland, Ohio* (Cleveland: S. J. Clarke, 1910), 1:95–96. The original letter is in the Western Reserve Historical Society Library. See also James Harrison Kennedy, *A History of the City of Cleveland, 1796–1896* (Cleveland: Imperial, 1896), 37–39.

4. Orth, *A History of Cleveland, Ohio,* 1:96.

5. Whittlesey, *Early History of Cleveland, Ohio,* 181–83.

6. Orth, *A History of Cleveland, Ohio,* 1:95–96.

IV.9.   Ohio's First Road: Zane's Trace, 1796–1797

With the coming of peace in 1795 and the migration of thousands of settlers from the East that followed, it was soon evident that the host of new settlements in the Ohio country, virtually all of which were located along waterways, would need overland connections to tie them together. Water travel was often seasonally undependable, due to spring floods, summer droughts, and winter ice. Indian trails through the forests proved only marginally helpful. Needed were mile- and time-saving roads that directly connected the new communities mushrooming across the land.

The first of the new roads was Zane's Trace, at the outset little more than a bridle path through the forest, just wide enough to accommodate a single file of packhorses. Built in 1797 by Ebenezer Zane, it connected Wheeling, Virginia, with Limestone (later called Maysville) in Kentucky, via St. Clairsville, Cambridge, Zanesville, Lancaster, Chillicothe, West Union, and Aberdeen, settlements either already in being or soon to be built because of the very presence of the road. Of these, Zanesville, bearing the name of the builder, and Chillicothe were destined to become Ohio capitals, while the communities along the eastern portion of the trace would later be served by the famed National Road, which followed the route of the trace.

On 17 May 1796, Congress granted to Ebenezer Zane three tracts of land, each one-mile square, for the purpose of establishing ferry crossings over the Muskingum, Hockhocking, and Scioto Rivers, at the sites of Zanesville, Lancaster, and Chillicothe. In return, Zane was to survey and lay out the road in its entirety, from Wheeling to Limestone (Maysville).[1] Significantly, it was Zane who had taken the initiative in petitioning Congress for these grants,[2] without which the construction of the road would have been impractical. With its completion in 1797, Zane's Trace presaged the day when the future state of Ohio would be crisscrossed with roadways.

Petition to Congress by Ebenezer Zane

[March 25, 1796]

*T*o the Senate and House of Representatives of the United States. the petition of Ebenezer Zane of Wheeling on the Ohio River. —

Your petitioner confident that the public as well as individuals would derive great advantage from the opining of a road through the Territory North West of the Ohio. from Wheeling to Sioto River, & from thence to Limestone in the State of Kentucky, and also to Fort Washington, Hath given Himself trouble & incurred some expence, in exploring the rout and ascertaining the practicability of the undertaking. That from an actual view of the Ground He Has no Hesitation in saying that a good waggon Road may with facility be made between these places, & at a moderate expence. That the more fully to demonstrate the practicability of the proposed road, He Hath at his own expence employ'd a number of labourers, and Hath actually made considerable progress in marking and opening the same in such manner as to be passible to travellers on Horseback; and is determined to Have the same compleated in that way in its whole distance previous to the last of April next. But as the proposed road must cross the Muskingum, Hockhocking and Sioto Rivers, streams fordable only in dry seasons; it must be obvious that it cannot be used by travellers with certainty and Safety without the establishment of Fer[ries] upon these rivers. These establishments cannot now be made without the permission and aid of Congress the land being the property of the United States. Your petitioner therefore prays that Congress will permit and authorize Him to locate military Bounty Warrants upon as much land at each of the crossings of the above Rivers as may in their Judgment be sufficient to support the desired establishments which He will engage to Have made in due time, & will also defray all expences which may be incurred in surveying and laying off such lotts of land. Your petitioner Holds land warrants of the above description and only requests the priviledge of locating them in situations which may be point out by the necessity of the case, He asks no other compensation for his trouble, nor any reimbursement of his expences. . . . — Your Petitioner submits His application to the wisdom & discretion of the National Legislature and doubts not but upon a candid examination his request will be deemed reasonable: & the undertaking He is engaged in admitted to be meritorious & deserving of encouragement.

EBENEZER ZANE.

[Endorsed] Legis: 1ˢᵗ Sess: 4ᵗʰ Cong: Petition of Ebenezer Zane praying liberty to locate military lands, at the crossings of certain rivers March 25ᵗʰ 1796. . . .

1. See "An Act to authorize Ebenezer Zane to locate certain lands in the territory of the United States, northwest of the river Ohio," approved May 17, 1796, 4th Cong., sess. 1, in Richard Peters, ed., *Public Statutes at Large of the United States of America* (Boston, 1848), 6:27.

2. See Clarence E. Carter, ed., *The Territorial Papers of the United States,* vol. 2, *The Territory Northwest of the River Ohio, 1787–1803* (Washington, 1934), 550-52.

IV.10. Division of the Old Northwest into the Indiana Territory and the Prospective State of Ohio, 1800

If one of the original thirteen states could lay claim to the title "Mother of Ohio" it was Virginia, for in the wake of the Treaty of Greene Ville and the opening of eastern and southern Ohio to the prospect of immediate settlement, the majority of the eager settlers who poured across the mountains and the Ohio River came from that state. Just across the river, Virginia was not only closer than Massachusetts, with its interest in the Ohio Company lands, or Connecticut, with its focus on the Western Reserve, or New Jersey, with its stake in Symmes's Miami Purchase, but it had an additional advantage over the others in its extensive Military District between the Scioto and Little Miami Rivers to be given away as bounty lands to its Revolutionary War veterans. The appeal of free land drew Virginians into southern Ohio in such numbers that Chillicothe, founded in 1796, was by 1798 the Northwest Territory's largest settlement and capital city!

In contrast to the Federalist supporters of Governor Arthur St. Clair, concentrated in areas of predominant New England influence such as Marietta and the Western Reserve, most of the Virginians coming into the Military District were Jeffersonian Republicans. Prominent among the latter were Edward Tiffin and his younger brother-in-law, Thomas Worthington, who, arriving in Chillicothe early in 1798, quickly emerged as key members of the Republican-dominated territorial legislature that took office for the first time on 2 February 1799, with Tiffin elected Speaker of the House of Representatives.

With the Republican majority behind Tiffin and Worthington pushing for statehood, opposed by the Federalist minority behind Governor St. Clair, whose territorial governorship, often exercised autocratically, would end with statehood, friction was soon abundantly evident. Enjoying the power of absolute veto, St. Clair exercised it eleven times over the first thirty bills passed by the Republican legislature. Yet the majority could not be denied when it came to the selection of the first territorial delegate to the Federal Congress, the Virginia-born Republican William Henry Harrison from North Bend being chosen in October 1799, over the governor's handpicked candidate, namely, his own son, Arthur St. Clair Jr.

Though Harrison could not vote, he could and did introduce legislation calculated to speed up the process of statehood. In December 1799 he introduced a measure to enable small farmers to buy land directly from the federal government in 320-acre lots (instead of the previous 640-acre minimum) and with four years to pay, enabling many to use their farming proceeds in those four years to help buy the land. Passed on 15 April 1800 by the Congress over the opposition of the Federalists, who feared for the future of their party when another Republican-dominated state would enter the Union, the measure came to be known as the Harrison Land Act.

Harrison was not finished. On 7 May 1800, another bill he proposed was passed by the Congress despite Federalist opposition.[1] Dividing the Northwest Territory into two parts by a line running from the mouth of the Kentucky River to Fort Recovery and then due north to the international boundary with Canada, it established the new Indiana Territory west of that line and continued what was left of the Northwest Territory, under that name, east of the line. Provision was made that when the state of Ohio was formed from the eastern division, the boundary would be established as a due north line running from the mouth of the Great Miami River. Following the passage of this act, Harrison was appointed governor of the Indiana Territory, with its capital at Vincennes, and relinquished his duties in Congress.

St. Clair had unsuccessfully attempted to counter the Harrison proposal with a plan of his own that had called for a division of the Northwest Territory into three parts, not one of which could be expected to reach the minimum population of sixty thousand required for statehood anytime soon. Specifically, he had proposed an eastern part, with Marietta as its capital; a central part, with its capital at Cincinnati; and a western part, with the capital at Vincennes. Had it been adopted by Congress, it would have eliminated Chillicothe and its bloc of Virginia Republicans as a seat of territorial power.

With the triumph of the Harrison proposal and the defeat of St. Clair's, Ohio statehood was on the horizon.

DIVISION OF THE TERRITORY NORTHWEST OF THE RIVER OHIO

[May 7, 1800]

*A*n act to divide the territory of the United States north-west of the Ohio, into two separate governments.

Be it enacted by the Senate and House of Representatives of the United States of America, in Congress assembled, That from and after the fourth day of July next all that part of the territory of the United States, north-west of the Ohio river, which lies to the westward of a line beginning at the Ohio, opposite to the mouth of Kentucky river, and running thence to Fort Recovery, and thence north until it shall intersect the territorial line between the United States and Canada, shall, for the purposes of temporary government, constitute a seperate territory, and be called the Indiana Territory.

SEC. 2 And be it further enacted, that there shall be established within the said territory a government in all respects similar to that provided by the ordinance of Congress, passed on the thirteenth day July one thousand seven hundred and eighty seven, for the government of the territory of the United States north-west of the river Ohio; and the inhabitants thereof shall be entitled to, and enjoy all and singular the rights, privileges and advantages granted and secured to the people, by the said ordinance.

SEC. 3. And be it further enacted, that the officers for the said territory, who by virtue of this Act shall be appointed by the President of the United States, by and with the advice and consent of the Senate, shall respectively exercise the same powers, perform the same duties, and receive for their services the same compensations, as by the ordinance aforesaid, and the laws of the United States, have been provided and established for similar officers in the territory of the United States north-west of the River Ohio. And the duties and emoluments of Superintendant of Indian affairs shall be united with those of Governor: Provided, That the President of the United States, shall have full power in the recess of Congress, to appoint and commission all officers herein authorized; and their commissions shall continue in force until the end of the next Session of Congress.

SEC. 4. And be it further enacted, That so much of the ordinance for the government of the territory of the United States north-west of the Ohio river, as relates to the organization of a General Assembly therein, and prescribes the powers thereof, shall be in force and operate in the Indiana Territory, whenever satisfactory evidence shall be given to the Governor thereof, that such is the wish of a majority of the freeholders, notwithstanding there may not be therein five thousand free male inhabitants of the age of twenty one Years and upwards: Provided, that until there shall be five thousand free male inhabitants of twenty-one Years and upwards in said territory, the whole number of Representatives to the General Assembly, shall not be less than seven, nor more than nine, to be apportioned by the Governor to the several Counties in said territory, agreeably to the number of free males of the age of twenty one Years and upwards, which they may respectively contain.

SEC. 5. And be it further enacted, That nothing in this Act contained, shall be construed so as in any manner to affect the government now in force in the territory of the United States north-west of the Ohio river, further than to prohibit the exercise thereof within the Indiana Territory, from and after the aforesaid fourth of July next: Provided, That whenever that part of the territory of the United States, which lies to the eastward of a line beginning at the mouth of the Great Miami river, and running thence due north to the territorial line between the United States and Canada, shall be erected into an independent State, and admitted into the Union on an equal footing with the original States, thenceforth said line shall become and remain permanently the boundary line, between such State and the Indiana Territory, any thing in this Act contained to the contrary notwithstanding.

SEC. 6. And be it further enacted, That until it shall be otherwise ordered by the legislatures of the said Territories respectively, Chillicothe, on Scioto river, shall be the seat of the government of the territory of the United States north-west of the Ohio river. And that Saint Vincennes, on the Wabash river, shall be the seat of the government for the Indiana Territory.

1. See Clarence E. Carter, *The Territorial Papers of the United States,* vol. 3, *The Territory Northwest of the River Ohio, 1787-1803* (Continued) (Washington, 1934), 86-88.

IV.11. The Ohio Constitution of 1802

After twelve years in power during the presidencies of George Washington and John Adams, the Federalists lost the election of 1800 to Thomas Jefferson, Aaron Burr, and the Republican Party. Though not conclusively known at the time, the Federalists would never again win a national election and would eventually disappear from the American political scene. Motivated by the fear that they might never again control the national government, particularly once the Republican-dominated western territories began to be admitted as states, the Federalists in the Ohio country, behind Governor Arthur St. Clair, worked zealously to delay Ohio statehood for as long as possible. For their part, the Republicans in the territory, led by Edward Tiffin and Thomas Worthington, worked just as hard to achieve statehood, and now they had the president of the United States on their side.

Backed by President Jefferson and the Republican majority in Congress, an Enabling Act was passed on 30 April 1802 "to enable the people of the eastern division of the territory northwest of the river Ohio to form a constitution and state government, and for the admis-

sion of such state into the Union, on an equal footing with the original states."[1] It was agreed that a convention would be elected to meet at Chillicothe on 1 November 1802 to begin work on the Ohio constitution. Though the population of the projected state had scarcely passed forty thousand, well short of the minimum sixty thousand mandated by the Northwest Ordinance for statehood, the rate of growth was such that it was projected that the minimal figure would be reached by the time the proposed new constitution would reach the Congress for its consideration. After charging in an emotional address before the convention that Jefferson and the Congress had no right to change the mandate of the ordinance, Governor St. Clair was removed from office by the president on 22 November and replaced by the territorial secretary, Charles W. Byrd, who would serve only a few months until succeeded by the first elected governor of the state under the constitution then being drafted.

The delegates, elected by districts to the constitutional convention, were thirty-five in number, of whom twenty-six were Republicans, seven were Federalists, and two identified themselves with neither party. When work on the constitution had been completed, the document was entrusted to Thomas Worthington, who carried it on horseback to Washington to deliver it personally to President Jefferson on 20 December and to Congress two days later.[2] With the approval of both houses of Congress, a bill to admit Ohio as the seventeenth state in the Union was signed into law by Jefferson on 19 February 1803.

After years of frustrating experience under the autocratic, often dictatorial territorial governor, Arthur St. Clair, the new Ohio Constitution relegated the status of the state's governor to that of a figurehead, without veto power, unable even to appoint the other state executive officers. Instead, power was concentrated in a bicameral legislature consisting of a Senate and a House of Representatives. Even the third branch of government, the judiciary, was subordinate to the legislature, which had the power to appoint and remove all judges.

The right to vote was restricted to white males, twenty-one years of age or older, who were taxpayers. Though the prohibition against slavery contained in the Northwest Ordinance was reinforced in the new Ohio Constitution, the right of blacks to vote in the new state failed to be included in the constitution by a narrow 18 to 17 vote.

Although not without flaws, the Ohio Constitution was widely regarded as the most democratic state constitution that had yet appeared. For almost half a century, until 1851, it would serve Ohio as the foundation of its government.

CONSTITUTION OF THE STATE OF OHIO—1802

*W*e, the people of the eastern division of the territory of the United States, northwest of the river Ohio, having the right of admission into the general government, as a member of the Union, consistent with the constitution of the United States, [and] the ordinance of Congress of one thousand seven hundred and eighty-seven, . . . do ordain and establish the following constitution or form of government, and do mutually agree with each other to form ourselves into a free and independent State, by the name of the State of Ohio:

ARTICLE I.

Of the Legislative Powers.

Section 1. The legislative authority of this State shall be vested in a General Assembly, which shall consist of a Senate and a House of Representatives, both to be elected by the people.

Sec. 2. Within one year after the first meeting of the General Assembly, and within every subsequent term of four years, an enumeration of all the white male inhabitants, above twenty-one years of age, shall be made in such manner as shall be directed by law. The number of Representatives shall, at the several periods of making such enumeration, be fixed by the Legislature, and apportioned among the several counties according to the number of white male inhabitants above twenty-one years of age in each, and shall never be less than twenty-four, nor greater than thirty-six, until the number of white male inhabitants, above twenty-one years of age, shall be twenty-two thousand inhabitants; and, after that event, at such ratio that the whole number of Representatives shall never be less than thirty-six, nor exceed seventy-two.

Sec. 3. The Representatives shall be chosen annually by the citizens of each county, respectively, on the Second Tuesday of October.

Sec. 4. No person shall be a Representative who shall not have attained the age of twenty-five years, and be a citizen of the United States, and an inhabitant of this State; shall also have resided within the limits of the county in which he shall be chosen, one year preceding his election, unless he shall have been absent on the public business of the United States, or of this State, and shall have paid a State or county tax.

Sec. 5. The Senators shall be chosen biennially, by the qualified voters for Representatives; and on their being convened in consequence of the first election, they shall be divided by lot, from their respective counties and districts, as near as can be, into two classes; the seats of the Senators of the first class shall be vacated at the expiration of the first year, and of the second class at the expiration of the second year; so that one-half thereof, as near as possible, may be annually chosen forever thereafter.

Sec. 6. The number of Senators shall, at the several periods of making the enumeration beforementioned, be fixed by the Legislature, and apportioned among the several counties or districts, to be established by law, according to the number of white male inhabitants of the age of twenty-one years in each, and shall never be less than one-third, nor more than one-half, of the number of Representatives.

Sec. 7. No person shall be a Senator who has not arrived at the age of thirty years, and is a citizen of the United States; shall have resided two years in the county or district immediately preceding the election, unless he shall have been absent on the public business of the United States, or of this State; and shall, moreover, have paid a State or county tax.

Sec. 8. The Senate and House of Representatives, when assembled, shall each choose a speaker and its other officers, be judges of the qualifications and elections of its members, and sit upon its own adjournments; two-thirds of each house shall continue [constitute] a quorum to do business; but a smaller number may adjourn from day to day, and compel the attendance of absent members.

Sec. 9. Each house shall keep a journal of its proceedings, and publish them, the yeas and nays of the members, on any question shall, at the desire of any two of them, be entered on the journals.

Sec. 10. Any two members of either house shall have liberty to dissent from, and protest against, any act or resolution which they may think injurious to the public or any individual, and have the reasons of their dissent entered on the journals.

Sec. 11. Each house may determine the rules of the proceedings, punish its members for disorderly behavior, and with the concurrence of two-thirds, expel a member, but not a second time for the same cause; and shall have all other powers necessary for a branch of the Legislature of a free and independent State.

Sec. 12. When vacancies happen in either house, the Governor or the person exercising the power of the Governor, shall issue writs of election to fill such vacancies.

Sec. 13. Senators and Representatives shall, in all cases, except treason, felony or breach of the peace, be privileged from arrest during the session of the General Assembly, and in going to and returning from the same; and for any speech or debate in either house, they shall not be questioned in any other place.

Sec. 14. Each house may punish, by imprisonment during their session, any person not a member, who shall be guilty of disrespect to the house, by any disorderly or contemptuous behavior in their presence; provided that such imprisonment shall not, at one time, exceed twenty-four hours.

Sec. 15. The doors of each house, and of committees of the whole, shall be kept open, except in such cases, as in the opinion of the house, require secrecy. Neither house shall, without the consent of the other, adjourn for more than two days, nor to any other place than that in which the two houses shall be sitting.

Sec. 16. Bills may originate in either house, but may be altered, amended or rejected by the other.

Sec. 17. Every bill shall be read on three different days in each house, unless, in case of urgency, three-fourths of the house where such bill is so depending, shall deem it expedient to dispense with this rule, and every bill having passed both houses, shall be signed by the speakers of their respective houses.

Sec. 18. The style of the laws of this State shall be: Be it enacted by the General Assembly of the State of Ohio.

Sec. 19. The Legislature of this State shall not allow the following officers of government greater annual salaries than as follows, until the year one thousand eight hundred and eight, to wit: The Governor not more than one thousand dollars, the judges of the Supreme Court not more than one thousand dollars each, the presidents of the Court of Common Pleas not more than eight hundred dollars each, the Secretary of State not more than five hundred dollars, the Auditor of Public Accounts not more than seven hundred and fifty dollars, the Treasurer not more than four hundred and fifty dollars; no member of the Legislature shall receive more than two dollars per day during his attendance on the Legislature, nor more for twenty-five miles he shall travel in going to and returning from the General Assembly.

Sec. 20. No Senator or Representative shall, during the time for which he shall have been elected, be appointed to any civil office under this State, which shall have been created, or the emoluments of which shall have been increased, during such time.

Sec. 21. No money shall be drawn from the treasury, but in consequence of appropriation made by law.

Sec. 22. An accurate statement of the receipts and expenditures of the public money shall be attached to, and published with, the laws annually.

Sec. 23. The House of Representatives shall have the sole power of impeaching, but a majority of all the members must concur in an impeachment; all impeachments shall be tried by the Senate; and when sitting for that purpose, the Senators shall be upon oath or affirmation to do justice according to law and evidence; no person shall be convicted without the concurrence of two thirds of all the Senators.

Sec. 24. The Governor, and all other civil officers under this State, shall be liable to impeachment for any misdemeanor in office; but judgment in such case shall not extend further than removal from office, and disqualification to hold any office of honor, profit, or trust, under this State. The party, whether convicted or acquitted, shall nevertheless be liable to indictment, trial judgment and punishment, according to law.

Sec. 25. The first session of the General Assembly shall commence on the first Tuesday of March next; and, forever after, the General Assembly shall meet on the first Monday of December, in every year, and at no other period, unless, directed, by law, or provided for by this constitution. . . .

ARTICLE II.

Of the Executive.

Section 1. The supreme executive power of this State shall be vested in a Governor.

Sec. 2. The Governor shall be chosen by the electors of the members of the General Assembly, on the second Tuesday of October, at the same places, and in the same manner, that they shall respectively vote for members thereof. The return of every election for Governor, shall be sealed up and transmitted to the seat of government, by the returning officers, directed to the speaker of the Senate, who shall open and publish them, in the presence of a majority of the members of each house of the General Assembly; the person having the highest number of votes shall be Governor; but if two or more shall be equal and highest in votes, one of them shall be chosen Governor by joint ballot of both houses of the General Assembly. Contested elections for Governor shall be determined by both houses of the General Assembly, in such manner as shall be prescribed by law.

Sec. 3. The first Governor shall hold his office until the first Monday of December, one thousand eight hundred and five, and until another Governor shall be elected and qualified to office; and forever after shall the Governor hold his office for the term of two years and until another governor shall be elected and qualified, but he shall not be eligible more than six years in any term of eight years. He shall be either thirty years of age and have been a citizen of the United States twelve years and an inhabitant of this State four years next preceding his election.

Sec. 4. He shall, from time to time, give to the General Assembly information of the state of the government and recommend to their consideration such measures as he shall deem expedient.

Sec. 6. The Governor shall, at stated times, receive for his service a compensation, which shall neither be increased nor diminished during the term for which he shall have been elected.

Sec. 7. He may require information, in writing, from the officers in the executive department upon any subject relating to the duties of their respective offices, and shall take that the laws be faithfully executed.

Sec. 8. When any officer, the right of whose appointment is, by this constitution, vested in the General Assembly, shall during the recess, die, or his office by any means become vacant, the Governor shall have power to fill such vacancy by granting a commission, which shall expire at the end of the next session of the Legislature.

Sec. 9. He may, on extraordinary occasions, convene the General Assembly, by proclamation, and shall state to them, when assembled, the purposes for which they shall have been convened.

Sec. 10. He shall be commander-in-chief of the army and navy of this State, and of the militia, except when they shall be called into the service of the United States.

Sec. 11. In case of disagreement between the two Houses, with the respect to the time of adjournment, the Governor shall have the power to adjourn the General Assembly to such time as he thinks proper: provided it is not a period beyond the annual meeting of the Legislature.

Sec. 12. In case of the death, impeachment, resignation or removal of the Governor from office, the Speaker of the Senate shall exercise the office of Governor until he be acquitted or another Governor shall be duly qualified. In case of the impeachment of the Speaker of the Senate, or his death, removal from office, resignation or absence from the State, the Speaker of the House of Representatives shall succeed to the office and exercise the duties thereof until a governor shall be elected and qualified. . . .

ARTICLE III.

Of the Judiciary.

Section 1. The judicial power of this State, both as to matters of law and equity, shall be vested in a Supreme Court, in Courts of Common Pleas for each county, in Justices of the Peace, and in such other courts as the Legislature may, from time to time, establish.

Sec. 2. The Supreme Court shall consist of three Judges, and two of whom shall be a quorum. They shall have original and appellate jurisdiction both in common law and chancery, in such cases as shall be directed by law; provided, that nothing herein contained shall prevent the General Assembly from adding another Judge to the Supreme Court after the term of five years; in which case the Judges may divide the State into two circuits, within which any two of the Judges may hold a court.

Sec. 3. The several Courts of Common Pleas shall consist of a President and Associate Judges. The State shall be divided, by law, into three circuits; there shall be appointed in each circuit a President of the Courts who, during his continuance in office, shall reside therein. There shall be appointed in each county not more than three nor less than two Associate Judges who, during their continuance in office, shall reside therein. The President and Associate Judges, in their respective counties, any three of whom shall be a quorum, shall compose the Court of Common Pleas; which court shall have common law and chancery jurisdiction in all such cases as shall be directed by law; provided, that nothing herein contained shall be construed to prevent the Legislature from increasing the number of circuits and Presidents after the term of five years.

Sec. 4. The Judges of the Supreme Court and Courts of Common Pleas shall have complete criminal jurisdiction in such cases and in such manner as may be pointed out by law.

Sec. 5. The Court of Common Pleas in each county shall have jurisdiction of all probate and testamentary matters, granting administration, the appointments of guardians, and such other cases as shall be prescribed by law.

Sec. 6. The Judges of the Court of Common Pleas shall, within their respective counties, have the same powers with the Judges of the Supreme Court, to issue writs of certiorari to the Justices of the Peace, and to cause their proceedings to be brought before them, and the like right and justice to be done.

Sec. 7. The Judges of the Supreme Court shall, by virtue of their offices, be conservators of the peace throughout the State. The President of the Courts of Common Pleas shall, by virtue of their offices, be conservators of the peace in their respective circuits; and the Judges of the Courts of the Common Pleas shall, by virtue of their offices, be conservators of the peace in their respective counties.

Sec. 8. The Judges of the Supreme Court, the President and the Associate Judges of the Courts of Common Pleas shall be appointed by a joint ballot of both Houses of the General Assembly, and shall hold their offices for the term of seven years, if so long they behave well. The Judges of the Supreme Court and the President of the Court of Common Pleas shall, at stated times, receive for their services an adequate compensation, to be fixed by law, which shall not be diminished during their continuance in office; but they shall receive no fees or perquisites of office, nor hold any other office of profit or trust under the authority of this State or the United States. . . .

ARTICLE IV.

Of Elections and Electors.

Section 1. In all elections, all white male inhabitants above the age of twenty-one years, having resided in the State one year next preceding the election, and who have paid or are charged with a State or county tax, shall enjoy the right of an elector; but no person shall be entitled to vote, except in the county or district in which he shall actually reside at the time of the election.

Sec. 2. All elections shall be by ballot.

Sec. 3. Electors shall, in all cases except treason, felony or breach of the peace, be privileged from arrest, during their attendance at elections, and in going to and returning from the same.

Sec. 4. The Legislature shall have full power to exclude from the privilege of electing, or being elected, any person convicted of bribery, perjury, or other infamous crime.

Sec. 5. Nothing contained in this article shall be so construed as to prevent white male persons, above the age of twenty-one years, who are compelled to labor on the roads of their respective townships or counties, and who have resided one year in the State, from having the right of an elector. . . .

ARTICLE VII.

Official Oaths.

Section 1. Every person who shall be chosen or appointed to any office, or trust, or profit under the authority of this State shall, before the entering on the execution thereof, taking an oath or affirmation to support the constitution of the United States and of this State, and also an oath of office. . . .

Of the Seat of Government.

Sec. 4. Chillicothe shall be the seat of government until the year one thousand eight hundred and eight. No money shall be raised, until the year one thousand eight hundred and nine, by the Legislature of this State for the purpose of erecting public buildings for the accommodation of the Legislature.

Of Amendments to the Constitution.

Sec. 5. That after the year one thousand eight hundred and six, whenever two-thirds of the General Assembly shall think it necessary to amend or change this constitution, they shall recommend to the electors, at the next election for members to the General Assembly, to vote for or against a convention, and if it shall appear that a majority of the citizens of the State, voting for Representatives, have voted for a convention, the General Assembly shall, at their next session, call a convention, to consist of as many members as there shall be in the General Assembly; to be chosen in the same manner, at the same place, and by the same electors that choose the General Assembly; who shall meet within three months after the said election for the purpose of revising, amending or changing the constitution. But no alteration of this constitution shall ever take place, so as to introduce slavery or involuntary servitude into this State.

Boundaries of the State.

Sec. 6. That the limits and boundaries of this State be ascertained, it is declared that they are as hereafter mentioned; that is to say: bounded on the east by the Pennsylvania line; on the south by the Ohio River to the mouth of the Great Miami, aforesaid; and on the north by an east and west line and drawn through the southerly extreme of Lake Michigan, running east, after intersecting the due north line, aforesaid, from the mouth of the Great Miami until it shall intersect Lake Erie or the territorial line, and thence with the same, through Lake Erie, to the Pennsylvania line aforesaid; provided always, and it is hereby fully understood and declared by this convention, that if the southerly bend or extreme of Lake Michigan should extend so far south, that a line drawn due east from it should not intersect Lake Erie, or if it should intersect the said

Lake Erie, east of the mouth of the Miami River of the Lake [the Maumee River], then in that case, with the assent of Congress of the United States, the northern boundary of this State shall be established by, and extended to a direct line running from the southern extremity of Lake Michigan to the most northerly cape of the Miami Bay [the Maumee Bay], after intersecting the due north line from the mouth of the Great Miami River as aforesaid, thence northeast to the territorial line, and, by the said territorial line to the Pennsylvania line.

ARTICLE VIII.

Bill of Rights.

That the general, great and essential principles of liberty and free government may be recognized and forever unalterably established, we declare:

Section 1. That all men are born equally free and independent, and have certain natural, inherent and unalienable rights; amongst which are the enjoying and defending life and liberty, acquiring, possessing and protecting property, and pursuing and obtaining happiness and safety; and every free republican government, being founded on their sole authority, and organized for the great purpose of protecting their rights and liberties, and securing their independence; to effect these ends, they have at all times a complete power to alter, reform or abolish their government, whenever they may deem it necessary.

Sec. 2. There shall be neither slavery nor involuntary servitude in this State, otherwise than for the punishment of crimes, whereof the party shall have been duly convicted; nor shall any male person, arrived at the age of twenty-one years, or female person arrived at the age of eighteen years, be held to serve any person as a servant, under the pretense of indenture or otherwise, unless such person shall enter into such indenture while in a state of perfect freedom, and on a condition of a bona fide consideration, received or to be received, for their service, except as before excepted. Nor shall any indenture of any negro or mulatto, hereafter made and executed out of the State, or if made in the State, where the term of service exceeds one year, be of the last validity, except those given in the case of apprenticeships.

Sec. 3. That all men have a natural and indefeasible right to worship Almighty God according to the dictates of conscience; that no human authority can, in any case whatever, control or interfere with the rights of conscience; that no man shall be compelled to attend, erect or support any place of worship, or to maintain any ministry, against his consent, and that no preference shall ever be given, by law, to any religious society or mode of worship, and no religious test shall be required as a qualification to any office of trust or profit. But religion, morality and knowledge being essentially necessary to good government and the happiness of mankind, schools and the means of instructions shall forever be encouraged by legislative provision not inconsistent with the rights of conscience.

Sec. 4. Private property ought and shall ever be held inviolate, but always subservient to the public welfare, provided a compensation in money be made to the owner.

Sec. 5. That the people shall be secure in their persons, houses, papers, and possessions, from unwarrantable searches and seizures; and that general warrants, whereby an officer may be commanded to search suspected places, without probable evidence of the fact committed, or to seize any person or persons not named, whose offenses are not particularly described, and without oath or affirmation, are dangerous to liberty, and shall not be granted.

Sec. 6. That the printing presses shall be open and free to every citizen who wishes to examine the proceedings of any branch of government, or the conduct of any public officer, and no law shall ever restrain the right thereof. Every citizen has an indisputable right to speak, write or print, upon any subject, as he thinks proper, being liable for the abuse of that liberty. In prosecutions for any publication respecting the official conduct of men in a public capacity, or where the matter published is proper for public information, the truth thereof may always be given in evidence; and in all indictments for libels, the jury shall have the right to determine the law and the facts, under the direction of the court, as in other cases.

Sec. 7. That all courts shall be open, and every person, for an injury done him in his lands, goods, person or reputation, shall have remedy by the due course of law, and right and justice administered, without denial or delay.

Sec. 8. That the right of trial by jury shall be inviolate. . . .

Sec. 28. To guard against the transgressions of the high powers, which we have delegated, we declare, that all powers, not hereby delegated, remain with the people. . . .

1. See Daniel J. Ryan, ed., "Enabling Act for Ohio—1802," 7th Cong., 1st sess., in *Ohio Archaeological and Historical Publications* (Columbus, 1897), 5:74–78.

2. See Daniel J. Ryan, ed., "Constitution of the State of Ohio—1802," in *Ohio Archaeological and Historical Publications* (Columbus, 1897), 5:132–53.

V. The Frontier State

AFTER CONGRESS APPROVED THE ADMISSION of Ohio into the Union on 19 February 1803, government in the new state began to function on 1 March with meetings of the fourteen members of the Senate and the thirty members of the House of Representatives, resulting in the selection of Nathaniel Massie and Michael Baldwin as Speakers of the Senate and House, respectively. On 3 March Edward Tiffin was inaugurated as governor. All three men were from Chillicothe. By April the Senate had also chosen Thomas Worthington of Chillicothe and John Smith of Cincinnati as Ohio's first U.S. senators.

The distinction of election by popular ballot in June of the state's first congressman went to a Morrow County farmer from the Little Miami Valley, Jeremiah Morrow. The new governor, speakers, senators, and congressman were all Jeffersonian Republicans. Indeed, the Federalist Party was so impotent in Ohio at this time that Tiffin had no real opposition for the governorship, while in the only significant contest, for the seat in Congress, Morrow bested his Federalist opponent by a margin of two to one.

The first capital of the new state, from 1803 until 1808, was Chillicothe, which had also served as the last capital of the eastern division of the Northwest Territory. Zanesville was the seat of government from 1808 until 1810; then Chillicothe once more, from 1810 to 1816; and finally the newly platted Columbus, which became the permanent capital in 1816.

Ohio's role as a frontier state was comparatively brief, less than two decades. While there may have been 60,000 inhabitants in 1803, when Ohio became the seventeenth state, by the 1810 census Ohio's population had reached 231,000 and by 1820, 581,000, which placed the state fifth in size, exceeded only by New York, Pennsylvania, Virginia, and North Carolina. With the nation's westward growth bringing Indiana into the Union in 1816 and Illinois in 1818, Ohio's frontier years were over by 1820, only the Black Swamp in northwestern Ohio remaining unsettled.

During the period from 1803 to 1820, Ohio was confronted by a number of challenges. With 436 miles of common border with the slave states of Kentucky and Virginia, the free state of Ohio was faced early on with the need to clarify the legal status of its residents of color in the face of the fugitive slave laws of both the federal government and the slave states of the South. It also had to address the question of educational opportunities for the children of its settlers, particularly those coming in from the East, where opportunities for social, economic, and cultural advancement already were to be found at such well-established colleges and universities as Harvard, Yale, Princeton, William and Mary, Columbia, Pennsylvania, Brown, and Rutgers.

Not the least of the challenges facing the new state in these formative years was the Burr-Blennerhassett Conspiracy of 1804–7, involving Jefferson's first vice president and the threat of possible separation of Ohio and the rest of the West, including the newly purchased Louisiana Territory, from the United States. Another was the War of 1812 with Great Britain, much of it fought on Ohio soil and in Ohio water, with the future of the young nation in question. Sometimes called the Second War for American Independence, it marked one last effort on the part of the British to involve the Indians of the Old Northwest as allies in common cause against the United States. Though the war ended in stalemate, favorable outcomes for Ohio included the final end of British intrigue with the Indians and the permanent neutralization of the Great Lakes, including Lake Erie, paving the way for what ultimately would become the world's longest unfortified international boundary, between the United States and Canada.

V.1.   The New State Begins, 1803

On 11 January 1803, even before Congress had taken action on the proposed Ohio Constitution, statewide elections were held under it in Ohio. These resulted in a virtual clean sweep of offices in the new government by the Jeffersonian Republicans, led by Edward Tiffin, a thirty-six-year-old former Virginian from Chillicothe. With explicit recognition of the new state and its constitution by the Congress on 19 February[1] came implicit acceptance of the results of the election already held. The way was clear for the General Assembly of the State of Ohio to begin to function on 1 March in the little two-story stone building in Chillicothe designated as the state capitol. There, on 3 March 1803, Edward Tiffin was inaugurated as Ohio's first governor, and there he delivered what in retrospect was certainly one of the shortest, tersest inaugural addresses in the history not only of Ohio but of all the states.[2]

Act of Congress Recognizing the State of Ohio

An act to provide for the due execution of the laws of the United States within the State of Ohio.

Whereas the people of the eastern district of the territory northwest of the river Ohio did, on the twenty-ninth of November, one thousand eight hundred and two, form for themselves a constitution and State government, and did give to the said State the name of the "State of Ohio," in pursuance of an act of Congress entitled "An act to enable the people of the eastern division of the territory northwest of the Ohio to form a constitution and State government, and for the admission of such State into the Union on an equal footing with the original States, and for other purposes," whereby the said State has become one of the United States of America; in order, therefore, to provide for the due execution of the laws of the United States within the said State of Ohio—

Section 1. Be it enacted by the Senate and House of Representatives of the United States of America in Congress assembled, That all the laws of the United States which are not locally inapplicable shall have the same force and effect within the said State of Ohio as elsewhere within the United States. . . .

Approved February 19, 1803.

The Inaugural Address of Governor Edward Tiffin

Gentlemen of the Senate, and Gentlemen of the House of Representatives,

In obedience to the call of my Fellow-Citizens, communicated to me through your joint-committee [which had reported that morning a total vote cast for Tiffin in the general election of January 11, 1803, of 5,373, with none reported for an opposition candidate], I have attended to take and subscribe the necessary oaths, required by the Constitution, preparatory to administering the Government of this State. I cannot, on this occasion, but express to them, through their Representatives, the high sense I entertain of the obligations I am under for their partiality towards me, in the unanimity which they have manifested at the late elections, and to assure you and them, that so-far as my very limited talents and experience will enable, it shall be my study and care to keep the public weal constantly in view, and uniformly to endeavor to evidence that the confidence reposed in me has not been misplaced.

In order to divert as little of your time as possible from the important duties assigned you, and to avoid that unnecessary parade which has too often been made on occasions of this kind, I will, while I am here, observe, that to-morrow, at 11 o'clock, I shall make a communication to the Legislature, on the state of the Government, by message.

1. See Daniel J. Ryan, "Act of Congress Recognizing the State of Ohio—1803," in *Ohio Archaeological and Historical Publications* (Columbus, 1897), 5:163-64.

2. The text of the address by Governor Tiffin was contained in a letter to the editor of the *Boston Independent Chronicle* from Nathaniel Willis, then serving as the editor of the *Scioto Gazette* in Chillicothe and also as the newly elected printer to the Ohio General Assembly. Willis, a former editor of the *Independent Chronicle,* wrote his letter on 5 March 1803, and it was published in the 31 March issue of that paper. In his letter, Willis reported that "On Thursday, March 3, conformable to a previous resolution, the Senate attended and took their seats in the Representatives' Chamber, and both Houses being assembled, the Speaker of the Senate [Nathaniel Massie], pursuant to the Constitution, proceeded to open the Returns of the Election for Governor, from the different Counties, (Fairfield & Washington having made no return,) and declared that EDWARD TIFFIN, Esq. was duly elected. The two Houses then

separated. A Committee of both Houses was appointed to inform Mr. Tiffin of his election to
the office of Governor, and to know when and where he will attend the two Houses, to be qualified, and to request the hon. Judge [Return J.] Meigs to administer the oaths of office. At 1
o'clock, on the same day, the Senate attended and took their seats in the Representatives' Chamber, and both Houses being assembled, Edward Tiffin, Esq. came in, and after taking the oaths
as prescribed by the Constitution, addressed them as follows:—[Here followed the inaugural
address as noted above.] It was subsequently confirmed in the same letter that when the votes
came in from the counties of Fairfield and Washington "the whole number of votes for Governor Tiffin, . . . was 5373." See Robert C. Wheeler, ed., *Ohio Newspapers: A Living Record* (Columbus: Ohio History Press, 1950), 88–89.

V.2.   Ohio's Black Code

*In the first session of the Ohio General Assembly, which began on 1 March 1803, much of
the legislative agenda related to what might be called housekeeping details: putting into law
the provisions of the new state constitution; continuing the tax laws (primarily on property)
of the former territory, as well as all other territorial laws not in conflict with the constitution;
providing for the organization of counties and townships and the punishment of crime; and
creating an educational system and a state militia. Additional legislation sought to aid the
frontier state's farmers, who comprised the overwhelming majority of the citizenry, by providing a bounty on predatory wolves and panthers for protection of their livestock.*

*With the beginning of the second session of the assembly on 5 December 1803, however,
one of the questions of far-reaching significance that moved to the forefront of legislative
attention was the status of black residents in Ohio. The Ordinance of 1784, as originally proposed by Thomas Jefferson, would have prohibited slavery in the western territories, but only
after 1800. It never went into effect, being replaced by the Northwest Ordinance of 1787,
which explicitly stated: "There shall be neither slavery nor involuntary servitude in the said
[Northwest] territory, otherwise than in the punishment of crimes, whereof the party shall
have been duly convicted: Provided always, That any person escaping into the same, from
whom labor or service is lawfully claimed in any one of the original States, such fugitive may
be lawfully reclaimed, and conveyed to the person claiming his or her labor or service as aforesaid." By this ordinance the Ohio River was made the historic boundary line between free soil
and slave. With the slave states of Kentucky and Virginia sharing a common boundary with
the free state of Ohio, the status of persons of color in the new state was of major importance.*

*By a vote of 18 to 17 in the convention that shaped the Ohio Constitution of 1802, the
right to vote was denied to black males; instead, it was restricted to white males only. Significantly, on the floor of the convention the vote on the issue of black suffrage had been tied, 17
to 17, necessitating the breaking of the tie by the presiding officer, Edward Tiffin, soon to be the
first Ohio governor. A former slaveholder in Virginia who had freed his slaves on coming to the
Northwest Territory, Tiffin broke the tie by casting his vote against black suffrage. Though
blacks at the time constituted but a tiny minority in the total Ohio population, one is moved
to wonder whether the history of race relations in the new state might have been substantially
different had the vote for black suffrage passed in 1802 rather than having been defeated.*

Stephen Middleton has written, in his Black Laws in the Old Northwest, A Documentary History, *that, "Although the majority of white Americans in the Northwest never owned slaves, the enslavement of Africans reinforced the color prejudice of whites. . . . The states formed from the region denied African Americans suffrage, public education, benefits of welfare, testimony against a white, freedom to marry a white, and imposed restrictions on militia service, immigration, and employment. By enacting discriminatory statutes, white lawmakers intended to reserve their states for whites only. They went to great lengths to make blacks unwelcomed in their respective states. Yet the African-American population boomed throughout the region in spite of the laws. African Americans considered racial discrimination more tolerable than slavery."*[1]

The first of the black laws passed by the General Assembly in the new state of Ohio was adopted on 5 January 1804.[2] *It sought to compel residents to comply with the federal Fugitive Slave Law of 1793 and to assure Virginia and Kentucky neighbors across the river that Ohio would not offer refuge to runaway slaves. Not until the 1840s and 1850s, when Ohio became a leader among the states in the abolitionist crusade, were the black laws (collectively called the "Black Code") substantially modified.*

An act, to regulate black and mulatto persons.

Sec. 1. Be it enacted by the general assembly of the state of Ohio, That from and after the first day of June next, no black or mulatto person, shall be permitted to settle or reside in this state, unless he or she shall first produce a fair certificate from some court within the United States, of his or her actual freedom, which certificate shall be attested by the clerk of said court, and the seal thereof annexed thereto, by the said clerk.

Sec. 2. And be it further enacted, That every black or mulatto person residing within this state, on or before the first day of June, one thousand eight hundred and four, shall enter his or her name, together with the name or names of his or her children, in the clerk's office in the county in which he, she or they reside, which shall be entered on record by said clerk, and thereafter the clerk's certificate of such record shall be sufficient evidence of his, her or their freedom; and for every entry and certificate, the person obtaining the same shall pay to the clerk twelve and an half cents: Provided nevertheless, That nothing in this act contained shall bar the lawful claim to any black or mulatto person.

Sec. 3. And be it further enacted, That no person or persons residents of this state, shall be permitted to hire, or in any way employ any black or mulatto person, unless such black or mulatto person shall have one of the certificates as aforesaid, under pain of forfeiting and paying any sum not less than ten nor more than fifty dollars, at the discretion of the court, for every such offense, one-half thereof for the use of the informer and the other half for the use of the state; and shall moreover pay to the owner, if any there be, of such black or mulatto person, the sum of fifty cents for every day he, she or they shall in any wise employ, harbor or secrete such black or mulatto person, which sum or sums shall be recoverable before any court having cognizance thereof.

Sec. 4. And be it further enacted, That if any person or persons shall harbor or secrete any black or mulatto person, the property of any person whatever, or shall in any wise hinder or prevent the lawful owner or owners from retaking and possessing his or her black or mulatto servant or servants, shall, upon conviction thereof, by indictment or information, be fined in any sum not less than ten nor more than fifty dollars, at the discretion of the court, one-half thereof for the use of the informer and the other half for the use of the state.

Sec. 5. And be it further enacted, That every black or mulatto person who shall come to reside in this state with such certificate as is required in the first section of this act, shall, within two years, have the same recorded in the clerk's office, in the county in which he or she means to reside, for which he or she shall pay to the clerk twelve and an half cents, and the clerk shall give him or her a certificate of such record.

Sec. 6. And be it further enacted, That in case any person or persons, his or their agent or agents, claiming any black or mulatto person that now are or hereafter may be in this state, may apply, upon making satisfactory proof that such black or mulatto person or persons is the property of him or her who applies, to any associate judge or justice of the peace within this state, the associate judge or justice is hereby empowered and required, by his precept, to direct the sheriff or constable to arrest such black or mulatto person or persons and deliver the same in the county or township where such officers shall reside, to the claimant or claimants or his or their agent or agents, for which service the sheriff or constable shall receive such compensation as they are entitled to receive in other cases for similar services.

Sec. 7. And be it further enacted, That any person or persons who shall attempt to remove, or shall remove from this state, or who shall aid and assist in removing, contrary to the provisions of this act, any black or mulatto person or persons, without first proving as hereinbefore directed, that he, she or they, is, or are legally entitled so to do, shall, on conviction thereof before any court having cognizance of the same, forfeit and pay the sum of one thousand dollars, one-half to the use of the informer and the other half to the use of the state, to be recovered by action of debt, *qui tam,* or indictment, and shall moreover be liable to the action of the party injured.

ELIAS LANGHAM,

Speaker of the house of representatives.

NATH. MASSIE,

Speaker of the senate.

January 5th, 1804.

1. Stephen Middleton, *The Black Laws in the Old Northwest, A Documentary History* (Westport, Conn.: Greenwood, 1993), xxvii, 3–7.

2. See General Assembly, *Acts of the State of Ohio, Second Session* (Norwalk, Ohio, 1901), 2:63–66.

V.3.   The First University Is Chartered

One of the inducements for settlers to cross the mountains and the river into the Ohio country was the promise of educational opportunity for their children. Article 3 of the Northwest Ordinance of 1787, authored by the Reverend Manasseh Cutler, Yale graduate and agent for the Ohio Company, defined that promise: "Religion, morality, and knowledge, being necessary to good government and the happiness of mankind, schools and the means of education shall forever be encouraged."

Even before the American Revolution, a mission school, with classes taught in German, had been established in the Moravian village of Schoenbrunn. By the 1790s, schools had emerged in Marietta, Cincinnati, Gallipolis, and elsewhere as settlements sprang up along the course of the Ohio River and its tributaries.

The first universities were not far behind. Commitments by the Congress of the United States for the establishment of the first two were made with the set aside in 1787 of two townships in the Ohio Company lands in the Hocking Valley for the support of one, and the designation in 1788 of a single township in the Symmes Purchase in the Miami Valley for the support of the other. With the chartering of Ohio University in 1804 and Miami University in 1809, these commitments were fulfilled.

Ohio University almost came into being as the American Western University. On 9 January 1802 an act was passed by the territorial legislature to establish a university with that name in the town of Athens and with a charter modeled on one prepared earlier by Manasseh Cutler. Before the trustees of the American Western University could do much more than hold their organizational meeting, however, the energies of a number of them as well as of other territorial leaders were diverted to the process of constitution-making for the proposed new state of Ohio. The decision was made, and wisely, for the prospective university to start afresh with the name of the new state and with a charter by the state legislature.

On 18 February 1804 the Ohio General Assembly passed an act to establish a university in the town of Athens "by the name and stile of the Ohio University."[1] The new charter was much like the one adopted two years earlier by the territorial legislature but with the provision that the lands in the two college townships were to be leased for ninety-nine years, renewable forever, with a yearly rent of 6 percent of their original appraisal and with proceeds to be used for the support of the university. With the establishment of Ohio's first university, settlers in the young frontier state could be assured that opportunities for advanced learning in the arts and sciences were no longer the province solely of the original states. Over time, the state of Ohio would come to be called the "mother of colleges." The first had its birth on the banks of the Hocking.

The Charter of the Ohio University

*W*hereas, institutions for the liberal education of youth are essential to the progress of arts and sciences, important to morality, virtue and religion; friendly to the peace, order and prosperity of society, and honorable to the government that encourages and patronizes them: therefore

Sec. 1. Be it enacted by the general Assembly of the State of Ohio, That there shall be an University instituted and established in the town of Athens in the ninth township of the fourteenth range of townships within the limits of the trace of land purchased by the Ohio company of associates by the name and stile of the Ohio University, for the instruction of youth in all the various branches of liberal arts and sciences, for the promotion of good education, virtue, religion and morality, and for conferring all the degrees and literary honors granted in similar institutions.

Sec. 2. And be it further enacted that there shall be and forever remain in the said University a body politic and Corporate by the name and stile of "The President and trustees of the Ohio University," which body politic and corporate shall consist of the governor of the state, (for the time being) the President, and not more than fifteen nor less than ten trustees to be appointed as herein after is provided.

Sec. 3. And be it further enacted, That Elijah Backus, Rufus Putnam, Dudley Woodbridge, Benjamin Tappan, Bazaleel [Bezaleel] Wells, Nathaniel Massie, Daniel Symmes, Daniel Storey, Samuel Carpenter, the Reverend James Kilbourn[e], Griffin Green[e], Senior, and Joseph Darlington, Esquires, together with the governor as aforesaid and the president of the said University (for the time being) to be chosen as herein after directed be and they are hereby created a Body politic and Corporate by the name of "The President and Trustees of the Ohio University" and that they and their successors and such others as shall be duly elected members shall be and remain a body politic and corporate, in law, by that name forever. . . .

1. See Thomas N. Hoover, *The History of Ohio University* (Athens: Ohio University Press, 1954), 16–19; also, Ohio Historical Society, *Fundamental Documents of Early Ohio* (Columbus, n.d.).

V.4.   Conspiracy on the River

Did the Burr-Blennerhassett conspiracy have as its central goal an invasion and conquest of that part of Mexico that we now know as Texas, or was its intent the ultimate separation from the American Union of the new state of Ohio and the rest of the West, including the newly acquired Louisiana Territory? Was it Burr's ambition to become the New World's Emperor Aaron I, ruling over a vast empire larger even than the one then being conquered by the Old World's Napoleon Bonaparte? For his part, was it Harman Blennerhassett's dream of becoming the "Grand Potentate of the Imperial Court of the Emperor Aaron I" that prompted the wealthy Irish exile and descendant of British kings, then living in a sumptuous mansion on an island in the Ohio River, to agree to finance the assembling of an army and the construction of a flotilla of flatboats to launch Burr's ambition of empire-building? To what degree was Ohio's Senator John Smith, a close friend of Burr, involved in the conspiracy?

These and myriad other questions continue to be asked, and the answers may never be entirely known. What is known is that after Burr had made two trips down the Ohio and Mississippi Rivers, in 1805 and 1806, when he had stopped at Blennerhassett's island and at the home of Senator Smith in Cincinnati, rumors abounded throughout the region that the former vice president, now ostracized from eastern society following his duel with Alexander Hamilton, was engaged in a conspiracy involving the territorial integrity of the nation. Lending credulity to the rumors was a series of articles that appeared in Marietta's Ohio Gazette *in the fall of 1806, written by Blennerhassett under the penname of "Querist," which openly discussed the possibility of the ultimate separation of the West, including Ohio and the Louisiana Territory, from the rest of the Union. Seeking recruits for a proposed expedition down the Mississippi, ostensibly for the purpose of invading Mexico, Blennerhassett's articles inevitably came to the attention of both Governor Edward Tiffin and President Thomas Jefferson. With reports of armed men coming and going with increasing frequency in and around Blennerhassett's island mansion, with the revelation that a flotilla of fifteen flatboats was under construction at the Judge Dudley Woodbridge farm six miles north of Marietta on the Muskingum River, and following receipt of a blunt warning from General James Wilkinson in New Orleans, all indicating the probability of a plot against the United States, President Jefferson on 27 November 1806 issued an order for the arrest of his former vice president on conspiracy charges. This was soon followed by an order to Ohio militiamen from Governor Tiffin for the confiscation of the flatboats on the Muskingum. Aware that their plans were unraveling and arrest was imminent, Blennerhassett and another arch conspirator, Comfort Tyler, fled from the island mansion under cover of darkness on 10 December with thirty men and four boats for a rendezvous with Burr in the Mississippi Territory. There Burr and Blennerhassett were apprehended in January 1807 and subsequently brought to trial in Richmond, Virginia, with Chief Justice John Marshall presiding. Marshall, who detested Jefferson, ordered both Burr and Blennerhassett released, ruling that since no overt act of war against the United States had yet occurred, the evidence of Blennerhassett's newspaper articles, the armed men, the flotilla of flatboats, the quantities of confiscated munitions, and reports from General Wilkinson and others did not conclusively prove the charge of treason.*

As for Senator Smith, when Burr was brought to trial the Ohio legislature called upon him to resign. A Senate committee in Washington, chaired by John Quincy Adams, recommended his expulsion, but the Senate failed to reach the two-thirds necessary for his removal by the margin of a single vote. Smith then voluntarily resigned and left Ohio for a new home in Louisiana.

Among those voting for Smith's expulsion was a new U.S. senator from Ohio, Edward Tiffin, who, after two terms as governor, had gone to Washington to take the place of his brother-in-law, Thomas Worthington, in the Senate. In turn, Worthington came back to Ohio, soon to take the place of Tiffin as governor.

Two documents shed particularly interesting light on the Burr-Blennerhassett conspiracy. The first, a report dated 15 December 1806 to the General Assembly by Tiffin, one of his last as governor, describes the confiscation of the flatboats and supplies on the Muskingum as authorized by the assembly on 6 December 1806 and also details the escape of Blennerhassett.[1] The second, a letter from Lewis Cass, then a member of the assembly and later (in 1848) a candidate for the presidency, addressed to Thomas Worthington on 21 December 1806, relates the possibility that it might have been Senator Smith's own son who enabled Blennerhassett to avoid capture.[2]

Governor Tiffin's Message on the Successful Arrest of the Expedition but the Escape of Blennerhassett

*T*o the General Assembly of the state of Ohio. I now communicate to the representatives of the people such operations as have taken place under the act passed this session [on 6 December 1806], to prevent certain acts hostile to the peace & tranquility of the United States, within the jurisdiction of this State, that they may be fully possessed of what has already occurred, & is still in train.

Immediately upon receiving the law, after its passage, I dispatched an express to Marietta, with orders to arrest the flotilla on the Muskingum river, & the agents engaged in its preparation, & to make due enquiry after such proof as would lead to their conviction; as also to prevent any armaments proceeding, that might be descending the Ohio, if possible. The execution of the operations at Marietta was entrusted to Judge Meigs & Major General Buell, I also dispatched orders to Cincinnati, to plant one or more pieces of artillery on the banks of the Ohio, to keep patroles up the river at proper distances, in order to give notice in due time, of the approach of all boats, either singly or in numbers, & to call out a sufficient force to be able to meet 300 men; the number I expected might probably be with Blennerhassett's & Comfort Tyler's flotillas, if they should effect a junction; & lest they might attempt to pass in detachments of one boat at a time, not to suffer a single boat to pass without an arrest & examination—The execution of these operations were entrusted to generals Gano, Findley & judge Nimmo. I have also given authority to Jacob Wilson esq. of Stubenville to act, if occasion offers for his interposition, in that quarter—and it gives me great pleasure to inform you that I have, last night, received a communication from judge Meigs of Marietta, announcing the complete success of the operations intrusted to him & Gen. Buell, & whose patriotic efforts entitled them both, to my warmest thanks.

It is suspected notice was conveyed to Blennerhassett's island of the passage of the law, & the preparations making here to carry it into immediate effect; for it appears that in the night of the 9th inst., Comfort Tyler passed Marietta with a number (not yet ascertained) of fast rowing boats, with men armed indiscriminately with muskets, pistols & cutlasses, & anchored at the island; & immediately sent an express after Blennerhassett who was hurrying on his flotilla: that upon discovering the movements of our militia they fled full speed to the island, which was guarded at night by sentinals & lighted lanterns at proper distances, & none suffered to pass to it except by countersign or watch word—Spies were also placed at Marietta, to give notice of the movements there; in the mean time Gen. Buell, by direction of Judge Meigs, with a detachment of militia, proceeded up the Muskingum river in the night, & arrested ten of the batteaux as they were descending the river to join Tyler's forces; they were so hurried that four more of the batteaux were not got ready to embark & would also be seized, which is, I believe, the whole of the Muskingum flotilla. There were 100 barrels of provisions seized on board, & 100 more which had not been put on board; & which I expect he also seized with the same remaining batteaux; these batteaux are each 40 feet long; wide & covered; & calculated each to carry one company of men. It is believed notice was immediately given to the island, of this seizure; for in about three hours afterwards, on the same night, Blennerhasset & Tyler made their escape from the island, & have pushed, it is said, through Kentucky—Col. Phelps of Virginia with a few mounted men are in pursuit of them.

I expect Tyler's boats will descend the Ohio, to meet him & Blennerhasset at some point low down on that river; & I have no doubt but that Gen. Gano will render a good account of them as they attempt to pass Cincinnati.

I also received last night, a communication from the Sec. of War of the United States, by direction of that Government; requiring me without delay, to raise 150 or 200 volunteer militia to be formed in companies with one field officer, one captain two subalterns and 70 men, commissioned officers, privates & musicians, to each company, in the pay of the United States; & direct them to march to Marietta, with orders to seize the Muskingum flotilla & prevent it from being removed until further orders from the President. But finding that this service was in part effected, I have ventured from the necessity of the case, to vary in some degree, from these instructions, & which I hope will meet the approbation of the General Government, and also of your's. I have sent on orders last night to Marietta, to raise one company of volunteers, to be composed of one Major, one Capt. two subalterns and 60 men, commissioned officers, privates & musicians, which I have thought sufficient to guard & keep safe the flotilla & stores already arrested; & have also dispatched an express to Cincinnati with orders to raise two companies as above, each—as I thought the most force wanted there to relieve the militia previously ordered out, & to secure Comfort Tyler's flotilla while descending the Ohio, if it was not already done. I have no doubt that these three companies will be instantly under arms, & that this hitherto mysterious enterprise will be completely frustrated; & the intended evil levelled at the peace and tranquillity of the United States, will fall with all its weight on its projectors.

Chillicothe Dec. 15th 1806.   Edward Tiffin.

Lewis Cass's Letter to Senator Worthington Concerning the Involvement of Senator Smith's Son in the Escape of Blennerhassett

Sir,

. . . . Presuming you would wish to be informed respecting those objects of general importance, which happens here, I have taken the liberty of communicating to you a singular event, which has happened in our Legislature.

About two weeks since, young Smith a son of your Colleague in the Senate passed thru' this place way on his way to Marietta. That Town being then the rallying point of Burr's adherents, and the members from that quarter being perfectly aware that Mr Smith could have no business in that part of the Country, so unusual a circumstance excited considerable agitation. The Young Man arrived here on the evening that our law was passed, and incidentally proceeded on with the express, whom the Governor dispatched to carry the law into affect.

When Smith arrived at the point, where the roads to Marietta and to Bel-pre parted he informed the express that his business was at Bel-pre, and immediately, according to information, proceeded to Blennerhassett's Island opposite to Bel-pre. Blennerhassett at that time was at Marietta, but his wife on receiving intelligence of the menacing danger dispatched a messenger to him, and he effected his escape. Owing to this circumstance we have not been able to arrest Blennerhassett.

This fact, together with the knowledge, which m[any] of the members possessed of Burr's having, . . . Smith some time last Summer excited an unusual agitation among them. The consideration of the business was procrastinated until yesterday, when a resolution was introduced, commencing with a preamble, that whereas at this time all public officers ought to possess the confidence of their Constituents, and whereas John Smith neglects his duty in Congress, therefore Resolved &c that it be and is hereby recommended to John Smith to resign. The word Confidence was inserted for the purpose of shewing the intention of the framer and the expressions of having failed to neglect his duty, to save in some measure his feelings. An amendment was proposed to insert, unless he proceed immediately to his post, and with this alteration it would have passed unanimously. It did not however prevail and it was carried 13 to 10. In the Senate it passed without a dissenting voice. I believe everyman [in] the Legislature was in favour of taking some novel step, yet I thought the resolution as it now stands rather too harsh. The Governor has been requested to transmit to Mr Smith a copy of the resolution. . . .

You will, I trust, excuse the liberty I have taken in communicating to you the above intelligence. It is so novel and important as to render it interesting. It seems to be the general opinion that Mr Smith will resign. There is no doubt but the Gov. will be your successor, which I presume is with your concurrence, and will be pleasing to you.

With esteem I am Sir
Your ob^r. St.
Lew Cass.

Hon. Thomas Worthington
Senator in Congress
City of Washington
  via Marietta

1. See "Blennerhassett's Escape," *Detroit Historical Monthly* 1, no. 2 (April 1923): 27-29; Thomas H. Smith, ed., *An Ohio Reader: 1750 to the Civil War* (Grand Rapids, Mich.: Eerdmans, 1975), 1:132-33; Norris F. Schneider, *Blennerhassett Island and the Burr Conspiracy* (Columbus: Ohio Historical Society, 1966).

2. See "Blennerhassett's Escape," 29-31.

V.5. A Traveler's View of the Western Reserve, 1811

From the Treaty of Greene Ville in 1795 until the mid-nineteenth century, "Ohio Fever" spread across the older settled regions of the eastern United States, drawing thousands of settlers and investors to the fertile soil and temperate climate of the Ohio country. The contagion was felt keenly in New England and most particularly in Connecticut, with its special interest in the Western Reserve or "New Connecticut" in northeastern Ohio.

One of the principal investors in the Connecticut Land Company was Oliver Ellsworth, one of the Founding Fathers of the Constitution (indeed, the one who proposed the name "United States" for the new nation) and author of the first ten amendments, known as the Bill of Rights. After service as a U.S. senator from Connecticut, he was appointed chief justice by President George Washington in 1796 and held that position until 1801, when he was replaced by John Marshall.

After his death in 1807, his family grew concerned about the vast estate of 41,335 acres to which he had title in the Western Reserve and decided that one of his sons, Henry Leavitt Ellsworth, and a son-in-law, Ezekiel Williams, should make a trip to the Reserve to see first-hand how their father's estate was being administered. Henry, not yet twenty years of age, had just graduated from Yale. Ezekiel, forty-five, was a Hartford lawyer. Together the two would make a grueling fourteen-hundred-mile horseback ride out to the Reserve and back from May to August 1811. In a leather-bound journal he kept in his saddlebag, Henry Leavitt Ellsworth kept a daily record of the people and places they encountered and the impressions made upon them of the country through which they were passing. His entries for the days from 23 June until 9 July, when they were in the Reserve and visiting such tiny frontier settlements as Poland, Youngstown, Warren, Aurora, Hudson, Boston, and Cleveland, as well as isolated cabins in remote wilderness areas, provide a kaleidoscope of life as it was in the formative years of one of Ohio's most interesting and attractive regions.[1]

The Narrative of Henry Leavitt Ellsworth

June 23d. [1811] . . . Poland was the first town we entered on the Western Reserve, the place of our destination. This town is new and flourishing. The houses are quite scattered, each farmer living near the centre of his farm.

Judge [Turhand] Kirtland being our agent we expected to pass a number of days in Poland to gain the necessary information respecting our land. But our Agent was summoned on a jury at Warren the monday following so we concluded to start for Warren the same day for the sake of Judge Kirtland's company. We had a pleasant sociable ride.

Youngstown lies half way between Poland and Warren. This town is considerably settled—the land is selling for 5 dollars per acre. Here we took a *check* and rode on to Warren to dine. Perhaps you may not understand the meaning of the word *check*—it is nothing more than what the Yankeys mean by *lunchon*.

Warren is a county town. The streets are laid out at right angles. The houses are very handsome for so new a settlement. I was very desireous to reach this place as I here expected to meet some of my friends, nor were I dissappointed for I had the pleasure of seeing a number. We saw Ephraim Root, Esq., Genrl [Simon] Perkins, and Mr. [John] Leavitt who appeared very glad to see us nor was our joy less than thirs.

And here too I met with *my good old friend Margaret Dwight*. So unexpected was my presence to her that she for a moment seemed not to recollect me. But she soon recognized me and we sat down and passed a few hours in *social chat*. Margaret is pleased with her new situation and lives perfectly contented, in the enjoyment of good health.

Tuesday morning we left Warren for Aurora. We dined at Widow Garricks [Garrett] and . . . we put up at Mr. [Oliver] Snows. Our admission shewed too well the fare we must have. His house was small and scantily contrived to accommodate even his own family. It was well nigh 10 o'clock before we could get anything to eat, and when it was provided no mortal could taste of it who saw the sluttish manner in which it was cooked. In all my life I never see so much dirt and filth in any human habitation as in this mans hut. The landlady said "she was out of eatibles of present but would knock up a custard." And so she did and then hung on her bake pan to make something which she called cake merely because it had sweetning in it. Finally the banquet was ready and we set down and performed the ususal exercises of eating and drinking, without any pleasure and with little refreshment.

Being a good deal fatigued we told the *lady* of the house we would retire as soon as our bed was prepared. She was not able to furnish us but one bed and that very narrow. It was of no use to complain since we could not better our condition. We retired and had no sooner got into the bed and extinguished our light than a horde of flas infested the bed and rendered it seemingly impossible to lie another moment. Nor were the bed bugs far behind in the chace. I have heard travellers complain of *fleas* and *bedbugs* and I thought I knew full well the dissagreeable sensation they produced, but before this I have had an inadequate conception. I had lain only 30 minutees before my whole body was covered with *bloches*. My *uneasiness* I may add pain forced me to get up and putt on my clothes, hoping that these would prevent their torture and afford me a few minutes respit. The experiment was useless. The vermin grew worse and worse every minute, and I jumped out bed determined not to lie there any longer. I went to the fire, and, after sitting up by the dim light reflected from a few coals an hour or more, I put on my great coat and lay down on the hearth in the same small room where the whole family lodged, consisting of man and wife, a hired man, and 4 daughters. As for Mr. Williams, who had the foresight to sleep with his clothes on, he thought my torments the effect of imagination. I concluded the best way to convince him of the reality was to let him lie a few minutes longer.

I had not lain by the fire more than 20 minutes before I heard him *groaning*, one symptom (thought I) of at least *imaginary* distress. Wishing to give him a fair trial of his invulnerability I let him lie some time without *my* disturbance. At last I went in to hold consultation upon the subject. By this time he was fully convinced that some carnivorous creature infested the bed, and he wished me to light a candle and discover the enemy.

It was ½ past 12. I stumbled across the room (and they lay so thick on the floor that I could scarcely take a single step without running against somebody) and lighted a candle by which the vermin were discovered. Mr. W. started up and we resolved to go out into the barn and "turn in" upon the straw.

The noise and the light about the house awakened the man and wife. The woman affected to be extremly mortified. I *hope it was real*. The only consolation left us was that day light must come when we should leave this place of affliction.

> "Yes, in scratches and in bites
> We pass'd away our nights."

We rode to Sqire [Ebenezer] Sheldons to breakfast. This family is from Suffield Conn. They have a good framed house and all thing convenient around it. We felt ourselves quite at home and had evry favour confered upon us that was possible from Mr. and Mrs. Shelden. After being greatly refreshed by the kindness of our friends we rode on to Mr. Kennady's [David Kennedy]. We stopped here not because we expected good accommodations but because it was the nearest settlement to the township we intended to explore.

26 June. After breakfast we started with our guide to view the tract called "Milan" [Solon]. This employment is not very agreeable (and particularly today) since the late rain had made the bushes very wet which upon the least motion would sprinkle us entirely. However we were determined not to be discouraged upon the outset and we spent most of day in exploring a tract of 6,000 acres. Our guide went on foot while we rode on horseback. We all returned after our excursion quite fatigued. We dined at the house of our guide and then set out for Hudson where I now am at Mr. Oviats [Heman Oviatt] an Inkeeper.

Hudson is quite settled. The houses are many of them framed, and the tavern where we lodge is *painted* white, a novelty in this western country. Land in this town is selling for 4 dollars per acre. We are obliged now to give our horses wheat (which is 87-½ cents per bushell) as we can find no oats.

From Hudson we passed on to the Portarge on the Caiahugua [Cuyahoga] river in the town of Northhampton. We left our horses here to go over to Hammondsburgh to see Mr. Hammond, a person who once lived in East Hartford. We were welcomed to his house and furnished with everything his new habitation afforded. Our chief intention in visiting Mr. Hammond was to obtain his assistance in finding a certain millseat on Mr. Williams land. He gave us all his knowledge respecting it and accompanied us to the place which was 3 miles distant. . . .

Mr. H. moved here last summer. A log hut imperfectly finished is his dwelling. Though his habitation is new and exposed to the damps of a new country we slept undisturbed, rejoicing we had *once* found clean sheets and a respit from the vermin. . . .

July 1st. This morning at ½ past 4 we started for No. 1 in the 18 range, the southeast [Ellsworth erred—it was southwest] township in the Western Reserve. Being informed the first house on our road was 33 miles and that a new establishment, we found it necessary to carry our own provision as well as something for our horses. So we engaged the landlady to bake us some buiscuit while we took all our clothes from the portmanteaus and filled them with wheat for the horses.

Where the country is not cleared up you will generally find poor water. To avoid this inconvenience we carri'd a bottle of water, and, I must add, a bottle of Whiskey which we were advised to drink occasionally to keep off the fever. Whether this is ever a preventitive I cannot say, the people drink a great deal whether from *fear* or *love* you may judge. What little I sipped was from the fear of the fever without the least prejudice in its favour, for to me it is *"disagreeable stuff."* . . .

July 4th. By this [time] you are engaged in the celebration of the anniversary of the commencement of our independence. I would fly on the wings of speed and pass a few jovial hours with you, but I cannot. Accept therefore my earnest wish for your enjoyment. In the meantime I shall celebrate the day by drinking "peace and prosperity to the nation" over a glass of Whiskey.

In these desolate woods the gospel is not unrevealed. A missionary from Mass. preached at the portage yesterday. The people seem very desireous to hear the word of truth but are unable yet to hire a regular minister. Many of the inhabitants are confined around the Portage with the fever and ague. I consider we are exposed, but what good will it do to anticipate evil. *He* only who wields the destinies of men can preserve us from disease.

Hooping cough is a disorder common among children. The distress which it occasions is a sufficient apology for mentioning a supposed infallible cure even in the most inveterate cases. The cure came from an old woman; you may therefore conjecture the effecacy. Simply, this is the proscription. Taking the person who is afflicted with this disorder and carry him to some grist mill. Then put him into the hopper while the mill *is going* and let him stay there just *30 minutes exactly and no more.* This whim has taken deep hold on the people and many have practiced upon it during my stay at the Portage, and they all say their children are recovering. Quere, would they have died without this experiment?

I suppose the magical operation of a hopper jarred by the running of a mill stone is similar to the wonderful efficacy of some mineral waters whose good qualities increase in proportion to the *distance.* Hence we may conclude it is owing more to the exercise of *going* and *returning,* than to any intrinsick quality in the experiment itself.

5th. Thursday afternoon we left Mr. [Samuel] Kings for Boston. We heard this town was considerably settled; we therefore expected to find better accommodations. But I was wretchedly dissappointd. We fared worse if possible than at Mr. *Snows.* . . .

We arrived at Cleavland to dinner where we stay untill tomorrow. Cleavland was originally laid out in small lots for the city. Whether it ever will be populous time alone can determine. I think its situation favourable being situated of the Mouth of the river where it empties into the lake.

Few views are more pleasant than the one at Cleavand viz. of a Lake—your view is terminated by an horizon formed on the water. The lake is 60 miles wide at this place. The Canadians pass it frequently on the ice in the Winter, not without some danger in my opinion. the river Caiahugua is not navigable but with small boats. The unhealthyness of Cleaveland will be a great hindrance to its settlement. However, we may suppose the fever and ague to abate here as well as in other towns which were visited with the same affliction before they were cleared up and settled. . . .

July 7th. From Cleavland we rode east to Grandriver where we intended to put up over the Sabbath. It *happened* there was preaching here on Sunday so we attended at the court house where the meeting was held. The preacher, though a man of a *good heart,* was inferior as to talents and laboured under the disadvantages of a poor education. . . .

July 9th. . . . We left the Reserve at the east end of Salem. As I have now passed through New Connecticut you may expect I shall give you some account of the appearance of the country. The tract called the Western Reserve or New Connecticut contains 3,500,000 acres. The surface is very level. You can scarcely find a hill in the whole purchase and yet it is well watered, much better than the Holland Purchase [in western

New York] which lies east of it. Some of the towns in New Conn. are quite settled, though there are yet many townships without a single inhabitant. The market of New Con. will always be tolerable since the south eastern part is within 60 miles of Pittsburgh and the northern boundary is lake Erie. Almost every hut is a tavern as it brings in a *little cash* which is in great demand among the first settlers who, generally speaking, are poor and destitute.

In my opinion there is no country where an equal number of acres (say 10,000) will support so great a population—I mean if they devote their attention to agriculture. For the land itself is remarkably fertile, and being level it has but little waste. . . .

1. See Phillip R. Shriver, ed., *A Tour to New Connecticut in 1811: The Narrative of Henry Leavitt Ellsworth* (Cleveland: Western Reserve Historical Society, 1985), 56–74.

V.6.   Ohio and the War of 1812: The First Siege of Fort Meigs

On 18 June 1812, the United States under the leadership of President James Madison formally declared war against Great Britain. In his message to Congress on 1 June, Madison affirmed that the British were already waging a de facto war against the United States through actions that violated its rights as a neutral nation, including searching and seizing U.S. vessels on the high seas, impressing U.S. seamen into British naval service, blockading U.S. shores, and inciting the Indians into attacks against American citizens and the U.S. government. Madison's call for war was supported in the House by a vote of 79 to 49, and in the Senate by a vote of 19 to 13. The close votes revealed that support for the president was the strongest in the South and West, the weakest in the Northeast.

Most Ohioans favored war with Britain in 1812 for three reasons: a belief that the only way stagnant farm commodity prices would rise was through war to compel the British to stop interfering with U.S. maritime trade; a conviction that Canada, the neighbor on the other side of the Lake Erie "fence," was destined someday to become part of the United States and that the best time to take it was when Britain was tied down by a struggle with France's Napoleon Bonaparte in Europe and around the world; and, finally, the belief that Britain's continuing intrigue with America's Indians, evident in the Indian Wars of the 1790s and then reinforced by the revelation that British-made arms had been used by the Indians in the Battle of Tippecanoe Creek on 7 November 1811, could only be ended once and for all with a decisive military victory over the former mother country.

What started out as an offensive war to drive the British out of Canada, however, soon turned into a defensive struggle to keep the young nation from being swallowed up by the greatest power in the world at that time, whose military and naval strength far surpassed that of the United States. As a consequence, the War of 1812 became in effect "The Second War for American Independence," with its most important battles fought on American, not Canadian, soil and water. And many of those battles were fought in Ohio.

Following the abortive campaign of General William Hull and the Ohio militia in western Ontario in July 1812 came the invasion of southeastern Michigan and the capture of Detroit by British and Canadian forces under the command of General Isaac Brock on 16 August 1812. After the surrender of Detroit, Hull was replaced as commander of U.S. forces in the northwest by William Henry Harrison, then governor of the Indiana Territory and one-time aide to Anthony Wayne at Fallen Timbers and Greene Ville. After the disastrous massacre of an American army under General James Winchester at the River Raisin near Monroe, Michigan, in late January 1813, Harrison determined to anchor his "Northwestern Army" at a new post whose construction he personally supervised, a fort he named Meigs in honor of Return Jonathan Meigs Jr., then governor of Ohio.

Located on the southeastern bank of the Maumee River near present-day Perrysburg, Ohio, Fort Meigs was twice besieged by British, Canadian, and Indian forces under the command of General Henry Proctor, successor to Brock. Regarding Fort Meigs as a challenge to British control over Detroit and southern Michigan, Proctor began the first siege in late April 1813, with a flotilla of gunboats and an army of three thousand, about twice the size of the defensive forces under the command of Harrison. So well was the fort constructed, with earthen revetments providing a shield against the shells from the British gunboats and artillery pieces, that Proctor withdrew his troops on 9 May. Helping him reach that decision was the arrival five days earlier of additional American reinforcements, primarily General Green Clay and a brigade of Kentucky militia, which, despite a Tecumseh-led Indian ambush that killed or captured nearly two hundred of them, brought the opposing armies nearer to equivalence and ended any prospect of a quick British victory.

In the pages of his personal diary, Captain Daniel Cushing of the U.S. Army, one of the defenders, has left an eyewitness account of the first siege of Fort Meigs.[1]

British Forces Gathering

Wednesday, 28th. [of April, 1813] — Last night we had the heaviest rain that I ever knew and very hard thunder. This morning we had the pleasure of seeing about 300 British down the river and a number of Indians and British came opposite to our fort and fired at our men that were on the river bottom. I gave them one shot with an eighteen pounder which made them leave their stations. Capt. Hamilton was sent down the river this morning—he reported that the British had landed on the other side about 1,500 or 2,000. We expect a hard fight this night. I have completed the abatis this evening in front of the grand battery. The whole army was at work this day, one third at a time, heaving up a traverse through the camp. A party of dragoons rode out a short distance from camp this evening; one of them received a ball in his arm from the rifle of an Indian—there was a party watching for our men.

Thursday, 29th.—This day we are employed in finishing the traverse and making ready for battle, for we have been surrounded by British and Indians for two days. We let loose our cannonade on them yesterday and have kept it up by spells all this day, and shall let loose upon them this evening with an eighteen pounder that is already elevated.

Friday, 30th.—We have been all day employed in traversing through the camp, playing upon their batteries with our eighteen pounders and throwing grape and cannister shot at the Indians which are in our rear and on our flanks. We have had one man killed and 6 or 7 wounded by the Indians this day.

The Battle Begun

Saturday, May 1st. — At 2 o'clock in the morning the British opened their artillery upon our garrison from their gun-boats, which lay one and one-half miles below us, but it was without effect. At 8 o'clock they hoisted the red flag at their lower battery and commenced firing with 24, 12 and 6 pounders, and eight inch mortars. They fired at us this day 240 shot and shells; did very little damage. They continued firing shells through the night but not often, just enough to keep our camp from rest. We keep up a heavy fire on them all day from different parts of our camp, the Indians are very thick on our flank and in our rear. We have not more than two killed and four wounded today.

Sunday, 2nd. — They kept up their bombardment all night, but not very often, enough to keep the men on the watch. This morning they commenced a heavy fire from all their batteries both with cannonade and bombs, and our camp is completely surrounded with Indian and British keeping up a heavy fire of musketry and rifles. They threw at us this day about 350 shot, a large proportion of them red hot; we had about 4 killed, 7 wounded this day, they keep up the business of sending over their shells this evening.

Monday, 3rd. — This morning I gave them a morning gun at break of day, which passed through their upper battery. They returned pretty much the same, and that all day. This day we discovered that they had a small battery on this side of the river, about 300 yards on our right flank. The Indians had been for two days firing at our men from that direction which kept us from noticing what they were about. They opened on us from that battery one six pounder and one five and a half inch howitzer which made a complete cross-fire through our camp. This day we received about 516 shots from them and lost about the same number of men as we did yesterday, killed and wounded.

Tuesday, 4th. — They still keep up their fire with shot hot and cold and bombs; killed a few men, wounded some. This evening Mr. Oliver who was sent out to meet Gen. Clay came down the river in a boat; arrived here tonight about 12 o'clock. He brought the news that Gen. Clay with his brigade would be here by break of day; this put our camp in motion. Every man was up and preparing for battle.

Gen. Clay's Arrival

Wednesday, 5th. — This morning about 3 o'clock Gen. Harrison sent Capt. Hamilton, Capt. Shaw and one other up the river to meet Gen. Clay with orders for him to land about 700 men two miles above camp on the other side of the river, proceed down to their batteries, spike their cannon and retreat immediately back to their boats, but to come down under the cover of my battery. They complied so far as to land the men, march them down to their battery, drive them from their guns, spike some of them, take down their colors, but did not retreat as ordered; pursued the Indians into the woods until about 200 of them fell into the enemies' hands and 100 supposed to be killed — the rest made their escape up to their boats and arrived safe at camp. At the time the balance of the brigade was floating to camp from where the men landed. The Indians and British kept up a heavy fire on them from the woods; then men left their boats fighting them. The cavalry with Major Alexander's battalion sallied out and drove them into the woods and then retreated into the garrison. There were several killed and several wounded, the Indians followed them within 150 yards of the gate. This sally was made from the left wing of our camp. Another sally was made at the same time from the right wing by Col. Miller. He drove the British and Indians from their little battery, spiked their guns and howitzer, took about 42 prisoners of which 2 were officers. We had several killed and wounded. After the battle ceased the British sent into our camp a flag of truce the bearer of which was Major Chambers. Gen. Harrison permitted the two regular officers to return back to their camp; they gave us but two shots after the battle was over. . . .

British Give Up the Fight

Sunday, 9th. — Last night two men deserted from the British and swimming the river came into our camp. They state on being examined that the enemy moved off the greater part of their cannon the night before last, and the rest last night. They also state that the British and the Indians have all cleared out; they state further that news had arrived in their camp within 24 hours that Little York had fallen into the hands of the Americans. They state that the Indians had got mad and would not stay any longer in consequence of the British not letting them have a share in the plunder that was given up in this fort, for they supposed that we had surrendered, as the white flag had been passing so very often. I have been out on the battle ground this day; found several dead men, the most of them scalped and tomahawked. The British took down their colors about 10 o'clock this morning, went aboard of their boats and cleared themselves for Malden. We gave them a few stern shots as they left their camp, and three cheers when they lowered their colors. Also we fired a salute at 12 o'clock three times around the fort. The sight of dead men has become no more terrifying than the sight of dead flies on a summer day. . . .

1. Originally published as *Captain Cushing in the War of 1812*, vol. 11, *Ohio Historical Collections* (Columbus: Ohio State Archaeological and Historical Society, 1944), this excerpt has been taken from Harlow Lindley, ed., *Fort Meigs and the War of 1812*, 2nd ed. (Columbus: Ohio Historical Society, 1975), 115–19.

V.7.   "We Have Determined to Maintain This Place and by Heaven We Can": George Croghan and the Defense of Fort Stephenson

In the wake of the unsuccessful British/Indian siege of Fort Meigs, some fifty Indian chiefs of the Delaware, Wyandot, Shawnee, and Seneca tribes met at Franklinton (Columbus), where on 21 June 1813, led by Tarhe the Crane, aged chief of the Wyandots, they signed an agreement with General William Henry Harrison pledging to join forces with him in common cause against the British. Though Tecumseh and most of his followers remained loyal to the British, thereafter they would have opposition from some of their own people.

To the British General Henry Proctor, the defections in the Indian ranks meant only one thing: he was going to have to demonstrate, and quickly, that the British still had the necessary strength to win. He looked about for a sure thing, an easy victory, and concluded that tiny Fort Stephenson at Lower Sandusky (now Fremont) on the banks of the Sandusky River should be his next target.

Defended by fewer than two hundred soldiers under the command of twenty-one-year-old Major George Croghan, named for his great uncle who had been a well-known fur trader in the Ohio country in the 1740s, Fort Stephenson was one of the smallest outposts in the Old Northwest. Proctor's strategy called for a return to the Maumee Valley for a second, abbreviated siege of Fort Meigs, 20–28 July, as a feint to draw American forces from the surrounding area to its defense, then a quick redeployment (mostly by boat) of his twelve hundred men, about half of them Indians, for the attack on Fort Stephenson in the Sandusky Valley.

When Harrison learned of the British ruse, he sent orders to Croghan to set fire to Fort Stephenson and escape to Fort Seneca (Tiffin) with his troops. But the young major, in his first command, averred that the orders arrived too late, that his fort was already surrounded. Whether or not he had time to follow Harrison's orders, Croghan was determined to fight and rejected a Proctor ultimatum implying a massacre of the fort's defenders by the Indians if he did not surrender. The siege was brief, lasting only from 1 to 3 August. Cleverly maneuvering the fort's single small cannon, affectionately dubbed "Old Betsy," from place to place inside the fort to give the impression that he had several cannons and not just one, and skillfully deploying his men to create the illusion they were far more numerous than they were, Croghan outfoxed the British general. The decisive moment of the siege came on the evening of 2 August, when, following a concentrated bombardment from their gunboats and artillery pieces on the corner of the fort closest to the Sandusky, the British made a charge from the woods on the opposite side. Anticipating that such would be the case, Croghan had his men concentrated on that side, along with Old Betsy, whose muzzle had been crammed with nails, scraps of iron and lead, broken glass, and other debris. The American defenders held their fire until the charging red-coated soldiers were at nearly point-blank range at the ditch that surrounded the fort. Then, on Croghan's command, his troops fired their weapons and Old Betsy spoke. The toll on the attackers was such that the British lifted the siege before dawn the next morning, retreating to Lake Erie and then to Detroit, leaving 150 dead and many injured, while American losses totaled only 1 killed and 7 wounded.

Though Fort Stephenson was small, Croghan's victory was significant, both for the demoralization that followed among British forces in and about Detroit and the western Lake Erie basin and as a morale builder for Ohioans and the nation. But speculation remains to this day concerning the inability or refusal of Major George Croghan to follow the orders of General William Henry Harrison and its meaning to the ultimate outcome of the war in the Old Northwest. Pertinent correspondence between the two men is reproduced below, with Croghan writing from Fort Stephenson at Lower Sandusky (Fremont) and Harrison writing from his headquarters at Fort Seneca at Seneca Town (Tiffin), about twenty miles away.[1]

Major Croghan to General Harrison

Lower Sandusky, 25th July, 1813.

General Harrison:

  Dear Sir:—. . . I have unloaded the boats which were brought from Cleveland, and shall sink them in the middle of the river (where it is ten feet deep) about one-half mile above the present landing. My men are engaged in making cartridges and will have in a short time more than sufficient to answer any ordinary call. I have collected all the most valuable stores in one house. Should I be forced to evacuate the place, they will be blown up.

> Yours with respect,
> Major G. Croghan,
> Commanding at Lower Sandusky.

General Harrison to Major Croghan

July 29, 1813.

Sir:—Immediately on receiving this letter you will abandon Fort Stephenson, set fire to it and repair with your command this night to headquarters [Fort Seneca]. Cross the river and come up on the opposite side. If you should deem and find it impracticable to make good your march to this place, take the road to Huron and pursue it with the utmost circumspection and dispatch. . . .

Major Croghan to General Harrison

July 30, 1813.

Sir:—I have just received yours of yesterday, 10 o'clock P.M., ordering me to destroy this place and make good my retreat, which was received too late to be carried into execution. We have determined to maintain this place and by Heaven we can. . . .

Assistant Adjutant General Holmes to Major Croghan

July 30, 1813.

To Major Croghan:

Sir:—The General has just received your letter of this date informing him that you had thought it proper to disobey the order issued from this office and delivered to you this morning. It appears that the information which dictated this order was incorrect, and as you did not receive it in the night, as was expected, it might have been proper that you should have reported the circumstances and your situation before you proceeded to its execution. This might have been passed over; but I am directed to say to you that an officer who presumes to aver that he has made his resolution and that he will act in direct opposition to the orders of his General, cannot longer be entrusted with a separate command. Colonel [Samuel] Wells is sent to relieve you. You will deliver the command to him and repair with Colonel [James V.] Ball's squadron to this place.

> By command, etc.,
> A. H. Holmes
> Assistant Adjutant General

Major Croghan to General Harrison

Lower Sandusky, 3d Aug., 1813.

General Harrison!

Dear Sir:—The enemy made an attempt to storm us last evening, but was repulsed with the loss of at least 200 killed, wounded and prisoners. One Lieut.-Colonel (Short), a major and a lieutenant, with about forty privates are dead in the ditch. I have lost but one killed and but few wounded. . . .

P.S.—Since writing the above, two soldiers of the Forty-first Regiment have gotten in who state that the enemy have retreated—in fact, one of their gunboats is within three hundred yards of our works, said to be loaded with camp equipage, etc., which they have in their hurry left. . . .

General Harrison to Secretary of War John Armstrong

Headquarters, Seneca Town, 4th August, 1813.

Sir:—In my letter of the first instant [August 1], I did myself the honor to inform you that one of my scouting parties had just returned from the Lake Shore and had discovered the day before, the enemy in force near the mouth of the Sandusky Bay. The party had not passed Lower Sandusky two hours, before the advance, consisting of the Indians, appeared before the Fort, and in half an hour after a large detachment of British troops; and in the course of the night commenced a cannonading against the fort with three six-pounders and two howitzers, the latter from gun boats. The firing was partially answered by Major George Croghan, having a six-pounder, the only piece of artillery. . . .

I am sorry that I cannot transmit you Major Croghan's official report. He was to have sent it to me this morning, but I have just heard that he was so much exhausted by thirty-six hours of continued exertion, as to be unable to make it. It will not be amongst the least of General Proctor's mortifications to find that he has been baffled by a youth who has just passed his twenty-first year. He is, however, a hero worthy of his gallant uncle, Gen. G. R. Clarke [George Rogers Clark], and I bless my good fortune in having first introduced this promising shoot of a distinguished family to the notice of the government. . . .

In a letter I informed you, sir, that the post of Lower Sandusky could not be defended against heavy cannon, and that I had ordered the Commandant, if he could safely retire upon the advance of the enemy to do so after having destroyed the fort, as there was nothing in it that could justify the risk of defending it, commanded as it is by a hill on the opposite side of the river within range of cannon and having on that side old and illy constructed blockhouses and dry, friable pickets. The enemy ascending the bay and river with a fine breeze, gave Major Croghan so little notice of their approach that he could not execute the order for retreating. Luckily they had no artillery but six pounders and five and a half inch howitzers. . . .

Major Croghan's Official Report to General Harrison

Lower Sandusky, August 5, 1813.

Dear Sir:—I have the honor to inform you that the combined force of the enemy amounting to at least 500 regulars and seven or eight hundred Indians under the immediate command of General Proctor, made its appearance before this place early on Sunday evening last; and so soon as the General had made such disposition of his troops as would cut off my retreat, should I be disposed to make one, he sent Colonel Elliott, accompanied by Major Chambers, with a flag to demand the surrender of the fort as he was anxious to spare the effusion of blood which he should probably not have in his power to do should be he reduced to the necessity of taking the place by storm.

My answer to the summons was that I was determined to defend the place to the last extremity and that no force however large, should induce me to surrender it. So soon as the flag was returned a brisk fire was opened upon us from the gun boats in the river and from a five and one-half inch howitzer on shore, which was kept up with little intermission throughout the night. At an early hour the next morning, three sizes (which had been placed during the night within 250 yards of the pickets) began to play upon us but with little effect. About 4 P.M., discovering that the fire from all his guns was concentrated against the northwestern angle of the fort, I became confident that his object was to storm the works at that point. I therefore ordered out as many men as could be employed for the purpose of strengthening that part which was so effectually secured by means of bags of flour, sand, etc., that the picketing suffered little or no injury, notwithstanding which the enemy, about 500, having formed in close column, advanced to assault our works at the expected point, at the same time making two feints on the front of Captain Hunter's lines. The column which advanced against the northwestern angle consisting of about 350 men was so completely enveloped in smoke as not to be discovered until it had approached within fifteen or twenty paces of the lines, but the men being all at their posts and ready to receive it, commenced so heavy and galling a fire as to throw the column into a little confusion. Being quickly rallied it advanced to the center works and began to leap into the ditch. Just at that moment a fire of grape was opened from our six-pounder (which had been previously arranged so as to rake in that direction) which together with the musketry, threw them into such confusion that they were compelled to retire precipitately into the woods. During the assault which lasted about half an hour, an incessant fire was kept up by the enemy's artillery (which consisted of five sixes and a howitzer) but without effect. My whole loss during the seige was one killed and seven slightly wounded. The loss of the enemy in killed, wounded and prisoners must exceed one hundred and fifty. One Lt. col., a Lt. and fifty rank and file were found in and about the ditch, dead or wounded. Those of the remainder who were not able to escape, were taken off during the night by the Indians. Seventy stand of arms and several brace of pistols have been collected near the works. About three in the morning the enemy sailed down the river leaving behind them a boat containing considerable military stores.

Too much praise cannot be bestowed upon the officers, non-commissioned officers and privates under my command for their gallantry and good conduct during the siege.

Yours with respect,
G. Croghan,
Major 17th U.S. Inf., Commanding Lower Sandusky.
Major General Harrison, Commanding Northwestern Army.

Public Statement of Major Croghan

Lower Sandusky, August 27, 1813.

I have with much regret seen in some of the public prints such misrepresentations concerning my refusal to evacuate this post, as are calculated not only to injure me in the estimation of military men, but also to excite unfavorable impressions as to the propriety of General Harrison's conduct relative to this affair.

His character as a military man is too well established to need my approbation or support, but his public services entitle him at least to common justice. This affair does not furnish cause of reproach. If public opinion has been lately misled respecting his late conduct, it will require but a moment's cool, dispassionate reflection to convince them of its propriety. The measures recently adopted by him, so far from deserving censure, are the clearest proofs of his keen penetration and able generalship. It is true that I did not proceed immediately to execute his order to evacuate this post, but this disobedience was not as some would wish to believe, the result of a fixed determination to maintain the post contrary to his most positive orders, as will appear from the following detail, which is given in explanation of my conduct:

About ten o'clock on the morning of the 30th ult. a letter from the Adjutant General's office dated Seneca Town, July 29, 1813, was handed me by Mr. Connor, ordering me to abandon this post, burn it and retreat that night to headquarters. On the reception of this order of the general I called a council of officers, in which it was determined not to abandon the place until the further pleasure of the General should be known, as it was thought an attempt to retreat in the open day, in the face of a superior force of the enemy would be more hazardous than to remain in the fort, under all its disadvantages. I therefore wrote a letter to the General Council in such terms as I thought were calculated to deceive the enemy should it fall into his hands, which I thought more than probable, as well as to inform the General should it be so fortunate as to reach him that I would wait to hear from him before I should proceed to execute his order. The letter, contrary to my expectations was received by the General, who, not knowing what reasons urged me to write in a tone so decisive, concluded very rationally that the manner of it was demonstrative of the most positive determination to disobey his orders under any circumstances. I was therefore suspended from the command of the fort and ordered to headquarters. But on explaining to the General my reason for not executing his orders, and my object in using the style I had done, he was so perfectly satisfied with the explanation that I was immediately reinstated in the command. . . .

1. See Charles R. Williams, ed., "George Croghan," in *Ohio Archeological and Historical Publications* (Columbus, 1903), 12:395–409.

V.8. "We Have Met the Enemy and They Are Ours"

Following their unsuccessful sieges at Fort Meigs and Fort Stephenson, the British soon suffered their most humiliating defeat in the war in the Old Northwest in the naval Battle of Lake Erie on 10 September 1813. Though blockaded by a British fleet commanded by Commodore Robert H. Barclay, Oliver Hazard Perry had supervised the construction of an American fleet of nine vessels in the harbor at Presque Isle (Erie, Pennsylvania) behind the protective barrier of a long, low sandbar that kept the British vessels at bay. Then, in early August 1813, Barclay abruptly ended the blockade to sail to Detroit to reprovision his ships and their crews. This move enabled Perry to get his own ships out of the harbor and over the sandbar to a nearby shore, where they were armed, provisioned, and manned. Ready to fight, Perry sailed to Sandusky Bay, where he met with General William Henry Harrison on 17 August and learned that the British fleet, augmented by a new flagship, the Detroit, *was preparing to leave Malden on the Detroit River for the open waters of western Lake Erie.*

On the morning of 10 September the two fleets met ten miles northwest of Put-in-Bay, near West Sister Island. Though Perry had nine vessels to Barclay's six, the British outgunned the Americans sixty-three to fifty-four, with clear superiority in long-range firepower. On the other hand, if there were sufficient breeze to assure maneuverability, Perry's close-range weapons would give him an advantage. Unfortunately, there was so little breeze that morning that though the two fleets were in visual contact shortly after daybreak it was nearly noon before they were close enough to open fire.

Perry's battle plan called for his two brigs, the Lawrence *and the* Niagara, *to duel the two largest British vessels, the* Detroit *and the* Queen Charlotte, *with the smaller ships of both fleets primarily engaged in their own combat. The captain of the* Niagara, *Jesse Elliott, however, chose not to close with the enemy, to make more effective use of his long-range guns he testified later at his court-martial. Though the pennant above the* Lawrence *read "Don't Give Up The Ship," Perry had no other choice after his flagship was devastated by the combined fire of the* Detroit *and the* Queen Charlotte. *With masts broken and the deck slippery with the blood of the dead and dying, the* Lawrence *was dead in the water when Perry was rowed to the* Niagara, *from which he could continue the battle.*

Fortunately for Perry, shortly after two o'clock in the afternoon, a fresh breeze began to stir, filling sails and giving his fleet the maneuverability it had to have to take advantage of its superiority in short-range weapons. At about this time, a shot from one of Perry's ships struck Barclay, the British commodore, shattering his one remaining arm. (He had lost the other one earlier in the Battle of Trafalgar.) In the ensuing confusion, a missed signal for a change of course caused the two largest British ships to collide. Stuck fast together, the two drifted helplessly between the opposing lines of fire. British gunners on the smaller ships had to hold their fire; American gunners now could hardly miss. Soon a white flag of surrender was flying above the British flagship Detroit. *The Battle of Lake Erie was over. For the only time in history an entire British fleet had been captured, and with it went control of the Great Lakes.*

Before taking the captured British ships to the harbor at Put-in-Bay, Perry hastily scrawled a message on the back of an old envelope to be carried to General William Henry Harrison, the commander of all U.S. forces in the Northwest. Though one of the briefest documents in Ohio and American history, it has been and is still one of the best known.[1]

U.S. Brig Niagara, off the Western Sister, Head of Lake Erie:

Sept. 10, 1813, at 4 p.m.

Dear General: — We have met the enemy and they are ours! Two ships, two brigs, one schooner and one sloop.

Yours with great respect and esteem,

O. H. Perry.

1. See Mrs. John T. Mack, "The Battle of Lake Erie," *Ohio Archaeological and Historical Publications* (Columbus, 1902), 10:38–43; also, National Park Service, Department of the Interior, *Perry's Victory and International Peace Memorial National Monument* (Washington, 1970); Robert J. Dodge, *The Battle of Lake Erie* (Fostoria, Ohio: Gray Print, 1967).

V.9.   Tecumseh Implores the British to Stay and Fight

With his army repulsed at Fort Meigs and Fort Stephenson and the captured British fleet immobilized in Put-in-Bay, British General Henry Proctor concluded the time had come to pull his forces out of Fort Malden and the Detroit area and head east across Ontario to the Niagara frontier, in advance of the pursuing army of William Henry Harrison. Dismayed by Proctor's preparations to withdraw from U.S. soil after earlier assurances that Britain would not stop fighting until the Indians' lands had been returned to them, Tecumseh called on the British general to stay and fight, or at least give the weapons of war to the Indians to enable them to continue to fight. Tecumseh concluded his impassioned plea with a prophetic death wish: "We are determined to defend our lands, and if it is . . . [the will of the Great Spirit], we wish to leave our bones upon them."[1]

Despite the pleas of the great Indian leader, Proctor abandoned Fort Malden and Detroit and began the long retreat across southern Ontario, with Tecumseh and his followers accompanying. At Moravian Town on the Thames River, Harrison's army caught up with the British and Indians, and in the ensuing battle, on 5 October 1813, the Ohio-born Shawnee chief, the "greatest Indian of them all," was killed.

Father, listen to your children! you have them now all before you. The war before this our British father gave the hatchet to his red children, when old chiefs were alive. They are now dead. In that war our father was thrown on his back by the Americans, and our father took them by the hand without our knowledge; and we are afraid that our father will do so again at this time.

Summer before last, when I came forward with my red brethren, and was ready to take up the hatchet, in favor of our British father, we were told not to be in a hurry, that he had not yet determined to fight the Americans.

Listen! When war was declared, our father stood up and gave us the tomahawk, and told us he was ready to strike the Americans; that he wanted our assistance, and that he would certainly get our lands back, which the Americans had taken from us.

Listen! You told us, at that time, to bring forward our families to this place, and we did so — and you promised to take care of them, and that they should want for nothing, while the men would go and fight the enemy; that we need not trouble ourselves about the enemy's garrisons; that we knew nothing about them, and that our father would attend to that part of the business. You also told your red children that you would take good care of your garrison here, which made our hearts glad.

Listen! When we were last at the Rapids [the siege of Fort Meigs at the Maumee Rapids], it is true we gave you little assistance. It is hard to fight people who live like ground hogs.

Father, listen! Our fleet has gone out; we know they have fought; we have heard the great guns, but know nothing of what has happened to our father with one arm [British Comdr. Robert H. Barclay]. Our ships have gone one way, and we are much astonished to see our father tying up everything and preparing to run away the other, without letting his red children know what his intentions are. You always told us to remain here and take care of our lands. It made our hearts glad to hear that was your wish. Our great father, the King, is the head, and you represent him. You always told us that you would never draw your foot off British ground; but now, Father, we see you are drawing back, and we are sorry to see our father doing so without seeing the enemy. We must compare our father's conduct to a fat animal that carries its tail upon its back, but when affrighted, it drops it between its legs and runs off.

Listen, Father! The Americans have not yet defeated us by land; neither are we sure that they have done so by water — we therefore wish to remain here and fight our enemy, should they make their appearance. If they defeat us, we will then retreat with our father.

At the battle of the Rapids, last war [Battle of Fallen Timbers, 1794], the Americans certainly defeated us; and when we retreated to our father's fort [Fort Miami] in that place, the gates were shut against us. We were afraid that it would now be the case, but instead of that, we now see our British father preparing to march out of his garrison.

Father! You have got the arms and ammunition which our great father sent for his red children. If you have an idea of going away, give them to us, and you may go and welcome, for us. Our lives are in the hands of the Great Spirit. We are determined to defend our lands, and if it is His will, we wish to leave our bones upon them.

1. Frank Moore, ed., *American Eloquence: A Collection of Speeches and Addresses by the Most Eminent Orators of America* (New York: Appleton, 1857), 2:856. See also R. David Edmunds, *Tecumseh and the Quest for Indian Leadership* (Boston: Little, Brown, 1984), 202–12.

V.10. The Peace of Ghent, 1814

With the defeat of the British and the death of Tecumseh in the Battle of the Thames, 5 October 1813, the war in the west, to all intents and purposes, was over. Though significant battles would continue to be fought in the east and the south, it was clearly evident that the

United States had failed in its initial ambition to wrest Canada from the British, and equally evident that the British would fail in their effort to restore the lost colonies to the empire, though they did succeed in burning the national capital, Washington, in 1814. Despite the fact that America's greatest military victory of the war, under General Andrew Jackson at New Orleans, did not come until January 1815, a peace had already been agreed upon at Ghent in Belgium by U.S. commissioners, including Henry Clay and John Quincy Adams, and British commissioners, including Lords Kenyon and Gambier. The peace agreement could be summarized in four Latin words: Status quo ante bellum — *that is, the state of things before the war. The War of 1812 ended in a draw.*

Did Ohio and the rest of the Old Northwest get anything out of a war that ended in stalemate? Yes. Never again would there be serious intrigue by British agents among Ohio's and America's Indians. Military roads would hasten postwar commercial and agricultural development. From the prewar Battle of Tippecanoe and the siege at Fort Meigs would come a future president of the United States, William Henry Harrison, a resident of North Bend, Ohio. And, after the war would come agreement for the permanent neutralization of the Great Lakes and the nonfortification of the international boundary between Canada and the United States.

TREATY OF PEACE AND AMITY BETWEEN HIS BRITANNIC MAJESTY AND THE UNITED STATES OF AMERICA. CONCLUDED DECEMBER 24, 1814: RATIFICATIONS EXCHANGED FEBRUARY 17, 1815; PROCLAIMED FEBRUARY 18, 1815.[1]

Article I.

There shall be a firm and universal peace between His Britannic Majesty and the United States, and between their respective countries, territories, cities, towns, and people, of every degree, without exception of places or persons. All hostilities, both by sea and land, shall cease as soon as this treaty shall have been ratified by both parties, as hereinafter mentioned. All territory, places, and possessions whatsoever, taken by either party from the other during the war, or which may be taken after the signing of this treaty, . . . shall be restored without delay, . . .

Article II.

Immediately after the ratifications of this treaty by both parties, as hereinafter mentioned, orders shall be sent to the armies, squadrons, officers, subjects and citizens of the two Powers to cease from all hostilities. . . .

Article III.

All prisoners of war taken on either side, as well by land as by sea, shall be restored as soon as practicable after the ratification of this treaty, . . .

Article IX.

The United States of America engage to put an end, immediately after the ratification of the present treaty, to hostilities with all the tribes or nations of Indians with whom they may be at war at the time of such ratification; and forthwith to restore to such tribes or nations, respectively, all the possessions, rights, and privileges which they may have enjoyed or been entitled to in one thousand eight hundred and eleven, previous to such hostilities: Provided always that such tribes or nations shall agree to desist from all hostilities against the United States of America, their citizens and subjects, upon the ratification of the present treaty being notified to such tribes or nations, and shall so desist accordingly. And His Britannic Majesty engages, on his part, to put an end immediately after the ratification of the present treaty, to hostilities with all the tribes or nations of Indians with whom he may be at war at the time of such ratification, and forthwith to restore to such tribes or nations respectively all the possessions, rights, and privileges which they may have enjoyed or been entitled to in one thousand eight hundred and eleven, previous to such hostilities: Provided always that such tribes or nations shall agree to desist from all hostilities against His Britannic Majesty, and his subjects, upon the ratification of the present treaty being notified to such tribes or nations, and shall so desist accordingly.

Article X.

Whereas the traffic in slaves is irreconcileable with the principles of humanity and justice, and whereas both His Majesty and the United States are desirous of continuing their efforts to promote its entire abolition, it is hereby agreed that both the contracting parties shall use their best endeavours to accomplish so desirable an object. . . .

1. U.S. Sen. Ex. Doc. No. 36, 41st Cong., 3d sess., *Treaties and Conventions Concluded between the United States of America and Other Powers since July 4, 1776* (Washington, 1871), 338-44.

V.11.   The Rush-Bagot Agreement

In 1913, on the occasion of the centennial of Perry's victory in the Battle of Lake Erie in the War of 1812, there was dedicated at Put-in-Bay on Ohio's South Bass Island a monument to international peace as well as to a great naval victory. For out of the War of 1812 came an agreement, reached in 1817 by Richard Rush, the American acting secretary of state, and Charles Bagot, Britain's envoy to the United States, that neutralized the waters of the Great Lakes and paved the way for the permanent nonfortification of the nearly four thousand miles of international border between the United States and Canada. By limiting the size and numbers of naval vessels on waters shared by the two neighbors, the Rush-Bagot Agreement assured an unbroken peace that has continued for nearly two centuries.[1]

EXCHANGE OF NOTES RELATIVE TO NAVAL FORCES ON THE AMERICAN LAKES, SIGNED AT WASHINGTON APRIL 28 AND 29, 1817. SUBMITTED TO THE SENATE APRIL 6, 1818. RESOLUTION OF APPROVAL AND CONSENT APRIL 16, 1818. PROCLAIMED APRIL 28, 1818.

Washington
April 28, 1817

*T*he Undersigned, His Britannick Majesty's Envoy Extraordinary and Minister Plenipotentiary, has the honour to acquaint Mr Rush, that having laid before His Majesty's Government the correspondence which passed last year between the Secretary of the Department of State and the Undersigned upon the subject of a proposal to reduce the Naval Force of the respective Countries upon the American Lakes, he has received the Commands of His Royal Highness The Prince Regent to acquaint the Government of the United States, that His Royal Highness is willing to accede to the proposition made to the Undersigned by the Secretary of the Department of State in his note of the 2^d of August last.

His Royal Highness, acting in the name and on the behalf of His Majesty, agrees, that the Naval Force to be maintained upon the American Lakes by His Majesty and the Government of the United States shall henceforth be confined to the following Vessels on each side—that is

On Lake Ontario to one Vessel not exceeding one hundred Tons burthen and armed with one eighteen pound cannon.

On the Upper Lakes to two Vessels not exceeding like burthen each and armed with like force.

On the Waters of Lake Champlain to one Vessel not exceeding like burthen and armed with like force.

And His Royal Highness agrees, that all other armed Vessels on these Lakes shall be forthwith dismantled, and that no other Vessels of War shall be there built or armed.

His Royal Highness further agrees, that if either Party should hereafter be desirous of annulling this Stipulation, and should give notice to that effect to the other Party, it shall cease to be binding after the expiration of six months from the date of such notice.

The Undersigned has it in command from His Royal Highness the Prince Regent to acquaint the American Government, that His Royal Highness has issued Orders to His Majestys Officers on the Lakes directing, that the Naval Force so to be limited shall be restricted to such Services as will in no respect interfere with the proper duties of the armed Vessels of the other Party.

The Undersigned has the honour to renew to Mr Rush the assurances of his highest consideration.

Charles Bagot

1. Hunter Miller, ed., *Treaties and Other International Acts of the United States of America,* vol. 2 (1776-1818) (Washington, 1931), 645-47. Only the note from Charles Bagot to Richard Rush has been reproduced above. The note from Rush to Bagot, dated 29 April 1817, affirms the approval of President James Monroe to the identical limitations stipulated in Bagot's note of 28 April and is not reproduced above.

VI. **From Trails to Rails**
The Passing of Pioneer Life

WITH THE END OF THE WAR OF 1812 and with it the end of British intrigue with the Indians of the Old Northwest, migration into Ohio surged once again. From a census count of 231,000 in 1810, the figures jumped to 581,434 in 1820, to 937,903 in 1830, and to 1,519,467 in 1840, by which year Ohio was exceeded in population only by New York and Pennsylvania among the American states. With this rapid growth in population, better access to distant markets was mandated if Ohio's produce was to sell and its people to prosper, a harsh reality underscored by the Panic of 1819. And with the advent of better transportation and access to markets, still greater numbers poured into the young state.

Crucial to the economic development of Ohio was access to its interior as well as to markets. A key decision immediately following the war was the identification of a permanent capital near the geographic center of the state. The territorial capitals and the first state capitals had all been in the south or southeast—Marietta, Cincinnati, Chillicothe, and Zanesville. The selection of Columbus as permanent capital, effective in 1816, assured the future growth and development of the center of the state.

The construction of a National Road from the Cumberland Gap in Maryland (not far from Washington and Philadelphia) to Wheeling in western Virginia had been authorized by Congress in 1806 to link the East Coast with the Ohio Valley. After the road reached Wheeling in 1817, Congress was pressured by western interests to consent to its extension across Ohio, with ground broken at St. Clairsville on 4 July 1825. Following the route of Zane's Trace to Cambridge and Zanesville, it left the trace to go on to the new capital at Columbus, which it reached in 1833. Continuing to Springfield and passing north of Eaton, it reached the Ohio-Indiana border in 1840. Eventually, the National Road would be continued to the Mississippi Valley and then on to the Pacific Coast.

Like spokes from the hub of a wheel, connecting roads soon reached out across Ohio, linking Columbus with Sandusky, Cleveland, Portsmouth, and Cincinnati. To pay for their construction and maintenance, tollgates were erected, at first twenty miles apart, and then, when revenues were insufficient, only ten miles apart. Typical tolls in the 1820s were two cents for each stage-coach passenger; one cent for each horse or cow; four hogs for one cent; while schoolchildren, workers going to work, clergymen, schoolteachers, and paupers were free. The gate at each tollhouse consisted of two poles, or pikes, at right angles. These were turned when the toll was paid, hence the word *turnpike*. In contrast to present-day images of turnpikes, however, those of the 1820s and 1830s were dirt roads, often impassible in inclement weather.

Even before the National Road was built across the state, Ohioans were getting excited about the possible construction of canals to link Lake Erie with the Ohio River. Their excitement was due in no small measure to the success of the state of New York in the construction of the Erie Canal connecting the Hudson River near New York City with Lake Erie at Buffalo. Started in 1817, the Erie Canal was completed by 1825. With the prospect of access by water to the markets of the world, via Lake Erie and the Erie Canal to New York City or via the Ohio River to New Orleans, the General Assembly in 1825 appropriated funds to begin the construction of two canals across Ohio: the Ohio and Erie, to connect Portsmouth with Cleveland, and the Miami and Erie, to connect Cincinnati ultimately with Toledo. But before Toledo was assured as a canal terminal, a boundary dispute with the Territory of Michigan first had to be resolved. A short-lived boundary "war," with armies from Ohio and Michigan facing each other across the Maumee River, forced a decision, with President Andrew Jackson and Congress ultimately assuring Ohio not only Toledo but also some four hundred square miles of what is now northwestern Ohio, in compensation for which Michigan was awarded the "Upper Peninsula," this at the expense of the Territory of Wisconsin! By 1845, when Ohio's canal system was finally completed, 813 miles of canals had been built with state funding, 210 more (as spur lines) by private capital.

The peak year for both use and income of the Ohio canals was 1851. Though they would continue in use until 1913, the canals could not compete in speed and efficiency with the railroads, the first of which was under construction in Ohio as early as 1832. Nor could they compete in severe winter weather, when the canals would freeze over while the railroads could continue operating.

That Ohio was emerging as a mature, major state in the Union by the 1840s was evident not only in its fast-growing population and thriving economy, buttressed by a rapidly changing transportation system, but also in the election of the first of an ultimate eight Ohio presidents of the United States, William Henry Harrison of North Bend. Though the passing of the frontier and with it pioneer life was not apparent in all parts of the state simultaneously, as revealed in 1842 in the notes of a well-known English visitor, the eminent author Charles Dickens, it was evidenced, sadly and regrettably, with the removal of the Wyandots, the last of the great Indian nations that had once called the Ohio area home, from their lands in the Sandusky Valley in 1843.

In no respect was the transformation of Ohio more evident than in the emergence of a number of cities as centers of commerce and even some industry. In his visit to Cleveland, Columbus, and Cincinnati in 1847, the best known of Ohio's historians of the nineteenth century, Henry Howe, recorded his impressions of three that particularly attracted his attention as cities with promising futures, not only for Ohio but for the nation.

VI.1. Columbus Is Chosen as Ohio's Capital

Though the Constitution of 1802 stipulated that Chillicothe was to be the first state capital, it also prohibited any immediate expenditure for a statehouse. In so doing, it recognized the need for a more central location within the state for a permanent capital. Consequently, the first General Assembly met temporarily in the Ross County courthouse, a two-story stone building that earlier had housed the territorial government.

Aware of the impermanence of the first capital, a number of settlements in the central Ohio counties began to petition the legislature for consideration as the permanent capital, among them Zanesville, Worthington, Delaware, Franklinton, Lancaster, and Newark. On 20 February 1810, the General Assembly established a five-member commission to inspect the interested communities, hear their arguments, and make a final recommendation as to the most desirable site.

One of the towns visited by the commission was Franklinton, which had been laid out on the west bank of the Scioto River near the junction of the Olentangy by the surveyor Lucas Sullivant in 1797. Part of the Virginia Military District, Franklinton was rejected as a possible site because of its low elevation, which made it subject to flooding, and because of its irregularly shaped streets and lots, typical of most of the Virginia lands. Not far distant was another tract of undeveloped land, owned by John and Peter Sells, which the commissioners thought most attractive and which they accordingly recommended to the General Assembly. That body took no action on the recommendation, however, and the Sells tract, which later became the town of Dublin, missed becoming the state's permanent capital.

Persuaded by political rather than geographic considerations, late in 1810 the General Assembly did agree to move the capital to Zanesville. While there, it received a proposal from four landowners on the east side of the Scioto, opposite Franklinton, calling for the permanent capital to be located on their site, on lands yet undeveloped, on what was known as the Refugee Tract. Granted by Congress to Canadians who had sympathized with the Patriot cause during the American Revolution and had taken refuge in the United States during and after the war (in contrast to the more numerous British Loyalists who had fled from the thirteen colonies to take refuge in what would become the Canadian province of Ontario), the Refugee Tract extended in a narrow strip eastward from the Scioto River some forty-eight miles. Subject to federal survey, in contrast to the Virginia lands on the west bank of the Scioto, the refugee lands were laid out in ranges and townships on a perpendicular grid. The four landowners, Lyne Starling, John Kerr, Alexander McLaughlin, and James Johnston, had acquired the land they proposed as site for the permanent capital from intermediaries who had purchased it from Canadian refugees. Higher in elevation than Franklinton (and thus not as susceptible to flooding) the as yet undeveloped land on the east side of the Scioto caught the fancy of the General Assembly. On 14 February 1812, the assembly voted to accept the proposals of Starling, Kerr, McLaughlin, and Johnston, and on 20 February 1812, by joint resolution, directed that the land be surveyed and that a town be laid out on it by the name of Columbus.[1] Further, the assembly agreed that beginning on 1 May 1812, Chillicothe again should be the temporary capital, but that after 1816 Columbus should serve as the state capital and continue as such until 1 May 1840, "and from thence until otherwise provided for by law." Ohio had found its permanent capital.

AN ACT FIXING AND ESTABLISHING THE PERMANENT AND TEMPORARY SEATS OF GOVERNMENT.

Sec. 1. Be it enacted by the General Assembly of the State of Ohio, That the proposals made to this legislature by Alexander McLaughlin, John Kerr, Lyne Starling and James Johnston, (to lay out a town on their lands, situate on the east bank of the Scioto River, opposite Franklinton, in the county of Franklin, and [on] parts of half sections number nine, ten, eleven, twentyfive and twentysix, for the purpose of having the permanent seat of government thereon established; also, to convey to this state a square of ten acres and a lot of ten acres, and to erect a state house, such offices, and a penitentiary, as shall be directed by the legislature), are hereby accepted and the same and their penal bond annexed thereto, dated the tenth of Feb. one thousand eight hundred and twelve, conditioned for their faithful performance of said proposals shall be valid to all intents and purposes, and shall remain in the office of the treasurer of state, there to be kept for the use of this state.

Sec. 2. Be it further enacted, that the seat of government of this state be, and the same is hereby fixed and permanently established on the land aforesaid, and the legislature shall commence their sessions thereat on the first Monday of December one thousand eight hundred and seventeen, and there continue until the first day of May, one thousand eight hundred and forty, and from thence until otherwise provided for by law.

Sec. 3. That there shall be appointed by a joint resolution of this general assembly a director who shall, within thirty days after his appointment, take and subscribe an oath faithfully and impartially to discharge the duties enjoined on him by law, and shall hold his office to the end of the session of the next legislature: Provided, That in case the office of the director aforesaid shall by death, resignation, or in any other wise become vacant during the recess of the legislature the Governor shall fill such vacancy.

Sec. 4. That the aforesaid director shall view and examine the lands above mentioned and superintend the surveying and laying out of the town aforesaid and direct the width of streets and alleys therein; also, to select the square for public buildings, and the lot for the penitentiary and dependencies according to the proposals aforesaid; and he shall make a report thereof to the next legislature; he shall moreover perform such other duties as will be required of him by law.

Sec. 5. That said McLaughlin, Kerr, Starling, and Johnston shall, on or before the first day of July next ensuing, at their own expence, cause the town aforesaid to be laid out and a plat of the same recorded in the recorder's office of Franklin County, distinguishing therein the square and lot to be by them conveyed to this state; and they shall moreover transmit a certified copy thereof to the next legislature for their inspection.

Sec. 6. That from and after the first day of May next, Chillicothe shall be the temporary seat of government until otherwise provided by law.

Matthias Corwin,
Speaker of the House of Representatives.
Thos. Kirker,
Speaker of the Senate.

1. From Ohio Laws, vol. 10, chapter 34, cited in Alfred E. Lee, *History of the City of Columbus, Capital of Ohio* (New York: Munsell, 1892), 1:201–10.

VI.2.   "An Immense Distance from a Market"

With most Ohioans engaged in farming, the very real problem almost all faced in the early decades of the nineteenth century was getting their produce to distant markets. With local markets glutted with surpluses, Ohio's farm commodity prices were often abysmally low — wheat at 25¢ per bushel, corn at 12½¢, pork at 2¢ per pound, beef at 3¢, butter at 6¢, and chickens at 5¢ apiece were prices that were not at all unusual. The scarcity of gold and silver coins and the overabundance of nearly worthless paper currency issued by local and state banks often led to a system of barter rather than cash sales for many items.

Periodic panics induced by near-worthless currency, unsold commodity surpluses, and overextended credit brought financial ruin for many. For these, the only hope of improvement lay in new or extended systems of transportation, whether by land or water, that could get their farm surpluses to distant markets, where prices were usually significantly better than they were locally.

In two letters written in 1818 from Zanesville to his brother John in Salem, Massachusetts, Nathaniel Dike, a young Yale graduate and prospective lawyer, reflected the belief of many that if Ohio were to prosper, the construction of a network of roads and canals across the state linking the Lake Erie–Erie Canal route to New York and the Ohio-Mississippi River system to New Orleans was imperative.[1]

Zanesville Jan. 10th, 1818.

My Dear Brother,

Zanesville is the seat of Justice for the county of Muskingum. It is situated on the Left bank of the Muskingum river about 70 ms. above its mouth. It contains about 2,500 in [inhabitants] — and is a very thriving place.

There are 2 good bridges across the river at this place. Iron and stone coal are found in the neighborhood, in exhaustless quantities. In 1814 a company was incorporated under the name of the Zanesville Canal & Manufacturing Company whose object it was to cut a canal round the falls of the Muskingum at this place, for the improvement of the navigation, and to enable the company to use the waters of the river for turning water-works for manufacturing purposes. A dam has already been built across the river, and the canal is almost completed. It is about 120 or 30 poles long, 30 ft. wide at the bottom, 24 or 6 ft. deep, a great part of it thro' solid rock. From this canal, when completed, water may be drawn for the purpose of driving mill works to almost any extent. The Muskingum is navigable above Zanesville with small batteaux to within eight miles of the navigable waters of the Cuyahoga river which empties into lake Erie. Some trade is already carried on in the produce of the country, from this place to New-Orleans. Salt made at the Onondaga Salt-works in the state of New-York, has been brought to this place by the way of lake Erie, and sold lower than any other Salt then in market. On the opposite side of the river lies the town of Putnam, which is a well-built, flourishing little town. Many New-Englanders are settled in and about Zanesville.

The great N. Y. canal, by which it is contemplated to connect lake Erie with Hudson river, when completed will operate very advantageously to Zanesville, and all the settlements on the Muskingum river.

There is a portage of only 8 ms between the navigable waters of the Tuscarawas the principle branch of the Muskingum, and the navigable waters of the Cuyahoga; and it is said to be very practicable to unite them by a canal. Whenever the Great N. York canal is finished, it will be the channell through which the surplus produce of the Northern half of this State will find its way to market, and through which the inhabitants of the same section of country will receive all the foreign merchandise they consume—It is for this reason that I should consider the tract in the N. W. part of this State lately purchased of the Indians, to be the most eligible part of the state for emigrants to fix on as their place of settlement. This tract embraces between 3 & 4 millions of acres—In the event of the canal being finished, N. York would be preferred to New Orleans for a market, on every account. N. O. is unhealthy, the passage to it is dangerous, the markets there are fluctuating. And the country merchants cannot find there such extensive assortments of merchandise, nor can he purchase on as good terms, as he could in N. York.

The steam boats now on the Ohio and Missisippi greatly facilitate the trade on those rivers. There are about 4000 tons of steam-boat craft between Pittsburgh & N. Orleans. 11 steamboats are already floating on the above mentioned waters, and 9 more building. The Steam-boat Washington lately arrived at Louisville in 24 days from N. Orleans with 155 tons of merchandise. The distance is about 1700 miles. A trip from Louisville to N. Orleans, and back, may be performed in 37 & 40 days. The freight of the Washington amounted to about 25,000 dollars.

Adieu—

Zanesville Feby. 1818

My Dear Brother

There is as much distress at present in the Western country as there ever was in any of the old states. This distress has been brought about in various ways. In the first place the country has been flooded with paper money. There has been a great multitude, which no man can number, of Banks, which have loaned their paper to anybody that applied, in fact some of them have *urged* individuals to accept loans. Beside this, every county, town, Bridge Co., Turnpike Co., every manufacturing company, library company and almost every shopkeeper have issued bills beyond their ability to redeem. This the people encouraged, because "it made money plenty." Our whole circulating medium is composed, at this very moment, of rich trumpery. A piece of gold or silver is a very rare object—Some of this paper is worth nothing at all, some 25, & some 50 cts on a dollar. And the best of it is at 10 pr. ct. discount in the Eastern cities. Immense quantities of merchandise have been sold at enormous prices, while produce was low. Indeed the expense of transportation of goods to this country, & the discount on its paper are enough to ruin it. Now the merchants are pressing the banks to redeem their notes, and the banks are pressing individuals to pay up their loans. So that Lawyers and Sheriffs are doing all the business at present. The groans of poverty are frequent & audible, and still thickening—

The distance of this part of the country from a market is very much against it. The surplus produce is usually sent to N. Orleans almost 2000 ms. by a course of navigation always somewhat dangerous, in a climate often very unhealthy also always acting with an unfavourable influence on the products of this country. The principal articles taken down the river from this state are flour and Whiskey. There is carried also some butter & lard. The price of wheat at this time is from 62-1/2 cts. to 75 pr. Bush. The nominal price of flour 4.50 cts pr. BBI. Whiskey about 37 & 40 cts pr. gal. Butter for exportation is bought at about 12-1/2 cts pr. lb. Salt is so expensive an article as to forbid the exportation of salted provisions.

As the distance of this part of the country from the Sea-board diminishes the value of its products, so it enhances the cost of all foreign merchandise. Foreign merchandise sells from 50 to 100 pr. ct. higher here than it does in Boston. For instance French brandy is $5 & Lisbon wine $4 pr. gal. Coffee 45 cts, and young hyson tea $2 pr. lb. — Still people will consume it; so that the stores have already drained the country of its money, and brought it immensely in debt. Much of the real estate of the country is already under execution, or tending inevitable to that condition. At this time real estate cannot be fairly valued at more than 1/2 what it would have sold for 4 years ago.

What then are the inducements to the people of the Eastern States to emigrate to this country? — I can see but two — the cheapness of land; and a climate perhaps somewhat more favourable to vegetation. — Against these advantages must be offsett the following considerations. — The land is at an immense distance from a market for its products. . . . Roads here as yet are very miserable. — Schools & churches are extremely scarce, and wretchedly supported. — There are very few respectable physicians. The health & lives of the in. are at the mercy of ignorant and impudent quacks. . . .

1. See Dwight L. Smith, ed., "Nine Letters of Nathaniel Dike on the Western Country, 1816-1818," in *The Ohio Historical Quarterly* 67, no. 3 (July 1958): 214-17.

VI.3. The National Road Reaches Ohio

If the thirteen original states, in effect the "Mother Country," were to bind the western territories to the Federal Union, the first step was to create a transportation linkage across the mountains by which travelers could reach the Ohio country and the produce of their labors could reach eastern markets. By the terms of the Enabling Act of 30 April 1802, which empowered the people of Ohio to hold a constitutional convention to prepare for statehood, 3 percent of the income from federal land sales in Ohio was committed for the construction of roads within the state and 2 percent for the construction of a road or roads to link Ohio with the eastern seaboard. An act to lay out and construct a National Road from Cumberland, Maryland, to Ohio was passed by Congress and approved by President Jefferson on 29 March 1806.[1]

Construction of the National Road (also called the National Pike) was commenced in 1811 at Cumberland, and by 1817 it had reached Wheeling on the Ohio River. At once a flood of traffic swept over it. So heavy became the stream of wagons, carts, coaches, humans, and animals that by 1822 a bill cleared Congress looking to the necessary repair and upkeep of the road, over much of which only a shallow layer of broken stone had been laid. Calling for the establishment of gates and tolls to secure the funds to maintain the road, the bill was vetoed by President James Monroe on the grounds that Congress did not have the power under the Constitution "to adopt and execute a complete system of internal improvements."[2] In 1824, however, with much of the road in wretched condition, President Monroe reversed his thinking and signed into law the first of a number of federal appropriations for further construction as well as maintenance, to be supplemented by the establishment of gates and tolls to collect revenues from the road's users.

Though Congress had appropriated funds as early as 1820 for the survey of the route to be followed from Wheeling across Ohio, Indiana, and Illinois to the Mississippi River, the challenge of unconstitutionality had blocked their expenditure. With President Monroe finally persuaded that sweeping internal improvements were both constitutional and necessary, on 3 March 1825, a bill was passed by Congress appropriating $150,000 to take the road across the Ohio River from Wheeling as far as Zanesville, Ohio, and to conduct a survey of the route to be followed to connect the state capitals of Ohio, Indiana, and Illinois, and eventually Missouri.[3]

On 4 July 1825, a ceremony was held in front of the Belmont County courthouse in St. Clairsville, Ohio, to mark the beginning of the construction of the National Road in Ohio. Following the route of Zane's Trace to Cambridge and Zanesville, it would continue on to Columbus by 1833, to Springfield by 1838, and would reach the Indiana border by 1840. Essentially the route followed by U.S. 40 today, the National Road has been closely paralleled by present Interstate 70 and has been called the most historic highway of America!

AN ACT TO REGULATE THE LAYING OUT AND MAKING A ROAD FROM CUMBERLAND, IN THE STATE OF MARYLAND, TO THE STATE OF OHIO.

Section 1. Be it enacted by the Senate and House of Representatives of the United States of America in Congress assembled, That the President of the United States be, and he is hereby authorized to appoint, by and with the advice and consent of the Senate, three discreet and disinterested citizens of the United States, to lay out a road from Cumberland, or a point on the northern bank of the river Potomac, in the state of Maryland, between Cumberland and the place where the main road leading from Gwynn's to Winchester, in Virginia, crosses the river, to the state of Ohio; whose duty it shall be, as soon as may be, after their appointment, to repair to Cumberland aforesaid, and view the ground, from the points on the river Potomac hereinbefore designated to the river Ohio; and to lay out in such direction as they shall judge, under all circumstances the most proper, a road from thence to the river Ohio, to strike the same at the most convenient place, between a point on its eastern bank, opposite to the northern boundary of Steubenville, in said state of Ohio, and the mouth of Grave Creek, which empties into the said river a little below Wheeling, in Virginia. . . .

Sec. 5. And be it further enacted, That said commissioners shall each receive four dollars per day, while employed as aforesaid, in full for their compensation, including all expenses. And they are hereby authorized to employ one surveyor, two chainmen and one marker, for whose faithfulness and accuracy they, the said commissioners, shall be responsible, to attend them in laying out said road, who shall receive in full satisfaction for their wages, including all expenses, the surveyor, three dollars per day, and each chainman and marker, one dollar per day, while they shall be employed in said business, of which fact a certificate signed by said commissioners shall be deemed sufficient evidence.

Sec. 6. And be it further enacted, That the sum of thirty thousand dollars be, and the same is hereby appropriated, to defray the expenses of laying out and making said road. And the President is hereby authorized to draw, from time to time, on the treasury for such parts, or at any one time, for the whole of said sum, as he shall judge the service requires. Which sum of thirty thousand dollars shall be paid, first, out of the fund of two per cent. reserved for laying out and making roads to the state of Ohio, and by virtue of the seventh section of an act passed on the thirtieth day of April, one thousand eight hundred and two, entitled, "An act to enable the people of the eastern division of the territory northwest of the river Ohio to form a constitution and state government, and for the admission of such state into the Union on an equal footing with the original states, and for other purposes." Three per cent. of the appropriation contained in said seventh section being directed by a subsequent law to the laying out, opening and making roads within the said state of Ohio; and secondly, out of any money in the treasury not otherwise appropriated, chargeable upon, and reimbursable at the treasury by said fund of two per cent. as the same shall accrue. . . .

Approved March 29, 1806.

Th. Jefferson.

AN ACT TO APPROPRIATE FUNDS "FOR OPENING AND MAKING A ROAD . . . IN THE STATE OF OHIO"

*A*ct of March 3, 1825, appropriates for opening and making a road . . . in the State of Ohio, opposite Wheeling, to Zanesville, and for the completion of the surveys of the road, directed to be made by the act of May 15, 1820, and orders its extension to the permanent seat of government of Missouri, and to pass by the seats of government of Ohio, Indiana and Illinois, said road to commence at Zanesville, Ohio; also authorizes the appointment of a superintendent by the President, at a salary of $1,500 per annum, who shall make all contracts, receive and disburse all moneys, &c.; also authorizes the appointment of one commissioner, who shall have power according to provisions of the act of May 15, 1820; $10,000 of the money appropriated by this act is to be expended in completing the survey mentioned. The whole sum appropriated to be advanced from moneys not otherwise appropriated, and replaced from reserve fund, acts admitting Ohio, Indiana, Illinois and Missouri. $150,000.00

1. Archer Butler Hulbert, "The Old National Road—The Historic Highway of America," in *Ohio Archaeological and Historical Publications* (Columbus, 1901), 9:419–21.

2. Ibid., 426–27.

3. Ibid., 513.

VI.4.   Canals across Ohio: "Safe, Easy, and Cheap"

On 4 July 1825, at the same time that ground was broken for the start of construction of the Ohio portion of the National Road at St. Clairsville, the earth was turned at Newark, Ohio, for the beginning of construction of the first of two major Ohio canals, the Ohio and Erie, with New York Governor DeWitt Clinton wielding the spade. Clinton, who had been the leader in the building of the Erie Canal across his home state to connect Buffalo on Lake Erie with the Hudson River and the worldwide markets of New York City, was clearly the central figure in the canal-building era then commencing. With the completion of the Erie Canal in October 1825, New York City would double its population within a decade and would supplant Philadelphia as America's leading city.

What Clinton was to New York, Ethan Allen Brown was to Ohio. Called the "Father of the Ohio Canals," Brown served as Ohio's governor from 1818 to 1822, during which time he pushed vigorously for an engineering study to ascertain the feasibility and potential cost of constructing a canal or canals across the state to connect the Ohio River with Lake Erie. Though the Ohio General Assembly passed an act in February 1820 that was supportive of such a study, the failure of Congress to agree in advance to donate or sell public lands along the route to be ultimately recommended effectively killed it. Refusing to accept defeat, Governor Brown did succeed in getting the Ohio House to appoint a Committee on Canals, which, on 3 January 1822, issued a lengthy report that concluded with the recommendation "that the Governor be authorised to cause the route of a practicable canal between Lake Erie and the Ohio river to be explored, and its cost estimated, and for this purpose report a bill."[1] Such a bill was enacted the following month, and a seven-member Canal Commission was appointed and one of the best of the engineers on the Erie Canal project, James Geddes, was employed to investigate three possible canal routes across Ohio: an eastern route via the Muskingum and Cuyahoga Valleys; a central route via the Scioto and Sandusky Valleys; and a western route via the Great Miami and Maumee Valleys. Though the central route had the most political and popular support, since it would serve both the new state capital at Columbus and the old one at Chillicothe, Geddes found an insufficiency of water in the Sandusky and Scioto watersheds to sustain a canal in that location.

After much delay caused by a legislative mandate to reexamine the Scioto-Sandusky route and by lengthy politicking over possible canal terminals, the Canal Commission in 1824 finally recommended the construction of two canals. One in the east would combine the watercourses of both the earlier proposed eastern and central routes, namely by following the valleys of the Cuyahoga, the Tuscarawas, the Muskingum, the Licking, and the Scioto, connecting Cleveland on Lake Erie with Portsmouth on the Ohio River. The second, to the west, would follow the Maumee and Great Miami Valleys, with the identity of the lake terminal in the Maumee watershed left indefinite owing to an ongoing boundary dispute with the Territory of Michigan, but with the Ohio River terminal definitely identified as Cincinnati. The eastern canal would come to be called the Ohio and Erie; the western, the Miami and Erie, though at first it would be known simply as the Miami Canal. Because of the lack of identification of a lake terminal, the act adopted by the Ohio General Assembly on 4 February 1825 provided for the construction of both canals but indicated Dayton as the initial northern terminal for the Miami Canal.[2]

While ground was broken on 4 July 1825 at Newark for the beginning of construction of the Ohio and Erie, it was on 21 July 1825 at Excello near Middletown that ground was broken for the Miami Canal. At both places it was Governor DeWitt Clinton of New York who was the guest of honor. Though the Ohio and Erie would be completed by 1835, an additional decade would be required to complete the Miami Canal to Lake Erie and an ultimate terminal at Toledo. A bitter boundary controversy with Michigan was responsible for the long delay.

All told, when completed by 1847, 813 miles of canal would be constructed under state contract at a cost of $15,369,000, and an additional 210 miles of spur lines would be built by private investors. The Ohio and Erie would cover 309 miles between Cleveland and Portsmouth and would be serviced by 152 locks and by principal reservoirs at the Portage Lakes, Buckeye Lake, and Guilford Lake. The Miami and Erie would cover an ultimate 266 miles between Cincinnati and Toledo and would be serviced by 105 locks and by principal reservoirs at Indian Lake and Grand Lake St. Marys, the latter for many decades the largest manmade body of water in the world.[3]

Thanks to the canals, the produce of Ohio's good earth could more readily reach the markets of the world, and Ohio's people could thrive and prosper as never before.

REPORT OF THE COMMITTEE ON CANALS OF THE OHIO HOUSE OF REPRESENTATIVES, January 3, 1822.

Mr. [Micajah T.] Williams, from the committee to whom was referred so much of the Governor's message as relates to canals, made the following REPORT—

That the superior importance of improving the means of intercourse between different parts of a country, being a well established principle in political economy, it will not be necessary to adduce to the House the evidences of its illustration, which are afforded in the examples of the most illustrious countries of the old world, and in parts of our own; neither have they occasion, in the performance of their present duty to urge with the intelligent members of this body, the peculiar applicability of this doctrine to an agricultural state so remote from the sea as our own. It is a well established fact, that man has not yet devised a mode of conveyance so safe, easy, and cheap, as canal navigation; and although the advantage of easy and expeditious transportation, is not so likely to be perceived when prices are high and trade most profitable, yet the truth is familiar to every person of observation, that the enormous expense of land carriage has frequently consumed nearly, and some times quite, the whole price of provisions at the place of embarkation for a distant market. This is essentially the case in relation to all commodities of a cheap and bulky nature, most of which will not bear a land transportation many miles, and consequently are rendered of no value to the farmer, and are suffered to waste on his hands. The merchant who engages in the exportation of the produce of the country, finding it a loosing commerce abandons it, or is ruined; and crops in the finest and most productive parts of the state, are left to waste on the fields that produced them, "or be distilled to poison and brutalize society."

The profits of agriculture and the reward of labour failing, industry must languish, and the train of evils must succeed, always consequent on such a state of things. . . .

Although the members of this committee have on other occasions, heard much of sectional jealousies, they have lent an unwilling ear to the degrading sentiment; and consider it would be highly derogatory to any part of the state to suspect they would be envious of an immense benefit to a portion of their fellow citizens, procured without expense to themselves, by an operation which cannot fail to enrich the whole community, and place at their disposal most ample resources for education and for every kind of internal improvements.

Your committee in their inquiries on this part of the subject have not been unmindful of the manufacturing interests, which in some part of Europe are thought to receive at least equal benefit with agriculture, from this species of improvement. It is conceived that the advantage of both, from the execution of the project, may be blended in many particulars, and that they may thereby be rendered mutually subservient to each other, and to the best interests of our country. . . .

Your committee have not exhausted this interesting subject; they have omitted numerous important particulars, tending to strengthen the position they have taken, and to shew the advantages that would result to the state of Ohio and to the Union, from the contemplated improvement. Their calculations are adapted to a state of profound peace with the rest of the world, and they hope that state may be long preserved; but should the injustice and aggression of other nations produce a maratime war, obstructing our commerce through the Gulph of Mexico, and with the Atlantic ports, the freights that would be borne on the bosom of our canal would exceed any calculation that can be made, and would increase the revenues in the same proportion; or should our country again be scourged with a war with Great Britain, the facilities a canal would afford to the operations of war, by its expeditious and cheap transportation of military stores and munitions to the frontier posts, would save to the nation in money more than its whole cost, and in the lives of her citizens, immense worth and blood. The committee leave to the imagination of the members of this house to picture the political importance the state would derive from such an enterprize and its consequences. They are convinced that if the scheme of uniting Lake Erie and the Ohio by a navigable communication shall be found practicable, it cannot be too soon commenced. They are unable to perceive the probability that the state will be better prepared, in the course of fifty years, than within the next five, to accomplish the project. Perhaps a century may not witness a similar stagnation of commerce in all parts of the world, and so much capital, in consequence disengaged from that employment. The present cheapness of labor and subsistence, mark this as the auspicious period for the undertaking; the consumption by the workmen will furnish a considerable market for provisions; and we may add, a consideration of some importance in the actual state of the country, that the expenditure on this great object of lasting utility will more effectually relieve the citizens of Ohio from pecuniary distress, than all the schemes of paper credit that our sister states have adopted. The year 1823 will witness the completion of the New York canal, when the experience of their engineers and their contractors — their improvement in labor saving machinery, and implements for the execution of the work, with the laborers now employed in that undertaking, may be brought in aid of ours, should the state think proper to embark in the enterprize.

Your committee therefore confidently recommend that the Governor be autho-rised to cause the route of a practicable canal between Lake Erie and the Ohio river to be explored, and its cost estimated, and for this purpose report a bill.

AN ACT TO PROVIDE FOR THE INTERNAL IMPROVEMENT OF THE STATE OF OHIO BY NAVIGABLE CANALS, February 4, 1825.

Sec. 1. Be it enacted by the General Assembly of the state of Ohio, That the board of canal commissioners, created by the act entitled "an act, authorizing an examination into the practicability of connecting Lake Erie with the Ohio river by a canal," and the several acts supplementary, and in addition thereto, shall hereafter consist of seven members, to be appointed by joint resolution of the senate and house of representa-tives, and shall hold their respective offices during the pleasure of the general assembly, . . . and further the said commissioners shall have power to employ such and so many agents, engineers, assistants, surveyors, draftsmen and other persons, as in their opin-ion may be necessary to enable them to fulfil and discharge the duties imposed upon them by this act, and allow and pay said agents, engineers, assistants, surveyors, drafts-men and other persons for their respective services, such sum or sums as may be ade-quate thereto.

Sec. 2. That the said canal commissioners are hereby authorized and empowered in behalf of this state, and on the credit of the fund hereby pledged to commence and prosecute the making of a navigable canal on the Muskingum and Scioto route, so called, from the Ohio river, at or near the mouth of the Scioto river by the way of the Licking summit and the Muskingum river to lake Erie, commencing at the most eligible point on the Licking summit, and such intermediate point or points between said sum-mit and lake Erie, and said summit and the Scioto river, as in the opinion of said com-missioners will best promote the interest of the state, and likewise a navigable canal on so much of the Maumee and Miami line, as lies between Cincinnati and Midriver, at or near Dayton.

Sec. 3. That for the purpose of carrying into effect the object hereby contem-plated, there shall be constituted a fund, to be denominated the "Canal fund," which shall consist of such appropriations, grants and donations, as may be made for that pur-pose, by the legislature of this state and by any individuals, and also all monies which may be raised by the sale of stocks as hereinafter provided, and the taxes by this act specifically pledged for the payment of the interest upon such stocks.

Sec. 4. That there shall be a board of commissioners to be denominated the "com-missioners of the canal fund," which board shall consist of three members, each of whom shall take an oath or affirmation, well and faithfully to execute the duties re-quired of him by law, who shall continue in their appointment six years, and until their successors are appointed and qualified, which board shall continue until the stock which shall be created, as hereinafter provided, shall be wholly paid and redeemed, and that the terms of service of the three persons first appointed, shall be so arranged that one of their terms shall expire at the end of two years, one at the end of four years, and one at the end of six years, to be decided by lot, so that one of said commissioners shall be appointed every two years, and should a vacancy happen in said board by death, resignation or otherwise, during the recess of the legislature, the governor for the time being, shall appoint a person or persons to fill such vacancy until the legislature shall act in the premises: Provided, That any of said commissioners may be removed by joint resolution of both branches of the legislature, and that the following persons, and their successors shall constitute said board, to wit: Eathan A. Brown, Ebenezer Buckingham and Allen Trimble. . . .

Sec. 5. That for the payment of interest, and the final redemption of the principal of the sums of money to be borrowed under the provisions of this act, there shall be, and are hereby irrevocably pledged and appropriated, all the nett proceeds of tolls collected on the canals herein described, and of the rents and profits of all works and privileges, connected with, or appertaining to said canals, and belonging to the state; . . .

Sec. 6. That the sum of money hereby specifically pledged and appropriated, together with the nett proceeds of all tolls, and of the rents and profits of all works and privileges connected with said canals, shall be paid into the state treasury, and shall be kept distinct and apart from the other monies belonging to the state, and the accounts thereof shall be entered by the treasurer, in a separate book, to be kept for that purpose, and all monies appropriated or pledged, that now are, or that hereafter shall be paid into the treasury for, or on account of the canal fund, shall be paid over by the treasurer of state on the order of the commissioners of the canal fund.

Sec. 7. That the Canal Commissioners shall be authorized to receive from time to time from the Commissioners of the Canal fund, such monies as may be necessary for, and applicable to the objects hereby contemplated under such rules and restrictions, and on such security as the Commissioners of the Canal fund may deem necessary and proper, and to cause the same to be expended in the most economical manner, in all such works as may be proper to make the said canals; and on completing any part or parts of the works or canals contemplated by this act, to establish reasonable tolls, and adopt all measures necessary for the collection and payment thereof to the Commissioners of the Canal fund; and the said Canal Commissioners shall report to the legislature at each session thereof, the state of said works with an account of expenditures, together with their proceedings under this act, and recommend such measures as they may think advisable for the objects intended by this act; and likewise, when called upon by the Governor, to report to him from time to time, such information as he may require.

Sec. 8. That it shall and may be lawful for the said Canal Commissioners, and each of them by themselves, and by any and every Superintendent, Agent and Engineer, employed by them to enter upon, and take possession of, and use all and singular any lands, waters, streams, and materials, necessary for the prosecution of the improvements intended by this act; and to make all such canals, feeders, dykes, locks, dams, and other works and devices as they may think proper for making said improvements; doing nevertheless, no unnecessary damage; and that in case any lands, waters, streams or materials, taken and appropriated for any of the purposes aforesaid, shall not be given or granted to this state, it shall be the duty of the Canal Commissioners, on application being made to them by the owner or owners of any such lands, waters, streams or materials, to appoint by writing not less than three nor more than five discreet disinterested persons as appraisers, who shall before they enter upon the duties of their appointment, severally take an oath or affirmation, before some person authorized to administer oaths, faithfully and impartially to perform the trust and duties required of them by this act, a certificate of which oath or affirmation, shall be filed with the Secretary of the Canal Commissioners, and it shall be the duty of said appraisers, or a majority of them, to make a just and equitable estimate and appraise of the loss or damage, if any over and above the benefit and advantage to the respective owners and proprietors, or parties interested in the premises, so required for the purposes aforesaid, and the said appraisers or a majority of them, shall make regular entries of their determination and appraisal, with an apt and sufficient description of the several premises, appropriated for the purposes aforesaid, in a book, or books, to be provided and kept by the Canal Commissioners, and certify and sign their names to such entries and appraisal, and in like manner certify their determination as to those several premises which will suffer no damages, or will be benefited more than injured by, or in consequence of the works aforesaid, and the Canal Commissioners shall pay the damages so to be assessed and appraised and the fee simple of the premises so appropriated shall be vested in this state: Provided however, That all such applications to the board of Canal Commissioners, for compensation for any lands, waters, streams, or materials so appropriated, shall be made within one year after such lands, waters, streams, or materials, shall have been taken possession of, by the said Commissioners, for the purposes aforesaid.

Sec. 9. That every person actually engaged in laboring on either of the canals, authorized by this act, shall be exempt from doing militia duty, in this state, except in cases of insurrection or invasion during the time he is actually engaged, and the certificate of one of the canal commissioners, or contractors, who shall employ such men so liable to perform militia duty in performance of their contracts, shall be prima facia evidence of such engagements, and no acting Commissioner, or principal, or assistant engineer, employed on either of said canals shall be liable to be taken by capias, or warrant in any civil suit, arising out of, or connected with their official duties, but that such persons may be proceeded against by summons in all such cases.

Sec. 10. That the said Canal Commissioners, or a majority of them shall be, and they are hereby authorized to make application in behalf of this state, to the Congress of the United States, and to the proprietors of lands through, or near which the said canals or either of them, may be proposed to pass; to all bodies politic, or corporate, public or private; and all citizens or inhabitants of this or any other of the United States, for cessions, grants, or donations of land, or money, for the purpose of aiding in the construction of both, or either of said canals, according to the direction of the several grantors or donors, and to take to this state, such grants and conveyances, as may be proper and competent, to vest a good and sufficient title in the said state, to the lands so to be ceded, or granted as aforesaid.

Sec. 11. That it shall be the duty of the Canal Commissioners, on or before the first Monday of December, in each and every year, to settle and account with the Commissioners of the Canal fund, for all monies received by them from the Commissioners of the canal fund, and it shall be the duty of the Commissioners of the canal fund, to report the settlement so made to the Legislature, as soon thereafter as may be, detaining the sums allowed by them to the engineers, agents and laborers respectively employed in the superintendence and construction of said canals, and the works connected therewith.

M. T. Williams,

Speaker of the House of Representatives.

Allen Trimble,

Speaker of the Senate.

February, 4, 1825.

1. *Journal of the House of Representatives of the State of Ohio, First Session, Twentieth General Assembly* (Columbus, 1821–22), 176–87.

2. See *Acts of a General Nature, First Session, Twenty-Third General Assembly* (Columbus, 1825), 50–58.

3. See C. C. Huntington and C. P. McClelland, *History of the Ohio Canals, Their Construction, Cost, Use, and Partial Abandonment* (Columbus, 1905), passim.

VI.5. The Ohio-Michigan Boundary War, 1835

The boundary dispute between Ohio and Michigan, which reached crisis proportions in September 1835 with rival armies facing each other across the Maumee River, had its origins in fallacious maps drawn in the eighteenth century by European cartographers. The maps showed Lake Michigan in a more northerly location than it actually was and is. In the Northwest Ordinance of 13 July 1787, the northern boundaries of what are now the states of Ohio, Indiana, and Illinois were defined as the line separating the United States from British possessions in Canada. But the ordinance also contained a proviso "that the boundaries of these three States shall be subject so far to be altered, that, if Congress shall hereafter find it expedient, they shall have authority to form one or two States in that part of the said territory which lies north of an east and west line drawn through the southerly bend or extreme of Lake Michigan." In the Enabling Act of 30 April 1802, Congress authorized the creation of a constitution and government for the proposed new state of Ohio and defined its northern boundary as "an east and west line drawn through the southerly extreme of Lake Michigan, running east after intersecting the due north line from the mouth of the Great Miami [the Maumee] . . . through Lake Erie, to the Pennsylvania line."

Quite obviously, it was Congress's intent that the entire western half of the south shore of Lake Erie, including the Maumee Bay, would be Ohio's. That some doubt was beginning to appear concerning the exact latitude of the southern tip of Lake Michigan, however, was evident in a caveat written into the Ohio Constitution of November 1802: "Provided always, and it is hereby fully understood and declared by this convention, that if the southerly bend or extreme of Lake Michigan should extend so far south, that a line drawn due east from it should not intersect Lake Erie, or if it should intersect the Lake Erie east of the mouth of the Miami River of the Lake [the Maumee], then and in that case, with the assent of the Congress of the United States, the northern boundary of this State shall be established by and extend to a direct line running from the southern extremity of Lake Michigan to the most northerly cape of the Miami Bay, after intersecting the due north line from the mouth of the Great Miami River aforesaid; thence north-east to the territorial line, and, by the said territorial line, to the Pennsylvania line." Unfortunately, Congress took no immediate cognizance of this provision of the Ohio Constitution, and the boundary ambiguity was unresolved when Ohio began to function as a state on 1 March 1803.

The problem was further compounded two years later when Congress created the Territory of Michigan on 11 January 1805 and defined her southern boundary as *"all that part of the Indiana territory which lies north of a line drawn east from the southerly bend or extreme of Lake Michigan, until it shall intersect Lake Erie,"* thus repeating the faulty language of the Northwest Ordinance and the Enabling Act.

It was not long before Michigan laid claim to the territory south to the latitude of the southernmost tip of Lake Michigan, including Toledo and the Maumee Bay, and some four hundred square miles of what are now Williams, Fulton, and Lucas Counties in Ohio. Nor was Ohio silent in response, pointing out that the line defined by Congress as the northern boundary of Ohio was an impossible line, not only cutting off the mouth of the Maumee from the rest of the river but also lopping off much of northeastern Ohio, including most of Cuyahoga, Lake, Geauga, and Ashtabula Counties, when carried eastward to the Pennsylvania line. It was argued that Congress would never have done such a thing had it had correct geographical information on which to base its decisions, and that the only boundary that made sense was one established by a direct line running northeasterly from the southern extremity of Lake Michigan to the most northerly cape of the Miami (or Maumee) Bay, in accord with the Ohio Constitution of 1802.

Despite repeated petitions from the Ohio General Assembly, Congress refused to intervene in the boundary dispute. Though much of the War of 1812 in the West was fought in and around the disputed tract, and notwithstanding a postwar survey ordered by President Madison that defined a boundary known as the Harris Line, which was favorable to Ohio, and one ordered by President Monroe (the Fulton Line) that was sympathetic to Michigan, Congress took no action until forced to do so by a warlike crisis that erupted between the two neighbors.

Three congruent forces brought the crisis to a head in 1835. The first was the need to resolve the question of a terminal for the Miami Canal. Initial construction had taken the canal as far north as Dayton. A second took it as far as Piqua. With growing clamor for a major canal to cut across Indiana, linking the Wabash River with the Maumee River, and with the towns of Perrysburg and Maumee deemed unsuitable as terminals, it was evident that the city of Toledo at the mouth of the Maumee was the only logical terminal with potential to handle the freight and passenger traffic of both the Miami and Wabash canals. But did Toledo belong to Ohio or Michigan? The question had to be resolved before the canals could be completed.

The second factor precipitating the crisis of 1835 was the beginning of settlement of the "Black Swamp" through which the Maumee passed on its way to Lake Erie. Old lake bottom for centuries, the swamp, once drained, was fast proving to contain some of the richest farm land in America and the world. As settlers began to arrive in numbers, the question of jurisdiction demanded an answer. Was it Ohio's land, or was it Michigan's?

A third factor was the approach of statehood for the Territory of Michigan. As Ohio saw it, it would be better to have the boundary dispute resolved when Ohio had voting representatives in both houses of Congress while the Territory of Michigan was still limited to a single *nonvoting delegate in the lower house. Then, too, Ohio could expect to have the support of the voting delegations of both Indiana and Illinois, states that would also be advantaged if the boundary with Michigan were "tilted" to the northeast, from the southern extremity of Lake Michigan to the most northerly cape of the Maumee Bay, instead of running due east.*

To force the issue while time was still on Ohio's side, Governor Robert Lucas in late January 1835 appealed to the Ohio General Assembly to authorize the survey of the entire four-hundred-square-mile tract of disputed land prior to its distribution under Ohio law, an appeal that resulted in such authorization on 23 February 1835. In the meantime, hearing of this, the acting governor of the Territory of Michigan, twenty-four-year-old Stevens T. Mason, secured passage by the territorial council on 11 February 1835 of an act "to prevent the organization of a foreign jurisdiction within the limits of the Territory of Michigan," with fines of $1,000 or up to five years at hard labor in Michigan prisons for agents of such foreign jurisdictions that might trespass on Michigan soil.[1] When Ohio surveyors reached the disputed land and began laying it out in ranges and townships, nine of them were arrested under the Michigan act of 11 February and taken to jail in Tecumseh, Michigan. (See report of 1 May 1835 below.[2])

With news of their arrest, Ohio Governor Robert Lucas called a special session of the General Assembly to respond to the crisis. The Ohio legislature responded by appropriating three hundred thousand dollars to extend Ohio's jurisdiction over the disputed tract. It also provided a penalty of three to seven years imprisonment for any future "abductions" of Ohio citizens; created the County of Lucas (in honor of the Ohio governor), made up in large part of the disputed land; and stipulated that county government should begin to function in Lucas County, Ohio, in the county seat of Toledo on 7 September 1835.

On 6 September 1835, both Michigan and Ohio had armies drawn up on opposite sides of the Maumee River. The Michigan army, 1,200 men strong under General Joseph W. Brown, was firmly encamped within the city of Toledo on the west bank of the river. The Ohio army (numbering only 600 out of some 12,361 who had signed up originally when it had appeared the whole matter would be an adventurous lark) took position on the east side of the river, under the command of General John Bell. The Michigan camp had artillery; the Ohio camp had none. In the face of these odds, which appeared overwhelming to the disheartened Ohioans, a colonel by the name of Van Fleet hit upon a strategy that might save the day. Nothing in the Ohio law that had appropriated funds to help establish county government in Toledo, Lucas County, Ohio, on 7 September 1835 had cited the time of day when all this was supposed to take place. Argued Van Fleet, if he could have twenty brave volunteers as escort for the three appointed Ohio judges, a court clerk, and a sheriff, the party could slip across the Maumee after midnight and organize county government in a schoolhouse on Washington Street while the Michigan army slept.

The plan worked to near perfection, with Judge J. H. Jerome holding court by candlelight in the empty schoolhouse at 3:00 A.M. Despite a practical joke during a short-lived celebration in a nearby all-night tavern, the Ohio group managed to return undetected to their side of the Maumee, a good night's work behind them. County government had indeed gotten under way on 7 September 1835 in Lucas County, Ohio.[3]

Though no lives were lost in the boundary "war," President Andrew Jackson and the Congress were very mindful of how close to catastrophe the dispute had taken Ohio, Michi-

gan, and the nation. With a presidential election looming in 1836 and Ohio's William Henry Harrison the likely Whig nominee in opposition to Jackson's good friend, vice president, and fellow Democrat, Martin Van Buren, Jackson prevailed on Congress on 25 June 1836 to pass an act admitting Michigan as a state, but with the boundary desired by Ohio as well as Indiana and Illinois. To compensate Michigan for its loss of the four hundred square miles in dispute with Ohio, the act granted Michigan some nine thousand square miles of the Upper Peninsula, this at the expense of the Territory of Wisconsin, still some years away from statehood. Though Michigan thought itself robbed, it would eventually realize great wealth from the iron ore, copper, and timber resources in the Upper Peninsula. As for Ohio, with Toledo and the Maumee Bay now officially part of the Buckeye State, the Miami Canal could now be completed all the way to Lake Erie and given a new name, the Miami and Erie. Greater prosperity for western Ohio was assured even as it had been earlier for the eastern part of the state with the completion of the Ohio and Erie. But relations between the two neighbors, Ohio and Michigan, have never fully recovered from the strains of the boundary "war," though thankfully the competition in recent decades has been played out by rival teams on football fields and not by rival armies facing each other across the Maumee River.

Letter from Acting Governor Stevens T. Mason to General Joseph W. Brown Advising That "A Collision between Ohio and Michigan Is Inevitable"

Executive Office, Detroit, March 9, 1835.

Sir: You will herewith receive a copy of a letter just received from Columbus. You now perceive that a collision between Ohio and Michigan is inevitable, and will therefore be prepared to meet the crisis. The Governor of Ohio has issued a proclamation, but I have neither received it nor have I ever been able to learn its tendency. You will use every exertion to obtain the earliest information of the military movements of our adversary, as I shall assume the responsibility of sending you such arms, etc., as may be necessary for your successful operation, without waiting for an order from the Secretary of War, so soon as Ohio is properly in the field. Till then I am compelled to await the direction of the War Department.

Very respectfully your obedient servant,
Stevens T. Mason

General Jos. W. Brown.

Report to Governor Robert Lucas of the Arrest and Incarceration of an Ohio Boundary Survey Team by Michigan Troops

Perrysburg, May 1, 1835.

To Robert Lucas, Esq., Governor of the State of Ohio:

Sir: In the discharge of the duties which devolve upon us as commissioners appointed by your Excellency for re-marking the northern boundary line of this State, which is known and distinguished as Harris's line, we met at Perrysburg on Wednesday,

April 1, last, and after completing the necessary arrangements, proceeded to the northwest corner of the State, and there succeeded in finding the corner as described in the field notes of the Surveyor Harris, a copy of which we had procured from the Surveyor-General's office. Thence your commissioners proceeded eastwardly along said line, which they found with little difficulty, and re-marked the same as directed by law in a plain and visible manner, to the distance of thirty-eight miles and a half, being more than half the length of the whole line.

During our progress we had been constantly threatened by the authorities of Michigan, and spies from the territory, for the purpose of watching our movements and ascertaining our actual strength, were almost daily among us.

On Saturday evening, the 25th ult., after having performed a laborious day's service, your commissioners, together with their party, retired to the distance of about one mile south of the line, in Henry county, within the State of Ohio, where we thought to have rested quietly and peacefully enjoy the blessings of the Sabbath—and especially not being engaged on the line, we thought ourselves secure for the day. But contrary to our expectations, at about twelve o'clock in the day an armed force of about fifty or sixty men hove in sight, within musket-shot of us, all mounted upon horses, well armed and muskets and under the command of General Brown, of Michigan. Your commissioners, observing the great superiority of force, having but five armed men among us, who had been employed to keep a lookout and as hunters for the party, thought it prudent to retire, and so advised our men. Your commissioners, with several of their party, made good their retreat to this place. But, sir, we are under the painful necessity of relating that nine of our men, who did not leave the ground in time after being fired upon by the enemy, from thirty to fifty shots, were taken prisoners and carried away into the interior of the country. Those who were taken were as follows, to-wit: Colonels Hawkins, Scott and Gould, Major Rice, Captain Biggerstaff, and Messrs. Elsworth, Fletcher, Moale and Rickets.

We are happy to learn that our party did not fire a gun in turn, and that no one was wounded, although a ball from the enemy passed through the clothing of one of our men.

We have this day learned by some of the men who were arrested and have just returned, that they were taken to Tecumseh under the escort of the armed force, were there brought before a magistrate for examination, that they denied the jurisdiction; but that six entered bail for their appearance; two were released as not guilty, and one, to-wit: Mr. Fletcher, refused to give bail and is retained in custody.

We are also further informed, by unquestionable authority, that on the Sabbath day an armed force of several hundred men were stretched along the line to the east of us, with a view to intercept us on our way.

Under existing circumstances and in the present threatening attitude of affairs, your commissioners have thought it prudent, for the interest of the State, as also for the safety of her citizens and to prevent the threatened effusion of blood, to withdraw from the line at present and suspend the further prosecution of the work, until some efficient preparatory measures can be taken which will insure the completion of the undertaking.

All of which is respectfully submitted.
                    [Signed]   Jonathan Taylor,
                                                                    J. Patterson,
                                                                    Uri Seeley,
                                                                        Commissioners.

Organizing County Government in Lucas County, Ohio, at 3:00 A.M., September 7, 1835: The Memoir of Hon. W. V. Way of Perrysburg, Ohio

"He, Colonel Van Fleet, told the judges that September 7 would commence immediately after midnight, and that there was no hour specified in the law when the court should be opened. Governor Lucas wants the court held, so that by its record he can show to the world that he has executed the laws of Ohio over the disputed territory, in spite of the vapouring threats of Governor Mason. If we furnish him that record, we shall accomplish all that is required. Be prepared to mount your horses to start for Toledo at precisely one o'clock A.M. I will be ready with an escort to protect you."

"At the hour named, the judges and officers of court were promptly in the saddle. Colonel Van Fleet was ready with his twenty men, mounted and completely armed. Each man had a rifle in addition to his two cavalry pistols. They proceeded to Toledo, reaching there about three o'clock A.M., and went to the school house that stood near where Washington street crosses the canal, and opened court in due form of law. Junius Flagg acted as sheriff. The proceedings were hastily written on loose paper, and deposited in the clerk's hat. When the court adjourned, the officers and escort went to the tavern, then kept by Munson H. Daniels, not far from where the American House now stands, kept by J. Langderfer, registered their names and took a drink all round; while filling their glasses for a second drink, a mischievious wag ran into the tavern and reported that a strong force of Michigan men were close by, coming to arrest them. They dropped their glasses, spilling the liquor they intended to have drunk, and sprang for their horses with all possible haste, leaving bills to be settled at a more leisure time. As they had accomplished the work intended, speed was of more importance than valor. A backward charge from the enemy was made at the top of the speed of their horses."

"They took the . . . [trail] that led to Maumee, by way of the route nearest the river. They went at such furious speed that, if their charge had been made in the opposite direction towards the enemy, they would have pierced the most solid columns. When they arrived at the top of the hill, near where the Oliver House now stands, not discovering the enemy in pursuit, they came to a halt and faced about. It was then discovered that the clerk had lost his hat, and with it the papers containing the proceedings of the court, from which the record was to be made up. The clerk wore one of those high bell-crowned hats, fashionable in those days, and which he used for carrying his papers as well as covering his head. It was then the custom in traveling to carry everything in the top of hats, from a spare collar and dickey to court papers. The hat of the clerk, reaching high above his head, burdened with its load of papers and other incumbrances, was steadied on by the left hand for greater safety, while the right held the reins. But in spite of this precaution, it struck against an overhanging limb of a tree with such violence, that it was knocked off and fell to the ground. Having succeeded in holding the court without molestation or bloodshed, and now losing the papers, would leave them in as bad condition, or worse, than if they had done nothing, in case they should fall into the hands of the enemy. Notwithstanding, they all believed they had been discovered and pursued, and might be surrounded by superior numbers and taken, if they delayed; yet the importance of recovering the papers was such as to nerve them to the boldest daring. Colonel Van Fleet's courage and tact did not desert him in this emergency. He had succeeded in accomplishing what had been contemplated; and now their labor would be lost, and the expedition be an entire failure, without a recovery of the papers. With him, to will, was to do. He directed the clerk and two of the guards to dismount, and feel their way back carefully in search of the papers, while the balance of the posse kept watch, to cover retreat. He cautioned them to move with as little noise as possible, and if likely to be discovered by the enemy, to conceal themselves, and watch their movements so that they could use the best possible advantage to accomplish their object. The orders were that nothing but utter impossibility would excuse a failure to recover them. The search proved safe and successful; the hat was found and the papers recovered. The party reported no enemy in sight. The State of Ohio was now triumphant; a record could be, and was made up, and still exists, to prove that the State of Ohio, on September 7, 1835, exercised jurisdiction over the disputed territory, by holding a Court of Common Pleas in due form of law. . . ."

"The feeling of joy at recovering the papers was so great that Colonel Van Fleet ordered two salutes to be fired on the spot. He well knew that the distance to the line of the State, where there was no dispute about jurisdiction, was but small, and that if pursued, they could reach there before being overhauled. The party proceeded to Maumee at a leisure pace, reaching there a little after daylight."

1. Quoted in Tod B. Galloway, "The Ohio-Michigan Boundary Line Dispute," in *Ohio Archaeological and Historical Publications* (Columbus, 1895), 4:213.

2. Ibid., 217–18.

3. Ibid., 225–27.

VI.6. Ohio's First Railroads

Even as the National Road was under construction across Ohio and canals were being dug to link the Ohio River with Lake Erie, another form of transportation that promised much faster and more efficient service for both passengers and freight was already making its presence felt. On 4 July 1828, Charles Carroll, the last surviving signer of the Declaration of Independence, broke ground in Maryland to begin the construction of the first commercially successful railroad in the United States, the Baltimore and Ohio. Caught up in the excitement of "railroad fever," the Ohio General Assembly in 1830 chartered the Ohio and Steubenville, but that railroad quite literally never got off the ground. By 1836 horse-drawn cars operating on rails of wood connected Toledo with Adrian, Michigan, on what was called the Erie and Kalamazoo. But the first steam-powered locomotive drawing cars on rails capped with iron and operating wholly within Ohio was on a railroad chartered by the General Assembly in 1832 as the Mad River and Lake Erie, which in the spring of 1838 made its initial run in forty minutes over the first sixteen miles of track between Bellevue and Sandusky, an event that was widely covered by Ohio newspapers.[1]

Cheaper to construct, not frozen over in cold winter months, and not confined to low land as were the canals, railroads signaled the dawn of a new era in transportation. But not everyone was persuaded that railroads represented a positive step forward. One who seriously questioned their feasibility was General Samson Mason of Springfield, Ohio, who, after service in the War of 1812 and later in the House and Senate of Ohio, was elected to the Congress in 1834 to begin the first of four consecutive terms in that office. In an 1836 letter to a constituent identified only as "Cush," he derided the railroad "experiment."[2] *Yet despite his opposition and the opposition of others, the railroads were here to stay. By the Civil War, Ohio was crisscrossed with rail lines connecting virtually every town of importance. Soon the county seats of every Ohio county except Adams had rail connections. The heyday of the canal was fast passing.*

The rapid expansion of Ohio's rail network, by century's end exceeded by only two other states, was summarized in a report by Ohio's commissioner of railroads, R. S. Kayler.[3] *The report evidenced how dramatically the state's reliance on rail transport had become in little more than six decades.*

The *Cleveland Herald and Gazette* Reports on the Mad River and Lake Erie Railroad, 22 May 1838

*W*e learn by the Sandusky Clarion, that business has fairly commenced on 16 miles of this road. The locomotive has been put on, and a train of freight and passenger cars are now making regular trips between Sandusky city and Bellevue. The first run from Bellevue to Sandusky was made in 40 minutes, to the great enjoyment of passengers and spectators, and fright of cattle and dogs, who had no ear for the music of the shrill steam-whistle.

General Mason Opposes the "Wild and Visionary" Railroad Experiment

Washington, D.C., Feb. 6, 1836.

Dear Cush:—The Committee on Roads and Canals has come to a decision in favor of a change of the [National] road from Springfield [Ohio] to Richmond [Indiana], according to the prayers of the petitioners. . . . This is a sorry business. It will give me a great deal of trouble. I availed myself of the permission of the committee to lay before it a written argument against the change. I shall give the friends of this measure considerable trouble before they are done with it. . . . The same committee has, under consideration, the project of substituting a railway for the present road from Columbus to the Mississippi. . . .

There is a great danger, in my opinion, that the road will be overlaid by one scheme after another. I am opposed to all these experiments, and as a railroad in lieu of the present McAdamized road I have no idea that it will answer the purpose at all. No one can travel on horseback or in a carriage of any description on a railroad, no matter how wide it may be, nor how finished. The steam engines and cars would scare any animal and drive it out of sight. Could you drive live stock on such a road? No; not within a half mile of it. The few that might escape being slaughtered by the engine in its passage through the drove would be frightened and driven into the woods, where they would not be heard from again that season. A new road would have to be opened, immediately, to accommodate the people on the line. They could not get to market nor go anywhere else in the direction of the road. Besides, how is it to be kept up? Who is to superintend it? How long must people wait at the point where the cars start, after they arrive there and are ready to pursue their journey? Would not the whole affair soon become a monopoly in the hands of a few enterprising capitalists? Is not the whole scheme wild and visionary? The United States will not make this road if the States refuse to take it after it is finished. The State of Ohio cannot therefore proceed too cautiously in this business—the untried experiment. In connection with this project, it is said, there is great danger that the States will suffer the present [National] road to get out of repair, and by neglecting it a short time, it will soon fall into decay, so that the resources of the State will be inadequate to put it again into complete repair. It is said by those who have recently traveled on the road from Zanesville to Wheeling, that the road between those points is greatly injured, and now needs very considerable repairs. I hope the Legislature will not permit this. Will you not amend the law so as to increase the tolls. There are too many exemptions, that the road should not be suffered to dilapidate. It would be wanton negligence in the Legislature. The Superintendent is a poor devil, I am told. We want a board of public works with a man just as vigorous and unpopular as Kelly [Alfred Kelley, state canal commissioner] at the head of it. . . .

Yours with esteem,
S. Mason.

State Commissioner of Railroads Kayler Reports on Ohio Railroads

. . . . We had (June 30, 1899) ninety-nine railroad and railway companies incorporated under the laws of Ohio, ninety-five of which are in operation, and four in process of construction. Seventy of these corporations are entirely within the State, and twenty-five are incorporated under the laws of Ohio and adjoining States. . . .

Ohio had . . . a total of 13,386.35 miles [of track] . . . 5,410 locomotives . . . 4,080 passenger cars and 227,771 freight cars . . . to do the business of the roads.

In order to appreciate the progress that has been made in the railroad business in Ohio one must contrast a track made of wooden rails covered with strap iron with modern "T" rails made of steel, weighing 100 pounds to the yard; wooden bridges set on wooden piling, driven into the earth, with steel bridges set on best of stone masonry;

double-deck coaches, built like an old-fashioned stage coach, with modern vestibule and Pullman palace cars; a small ten-ton engine, built like a modern thresher engine, with a 280-ton engine with a tank capacity of 7,000 gallons of water and ten tons of coal, with a hauling capacity of 2,000 tons up a grade of 42 feet to the mile at a much higher rate of speed than the first engines were able to make on a level; a wooden freight car, ten ton capacity, with a car made entirely of steel, with a capacity of 50 tons. And finally, an engine and a couple of cars, coupled together with link and pin, braking done entirely by hand, lumbering along at a speed of about ten miles per hour, with a service each way once in twenty-four hours, with a train of thirteen cars, each a palace within itself, with every convenience, coupled together with automatic couplers, which admit of the smallest amount of slack, and handled entirely by air brakes, running at a speed of a mile a minute, and so smoothly that the great speed is hardly perceptible to the passengers, with service in either direction, in the most densely populated districts, every half hour.

1. See Robert C. Wheeler, *Ohio Newspapers: A Living Record* (Columbus: Ohio History Press, 1950), 138–39.
2. See B. F. Prince, "General Mason and His Letter on Railroads," *Ohio Archaeological and Historical Publications* (Columbus, 1908), 17:257–58.
3. See R. S. Kayler, "Ohio Railroads," *Ohio Archaeological and Historical Publications* (Columbus, 1901), 9:189–92.

VI.7. "Tippecanoe and Tyler Too": The Election of 1840

By acknowledging Ohio's claim to the disputed four-hundred-square-mile tract along the Michigan border and by granting smaller though similar concessions to Indiana and Illinois, the Jackson administration helped secure the election of Martin Van Buren over William Henry Harrison in 1836. Following the Panic of 1837, however, the Van Buren years were marked by economic depression, which gave opportunity to the Whig Party to win its first national election in 1840.

Returning to his farm at North Bend and his position as county recorder of Hamilton County, Ohio, Harrison remarked after the 1836 presidential election that "some folks were silly enough to have formed a plan to make a president of the United States out of this clerk and clodhopper." Yet when the Whigs held their next national convention in December 1839 at Harrisburg, Pennsylvania, it was Harrison, still remembered as the hero of Tippecanoe, Fort Meigs, and the Thames, who again received the nomination, this despite his poor health and advanced years. (He was nearly sixty-seven and was the oldest presidential candidate until Ronald Reagan.) To balance the ticket with a southerner, John Tyler of Virginia was nominated for the vice presidency.

Though the Democrats were not aware of its potential significance at the time, one of their principal East Coast newspapers, the Baltimore Republican, *inadvertently set the stage for the Whig campaign when it sneeringly editorialized, "Give him [Harrison] a barrel of hard cider and settle a pension of 2000 on him, and our word for it, he will sit the remainder of his days content in a log cabin." The sneer boomeranged as no other jibe in our political history. For long decades the Hamiltonian Federalists and their successors, the Whigs, had suffered under the accusation of being the party of the rich and the well-born, while the Jeffersonian Republicans and their successors, the Democrats, had been portrayed as the party of the common man. With a leading opposition newspaper characterizing Harrison as a humble pensioner, content with hard cider and a log cabin, the Whigs eagerly endorsed the jibe of the Democrats. Ignoring Harrison's seventeen-room country home in North Bend, they agreed that their candidate was indeed a poor man, a western farmer with a common touch—a log cabin, hard cider candidate. In contrast, they portrayed Van Buren as a rich, aristocratic easterner who was out of touch and out of sympathy with those experiencing the hard times of the depression.*

The campaign of 1840 brought showmanship, songs, and slogans to the fore as never before. Of more than eighty Whig campaign songs, two in particular attracted attention. "The Buckeye Cabin," by Otway Curry of Marysville, depicted Harrison's fictitious log cabin as made from buckeye logs, thus helping to establish the buckeye as an Ohio state symbol. The other was written by Alexander C. Ross of Zanesville. Entitled "Tippecanoe and Tyler Too," it provided a catchy, alliterative slogan that soon echoed across the land.

With Harrison as Ohio's favorite son, a number of new Whig newspapers made their appearance across the state: the Harrisonian *in Zanesville,* The Log Cabin Herald *in Chillicothe,* Hard Cider for Log Cabins *in Cleveland, and the* Log Cabin *in Dayton. It was in Dayton that the campaign reached its zenith, when, on 10 September 1840, a crowd estimated by some to be in excess of one hundred thousand and described as the largest political gathering ever held in the United States to that time, assembled on the anniversary of Perry's victory at Put-in-Bay to recall Perry's celebrated "We have met the enemy" message to Harrison and to "whoop it up" for the old general. The* Dayton Log Cabin, *in its issue of 18 September 1840, captured the essence of that rally, as victory in the election the following month was beginning to look more certain.*[1]

10ᵀᴴ OF SEPTEMBER, 1840
DAYTON CONVENTION.

Memorable and ever to be remembered as is the glorious triumph achieved by the immortal Perry on the 10th of September, 1813, scarcely less conspicuous on the page of history will stand the noble commemoration of the event which has just passed from before us. Who shall describe the magnificence of the display? Who can portray the swelling spirit of the thousands of freemen whose shouts, rending the very heavens, gave an earnest of the ardor with which the holy flame of liberty burned within their bosoms! What pen will not be laid down in despair, when the full magnitude of the task is made apparent by an effort to depict the grandeur of a scene, the magnificence of which is utterly indescribable! If there is power in language to convey to the mind a just idea of the overpowering manifestation of feeling and display, the man does not live who can put it to that use. No description however animated, will seem otherwise than tame to those who witnessed the splendid reality of that wonderful assemblage. And the tens of thousands who long to see a record of the glory with which Dayton shone on the never to be forgotten Tenth, will each notice the omission of interesting scenes and incidents which came within their own observation.

Wednesday the 9th.

Dayton was all activity on the 9th. Flags were seen to float in every part of town, early in the morning. As the day advanced, the number rapidly increased, till near seven hundred of these Tippecanoe signals decorated our beautiful place. Across Main st. at the corner of 2nd, was stretched a banner 150 feet long, bearing conspicuously these inscriptions: "Harrison and Tyler, Corwin [Thomas Corwin, candidate for governor] and Goode [Patrick G. Goode, candidate for Congress];" with a log cabin in the midst, and an appeal to "Roll on the Ball" [Alexander Ross's song also had included another catchy slogan, "Keep the Ball Rolling," as an appeal to Harrison supporters to sustain the campaign's momentum.] — . . . .

And again; over Main and below fifth was suspended 150 feet of canvass, upon which was inscribed "The People's candidates, Harrison Tyler and Corwin."

From Pense's Mill to Gilmore's large building, on Third street, was stretched a banner, 150 feet long, on one side of which was inscribed "No Standing Army, Resistance to tyrants is obedience to God," on the other side, "Eternal Vigilance is the price of liberty."

Over first street, at the Head of the Basin, floated a banner 100 feet long, on one side of which was inscribed, "Our Country — In Union is strength," on the other, "The Constitution, Don't give up the ship."

The factories were dressed out with appropriate flags and banners. The Carpet Factory had a banner upon the roof 42 feet in length, inscribed "Cuba prices can't come it." "Domestic carpets for Log Cabins." The Cooper Cotton Factory exhibited a banner 100 feet in length upon its roof, with these sound sentiments, "Success to American Manufactures & Farmers. A protective Tariff, and No Sub Treasury Wages;" "Live and let Live."

Upon Estabrook's Oil Mill, was a banner with these words, "Press Seed — but not the People." Between Curtis' Mill and the Rifle Factory was one inscribed — "Protect us and we'll clothe you." Another, with the words — "Old Green never tire — good for 1500 majority" On the reverse — "Agriculture, Manufactures and Commerce." The new Saw Mill was decorated with a flag inscribed — "Harrison and Tyler — the Tyrant's Foe's — the People's Friends." A bale of Cotton was suspended at the gable of Clegg's new Factory, upon which was painted — "Harrison and Tyler, Corwin and Goode. . . ."

The Procession.

Early on the morning of the 10th, carriages and horsemen were making their way to the place from whence Gen. Harrison was to be escorted into town. The beginning made by individuals only, was followed up by whole delegations with their Canoes, Cabins, Flags and Banners until every foot of the road between the town and that point, was literally choaked up with people, — all anxious to look upon and to honor him who had been selected as their champion against the minions of power upon the political battle field. Long before the General was expected to appear, the streets and houses on the route were crowded with anxious spectators. The Head of the Basin was literally jammed with people, and for some distance out in the direction the procession was to come as far as we saw, the sidewalks were filled. At last the eager expectation of the people was gatified. The discharge of cannon, announced the moving of the triumphal entry, and on came the immense array, with "banner and bugle, trump and drum." In advance were the military, formed in a hollow square with Gen. Harrison, Gov. Metcalfe, and Col. Johnson as above stated. Then followed a boat on wheels in which twenty six little girls, dressed in white, each carrying a satin flag, upon which the name of a State was inscribed — New Jersey bound with crape, the garb of mourning. Next, in a carriage thirty two boys in blue caps and hunting shirts, with blue silk flags, inscribed "Hail to the Hero." Then came bands of music, canoes and skiffs and cabins, and Trappers lodges, with banners and flags innumerable. The variety and number of the devices defy all attempts at description — To speak of the delegations as they appeared in procession and describe the many strange devices they exhibited, would be altogether impossible. Even to look upon that wonderful scene which was exhibited before you, for the purpose of gathering materials for description to be written afterwards, was vain and futile. You could not tell where one delegation ended and another began, or locate the Cabins, Canoes and Banners in their proper counties. Clark, had her band of music, and a trapper's lodge with Cabins and Canoes and a host of delegates. Warren, with the Lebanon Band, and various Log Cabin devices; one of the canoes, built at Morrow's Mill, on the Miami and drawn by six horses brought 102 delegates to the convention. Warren was well represented. Green came over with rising delegates in one procession, accompanied by the fine band from Xenia; their display of flags and emblems was imposing. Miami, with a crowd of true hearts was among us; cabins, banners and flags were conspicuous in her line. . . .

1. See Robert C. Wheeler, ed., *Ohio Newspapers: A Living Record* (Columbus: Ohio History Press, 1950), 118-21.

VI.8.   Charles Dickens Visits Ohio, 1842

In the course of a trip to the United States with his wife in April 1842, the celebrated English novelist, Charles Dickens, visited Ohio and later recalled his experiences and impressions in his American Notes, *published in 1844. His commentary on road conditions and on the Ohio towns where they stayed and through which they passed reflect a state still in process of transformation from its pioneer and frontier roots. Particularly illuminating are his descriptions of their trip from the state capital of Columbus to Sandusky, the lake port where they would board a steamer for Buffalo.*[1]

*W*e reached Columbus shortly before seven o'clock, and staid there, to refresh, that day and night: having excellent apartments in a very large unfinished hotel called the Neill House, which were richly fitted with the polished wood of the black walnut, and opened on a handsome portico and stone verandah, like rooms in some Italian mansion. The town is clean and pretty, and of course is "going to be" much larger. It is the seat of the State legislature of Ohio, and lays claim, in consequence, to some consideration and importance.

There being no stage-coach next day, upon the road we wished to take, I hired "an extra," at a reasonable charge, to carry us to Tiffin; a small town from whence there is a railroad to Sandusky. This extra was an ordinary four-horse stage-coach, . . . changing horses and drivers, as the stage-coach would, but was exclusively our own for the journey. To ensure our having horses at the proper stations, and being incommoded by no strangers, the proprietors sent an agent on the box, who was to accompany us the whole way through; and thus attended, and bearing with us, besides, a hamper full of savoury cold meats, and fruit, and wine; we started off again, in high spirits, at half-past six o'clock next morning, very much delighted to be by ourselves and disposed to enjoy even the roughest journey.

It was well for us, that we were in this humour, for the road we went over that day, was certainly enough to have shaken tempers that were not resolutely at Set Fair, down to some inches below Stormy. At one time we were all flung together in a heap at the bottom of the coach, and at another we were crushing our heads against the roof. Now, one side was down deep in the mire, and we were holding on to the other. Now, the coach was lying on the tails of the two wheelers; and now it was rearing up in the air, in a frantic state, with all four horses standing on the top of an insurmountable eminence, looking cooly back at it, as though they would say "Unharness us. It can't be done." The drivers on these roads, who certainly get over the ground in a manner which is quite miraculous, so twist and turn the team about in forcing a passage, corkscrew fashion, through the bogs and swamps, that it was quite a common circumstance on looking out of the window, to see the coachman with the ends of a pair of reins in his hands, apparently driving nothing, or playing at horses, and the leaders staring at one unexpectedly from the back of the coach, as if they had some idea of getting up behind. A great portion of the way was over what is called a corduroy road, which is made by throwing trunks of trees into a marsh, and leaving them to settle there. The very slightest of the jolts with which the ponderous carriage fell from log to log, was enough, it seemed, to have dislocated all the bones in the human body. It would be impossible to experience a similar set of sensations, in any other circumstances, unless perhaps in attempting to go up to the top of Saint Paul's in an omnibus. Never, never once, that day, was the coach in any position, attitude, or kind of motion to which we are accustomed in coaches. Never did it make the smallest approach to one's experience of the proceedings of any sort of vehicle that goes on wheels.

Still, it was a fine day, and the temperature was delicious, and though we had left Summer behind us in the west, and were fast leaving Spring, we were moving towards Niagara, and home. We alighted in a pleasant wood towards the middle of the day, dined on a fallen tree, and leaving our best fragments with a cottager, and our worst with the pigs (who swarm in this part of the country like grains of sand on the sea-shore, to the great comfort of our commissariat in Canada), we went forward again, gaily.

As night came on, the track grew narrower and narrower, until at last it so lost it-self among the trees, that the driver seemed to find his way by instinct. We had the comfort of knowing, at least, that there was no danger of his falling asleep, for every now and then a wheel would strike against an unseen stump with such a jerk, that he was fain to hold on pretty tight and pretty quick, to keep himself upon the box. Nor was there any reason to dread the least danger from furious driving, inasmuch as over that broken ground the horses had enough to do to walk; as to shying, there was no room for that; and a herd of wild elephants could not have run away in such a wood, with such a coach at their heels. So we stumbled along, quite satisfied. . . .

At length, between ten and eleven o'clock at night, a few feeble lights appeared in the distance, and Upper Sandusky, an Indian village, where we were to stay till morning, lay before us. . . .

It is a settlement of the Wyandot Indians who inhabit this place. Among the company at breakfast was a mild old gentleman [John Johnston], who had been for many years employed by the United States Government in conducting negotiations with the Indians, and who had just concluded a treaty with these people by which they bound themselves, in consideration of a certain annual sum, to remove next year to some land provided for them, west of the Mississippi, and a little way beyond St. Louis. He gave me a moving account of their strong attachment to the familiar scenes of their infancy, and in particular to the burial-places of their kindred; and of their great reluctance to leave them. . . .

1. Charles Dickens, *American Notes* (London, 1844), 160-70.

VI.9. Farewell to the Sandusky: The Wyandot Removal of 1843

In his memorable visit to Ohio in April 1842, the famed English writer Charles Dickens stopped at Upper Sandusky at a historic moment in that community's history. Only a month before, agreement had been reached to effect the removal of the Wyandots from the last of the Indian reservations in Ohio. The relinquishing of tribal claims of nearly a dozen Indian nations, begun at Greene Ville in August 1795, would reach a final conclusion in Ohio with the departure of the Wyandots from Upper Sandusky in July 1843.

In the Treaty of Greene Ville, Indian claims to some seventeen million acres of eastern and southern Ohio had been ceded to the United States. A decade later, at Fort Industry (Toledo) on 4 July 1805, remaining Indian claims to lands in the Western Reserve and immediately south of the Reserve and west of the Cuyahoga and Tuscarawas Rivers were also relinquished. A tract northwest of the Maumee River was ceded by the Ottawa, Chippewa, Wyandot, and Potawatomi tribes in the Treaty of Detroit, 17 November 1807, while some 4.5 million acres east of the Maumee were relinquished by the Delawares, Wyandots, Senecas, Shawnees, Potawatomis, Ottawas, and Chippewas in a treaty concluded at the Maumee Rapids on 29 September 1817. The following year, on 6 October 1818, the Miamis ceded to the United States nearly three hundred thousand acres of west central Ohio, including most of Mercer and parts of Shelby and Auglaize Counties, in the Treaty of St. Marys. Save for a handful of small reservations in the northwestern counties, primarily in the Sandusky Valley, Indian claims in Ohio were at an end.

But even these reservations proved short lived, for relocation of America's eastern Indians to lands west of the Mississippi, proposed by Jefferson as early as 1803, became national policy in the Jackson administration with the passage by Congress of the Indian Removal Act of 1830. Though the Delawares had already ceded the remainder of their reservation lands in the Sandusky Valley in 1829, they were soon followed by the Senecas in 1831, the Ottawas in 1837 and 1839, and the Wyandots in 1842. By the terms of a treaty negotiated by Indian agent John Johnston on 17 March 1842, the Wyandots agreed to cede the last remaining Indian reservation in Ohio in exchange for which the United States proposed to grant them 148,000 acres west of the Mississippi. Leaving Upper Sandusky on 12 July 1843, the Wyandots passed through Bellefontaine, Urbana, Springfield, Xenia, and Lebanon, arriving at Cincinnati on 19 July. There they boarded two Ohio River steamboats that carried them to St. Louis, where they transferred to two Missouri River steamers that took them to their new home in the valley of the Kansas River.[1]

A Xenia newspaper, the Torch-Light, *in its issue of 20 July 1843, captured the melancholy pathos of a people uprooted from their Ohio homes as the Wyandots passed through that community on their way to the West.*[2] *With their departure, Indian tribal life in Ohio would be no more.*

The Wyandots.

The remains of this once flourishing tribe of Indians passed through our town on Sunday morning last. They encamped about three miles north of town on Saturday evening, where they had intended to remain over the Sabbath, but some person or persons, having injudiciously furnished the intemperate among them with ardent spirits, it was thought best to leave in the morning, for fear that their peace would be seriously disturbed by those few who had become intoxicated. The general appearance of these Indians was truly prepossessing. Every one of them, we believe, without an exception, was decently dressed, a large proportion of them in the costume of the whites. Their deportment was quite orderly and respectful. We are informed that nearly one-half of them make a profession of the Christian religion. They appeared to be well fitted out for their journey, having a convenient variety of cooking utensils, and provisions in abundance. The whole number of persons in the company, so far as we could learn, was about 750. The number of wagons, carriages and buggies owned by the tribe, about 80. Hired wagons 55. Horses and ponies near 300.

Our citizens seemed to look upon the scene of their departure from among us with feelings of melancholy interest. To reflect that the last remnant of a powerful people, once the proud possessors of the soil we now occupy, were just leaving their beloved hunting grounds and the graves of their ancestors—that their council fires had gone out and their wigwams were deserted—was well calculated to awaken the liveliest sympathies of the human heart. No one, we are sure, who felt such emotions, could refrain from breathing a devout aspiration to the "Great Spirit," that he would guide and protect them on their journey, and carefully preserve them as a people after they shall have arrived at their new home in the far, far west.

1. See Carl G. Klopfenstein, "The Removal of the Indians from Ohio," in Randall Buchman, ed., *The Historic Indian in Ohio: A Conference to Commemorate the Bicentennial of the American Revolution* (Columbus: Ohio Historical Society, 1976), 28-38. Also, Dwight L. Smith, ed., "An Unsuccessful Negotiation for Removal of the Wyandot Indians from Ohio, 1834," in *Ohio State Archaeological and Historical Quarterly* 58 (Columbus, 1949), 305-31; and Leonard U. Hill, *John Johnston and the Indians in the Land of the Three Miamis* (Piqua, 1957), 119-38.

2. See Robert C. Wheeler, ed., *Ohio Newspapers: A Living Record* (Columbus: Ohio History Press, 1950), 112-13.

VI.10. Henry Howe Visits Cleveland, Columbus, and Cincinnati, 1846–1847

Among a handful of noteworthy historians of Ohio's principal towns and villages in the pre-Civil War years, Henry Howe was and still is the best known. As a young man but thirty years of age, in 1846 and 1847 he visited all of Ohio's counties and most of their localities and historic spots, gathering information from longtime residents and community leaders from which he compiled the first of his famed Historical Collections of Ohio. *Rambling and often disjointed, his writings more closely resemble the notes of a visiting tourist rather than the polished narratives of a professional historian. Yet, as a source of information about Ohio's towns and villages in the nineteenth century, Howe's* Historical Collections *are invaluable even to the present day.*

Particularly insightful are his comments concerning three Ohio communities that were fast becoming centers of political, economic, social, and cultural activity. As terminal of the Ohio and Erie Canal and an important lake port, Cleveland was emerging as northeastern Ohio's key commercial center.[1] As Ohio's capital, Columbus was the focus of the state's political life,[2] while Cincinnati, the Ohio River terminal of the Miami and Erie Canal, was already heralded as the "Queen City of the West" and one of America's most important cultural centers.[3]

CLEVELAND

Cleveland is at the northern termination of the Ohio canal, 139 miles ne. from Columbus, 255 from Cincinnati, 130 from Pittsburg, 190 from Buffalo, 455 from New York, and 130 from Detroit. It was incorporated as a village in 1814, and as a city in 1836. Excepting a small portion of it on the river, it is situated on a gravelly plain, elevated about 100 feet above the lake, of which it has a most commanding prospect. Some of the common streets are 100 feet wide, and the principal business one, Main street, has the extraordinary width of 132 feet. It is one of the most beautiful towns in the Union, and much taste is displayed in the private dwellings and disposition of shrubbery. "The location is dry and healthy, and the view of the meanderings of the Cuyahoga river, and of the steamboats and shipping in the port, and leaving or entering it, and of the numerous vessels on the lake under sail, presents a prospect exceedingly interesting, from the high shore of the lake.

"Near the center of the place is a public square of ten acres, divided into four parts, by intersecting streets, neatly enclosed, and shaded with trees. The court house and one or two churches front on this square.

"The harbor of Cleveland is one of the best on Lake Erie. It is formed by the mouth of the Cuyahoga river, and improved by a pier on each side, extending 425 yards into the lake, 200 feet apart, and faced with substantial stone masonry. Cleveland is the great mart of the greatest grain-growing state in the Union, and it is the Ohio and Erie canals that have made it such, though it exports much by the way of the Welland canal to Canada. It has a ready connection with Pittsburg, through the Pennsylvania and Ohio canal, which extends from the Ohio canal at Akron to Beaver creek, which enters the Ohio below Pittsburg. The natural advantages of this place are unsurpassed in the west, to which it has a large access by the lakes and the Ohio canal. But the Erie canal constitutes the principal source of its vast advantages; without that great work, it would have remained in its former insignificance." The construction of two contemplated railroads, the first connecting Cleveland with Wellsville, on the Ohio; and the last, with Columbus, will add much to the business facilities of the place.

The government of the city is vested in a mayor and council, which consists of three members from each of the three wards into which the city is divided, and also an alderman from each ward. The following is a list of the mayors of the city since its organization, with the time of their election: John W. Willey, 1836 and 1837; Joshua Mills, 1838 and 1839; Nicholas Dockstader, 1840; John W. Allen, 1841; Joshua Mills, 1842; Nelson Hayward, 1843; Saml. Starkweather, 1844 and 1845; George Hoadley, 1846, and J. A. Harris, 1847.

The Cleveland medical college, although established but four or five years, is in a very flourishing condition, and has gained so much in public estimation, as to be equalled in patronage by only one or two similar institutions in the west. It has seven professors, and all the necessary apparatus and facilities for instruction.

In 1837, the government purchased nine acres on the height overlooking the lake, for the purpose of erecting a marine hospital; up to the present time, but little more than the foundation has been laid. It is to be of Ionic architecture, of hewn stone, and will combine convenience and beauty.

There are in Cleveland a large number of mercantile and mechanical establishments, 4 banks, 3 daily, 6 weekly, and 1 semi-monthly newspapers, and 21 religious societies, viz: 3 Episcopal, 2 Presbyterian, 1 Methodist Episcopal, 1 Baptist, 1 Catholic, 1 Bethel, 1 Wesleyan Methodist, 1 German Evangelical Protestant, 1 German Mission Society of the Protestant Episcopal Church, 1 German Evangelical Lutheran, 1 Evangelical Association of North America, 1 Associate Presbyterian, 1 Seceder, 1 Disciples, 1 Jewish, 1 Universalist and 2 Second Advent. The business of the port of Cleveland, both by canal and lake, is very heavy, and constantly increasing. The number of arrivals by lake, in 1845, was 2136; of these, 927 were steamers. The tonnage then owned at this port, amounted to 13,493, and number of vessels, of all kinds, 85. The total value of the imports and exports by the lake, was over $9,000,000.

The population of Cleveland, on the east side of the Cuyahoga, was, in the year 1796, 3; 1798, 16; 1825, 500; 1831, 1100; 1835, 5080; 1840, 6071, and 1846,

10,135. Of the last, 6780 were natives of the United States; 1472 of Germany; 808 of England; 632 of Ireland; 144 of Canada; 97 of the Isle of Man, and 96 of Scotland.

Ohio City is beautifully situated on a commanding eminence on the west side of the Cuyahoga, opposite Cleveland. It was incorporated as a city, March 3d, 1836, and its government vested in a mayor and council. The city is divided into three wards, and is well laid out and built. There are three churches, viz.: 1 Presbyterian, 1 Methodist Episcopal and 1 Episcopalian — the last of which is a Gothic structure of great beauty. The population of Ohio city, in 1840, was 1,577, and in 1845, 2,462.

COLUMBUS

From the first organization of the state government until 1816, there was no permanent state capital. The sessions of the legislature were held at Chillicothe until 1810; the sessions of 1810-11 and 1811-12, were held at Zanesville; after that, until December, 1816, they were again held at Chillicothe, at which time the legislature was first convened at Columbus.

Among the various proposals to the legislature, while in session at Zanesville, for the establishment of a permanent seat of government, were those of Lyne Starling, Jas. Johnston, Alex M'Laughlin and Jon Kerr, the after proprietors of Columbus, for establishing it on the "high bank of the Scioto river, opposite Franklinton," which site was then a native forest. On the 14th Feb., 1812, the legislature passed a law accepting their proposals, and in one of its sections, selected Chillicothe as a temporary seat of government merely. By an act amendatory of the other, passed Feb. 17th, 1816, it was enacted, "that from and after the second Tuesday of October next, the seat of government of this state shall be established at the town of Columbus."

On the 19th of Feb., 1812, the proprietors signed and acknowledged their articles at Zanesville, as partners, under the law for laying out, &c., of the town of Columbus. The contract having been closed between the proprietors and the state, the town was laid out in the spring of 1812, under the direction of Moses Wright. On the 18th of June, the same day war was declared with Great Britain, the first public sale of lots, by auction, was held. . . .

The first penitentiary was erected in 1813. The state house was erected in 1814; the brick of this edifice were partly made from a beautiful mound near by, which has given the name to a street. On the 10th of Feb., 1816, the town was incorporated as "the borough of Columbus." The first board of councilmen elected were Henry Brown, Michael Patton, Jarvis Pike, Robt. and Jeremiah Armstrong, John Kerr, John Cutler, Caleb Houston and Robt. M'Coy. About the year 1819, the United States or old court-house was erected. In 1824, the county seat was removed from Franklinton to Columbus. The present city charter was granted March 3d, 1834. The first newspaper in Columbus was commenced about the beginning of 1814, and was called "the Western Intelligencer and Columbus Gazette:" it was the foundation, the original of "the Ohio State Journal."

For the first few years Columbus improved rapidly. Emigrants flowed in, apparently, from all quarters, and the improvements and general business of the place kept pace with the increase of population. Columbus, however, was a rough spot in the woods, off from any public road of much consequence. The east and west travel passed through Zanesville, Lancaster and Chillicothe, and the mails came in cross-line on horseback. The first successful attempt to carry a mail to or from Columbus, otherwise than on horseback, was by Philip Zinn, about the year 1816, once a week between Chillicothe and Columbus. The years from 1819 to '26, were the dullest years of Columbus; but soon after it began to improve. The location of the national road and of the Columbus feeder to the Ohio canal, gave an impetus to improvements.

Columbus is beautifully situated on the east bank of the Scioto, about half a mile below its junction with the Olentangy. The streets are spacious, the site level, and it has many elegant private dwellings. Columbus has a few manufactories only; it does, however, a heavy mercantile business, there being many stores of various kinds. It contains 17 churches, viz.: 2 Methodist Episcopal, 1 German Methodist, 2 Presbyterian, 1 Baptist, 1 German Lutheran, 1 do. Evangelical Protestant, 1 do. Reformed, 2 Episcopal, 1 Catholic, 1 Welch Presbyterian, 1 United Brethren, 1 Universalist and 1 Bethel, and 1 Baptist for colored persons. The principal literary institutions in this city, are the Columbus institute, a flourishing classical institution for males, Mr. and Mrs. Schencks' female seminary, and the German theological Lutheran seminary, which last has been established about 17 years, Rev. Wm. Lehmann, professor of theology. There are in Columbus 6 weekly, 2 tri-weekly and 1 semi-monthly newspapers and several banks. Its population, in 1815, was about 700; in 1820, about 1,400; in 1830, 2,437; in 1840, 6,048, and in 1846, 10,016.

The great state institutions located at Columbus, do honor to Ohio, give great interest to the city, and present strong attractions to strangers. . . .

CINCINNATI

. . . . It is the largest city of the west, north of New Orleans, and the fifth in population in the United States. It is situated on the north bank of the Ohio river, opposite the mouth of Licking river, which enters the Ohio between Newport and Covington, Ky. The Ohio here has a gradual bend towards the south.

This city is near the eastern extremity of a valley, about twelve miles in circumference, surrounded by beautiful hills, which rise to the height of 300 feet by gentle and varying slopes, and mostly covered with native forest trees. The summit of these hills presents a beautiful and picturesque view of the city and valley. The city is built on two table lands, the one elevated from 40 to 60 feet above the other. Low water mark in the river, which is 108 below the upper part of the city, is 432 feet above tide water at Albany, and 133 feet below the level of Lake Erie. The population in 1800, was 750; in 1810, 2540; in 1820, 9602; in 1830, 24,831; in 1840, 46,338, and in 1847, over 90,000. Employed in commerce in 1840, 2,226; in manufactures and trades, 10,866: navigating rivers and canals, 1748; in the learned professions, 377. Covington and Newport opposite, in Ky., and Fulton and the adjacent parts of Mill creek township on the north, are in fact, suburbs of Cincinnati, and if added to the above population would extend it to 105,000. The shores of the Ohio at the landing, is substantially paved to low water mark and is supplied with floating wharves, adapted to the great rise and fall of river, which renders the landing and shipping of goods at all times convenient.

Cincinnati seems to have been originally laid out on the model of Philadelphia, with great regularity. North of Main street, between the north side of Front street and the bank of the river, is the landing, an open area of 10 acres, with about 1000 feet front. This area is of great importance to the business of the city, and generally presents a scene of much activity. The corporate limits include about four square miles. The central part is compactly and finely built, with spacious warehouses, large stores and handsome dwellings; but in its outer parts, it is but partially built up and the houses irregularly scattered. Many of them are of stone or brick, but an equal or greater number are of wood, and are generally from two to four stories high. The city contains over 11,000 edifices public and private; and of those recently erected, the number of brick exceeds those of wood, and the style of architecture is constantly improving. Many of the streets are well paved, extensively shaded with trees and the houses ornamented with shrubbery. The climate is more variable than on the Atlantic coast, in the same latitude. Snow rarely falls sufficiently deep, or lies long enough, to furnish sleighing. Few places are more healthy, the average annual mortality being 1 in 40. The inhabitants are from every state in the Union and from various countries in Europe. Besides natives of Ohio, Pennsylvania and New Jersey have furnished the greatest number; but many are from New York, Virginia, Maryland and New England. Nearly one fifth of the adult population are Germans. But England, Ireland, Scotland, France and Wales, have furnished considerable numbers.

The Ohio river at Cincinnati, is 1800 feet, or about one third of a mile wide, and its mean annual range from low to high water, is about 50 feet; the extreme range may be about 10 feet more. The greatest depressions are generally in August, September and October; and the greatest rise in December, March, May and June. The upward navigation is generally suspended by floating ice for eight or ten weeks in the winter. Its current at its mean height, is about 3 miles an hour; when higher and rising, it is more; and when very low, it does not exceed 2 miles. The quantity of rain and snow which falls annually at Cincinnati, is near 3 feet 9 inches. The wettest month is May, and the driest January. The average number of clear and fair days in a year, is 146; of variable, 114; of cloudy, 105. There have been, since 1840, from thirty to thirty eight steamboats annually built with an average aggregate tonnage of 6500 tons.

Among the public buildings of Cincinnati, is the court house on Main street; it is a spacious building. The edifice of the Franklin and Lafayette bank of Cincinnati, on Third street, has a splendid portico of Grecian Doric columns, 4 feet 6 inches in diameter, extending through the entire front, was built after the model of the Parthenon, and is truly classical and beautiful. The first and second Presbyterian churches are beautiful edifices, and the Unitarian church is singularly neat. There are several churches built within the last three years, which possess great beauty, either internally or externally. But the most impressive building is the Catholic Cathedral, which at far less cost, surpasses in beauty and picturesque effect, the metropolitan edifice at Baltimore. There are many fine blocks of stores, on Front, Walnut, Pearl, Main and Fourth streets, and the eye is arrested by many beautiful private habitations. The most showy quarters are Main street, Broadway, Pearl and Fourth street, west of its intersection with Main.

There are 76 churches in Cincinnati, viz.: 7 Presbyterian, (4 old and 3 new school); 2 Congregational; 12 Episcopal Methodist; 2 Methodist Protestant; 2 Wesleyan Methodist; 1 Methodist Episcopal south; 1 Bethel; 1 Associate Reformed; 1 Reformed Presbyterian, 6 Baptist; 5 Disciples; 1 Universalist; 1 Restorationist; 1 Christian; 8 German Lutheran and Reformed; English Lutheran and Reformed 1 each; 1 United Brethren; 1 Welch Calvinistic; 1 Welch Congregational; 1 Unitarian; 2 Friends; 1 New Jerusalem; 8 Catholic, 6 of which are for Germans; 2 Jews Synagogues; 5 Episcopal and 1 Second Advent.

There are 5 market houses and 3 theatres, of which 1 is German.

Cincinnati contains many literary and charitable institutions. The Cincinnati college was founded in 1819. The building is in the center of the city, and is the most beautiful edifice of the kind in the state. It is of the Grecian Doric order, with pilaster fronts and facade of Dayton marble, and cost about $35,000. It has 7 professors or other instructors, about 160 pupils, one quarter of whom are in the collegiate department. Woodward college, named from its founder, who gave a valuable block of ground in the north part of the city, has a president and five professors, or other instructors, and including its preparatory department, near 200 students. The Catholics have a college called St. Xavier's, which has about 100 students and near 5000 volumes in its libraries. Lane seminary, a theological institution, is at Walnut Hills, 2 miles from the centre of the city. It went into operation in 1833, has near 100 students, and over 10,000 volumes in its libraries. There is no charge for tuition. Rooms are provided and furnished at $5 per annum, and the students boarded at 90 and 62-1/2 cents per week. The Medical college was chartered and placed under trustees, in 1825. It has a large and commodious building, a library of over 2000 volumes, 7 professors and about 150 students. The Cincinnati law school is connected with Cincinnati college, has 3 professors and about 30 students. The mechanics' institute, chartered in 1828, has a valuable philosophical and chemical apparatus, a library and a reading room. The common free schools of the city are of a high order, with fine buildings, teachers and apparatus. In the high schools, there are not less than 1500 pupils; in the common and private 5000, and including the students in the collegiate institutions, there are 7000 persons in the various departments of education. In 1831, a college of teachers was established, having for its object the elevation of the profession, and the advancement of the interest of schools in the Mississippi valley, which holds an annual meeting in Cincinnati, in October. The young men's mercantile library association has a fine library and reading rooms. The library contains over 3800 volumes, and the institution promises to be an honor and a blessing to the commercial community. The apprentices' library, founded in 1821, contains 2200 volumes.

The charitable institutions of the city are highly respectable. The Cincinnati orphan asylum is in a building, which cost $18,000. Attached is a library and well-organized school, with a provision even for infants; and it is surrounded by ample grounds. It has trained up over 300 children for usefulness. The Catholics have one male and female orphan asylum. The commercial hospital and lunatic asylum of Ohio, was incorporated in 1821. The edifice, in the northwest part of the city, will accommodate 250 persons; 1100 have been admitted within a year. A part of the building is used for a poor house; and there are separate apartments for the insane.

The city is supplied by water raised from the Ohio river, by a steam engine, of 40 horse power, and forced into two reservoirs, on a hill, 700 feet distant; from whence it is carried in pipes to the intersection of Broadway and Third streets, and thence distributed through the principal streets in pipes. These works are now owned by the city.

Cincinnati is an extensive manufacturing place. Its natural destitution of water power is extensively compensated at present by steam engines, and by the surplus water of the Miami canal, which affords 3000 cubic feet per minutes. But the Cincinnati and White Water canal, which extends 25 miles and connects with the White Water canal of Indiana, half a mile south of Harrison, on the state line, will furnish a great increase of water power, equal to 90 runs of millstones. The manufactures of the city, already large, may be expected to greatly increase. By a late enumeration, it appears that the manufactures of Cincinnati of all kinds, employs 10,647 persons, a capital of $14,541,842, and produces articles of over seventeen millions of dollars value.

The trade of Cincinnati embraces the country from the Ohio to the lakes, north and south; and from the Scioto to the Wabash, east and west. The Ohio river line, in Kentucky, for 50 miles down, and as far up as the Virginia line, make their purchases here. Its manufactures are sent into the upper and lower Mississippi country.

There are six incorporated banks, with aggregate capital of $5,800,000, beside two unincorporated banks. Cincinnati is the greatest pork market in the world. Not far from three millions of dollars worth of pork are annually exported.

Cincinnati enjoys great facilities for communication with the surrounding country. The total length of canals, railroads and turnpikes which center here, completed and constructing, is 1125 miles. Those who have made it a matter of investigation predict, that Cincinnati will eventually be a city of a very great population. A writer [J. W. Scott, editor of the *Toledo Blade*] in Cist's "Cincinnati in 1841," in a long article on this subject, commences with the startling announcement: "Not having before my eyes the fear of men, 'who—in the language of Governeur Morris—with too much pride to study and too much wit to think, undervalue what they do not understand, and condemn what they do not comprehend,' I venture the prediction, that within one hundred years from this time, Cincinnati will be the greatest city in America; and by the year of our Lord, 2000, the greatest city in the world." We have not space here to recapitulate the arguments on which this prediction is based. The prediction itself we place on record for future reference.

1. Henry Howe, *Historical Collections of Ohio* (Cincinnati, 1848), 123–25.
2. Ibid., 171–72.
3. Ibid., 216–21.

VII. **Religion, Education, and Social Reform**

WHEN HISTORIAN HENRY HOWE VISITED Cincinnati in 1847, he found seventy-six churches of wide denominational diversity serving a community of ninety thousand people in buildings that ranged from simple one-story frame structures to the impressive downtown Catholic Cathedral, which, in beauty and picturesqueness, more than matched the much heralded Metropolitan Cathedral in Baltimore. In Cleveland he found twenty-one flourishing religious congregations in a city of ten thousand people, while in Columbus, a city of similar population, he found seventeen. Clearly, organized religion was playing a major role in the lives of many Ohioans by the middle of the nineteenth century.

Yet it had not always been thus. During the frontier years at the beginning of the century, most Ohioans had been unchurched. Thinly settled over a vast area that not long before had been wilderness, Ohio's pioneer families had to rely on the services of missionaries, such as the Congregationalist Joseph Badger, and circuit-riding preachers, such as the Methodist James B. Finley, to meet their religious needs. Occasionally revivalist camp meetings would bring them together, hundreds and sometimes thousands strong, drawn from miles around, but it was not until settlements became more populous that church buildings of log or frame construction were built and resident ministers employed.

In the absence of well-established religious traditions along the Ohio frontier, there appeared a number of religious groups that took root and flourished in the welcoming atmosphere of the young state. Among them were the Campbellites, or Disciples of Christ; the Mormons, or members of the Church of Jesus Christ of Latter Day Saints; and the Amish, who would establish in Ohio their largest concentration of members in the world.

Ohio's open society and abundance of rich, fertile land also proved attractive to a number of utopian societies, of which the Shakers (The United Society of Believers in Christ's Second Appearance) and the Zoarites (The Society of Separatists of Zoar) were the most consequential and long lasting. Appearing as early as 1805 at Union Village, near Lebanon, and in 1821 at North Union (now Shaker Heights) near Cleveland, the

Shakers would maintain an active presence in Ohio until the early years of the twentieth century. Establishing a communal village near Dover in 1817, the Society of Separatists of Zoar did not finally succumb to the attractions of capitalistic enterprise and dissolve their community until 1898.

Except for a small number of private academies, Ohio's schools, like its churches, were noticeably absent in most sections of the state during the first decades of the nineteenth century. Though the Land Ordinance of 1785 had stipulated that Section 16 in each township should be used for the support of schools, the General Assembly unwisely permitted revenues from the sale of these school lands for a number of years to be diverted for construction of the state's canal system and for payment of state debts. Not until 1821 did the legislature authorize the division of each township into school districts and the raising of funds for the construction of schoolhouses, and not until 1853 was a recognizable statewide system of public education finally put into place by legislative action.

A central figure in the move toward a statewide system of tax-supported schools was Samuel Lewis, a native of Falmouth, Massachusetts, who was selected in 1837 as Ohio's first state superintendent of common schools after noteworthy success in establishing accessible public schools of quality in Cincinnati. Traveling more than fifteen hundred miles on horseback into every part of Ohio and visiting some three hundred schools in his first year in office, Lewis submitted a lengthy report in 1837 to the legislature that did much to arouse awareness of the importance of free public education (accompanied by exacting standards) for all children regardless of family income. Though ill health forced him to leave the superintendency in 1839 and reaction to his uncompromising zeal prompted the temporary abolition of the office he had held, the movement for educational reform that he had led could not be stopped. A plan first proposed in Akron in 1847, which established a graded system of elementary and high schools under the control of an elected board of education, was adopted statewide in 1849, while in 1853 another state law assured the distribution of revenues from a uniform tax of two mills to all Ohio counties in proportion to their numbers of schoolchildren.

Significant improvement in the education of schoolchildren also was effected through the publication of a number of nineteenth-century schoolbooks written by Ohio authors. No state in the Federal Union produced writers of school texts that made greater impact on the education of America's youth than Ohio. Generations of schoolchildren learned arithmetic from books written by Joseph Ray of Cincinnati, or learned their penmanship from copybooks prepared by Platt R. Spencer of Geneva, or their grammar from books authored by Thomas W. Harvey of Painesville. But it was a series of graded readers and spellers first prepared in 1836 by William Holmes McGuffey, then a professor at Miami University in Oxford, that achieved significance unequaled by any other texts in the history of publishing. Frequently updated and revised, *McGuffey's Eclectic Readers* helped educate five generations of schoolchildren from the 1830s to the 1920s, not only in America but also overseas. With nearly 130 million copies sold, the *Readers* are still in print. Only the Holy Bible has surpassed them in number of copies published. Understandably, McGuffey came to be called the "Schoolmaster to the Nation."

While Ohio schoolbooks were helping to educate the nation, Ohio colleges and universities were helping prepare the future leaders of the Buckeye State and beyond.

As noted earlier (see document V.3), the first institution of higher learning in Ohio and the Old Northwest was Ohio University at Athens, chartered in 1804, with classes under way in 1809 and the first degree conferred (on Thomas Ewing) in 1815. Also chartered by the General Assembly was Miami University, in 1809, with classes delayed until 1824 (largely the consequence of the War of 1812) and first degrees conferred in 1826. Though created by the state, neither of these two venerable institutions received state financial support until late in the nineteenth century.

At Cincinnati the Medical College of Ohio was established in 1819, followed by the Cincinnati Law School in 1833. Both became part of the University of Cincinnati when it was established in 1871 as the first municipal university in Ohio.

Among the independent colleges and universities that emerged in the pre–Civil War years were Kenyon, founded in 1824 by Philander Chase, the first Episcopal bishop of Ohio, at Gambier; Western Reserve, founded with Presbyterian assistance in 1826 at Hudson; Capital, a Lutheran college established at Columbus in 1830; Denison, established by a group of Baptists in 1831 at Granville; Xavier, founded in 1831 by the first Catholic bishop of Cincinnati, Edward Fenwick; Oberlin, founded in the town of the same name in 1833 by Congregationalists; Marietta, established in 1835, also by Congregationalists; Ohio Wesleyan, founded by Methodists in 1842 at Delaware; the school now known as Baldwin-Wallace, founded by Methodists, in 1845 at Berea; Mount Union, established in 1846 at Alliance, also with Methodist support; Wittenberg, established by Lutherans at Springfield in 1845; Otterbein, organized by United Brethren in 1847 at Westerville; Heidelberg, established in Tiffin by the Evangelical and Reformed Church in 1850, the same year Hiram College was founded by Disciples of Christ, and Urbana College by the Swedenborgians; Dayton, established in 1850 by Catholic Marianists; Antioch, founded in 1853 at Yellow Springs as a nonsectarian college by Horace Mann, one of America's foremost educators; Western and Lake Erie, colleges for women at Oxford and Painesville, which opened in 1853 and 1856, respectively; and Wilberforce, founded in 1856 by the Methodist Episcopal Church and later supported by the African Methodist Episcopal Church as the first American college primarily serving black students.

Of the church-related colleges, it was Oberlin that attracted particular attention when it opened its doors in the 1830s to both women and blacks, becoming the world's first coeducational and coracial college. By so doing it became prominently identified with two emerging social reform movements: the quest for women's rights and the crusade to abolish slavery. The women's rights movement will be treated in the final two documents of this chapter, while abolitionism and the coming of the Civil War will be the focus of chapter VIII.

VII.1. Missionaries, Camp Meetings, and Circuit Riders

Though the third article of the Northwest Ordinance had stressed the need to undergird "schools and the means of education" with "religion, morality, and knowledge" in order to achieve "good government and the happiness of mankind," and though Congress had purposely reserved "ministerial lands" for the support of organized religious groups in both the Symmes Purchase and the Ohio Company grant, neither churches nor schools were in abundant evidence during Ohio's formative years as a state. The diversity of backgrounds of the early settlers; their adverse reaction to compulsory taxation, which they had experienced in many of the older eastern states to support established churches; and their sparse diffusion over the large area that was Ohio combined to keep most of them unchurched. Challenged by this circumstance, church groups on the eastern seaboard sent missionaries and circuit-riding preachers into the Ohio country to reach those in isolation and rekindle their faith. On occasion, revivalistic camp meetings were held, drawing hundreds, sometimes thousands, to open-air services in wooded groves.

Among the more successful missionaries was Joseph Badger, a New England Congregationalist who was sent to the Western Reserve by the Missionary Society of Connecticut in 1800. Not only was he the first missionary to reach the Reserve, but he was also the founder of its first Congregational Church, at Austinburg, in 1801. A Yale graduate and Revolutionary War veteran, Badger served the Missionary Society of Connecticut until 1806, when he accepted appointment from the Western Missionary Society to work among the Wyandot Indians of the Sandusky Valley. In 1810 he took yet another position, this in behalf of the Massachusetts Missionary Society in its work in Ohio, a position he held until the outbreak of the War of 1812, when he accepted an army appointment from General William Henry Harrison as brigade chaplain. After the war he again served his church as minister and missionary in the Western Reserve, continuing in this work until his retirement in 1835. He passed away in Perrysburg, Ohio, in 1846, at the age of eighty-nine.

Because he was obligated to keep a detailed record of his missionary activities for the sponsoring societies in New England, much is known of the vicissitudes and challenges, successes and setbacks that Badger experienced in planting and nourishing the seeds of Congregationalism in early Ohio.[1]

Among the several denominations active in reaching out to and serving the needs of the unchurched in the Ohio Valley through the medium of camp meetings and circuit riders, the Methodists were particularly zealous. While for a time Presbyterian and Baptist clergymen also used camp meetings and circuit riders as effective means of gaining new converts, the leading exponent of their use was Bishop Francis Asbury, general superintendent of the Methodist Church in America. Beginning in the late 1790s in Kentucky, then in Ohio after 1804, the camp meeting became an integral part of Methodism's appeal to frontiersmen and their families. In Ohio one of its foremost advocates was the Reverend James B. Finley, whose father, the Reverend Robert W. Finley, a Princeton graduate, had earlier been a Presbyterian preacher in the Carolinas, Georgia, and Kentucky. In his autobiography, published in 1853, James Finley recalled the enthusiasm and excitement engendered by Methodist camp meetings in Ohio, particularly in 1818–19, when he was serving as presiding elder of the Ohio District of the Methodist Church. As he remarked on one occasion, "Much may be said about camp meetings, but, take them all in all, for practical exhibition of religion, for unbounded hospitality to strangers, for unfeigned and fervent spirituality, give me a country camp meeting against the world."[2]

While camp meetings were seasonally most effective in reaching the unchurched in late summer and early fall, a year-round contact with converts was often necessary to keep them *"saved," and the most effective means of reaching these on a regular basis were the circuit riders. Itinerant Methodist preachers were assigned to circuits defined by the river valleys, through which they rode on horseback, and by the weeks required to make their rounds (for example, six-week circuits, four-week circuits, three-week circuits, etc.). James Finley not only served his church as a preacher at camp meetings, but he also accepted assignment as a rider on the four-week Cross Creek circuit in eastern Ohio, which he described as follows: "Our circuit included the towns of Steubenville, Cadiz, Mount Pleasant, Smithfield, and several other villages, embracing all the country in Jefferson, part of Harrison, and Belmont Counties. It took four full weeks to travel round it, with an appointment for every day and two for the Sabbath. The membership was large, amounting to nearly one thousand. We had to preach thirty-two times every round, and meet fifty classes."³*

William W. Sweet has written, "By the year 1812 Methodism had achieved a firm and dominant grip upon all the settled territory west of the mountains. During the twelve years of the life of the old Western Conference the membership in the west had increased from less than 3,000 in 1800 to over 30,000 in 1811. The number of circuits had grown from nine to sixty-nine, while the circuit riders had likewise increased from fourteen to one hundred."⁴ With the surge of population across the mountains into the Ohio country after the War of 1812, and with the appearance of scores of settlements of sufficient size to warrant the establishment of permanent churches with their own buildings and full-time ministers, the day of the circuit rider, like that of the camp meeting, began to pass. Yet as late as the 1820s their presence was still felt in remote valleys and along isolated ridges where settlement was insufficient to sustain formal church organization. Typical of these remnant circuits was that of the Muskingum Valley, the schedule for which from 21 September through 19 October 1823 identified twenty-three preaching sites, all but two of them the cabins of settlers.⁵ Only two were identified as chapels, fittingly named Wesleyan and Asbury. For all their limitations the circuit riders, like the camp meeting revivalists and the missionaries, had played a major role in bringing religion to backwoods Ohio and ending the spiritual poverty of many of its people.

THE MEMOIR OF A MISSIONARY, JOSEPH BADGER.

....[January] 8ᵗʰ, [1804] —Rode to Harpersfield, and preached twice on the Sabbath, and again in the evening. Spent Monday, Tuesday, and Wednesday, visiting from house to house: preached Thursday afternoon and in the evening.

Saturday, rode to Painesville, sixteen miles, without a house; pretty cold.

15ᵗʰ, —Sabbath, preached twice to about seventy people, who gave decent attention, from Romans vii: 9; in the afternoon from Luke xi: 21, 22. The strong man armed is the devil; his palace, the carnal heart; his goods, the careless sinner; the one stronger then he, the Holy Spirit.

On Monday returned to Harpersfield, and preached in the evening.

Tuesday, returned to the north end of Austinburg, and attended conference.

Wednesday, made several family visits, and returned home on Thursday.

Saturday morning, heard that George Beckwith was lost: he was found some time after night, by his tracks in the snow; had perished by frost.

22d,—Sabbath morning, went with others to where the body lay. Returned to Judge Austin's, and preached in the afternoon.

Monday, preached at the funeral of Mr. Beckwith, and returned home.

Wednesday, rode to Conneaut, 24 miles.

Thursday, wrote journals and letters.

Friday, preached. Saturday, made family visits, and examined Thomas Montgomery and his wife for admission to the Church. Sabbath, preached twice, admitted the two persons into the Church, and baptized five of their children. The transaction was attended with a good degree of solemnity.

Monday, rode to Ashtabula settlement, and preached to about twenty people.

Tuesday, returned to Conneaut and preached again. . . .

March 13,—Tuesday, Rode to Vernon, thirty-two miles; the day tedious, with squalls of snow. Found two of Esquire Smith's daughters, one thirteen, and the other eight years old, exercising a hope. Saw another young woman who had exercised a hope several weeks past; appeared remarkably comfortable with views of the glory of God, in the plan of salvation by grace. She often fell when at her wheel. I asked her if she could give any reason why she fell. She said, when she reflected on the glory of God there appeared such soul delight in the discovery, that it overcame all her natural strength.

14th,—Wednesday, Rode to Warren, transacted some business, and on Friday made several family visits, attended a meeting of the Church. . . . Preached in the evening.

Saturday, rode to Mantua, crossing the Mahoning, the water up over my saddleskirts; got my boots full of water. At the other crossing swam my horse and crossed myself on a glade of ice. Led my horse on the ice across the Cuyahoga; agreed, as I came through Nelson, to return there on Monday.

Sabbath, preached twice to a stupid, unfeeling company; appointed to preach again on Wednesday, and at Aurora on Thursday. . . .

JAMES FINLEY RECALLS FRONTIER CAMP MEETINGS

. . . . The camp meetings during the latter part of the year [1819] were attended with success. In many places the novelty of such scenes as are presented by worshiping God in the grove attracted the attention of many, and produced a good impression. But few can look upon a camp meeting scene and not be moved. Such a scene as is presented by an encampment at night, to one who has never witnessed any thing like it before, must be impressive. To look upon the long ranges of tents surrounding a large area, in each corner of which bright fires are lighted up, and then from tent and tree to see innumerable lamps hung out, casting their lights among the branches and illuminating all the ground, would remind one of the descriptions given of an oriental wedding scene, when, at midnight, the cry is heard, "Behold, the bridegroom cometh! Go ye forth to meet him." Then the sound of the trumpet, and the gathering together of thousands, who pass to and fro with lights and torches, all has a tendency to awaken the most solemn reflections. And when the holy song rises from a thousand voices, and floats out upon the stillness of the night air, the listener must feel that surely such a place is holy ground. These camp meetings were seasons of special mercy to thousands, and many who came to curse remained to pray for salvation and seek an interest in the blessed Savior. . . .

We wound up our year's work with a round of [such] camp meetings. Some of these were attended with unusual manifestations of Divine power. Of such were Rattlesnake, Honey creek, and Union camp meetings. . . . The gathering of the people was immense. They came together in the spirit of prayer, and not for the purpose of making a display, such as might be called a religious picnic, where families vie with each other in showing off to the best advantage, but to worship God exclusively, without any regard to "visits, modes, and forms." And such realized the desire of their hearts. The work commenced at once, and continued day and night with increasing power, and over one hundred and fifty were soundly converted to God. Milford camp meeting was also a time of great power, there was a mighty shaking among the dry bones. A leader of infidelity, renowned for his advocacy of error, was awakened and converted, and sent out by the Spirit to bear testimony to the truth of that religion which he had reviled. White-oak camp meeting was held at Indian hill, and was the most powerful one I had attended on the district. How many were converted I am not able to say, but the number was large. On Sabbath I baptized one hundred persons before nine o'clock, by sprinkling and pouring. Brother G. W. Light wrote down the names as I announced them, and gave them to me. . . .

Strait creek camp meeting was held soon after, and was attended with mighty power. On Sabbath morning, while brother John Collins was praying, the Holy Spirit came down on us as a rushing, mighty wind, and more than one hundred fell under the power of God; and such a time of weeping and rejoicing I never saw before. . . .

RIDING THE MUSKINGUM CIRCUIT: A FOUR-WEEK SCHEDULE IN 1823

*W*hen the [circuit-riding] pastor went to the annual conference, he, by the law of the [Methodist] Church, was required to bring a plan of his circuit to be handed to his successor. The following schedule is the Plan of the Muskingum Circuit, [prepared] August 29, 1823:

Day of the week.	Day of the month.	Preaching place.	Preaching hour.	Distance in miles.	Official list.
Sunday	Sept. 21	Putnam	11	....	Alexander McCraken,) Elders
Monday	Sept. 22	Rest	....	....	John Wilson,)
Tuesday	Sept. 23	Headley's	12	5	Samuel Wilson,) Teachers.
Wednesday	Sept. 24	Simpson's	12	4	Samuel Aikins,)
Thursday	Sept. 25	Rest	....	....	John Goshen,)Deacons.
Friday	Sept. 26	Rest	....	....	Martin Tate,)
Saturday	Sept. 27	Rest	....	....	John Wilson,)
Sunday	Sept. 28	Dickerson's	11	10	Thomas Ijams,)
Monday	Sept. 29	Rest	....	....	Elijah Ball,)
Tuesday	Sept. 30	Gard's	12	4	Samuel Chapman,)
Wednesday	Oct. 1	Wigginbottom's	12	4	John Jordon,)

Day of the week.	Day of the month.	Preaching place.	Preaching hour.	Distance in miles.	Official list.
Thursday	Oct. 2	Sain's	12	6	Wm. Armstrong, Stewards.
Friday	Oct. 3	Springer's	12	6	Wm. Heath,)
Saturday	Oct. 4	Lenhart's	12	4	Elijah Collin,)
Sunday	Oct. 5	Asbury Chapel	11	6	David Fate,)
Monday	Oct. 6	Hitchock's	12	12	Jona Witham,)
Tuesday	Oct. 7	Teals	12	7	Robert Aikins,)
Wednesday	Oct. 8	Fate	12	5	David Edwards,)
Thursday	Oct. 9	Chaplin	12	12	David Butt,) Exhorters.
Friday	Oct. 10	Harris'	2	12	M. Putnam,)
Saturday	Oct. 11	Hopkin's	12	6	David Sherard,)
Sunday	Oct. 12	Aikin's	11	12	James Kelly,)
Monday	Oct. 13	Sailors	12	7	
Tuesday	Oct. 14	Edwards	12	5	
Wednesday	Oct. 15	Wesleyan Ch.	12	8	
Thursday	Oct. 16	Wilson's	10	6	Number of members, 760.
Thursday	Oct. 16	Beall's	3	3	
Friday	Oct. 17	Hametta	12	6	
Saturday	Oct. 18	Butt's	11	5	
Sunday	Oct. 19	Putnam	11	6	

163

1. Joseph Badger, *A Memoir of Rev. Joseph Badger, Containing an Autobiography and Selections from His Private Journal and Correspondence* (Hudson, Ohio, 1851); the selection reprinted here is from pages 69–81.

2. W. P. Strickland, ed., *Autobiography of Rev. James B. Finley, or, Pioneer Life in the West* (Cincinnati, 1853), 315; the selection reprinted here is from pages 345–50. See also Charles A. Johnson,"Early Ohio Camp Meetings," *Ohio State Archaeological and Historical Quarterly* 61, no. 1 (January 1952): 49.

3. William W. Sweet, *Circuit-Rider Days along the Ohio, Being the Journals of the Ohio Conference from Its Organization in 1812 to 1826* (New York: Methodist Book Concern, 1923), 37. See also Charles Townsend, "Peter Cartwright's Circuit Riding Days in Ohio," *Ohio History* 74, no. 2 (spring 1965): 90–98.

4. Sweet, *Circuit-Rider Days*, 27.

5. Ibid., 56; I. F. King, "Introduction of Methodism in Ohio," *Ohio Archaeological and Historical Publications* (Columbus, 1902), 10:189.

VII.2. Utopian Societies: The Shakers and the Zoarites

The vast expanse of inexpensive, fertile farmland and the social openness of the Ohio frontier proved inviting to a number of Utopian religious societies in the early nineteenth century. Principal among these were the groups known as the Shakers and the Zoarites.

Referring to themselves as the United Society of Believers in Christ's Second Appearance, the Shakers were founded by Ann Lee, a blacksmith's daughter in England, who claimed that it had been revealed to her that she was the second Christ, that God being both male and female had already appeared in masculine form as Jesus and was now appearing in feminine form as Ann Lee. Driven from England by persecution in 1774, "Mother" Ann Lee fled to the colonies and took residence in Watervliet, New York, where in 1776 she established the first Shaker colony with eight followers.

The nickname "Shakers" (they were also called "Shaking Quakers") stemmed from one of their ritualistic dances in which they shook all over in the manner of the heavenly hosts who an early leader, Joseph Meachem, claimed to have seen in a vision. Believing that pleasure was evil and that work and celibacy represented the highest good, the Shakers established communal villages in New England as well as in New York before coming west into Kentucky and Ohio. Living in the strictest celibacy in "family" units of thirty to ninety members, occupying large houses with upper floors divided between men and women, the Shakers depended on adult conversions and the adoption of orphans for new members. Operating their farms communally, the Shakers are remembered as the first to introduce the modern seed packaging industry, as the developers of the Poland China hog, the inventors of the clothespin and babbitt metal (an anti-friction alloy of copper, antimony, and tin), and as experimenters in crop rotation. They were also the first to introduce Merino sheep and Durham cattle in southwestern Ohio. This they did on the largest of their farms at Union Village, founded in 1805 some six miles west of Lebanon, and, of course, their name still remains at Shaker Heights, a Cleveland suburb, once the Shaker village of North Union founded in 1822. Other Ohio communities included Watervliet, near Dayton, and Whitewater, in northwestern Hamilton County, founded in 1813 and 1824, respectively.

Communalism and celibacy ultimately proved the undoing of the Shakers, particularly after the established religious denominations began to sponsor their own orphanages. As older members died off or were lured away by the temptations of enterprising individualism, one by one the Shaker villages were abandoned, North Union in 1889, Union Village in 1910 among them. But their legacy endures, not only in their unique style of furniture, seeds, and livestock, but also in the concept of the equality of the sexes that was fundamental to their faith.

Like the first Shakers, the Zoarites fled from the sting of persecution in Europe to come to the welcoming environment of the New World. Separatists whose ideas were at variance with the established Lutheran Church in the German kingdom of Wurttemberg, they came three-hundred strong to America in 1817, and with the help of Philadelphia Quakers purchased a tract of fifty-five hundred acres near Dover in the Tuscarawas Valley of eastern Ohio. There they established the village they called Zoar, named for the ancient Biblical town on the Dead Sea in which Lot took refuge to escape the wicked Sodom. Though they had had no original intention of forming a communal, celibate order, the heavy burden of indebtedness incurred with the purchase of their land, exacerbated by the Panic of 1819 and the economic depression that followed, convinced them that if they were to maintain themselves as a religious community, they could do so only through cooperative effort. Accordingly, under the leadership of a convert whom they had first met on shipboard on their way to America, Joseph Baumeler (or Bimeler), they organized themselves into the Society of Separatists of Zoar and agreed to pool all their property and wealth, at least until their debt had been paid off. Similarly, they also agreed to practice celibacy until the removal of their indebtedness, since there were many more women than men in the group, and their work in the fields and the village was essential if the society was to survive. Though celibacy ended with the last payment on the debt in 1834, their communal form of government and economy continued until the society was dissolved in 1898.[1]

More than a century later, Zoar is still an inhabited village, and, under the custody of the Ohio Historical Society, the beautiful Zoar Garden, based on the description of the New Jerusalem in the book of Revelation, and the Number One House, the former home of Joseph Baumeler, are preserved as properties of the State of Ohio in tribute to the founders.

UNION VILLAGE, THE SHAKER SETTLEMENT NEAR LEBANON

*I*n Cincinnati, Ohio, I met one day with a Shaking Quaker. He wore a broad-brimmed hat and shad-bellied coat of a bluish-gray homespun cloth, with his hair cropped short before and falling into the neck behind. He was mild in manner, simple in conversation, and his communications were "yea" and "nay." He conversed freely on the doctrines and polity of the society, and gave me a friendly invitation to visit the Shaker village of Lebanon, twenty miles distant.

The wisdom of the ruling elders could scarcely have selected a finer spot for the domain of a community. The land in the Miami valley is of a wonderful fertility, and the whole region is a rich and well-cultivated country; still the domain of the Shakers was marked by striking peculiarities. The fences were higher and stronger than those on the adjacent farms; the woods were cleared of underbrush; the tillage was of extraordinary neatness; the horses, cattle, and sheep were of the best breeds, and in the best condition.

In the Shaker village are no tavern or shops, but large, plainly-built dwelling houses, barns, workshops, and an edifice for meetings and religious exercises. Simple utility is the only rule of architecture. There is not, in the whole village, one line of ornament. The brown paint is used only to protect the woodwork of the buildings. I did not see so much as an ornamental shrub or flower in the whole domain.

One house is set apart for the entertainment of strangers, who receive attention, food, and lodging as long as they choose to remain. The brethren and sisters who are appointed to fulfill the duties of hospitality neither demand nor refuse payment.

The women, old and young, ugly and pretty, dress in the same neat but unfashionable attire. There are no bright colors, no ruffles or flounces or frills, no embroidery or laces, no ribbons or ornaments of any kind. The hair is combed smoothly back under a plain cap; a three-cornered kerchief of sober brown covers the bosom, and the narrow gored shirt has no room for crinoline.

The rooms and furniture are as plain and homely as the external architecture. There is not a molding nor any colored paper; not a picture nor print adorns the walls, nor is there a vase or statue. The only books are a few of their own religious treatises, collections of hymns, and works of education, science, and utility.

But there is everywhere the perfection of order and neatness. The floors shine like mirrors. Every visible thing is bright and clean. There is a place for everything, and everything is in its place. This order and neatness is carried out in the workshops, the farmyards, everywhere.

A community of two or three hundred industrious persons, all engaged in agriculture and useful manufactures, paying no rents, having no costly vices, producing for themselves all the necessaries of life, and selling their surplus produce, cannot fail to grow rich. I found this community living in comfort and abundance, surrounded with a great wealth of houses and lands, flocks and herds and, as I was told, with large sums invested in the best securities. Men, women, and children all work. There are no idlers, and no time is lost. As the honesty of the Shakers is proverbial, they have the command of the best markets for their wooden wares, agricultural implements, brooms, garden seeds, preserved fruits and vegetables, and the surplus of their cloth, leather, etc. There is nothing, therefore, to hinder them from accumulating property to an immense extent, as can easily be done by an honest community in any country.

As there are no marriages, all the men and women living together like brothers and sisters, their only increase is by the accession of new members from "the world," or by taking orphan and destitute children, sometimes children from the workhouse. People with whom the world has dealt hardly, widows, or wives deserted by drunken husbands, with families of children, go to the Shakers. They are never turned away. So long as they choose to remain and comply with the rules of the society, they have the full enjoyment of all its material and spiritual goods. So the Shakers slowly increase, and new domains are purchased and brought under cultivation.

ARTICLES OF ASSOCIATION OF THE SOCIETY OF SEPARATISTS OF ZOAR

[Dated 19 April 1819, the articles of association were signed by 53 males and 104 females and were prefaced by the following preamble:][2]

The undersigned, members of the Society of Separatists of Zoar, have, from a true Christian love towards God and their fellow men, found themselves convinced and induced to unite themselves according to the Christian Apostolic sense, under the following rules through a communion of property; and they do hereby determine and declare that from the day of this date, the following rules shall be valid and in effect:

1. Each and every member does hereby renounce all and every right of ownership, of their present and future movable and immovable property; and leave the same to the disposition of the directors of the society elected [annually] by themselves.

2. The society elects out of its own members their directors and managers, who shall conduct the general business transactions, and exercise the general duties of the society. They therefore take possession of all the active and passive property of all the members, whose duty it shall be at the same time to provide for them; and said directors are further bound to give an account to the society of all their business transactions. . . .

1. The description of Union Village is from Thomas Low Nichols, *Forty Years of American Life, 1821–1861* (London, 1874; reprinted, New York, 1937), and excerpted in Henry Steele Commager and Allan Nevins, eds., *The Heritage of America* (Boston: Little, Brown, 1945), 438–40. See also, Harvey L. Eads, *Condition of Society; and Its Only Hope, in Obeying the Everlasting Gospel, as Now Developing among Believers in Christ's Second Appearing* (Union Village, Ohio, 1847), 2–5.

2. See E. O. Randall, "The Separatist Society of Zoar," *Ohio Archaeological and Historical Publications* (Columbus, 1900), 8:7–8.

VII.3. In Search of a Statewide System of Public Education

It can be argued that no issue consumed more legislative time in Ohio in the course of the nineteenth century than public education. It can also be argued that not until the appointment of Samuel Lewis as the state's first superintendent of common schools in 1837 was there finally an experienced educator of proven ability in a position to conduct a statewide study and make necessary recommendations for action to the General Assembly. Key problems included widespread apathy, a three-month school "year" in some districts, inadequate or nonexistent school buildings, lack of attention to the educational needs of poor children, salaries too low to attract and keep good teachers, the diversion of revenues from the sale of federally granted school lands to nonschool uses, and the division of opinion over who should bear the burden of school finance, the taxpayers of the local school district or the state from its general revenues.

Lewis, a protege of Horace Mann in Massachusetts and a man of almost fanatical zeal, spent an exhausting year in 1837 traveling the length and breadth of Ohio and visiting more than three hundred of its existing schools before making his landmark report to the legislature.[1] Though a fair and adequate system of public education did not immediately result from it, a long step toward such a system was taken with its publication. More than any other it was Lewis who popularized the idea of free public education in Ohio and demanded that its standards be high.

THE REPORT OF SAMUEL LEWIS

To the Honorable, the Legislature of Ohio.

. . . . The legal foundation of common schools in this State, may be laid in the ordinance of Congress passed in 1787, providing for the government of the Territory, of which Ohio formed a part. In that document certain great principles are laid down, which must, of necessity, be incorporated into the constitutions of the States; and the third article has these words: "Religion, morality, and knowledge, being necessary to good government, and the happiness of mankind, schools and the means of education shall forever be encouraged." . . . .

The bill of rights in our constitution [of 1802] (after providing that certain rights shall be enjoyed,) declares: "But religion, morality, and knowledge, being essentially necessary to good government and the happiness of mankind, schools and the means of instruction shall forever *be encouraged by legislative provision.*" These provisions cannot be taken to mean any thing less, than that the Legislature should encourage education by *such legislative enactments* as might be required to effect the object thus recognized as of primary importance.

If no obligation rested on the Legislature in reference to education, other than toleration, there must have been a strange effort to select such language to convey the sentiment. The constitution seems to have imposed upon the State the duty of *effectually* promoting education by legislative *provision.*

The great question then is to determine what means are best adapted to the end. Nor are we now, (if we ever were) trammeled with fears that public opinion will not sustain an enlightened legislation on this subject.

The thousands with whom I have conversed, of all classes, and in all departments of life, are unanimous; and they represent their neighbors as unanimous in favor of efficient and active measures, on the part of the legislature, for the promotion of common schools. I have heard of persons and of neighborhoods, that were said to be opposed to such a course, but on visiting such persons and places, the objections were found to be not against proper legal provision for these schools, but against particular details in the law. Complaints against defects are often erroneously put down by lookers on, as opposition to the law, when, in fact, the complainers are frequently the most ardent friends, and in favor of the most active measures. It is one way of making a friend of reform odious, by representing his complaints as opposition. I have not found an individual that, for himself, objected to the expense, provided the schools are made good.

Of the particular enactments required, but few express decided opinions, except the want of funds, in which all agree. The general language is, "We are impatient to see and feel the benefits of the school law, so long promised, and so much praised; we must have common schools made better, and more abundant. The present law, for some reason, does not bring with it the means of education to supply our wants. Let a law be passed that will be felt in its benefits, as well as in its burdens, and we will not complain. We object now to the defects, to the complicated machinery, the inadequacy of the means, the crowded schools, the short time a school is taught. Either leave us to depend wholly on our own efforts, or give us something worth our attention; at present, the law hinders private schools, without supplying public schools." Some say, "If you cannot make the system better, abandon the whole." This is the language of men in every county in our State, all agreeing in the one general and enlightened sentiment; so that we can approach the subject with cheerful confidence, and backed by such a public opinion, profiting by past experience, erect a national institution, that shall be at once our strength, our pride, and our happiness.

The first law assessing a school tax, in 1825, is generally considered the commencement of the system. This was frequently altered, until, in 1836, the present law was passed. The tax, which commenced at half a mill on the dollar, has gradually risen to a mill and a half, and power is given to increase it by townships; some have done so. The history of the different enactments would be tedious, and perhaps of little use. All the legislation on the subject has aimed at the same end, viz: to secure certainly the proper education of all the children in the State, on terms of the greatest possible equality.

It may take some years to secure a perfect uniformity in the system of teaching and conducting school business, with a people so varied in their origin, habits, and prejudices. It is not supposed that any direct legislative enactment can be made, to prescribe rules for the internal regulations of the schools. This would produce great discontent, if at all practicable. These must be left to officers and teachers, in a great degree, after the schools are established. The internal improvement must be effected by those who exercise an influence in the different departments of the work, and it must take time. But as to what shall be taught, there is less difference of opinion. The future fathers and mothers of Ohio, it is agreed, must be so instructed as to enable them to discharge the high and important responsibility of hereditary rulers of a mighty nation. This requires, to be sure—that they learn to *read, and write, and cypher,* according to the old standard. But this, added to the other branches usually required in common schools, is not all; and, while its importance is admitted, it is not the most important:—there are high and noble departments of education, besides merely learning how to make money.

The sound principles of our government are to be taught—that lesson that Washington gave, viz: that "next to our God, we owe our highest duty to our country;" and that this duty does not in chief, consist in splendid efforts in battles or Senates; but that real patriotism consists in a proper cultivation of those arts and principles that adorn society, and make in practice, what we claim in theory; viz: the cottage equal to the palace. The natural impetuosity of unrestricted liberty, is to be tempered by a well grounded conviction that obedience to the law is real liberty. The great point, that majorities must govern by a peaceable expression of opinion, (here for the first time admitted,) must be engraven upon the memory and judgment of all our sons. Patience, until legal and constitutional redress can be had, for all wrongs, public and private, must be inculcated; habits of self-government, economy, and industry, must be enforced. These must all be taught by men who know how to exhibit the proper facts and principles, in all their bearings, and with all their advantages.

It cannot be too deeply impressed on all minds, that we are a christian, as well as republican people; and the utmost care should be taken to inculcate sound principles of christian morality. No creed or catechism of any sect should be introduced into our schools; there is a broad, common ground, where all christians and lovers of virtue meet. On this should every teacher take his stand, and make it a paramount work, to train up the rising generation in those elevated moral principles of the Bible; and here should be taught all the social and relative duties, with proper inducement to correct action. . . .

The branches of learning and science to be taught in these schools, will readily occur to every man. They must be such as will qualify our children to perform the different duties of life, that, by the laws of our country, they may be called to discharge, whether public or private; keeping in view, that an early introduction to nature is important in popular education, and that the whole system should be directed to a proper development of the powers of the mind. Nor should we any longer delay the time. Every year's delay is adding mountains of obstacles to be overcome. We need no longer direct public attention to the future—to our children's children—to the third and fourth generation, before the promised blessings are realized. Nothing will be more hurtful than procrastination, in a work like this. If we would render succeeding generations virtuous and happy, we must begin with the present. At the same time, care must be taken to prevent any relaxation of effort on the part of parents, and others interested in the care of the young; and whatever the State does, should, if possible, be so arranged as to increase, rather than diminish, other efforts to effect the same object.

This, then, is the standard of education fixed by ordinance—by constitution—by sundry legal enactments, and is now demanded by the almost unanimous voice of the people in our State; this must be so provided as to secure the participation of all the children in the State; and if we have peculiar difficulties to surmount, we must adapt our means to the ends. Neither the expense nor the labor is to be an objection, when the object to be accomplished is paramount. This supposes that a suitable number of convenient school houses shall be furnished, and supplied with a sufficient number of competent male and female teachers, with all other conveniences required, to make the school an agreeable, as well as useful place for children. And by a suitable number is meant, such a proportion of children to a teacher, as will allow time for proper instruction, according to the outlines laid down, certainly not more than forty to a teacher; for it is mockery to crowd from fifty to eighty children into a room, under one teacher, who has little of learning or experience, and call that a school. . . .

Our State has more children under sixteen years of age than any other equal amount of population; our people must soon number 3,000,000. On roads, where a very few years since, I traveled whole days in unbroken forests, I could, last fall, scarcely find shade trees to rest under. Houses are in almost, speaking distance, and villages are springing up and flourishing until they almost join, while the noise and cheerful halloo of numerous children scarcely dies upon the ear of the traveler from morning until night; and with all this we have hardly begun to appreciate our wants or our resources. We must be a great manufacturing people, and it is highly important to have this principle of good moral education well grounded in the affections and habits of the people, before a counter influence is among us. Massachusetts could not have retained her elevated character amid her thousand factories, if her free schools had not been before them.

By adopting this plan, we shall bring into the field in a few years, an amount of industry, talent and enterprise, that will return to our coffers an hundred fold on the amount expended. It will furnish so much light to every one, that the true policy will be seen and adopted, and on the foundation of good common schools will be erected, in seven years, hundreds of county and township high schools and academies. Farmers will prove the full benefit of education; they will repudiate that vulgar opinion, that learning begets idleness; and it will no longer be said, "this school is good enough for my son, he is only to be a farmer," or "for my daughter, she will always live in the country." But learning, as in other days, will make her peculiar home, and diffuse her choicest blessings in the farmer's circle.

The importance of sustaining and elevating colleges, and all the higher institutions of learning, is admitted by all enlightened men. But to support our numerous colleges, is now known to be up hill work, and so it always will be, until we lay the foundation in general education; but this done, and it will furnish for them an easy and natural support. High schools and colleges will, as a natural consequence, grow out of good common schools. At present, (I speak advisedly when I say that) our graduates have, in many cases, been deprived of proper early education; and it is found that of those who go to college, not one-half have been properly educated in the branches of common school learning, before going to college. . . .

SCHOOL HOUSES.

*C*losely connected with the foregoing subject, is another only second in importance, viz: that of securing the erection of good school houses. The difficulty on this subject is now immense. There are now 3,370 districts without school houses, and in many places the houses now provided are wholly unfit.

No tax is so heavy as school house tax. In the country, the difficulty is so great, that in many places temporary buildings are resorted to, which are really unfit, and in the end are the most expensive.

In towns and villages the want of good school houses is felt the most. Some places containing from 500 to 6,000 inhabitants, have no common school houses. To build at once what ought to have been in progress for many years, would be difficult. Power could be given to corporate towns to borrow money for this purpose; but that relief would be partial, and in such small loans would be more troublesome and expensive than if the whole were consolidated. If the separate action of each district, is relied on wholly for the erection of these buildings, the present generation will have passed away before the work is done. . . .

The money for tuition must be raised by annual supply; but that for building, as it is required usually but once in an age, may, with propriety, be raised by loan; and in twenty years, the districts will be better able to pay the principal, than they are now to pay the interest.

I therefore respectfully suggest the propriety of raising by loan, such sum as may be required to aid the towns and districts in securing lots and building school houses. This does not involve any further appropriation; let the towns and districts signify in such manner as may be directed, their desire to borrow from $200 to $10,000, as the case may be; and if enough should be wanted to make the sum $100,000 or more, let the State borrow the amount required. . . .

The plan I have proposed is general, and includes every class — the poorest equal to the richest child of Ohio. Poverty and pride, it is well said, go together, and so far from condemning the sentiment, we should cherish the laudable aspirations of the young. First furnish proper objects of emulation, and then give a nation's energy, if required, to stimulate them onward to the goal. And if parents should ever in Ohio forget their high responsibilities to their offspring, we should take them in, give them proper instruction, and by the influence of the child, open a door for the (perhaps) repenting parent to return to the confidence of the world and the affections of his family. These, however, are incidental advantages; the institution to be thus established would include all, benefit all, and, with very few exceptions, save all the rising generation.

SAMUEL LEWIS,
Superintendent of Common Schools.

COLUMBUS, January 9, 1838.

1. Samuel Lewis, "First Annual Report of the Superintendent of Common Schools, Made to the Thirty-Sixth General Assembly of Ohio, January, 1838" [for the year 1837], *Ohio Executive Document No. 17* (1838), 3–34.

VII.4. William Holmes McGuffey: "Schoolmaster to the Nation"

Born in Washington County, Pennsylvania, in 1800, William Holmes McGuffey was brought to Ohio's Trumbull County in 1802 by his parents, Alexander and Anna Holmes McGuffey. Imbued with the Scotch-Irish zest for learning, he early mastered Latin and mathematics and began teaching school at the age of fourteen. After graduation from Washington College near his birthplace in Pennsylvania, he opened a private school in a converted smokehouse in Paris, Kentucky, where his success as a teacher prompted Robert Hamilton Bishop, president of Miami University at Oxford, Ohio, to tender him appointment in 1826 as professor of ancient languages and literature and librarian. While at Miami he was ordained a Presbyterian minister, but it was his work in compiling a set of graded readers with lessons determined for suitability by testing them on his front porch with neighborhood schoolchildren (some would call it the first laboratory school) that destined him for immortality as an educator. First published in 1836 in Cincinnati, the McGuffey Readers *would run through innumerable editions and printings and would become the most popular schoolbooks in America's history, helping to educate five generations of Americans from the 1830s to the 1920s, and they are still in print. What set them apart from other books was McGuffey's insistence that values were as meaningful as elocution and ciphering, that it was as important to learn how to behave as it was to learn how to read and write. Because McGuffey's lessons "were alive with children at work, at play, at school; boys with hoops, kites, skates; girls with dolls, sleds and jumping ropes," he made reading fun.*[1]

In 1836 McGuffey left Miami to accept the presidency at Cincinnati College, a position he held but three years before leaving to become president of Ohio University. In Athens until 1843, he resigned to return to Cincinnati to become a professor at Woodward College, in reality a "good, classical high school." In 1845 he accepted a position at the University of Virginia as professor of moral philosophy and political economy, a position he held until his death in 1873.

For countless millions of Americans, McGuffey was not remembered for his lectures or his sermons but rather for his readers and their lessons and sayings: "The Boy Who Cried Wolf," "Mary Had a Little Lamb," "Twinkle, Twinkle, Little Star," "Lazy Ned," "Mr. Toil," "Where There's a Will There's a Way," "If at First You Don't Succeed"—the list goes on and on. The two lessons that follow, drawn from the original 1836 Eclectic Second Reader for the Younger Classes in Schools,[2] *are illustrative of the work of the man who came to be called the "Schoolmaster to the Nation."*

LESSON XIX.

The Boys Who Did Mischief for Fun.

1. I will tell you another story. William and Edward were two clever little boys, and not at all ill-natured. They were very fond of sport, and they did not care whether people were hurt or not, provided they could have a laugh.

2. One fine summer's day, when they had said their lessons, they took a walk through the long grass in the meadows. William began to blow the dandelions, and the feathered seeds flew in the wind like arrows.

3. But Edward said, "Let us tie the grass. It will be very good sport to tie the long grass over the path, and to see people tumble upon their noses as they run along, and do not suspect any thing of the matter."

4. So they tied it in several places, and then hid themselves to see who would pass. Presently a farmer's boy came running along, and down he tumbled, and lay sprawling on the ground. He had nothing to do but to get up again, so there was not much harm done this time.

5. Then there came Susan the milkmaid, tripping along with her milk upon her head, and singing like a lark. When her foot struck against the place where the grass was tied, down she came with her pail rattling about her shoulders, and her milk was all spilled upon the ground.

6. Then Edward said, "Poor Susan! I think I should not like to be treated like that, let us untie the grass." — "No, no," said William, "If the milk is spilled, there are some pigs that will lick it up, let us have more fun. I see a man running along as if he were running for a bet. I am sure he will fall upon his nose."

7. And so the man did. William and Edward both laughed, but when the man did not get up again, they began to be frightened, and went to him, and asked him if he were hurt.

8. "Oh, masters," said the man, "some thoughtless boys I do not know who they are, have tied the grass together over the path, and as I was running with all my might, it threw me down, and I have sprained my ankle so that I shall not be able to walk for a month."

9. "I am very sorry," said Edward; "Do you feel much pain?" — "Oh, yes," said the man, "that I do not mind, but I was going in a great hurry to bring a surgeon to save a man's life."

10. Then Edward and William both turned pale, and said, "Where does the surgeon live? We will go for him, we will run all the way." — "He lives at the next town," said the man, "but it is a mile off, and you cannot run so fast as I should have done, you are only boys."

11. "Where must we tell the surgeon to come to?" said William. "He must come to the white house, at the end of the long chestnut avenue," said the man. "He is a very good gentleman that lives there."

12. "Oh, it is our dear father! It is our dear father!" said the two boys, "Oh, father will die, what must we do?"

13. I do not know whether their papa died or not. I believe he got well again, but I am sure of one thing, that Edward and William never tied the grass to throw people down again as long as they lived.

LESSON LXI.

The Little Boy and the Hatchet.

1. Never, perhaps, did a parent take more pains than did the father of George Washington to inspire his son George with an early love of Truth. "Truth, George," said he, "is the most lovely quality of youth. I would ride fifty miles, my son, to see the boy whose heart is so honest, and whose lips so pure, that we may depend on every word he says.

2. "How lovely does such a child appear in the eyes of everybody! His parents dote on him. His relations glory in him. They praise him before their children, and wish them to follow his example. They often invite him to visit them, and when he comes, they receive him with joy, and treat him as one whose visits they enjoy most.

3. "But oh, George, how far from this is the case with the boy who is given to lying! Good people avoid him wherever he goes, and parents dread to see him in company with their children.

4. "Oh, George, my son, rather than see you come to this pass, dear as you are to me, gladly would I assist to nail you up in your little coffin, and follow you to your grave.

5. "Hard, indeed, it would be to me to give up my son, whose feet are always so ready to run about with me, and whose smiling face and sweet prattle make so large a part of my happiness. But still I would give him up, rather than see him a common liar."

6. "Father," said George, with tears in his eyes, "do I ever tell lies?"

7. "No, George: I thank God you do not, my son; and I rejoice in the hope you never will. Whenever by accident you do anything wrong, which must often be the case, as you are but a little boy yet, you must never say what is not true to conceal it, but come bravely up, my son, like a little man, and tell me of it."

8. When George was about six years old, he was made the owner of a little hatchet, with which he was much pleased, and went about chopping everything that came in his way. One day, when in his garden, he unluckily tried the edge of his hatchet on the body of a fine young English cherry tree, which he barked so badly that he destroyed it.

9. The next morning, the old gentleman, finding out what had befallen his favorite tree, came into the house, and angrily asked who had destroyed the tree. Nobody could tell him anything about it. At this moment in came George, with his hatchet.

10. "George," said his father, "do you know who killed that fine cherry tree in the garden?" This was a hard question. George was silent for a moment, and then, looking at his father, his young face bright with conscious love of truth, he bravely cried out, "I can't tell a lie, father. You know, I can't tell a lie. I did cut it with my hatchet."

11. "Come to my arms, my dearest boy!" cried his father, happily; "come to my arms! You killed my cherry tree, George, but you have now paid me for it a thousand fold. Such proof of heroic truth in my son is of more value than a thousand trees, though they were all of the purest gold."

1. Walter Havighurst, *The Miami Years* (New York: Putnam, 1984), 69.

2. William H. McGuffey, *The Eclectic Second Reader; Consisting of Progressive Lessons in Reading and Spelling, for the Younger Classes in Schools.* (Cincinnati, 1836; reprinted, Milford, Mich.: Mott Media, 1982), 41–44; 158–61.

VII.5. College Days at Old Miami

What was college life like in the years before the Civil War? At the beginning of the nineteenth century there were only colleges for men, none for women until well into the century. Most were residential, expecting their students to attend full time, except for the months of summer, when farm families especially needed the help of their sons. The classical curriculum still prevailed, with emphasis on the ancient languages, moral and natural philosophy, rhetoric, mathematics, and science. Residence halls were small, with wood-burning fireplaces in individual rooms providing heat, stoves the means of cooking, and oil-burning lamps the means for study in the hours of darkness. Water was drawn from wells and outdoor privies were commonplace. Students and faculty were few in number but close in friendship. By 1838, when Miami University in Oxford reached an enrollment of 250 students and a faculty (including the president) of seven, it was the fourth largest university in the nation, exceeded only by Harvard, Yale, and Dartmouth. Not unlike most of America's other colleges of that time, Miami expected its faculty and students to attend chapel services daily. (Indeed, Miami's first seven presidents were all clergymen.) Miami's students were also encouraged to participate actively in campus organizations, especially the literary and debating societies (the Erodelphian, Eccritean, and the Union), while those that wished might also join Greek letter fraternities already making their presence felt on campus.

Though most Miami students came from Ohio, many were drawn from other states. One with the unlikely name of Theophilus Cannon Hibbett arrived in Oxford as a seventeen-year-old freshman in the late summer of 1851, following a five-day trip by railroad, stagecoach, steamboat, and horse-drawn omnibus from his family's farm near Lavergne, Tennessee. Because of the distance that separated them, his father asked "T.C." (understandably the young man preferred to be called by his initials) to keep a diary of his experiences at Miami, to be shared with his family after his return home. With fellow students including such future national leaders as Benjamin Harrison, David Swing, Whitelaw Reid, and John Shaw Billings, it was a heady time for T.C. to be at Old Miami.

Naturally gregarious, Hibbett joined the Union Literary Society in his first year and the Phi Delta Theta fraternity his second, and would ultimately serve the society as secretary and the fraternity as president in his third year. Both groups offered him opportunity to grow and mature in sociability and intellect, particularly important dimensions when considering that he would graduate from Miami in three years among the top students in his class. Through the pages of his diary, the first semester of the third year of which is printed below,[1] the reader is struck by the many changes that have taken place in higher education (and, yes, in the state and nation) since Hibbett was a student a century and a half ago.

THE DIARY OF T. C. HIBBETT

Aug. 23rd [1853].
After saying "farewell" at home, I took a seat in a buggy with Mr. J. B. Buchanan, and once more set out for College. Spend the day in surveying the City of Nashville.
Aug. 24th & 25th.
Took the stage for Louisville, at 2 o'clock a.m., and although it was raining exceedingly hard, we had quite a pleasant berth inside. We went the Bardstown route, and had very pleasant weather, so that we enjoyed ourselves very well, considering that so many were both inside and on top of the stage. Arrived at Louisville about sundown, and put up at the Exchange House. 26th. Was up very early and found my friend and classmate Ed. T. Shields, in company with whom I engaged passage on the steamer *Telegraph No. 3* to Cin-

cinnati, where we arrived at 4 o'clock the next morning. 27th. Found no difficulty nor met with any accident on our way hence to Oxford, where I found but few of our old students but almost all new ones. My roommate has concluded not to return, and left orders for me to dispose of his property to his and my own advantage. Spent the afternoon in arranging my room, as I found it in a terribly dilapidated condition. As there will of necessity be much monotony in college life, I shall hereafter only attend to my manual once or twice per week.
Sept. 3rd.

As there have been about 100 new students to be examined, but little has been done in the way of either study or recitation. Wrote a letter home, informing them of my safe arrival. Gave $150 of my money over to Prof. Bishop for safekeeping, reserving $50 to bear my expenses this session. Wrote to A. W. Cannon in West Tennessee, and also to R. P. Adams of Georgia, to inform me as to the chances in each place for obtaining a profitable school. As my former roommate, E. M. McCartey of Brookville, Indiana, is not coming back this year, I am rooming alone. On account of the cold which I took coming up the river, I have not been very well.
Sept. 10th.

My attention has been entirely occupied this week, as my studies have been somewhat onerous, and besides, the Miami Union Hall is at present at a rather low ebb, and consequently electioneering spirits are running high. Our Society has held no meeting as yet, as we are having a new Hall fitted up which will cost us at least $600. The Eccriteans and Erodelphians have joined hands against us, but our prospects among the new students are cheering. Our chapel performance this morning was exceedingly good; all the participants were members of the senior class. My name was read out as one of the performers for two weeks hence. I pled to get off, but did not succeed.
Sept. 17th.

Although I have been confined very close to my room this week, yet I feel none the worse for it. Our new Hall is finished and splendidly furnished. We took in 12 new members, at this our first meeting. My speech, to be delivered in chapel next Saturday, is written and has been submitted. My subject is "True Greatness in Poverty."
Sept. 24th.

This week has been one of great anxiety to me, especially when I would look forward to my speech; however, this passed off very well indeed, and the most sanguine hopes of my friends were fully realized. I have also been troubled for fear that something unfortunate has happened at home, as I have rarely fallen to sleep but that I've had some unpleasant dream connected with the family.
Oct. 1st.

No letter has been received from home as yet. Our election of officers came off in Hall this week. My duty in said ranks in Corresponding Secretary. Our exhibition came off yesterday evening, and the Hall was crowded with visitors, who seemed quite disappointed, as the speeches were very common. E. E. Hutcheson (Phi) and E. T. Shields (Phi) were both good, but the latter was badly delivered and the former was an old one which some of us had heard before. Charles E. Brown and Mr. Bruce were the other two performers, and neither of them were very good. We took in only one new member this meeting, Mr. Crane of the senior class, nicknamed Judge.

Oct. 8th.

No letter from home yet. I have gotten along as well as usual with my lessons. Weather cool, but clear and healthy. Society met and elected Thomas Williams, Jr., of Pittsburgh, Pa., as our speaker at Commencement, also William Dennison, diploma speaker. I have informed the gentlemen of their election.

Oct. 18th.

The long looked for letter came this week, but contained nothing peculiarly distressing or interesting. Hall met and the following gentlemen were elected speakers for our exhibition in December, viz., E. E. Hutcheson (Phi), Thomas Williams (Phi), Theo. C. Hibbett (Phi), Crane, William Owens, and Henry Woodruff. Weather still cool. Answered Ira's letter. Also, in conjunction with Mr. Hutcheson, wrote to New York for *Le Courier des Etas Unis.*

Oct. 22nd.

Much excitement has been gotten up by the outsiders in our hall about the Phis "ruling." So Charles Brown has been nominated as their candidate for the next presidency, and as no opposing candidate came out, they of course thought that victory was perched on their banner. But when we met for the election, "Billy" Owens ran and was elected by one vote. How they tore! Today was given as a rest day, i.e., we had no chapel this morning. Winter has set in.

Oct. 29th.

The weather has been quite cool. Besides my regular recitations, and French, I have read *David Copperfield* by Charles Dickens. By a vote passed in Hall, we who are on the coming exhibition will be excused from attendance in Hall until next session. I have begun to saw and pack away my wood for this winter, but I find it very tiresome work, and am almost resolved to hire the sawing of it.

Nov. 5th.

Read the first volume of the *Life of Columbus* by Washington Irving, and study but little, as my duties were not very onerous. There was a show in town, but I did not attend it. There was also a woman's rights lecture by Mrs. Jenkins in the Masonic Hall, but instead of going there, I commenced writing my speech for exhibition. Thomas Williams, Jr., made a "nailing" speech in chapel this morning on "Chivalry."

Nov. 12th.

In addition to my regular duties for this week, I have written my speech to be delivered at our exhibition next month. Subject, "Means and Extremes." Wrote some letters, also. Minor Milliken of the senior class dismissed from College for impudence to the President, but was taken back after having made the necessary acknowledgments and confessions. Jonathan (Muddy) Stewart of the same class was also dismissed by Prof. Bishop for the same offense, but taken back in the same manner. Weather cold, health but moderate.

Nov. 19th.

Weather quite warm for the season. Read the second volume of *Columbus*. Gave my speech to Prof. Elliott to be criticized, with which he found but a few mistakes, and was much pleased with the sentiment. As I have not felt very well this week, I have turned my attention to taking exercise in the way of sawing wood.

Nov. 26th.

Weather cooler. Read the third and last volume of *Columbus*. Have not studied very diligently, but have managed to get along tolerably well with the professors. Thanksgiving Day was observed on the 24th, and we had such a good dinner that I have made myself almost sick with eating entirely too much.

Dec. 3rd.

Weather damp and cool, so that I have taken a desperately bad cold; put on my flannel shirt. Read the life of James the First of England by Lingard. Elected and inaugurated President of the Phi Delta Theta Society. Made a terrible effort in the way of a speech in Hall on the non-extension of the bounds of our territory and lost the question.

Dec. 10th.

My cold has become much worse, so much so that I'm kept awake almost the whole night by excessive and almost unremitting spells of coughing, so that by this time my lungs are very sore indeed. Have not been able to study much in consequence. Received a letter from my old friend James H. Brookes, who is studying Divinity at Princeton. He fears that consumption will soon decide his case. Read the biography of Charles the First of England.

Dec. 17th.

As I have not felt well this week, my studies have not been overly well attended to. Examinations commenced the 12th, and the senior class have sent in a petition to be examined first, which has been granted on the grounds that the speakers are from said class and ought to have some time to prepare. Read biography of James the First of England by Hume. Examinations of our class all went off better than usual.

Dec. 20th.

As I have been in a great bustle about the exhibition, little else has occupied my attention.

[Announcement pasted in diary:]

ANNUAL EXHIBITION
OF THE MIAMI UNION LITERARY SOCIETY
Miami University
Tuesday Evening, Dec. 20th, 1853

Order of Exercises

Music

PRAYER

Music

Oration.. H. M. Woodruff
"What is Life?... Chas. E. Brown
"Render the Fallen Genius His Deserts .... S. Crane
"Means and Extremes... T. C. Hibbett
"The Anglo Saxons... Thos. Williams, Jr.
"The Titans, with an Address to the Society .... E. E. Hutcheson

Music

BENEDICTION

The evening came at last; and decking myself in the best finery I had (which, after all, was my everyday suit, with a little of the lint, feathers, etc., abolished), and having received the best wishes of Mrs. Hughes and Ann Reagan, my boarding ladies, and the rest of my friends, we marched on the platform erected in one end of the Old School Presbyterian Church, accompanied by the best music the Acton Brass Band could give us: whilst thus mounting the stand at the sound of such delightful music, my feelings were so patriotic that I was almost beside myself, but when I came to take my seat and gaze over such a large audience (about 1,000), and especially when I came to think of what my friends had expressed a desire that I should do, my patriotic feelings were soon transformed into dismal forebodings that I was going to make a failure. Woodruff (Delta) came first, and made a complete failure: for he did not quite get through with his speech (which, by the way, was very soft), and, besides, he spoke so low that only a few near the stand could hear him. Brown came next, and had a very well-written speech but had spoken it over so often to himself that he lost all interest in the delivery of it. Crane came next, and got up and made a first-rate beginning, but became frightened after speaking about three minutes, and had to refer to his manuscript, but as he was very much excited, and so near-sighted that he can scarcely read coarse print in daylight, he could not find the place on the manuscript and consequently had to sit down. In the meantime, I stopped thinking of my own speech to sympathize with Crane, and after listening to a very lively piece of music from the band, I got up and did the best I could possibly have done under any circumstances, for which I have since received universal applause. Williams did first rate, and so did Hutcheson, if his had not been 50 minutes long, when the audience was wearied out.

Mrs. Hughes went to Cincinnati on Friday, and will be gone one or two weeks. I have been to the bakery and bought some crackers, light bread, tea and butter, and will do my own cooking until she comes back. The weather has been so cold for two or three weeks past that, although the sun shines out prettily every day, yet the little snow which is on the ground has shown no sign of melting. I leaped out of the room and strained my ankle so very badly that I can scarcely walk, which together with my bad cold (made worse by speaking) has given me the blues. Assisted Prof. Elliott in collecting books, and there is a prospect of my being appointed "Sub" in the Library department. Received a letter from home which I answered "instanter." Phis had their supper in Clute's Ladies Saloon on Tuesday night, after our speeches. A full attendance was had, and Clute had prepared us a nice supper, equal to any wedding supper I was ever at. It will cost us about $30 or $40, and there were only about 10 or 12 of us. The speeches of the Eccritean and Erodelphian Societies went off tolerably well. All the boys except a few who have remained to study have either gone home or are visiting their college mates. I was solicited to go home with several of them, but refused, as I have more reading than I can possibly get through with.

Dec. 31st.

The vacation so far has passed quite pleasantly. I have been entirely by myself, except one afternoon in company with David Swing. I went to the creek to see the boys skate. I have scarcely been out of my room more than twice per day, and then only to stay five minutes. Have not been up town this week. Have read the first volume of the

History of Greece by Grote, and one volume of *Don Quixote,* also the translation of Goethe's *Faust,* besides writing five or six long letters. Went to hear David Swing preach on last Sabbath. . . .

1. See William Pratt, ed., *College Days at Old Miami: The Diary of T. C. Hibbett, 1851-1854* (Oxford, Ohio: Miami University, 1984), 110-17. The original diary is now in the Walter Havighurst Special Collections of the King Library at Miami.

VII.6. Oberlin, the First College to Admit Women

Oberlin College historian Robert S. Fletcher has written:

Early Oberlin is best understood as the experimental college of its day. For the most part, the colleges of the middle third of the nineteenth century [Oberlin was founded in 1833] sternly resisted the assaults of innovation. A monastic unworldliness and timelessness characterized the great majority; they stood barrenly and stubbornly isolated amidst the pounding surf of romantic reformism. . . . But innovation, barred elsewhere, was always welcomed at Oberlin. Oberlin embraced the heretical theology of President Charles Grandison Finney and every reform which could be reconciled with that form of revolt against Calvinism. Oberlin was the chief center of the peace movement beyond the Appalachians. Students and faculty embraced Graham vegetarianism and expelled meat from the commons. The largest chapter of the American Moral Reform Society in the West was at Oberlin. Negroes were welcomed as students at Oberlin when they were scarcely or not at all tolerated elsewhere. Of course, Oberlin was a focus of antislavery sentiment and Underground Railroad activity. . . .

[From 1834 to 1837] Oberlin combined a college, a preparatory school, and a female seminary as well as a theological school in one institution and so it is not surprising to find experiments tried in the elementary course extended to the 'Collegiate Department.'. . . . Young women taking the Ladies' (Seminary) Course were admitted to classes with college men. And finally in 1837 the system of 'joint education of the sexes' was carried to the point where four 'females' were admitted along with [thirty] young men to the classical course and to candidacy for the baccalaureate degree. Thus, naturally enough, college co-education began at Oberlin. . . . Though the matriculation of Mary Hosford, Mary Kellogg, Elizabeth Prall, and Caroline Mary Rudd in the full college course was largely on their own initiative and the faculty was divided on the advisability of their action [indeed, Professor John P. Cowles was forced out of the college because of his vehement opposition], the important fact is that *they were admitted,* as they could not have been at any other college.[1]

Reactions to the coeducational "Oberlin Experiment," as it came to be called, were understandably mixed. Critics, and there were many, were quick to predict gross immorality, licentious language, excessive distraction, a decline of piety, dangers to women's health, and a distaste for study as inevitable outcomes of "a doubtful and dangerous experiment." Proponents argued that the manners of both sexes would be improved, that women's health would not be affected, and that there would be "a wholesome incitement to effort to study." Professor John F. Stoddard, in speaking of the moral advantages of coeducation, went so far as to declare, "At Oberlin College, where both sexes are admitted, not an oath is uttered, nor a segar smoked, nor a glass of liquor drunk. What other college can make the same boast?"[2]

One of the strongest and most oft-quoted endorsements of Oberlin's experiment came from Dr. William A. Alcott, editor of the prestigious American Annals of Education, *who was also president of the American Physiological Society and editor of a monthly magazine,* Moral Reformer. *Calling the Oberlin experiment "unequivocally successful," he predicted that "the benefits which are likely to flow from it are immense. Woman is to be free. The hour of her emancipation is at hand. Daughters of America, rejoice!"[3]*

Though not a single New England or eastern college was quick to follow the Oberlin example, a number of privately supported midwestern schools did, including among others Antioch, Otterbein, and Wilberforce in Ohio; Olivet, Hillsdale, and Adrian in Michigan; Beloit, Lawrence, and Ripon in Wisconsin; and Knox and Wheaton in Illinois. With a number of state universities, including Michigan, Wisconsin, and Ohio State, following suit in the 1870s, the "Oberlin Experiment" was well on its way to becoming the rule rather than the exception in higher education.

When Dr. Sophia Louisa Jex-Blake, a pioneer in the cause of higher education for women in England and that nation's first female physician, made a tour in 1865 of a number of American schools and colleges whose doors were open to women, she first visited Oberlin. "Whatever shortcomings or errors," she later wrote, "may be recorded against Oberlin, it should ever be remembered in her favour that she took the initiative before all the world in opening a college career to women."[4]

DAUGHTERS OF AMERICA, REJOICE!

We have received a Catalogue of the Trustees, Officers and Students of the Oberlin Collegiate Institute, for 1838, of which an account has been given, from time to time, in this Journal. We perceive that the whole number of names in the Catalogue, is 391. Of these, 255 are males, and 126 are females. Of the males, 97 belong to the preparatory department, 44 to the [theo]logical school, 9 are attending a shorter course of study, 2 are irregular students, and 213 are attending the collegiate course. Of the females, 21 belong to the preparatory department, and 105 to the collegiate school.

There are many things in regard to this Institution to render it interesting to every friend of education. Its moral tone and standing — its broad temperance principles — its banner of freedom — the large benevolence it inculcates and encourages, and the habits of industry, in both sexes, which it enjoins and secures, give it a prominence in the view of the Christian philanthropist, which few literary or religious institutions can claim.

But its most interesting feature — to us, — is the uniting of the sexes in a course of liberal study, and the unexpected results which have followed. Many good men among us, when they heard that males and females were to recite together in some measure on the principle of a well-ordered Christian household, — did not fail to predict a failure. Yet the Institution has flourished, and the experiment is unequivocally successful. We consider it now fully established, that the sexes may be educated together.

This discovery is one of the most important ever made. The benefits which are likely to flow from it are immense. Woman is to be free. The hour of her emancipation is at hand. Daughters of America, rejoice!

1. See Robert S. Fletcher, "Oberlin and Co-education," *Ohio Archaeological and Historical Quarterly* 47 (January 1938): 1–3. Of the four young women admitted as Oberlin freshmen in 1837, three completed the course of study and received baccalaureate degrees at commencement exercises on 25 August 1841. Only Mary Kellogg, who had moved with her family to Louisiana, did not graduate.

2. Ibid., 7.

3. William A. Alcott, ed., *American Annals of Education for the Year 1838* (Boston, 1838), 477; the quotation is from the selection reproduced in this section. Alcott, whose *Moral Reformer* decried gluttony and advocated physical education among other causes, had become attracted to Oberlin, where the largest chapter of the American Moral Reform Society in the West could be found. When he visited the college in 1840, he lectured on "dress, diet, and marriage, and seriously considered moving his residence and his magazine to that promising community." See Robert S. Fletcher, "Bread and Doctrine at Oberlin," *Ohio State Archaeological and Historical Quarterly* 49 (1940): 60.

4. Quoted in Fletcher, "Oberlin and Co-education," 11.

VIII. The Antislavery Crusade

CLOSELY PARALLELING AND OFTEN intertwined with the movement for women's rights in the pre-Civil War years was the crusade to end slavery and achieve for persons of color the full measure of civil rights and equal protection under the law. Just as Quakers had initiated the abolitionist movement in Pennsylvania and other eastern states during and after the Revolution, so it was Quakers, primarily concentrated in eastern and southern parts of the state, who launched the antislavery crusade in Ohio. Though slavery had been prohibited north and west of the Ohio River by the Ordinance of 1787, Ohio was confronted by two slave-holding states, Kentucky and Virginia, on the other side of the river. Thus it was no accident that concern over the slavery question would be most pronounced among those living near the river that separated free soil from slave.

It was Benjamin Lundy—a nineteen-year-old Quaker who was shocked at the sight of a long line of slaves, each chained to the next, being driven like cattle to an auction block to be sold—who organized Ohio's first abolitionist society in St. Clairsville in 1815 and called it the Union Humane Society. Starting with six charter members it soon grew to nearly five hundred. Among them was a fellow Quaker, Charles Osborn, who in 1817 started the first abolitionist newspaper, the *Philanthropist,* in nearby Mount Pleasant. Though Osborn's paper proved short lived, Lundy founded another in 1821, which he called the *Genius of Universal Emancipation.* Determined to extend its outreach beyond eastern Ohio, which he had earlier attempted to do with Osborn's paper, Lundy moved about the nation, preaching abolitionism and printing and distributing copies of the *Genius* in city after city.

With only limited success in persuading slave owners to voluntarily free their slaves, it was not long before the antislavery crusade turned to direct action to help slaves escape to freedom, primarily through the medium of what came to be called the Underground Railroad.

As its name implies, the Underground Railroad was a covert network of "stations," or homes of abolitionist sympathizers, linked together by ever-changing routes over which "conductors" would guide runaways (often hidden in farm wagons under loads of hay or produce) ever northward toward the "promised land," the name given by escaping slaves to Canada. Because fugitive slave laws made it a federal offense to help the runaways, detailed records concerning the exact identities of stations, routes, and conductors are virtually nonexistent. One who left a record of his escape to freedom through Ohio to Canada was Josiah Henson, a Methodist preacher who helped establish in 1841 in Dresden, Ontario, a vocational school, the British American Institute for Fugitive Slaves.

Since Ohio represented the shortest distance between slavery (the states south of the Ohio River) and freedom (Canada, where federal fugitives slave laws did not apply), a disproportionate number of stations, routes, and conductors had Ohio identities in contrast to other northern states. And, of the estimated total of fifty thousand who escaped via the underground, Ohio was the leader in the proportion of fugitive slaves passing through it. In Cincinnati lived Levi Coffin, a Quaker from North Carolina who came to be called the "president" of the Underground Railroad. Upriver in Ripley lived the Reverend John Rankin, a Presbyterian minister through whose home nearly three thousand slaves passed on their way to freedom, including Eliza Harris, immortalized in Harriet Beecher Stowe's *Uncle Tom's Cabin.* Another who lived in Ripley was John Parker, a former slave said to have single-handedly ferried nearly a thousand fugitives across the Ohio River from Kentucky.

Cincinnati not only was the home of Levi Coffin and Harriet Beecher Stowe but also the city where a one-time Kentucky slave owner turned abolitionist, James G. Birney, in 1836 began to publish another newspaper called *The Philanthropist,* only to have its printing presses destroyed by a mob. In 1840 he emerged as the presidential candidate of the nation's first antislavery political party, the Liberty Party. From the Liberty Party and its successor, the Free Soil Party, came the movement that in 1849 achieved at least a partial repeal of the Black Codes that had been in effect in Ohio since 1804 and that, though not immediately successful in achieving the right to vote for Ohio's black citizens, did help create the impetus for a new state constitution in 1851, replacing the one adopted in 1802.

In the Western Reserve in northern Ohio abolitionism burned with particular passion, producing Ashtabula County's Joshua Reed Giddings and Benjamin F. Wade, law partners in Jefferson. It was the Whig Giddings who, with Liberty Party and Free Soil support, served as abolition's principal spokesman in Congress in the 1840s and 1850s, and it was Wade who would subsequently emerge as the leader of the "Radical Republicans" in the U.S. Senate. Out of Oberlin in 1858–59 came the classic litigation involving the Underground Railroad and the enforcement of federal fugitive slave laws, the "Oberlin-Wellington Rescue Case," while from his background in Hudson, Akron, and Kent came the best known of all the militant abolitionist leaders, John Brown of Harpers Ferry fame. Little wonder that Ohio came to be called by some "Freedom's Proving Ground."

VIII.1. The Quakers Take the Lead

It is sometimes difficult for Ohioans to appreciate that until the Civil War their state shared 436 miles of common boundary with the slave states of Virginia and Kentucky, and that river communities such as Steubenville, Martins Ferry, and Bridgeport looked out on towns

such as Follansbee, Wellsburg, and Wheeling, where slavery was not only condoned but prac-
ticed. There was no West Virginia until that war, only Virginia, which poked a long finger
northward between Pennsylvania and Ohio all the way to the portals of East Liverpool.

It was in the eastern Ohio counties of Belmont and Jefferson, bordering the Ohio River,
that concentrations of Quakers could be found in the early nineteenth century in and around
such settlements as St. Clairsville and Mount Pleasant. It was the Quaker Benjamin Lundy,
sometimes called "the Father of Abolitionism," who organized Ohio's first antislavery society
at St. Clairsville in 1815. He called it the "Union Humane Society." And it was a fellow
Quaker, Charles Osborn, who began publication of the first abolitionist newspaper, the Phi-
lanthropist, at Mount Pleasant in 1817.

With Quaker and other abolitionists on one side of the Ohio River and Virginia slave-
holders on the other, it was not long before reports of runaway slaves were filling the columns of
area newspapers, along with allegations on the part of slave owners that antislavery advocates
were aiding and abetting the fugitives. What follows is an account by Benjamin Lundy describing
his part in getting the abolitionist movement under way in eastern Ohio,[1] followed by a slave
owner's advertisement that appeared in a Steubenville paper in 1817 calling for the arrest and
return of "My copper color'd BEN" and a response to that ad from Mount Pleasant abolitionists.[2]

ANTI-SLAVERY LABOURS IN OHIO.

I had lamented the sad condition of the slave, ever since I became acquainted with his
wrongs and sufferings. But the question, "What can I do?" was the continual response to the impulses of my heart. As I enjoyed no peace of mind, however, I at length
concluded that I *must* act; and shortly after my settlement at St. Clairsville, I called a few
friends together, and unbosomed my feelings to them. The result was the organization
of an anti-slavery association, called the Union Humane Society. The first meeting,
which was held at my own house, consisted of but five or six persons. In a few months
afterwards, the Society contained nearly five hundred members, among whom were
most of the influential preachers and lawyers, and many respectable citizens of several
counties in that section of the state.

I also wrote an appeal on the subject of slavery, addressed to the philanthropists
of the United States, and circulated five or six copies in manuscript. I was urged to publish it by some of my friends, and by persons from a distance whom I met at the Yearly
Meeting of the Society of Friends, held at Mount Pleasant. I consented, on condition
that it should appear with a *fictitious signature*. [Philo Justitia]. Since that time my modesty has much worn off.

Soon after this occurrence, proposals were issued by Charles Osborne, for publishing a paper at Mount Pleasant, to be entitled the Philanthropist. He stated in his pro-
spectus, that he should discuss the subject of slavery in the columns of the paper. The idea
now occurred to me, that I might act efficiently for the cause of emancipation—that I
could select articles, (for I did not think of writing myself,) and have them published in
the Philanthropist, and that I could also get subscribers to the publication. Engrossed
with these thoughts, I went to work with alacrity.

My leisure moments were now fully employed. When I sent my selections to Charles, I sometimes wrote him a few lines. After he had published the Philanthropist a few months, I was surprised at receiving from him a request that I should assist in editing it. The thought that I could do such a thing had not then even occurred to me. But on his repeating the request, I consented to try:—and from that moment, whenever I have thought that something ought to be done, my maxim has been, though doubtful of my ability—"*try.*" Although I resided ten miles from the office, and was extensively engaged in other business, I continued, for some time, to write editorial articles for the paper.

At length, Charles proposed to me to join him in the printing business, and to take upon myself the superintendence of the office. After some deliberation, I consented to accept the offer, and, with that view, prepared to diminish my other business. I discharged some of my workmen, and took a portion of the articles which had been made in my shop, to Missouri, in order to sell them. I returned in about six months, when finding business more dull than before, I determined to break up my establishment at St. Clairsville, altogether, and remove to Mount Pleasant. . . .

Fifty Dollars Reward.

————————

The above reward will be given to any person or persons who will apprehend and deliver into my possession, or deliver into the hands of the keeper of the jail in Steubenville,
My copper color'd BEN,
A man of color, who is a slave of mine.
BEN is about thirty years of age, five feet and better, high; chunky made, and not quite so impudent as men of color generally are—he was prevailed upon by a mob in the town of Mountpleasant, Jefferson Co. O. to leave my service, stating to them that he was as free as I was:—I advise emigrants from any of the slave-holding states, to avoid the rout by Mountpleasant.
Griffith Davis
January 19th, 1817.

Base Calumny Refuted.

————————

Mr. Wilson [the editor]—Whereas a certain *Griffith Davis* has caused to be inserted in your last week's paper an advertisement, headed 'Fifty dollars reward,' for the apprehension of his *copper color'd BEN,* as he calls him, and stating that said Ben had been enticed from his service 'by a mob in the town of Mountpleasant, Jefferson county,

Ohio, and cautions all 'emigrants from the slave-holding states to avoid the rout through said town: In justice to the citizens of Mountpleasant, as also to those of the state of Ohio generally, we deem it our duty, who were eye-witnesses of the circumstances relative to the said Davis and his copper color'd Ben, as he calls him, to make a candid statement of the facts and leave an impartial public to judge who was the mob and who endeavored to suppress the riot.

About two weeks ago said Davis came with his family into the town of Mountpleasant—became much intoxicated with liquor; and, in a fit of rage, without any previous provocation, began to beat said Ben on the head with an unlawful weapon, in a shocking and inhuman manner—he was requested to desist, which only tended to increase his rage; and when all intreaty had proved ineffectual, and he had threatened to serve the citizens who interfered in the same manner he was treating the black man, a complaint was entered against him for a breach of the peace—he was brought before a justice and bound over to answer at the next court for his conduct—mean time, before the warrant was put into the hands of the officer, the black man disappeared.

These are the facts as they took place in this town, and if any mob was raised, the public will not hesitate to say who composed it.

Wm. Hamilton   Neh'h Wright,
Jesse Newport,   Thomas Emory,
James Johnson,   Daniel Strahl.
Mountpleasant, Jan'y 29, 1817.

1. From Thomas Earle, ed., *The Life, Travels and Opinions of Benjamin Lundy* (Philadelphia, 1847), 16-20.

2. From the *Western Herald and Steubenville Gazette,* Steubenville, Ohio, 7 February 1817, reproduced in Robert C. Wheeler, ed., *Ohio Newspapers: A Living Record* (Columbus: Ohio History Press, 1950), 152, 154.

VIII.2. James G. Birney and *The Philanthropist*

A native of Kentucky and a one-time slaveholder, James G. Birney became a convert to abolitionism and sought to establish an antislavery paper at Danville in his home state in an effort to persuade his fellow Kentuckians to join him in common cause. Failing in that endeavor, he moved to Cincinnati and announced his intention to publish his paper in that city, an announcement that was quickly denounced by some of that city's leading businessmen, who, more interested in developing trade with the South and a Cincinnati-to-Charleston railroad than they were in freeing the slaves, warned Birney that he could expect mob action against himself and his paper were he to proceed with his publication in that city.

Though printed in Cincinnati, Birney's paper, The Philanthropist *(the same name earlier used by the Quaker Charles Osborn for his paper published at Mount Pleasant in 1817), was distributed weekly from New Richmond in neighboring Clermont County. Its first issue, on 1 January 1836, explained the difficulties Birney had encountered in getting it under way and also his intent to open it as a medium of expression to slaveholders and abolitionists alike. Yet in unmistakable language, abolitionist that he was, Birney asserted his belief that "Liberty and Slavery . . . when roused into strife, know neither truce nor reconciliation. . . . They are in actual conflict—theirs is the struggle of death;—there can be but one triumph, and this in the utter destruction of the adversary."[1]*

The prediction by the Cincinnati naysayers that mob violence could be anticipated if the paper were published proved all too true. On 30 July 1836, a mob attacked the press of Achilles Pugh, Birney's printer in Cincinnati, scattered the type in the streets, and left the place a shambles.[2] Undaunted, Birney and Pugh continued publishing in Springboro, north of Cincinnati. In recognition of his courage as well as his fervent abolitionism, Birney in 1840 was nominated for the office of president of the United States on the ticket of the Liberty Party, the first antislavery party in the nation. Though soundly defeated, Birney and his party had brought the issue of abolition to the forefront of American politics. And there it would remain until resolved by civil conflict two decades later.

THE PHILANTHROPIST

NEW-RICHMOND, OHIO, JAN. 1, 1836.

After long delay, occasioned by difficulties which we have not been slow to overcome, we are enabled to issue our first number. It may be satisfactory to our friends to give them—though we shall do it very briefly and in very general terms—the reasons for issuing our paper at New-Richmond, rather than at Cincinnati, where we reside.

When the opposition of slaveholders had succeeded in defeating our *first* purpose, of publishing the Philanthropist in Kentucky, and in virtually expelling us from the very village in which we had our birth, by rendering our residence in its neighborhood disagreeable, if not dangerous, to ourself and our family, our attention was turned to this city;—not only as a pleasant place to dwell in, to a person who could find inducements in the intelligence of those around him, and in the religious influence which, it was supposed, prevailed in it—but as a town of safety, to any one engaged in the pursuit of truth, and who might be disposed to make publication of its results.

The people of this State, remembering, in all probability, at the time they formed their Constitution, the attack, which, but a short time before, had been made under the sanction of a law of Congress, on the freedom of Speech and of the Press, put this right—so far as human language could do so—beyond all doubt or question in their own case, when they declaired with a force of expression, peculiar to the Constitution of Ohio, that "*the right to speak, write or print* ON ANY SUBJECT" *was* "INDISPUTABLE." Furnished with such an Egis as this, it might have been supposed, that any advocate of Liberty could carry on war even to the death, against her adversary—especially, as Ohio, to her great honor, was the *first* of the States, which had, in its primary organization, placed the seal of utter condemnation on Slavery, forbidding its existence in any shape, or under any guise or pretence whatever, within her limits;—and this, too, after the most mature consideration, and in the very view of her *elders*, who in the warm embraces, with which they hugged the delusion to their own breasts, gave

it the highest recommendation to their younger and less experienced sisters. Such was
the noble and dignified rebuke of slavery by the PEOPLE of Ohio, more than thirty
years ago.

Judge, then, of our astonishment, when, on the occurrence of a very trivial circumstance, in which we had no agency, and almost before we had made an orderly adjustment of our domicil, we were waited on (it gives us pleasure to say, *very politely,*) by
official gentlemen, and assured, that the issue, in Cincinnati, of a paper, favorable to
emancipation, would produce an explosion of mobocratic elements more violent and
destructive than had been known before; so much so, that any attempt, on the part of
the city-authority to suppress, or restrain it, would be altogether useless and unavail-
ing;—for, that respectable and influential men, such as might be relied on to aid in ar-
resting a riotous outbreak proceeding from any other cause, would in this case,—
encourage it by their silence, or their acquiescence,—if respect for themselves should
prevent them from actual co-operation with the mob.—Although we did not, at the
time, place entire confidence in those opinions, however sincerely entertained by the
gentlemen alluded to; and are yet incredulous as to statements going to show a disre-
gard, on the part of any respectable portion of our population, of the most precious
rights of their fellow-citizens secured, as they have been attempted to be, by the Constitution and laws of the State;—yet so desirous were we of peace, and to escape the im-
putations of furnishing, by any act of ours, however innocent, even an *occasion* for its
breach, that we determined (keeping in view, that our main object was not thereby defeated,) to defer our own "indisputable" rights, to the supposed state of public feeling,—and, though with great inconvenience, and at no small additional expense, to
establish the press at some other point where investigation would rather be welcomed
than repelled. . . .

It is our intention to make the *Philanthropist* a repository of facts and arguments
on the subject of Slavery as connected with Emancipation. The discussion we invite,
and the aid we desire, we are willing to accept from any quarter that will furnish it. To
the south, we have offered in our main editorial article to day, the free use of our columns, to defend a system which they seem determined to continue. We here repeat this
offer,—and we will hope, that it may be accepted in the spirit of kindness which
prompts us to make it.

It is not our design to pour out our publications on the south, unasked. Courtesy
will require of us to send a No. of this date to each of the members of the *Athens Vigilance Committee.* Four consecutive Nos. beginning with the present, will be sent—as we
trust without giving offence or provoking abuse—to several of the principal journals in
the slave States. Should *they* not be sent in exchange, ours will be discontinued. To the
subscribers in slave States, their paper will be regularly transmitted by the mail. We have
no wish to obtrude our lucubrations on those, who—unknown to us personally or by
reputation—may, in the spirit of the south, scornfully reject our well meant efforts to
benefit them, and to conduct the existing controversy to a happy termination. To several of our southern acquaintances, whose names we have no desire, because of our
widely differing views on the subject of Slavery, to erase from the list of our friends, we
shall take the liberty of sending an occasional number; because, we believe, they will

cheerfully receive and read it, to be informed of what is doing abroad;—and further, because, if our publications contain in them any incendiary ingredient, they will be as safe in their hands and as well restrained from the work of mischief, as if in the immediate custody of the distinguished gentlemen who executed the patriotic office of superintending the burning of the effigies of our friends, Tappan, Cox, & c., in the public square in Charleston.

Beside this, if not a single number should ever find its way into the hands of any one south of the Ohio river, such publications as the Philanthropist purposes to be, have become absolutely necessary for the preservation of liberty in what are called the Free States. Whilst the spirit of Freedom which was awaked up in the north by the principles of the American Revolution, and which accomplished the liberation of her own slaves, has been almost dormant and unaggressive till within a short time past, it has not been so with the spirit of Slavery. It has been wide awake, ever on the alert, and busy with its concentrated energies and mighty resources, in pushing its victories and extending its conquests over the domains of her unsuspecting and listless antagonist. The free States must, for their own sakes, have the subject of slavery discussed anew,—they must have the secrets of this prisonhouse of both soul and body laid open before them; its horrors exposed before the sun;—they must be brought to see its almost universal effects on the character of the offspring and family of the slaveholder, and on the slaveholder himself; how, by the very laws of our being, the habit of uncontrolled domination over slaves, will, when occasion offers, show itself in our intercourse with *equals*; how the temper, formed by despotic rule, denying that laws were made for it, spurns the restraints of governments and the ordinances of constitutions, vents itself in deeds of blood and death, and is ready to prostrate every barrier to the accomplishment of its own will, or the gratification of its own pleasure. These, the legitimate fruits of slavery every where, must be made known—must be examined, and marked with a fresh brand of condemnation; or we, of the States yet free, and our children, will soon be compelled to partake of them, as our daily repast, in all their bitterness.

The truth is, Liberty and Slavery cannot, both, live long in juxtaposition. They are antagonist elements, and when roused into strife, know neither truce nor reconciliation. This is their condition now. They have met, fiercely disputing each other's reign. They are in actual conflict—theirs in the struggle of death;—there can be but one triumph, and this in the utter destruction of the adversary. Either Liberty will stand on the lifeless body, rejoicing in the everlasting overthrow, of her great enemy,—or Slavery, with its chains and its scourges, its woes, its curses, and its tears, will overspread our favored land. . . .

1. In this same issue of *The Philanthropist* there appears on page 1 a quotation from the *Cincinnati Whig* of 21 December 1835: "We perceive by a notice in the Christian Journal, that James G. Birney, is about to commence his Abolition paper, at New Richmond, Clermont County. Finding that his fanatical project would not be tolerated at Danville, Ky., nor in this city, he has at length settled himself on the border of Kentucky, and so near Cincinnati as to make the pestiferous breath of his paper, spread contagion among our citizens. We deem this new effort an insult to our slaveholding neighbors, and an attempt to browbeat public opinion in this quarter. We do therefore hope, notwithstanding the alleged respectability of the editor,

that he will find the public so inexorably averse to his mad scheme, that he will deem it his interest to abandon it."

2. Henry Howe, *Historical Collections of Ohio* (Cincinnati, 1848), 225-26, noted: "As early as the 14th of July [1836], the press room [of *The Philanthropist*] was broken open and the press and materials defaced and destroyed. July 23d, a meeting of citizens was convened at the Lower Market house 'to decide whether they will permit the publication or distribution of abolition papers in this city.' . . . On Saturday night, July 30th, very soon after dark, a concourse of citizens assembled at the corner of Main and Seventh streets, in this city [Cincinnati], and upon a short consultation, broke open the printing office of the Philanthropist, the abolition paper, scattered the type into the streets, tore down the presses and completely dismantled the office."

VIII.3. The Constitutional Convention of 1850–1851: Issues of Race, Gender, and Governmental Reform

With the movement for social justice accelerating, the Ohio General Assembly in 1849 partially repealed the "Black Laws," or "Black Codes," in effect since the first years of statehood. Specifically removed were the mandates that all blacks moving into the state had to post bond, register their "freedom papers" to show they were not fugitive slaves, and secure the endorsement of white citizens who would accept responsibility for them. At the same time, Ohio voters overwhelmingly approved a proposal from the legislature to call a constitutional convention to address deficiencies in the existing Constitution of 1802.

In sessions held from May to July 1850 in Columbus, and then in Cincinnati from December until March 1850-51, following an outbreak of cholera in the state capital, delegates agreed on a number of important changes in state government. The supreme court would no longer be required to meet annually in each county, and judges would be chosen henceforth not by the legislature but by popular vote. In addition to the governor all other principal executive officers would be elected by the voters. To assure that the constitution in the future would remain viable and up to date, the voters would be given the opportunity every twentieth year to decide whether or not another constitutional convention should be called, with amendments possible in the meantime if approved by voters following endorsement by at least three-fifths of each house of the General Assembly.

What the convention of 1850-51 did not do was also significant. It did not give the governor the veto power, instead continuing the inheritance of legislative supremacy from the Constitution of 1802. And it failed to grant the franchise to either women or blacks despite strenuous efforts on the part of social reformers to achieve these goals. Federal constitutional amendments would be needed to assure these changes in the years to come.

Ratified by the voters in June 1851, the Ohio Constitution of 1851 is still in effect, though many times amended. Twice since then voters have approved the holding of a constitutional convention in the routine twentieth-year cycle, in 1873 and again in 1912. The amendments produced in the latter year would prove particularly significant.

A Debate on Education and Race at the Constitutional Convention

The third section was then taken up, and is as follows:[1]

> The General Assembly shall make such provision by taxation
> and other means (in addition to the income arising from the
> irreducible fund) as will secure a thorough and efficient system
> of Common Schools, free to all the children in the State.

MR. SAWYER.[2] I move to insert the word "white" between the word "the" and the word "children," so that the section will provide for the education of all the *white* children in the State. That is the only class of children in the State of Ohio for whose education I am willing to make provision in this Constitution.

MR. TAYLOR.[3] I confess, sir, that I am surprised. I did not expect that a motion of this kind would be made by any gentleman on this floor. I did not, on the other hand, suppose that any proposition to extend the political rights of the colored citizens of Ohio would be adopted; but I had supposed that a knowledge of the law of self-preservation would have suggested to the gentleman from Auglaize [Mr. Sawyer], and to every gentleman upon the floor, that it would be good policy to give to all within the reach of our laws a good moral and intellectual training. I knew that this Convention was not prepared to increase the political rights of the black man; but I had hoped that all were willing to provide against his becoming the pest of society, by being deprived of all opportunities for education. Shall we not secure protection to ourselves and our children by relieving the colored population of Ohio, from the absolute necessity of growing up in vice and ignorance? Shall we, by the adoption of the amendment of the gentleman from Auglaize, constitute a class who will become the inmates of our poor houses, and the tenants of our jails? I think it must be clear to every reflecting mind that the true policy of the statesman is to provide the means of education, and consequent moral improvement, to every child in the State, the offspring of the black man equally with that of the white man, the children of the poor equally with the rich. But I am told that the Negro belongs to a degraded and inferior race; so much the more reason, sir, for their education and improvement. Leave them to grow up without moral and intellectual training, and they become a positive curse as well as burthen upon society. Educate them, and they become useful members of the community that has cared for them.

I repeat that I had not heard that we were positively to retrograde in this matter by commencing a system of persecution upon the colored population of the State, already, one would think, sufficiently unfortunate. I beg gentlemen to be consistent in this regard—let them proclaim their real designs—if the black man is to be driven across our borders at the point of the bayonet, let them say so.

I believe that a majority of the members of this Convention are not prepared to deny to our colored population all opportunities for moral and intellectual training for the duties of life; although they may not be willing to extend to that class the right to exercise the elective franchise. Education will tend to make men moral and useful members of society, therefore let us provide for the education of every child in the State.

Mr. SAWYER. I have but a few words to say, sir, upon this subject. I am sure that I would go quite as far as the gentleman from Erie, (Mr. Taylor), to do justice to the negro race. When he hears my views upon the subject, he may find that we do not differ very widely. Under our present laws, the negro is not taxed for the support of schools to which his children are denied admittance. True, the negro is taxed for school purposes, but it is exclusively for the benefit of his own children, when he desires it should be thus applied. There is therefore no injustice, no inhumanity, if gentlemen choose to place the matter upon that ground. And, sir, I am willing to extend to the negro the same exemption from taxation for the support of white schools, for all time to come. But, sir, while I will oppose any measures for the oppression of the blacks now in the State, I will as strenuously oppose every proposition which, in its practical effect, will tend to encourage the emigration of blacks into the State. And, sir, while I would desire to injure the feelings of no gentleman who holds sentiments opposite to my own, I must say that I rejoice in the passage of the fugitive slave bill; for I believe it will have the effect to rid the free States of the curse of a negro population, intermixed with the whites. Nor shall I be deterred from frankly expressing this opinion. . . .

The people of Canada are now reaping the bitter fruits of the seed sown by themselves. They are now overrun with an impoverished, if not a vicious, negro population. And because the fugitive slave bill has had the effect, in so great a measure, to rid us of the negroes which were everywhere a pest in society, and has accumulated them upon the soil of Canada, I rejoice in its passage.

Mr. President, while I sit here, to assist in framing a Constitution for the people of Ohio, I must look first, to the interests of the white race. With this view, I will not encourage the emigration of blacks into this State, nor will I make it so much the interest of that class to remain here, that there will be no disposition for them to emigrate to Liberia. And, in this I am actuated by no hatred of the negro race—no desire to oppress them. I have declared before, and I repeat it now, that I am willing that the negro shall have every privilege and every right that I myself enjoy. I am willing that he shall vote; I am willing that he shall be a justice of the peace, or governor, a judge, or a member of Congress. Aye, sir, I am willing that he shall be President of a Republic. I am willing that the language of our sublime Declaration of Independence, shall apply to the negro as well and as fully as to myself. But sir, I am unwilling that he shall enjoy these privileges in this country, preoccupied as it is, by a different and a higher race. I am willing that he shall enjoy all these rights and privileges in his native country. Is there anything either unjust or inhumane in this? . . .

One other remark, and I will take my seat. If you will look at the statistics furnished by the recent census, you will find that in those counties of this State, where abolitionism or free-soilism predominates, there are the fewest negroes. It is in the Southern counties, bordering on Kentucky, where there is the largest proportion of negroes and mulattoes; and those counties are the least friendly to provisions for the encouragement of their emigration or remaining in the State. Either the negroes do not know their friends, or else they will not go to them.

I hope that the word "white" will be inserted in this section, so that it will provide for the education of "all white children."

Mr. TOWNSHEND.[4] I did not rise, Mr. Chairman, to reply to the remarks of the gentleman from Auglaize on the Fugitive Slave Bill. I don't see what that bill has to do with Common Schools in Ohio; but sir, as that gentleman has kindly given us his opinion, I will just take the opportunity to give mine, which is, that the Fugitive Law in all its distinctive features, is utterly and teetotally damnable.

But I rose, Mr. Chairman, to correct one or two mistakes into which that gentleman has unfortunately fallen. The first relates to the feelings with which the people of Canada regard the fugitives who escape from this country. I do not believe that the people there are alarmed at the "black cloud" of fugitives that comes up from the States. On the contrary, know that they treat them with great humanity, furnishing them with food, clothing, and employment. But, sir, Canadians feel, and have a right to feel indignation and contempt for the government and people, that, in spite of the loudest pretentions to freedom and justice, nevertheless drives a portion of the human family to take refuge under the protection of Monarchical Institutions. . . .

The other mistake I wish to notice, is the assertion of the gentleman, that there are, comparatively, no colored persons in the free soil counties, and that therefore, all the sympathy felt in those counties, is for a class of persons, which we, in such counties, don't have among us; and of the evils of whose presence we know nothing. Now, sir, I think it will be conceded that we have *some* free soil in Lorain, and there, sir, we have quite a sprinkling of colored persons. I don't pretend to know the exact number, but I should think but little, if any, less than one hundred in the village where I live, and a still larger number in another village but a few miles off. The census of 1840 is in error on that subject, possibly because with us we don't call a man black, unless he is absolutely and unequivocally so; nor a man a mulatto unless we know enough of his pedigree to satisfy us that he is exactly half and half. But, sir, we have less prejudice against colored persons, not because we don't know them, but because we do. In Lorain county there is a Collegiate Institution, [Oberlin], which has, in its several departments, about six hundred students, and to all the privileges of that Institution colored youth are admitted as freely as white. And, sir, I have attended the Commencement Exercises of that College for several years, and I know that the young colored men who have graduated have stood as high and acquitted themselves as well as the other students in the same class. This year one colored young lady graduated from the Ladies' Department, who was second to none of the ladies that graduated at the same time, and the address delivered by her on that occasion, would, I think, have done good even to the gentleman from Auglaize, could he have heard it. Our sympathy, sir, for colored persons does not spring from our ignorance of them, but from the conviction that they are human beings, and therefore entitled to all the rights and privileges and sympathies due to humanity, and from the conviction that they, equally with other men, are susceptible for intellectual and moral elevation. . . .

A Constitutional Debate: Should Blacks and Women Be Entitled to Vote?

ARTICLE V—ELECTIVE FRANCHISE.[5]

Section 1. Every white male citizen of the United States, of the age of twenty-one years, who shall have been a resident of the state one year next preceding the election, and of the county, township, or ward, in which he resides, such time as may be provided by law, shall have the qualifications of an elector, and be entitled to vote at all elections. . . .

EXTENSION OF THE ELECTIVE FRANCHISE.[6]

On motion of Mr. GREEN[7] of Ross, the Convention took up the Report of the committee on the Elective Franchise.

The question pending being on the motion to strike out the word "white" where it occurs in the first line of the first section.

Mr. TOWNSHEND. It will be seen that my name is not affixed to the Report of the committee on the Elective Franchise, of which committee I am a member. I could not sign that Report consistently with my own views of right, nor consistently with the known wishes of a large proportion of my constituents. . . .

I am opposed, Mr. President to the insertion of the word *white* in this Report. The first reason I have to offer for my opposition is the belief that the intended restriction of the right of suffrage is *unjust.*

Sir, I not only say, but I believe that "*all* men are created equal," that is they are equally endowed by their Creator with certain inherent rights. These rights are essential to our existence, they spring from the necessities of our being. In order to live we must have a place somewhere, we must have air and food, and each of these and every other necessity imposed on us by our maker, involves a corresponding right whether it pertain to our physical or to our intellectual or moral nature. Some of our rights grow directly out of the relations we sustain, such as husbands or fathers, &c., each of these relations imposing certain obligations or duties, and these involving corresponding rights. All men have by nature the same necessities and may sustain the same or equal relations, consequently all men must have the same natural rights. For the protection of these natural rights governments are instituted among men, and this single purpose of protection is the only legitimate function of government. All the human governments on earth cannot create a right, nor can they take a right away, and the idea that man on entering into jural or civil relations with these, surrenders any part of his natural rights, is only one of the grand but mischievous blunders of the past. Human governments derive all their just authority from the consent of the governed; all persons have the same rights to protect, and are therefore equally interested, and equally entitled to share as principals in government, and the consent of one person is just as necessary as the consent of another person, in order to constitute just authority.

To attempt to govern men without seeking their consent is usurpation and tyranny, whether in Ohio or in Austria. There is a portion of the people of this State who have the same right to stand upon this part of God's earth, and to breathe this free air, that you or I have, and yet you seek to impose a government upon them without consulting them. I can only say that they are under no obligation to obey your laws or to submit to your authority. You burthen them with taxation without representation, and thus inflict upon them the identical wrong for which the thirteen United Colonies threw off the yoke of the mother country. To establish a government over them, not based on their consent; to subject them to laws they have had no voice in framing; to tax them while you deny them representation is clearly and manifestly unjust; and I might stop here without urging any further objections to the Report, for with governments there should be really but one enquiry, what is just?

Another objection I have to this limitation of the right of suffrage, I believe it is *anti-democratic*. I desire to speak on this point with becoming modesty, for I am but a young man, while I see around me many whose hair has grown gray in the study of democratic principles. One of these gentlemen has said with Jefferson that democracy consists in doing "equal and exact justice to all men," another gentleman has said that democracy concedes to others all it demands for itself, and demands for itself all it concedes to others. If the restriction of the elective franchise is tested by either of these rules it will be found anti-democratic. To justify the practice the report recommends, Jefferson's rule should be amended so as to read "equal and exact justice to all *white* men — or to all men *except negroes.*" If I understand genuine democracy it is neither more nor less than the golden rule of christianity applied to politics, or to our civil relations — that is doing unto others as we would have others to do unto us and I see no reason why democracy is not like christianity, comprehensive enough to embrace the whole family of man. . . . .

I believe it to be our duty here to erect a civil platform upon which the foot of every person in the State may stand and on exactly the same level. I have not intentionally given in this body, one vote, nor do I intend to give one vote, to place any man, or set of men, above the common level. . . . But sir, the same sense of justice, which will not permit me to place another man's foot higher than my own, will also prevent me from consenting to place any man a hair's breadth below the common level. If the government of Ohio is to be in the hands of a privileged class, whether that class be large or small, it will be an aristocracy, a form of government for which I have no partiality; this government ought to be democratic — a government shared by all, for the good of all. Let us then have no limitations of suffrage — for who does not know that all such limitations are anti-democratic?

We have already stated that the true function of government is to protect rights, or in other words, to prevent wrongs. Experience has taught us that ignorance is one of the most fruitful sources of crime, and it has therefore been found to be good policy to secure the education of the whole people, as a means of preventing crime, which it does at less expense and more effectually than all the jails or penitentiaries, or scaffolds, that were ever erected. I was surprised, when we were considering the subject of education, to hear some gentleman propose to exclude the children of colored persons from the benefits of our common school system. Surely, after what we know of the good influences of education, to provide for keeping one class of our inhabitants in ignorance, would be most miserable policy. But it is not enough that all should have the means of education; we ought to give to all the inhabitants of the State the full benefit of the powerful stimulus of hope and ambition. Let no man feel that the law which ought to be his protector, interposes a barrier to his progress, by saying to him, "thus far shalt thou come, but no farther." Rather let us offer the strongest inducements to the intellectual and moral elevation of every person, of whatever class or condition, by opening the race and offering every prize of wealth, or honor, or usefulness, alike to all.

If, on the other hand, we make it impossible for any class of our people to rise—if we consign them to ignorance, and want, and degradation, we ought to consider ourselves responsible for whatever invasion of our rights may be the consequence; we shall reap exactly what we sow. To my view, the political degradation of any portion of our people is the highest degree impolitic. . . .

Mr. HITCHCOCK of Cuyahoga.[8] . . . I would sustain the motion to strike out this word, because I hold, that the distinction which it indicates is diametrically opposed to the great principle upon which our government is based—that great principle of action which animated over revolutionary fathers—which was acknowledged as a principle of action by the framers of all the early constitutions of this country, even of some of the Slave States, in those times which tried men's souls—because that distinction is opposed to the principle of equality amongst men, which this constitution recognizes; because it is opposed to the principles of justice and state policy, and humanity, and hostile to everything that elevates and dignifies the name of man; and because it is the indication of a principle, which, if carried out, as it might be, it would divest every man in the state of his rights. . . .

Mr. HUMPHREVILLE.[9] I had intended, (as I believe I declared when I made this motion,) to give a silent vote in favor of striking out. But, since the adoption of the rule which precludes members who desire to speak upon this question, and since, on account of the adoption of that rule, the question is not likely to be fully discussed, I will beg the indulgence of the Convention, whilst I offer a very few remarks.

In addition to what has been just summed up by the gentleman from Cuyahoga, [Mr. Hitchcock,] as a synopsis of the reasons why he should vote for striking out this word "white," I will say that I shall vote for striking out, because I believe it is against the constitution of the United States. If this word should be retained, I believe it would be, substantially, a violation of the constitution of the United States, because it makes distinctions amongst citizens. . . .

Mr. SAWYER. I have given my views upon this subject, and shall not repeat them. I have now merely to say, that I have changed my opinion somewhat, of gentlemen, who advocate these peculiar views. I believe now, that they are honest—and according this to them, I ask the same consideration for myself, when I oppose their views. Moreover, I am willing now, to vote for submitting the question of negro suffrage, to the people, in a separate clause. But I cannot consistently, with my sense of duty, vote for negroes to approach the ballot box, so long as I remember that we citizens are white men, and that we have acquired this country, (whether by fair, or foul means,) and it belongs to us. At the same time, I adhere to the motto of "equal rights to all, exclusive privileges to none." I am willing that the colored race should be colonized, and will go as far as any man to effect that object, for I believe, it is the only proper method of elevating them to their just position. But that negroes have the same rights with white men, in this country, I utterly deny. . . .

Mr. WOODBURY.[10] I am pleased to see those who are opposed to this amendment treat the subject with so much candor—feeling no disposition, apparently, to prevent a direct vote upon the question. I find no fault with any man for opposing the amendment, for I am satisfied that there are members who are individually in favor of the amendment, but whose duty it will be to vote against it, on account of the known will of their constituents. . . .

The question pending, being on the motion to strike out the word, "white," where it occurs the first time, in the first section. . . .

Mr. WOODBURY demanded the yeas and nays, and being ordered, resulted, yeas 12, nays 66. . . . So the motion to strike out [the word "white"] was rejected.

Mr. WOODBURY moved to further amend the report, by striking out the word, "male," where it occurs in the first section.

Mr. TOWNSHEND. Mr. President, notwithstanding the manifest impatience of the Convention, I will make a remark or two before giving my vote on the motion of the gentleman from Ashtabula to strike out the word *male*.

It is known to gentlemen that many petitions have been presented to this body asking that females may be permitted to exercise the right of suffrage. Their petitions have been signed by several hundred ladies, the precise number of these signatures I am not able to state in consequence of the resignation of the chairman of the committee to whom they were entrusted. They were sent from several different counties, and set forth in a respectful and forcible manner the claims and wishes of the petitioners. I believe none of these petitions came from the counties I have the honor to represent, but I have the happiness to be acquainted with many ladies who entertain similar views, and I take this occasion to say that I know of none who are more refined or more intelligent, nor do I know of any who more faithfully discharge all the duties that pertain to their families and homes.

I shall not repeat what I have heretofore said of the injustice of limitations of the right of suffrage. I will only say that woman has, by nature, rights as numerous and as dear as man. She shares equally with man in all the rights that pertain to our common humanity, and therefore has the same or an equal interest in all that pertains to civil government. I say further that she is man's equal in intelligence and virtue, and is therefore as well qualified as man to share in the responsibilities of government; and I can see no justice in making her merely a subject of government, rather than a party to it, especially if she desires such participation.

I know it is said that woman is even now represented, and that her interests are safer in the hands of fathers, husbands, brothers and sons, than they could be in her own. If this is true, how comes it to pass that woman is now, in this enlightened age and in this Christian country, subject to so many legal disabilities. Every one knows, or ought to know, that under the common law, woman has scarcely any legal existence, and under some circumstances, her rights of person and property are utterly disregarded. If woman's interests have suffered so much, even in the hands of fathers and brothers, I think it is high time they were entrusted to her own keeping.

We hear it said, that woman's sense of propriety would be outraged by giving to her political rights; I would respectfully suggest, that women themselves are the best judges of what comports with female propriety, and I see no difficulty or inconvenience in leaving the matter entirely to their own taste, and sense of duty. Leave out the word *male*, then those ladies who think proper, can go to the polls, and those who do not choose to go, can stay at home; in this respect placing them on the same footing with ourselves. I know it is also said, that there is something so essentially bad and corrupting in politics, and especially that at the places of holding elections, such angry passions are exhibited, and such vulgar and indelicate language employed, that no woman possessed of feminine delicacy could mingle in politics, or go to the polls. I do not believe in the corrupting tendency of political duties, or associations, but if what is said, be true, it furnishes an equally strong reason, why men should abstain from every thing political, and fathers should exhort their sons, neither to handle nor touch the unclean thing. I do admit that there is much that is improper in political strife, and much that is unbecoming said, and done in political meetings, and at the polls, and this to my mind, furnishes the strongest proof of the necessity of woman's influence and presence, for men always behave like barbarians, when deprived of the refining and moralizing influence of woman. I wish then to admit woman to political life, not to make woman worse, but to make politics better of which it is confessed there is some necessity. At the present time, ladies can accompany their husbands or fathers or brothers to church, or public lectures, or entertainments, without fear of receiving any offence or molestation, and I do not see why they could not as safely accompany the same persons to the ballot box.

I do not suppose that the ballot box is the sole panacea for all the sufferings to which woman is exposed; for she suffers from social, as well as from political wrongs. She ought to be admitted by custom, to receive an equal education, with her brother man; and various kinds of profitable employment ought to be opened to her, from which she is now by custom excluded; but for such evils this convention cannot directly provide no remedy, we may however, restore to her, the rights of which she has heretofore been deprived; with such intention I shall vote for the motion.

Mr. WOODBURY demanded the yeas and nays, which were ordered, and resulted, yeas 7, nays 72. . . .

So the amendment was rejected. . . .

1. See J. V. Smith, Official Reporter to the Convention, *Report of the Debates and Proceedings of the Convention for the Revision of the Constitution of the State of Ohio, 1850-51* (Columbus, 1851), 2:11–13. Also, Thomas H. Smith, ed., *An Ohio Reader, 1750 to the Civil War* (Grand Rapids, Mich.: Eerdmans, 1975), 176–78.

2. A delegate from Auglaize County, William Sawyer was a blacksmith by trade.

3. James W. Taylor, a delegate from Erie County, was a newspaper editor.

4. A physician by profession, Dr. Norton S. Townshend was a delegate from Lorain County.

5. Isaac F. Patterson, *The Constitution of Ohio: Amendments, and Proposed Amendments* (Cleveland, 1912), 135. This was the wording proposed by the Committee on the Elective Franchise at the Ohio Constitutional Convention of 1851 and ultimately incorporated in the Constitution of 1851.

6. See Smith, *Report of the Debates and Proceedings,* 2:550–55.

7. John L. Green, a delegate from Ross County, was a lawyer.

8. Reuben Hitchcock, one of two delegates from Cuyahoga County, was another lawyer.

9. Delegate S. Humphreville, also a lawyer, represented Medina County.

10. E. B. Woodbury, yet another attorney, represented Ashtabula County.

VIII.4. Following the North Star: The Narrative of a Fugitive Slave, Josiah Henson

"I knew the North Star—blessed be God for setting it in the heavens! Like the Star of Bethlehem, it announced where my salvation lay. Could I follow it through forest, and stream, and field, it would guide my feet in the way of hope. I thought of it as my God-given guide to the land of promise far away beneath its light. I knew that it had led thousands of my poor, hunted brethren to freedom and blessedness."[1]

So wrote the Reverend Josiah Henson in a later reflection on the planning and dreaming that had preceded his decision to leave behind a life of bondage and, with his wife and four children, follow the Underground Railroad to a new life in Canada. Of the thousands of fugitive slaves who passed through Ohio on the "freedom road," Henson is certainly one of the best known. With the aid of Hiram Wilson, an Oberlin College graduate who had earlier transferred from the Lane Seminary in Cincinnati in protest to that institution's restrictions on antislavery protests and had then moved to Canada to help found schools for the growing free black community, Henson helped establish (with others) the British American Institute for Fugitive Slaves in 1841 in Dresden, Ontario. But it was the several editions of his autobiography (first published in 1849) that earned for Henson his greatest measure of fame.

Yale historian Robin W. Winks has noted: "Of the many narratives written for, and on occasion by, fugitive slaves who fled from the United States to the provinces of British North America before the Civil War, no single book has been so widely read, so frequently revised, and so influential as the autobiography of Josiah Henson. For Henson came to be identified with one of the best known figures in Nineteenth Century American literature, the venerable and self-sacrificing Uncle Tom of Harriet Beecher Stowe's most famous novel. To the popular mind then, and to many people now, Henson was undeniably Tom, the very figure from whom Mrs. Stowe borrowed large elements of plot and characterization, the figure who came to symbolize the successful fugitive, the man who permanently settled in Canada and there won fame, if not fortune, and a permanent place in the history of the abolitionist struggle."[2]

Born a slave in Charles County, Maryland, on 15 June 1789, Josiah Henson was owned at various times by three different individuals. Crippled for life as a youth when beaten by an enemy of one of his masters, he became a Methodist preacher while still a slave and served churches in Kentucky for three years, hoping thereby to earn enough money to buy his freedom. When his master more than doubled the previously agreed-on price for his freedom, however, Henson determined to leave Kentucky with his wife and four children and make his way to Canada. In his autobiography he details their experience in crossing Ohio from Cincinnati to Sandusky and crossing Lake Erie by steamer to Buffalo and then on to Canada.[3]

JOURNEY TO CANADA.

[On reaching Cincinnati] I now felt comparatively at home. Before entering the town I hid my wife and children in the woods, and then walked on alone in search of my friends [abolitionists involved in the Underground Railroad]. They welcomed me warmly, and just after dusk my wife and children were brought in, and we found our-selves hospitably cheered and refreshed. Two weeks of exposure to incessant fatigue, anxiety, rain, and chill, made it indescribably sweet to enjoy once more the comfort of rest and shelter.

I have sometimes heard harsh and bitter words spoken of those devoted men who were banded together to succour and bid God speed to the hunted fugitive; men who, through pity for the suffering, voluntarily exposed themselves to hatred, fines, and im-prisonment. If there be a God who will have mercy on the merciful, great will be their reward. In the great day when men shall stand in judgment before the Divine Master, crowds of the outcast and forsaken of earth, will gather around them, and in joyful tones bear witness, "We were hungry and ye gave us meat, thirsty and ye gave us drink, naked and ye clothed us, sick and ye visited us." And He Who has declared that, "in-asmuch as ye have done it unto the least of these My brethren, ye have done it unto Me," will accept the attestation, and hail them with His welcome, "Come ye blessed of My Father." Their glory shall yet be proclaimed from the house-tops, and may that "peace of God which the world can neither give nor take away" dwell richly in their hearts!

Among such as those—good Samaritans, of whom the Lord would say, "Go ye and do likewise,"—our lot was now cast. Carefully they provided for our welfare until our strength was recruited, and then they set us thirty miles on our way by waggon.

We followed the same course as before—traveling by night and resting by day—till we arrived at the Scioto, where we had been told we should strike the military road of General Hull, made in the last war with Great Britain, and might then safely travel by day. We found the road, accordingly, by the large sycamore and elms which marked its beginning, and entered upon it with fresh spirits early in the day. Nobody had told us that it was cut through the wilderness, and I had neglected to provide any food, thinking we should soon come to some habitation, where we could be supplied. But we travelled on all day without seeing one, and lay down at night, hungry and weary enough. The wolves were howling around us, and though too cowardly to approach, their noise terrified my poor wife and children. Nothing remained to us in the morning but a little piece of dried beef, too little, indeed, to satisfy our cravings, but enough to afflict us with intolerable thirst. I divided most of this amongst us, and then we started for a second day's tramp in the wilderness. A painful day it was to us. The road was rough, the underbrush tore our clothes and exhausted our strength; trees that had been blown down, blocked the way; we were faint with hunger, and no prospect of relief opened up before us. We spoke little, but steadily struggled along; I with my babes on my back, my wife aiding the two other children to climb over the fallen trunks and force themselves through the briers. Suddenly, as I was plodding along a little ahead of my wife and the boys, I heard them call me, and turning round saw my wife prostrate on the ground. "Mother's dying," cried Tom; and when I reached her, it seemed really so. From sheer exhaustion she had fallen in surmounting a log. Distracted with anxiety, I feared she was gone. for some minutes no sign of life was manifest; but after a time she opened her eyes, and finally recovering enough to take a few mouthfuls of the beef, her strength returned, and we once more went bravely on our way. I cheered the sad group with hopes I was far from sharing myself. For the first time I was nearly ready to abandon myself to despair. Starvation in the wilderness was the doom that stared me and mine in the face. But again, "man's extremity was God's opportunity."

We had not gone far, and I suppose it was about three o'clock in the afternoon, when we discerned some persons approaching us at no great distance. We were instantly on the alert, as we could hardly expect them to be friends. The advance of a few paces showed me they were Indians, with packs on their shoulders; and they were so near that if they were hostile it would be useless to try to escape. So I walked along coldly, till we came close upon them. They were bent down with their burdens, and had not raised their eyes till now; and when they did so, and saw me coming towards them, they looked at me in a frightened sort of way for a moment, and then, setting up a peculiar howl, turned round, and ran as fast as they could. There were three or four of them, and what they were afraid of I could not imagine. There was no doubt they were frightened, and we heard their wild and prolonged howl, as they ran, for a mile or more. My wife was alarmed, too, and thought they were merely running back to collect more of a party, and then would come and murder us; and she wanted to turn back. I told her they were numerous enough to do that, if they wanted to, without help; and that as for turning back, I had had quite too much of the road behind us, and that it would be a ridiculous thing that both parties should run away. If they were disposed to run, I would follow. We did follow, and the noise soon ceased. As we advanced, we could discover Indians peeping at us from behind the trees, and dodging out of sight if they thought we were looking at them. Presently we came upon their wigwams, and saw a fine-looking, stately Indian, with his arms folded, waiting for us to approach. He was, apparently, the chief; and saluting us civilly, he soon discovered we were human beings, and spoke to his young men, who were scattered about, and made them come in and give up their foolish fears. And now curiosity seemed to prevail. Each one wanted to touch the children, who were as shy as partridges with their long life in the woods; and as they shrunk away, and uttered a little cry of alarm, the Indian would jump back too, as if he thought they would bite him. However, a little while sufficed to make them understand whither we were going, and what we needed; and then they supplied our wants, fed us bountifully, and gave us a comfortable wigwam for our night's rest. The next day we resumed our march, having ascertained from the Indians that we were only about twenty-five miles from the lake. They sent some of their young men to point out the place where we were to turn off, and parted from us with as much kindness as possible.

In passing over the part of Ohio near the lake, where such an extensive plain is found, we came to a spot overflowed by a stream, across which the road passed. I forded it first, with the help of a sounding-pole, and then taking the children on my back, first the two little ones, and then the others, one at a time, and, lastly, my wife, I succeeded in getting them safely across. At this time the skin was worn from my back to an extent almost equal to the size of the knapsack.

One more night was passed in the woods, and in the course of the next forenoon, we came out upon the wide, treeless plain which lies south and west of Sandusky city. The houses of the village were in plain sight. About a mile from the lake I hid my wife and children in the bushes, and pushed forward. I was attracted by a house on the left, between which and a small coasting vessel, a number of men were passing and repassing with great activity. Promptly deciding to approach them, I drew near, and scarcely had I come within hailing distance, when the captain of the schooner cried out, "Hollo there, man! you want to work?" "Yes sir!" shouted I. "Come along, come along; I'll give you a shilling an hour. Must get off with this wind." As I came near, he said, "Oh, you can't work; you're crippled." "Can't I?" said I; and in a minute I had hold of a bag of corn, and followed the gang in emptying it into the hold. I took my place in the line of labourers next to a coloured man, and soon got into conversation with him. "How far is it to Canada?" He gave me a peculiar look, and in a minute I saw he knew all. "Want to go to Canada? Come along with us, then. Our captain's a fine fellow. We're going to Buffalo." "Buffalo; how far is that from Canada?" "Don't you know, man? Just across the river." I now opened my mind frankly to him, and told him about my wife and children. "I'll speak to the captain," said he. He did so, and in a moment the captain took me aside, and said, "The Doctor says you want to go to Buffalo with your family." "Yes, sir." "Well, why not go with me!" was his frank reply. "Doctor says you've got a family." "Yes, sir." "Where do you stop?" "About a mile back." "How long have you been here?" "No time," I answered, after a moment's hesitation. "Come, my good fellow, tell us all about it. You're running away, ain't you?" I saw he was a friend, and opened my heart to him. "How long will it take you to get ready?" "Be here in half an hour, sir." "Well, go along and get them." Off I started; but before I had run fifty feet, he called me back. "Stop," said he; "you go on getting the grain in. When we get off, I'll lay to over opposite that island, and send a boat back. There's a lot of regular nigger-catchers in the town below, and they might suspect you if you brought your party out of the bush by daylight." I worked away with a will. Soon the two or three hundred bushels of corn were aboard, the hatches fastened down, the anchor raised, and the sails hoisted.

I watched the vessel with intense interest as she left her moorings. Away she went before the free breeze. Already she seemed beyond the spot at which the captain agreed to lay to, and still she flew along. My heart sank within me; so near deliverance, and again to have my hopes blasted, again to be cast on my own resources! I felt that they had been making sport of my misery. The sun had sunk to rest, and the purple and gold of the west were fading away into grey. Suddenly, however, as I gazed with a weary heart, the vessel swung round into the wind, the sails flapped, and she stood motionless. A moment more, and a boat was lowered from her stern, and with a steady stroke made for the point at which I stood. I felt that my hour of release had come. On she came, and in ten minutes she rode up handsomely on to the beach.

My black friend and two sailors jumped out, and we started off at once for my wife and children. To my horror, they were gone from the place where I left them. Overpowered with fear, I supposed they had been found and carried off. There was no time to lose, and the men told me I would have to go alone. Just at the point of despair, however, I stumbled on one of the children. My wife, it seemed, alarmed at my long absence, had given up all for lost, and supposed I had fallen into the hands of the enemy. When she heard my voice, mingled with those of the others, she thought my captors were leading me back to make me discover my family, and in the extremity of her terror

she had tried to hide herself. I had hard work to satisfy her. Our long habits of conceal-
ment and anxiety had rendered her suspicious of every one; and her agitation was so
great that for a time she was incapable of understanding what I said, and went on in a
sort of paroxysm of distress and fear. This, however, was soon over, and the kindness of
my companions did much to facilitate the matter.

And now we were off for the boat. It required little time to embark our baggage—
one convenience, at least, of having nothing. The men bent their backs with a will, and
headed steadily for a light hung from the vessel's mast. I was praising God in my soul.
Three hearty cheers welcomed us as we reached the schooner, and never till my dying
day shall I forget the shout of the captain—he was a Scotchman—"Coom up on deck,
and clop your wings and craw like a rooster; you're a free nigger as sure as you're a live
mon." Round went the vessel, the wind plunged into her sails as though innoculated
with the common feeling—the water seethed and hissed past her sides. Man and nature,
and, more than all, I felt the God of man and nature, who breathes love into the heart
and maketh the winds His ministers, were with us. My happiness that night rose at
times to positive pain. Unnerved by so sudden a change from destitution and danger to
such kindness and blessed security, I wept like a child.

The next evening we reached Buffalo, but it was too late to cross the river that
night. "You see those trees," said the noble-hearted captain, next morning, pointing to
a group in the distance; "they grow on free soil, and as soon as your feet touch that,
you're a *mon.* I want to see you go and be a freeman. I'm poor myself, and have nothing
to give you; I only sail the boat for wages; but I'll see you across. Here, Green," said he
to a ferryman, "What will you take this man and his family over for—he's got no
money?" "Three shillings." He then took a dollar out of his pocket and gave it to me.
Never shall I forget the spirit in which he spoke. He put his hand on my head and said,
"Be a good fellow, won't you?" I felt streams of emotion running down in electric
courses from heat to foot. "Yes," said I; "I'll use my freedom well; I'll give my soul to
God." He stood waving his hat as we pushed off for the opposite shore. God bless him!
God bless him eternally! Amen!

It was the 28th of October, 1830, in the morning, when my feet first touched the
Canada shore. I threw myself on the ground, rolled in the sand, seized handfuls of it and
kissed them, and danced around, till, in the eyes of several who were present, I passed
for a madman. "He's some crazy fellow," said a Colonel Warren, who happened to be
there. "Oh, no, master! don't you know? I'm free!" He burst into a shout of laughter.
"Well, I never knew freedom make a man roll in the sand in such a fashion." Still I could
not control myself. I hugged and kissed my wife and children, and, until the first exu-
berant burst of feeling was over, went on as before.

1. John Lobb, ed., *An Autobiography of the Rev. Josiah Henson* (London, Ontario, 1881),
59. See Robin W. Winks, gen. ed., *Four Fugitive Slave Narratives* (Reading, Mass.: Addison-
Wesley, 1969), in which the 1881 edition of the Henson autobiography has been reprinted.

2. Winks, *Four Fugitive Slave Narratives,* v (introduction).

3. Ibid., 64–70.

VIII.5. Harriet Beecher Stowe and *Uncle Tom's Cabin*

Of all the activists in the antislavery crusade, few if any caused as much stir as did Harriet Beecher Stowe when in 1852 her novel Uncle Tom's Cabin *was published. With sales reaching into the millions of copies, her book became one of the all-time best-selling novels, not only in the United States but also in England and Canada. Until it was published, the quarrel over slavery between northern and southern states had been expressed primarily in political and economic terms. It was Stowe's* Uncle Tom's Cabin *that made slavery a moral issue as well.*

Born and educated in New England and sister to one of abolitionism's foremost evangelists, Henry Ward Beecher, Harriet Beecher Stowe came out to Ohio when her father, Lyman Beecher, accepted the presidency of the Lane Theological Seminary in Cincinnati. There she met and married one of the seminary professors, Calvin Stowe, in 1836, and there, in close proximity to Kentucky, she had opportunity not only to witness firsthand the activities of the Underground Railroad in aiding fugitive slaves but also to visit homes in Kentucky from which some of them were trying to escape. From these experiences came many of the scenes and the characters described in her book. One of these, Eliza Harris, a young slave who feared possible separation from her young son were her master to sell him, escaped to the safety of the home of the Reverend John Rankin in Ripley, Ohio, her son in her arms, by hopping across floes of ice on the Ohio River in the dead of winter, her pursuers close behind. Rankin, a Presbyterian minister living high above the river in a house reached by a long flight of stairs dubbed "liberty's staircase," kept a lantern shining every night as a beacon to fugitive slaves. The busiest station on the underground, the Rankin home provided shelter to nearly three thousand runaways from the late 1820s to the Civil War. None was more famed than Eliza Harris, whose epic escape across the Ohio River was told to Harriet Beecher Stowe, a frequent visitor in the Rankin home, who then immortalized the brave young woman in the pages of Uncle Tom's Cabin.[1]

Mrs. Stowe's vivid character portrayals—Eliza, Little Eva, Topsy, the kindly Uncle Tom, and the villainous Simon Legree—together with her descriptions of the treatment the slaves endured, aroused the sympathies and antislavery feelings of many in the North while invoking howls of rage across the South. In recognition of the polarizing role her book had played in helping to bring on the Civil War, President Abraham Lincoln, when meeting Harriet Beecher Stowe for the first time, is reported to have said, "So this is the little woman who made this big war."

The Mother's Struggle.

It is impossible to conceive of a human creature more wholly desolate and forlorn than Eliza, when she turned her footsteps from Uncle Tom's cabin.

Her husband's suffering and dangers, and the danger of her child, all blended in her mind, with a confused and stunning sense of the risk she was running, in leaving the only home she had ever known, and cutting loose from the protection of a friend whom she loved and revered. Then there was the parting from every familiar object,—the place where she had grown up, the trees under which she had played, the groves where she had walked many an evening in happier days, by the side of her young husband, — everything, as it lay in the clear, frosty starlight, seemed to speak reproachfully to her, and ask her whither she could go from a home like that?

But stronger than all was maternal love, wrought into a paroxysm of frenzy by the near approach of a fearful danger. Her boy was old enough to have walked by her side, and, in an indifferent case, she would only have led him by the hand; but now the bare thought of putting him out of her arms made her shudder, and she strained him to her bosom with a convulsive grasp, as she went rapidly forward.

The frosty ground creaked beneath her feet, and she trembled at the sound; every quaking leaf and fluttering shadow sent the blood backward to her heart, and quickened her footsteps. She wondered within herself at the strength that seemed to be come upon her; for she felt the weight of her boy as if it had been a feather, and every flutter of fear seemed to increase the supernatural power that bore her on, while from her pale lips burst forth, in frequent ejaculations, the prayer to a Friend above, — "Lord, help! Lord, save me!"

If it were *your* Harry, mother, or your Willie, that were going to be torn from you by a brutal trader, to-morrow morning, — if you had been the man, and heard that the papers were signed and delivered, and you had only from twelve o'clock till morning to make good your escape, — how fast could *you* walk? How many miles could you make in those few brief hours, with the darling at your bosom, — the little sleepy head on your shoulder, — the small, soft arms trustingly holding on to your neck? . . .

The boundaries of the farm, the grove, the wood-lot, passed by her dizzily, as she walked on; and still she went, leaving one familiar object after another, slacking not, pausing not, till reddening daylight found her many a long mile from all traces of any familiar objects upon the open highway.

She had often been, with her mistress, to visit some connections, in the little village of T____, not far from the Ohio River, and knew the road well. To go thither, to escape across the Ohio River, were the first hurried outlines of her plan of escape; beyond that, she could only hope in God. . . .

An hour before sunset, she entered the village of T____, by the Ohio River, weary and footsore, but still strong in heart. Her first glance was at the river, which lay, like Jordan, between her and the Canaan of liberty on the other side.

It was now early spring, and the river was swollen and turbulent; great cakes of floating ice were swinging heavily to and fro in the turbid waters. Owing to the peculiar form of the shore on the Kentucky side, the land bending far out into the water, the ice had been lodged and detained in great quantities, and the narrow channel which swept round the bend was full of ice, piled one cake over another, thus forming a temporary barrier to the descending ice, which lodged, and formed a great undulating raft, filling up the whole river, and extending almost to the Kentucky shore.

Eliza stood, for a moment, contemplating this unfavorable aspect of things, which she saw at once must prevent the usual ferry-boat from running, and then turned into a small public house [tavern] on the bank, to make a few inquiries.

The hostess, who was busy in various fizzing and stewing operations over the fire, preparatory to the evening meal, stopped, with a fork in her hand, as Eliza's sweet and plaintive voice arrested her.

"What is it?" she said.

"Isn't there any ferry or boat, that takes people over to B_____, now?" she said.

"No, indeed!" said the woman; "the boats has stopped running."

Eliza's look of dismay and disappointment struck the woman, and she said, in-quiringly, —

"May be you're wanting to get over? — anybody sick? Ye seem mighty anxious?"

"I've got a child that's very dangerous," said Eliza. "I never heard of it till last night, and I've walked quite a piece today, in hopes to get to the ferry."

"Well, now, that's onlucky," said the woman, whose motherly sympathies were much aroused; "I'm re'lly consarned for ye. Solomon!" she called, from the window, to-wards a small back building. A man, in leather apron and very dirty hands, appeared at the door.

"I say, Sol," said the woman, "is that ar man going to tote them bar'ls over to-night?"

"He said he should try, if 't was any way prudent," said the man.

"There's a man a piece down here, that's going over with some truck this evening, if he durs' to; he'll be in here to supper to-night, so you'd better set down and wait. That's a sweet little fellow," added the woman, offering him a cake.

But the child, wholly exhausted, cried with weariness.

"Poor fellow! he isn't used to walking, and I've hurried him on so," said Eliza.

"Well, take him into this room," said the woman, opening into a small bedroom, where stood a comfortable bed. Eliza laid the weary boy upon it, and held his hands in hers till he was fast asleep. For her there was no rest. As a fire in her bones, the thought of the pursuer urged her on; and she gazed with longing eyes on the sullen, surging wa-ters that lay between her and liberty. . . .

. . . it was about three quarters of an hour after Eliza had laid her child to sleep in the village tavern that the [pursuing] party came riding into the same place. Eliza was standing by the window, looking out in another direction, when Sam's quick eye caught a glimpse of her. Haley [the white slave-trader] and Andy [a black slave] were two yards behind. At this crisis, Sam [a black slave] contrived to have his hat blown off, and ut-tered a loud and characteristic ejaculation, which startled her at once; she drew suddenly back; the whole train swept by the window, round to the front door.

A thousand lives seemed to be concentrated in that one moment to Eliza. Her room opened by a side door to the river. She caught her child, and sprang down the steps towards it. The trader caught a full glimpse of her, just as she was disappearing down the bank, and throwing himself from his horse, and calling loudly on Sam and Andy, he was after her like a hound after a deer. In that dizzy moment her feet to her scarce seemed to touch the ground, and a moment brought her to the water's edge. Right on behind they came; and, nerved with strength such as God gives only to the des-perate, with one wild cry and flying leap, she vaulted sheer over the turbid current by the shore, on the raft of ice beyond. It was a desperate leap, — impossible to anything but madness and despair; and Haley, Sam, and Andy instinctively cried out, and lifted up their hands, as she did it.

The huge green fragment of ice on which she alighted pitched and creaked as her weight came on it, but she stayed there not a moment. With wild cries and desperate energy she leaped to another and still another cake;—stumbling,—leaping,—slipping,—springing upwards again! Her shoes are gone,—her stockings cut from her feet,—while blood marked every step; but she saw nothing, felt nothing, till dimly, as in a dream, she saw the Ohio side, and a man helping her up the bank.

"Yer a brave gal, now, whoever ye ar!" said the man, with an oath.

Eliza recognized the voice and face of a man who owned a farm not far from her old home.

"Oh, Mr. Symmes!—save me,—do save me,—do hide me!" said Eliza.

"Why, what's this?" said the man. "Why, if 't an't Shelby's gal!"

"My child!—this boy!—he'd sold him! There is his Mas'r," said she, pointing to the Kentucky shore. "Oh, Mr. Symmes, you've got a little boy!"

"So I have," said the man, as he roughly, but kindly, drew her up the steep bank. "Besides, you're a right brave gal. I like grit, wherever I see it."

When they had gained the top of the bank, the man paused. "I'd be glad to do something for ye," said he: "but then there's nowhar I could take ye. The best I can do is to tell ye to go *thar*," said he, pointing to a large white house which stood by itself, off the main street of the village. "Go thar; they're kind folks. Thar's no kind o' danger but they'll help you,—they 're up to all that sort o' thing."

"The Lord bless you!" said Eliza earnestly.

"No 'casion, no'casion in the world," said the man. "What I've done 's of no 'count."

"And oh, surely, sir, you won't tell any one!"

"Go to thunder, gal! What do you take a feller for? In course not," said the man. "Come, now, go along like a likely, sensible gal, as you are. You 've arnt your liberty, and you shall have it, for all me."

The woman folded her child to her bosom, and walked firmly and swiftly away. . . .

1. Harriet Beecher Stowe, *Uncle Tom's Cabin; or, Life among the Lowly,* first published in serial form in the antislavery paper *National Era* of Washington, D.C., 1851–52, and in book form in 1852.

VIII.6. The Oberlin-Wellington Rescue Case, 1858–1859

Out of the Compromise of 1850 came the Federal Fugitive Slave Law of that same year, and from that law came a mounting number of incidents involving not only fugitive slaves but also freed blacks being seized by southern slave catchers supported by federal marshals or being aided by sympathetic abolitionists in their efforts to escape. With cotton culture dominant in the southern economy and with a good field hand bringing up to two thousand dollars in slave markets, careful distinction was not always made between the capture of fugitives and the kidnapping of free men.

The "Oberlin-Wellington Rescue Case" was called the classic case in litigation under the Federal Fugitive Slave Law. Dubiously claimed to be the property of John G. Bacon of

Maysville, Kentucky, one John Price, then living in Oberlin, was seized by Anderson Jennings, a slave hunter from Maysville, with the help of U.S. Deputy Marshal A. P. Dayton of Oberlin on 13 September 1858 and taken to a hotel in the nearby village of Wellington to await the five o'clock train heading south. Learning of the capture of Price, a crowd of Oberlin students, faculty, and townsfolk descended by buggy and wagon on Wellington. Augmented by citizens of that village, they surrounded the hotel and liberated the captive. Hidden overnight in Oberlin in the attic of the home of Prof. James H. Fairchild, John Price was taken the next day to a lake port, where he boarded a steamer and made the crossing to Canada.

Thirty-seven men were ultimately indicted for violation of the Fugitive Slave Law in what came to be called the "Oberlin-Wellington Rescue Case." Of these, twenty-one were from Oberlin and sixteen from Wellington. In the trial that followed in April 1859, in the federal district court in Cleveland, the first two to be tried, Simeon Bushnell, a white man, and Charles H. Langston, a man of mixed blood (described as "Anglo-Saxon, Native American, and African"), were found guilty and jailed. The cases were then appealed to the Ohio Supreme Court to determine whether the men were legally held. At issue was the constitutionality of the Federal Fugitive Slave Law of 1850, under which they had been tried and convicted. By a vote of three to two, the Ohio Supreme Court found the law to be constitutional and refused to intervene in behalf of the prisoners.

On 11 May 1859, Bushnell was sentenced to sixty days' imprisonment and ordered to pay a fine of six hundred dollars. Owing in large part to his impassioned plea on behalf of the poor and oppressed,[1] said by onlookers to be "the most eloquent and effective speech made during the entire proceedings," Charles Langston drew a fine of only one hundred dollars and imprisonment for only twenty days. Charges were then dropped against the remaining thirty-five defendants, enabling abolitionists across the state and nation to proclaim a great "victory" as the outcome of the rescue case.

Eulogizing Charles Langston, who emerged as a martyr in the cause of freedom in this celebrated case, the Cleveland Leader *on 13 May 1859 predicted that his eloquent statement before sentencing in the federal court "would live in history. The children of the Free will read it in their school books and will execrate the memory of the Court and the Jury who consigned such a man to fine and imprisonment for a crime so God like!"*

THE STATEMENT OF CHARLES LANGSTON.

*T*he law under which I am arraigned is an unjust one, one made to crush the colored man, and one that outrages every feeling of Humanity, as well as every rule of Right. . . . I remember the excitement that prevailed throughout all the free States when it was passed; and I remember how often it has been said by individuals, conventions, communities and legislatures, that it never could be, never should be, and never was meant to be, enforced.

But I have another reason to offer why I should not be sentenced. . . . I have not had a trial before a jury of my peers. . . . The Constitution of the United States guarantees—not merely to its citizens—but to *all persons* a trial before an *impartial jury.* I have had no such trial. The colored man is oppressed by certain universal and deeply fixed *prejudices.* Those jurors are well known to have shared largely in these prejudices, and I therefore consider that they were neither impartial, nor were they a jury of my peers. And the prejudices which white people have against colored men grow out of this fact; that we have, as a people, consented for two hundred years to be *slaves* of the whites. We have been scourged, crushed, and cruelly oppressed and have submitted to it all tamely, meekly, peaceably; I mean as a people, and with rare individual exceptions. . . . And while our people as a people submit, they will as a people be despised. . . . The jury came into the box with that feeling. They knew that they had that feeling and so the Court knows now, and knew then. The gentlemen who prosecute me have that feeling, the Court itself has that feeling and even the counsel who defended me have that feeling. . . .

Some persons may say that there is no danger of free persons being seized and carried off as slaves. No one need labor under such a delusion, sir, *four* of the eight persons who were first carried back under the act of 1850, were afterwards proved to be *free men.* The pretended owner declared that they were not his, after his agent had 'satisfied the Commissioner' that they were by his oath. They were free persons, but wholly at the mercy of the oath of one man. . . . A letter was not long since found upon the person of a counterfeiter when arrested, addressed to him by some Southern Gentleman in which the writer says: *'Go among the niggers; find out their marks and scars; make good descriptions and send to me, and I'll find masters for 'em.'*

That is the way men are carried *'back'* to slavery.

But I stand up here to say, that if for doing what I did on that day at Wellington, I am to go in jail for six months and pay a fine of a thousand dollars, according to the Fugitive Slave Law, and such is the protection the laws of this country afford me, I must take upon myself the responsibility of self-protection; and when I come to be claimed by some perjured wretch as his slave, I shall never be taken into slavery.

I stand here to say that I will do all I can, for any man thus seized and held, though the inevitable penalty of six months imprisonment and one thousand dollars fine for each offence hangs over me. We have a common humanity. You would do so; your manhood would require it; and no matter what the laws might be, you would honor yourself for doing it; your friends would honor you for doing it; your children through all generations would honor you for doing it; and every good and honest man would say, you had done *right!*

[Great and prolonged applause, in spite of the efforts of the Court and the Marshal.]

1. See William C. Cochrane, "The Oberlin-Wellington Rescue Case," in *The Western Reserve and the Fugitive Slave Law: A Prelude to the Civil War,* Publication No. 101, *Collections, The Western Reserve Historical Society* (Cleveland, Ohio, 1920), 152-57.

VIII.7. John Brown: "His Soul Goes Marching On"

With the markets of the world demanding more and more southern cotton, which in turn demanded more and more land, the burning issue of the 1850s came to be whether or not the territories of the west should be opened to "King Cotton" and the institution on which it rested, slavery. With the passage of the Kansas-Nebraska Act in 1854, territories made free "forever" from slavery by the Missouri Compromise of 1820 were now opened to the possibility of slavery if their people should so decide. Unleashed by the new law was a succession of events that led inexorably toward civil conflict. Political parties disappeared or were realigned. The Whig Party faded into memory, to be replaced by a new party with an old name, "Republican," a party primarily based in the North. It was in Ohio that the first governor would be elected under its banner, Salmon P. Chase, in 1855. And it was in the Kansas Territory that another Ohioan, John Brown, would help make the expression "Bleeding Kansas" a reality, as extremists from both sides of the slavery question flocked to the territory ostensibly to vote slavery up or down, but ultimately to turn to bullets rather than ballots to defend their points of view.

When the administration of President James Buchanan eventually sought to concede Kansas to the supporters of slavery, John Brown put in motion a plan he had formulated as early as 1851 to liberate southern slaves by seizing and holding a mountain stronghold in the South as a sanctuary for runaways. With eleven white and thirty-five black associates, Brown held a convention in the spring of 1859 in Chatham, Ontario, to adopt a "Provisional Constitution and Ordinance for the People of the United States," which proclaimed the end of slavery and under which Brown proclaimed himself commander in chief. The longtime resident of Hudson, Kent, and Akron then returned to Ohio, to headquarters in West Andover in Ashtabula County, where rifles and other materials of war were accumulated in a cabinet factory. From that base and from a farm he purchased not far from the federal arsenal at Harpers Ferry, Virginia, John Brown and a small group of followers conducted a raid on the night of 16 October 1859 which succeeded in capturing the arsenal. With sixty of the town's citizens as hostages, Brown and his men held off counterattacks until 18 October, when a detachment of U.S. Marines commanded by Colonel Robert E. Lee stormed the arsenal, killing ten of Brown's men (including two of his sons) and taking seven prisoners, one of whom was the wounded John Brown. U.S. losses included five men killed and nine injured.

Imprisoned at the Charlestown jail, Brown was convicted on 31 October 1859 of "treason and conspiring and advising with slaves and other rebels, and murder in the first degree." Despite appeals from abolitionists from across the North that his life be spared, and notwithstanding dire predictions that in death he would be far more dangerous to the cause of peace and national unity than he would be alive, John Brown "mounted the scaffold with the step of a conqueror" and was executed by hanging at Charlestown on 2 December 1859.

"Someone has said that if John Brown had been killed at the engine house at Harpers Ferry his epitaph would have been a score of lines in the newspapers to be forgotten in as many days, like the record of a desperado who dies by the law against which he raises a violent hand. He lived six weeks and by his bearing, his conversation and his letters won his great battle and the meed of martyrdom. In those forty-five days this son of Connecticut, this tanner, shepherd and farmer of Ohio, showed how he could fearlessly live for a principle and triumphantly die for it. That principle itself was soon to triumph in the Republic and give John Brown a permanent place in history." [1]

THE DEATH OF JOHN BROWN.

*W*hen he left the jail on his way to the place of execution, John Brown handed to a reporter his last written statement:

"I, John Brown, am now quite certain that the crimes of this guilty land will never be purged but with blood. I had, as I now think vainly, flattered myself that without very much bloodshed it might be done."

Victor Hugo, Edmund C. Stedman, William Dean Howells, Wendell Phillips, Ralph Waldo Emerson, Moncure D. Conway and scores of other prominent men united in declaring that the execution of Brown would ring the knell of slavery.

It is remarkable how that event brought together many of the actors in the mighty conflict soon to be. Over the gallows at Charlestown the hand of Fate wrought a paradox. Hither came to witness the execution Col. Robert E. Lee, in a uniform of blue, soon to be exchanged for one of gray and the rank of commander-in-chief of the armies of the southern Confederacy. There was Governor Henry A. Wise, and there in the ranks of the Virginia troops was his promising son, the former to rise to the rank of brigadier general and the latter to lose his life in the service of the Confederacy. At the head of the cadets from Lexington stood stalwart Thomas J. Jackson, destined to become the Stonewall Jackson of history and to fall on the field of Chancellorsville. . . .While there with the Richmond troops, that wayward evil genius, John Wilkes Booth, witnessed an act which was to pale into insignificance compared to his murderous deed that plunged the Republic into woe and shocked the civilized world. . . .

And all these were here to punish treason — to vindicate and uphold the majesty of the law of the United States and the commonwealth of Virginia.

Fate turned the kaleidoscope, and lo! all these by the same token became themselves traitors and boldly joined an insurrection to rend the Union asunder! . . .

Swiftly, with startling and dramatic sequence, the scenes shifted on the stage of history. Eighteen months after John Brown mounted the scaffold with the step of a conqueror and stood unawed with the hangman's rope around his neck, the Twelfth Massachusetts Regiment was on its way South to put down the rebellion and singing as it went:

> "John Brown's body lies a' moldering in the grave,
> But his soul goes marching on."

And the chorus of this battle song went on from Bull Run to Appomattox. . . .

1. Quoted in Charles B. Galbreath, *History of Ohio* (Chicago, 1925), 2:296; the selection is on pages 300–301 of the same source.

IX. Civil War and Reconstruction

It can be said that the martyrdom of John Brown did much to elect Abraham Lincoln to the presidency in 1860, even though Lincoln disapproved of Brown's radical stand on abolition and denounced his raid on Harpers Ferry. Brown's death left little room for neutrality on the question of slavery's extension into the territories and hastened the split in the Democratic Party between Northern (Douglas) and Southern (Breckenridge) wings. In turn it solidified Republican opposition to further concessions to the South. With the division of the Democrats, Lincoln was elected with a minority of the total vote cast, and with his election Southern leaders concluded their interests no longer could expect the protection of the federal government. Even before Lincoln was sworn in as president of the United States, Jefferson Davis of Mississippi had been inaugurated as president of the secessionist Confederate States of America. When Lincoln refused to withdraw federal forces from Southern stations, civil conflict was forced with the bombardment of Fort Sumter in Charleston Harbor by Confederate shore batteries on 12 April 1861.

Lincoln's decision to preserve the Union by suppressing the rebellion in the South was supported by a majority of Ohioans. His call on 19 April 1861 for seventy-five thousand volunteers for ninety days of service to put down the insurrection could have been met within the month by that many in Ohio alone, though the state's quota was only thirteen thousand. Governor William Dennison's challenging assertion to his fellow Ohioans that "Ohio must lead throughout the war!" was frank recognition of the significance of 436 miles of common border with the slave states of Kentucky and Virginia. Though Kentucky did not secede, tens of thousands of its residents served in the regiments of the South, while Virginia not only seceded but provided the Confederacy its capital, Richmond.

Not since 1812 had Ohio an enemy on its borders. Forming an army capable of fighting proved difficult in 1861, not only for Ohio but for all the states, as events at Bull Run soon evidenced. But Ohio regiments under General George B. McClellan (then living in Cincinnati), appointed by Governor Dennison to take command of

Ohio's volunteers and militia, were able to invade Virginia successfully and drive Confederate forces out of the thirty-four westernmost counties by July 1861. These in turn would enter the Union as the new state of West Virginia in 1863. Ohio's success in western Virginia partially offset the tremendous demoralization that set in after the defeat of Union forces at Bull Run in eastern Virginia and prompted Lincoln to replace General Irvin McDowell (of Columbus) with George McClellan in command of the Army of the Potomac.

The Battle of Bull Run (Manassas Junction) on 21 July 1861, just thirty miles from Washington, D.C., showed that early predictions of a short war with a quick Union victory had been in error. Now Lincoln called for 500,000 three-year enlistments. Ohio's quota of 67,000 was exceeded by the 77,844 who stepped forward, the excess then used to fill a large part of Kentucky's quota. That same month, Republicans and pro-war Democrats met in convention in Columbus, where, under the leadership of Thomas Ewing, the former Whig leader, they agreed to form a Union Party. As evidence of their determination to put aside earlier differences, the majority Republicans supported the nomination of David Tod of Youngstown, a "War Democrat," for the governorship. Elected that fall, he replaced the Republican William Dennison, who later accepted a position in the Lincoln cabinet.

With battlefield victories largely favoring the South in the first years of the war, Southern leaders concluded that the war could be dramatically shortened if Cincinnati were seized and the Ohio River supply line of the North severed. In late summer 1862, twenty thousand Confederate troops under the command of Generals Kirby Smith and John Hunt Morgan drove across Kentucky, captured Lexington and Frankfort, and advanced toward Covington and Newport. With most of Ohio's fighting men on other fronts, east and south, Governor Tod appealed for volunteers to come to the aid of Cincinnati. The response was overwhelming. From boys as young as twelve to old men in their seventies, they came from all sections of the state, fifty thousand strong, bringing their flintlocks and squirrel rifles with them. Under the command of General Lewis Wallace (later best known as the author of *Ben Hur*), they crossed the Ohio on pontoon bridges, dug trenches south of Covington and Newport, and transformed Ohio River steamers into gunboats. Dubbed the "Squirrel Hunters," they outmatched the advancing Confederates who soon withdrew. Cincinnati and the Ohio River supply line had been saved.

Not all Ohioans supported the war effort. Perhaps as many as 40 percent regarded Lincoln's decision to preserve the Union with force as wrong. Some four thousand Ohioans actually served in armies of the Confederacy, the most infamous of these the border raider, William C. Quantrill of Dover. Most who disagreed with Lincoln, however, did so politically as "Peace Democrats" (also called "Copperheads" or "Butternuts"). Best known of these was Clement L. Vallandigham, a congressman from Dayton who argued that slavery was protected by the Constitution, that the war was useless since the South was going to win anyway, and that the war was a partisan measure waged by Republicans to destroy the Democratic Party. Defeated for reelection in 1862, he was subsequently arrested and charged with sedition, jailed, then banished to Canada, from where in 1863 he ran as the Democratic Party's candidate for governor of Ohio against the Union Party candidate, John Brough, a War Democrat.

In the midst of the campaign of 1863, Ohio was invaded by a Confederate army, a cavalry division led by General John Hunt Morgan. From Hamilton County in the southwest to Columbiana County in the northeast, Morgan's raiders for two weeks drove their way across twenty-six Ohio counties until finally captured near Lisbon, the farthest northward advance of any Confederate force in the entire Civil War. Morgan's Raid had the unintended effect of dooming Vallandigham's bid for the Ohio governorship.

Throughout the war a number of Ohioans distinguished themselves as among the nation's foremost military and political leaders in the fight to preserve the Union and, after Lincoln's Emancipation Proclamation, to bring an end to slavery. Like Cornelia, the Roman matron of old who when asked the source of her wealth had turned to her seven sons and said, "These are my jewels," so Ohio, too, had sons who were her "jewels" in this time of cataclysmic struggle. Among literally dozens who could be so described, seven in particular stood out: Ulysses S. Grant, Philip H. Sheridan, William Tecumseh Sherman, James A. Garfield, Edwin M. Stanton, Salmon P. Chase, and Rutherford B. Hayes. It was fitting that after the war a statuary memorial depicting Ohio as Cornelia with these seven sons of Ohio clustered about her as her jewels was erected on the statehouse lawn in Columbus, where it stands to this day.

Well before Lee's surrender to Grant at Appomattox Court House brought the Civil War to a close, much thought had been given to the nature of the Reconstruction of the Union that would follow. From the beginning Lincoln had referred to the war as a rebellion by individuals against the authority of the national government and not as a war between states. Under the pardoning power granted the chief executive under the Constitution, he believed he had the ultimate authority to pardon rebels and restore them to citizenship in the nation they had tried to destroy. Under executive control, he argued, the wounds of war could be more readily healed if the program of Reconstruction were based on moderation and forgiveness rather than on harsh, vindictive punishment.

In the eyes of the radical wing of the Republican Party, however, Reconstruction was the responsibility of the Congress, not the president. Led by Senator Benjamin F. "Bluff Ben" Wade from Ashtabula County, Ohio, the "Radical Republicans" affirmed that the states of the South had voluntarily withdrawn from the Union and at war's end were no more than conquered territories subject to the control of Congress. They argued that Reconstruction of the defeated South should be punitive and should be made to fit the enormity of the crime of war that the South had precipitated. Drawn in large measure from the newly industrialized areas of Ohio and the rest of the North, the Radicals believed that a too-lenient peace for the South might well mean the return to power of the agrarian interests which had long dominated federal policies on trade, tariffs, currency, and banking. And, as Republicans, they were mindful that the very future of their party hung in the balance were the old Democratic coalition, North and South, to be restored to power. After all, they had never won a national election with a majority of the votes cast. Lincoln had been victorious in 1860 with 40 percent of the popular vote because of the split of the Democrats into Northern and Southern wings.

And he had been reelected in 1864, not as a Republican candidate but as the candidate of the *Union* Party, representing War Democrats as well as Republicans.

For twelve years the Reconstruction of the Union evolved against a tangled backdrop of discordant events that included the assassination of Lincoln; the ascension of a War Democrat, Andrew Johnson, to the presidency; the dissolution of the Union Party; the impeachment of Johnson, presided over by Chief Justice Salmon P. Chase of Cincinnati, following Johnson's removal of Edwin M. Stanton of Steubenville as secretary of war; the failure by a single vote to remove Johnson from office, thus blocking Ben Wade from becoming the president of the United States from his role as presiding officer of the Senate; the elections of Ulysses S. Grant in 1868 and 1872 and the unfortunate scandals that developed in his eight years in the White House; and finally the controversial election in 1876 of President Rutherford B. Hayes, a moderate Republican from Fremont, Ohio—from the dispute over which came the agreement to withdraw the last of the federal troops occupying the soil of the defeated South, bringing Reconstruction to an end.

IX.1. Forming an Army

When the Civil War began on 12 April 1861, the people of Ohio, like those of most of the states of the Union, were unprepared to fight. Following decades of peace and relative prosperity, they had been lulled into a sense of security that remained unbroken until news reached the state that Confederate shore batteries had fired upon the federal Fort Sumter in Charleston Harbor. For the next several months it was Governor William Dennison and the state government that had to recruit an Ohio army, build Ohio camps where troops might be trained, and provide for their food, shelter, and clothing from Ohio resources. Confronted by two slave states, one of which, the secessionist Virginia, was providing the Confederacy its capital at Richmond, Dennison boldly proclaimed that "Ohio must lead throughout the war!"

Until camps could be established, the governor directed that recruits be housed in hotels and private homes. When camps were established (Camp Jackson in Goodale Park, Columbus; Camp Chase, four miles west of Columbus; and Camp Dennison near Miamiville east of Cincinnati), tents, uniforms, and weapons had to be procured, not an easy task when there were few to be found and nineteen other states as well as the federal government competing for them. Little wonder that the governor, with a background in law and banking but with no previous military experience, was soon roundly if unjustly criticized for expensive delays and shortfalls. Yet, for all of his problems, it was Dennison who got an army in the field even before the federal government was able to do so, and, under the command of General George B. McClellan, that Ohio army managed in the early months of the war to drive Confederate forces not only out of the wedge of Virginia that separated Ohio and Pennsylvania but also out of the rest of Virginia west of the Blue Ridge Mountains. To his credit, Dennison appreciated that the mountains rather than the Ohio River provided the best natural defense for the state of Ohio.

Forming an effective army was not accomplished overnight. It took the shocking defeat of McDowell's Army of the Potomac at Bull Run on 20 July 1861 to convince President Lincoln, the Congress, and the nation that the war was going to be a long one and that the armed forces ultimately had to have coordinated and centralized control from Washington rather than the state capitals.

It was fortunate for Ohio's war effort that in the summer of 1861 an able and knowledgeable graduate of West Point, C. P. Buckingham, joined Governor Dennison's staff as adjutant general. In his annual report for that year he summarized the challenges that faced the state in its recruiting efforts as the pendulum of citizen response swung from the initial outburst of patriotism and volunteer enlistments following Fort Sumter, to the difficulties that developed from the lack of cohesion between the state and federal authorities in processing, provisioning, and paying the recruits, and finally to the development of a coordinated and equitable system by the last months of the year. "It may now be said with pride," Buckingham reported at year's end, "that in all that goes to constitute an army, in its personnel as well as in its material, the regiments of Ohio are second to none others in the army."[1]

THE REPORT OF ADJUTANT GENERAL C. P. BUCKINGHAM TO GOVERNOR WILLIAM DENNISON.

> Head Quarters, Ohio Militia,
> Adjutant General's Office,
> Columbus, Dec. 31ˢᵗ, 1861.

His Excellency, Wm. Dennison, Governor and Commander-in-Chief:

     . . . . The commencement of the present year found the country on the brink of a war in many respects, unexampled in the history of the world. With the exception of the short and inconsiderable war with Mexico, the nation had been, for nearly fifty years, in a state of profound peace. No one dreamed that a war could arise, demanding the utmost energies of the country, without a sufficient note of warning to afford opportunity for at least some preparation. Resting in this fancied security, the people of Ohio lost all interest in military matters, so that they not only neglected to cultivate among themselves anything like military taste and education, but had come to consider every effort in that direction as a fit subject for ridicule. Hence, on the breaking out of the present war, the State was found to be comparatively without arms, organization or discipline, to prepare her for the part it became her to take in the fearful struggle. Of the many thousand muskets received by the State from the Federal Government, with which to arm and drill the militia, nearly all had been lost or sold for a trifle. The cannon had been used for firing salutes, and left exposed to the weather, until rust and decay had rendered them and their equipments worthless.

     A few volunteer companies had been formed from time to time, and after a spasmodic existence for two or three years, had most of them been disbanded or had dwindled to nothing.

     Almost the entire organization of the militia was merely nominal. Very many of the high offices were vacant, and the system, if it could be called so, had no working power. The only bright spots in this melancholy picture were, less than a dozen independent companies of Volunteer Infantry, and seven or eight gun squads of Artillery, called by law, companies. Six of these called a Regiment, but really composing a single Battery, under the command of Col. James Barnet, took the field at once as then organized, and during the three months service, proved most efficient in the early part of the campaign in Western Virginia. One section of this Battery, under Lieut.-Col. Sturges, had the honor of opening war in that region, at the attack and capture of Phillippi.

Still it may be said with truth, that the war found the State in no condition whatever to meet its requirements. When the President of the United States demanded thirteen Regiments from Ohio to commence the work of putting down the rebellion, not one was ready to go into the field in a condition fit for service. There was no lack of willingness however on the part of the people, to volunteer for the defence of the Government. Within two weeks, instead of thirteen thousand, nearly thirty thousand had offered their services to meet the call of the President. So eager were they all to take part in the high duty of maintaining the integrity of the government, and the majesty of the law, that it became a task of serious and embarrassing difficulty, to decide which should be the favored ones. After the thirteen Regiments originally called for were selected, the Legislature decided that ten thousand more of the men, who had so promptly offered themselves to the country, should be retained in the service of the State, to defend her against invasion should it be threatened by the rebels.

Four thousand more were held in reserve in organized companies, under command of their respective captains, drilling and preparing to meet the next call. The remainder were disbanded.

Of the thirteen Regiments called for by the President for three months, two, viz. the First and Second, were ordered to Washington immediately. Within two days after receiving the proclamation of the 15th April, they were on their way to the field. They were, under an imperative order from the War Department, reluctantly sent without arms or clothing, except that with which they left their homes. After many delays, they finally reached Washington, and received their supplies of arms and uniforms, and served out their time in the army of the Potomac, participating in the battle of Bull's Run. Immediately after that battle, they were ordered home and mustered out of service, as their term of enlistment had expired. The other eleven Regiments were directed to rendezvous at Camp Dennison, and while there, by order of the President, were reorganized for three years, instead of three months. To effect this organization was a matter of considerable difficulty. By the State law, as three months men, they had elected their own officers. Under the order of the President, the officers were to be appointed by the Governor of the State; and the difficulty was to determine whether to break up the old organization and appoint officers without regard to their former positions, or to take the Regiments as they were, and confirm all the old commissions. It was at length decided to retain the general organization of the Regiments, together with the numbers, and to effect the change in the service as quietly as possible. Measures were taken to ascertain who would volunteer for three years, and the officers of the Regiments were appointed with due regard to their wishes. The vacancies, occasioned by the refusal of many of the three months men to enter the three years service, were filled by recruiting, for which purpose officers were sent out into the neighborhood, where the companies were originally raised.

When their recruits began to come in, it was found that the presence of the three months men, who had declined to re-enlist, was the cause of much inconvenience, and greatly tended to demoralize the entire force. The quarters were crowded, jealousies sprung up, doubts arose as to the rights of the different classes of troops, ill feeling was engendered, and general insubordination in most regiments was the result. It became absolutely necessary to separate the three months men from the others. Instead of mustering them out of the service however, as would seem to have been the proper method, no directions were received from the War Department as to the disposition to be made of them, though sought by the Governor and officers often and earnestly. At length the Colonels of the Regiments took the responsibility of sending these three months men home on furlough until further orders.

The results of this unfortunate step on the subsequent recruiting service, became apparent in a few weeks to a lamentable extent. Some two or three thousand men were scattered over the State, discontented and complaining because they were not paid. These feelings were participated in by their friends, until very many were led to believe that the promises of the Government were worthless, and bitterness and wrath succeeded to suspicion and disappointment. The influence of such men on the recruiting service may be easily imagined, and will account in part for the want of success in rapidly filling the regiments organizing in July and August. In the meantime, the troops had to be retained in Camp Dennison until the new recruits were drilled, and the whole clothed and armed for the field. This did not take place until the latter part of June, and even then two of the regiments were incomplete as to numbers, when they took the field in Western Virginia.

The general officers appointed under the act of April 23d, 1861, for the three months troops, were: Geo. B. McClellan, Major-General; Joshua L. Bates, J. D. Cox, and Newton Schleich, Brigadiers-General. Of these, Brigadier-General Cox remained in the three years service, under the appointment of the President, and General McClellan was transferred to the regular army. . . .

When the President called for these troops, no digested plan for raising them was presented by the War Department. The Governor was simply requested to furnish so many Regiments, organized in a specific manner, and to be commanded by officers of his appointment. Companies were to be completed before being mustered into service, and a regiment before the Field and Staff officers might be mustered, and its organization completed. No provision was made for the transportation nor subsistence while organizing, nor any authority given their officers to command them until they were filled and mustered. Field officers appointed to take charge of camps, to instruct, drill, and discipline the men, had no legal authority to enforce obedience to their commands. No provision was made for the clothing of recruits, or furnishing them with blankets, until the company was full; nor indeed until the last of August, could a Quartermaster be appointed and mustered into service, to provide for the wants of regiments, until a complete organization was perfected. Nothing was allowed as compensation to the men during the time they were awaiting the completion of their companies, nor to those who, by great exertions, and often at considerable expense, were endeavoring to recruit companies and regiments. Nor was any defined power given to the Governor to regulate the recruiting service, except that incidentally derived from the power to appoint officers. Indeed, it seemed as though the War Department supposed that companies would spontaneously flock together and organize themselves into regiments, and ask to be received into service. In the beginning the ardent patriotism of the people answered every purpose, but presently the work of organization and preparation became more difficult and protracted. . . .

Ohio has not meted out its contributions to the National forces with a stingy hand. Ohio has not inquired how much she was bound to do, and paused at that. The State owed 57,000 men to the service, our recruits number nearly 80,000. Ohio did not go into this war with arsenals filled, and materials provided. The preparations necessary for war had been studiously avoided, and she had nothing but her sons to offer, all else had to be created. The work was no small one, but it has been accomplished. It may now be said with pride, that in all that goes to constitute an army, in its personnel as well as its material, the regiments of Ohio are second to none others in the army. . . .

1. See *Annual Report of the Adjutant General to the Governor of the State of Ohio for the Year 1861* (Columbus, 1862), 3-29. See also Thomas H. Smith, ed., *An Ohio Reader, 1750 to the Civil War* (Grand Rapids, Mich.: Eerdmans, 1975), 295-305; and Harry L. Coles, *Ohio Forms an Army* (Columbus: Ohio State University Press, 1962), 3-23.

IX.2. The "Squirrel Hunters" Defend Cincinnati

In a bid to cut one of the Union's vital supply lines and shorten the war, Confederate Generals Kirby Smith and John Hunt Morgan and twenty thousand Southern troops entered Kentucky in August 1862, and after seizing Lexington and Frankfort, headed north toward Cincinnati and the Ohio River. Union General Lewis Wallace, in command of the defense of southern Ohio and northern Kentucky, appealed to Governor David Tod for help in this emergency. The governor turned to his fellow Ohioans and asked for volunteers to halt the advancing rebels. The response was overwhelming. Fifty thousand strong, they came from all parts of the state and from all age groups. And they brought with them their own weapons—pistols, carbines, flintlock muskets, anything that would shoot. But the predominant weapons were muzzle-loading squirrel rifles, and the name by which these volunteers would henceforth be remembered was the "Squirrel Hunters."

Converting and manning river steamers as gunboats, constructing a pontoon bridge across the Ohio, and digging trenches and rifle pits on the approaches to Covington and Newport, the tens of thousands of volunteers convinced the Confederates they should withdraw. Though Morgan and a division of Confederate calvary would return the next summer for a raid across southern and eastern Ohio, thoughts of frontal assault on Cincinnati were no more.

Following discharge from their volunteer service in defense of Cincinnati and the Ohio River supply line, each of the "Squirrel Hunters" received a certificate of commendation and copy of a resolution passed by the Ohio General Assembly and signed by Governor Tod. The resolution, a copy of which was received by Royal A. Smith, an Ashtabula County farmer, expressed not only the gratitude of the state but also the concern that he "keep the old gun in order" and the "powder horn and bullet pouch supplied" in case the Confederates might attempt to strike again.[1]

THE STATE OF OHIO

Executive Department
Columbus, March 4ᵗʰ, 1863.

To: R. A. Smith, Esqr. of Ashtabula County, O.

The Legislature of our State has this day passed the following Resolution: "Resolved by the Senate and House of Representatives of the State of Ohio, That the Governor be, and he is hereby authorized and directed to appropriate out of his contingent fund, a sufficient sum to pay for printing and lithographing discharges for the patriotic men of the State, who responded to the call of the Governor, and went to our Southern border to repel the invaders, and who will be known in history as the "SQUIRREL HUNTERS."

And in obedience thereto, I do most cheerfully herewith enclose a Certificate of your service. But for the gallant services of yourself and the other members of the corps of patriotic "Squirrel Hunters," rendered in September last, Ohio, our dear State, would have been invaded by a band of pirates determined to overthrow the best government on earth; our wives and children would have been violated and murdered, and our homes plundered and sacked. Your children, and your children's children, will be proud to know that you were one of this glorious band.

Preserve the Certificate of service and discharge, herewith enclosed to you as evidence of this gallantry. The rebellion is not yet crushed out and therefore the discharge may not be final: keep the old gun then in order; see that the powder horn and bullet pouch are supplied and caution your patriotic mothers or wives to be at all times prepared to furnish you a few days cooked rations so that if your services are called for (which may God in his infinite goodness forbid) you may again prove yourselves "Minute Men" and again protect our loved homes.

Invoking God's choicest blessings upon yourself and all who are dear to you.

I am very truly Yours,

David Tod, Governor.

1. The copy is in the possession of the author.

IX.3. Vallandigham and the Antiwar Movement

One of the most bizarre elections in the history of American politics occurred in 1863 when Clement L. Vallandigham, though banished from the United States, accepted the nomination of the Democratic Party and campaigned for the governorship of Ohio while living in exile in Canada. An outspoken critic of the Lincoln administration's decision to resist secession and to fight to save the Union, Vallandigham by his voice and vote fought every measure in the Congress to support the war effort.[1] After a gerrymander of his district, the "Peace Democrat" and arch Copperhead was defeated by Republican Robert C. Schenck for reelection to Congress in 1862 and returned to his home in Dayton. No longer enjoying congressional immunity, he was circumspect in his antiwar statements and actions until 1 May 1863, when in an address in Mount Vernon before a crowd of Copperhead partisans he attacked the pro-war policies of both Governor Tod and President Lincoln and denounced in particular the so-called General Order No. 38 recently issued by General Ambrose E. Burnside.[2]

After the Confederate march on Cincinnati, which had been repulsed by the "Squirrel Hunters" the fall before, Burnside had replaced Lewis Wallace as commander of the defensive forces guarding southern Ohio and Indiana and northern Kentucky. Sensing the danger of Copperhead agitation behind the Union lines, Burnside had issued his General Order No. 38, which called for the arrest and imprisonment of those actively opposing the war effort. In the crowd listening to Vallandigham's address at Mount Vernon were two soldiers in civilian garb who took copious notes of Vallandigham's diatribe against Tod, Lincoln, Burnside, and the war effort, and turned these over to Burnside, who promptly ordered the arrest of Vallandigham.

Vallandigham's arrest at his home in Dayton on 5 May and confinement in the Kemper Barracks in Cincinnati sparked immediate protest from his supporters. An angry mob descended on the office of the Dayton Journal, *the leading pro-Union newspaper of the area, and destroyed it. Downtown buildings were looted and burned. Telegraph wires were cut and railroad tracks torn up, temporarily isolating the city from the rest of the world. Learning of the riot in Dayton, Burnside rushed 150 troops from Cincinnati on 6 May to suppress it and summoned a military commission to court-martial Vallandigham on the charge of "Publicly expressing, in violation of General Order No. 38, from Headquarters Department of the Ohio, sympathies for those in arms against the Government of the United States, declaring disloyal sentiments and opinions, with the object and purpose of weakening the power of the Government in its efforts to suppress an unlawful rebellion."[3]*

Tried and found guilty of the charge, Vallandigham was ordered by Burnside to be confined in the military prison at Fort Warren in Boston Harbor, an order that was at once countermanded by President Lincoln. Fearful that the Copperhead leader would be more likely to emerge a martyr in the eyes of many were he to be jailed, Lincoln mandated that he be taken across the lines and turned over to Confederate authorities. The president's decision was at once challenged in a mass protest meeting at Albany on 16 May, by none other than the New York governor, Horatio Seymour, who in an open letter questioned Lincoln's constitutional authority to exile his principal critic. Lincoln replied with one of his classic statements of the war period. "Must I shoot a simple-minded soldier boy who deserts," he asked, "while I must not touch a hair of the head of the wily agitator who induces him to desert? I think that, in such a case, to silence the agitator and save the boy is not only constitutional but a great mercy."[4]

Banished by Lincoln, Vallandigham soon left the South for Bermuda and thence to Canada, where he took up residence on the Canadian side of Niagara Falls. There he accepted the nomination of the Democratic Party of Ohio, made on 11 June 1863, for the office of governor.[5] Viewed by many as a martyr to the cause of free speech, Vallandigham made a formidable candidate.[6] Had the election been held at the time of his nomination in June instead of October, he might well have won. The war had been going badly for the Union, both on the battlefield and on the home front. When voluntary enlistment failed to produce the number of recruits needed for the armed forces, a Draft Act had been passed that provoked protests across the North, including a brief insurrection in Holmes County, Ohio.

But military successes at Gettysburg and Vicksburg and the collapse of "Fort Fizzle" in Holmes County helped turn the corner for pro-Union sentiment.

Wisely, the Union Party in Ohio chose another "War Democrat," John Brough, to succeed David Tod and to oppose the "Peace Democrat" Vallandigham for the governorship, reducing the potential for charges of partisan politics. And then, in the hottest part of the campaign, the state was invaded by a Confederate army led by General John Hunt Morgan. For two full weeks and across twenty-six Ohio counties the raiders carried the war into southern and eastern Ohio. As many said, it became more difficult to talk about constitutional guarantees of free speech for antiwar protesters such as Vallandigham while dodging the bullets of Morgan and his Confederate raiders.

On 13 October 1863, the election was held. Brough carried the state with 246,907 civilian votes to 185,204 for Vallandigham. (When the soldier vote came in days later it was one-sided, as might have been expected, 41,467 to 2,288.) President Lincoln, who stayed up far into the night in the White House, anxiously awaiting the results of the Ohio election, sent a telegram of congratulations to John Brough just before dawn on 14 October: "Glory to God in the highest. Ohio has saved the Union!" And he meant it.

Vallandigham's Antiwar Speech in Congress, 14 January 1863

. . . . I have denounced, from the beginning, the usurpations and the infractions, one and all, of law and Constitution, by the President and those under him; their repeated and persistent arbitrary arrests, the suspension of *habeas corpus,* the violation of freedom of the mails, of the private house, of the press and of speech, and all the other multiplied wrongs and outrages upon public liberty and private right, which have made this country one of the worst despotisms on earth for the past twenty months; and I will continue to rebuke and denounce them to the end; and the people, thank God! have at last heard and heeded, and rebuked them, too. To the record and to time I appeal again for my justification. . . .

From the beginning the war has been conducted like a political campaign, and it has been the folly of the party in power that they have assumed, that numbers alone would win the field in a contest not with ballots but with musket and sword. But numbers, you have had almost without number — the largest, best appointed, best armed, fed, and clad host of brave men, well organized and well disciplined, ever marshaled. A Navy, too, not the most formidable perhaps, but the most numerous and gallant, and the costliest in the world, and against a foe, almost without a navy at all. Thus, with twenty millions of people, and every element of strength and force at command — power, patronage, influence, unanimity, enthusiasm, confidence, credit, money, men, an Army and a Navy the largest and the noblest ever set in the field, or afloat upon the sea; with the support, almost servile, of every State, county, and municipality in the North and West, with a Congress swift to do the bidding of the Executive; without opposition anywhere at home; and with an arbitrary power which neither the Czar of Russia, nor the Emperor of Austria dare exercise; yet after nearly two years of more vigorous prosecution of war than ever recorded in history; after more skirmishes, combats and battles than Alexander,

Caesar, or the first Napoleon ever fought in any five years of their military career, you have utterly, signally, disastrously—I will not say ignominiously—failed to subdue ten millions of "rebels," whom you had taught the people of the North and West not only to hate, but to despise. Rebels, did I say? Yes, your fathers were rebels, or your grandfathers. He, who now before me on canvas looks down so sadly upon us, the false, degenerate, and imbecile guardians of the great Republic which he founded, was a rebel. And yet we, cradled ourselves in rebellion, and who have fostered and fraternized with every insurrection in the nineteenth century everywhere throughout the globe, would now, forsooth, make the word "rebel" a reproach. Rebels certainly they are; but all the persistent and stupendous efforts of the most gigantic warfare of modern times have, through your incompetency and folly, availed nothing to crush them out, cut off though they have been, by your blockade, from all the world, and dependent only upon their own courage and resources. And yet, they were to be utterly conquered and subdued in six weeks, or three months! . . .

Sir, this war, horrible as it is, has taught us all some of the most important and salutary lessons which a people ever learned.

First, it has annihilated, in twenty months, all the false and pernicious theories and teachings of Abolitionism for thirty years, and which a mere appeal to facts and arguments could not have untaught in half a century. We have learned that the South is not weak, dependent, unenterprising, or corrupted by slavery, luxury, and idleness; but powerful, earnest, warlike, enduring, self-supporting, full of energy and inexhaustible in resources. We have been taught, and now confess it openly, that African slavery, instead of being a source of weakness to the South, is one of her main elements of strength; and hence the "military necessity," we are told, of abolishing slavery in order to suppress the rebellion. We have learned, also, that the non-slaveholding white men of the South, millions in number, are immovably attached to the institution, and are its chief support; and Abolitionists have found out, to their infinite surprise and disgust, that the slave is not "panting for freedom," nor pining in silent, but, revengeful grief over cruelty and oppression inflicted upon him, but happy, contented, attached deeply to his master, and unwilling—at least not eager—to accept the precious boon of freedom, which they have proffered him. I appeal to the President for the proof. I appeal to the fact, that fewer slaves have escaped, even from Virginia, in now yearly two years, than Arnold and Cornwallis carried away in six months of invasion, in 1781. Finally, sir, we have learned, and the South, too, what the history of the world ages ago, and our own history might have taught us, that servile insurrection is the least of the dangers to which she is exposed. Hence, in my deliberate judgment, African slavery, as an institution, will come out of this conflict fifty-fold stronger than when the war began. . . .

I have finished now, Mr. Speaker, what I desired to say at this time, upon the great question of the reunion of these States. I have spoken freely and boldly—not wisely, it may be, for the present, or for myself personally, but most wisely for the future and for my country. Not courting censure, I yet do not shrink from it. My own immediate personal interests, and my chances just now for the more material rewards of ambition, I again surrender as hostages to that GREAT HEREAFTER, the echo of whose footsteps already I hear along the highway of time. . . .

A Report in the Columbus *Crisis* on the Mount Vernon Meeting of 1 May 1863.

*I*n every point of view it was an unparalleled *county* meeting. Any fair estimate must put its numbers between fifteen and twenty thousand! . . . It being well known that Mr. Vallandigham had come, an immediate and general call was made for him, and he was at once introduced to the vast assembly, which saluted him with three hearty cheers. Mr. Vallandigham addressed the great multitude of people for about two hours, making a most able, eloquent, and truly patriotic speech. It was a noble and glorious effort in behalf of Liberty, Union and the Constitution, and was listened to with wrapt attention, interrupted only by frequent enthusiastic responses and applause. It must have left an ineffaceable impression upon the minds of all who heard it. He showed and established conclusively which was the true Union, and which the disunion party, by tracing the history and proceedings of each from its origin to the present moment. The contrast between the life-long Unionism of the Democratic party, and the original and continuous disunionism of the Abolition party, was so glaring and true, that an Abolitionist with any degree of conscience must have felt confounded and abashed at the recital. . . . Mr. V. spoke in words of burning eloquence of the arbitrary measures and monarchical usurpations of the Administration, the disgraceful surrender of the rights and liberties of the people by the last infamous Congress, and the conversion of the Government into a despotism. No candid man, after hearing Mr. Vallandigham, can for a moment doubt his sincerity and patriotism. These attributes of the man stand out in bold prominence, and are so palpable as not to be drawn in question by any honest man of common sense.

It being apparent during the delivery of Mr. Vallandigham's speech that it was quite impossible for even his strong and clear voice to reach the edges of the crowd, besides which Main street for several squares below was blocked with people, it was proposed to organise another meeting at the corner of Main and Vine streets, which was gladly accepted. A large meeting was there convened. This second meeting being found insufficient to accommodate the immense number of people, a third large meeting was organised farther down Main street, in front of the Franklin House. In the evening, about eight o'clock, still another large meeting, a considerable proportion of which was composed of ladies, filled the spacious Court-room.

FROM HIS ARREST AS A TRAITOR TO HIS NOMINATION FOR GOVERNOR: THE RECORD IS DETAILED.

No. XXIV. ARREST OF MR. VALLANDIGHAM. — From the meeting in Mt. Vernon Mr. Vallandigham went home, where he intended to remain a few days, then go to Norwalk, thence to other places, where appointments to speak had been made. Meantime Gen. Burnside had also concluded to take charge of Mr. Vallandigham's movements, and had marked out a different course. The first intimation of this determination on the party of the military commander was brought to the notice of the public, by the following announcement in the State Journal of May 4th:

"Watched. — Gen. Burnside sent up a portion of his staff, in citizen's dress, to report Vallandigham at Mount Vernon on Friday, and we should not be at all surprised to learn that he had got himself into a scrape."

A three o'clock the next morning, Tuesday, May 5th, Mr. Vallandigham was arrested — one hundred and fifty soldiers being sent up from Cincinnati for that purpose. The arrest, though not very brave, was exquisitely strategic. The night, the special train, houses guarded near the residence of Mr. V., and along the street to the depot, quick and cautious movements, doors broken, bed-room entered, prisoner captured, placed in the cars and gone, all inside of thirty minutes! The mind that planned and executed that movement must have been endowed with military genius equal to the emergency.

Mr. Vallandigham was hurried to Cincinnati, and consigned to prison. His arrest was announced, and the indignation of the people was deep and terrible.

The following letter, written in prison, on the day of his arrest, was handed to a visitor, and thus came to the public.

MILITARY PRISON, CINCINNATI, OHIO,
May 5th, 1863.

To the Democracy of Ohio:

I am here in a military bastile for no other offense than my political opinions, and the defense of them, and of the rights of the people, and of your Constitutional liberties. Speeches made in the hearing of thousands of you in denunciation of the usurpations of power, infractions of the Constitution and Laws, and of Military Despotism, were the sole cause of my arrest and imprisonment. I am a Democrat — for Constitution, for Law, for the Union, for Liberty — this is my only "crime." For no disobedience to the Constitution; for no violation of law; for no word, sign or gesture of sympathy with the men of the South, who are for disunion and Southern independence, but in obedience to *their* demand, as well as at the demand of Northern Abolition Disunionists and Traitors, I am here in bonds to-day; but

"Time, at last, sets all things even!"

Meantime, Democrats of Ohio, of the Northwest, of the United States, be firm, be true to your principles, to the Constitution, to the Union, and all will yet be well. As for myself, I adhere to every principle, and will make good, through imprisonment and life itself, every pledge and declaration which I have ever made, uttered or maintained from the beginning. To you, to the whole people, to TIME, I again appeal. Stand firm! Falter not an instant!

C. L. VALLANDIGHAM.

No. XXVIII. PARTING ADDRESS AND DEPARTURE. — Just before leaving, Mr. Vallandigham wrote and left for publication the following:

MILITARY PRISON, CINCINNATI, OHIO,
May 29, 1863.

To the Democracy of Ohio:

Banished from my native State for no crime save Democratic opinions and free speech to you in their defense, and about to go into exile, not of my own will, but by the compulsion of an arbitrary and tyrannic power which I cannot resist, allow me a parting word. Because despotism and superior force so will it, I go within the Confederate lines. I well understand the purpose of this order. But in vain the malice of enemies shall thus continue to give color to the calumnies and mis-representations of the past two years. They little comprehend the true character of the man with whom they have to deal. No order of banishment, executed by superior force, can release me from my obligations or deprive me of my rights as a citizen of Ohio and of the United States. My allegiance to my own State and Government I shall recognize, wheresoever I may be, as binding in all things, just the same as though I remained upon their soil. Every sentiment and expression of attachment to the Union and devotion to the Constitution—to my country—which I have ever cherished or uttered, shall abide unchanged and unretracted till my return. Meantime, I will not doubt that the people of Ohio, cowering not a moment before either the threats or the exercise of arbitrary power, will, in every trial, prove themselves worthy to be called freemen.

C. L. VALLANDIGHAM.

No. XXX. NOMINATED FOR GOVERNOR, AND RETURN DE-MANDED.—On the eleventh of June, 1863, Mr. Vallandigham, being still an *involuntary exile,* was nominated for Governor of Ohio. Those twenty thousand citizens of the State, elected and volunteer delegates, assembled at the Capitol for that purpose. The nomination was unanimous, and the enthusiasm unparalelled.

A committee of nineteen was also appointed to proceed to Washington, and respectfully but earnestly request the President to return Clement L. Vallandigham to his home in Ohio.

Thus stands the "RECORD OF VALLANDIGHAM." Thus twenty thousand freemen have returned to their homes, resolved to make his election sure on the second Tuesday in October.

1. Vallandigham's antiwar speech to Congress of 14 January 1863 is quoted in J. Walter & Co., publisher (no author indicated), *The Record of Hon. C. L. Vallandigham on Abolition, the Union, and the Civil War* (Columbus, 1863), 180–203; the excerpts from *The Record* labeled nos. XXIV, XXVIII, and XXX are from pages 252–56.

2. The selection in this section describing Vallandigham's Mount Vernon address is from a letter published in the *Columbus Crisis* and quoted in James L. Vallandigham, *A Life of Clement L. Vallandigham* (Baltimore, 1872), 252–53.

3. *The Record of Hon. C. L. Vallandigham,* 254.

4. Quoted in David W. Bowman, *Pathway of Progress: A Short History of Ohio* (New York: American Book Company, 1943), 273.

5. Before the October election, Vallandigham moved again, from Niagara to Windsor. See Frank L. Klement, "Vallandigham as an Exile in Canada, 1863–1864," *Ohio History* 74, no. 3 (summer 1965): 151–68.

6. *The Record of Hon. C. L. Vallandigham,* 252–56.

IX.4. Morgan's Raid

One of the events of July 1863 that helped turn the tide of the Ohio gubernatorial campaign from Clement L. Vallandigham to John Brough was the spectacular raid of General John Hunt Morgan and his division of 2,460 Confederate cavalrymen across twenty-six southern and eastern counties of the state. This so alarmed Ohioans that it convinced a good many to vote for Brough to protect their homes and their families.

Following as it did the defeat of Southern armies at Gettysburg just ten days before, the raid was intended by Morgan to recoup lost prestige and muster flagging spirits in the South, ease pressure on other fronts by compelling Northern troops to be pulled out to defend Ohio, and serve as a smoke screen for Confederate troop redeployment in Kentucky and Tennessee. Aware of the intense antiwar sentiment in many parts of Ohio, revealed by the nomination of the exiled Vallandigham for the governorship and by protests against the Federal Draft Act in Holmes County and elsewhere, Morgan also may well have hoped to enlist supporters for the Confederate cause.

Having been frustrated by his inability to sustain a frontal attack on Cincinnati the year before, Morgan this time crossed the Ohio River into southeastern Indiana and invaded Ohio on 13 July at Harrison near the state line northwest of Cincinnati. Sending soldiers disguised as civilians into both Hamilton and Cincinnati to spread rumors that his army was about to attack each city, Morgan was able to split Burnside's defensive forces and ride virtually unopposed across northern Hamilton County. There he divided the raiders into three groups to maximize the effectiveness of the raid by cutting rail lines and destroying bridges, trestles, and anything else of value to the Union war effort. One group headed northeast across Warren, Clinton, Fayette, and Ross Counties. A second proceeded eastward through Clermont, Highland, Pike, and Jackson Counties. The third took a southerly route through southern Clermont, Brown, and Adams Counties. Avoiding cities and foraging from the countryside, the three groups reunited at Jackson in Jackson County, and then as a full division moved to Vinton in Gallia County and northward to Wilkesville in Vinton County. There, mindful of mounting numbers of Union pursuers and increasing resistance from Home Guard units, Morgan determined the time had come to leave Ohio and return to the South.

Learning of a ford at Buffington Island on the Ohio River, Morgan made his way eastward across Meigs County, reaching the crossing place at dusk on 18 July. There he was fired upon by a small Home Guard unit that, anticipating his coming, had prepared defensive positions. Not knowing the size of the guard unit he was facing, Morgan determined to camp for the night and fight his way across the river into western Virginia in the morning.

At dawn the next day, Morgan found himself virtually surrounded by a Union army of federal soldiers and Ohio militia under General James M. Shackleford, who, on learning of Morgan's presence at the island crossing, had made a forced march through the night to catch up with him. In the battle that followed (known as the Battle of Buffington Island), Morgan fought his way out of the entrapment but lost 120 of his men killed and more than 700 others captured. Though some of his men managed to cross the river to the Virginia side, about 1,200 others remained with Morgan to seek another crossing about twenty miles upriver. There, about 300 were able to cross the Ohio before Union gunboats arrived to turn the rest back.

From that point on, Morgan was leading a flight, not a raid. He tried to make his way to Blennerhassett Island, but turned back when he learned that gunboats were already there waiting for him. He headed back to Gallia County but met a Union force at Addison, where more of his men were killed or captured. Northward he turned, through Vinton, Athens, and Hocking Counties. At Nelsonville, in Athens County, the raider came back in him when he found a dozen canal boats full of produce and destroyed them. Heading northeastward, he passed through Perry, Morgan, Muskingum, Noble, Guernsey, Harrison, and Jefferson Counties. He hoped to cross the river at Rayland but found both gunboats and high water in his path. Circling west of Steubenville, then north through Wintersville, Richmond, and Bergholz, he led the remnants of his division across Carroll County and on into Columbiana County, where at Salineville he was intercepted by the Seventh Michigan Cavalry on the morning of 26 July. After a short but sharp battle in which he lost 30 killed and 200 taken prisoner, he managed to escape to the north. Not far away, at a place called Power Point some six miles south of Lisbon and fifteen miles from the Pennsylvania border, the exhausted raiders (numbering only 336 by this time) were trapped and forced to surrender, ironically to the pro-Union Ninth Kentucky Cavalry under the command of Major George W. Rue. No other Confederate army in the entire war would get as far north.

Morgan's raid cost Ohio more than a million dollars in property damaged or destroyed and in wages to keep the militia in the field. On the other hand, the South lost one of its finest cavalry divisions, along with its commanding officer. But Morgan, taken with his staff officers to the Ohio Penitentiary in Columbus for confinement, managed to escape with six others on 27 November 1863 by digging a tunnel under the penitentiary walls. For the other officers and men of the raiding party, confined in military prisons at Camp Chase and Johnson's Island, the war was over.

The account that follows is from The Highland Weekly News *for 23 July 1863.[1] For the capture of Morgan's Raiders, Major George W. Rue provides a firsthand account.[2]*

MORGAN WITHIN 15 MILES OF HILLSBORO.

About 6 o'clock last Wednesday evening, news was brought to town, that Morgan was coming towards Hillsboro, and that his advance was but a few miles distant. The people of the town, and the militia of the surrounding country, several hundreds of whom had arrived during the day, immediately gathered at the public square, to consult upon the measures to be taken in the emergency. James H. Thompson, Esq., was called on, and made a few appropriate remarks, advising an immediate organization, and recommending the appointment of some military man to take the command and direction of all the measures for the defence of the town. On motion, Major J. K. Marlay, Provost Marshal of this District, was unanimously appointed, and Lieut. Col. Hixon, Major Buck, and Capt. Sloane were appointed as assistants.

The few arms which could be gathered up were hastily got together, ammunition prepared, and scouts sent out on the roads leading South and West, to ascertain whether the reports of Morgan's approach were true, and if so, to give notice of the fact. Night came on, and still no signs of the enemy were discovered. It was deemed prudent, however, to keep a vigilant look out. — A detail of four companies of 30 men each, was made from the militia, who were armed with guns and axes, and stationed at the bridges on the Western and Southern turnpikes, and the Danville and Marble Furnace roads, for a distance of five or six miles from town, with orders to tear up the bridges and cut down trees on the approach of the enemy. During the night it was ascertained that Morgan's forces, instead of coming this way had taken an easterly direction from Winchester, where they were at noon on Wednesday.

On Thursday morning, about 300 men, mounted and armed with muskets, rifles and shot guns, under command of Lieut Col. Hixon, and Major Buck, started out, and during the day overtook and joined Gen. Hobson's cavalry, who were in pursuit of Morgan towards the Scioto river. Most of them continued the pursuit until Saturday, and some went on still further, and have not yet returned.

Only small detachments of Morgan's force came within our county limits, the main body passing South of the line in the edge of Adams and Brown counties. They visited Winchester, Locust Grove, Youngstown and West Union, robbing stores, stealing horses and plundering as they went.

Great credit is due Major Marlay and his assistants for their prompt and skillful disposition of all the means they had at command, in view of an attack. From facts which have since come to light, it is highly probable that the presence of the few hundred militia who were gathered here, unarmed as they mostly were, and the measures taken for defence, induced Morgan to change his avowed purpose of visiting our town, and caused him to take a more southerly route.

THE SURRENDER OF GENERAL JOHN H. MORGAN: AN ACCOUNT BY MORGAN'S CAPTOR, MAJOR GEORGE W. RUE.

At Salineville, I learned from scouts and telegraph operators that Morgan had crossed the C. & P. railroad and that his column was leisurely moving down the West Beaver road, which ran along the north side of the creek, some ten or twelve miles distant from Salineville. I lost no time and took the road leading towards the creek. When I got on the high ground, near a church, I met a man on horseback riding a good horse. He looked like an intelligent fellow, and I inquired where he was going and from whence he came. He said he was looking for Morgan. I asked him if he was acquainted with the roads leading to West Beaver creek. He said he was, and stated that he was a physician, and had practiced medicine all along the West Beaver valley for a number of years. I told him he was just the fellow I was looking for, and that if he would go with me, and show me the shortest roads, leading to the creek, I would promise to find Morgan for him before noon. He sized me up, and looked over my men, and turning his horse around said, "Come on." When we got to the high ground which overlooks the broad valley for several miles, I saw a cloud of dust arising over a mile away. I asked the doctor, he told me his name, but I do not recall it now, if the West Beaver creek was over where we saw the cloud of dust. The doctor said the dust was rising from the West Beaver road. It follows the creek, down the north side for several miles, where it leaves the creek and leads to the Ohio river. When I first saw the cloud of dust it was rising slowly. Soon it began to move faster. The doctor told me the road over which we were traveling crossed the creek and intercepted the road down the creek about two miles away. Morgan was traveling towards the point where these two roads came together. I had much the greater distance to travel. I at once ordered my command into a brisk trot.

About this time my command commenced to throw some dust. Morgan evidently soon noticed the dust we were raising, and his guides must have informed him that the road over which we were traveling led into the road which was leading him towards the goal he was so anxious to reach, the Ohio river. Morgan's tired horses were spurred into a faster gait, and he beat me to where the roads came together. Most of his command had passed the point before I reached the creek. I could only fall in his rear and give him a chase. This I did not want to do. I wanted to meet Morgan and his raiders face to face, and fight him to a finish. Here the doctor suggested that by riding down the creek, along which he said was a private road, not very good, but over which horses could travel nicely. I found the creek bottom was level, almost with the road. It was not very rocky, and was suitable for fast riding, because there was but little water at most places.

We rode down that creek bottom at a gallop, probably a mile and a half or two miles, until we found a private road leading from the creek up through the fields, past a barn to the main road. It was a fast ride, with good horses. I remember it well. I shall never forget it. As soon as we reached the main road we wheeled to the left, and rode to the crest of the first hill, up the creek. I found we were ahead of Morgan. I knew than I had him. I formed my command in line of battle across the road, quickly. My right rested in a bit of timberland, with the left of the line below the road, down in the orchard. I had scarcely placed my troops in position for a fight, when over the crest of a hill about a quarter of a mile away, appeared the heads of the horses of Morgan's advance troops. As soon as they saw me, they halted and drew back, leaving one or two men to watch our movements.

Soon afterwards three troopers came riding over the crest of the hill and down into the little valley which lay between the two opposing lines. One of the men had a bit of white muslin tied on a saber, or on a ramrod, which he was waiving. This I supposed was intended for a flag of truce. I sent three of my men forward to find out what was wanted. My troopers came back and reported that General Morgan demanded my surrender. I at once recognized that as a John Morgan bluff. I sent word to Morgan that he must surrender or fight Major Geo. W. Rue, of the Ninth Kentucky cavalry. This must have been a surprise to Morgan, and no doubt was the first intimation to him that I was not still in Kentucky.[3]

He next tried a ruse and sent back his men with a flag of truce, informing me that he had already surrendered to Captain Burdick. I had never heard of Captain Burdick until that moment. I inquired who he was, and to whose command he belonged. One of Morgan's men told me that Captain Burdick was captain of a militia company from a nearby town. I then sent word back to Morgan that I recognized no surrender, only one to myself, and informed his men that he must surrender or fight at once. They then went back to report, and in a few moments returned with the announcement that Morgan was willing to surrender to me.

I at once, with an escort, rode over into Morgan's camp. His men were lying on both sides of the road and nearly every one of them asleep. It was a hot July day and they were the tiredest lot of fellows I ever saw in my life. I rode quite a little distance through his men before I reached Morgan. When I met him he was on a fine Kentucky, thoroughbred sorrel mare, one that Morgan said was the only horse that came through from Kentucky, and which had withstood the strain of travel for twenty-seven consecutive days. Morgan was very loth to part with that sorrel mare. He gave the mare to me, supposing probably that I would take her back to Kentucky where he might some day have a chance to steal her back. . . .

1. From the *Highland Weekly News,* 23 July 1863, reproduced in Robert C. Wheeler, ed., *Ohio Newspapers: A Living Record* (Columbus: Ohio History Press, 1950), 180–81.

2. George W. Rue, "Celebration of the Surrender of General John H. Morgan," *Ohio Archaeological and Historical Publications* (Columbus, 1911), 20:373–76.

3. Born and raised south of Lexington, which was Morgan's hometown, Rue came to Ohio after the Civil War. His remains are interred in the cemetery in Hamilton.

IX.5. "Ohio's Jewels"

It would be difficult if not impossible to find a state whose contributions to the winning of the Civil War and with it the preservation of the Union and the ending of slavery were greater than those of Ohio. While the only military action of consequence on Ohio soil came with Morgan's Raid, the contributions of Ohioans both military and governmental on distant battlefields and in the national capital made Ohio a leader among the Northern states throughout the war.

The Civil War Memorial in front of the statehouse in Columbus today, appropriately called "These Are My Jewels," depicts Ohio as Cornelia, the famous Roman mother, with arms outstretched to her seven sons clustered about her, her greatest assets, her jewels.[1] Ohio's seven jewels of the Civil War were Ulysses S. Grant, Philip H. Sheridan, William Tecumseh Sherman, James A. Garfield, Edwin M. Stanton, Salmon P. Chase, and Rutherford B. Hayes — outstanding generals, cabinet officers, a chief justice, and three future presidents among them. But so many more might have been included, from little Johnny Clem, the "Drummer Boy of Shiloh," to the fourteen "Fighting McCooks." Or the Andrews Raiders, the first to receive the Congressional Medal of Honor. And what about the war governors, William Dennison, David Tod, and John Brough? Or Benjamin Harrison, Jay Cooke, Don Carlos Buell, George A. Custer, James B. McPherson, Irvin McDowell, George B. McClellan,

William S. Rosecrans, Jacob D. Cox? Or the U.S. senators Benjamin F. Wade and John Sherman? The list of distinguished Ohioans of the war period goes on and on.

All told, 346,326 Ohioans served in the armed forces during the war. Of these, 24,591 made the supreme sacrifice, including 11,237 who were killed in battle or died from battlefield wounds, and another 13,354 who died from non-battlefield causes, primarily disease. Truly, all of these were also Ohio's Jewels.

Ohio Writer Walter Havighurst Reflects on "Ohio's Jewels"

To the World's Fair in Chicago in 1893 Ohio sent the monument—now on the State House grounds in Columbus—of seven leaders in the Civil War. On a granite pedestal stand the bronze figures of Ulysses S. Grant, William T. Sherman, Philip H. Sheridan, Edwin M. Stanton, Salmon P. Chase, James A. Garfield, and Rutherford B. Hayes. Two were generals who became presidents. Two were colleagues in Lincoln's cabinet. Three were Union generals who in the welter of war rose to greatness. All had grown up in Ohio.

On the pedestal they stand passive in rumpled army dress, but Sherman, Sheridan, and Grant were three men of action, wholly different from each other except in remorseless determination and a willingness to risk greatly for great ends.

Sherman, lean and wiry, hands clenched, eyes roving, with bristling red hair and stubble beard, had a lightning mind and volcanic emotions. In Georgia he broke all the rules of warfare. Without baggage and supply trains he marched through the heart of enemy country, cut off from reserves nowhere to fall back to. Tacticians abroad said he was undertaking the most brilliant or the most foolish feat in modern conflict. Week after week, month after month, summer and autumn and winter, his great column swept on, over mountains and across rivers, through villages, towns, and cities, driving the enemy before him and thrusting it aside, leaving a swath of ruin all the way to Savannah and the sea.

Little Phil Sheridan, one of six children of an Irish immigrant, grew up in Perry County where stagecoaches and freight wagons rumbled over the National Road. One morning in 1847 while Henry Howe sketched the courthouse in Somerset, he saw across the road a pink-faced boy lugging goods into a general store. On Munster Day the Irish had a free fight, with that scrappy boy in the middle. Seventeen years later, commanding the Army of the Shenandoah, he pounded up and down the battle lines, cheered by men whose lives he was gambling. A fiery, forceful leader on his black horse Rienzi, he put strength into exhausted men, will into the lagging, heart into the hopeless. Now a bronze Sheridan on horseback dominates the courthouse yard in Somerset.

Grant had neither the build nor the bearing of a commander. But he had a stubborn mind and unrelenting will. Stumpy, stocky, slouchy—only a horse could give him stature. His favorite mount was a big bay named Cincinnati; Grant had come from Brown County, just upriver from the Queen City. He never lost the look of a country man, even when he was spilling cigar ash in the White House and saluting to crowds in the great cities of Europe and Asia. The fiery Sheridan learned foresight from him and the voluble Sherman gave this closemouthed man his deepest devotion.

In 1893 when the monument was unveiled in the Court of Honor in Chicago, all seven of the bronze Ohio men were dead but not forgotten. The remarkable leadership that came from Ohio makes one wonder. What did these men have in common? In mind, character, and capabilities they were unlike each other. But they all, in a crucial time, seem to have believed in success. They believed in it enough to transmit that belief to others, and so to evoke from others the best that was in them.

1. The statuary group was the work of Levi T. Scofield of Cleveland, who also sculptured the Soldiers' and Sailors' Monument in that city.

The excerpt is from Walter Havighurst, *Ohio, A Bicentennial History* (New York: Norton, 1976), 105–7.

IX.6. "Bluff Ben" Wade and the Fight for Congressional Control of Reconstruction

Denounced as a tyrannical despot by Clement L. Vallandigham and the "Peace Democrats" for his efforts to preserve the Union through force and for his proclamation to emancipate the slaves of the South, President Abraham Lincoln also had his share of critics in the radical wing of his own party over issues of Reconstruction. Led by Senator Benjamin F. Wade from Ashtabula County, Ohio, the "Radical Republicans" challenged Lincoln's position that the war was a rebellion by disgruntled individuals and that under the pardoning power granted to the president by the Constitution, the postwar reconstruction of the defeated South was a presidential, not a congressional, matter. Rather, Wade and the Radicals argued, the defeated Southern states had voluntarily surrendered all rights and privileges as states when they seceded and, once conquered by force of arms, they became the territory or property of all the United States and thus, constitutionally, subject to the control of Congress. The argument was not a mere play on words. At issue was Lincoln's fundamental belief that, in the interest of long-range harmony and goodwill, Reconstruction of the Union should be based on reconciliation, not punitive vindication. To the Radical Republicans, a lenient peace could well mean an early return to power in the South of those who had precipitated the war and, across the nation, of the Democratic Party. They also foresaw a return to dominance of agrarian interests to the detriment of the newly industrialized areas of the North.

Well before the end of the war the clash between rival executive and congressional plans of Reconstruction had moved to the fore. On 8 December 1863, Lincoln issued his Proclamation of Amnesty and Reconstruction, in which he offered pardon to all except high-ranking Confederate military, civil, and diplomatic officers and former U.S. military and civil officials who had left the federal service to serve the Confederacy, provided they take the oath of allegiance and accept the recent laws and proclamation respecting the emancipation of slaves. Aimed at restoring loyal governments in the seceded states as soon as possible, Lincoln's Amnesty Proclamation directed that when the number taking the oath of allegiance amounted to 10 percent of the voting population of 1860, the loyal 10 percent could then organize a new, loyal state government and receive executive recognition. Shocked at the leniency of Lincoln's "10 percent plan," congressional Radicals responded with a plan of their own, embodied in the Wade-Davis Bill of 2 July 1864. Cosponsored by Senator Wade and Congressman Henry Winter Davis of Maryland, the bill authorized reestablishment of loyal state governments in the South only when at least half of their citizens had taken the oath of allegiance, but prohibited from voting or holding office all who had fought for the Confederacy. The practical result of this prohibition would have been the disfranchisement of most Southern white males and an indefinite postponement of the return of the Democratic Party to power in the former Confederate states. Believing this much too severe and likely to cause long-range racial problems in the South, particularly in light of the prospective enfranchisement of the black male population through constitutional amendment, Lincoln pocket vetoed the bill on 8 July 1864.

The response of Senator Wade was quick and to the point. The longtime abolitionist and staunch supporter of voting rights for blacks, who later would lead the fight to require all white males in the South to take an "iron-clad" oath that they had not borne arms against the Union as prerequisite for voting, issued a "Manifesto" with Congressman Davis that denounced Lincoln's "dictatorial usurpation" of power from the Congress in the president's bid to control Reconstruction. "A more studied outrage on the legislative authority of the people," it was asserted in the manifesto, "has never been perpetrated."[1]

Lincoln's fight with the radicals of his own party was cut short by his assassination the following April. Ironically, when the vice president, Andrew Johnson, replaced Lincoln, it was Benjamin Wade who replaced Johnson as president (pro tempore) of the Senate. When the fight over control of Reconstruction continued between Johnson and the Congress, culminating in the impeachment trial of Johnson in 1868, it was Ohio's Benjamin F. Wade who missed becoming the president of the United States by the margin of the single vote by which Andrew Johnson was saved from removal from office.

THE WADE-DAVIS MANIFESTO
August 5, 1864

*W*e have read without surprise, but not without indignation, the proclamation of the President of the 8th of July [vetoing the Wade-Davis Bill]. . . .

The President, by preventing this bill from becoming a law, holds the electoral votes of the rebel States at the dictation of his personal ambition.

If those votes turn the balance in his favor, is it to be supposed that his competitor, defeated by such means, will acquiesce?

If the rebel majority assert their supremacy in those States, and send votes which elect an enemy of the Government, will we not repel his claims?

And is not that civil war for the Presidency inaugurated by the votes of rebel States?

Seriously impressed with these dangers, Congress, *"the proper constituted authority,"* formally declared that there are no State governments in the rebel States, and provided for their erection at a proper time; and both the Senate and the House of Representatives rejected the Senators and Representatives chosen under the authority of what the President calls the free constitution and government of Arkansas.

The President's proclamation *"holds for naught"* this judgment, and discards the authority of the Supreme Court, and strides headlong toward the anarchy his proclamation of the 8th of December inaugurated.

If electors for President be allowed to be chosen in either of those States, a sinister light will be cast on the motives which induced the President to "hold for naught" the will of Congress rather than his government in Louisiana and Arkansas.

That judgment of Congress which the President defies was the exercise of an authority exclusively vested in Congress by the Constitution to determine what is the established government in a State, and in its own nature and by the highest judicial authority binding on all other departments of the Government. . . .

A more studied outrage on the legislative authority of the people has never been perpetrated.

Congress passed a bill; the President refused to approve it, and then by proclamation puts as much of it in force as he sees fit, and proposes to execute those parts by officers unknown to the laws of the United States and not subject to the confirmation of the Senate!

The bill directed the appointment of Provisional Governors by and with the advice and consent of the Senate.

The President, after defeating the law, proposed to appoint without law, and without the advice and consent of the Senate, *Military* Governors for the rebel States!

He has already exercised this dictatorial usurpation in Louisiana, and he defeated the bill to prevent its limitation. . . .

The President has greatly presumed on the forbearance which the supporters of his Administration have so long practiced, in view of the arduous conflict in which we are engaged, and the reckless ferocity of our political opponents.

But he must understand that our support is of a cause and not of a man; that the authority of Congress is paramount and must be respected; that the whole body of the Union men of Congress will not submit to be impeached by him of rash and unconstitutional legislation; and if he wishes our support, he must confine himself to his executive duties—to obey and execute, not make the laws—to suppress by arms armed rebellion, and leave political reorganization to Congress.

If the supporters of the Government fail to insist on this, they become responsible for the usurpations which they fail to rebuke, and are justly liable to the indignation of the people whose rights and security, committed to their keeping, they sacrifice.

Let them consider the remedy for these usurpations, and, having found it, fearlessly execute it.

1. The Wade-Davis Manifesto is quoted in Henry Steele Commager, ed., *Documents of American History,* 7th ed. (New York: Appleton-Century-Crofts, 1963), 1:439–40.

IX.7. Grant, Hayes, and the End of Reconstruction

Though the Radical Republicans in 1868 failed by a single vote at the end of his impeachment trial to remove Andrew Johnson from the presidency and to replace him with one of their own, the Senate president pro tempore, Benjamin F. Wade, they succeeded that fall in electing Ulysses S. Grant, the hero of Appomattox, as president, and in reelecting him in 1872. With Congress in firm control of Reconstruction by 1867, the Southern state governments recognized by Lincoln and Johnson were dismantled. The South was temporarily divided into five military districts, each headed by a major general. Readmission of the former Confederate states to the Union was possible only when newly elected state legislatures accepted the Fourteenth and (later) Fifteenth Amendments (guaranteeing citizenship and the right to vote irrespective of race, color, or previous condition of servitude) and when new state constitutions had been written to provide for black suffrage. In Ohio, the Fifteenth Amendment was finally ratified in 1870, and in that year, for the first time, black delegates attended the Republican state convention.

Though he had been the Union's foremost general, President Grant had little interest in political life and was ill suited to lead the nation in a critical period. Personally honest, he trusted too much in those who were not. Scandals soon tainted his administration and followed him to the end of his presidency.

In 1876 the Republicans turned to another son of Ohio and Civil War hero, Rutherford B. Hayes, as their candidate to succeed Grant. Ohio's first three-term governor, Hayes was a moralist in politics and untouched by personal or political scandal, hence regarded as one who could rid the national government of corruption. To oppose Hayes, the Democrats nominated Samuel J. Tilden, the reform governor of New York. Since the Grant scandals had occurred in a Republican administration, most voters believed the best hope for reform lay with the opposition party and hence gave Tilden a 250,000-vote majority in the fall election. In the electoral college, however, a dispute arose over the returns from three Southern states, South Carolina, Louisiana, and Florida, and over the qualifications of a single elector from Oregon. In all, a total of 20 votes in the electoral college were at stake. Without any of them, Tilden had 184 electoral votes. But he needed 185 to win. If all 20 disputed votes went to Hayes, the Ohioan would win.

A special electoral commission of five representatives, five senators, and five justices of the Supreme Court was agreed upon in the Congress to resolve the matter. There was no problem in getting five Republicans and five Democrats selected from the two houses of Congress, but it was not as easy when it came to selecting the five commission members from the Supreme Court, for there were only two known Democrats on the Court, and one other regarded as an independent. The rest were all Republicans. When the one independent accepted election to the Senate by the Democratic legislators of Illinois, the only ones remaining were Republicans. Thus, the special electoral commission to resolve the disputed election of 1876 finally consisted of eight Republicans and seven Democrats. By a strict party vote of 8 to 7, every one of the disputed electoral ballots was awarded to Hayes, who was declared the winner of the election in the electoral college by a final count of 185 to 184. For the second time in less than a decade, an Ohioan had won or lost the presidency by the margin of a single vote.

Asserting that the election had been "stolen," the Democrats in Congress threatened not to take their seats in the upcoming legislative sessions. At length a compromise was reached. If the Democrats would accept him as the next president, Hayes would withdraw the last of the federal troops still occupying Louisiana and South Carolina and propping up Republican-dominated governments in both states, in each of which electoral votes had been in dispute.

With executive orders from President Hayes directing the withdrawal of federal military support, the last of the so-called carpetbag governments collapsed. The political Reconstruction of the South was finally at an end, twelve long years after Appomattox.

President Grant Apologizes for His Errors of Judgment[1]

Executive Mansion
December 5, 1876.

To the Senate and House of Representatives:

In submitting my eighth and last annual message to Congress it seems appropriate that I should refer to and in some degree recapitulate the events and official acts of the past eight years.

It was my fortune, or misfortune, to be called to the office of Chief Executive without any previous political training. From the age of 17 I had never even witnessed the excitement attending a Presidential campaign but twice antecedent to my own candidacy, and at but one of them was I eligible as a voter.

Under such circumstances it is but reasonable to suppose that errors of judgment must have occurred. Even had they not, differences of opinion between the Executive, bound by an oath to the strict performance of his duties, and writers and debaters must have arisen. It is not necessarily evidence of blunder on the part of the Executive because there are these differences of views. Mistakes have been made, as all can see and I admit, but it seems to me oftener in the selections made of the assistants appointed to aid in carrying out the various duties of administering the Government—in nearly every case selected without a personal acquaintance with the appointee, but upon recommendations of the representatives chosen directly by the people. It is impossible, where so many trusts are to be allotted, that the right parties should be chosen in every instance. History shows that no Administration from the time of Washington to the present has been free from these mistakes. But I leave comparisons to history, claiming only that I have acted in every instance from a conscientious desire to do what was right, constitutional, within the law, and for the very best interests of the whole people. Failures have been errors of judgment, not of intent.

President Hayes Orders the Withdrawal of Federal Troops from the Vicinity of the Louisiana Statehouse[2]

Executive Mansion,
Washington, April 20, 1877.

Sir:

Prior to my entering upon the duties of the presidency there had been stationed, by order of my predecessor, in the immediate vicinity of the building used as a State house in New Orleans, Louisiana, and known as the Saint Louis Hotel, a detachment of United States Infantry. Finding them in that place I have thought proper to delay a decision of the question of their removal until I could determine whether the condition of affairs is now such as to either require or justify the continued military intervention of the National Government in the affairs of that State.

In my opinion there does not now exist in Louisiana, such domestic violence as is contemplated by the constitution, as the ground upon which the military power of the National Government may be invoked for the defense of the state. The disputes which exist as to the rights of certain claimants to the Chief Executive office of that State, are to be settled and determined; not by the Executive of the United States, but by such orderly and peaceable methods as may be provided by the constitution and laws of the State. Having the assurance that no resort to violence is contemplated, but, that on the contrary, the disputes in question are to be settled by peaceful methods, under, and in accordance with law, I deem it proper to take action in accordance with the principles announced when I entered upon the duties of the presidency. You are therefore directed to see that the proper orders are issued for the removal of said troops at an early date, from their present position, to such regular barracks in the vicinity as may be selected for their occupation.

(signed) R. B. Hayes

To Hon. Geo. W. McCrary
Secretary of War

1. Quoted in Henry Steele Commager, ed., *Documents of American History,* 7th ed. (New York: Appleton-Century-Crofts, 1963), 1:545.

2. From the microfilm copy of the 20 April 1877 handwritten executive order from President R. B. Hayes to George W. McCrary, secretary of war, in the Rutherford B. Hayes Presidential Center Library, Fremont, Ohio.

Part Two

The Gilded Age to the Present

Edited by Clarence E. Wunderlin, Jr.

X. Politics, Law, and Society in Ohio's Gilded Age

THE LAST FOUR DECADES of the nineteenth century constitute an important, formative era in Ohio history. Often dismissed as an insignificant period of speculative profiteering and corrupt political deal making sandwiched between the Civil War and the beginning of the twentieth century, the Gilded Age was an era of political, economic, and social development that transformed the state. From the 1870 to 1900, Ohio evolved from a state that was predominantly agricultural, rural, and traditional to one that was heavily industrialized, urban, pluralistic, and modern. During these years, Ohio's political parties did much to establish the parameters of that transformation; parties acted not merely as organizations that mobilized voters and financial contributors solely for competitive advantages, but also as vehicles for the debate and resolution of significant policy questions. The documents that follow provide a glimpse of how the two major political parties operated, how legislators attempted to order race and gender relations, and what impact modernization had on workers, farmers, women, and minorities. The next chapter will offer a closer look at Ohio's industrial transformation. As the research of recent historians demonstrates, Gilded Age businessmen combined new technical and organizational knowledge and massive amounts of capital to create productive enterprises that effectively exploited the region's abundant resources and ever-expanding workforce as the nineteenth century ended.

Throughout most of the Gilded Age, the two major parties, Republicans and Democrats, dominated Ohio politics. Only at the beginning and end did third-party efforts, by Greenbackers after Reconstruction and by Populists in the 1890s, have a significant impact on the conduct of political affairs. Those affairs were marked by the organization of powerful political machines that mobilized voters, financed campaigns, and constructed elaborate relationships between city bosses and big-business interests. But, just as significant, political machines performed key services that kept cities functioning and assimilated new arrivals, especially immigrants from central and eastern Europe.

Although they appeared to be ambitious, greedy politicos, jousting solely for competitive advantage, Republicans and Democrats differed significantly in their philosophy of government during the last quarter of the nineteenth century. Republicans at all levels of government were more inclined to use its authority in the public interest during the Gilded Age. At the national level, Republicans resorted to government intervention, especially trade policy, to promote economic development. At the state and local level, intervention might come in the form of social legislation, such as the advocacy of temperance laws favored by the native-born, skilled labor, and middle-class constituents in the Republican fold. In contrast, Democrats, with important agrarian and immigrant labor constituencies, usually opposed governmental paternalism. National leaders such as President Grover Cleveland rejected the economic policy of high protection in favor of low "revenue" tariffs. Gilded Age Democrats opposed most social legislation, or accepted only limited restraints on personal conduct, because they, like Thomas Jefferson, favored "the largest individual liberty consistent with public order."[1]

Consistent with their party's advocacy of reasonable state intervention in the private sector, Ohio's Republican governors supported a number of regulatory measures after 1880. During his four years as governor, Charles Foster advocated the creation of bipartisan boards of control for public agencies, the extension of coal mining regulations, the initiation of forest conservation measures, and the revision of state tax laws. Under Joseph B. Foraker's leadership, the state established boards of health and pardons, created a canal commission to recover land abandoned after operations on the waterways ceased, and enforced the laws against the vigilante "White Caps" in southern Ohio.[2] In the following decade, Republican William McKinley, architect of the nation's 1890 tariff act while in Congress, balanced the use of the state militia in the 1894 coal miners' strike with the organization of food relief to assist the economically depressed Athens County mining communities that teetered on the edge of starvation.[3]

Both major parties seemed compelled to demonstrate their economic conservatism to Ohio voters after 1885. Republicans opposed inflationary monetary schemes and refrained from proposing regulations on business practices that might damage their relationship with big corporations. Similarly, most Ohio Democrats, who had to prove themselves to business leaders, abandoned the currency schemes of the greenback movement that proved so popular in the state between the elections of 1877 and 1885. From the mid-1880s Ohio Democrats embraced the more respectable "free-silver" money program and supported protective tariffs that far exceeded the revenue tariff policy of President Grover Cleveland and the party's national leadership.

Rather than shrink from debate over controversial social issues, state legislators debated and acted on numerous measures that confronted Ohioans at the end of the century. Alcohol consumption, race relations, and relations between husbands and wives were three key areas where state government extended individual rights and attempted to regulate personal conduct.

Alcohol may have been the most hotly debated topic of the Gilded Age. It shaped Ohio's legislative agendas and political campaigns beginning in the early 1880s. Republican governors took strong positions on the regulation of liquor consumption during that decade. Governor Charles Foster became the first notable crusader against drink. Backed by Foster, the state legislature passed two constitutional amendments providing voters with taxation and local option prohibition schemes. Before voters decided on the amendments, legislators first enacted the Pond Bill, instituting a saloon taxation scheme, then the Scott Bill, a modified Sunday "Blue Law" that initiated retail sales taxes. The Ohio Supreme Court declared both laws unconstitutional, sending lawmakers back to the drawing boards.

The drink issue drowned Republican gubernatorial candidate Joseph B. Foraker and the party's majority in the state legislature in 1883. By the mid-1880s, both parties had staked out viable positions on the issue of drink. Republicans clearly defined themselves as advocates of liquor taxation. Finally elected in 1885, Foraker pressed for passage of the Dow Law that instituted state taxation of liquor sales in his first year in office. In contrast, Democrats adopted saloon licensing, a program that conferred legitimacy on alcohol consumption while condoning an acceptable form of regulation.

Ohio's legislators also confronted the controversial issue of civil rights in the late Gilded Age. Undoubtedly influenced by the tradition of relatively harmonious race relations in northern Ohio, lawmakers quickly stepped into the void created by the U.S. Supreme Court's 1883 decisions invalidating the existing federal civil rights law. In 1884, the General Assembly enacted legislation that declared a wide range of discriminatry actions in public facilities to be unlawful.

When race relations deteriorated into mob violence in southern Ohio in the early 1890s, the legislature again acted, passing a model antilynching law that placed the burden of lawlessness squarely on the shoulders of the surrounding community. Many states, on both sides of the Mason-Dixon line, followed Ohio's lead, enacting similar laws to stop the wave of lynching.

During the last half of the nineteenth century, women's rights activists lobbied the Ohio General Assembly to alter the legal status of women. During these years, state lawmakers enacted, then amended, numerous "married women's property laws." By the end of 1887, the year that the legislature codified the rights and liabilities of marriage partners, wives and widows possessed a broad range of married women's property rights, a bundle of rights entitling women to own and manage real and personal property and contract with others for the conduct of business.

The first five documents in this chapter address the political and legal themes discussed above. Two documents are impressions of political life and the work of political parties; the other three are texts of statutes that were meant to shape social relations within the state. The final two documents belong, more obviously, to the category of social history and offer readers a glimpse of life in the city and on the farm at the turn of the last century.

1. Charles W. Calhoun, "The Political Culture: Public Life and the Conduct of Politics," in Calhoun, ed., *The Gilded Age: Essays on the Origins of Modern America* (Wilmington, Del.: Scholarly Resources, 1996), 190-91.

2. Eugene H. Roseboom and Francis P. Weisenburger, *A History of Ohio* (Columbus: Ohio Historical Society, 1973), 243-45.

3. George W. Knepper, *Ohio and Its People* (Kent, Ohio: Kent State University Press, 1997), 182-83.

X.1.   "Bosses and Boodle" in the Gilded Age: De Chambrun's Story of Machine Politics in the Queen City

Cincinnati, one of the two great urban industrial centers in the state, was fortunate enough to possess not one, but two, political machines during the last quarter of the nineteenth century. The Democrats organized first, tightly knitting together an organization under the direction of John R. McLean. The Republicans responded, countering McLean's mobilization of immigrants, especially Catholics, with the organization of mostly native-born, skilled, Protestant, and more prosperous city dwellers.[1]

The success of machine politics in Cincinnati's Gilded Age can be attributed, in part, to the changing demographics of the city. As business enterprise took possession of those sections of the old antebellum "walking city" closest to the Ohio River, a growing wage-earning class spread out between the rail yards and the hills to the north. During the chaotic years of the Civil War, prominent local men, labeled "bummers"—often saloon keepers, brothel owners, even police officers and fire brigade captains—in the working-class neighborhoods gradually began to organize political activity and deliver votes for the major parties. McLean inherited and perfected the emerging system. He carefully wove together a coalition of these bummers into an organization that could mobilize voters, take advantage of any opportunity for election-day irregularities, and secure a comfortable victory for Queen City Democrats. Voters were not obligated to register, did not need to provide proof of identification, could repeat their choices at other polling places, and could, as in frontier days, carry firearms while exercising their franchise. By the mid-1870s, Republicans responded to these tactics in kind. Consider historian Philip D. Jordan's account of graft and corruption in Cincinnati during the crucial 1876 general election:

> *Both sides pulled every trick from their political poke. Money was lavishly spent. Gangs of repeaters were brought in from larger cities. Negroes were imported from Kentucky and bummers from Chicago. Negroes were rounded up by the Democratic police force and roughs by the Republican marshals. Votes were bought and ballot boxes stuffed. . . . An unusually high Democratic vote in some Queen City wards soon provoked an inquiry headed by the Cincinnati Gazette and the Cincinnati Commercial. By comparing the lists of voters as they registered at the polls with a city directory, investigators found many names which did not appear as residents. The Gazette found an excess of 1,766 voters in nine wards. Some of the names were found to be those of legal voters who had moved into these wards but a short time before. The greater part of these votes, however, gave evidence of being illegal. Several similar lists were drawn up within the next few weeks.[2]*

Clara Longworth de Chambrun, a Cincinnati native and the sister of Nicholas Longworth, member, and later Speaker, of the U.S. House of Representatives, viewed city and state politics from a unique vantage point. The following document, an excerpt from her Cincinnati: Story of the Queen City,[3] *emphasizes the competitiveness and corruption of the emerging political organizations in the city.*

*I*t took many years of civic corruption, graft, blackmail—and perhaps the stinging re-buke of a visiting foreigner—to awaken America—east, west, north, and south—to the fact brought forward by James Bryce, in the *American Commonwealth,* that the government of our cities was the one conspicuous failure of democracy in the United States.

Cincinnati seldom does things by halves: when bribery was the order of the day, few equaled her in applying such methods, and when she awoke to the realization that a city cannot prosper as a party enterprise but must be conducted with specialized professional skill on the lines of a business corporation and run by experts in organization, in housing, planning, and parking without regard for politics, keeping in view only the interest of her citizens, she reversed the machine completely. . . . In the eighties the city was generally ruled by the Democratic Party. The administration was notoriously corrupt. The patient public put up with the governing powers so long that outsiders supposed that it would never be stirred from lethargy to action. Nevertheless, as we have seen, the people possessed an unsuspected capacity for indignation. In 1884, following repeated denials of criminal justice, the courthouse was burned by an indignant mob.

For many years Republican votes were simply and radically eliminated. Several wagons of police-patrol passed through the precincts early on election day, arrested all would-be Negro voters, and kept them under lock and key until the polls were closed.

Many other Republican tickets were scrapped before reaching the ballot boxes, while Democratic tickets were manufactured wholesale. When John R. McLean was up for senatorial election there were more votes listed from one precinct than its entire population could show. Not much imagination went into the confection of fake ballots: for when the list of names began to run low, such samples were presented as William January, John February, James March, Alfred April, and William May!

Every ward captain held an official job, the one exception being a man who had no need of small emoluments for he was the happy possessor of a rich monopoly, that of the gambling establishments then numerous in our town.

Popular indignation stirred up by newspaper revelations suddenly caused a party overturn. The Democrats were ousted from power. Republicans came triumphantly to remain for a long time masters of the situation. Unfortunately the Grand Old Party did not bring with it more honest methods: civic virtue was at a particularly low ebb: skepticism reigned among the voters and, although politics were declared "too dirty to handle," they became increasingly unsavory. It is true that the Democratic *Enquirer* now thundered against "gang corruption," but the Republican *Commercial Gazette* took care not to criticize the people of their own party: *your* scamps and *our* scamps are rarely viewed by the same standards; thus, amidst revelations all around, public confidence was destroyed without bringing reform to political methods.

Such inertia among our citizens can be partially explained by the exodus to the neighboring heights. Progressively, as years went on, the best elements abandoned the center to business and having "moved up and out" our leading men felt morally remote from what was happening "downtown" where a smoke screen through which virtuous eyes could not pierce veiled the activities of gambling-houses and saloons.

In the light of after events, it is now apparent that neither of the two great parties can be held entirely accountable for the tide of corruption which submerged the city at the opening of the twentieth century. The practice of bribery, the prevalence of graft made the body politic an unresisting victim of organized public plunder. The base of the structure was prepared for the master builder who went by a less respectable name: the *boss*.

George B. Cox began his astonishing career in the seventies as a driver of a grocery wagon and proprietor of a beer saloon of such ill repute that he constantly got in trouble with the police. Cox developed the brilliant idea that if he could get himself elected to city Council he would be immune from attack.

This he effected in 1879 and, at once, his power and riches began to grow. The *Boss*-to-be had many of the elements which go into making a great leader: talent for organization, political acumen of exceptional nature, and three principles of conduct from which he did not swerve. He never broke a promise, never went back on a henchman who served him well, and always delivered the promised goods in lucrative city jobs all of which, by 1885, he held in the palm of his hand. . . .

At this time no obstacle was permitted to stand long in the paths of the bosses' ambition. Through political manipulation the Board of Public Works, elected by the people, was transformed into the Board of Public Affairs, appointed by the State governor. Thus, nearly two thousand more "jobs" were, from that time, duly distributed by George B. Cox. But being no fool, just as public patience neared the breaking point he would throw in his influence to get a good man elected to an important position, as for instance when he twice backed Julius Fleischmann for mayor, a man who did his work exceptionally well. Nor was this the only case when the astute boss found it good policy to back the right candidate.

1. Zane L. Miller, *Boss Cox's Cincinnati: Urban Politics in the Progressive Era* (New York: Oxford University Press, 1968), esp. 1–110.

2. Philip D. Jordan, *Ohio Comes of Age, 1873–1900* (Columbus: Ohio State Archaeological and Historical Society, 1943), 194–95.

3. Clara Longworth de Chambrun, *Cincinnati: Story of the Queen City* (New York: Charles Scribner's Sons, 1939), 291–94.

X.2.   The "Bloody Shirt" in Ohio Politics: Joseph B. Foraker and the Gubernatorial Campaign of 1885

Joseph B. Foraker, governor from 1886 to 1890, embodied the quintessential Gilded Age "politico." A Civil War veteran who drew considerable support from the Grand Army of the Republic, Foraker did not hesitate to resurrect the "bloody shirt of rebellion," reiterating the roles played by the Democratic Party in secession, war, and reconstruction. The document included below is a dramatic illustration of Foraker's rhetorical style. But it also reveals, in no uncertain terms, Foraker's interpretation of the Republican Party's stance on voting rights for African Americans in the South and, more generally, of the party's expansive view of government in the 1880s. The speech, given in Bellefontaine, Ohio, during the 1885 gubernatorial campaign, is taken from Foraker's memoirs.[1]

*T*he party of today believes that if the party of twenty years ago did right in giving to the colored people of the South the right to vote, it is the duty of the people of this country today to give them protection in the exercise of that right. (Applause.) And hence it is that, standing at the head of the resolutions adopted by the Springfield Convention is the declaration that the right to vote is a sacred right—that it must be protected and guaranteed by the Constitution and the laws, and that every man who has the right to vote must be accorded that right, free from all violence, fraud or intimidation, and that his ballot when cast must be counted as cast. (Applause.) The platform goes further than that, and says that if under the Constitution and the laws as now existing, it is not possible so to protect the right of suffrage, then the Constitution and the laws must be made so that the protection can be given. (Applause.) Why, my friends, in other words, to the Republican Party it is an infamous idea that the general government should have the right, as it unquestionably has, to cross over the lines of the States and draft you into its military service, compelling you to go out and stand up for the flag on the field of battle, and that when you have done this at the peril of your life you are mustered out and have returned home within your State, those State lines so easily crossed in one case should rise up so high about you that the general government that drafted you cannot cross over them to protect you in the enjoyment of your rights. (Loud applause.) We believe that a government that cannot defend its defenders and protect its protectors has something the matter with it. (Loud applause.) We intend to find out what that something is and mend it. We have a great contest in this country to establish these rights; it may be we have entered upon another long contest, but it is one in which we are bound to triumph. Sooner or later we shall surely secure the enforcement of these rights throughout the country. Now why do I talk like this? Why do I say anything about the right of people down South to vote? There are a great many people North, there are a great many newspapers here who, when they hear you talking about interference with the right of suffrage down yonder, dismiss the whole matter by saying, "That is waving the bloody shirt." Well, now if so, then let us talk a little about the bloody shirt.

Heretofore we have been electing our Presidents and Vice Presidents each time for twenty-four years. Heretofore we have had nothing to do—as hereafter we will not have—with the local State elections in the South, and inasmuch as the national result has been favorable to us anyhow, we have slipped along, paying very little attention to what was going on down there. But at last, by last year's election, we have forced upon us in a way we can understand and appreciate, the effect of the fact that when a man deposits his ballot in Mississippi, or Georgia, or any other State in this nation for President, he is voting not alone for himself and the people of his State, but he is voting for the people of the State of Ohio; and when a man goes to the ballot-box with a shotgun to keep somebody from putting his ballot in the box, he is interfering with the expression of the people that affects not only the citizens of his own State, but the citizens of Ohio as well. In other words, in the language of our platform, as adopted at Springfield, we have been taught that the right to vote is a right that concerns the whole people of this entire country. (Applause.) It is our matter. It is our affair. It is our concern what they do down there, as well as their concern what we do up here. Now what the Republican Party wants is of course that everybody will vote our principles, if they can make up their minds freely, willingly, so to do; but the Republican Party does not want to force anybody to vote our principles. If the colored or the white people of the South want to vote the Democratic ticket as a matter of preference, as a matter of free will or choice, the Republican Party has not one word to say. But what the Republican Party does say is that every man shall have the right to vote just as to him is his choice in that matter.

1. Joseph B. Foraker, *Notes of a Busy Life,* 2 vols. (Cincinnati, Ohio: Stewart & Kidd Company, 1916), 1:196–97.

X.3.   The Issue of Civil Rights: The State Legislature Confronts the Supreme Court's 1883 Rulings on Minority Rights

In a series of decisions at the end of the nineteenth century, the U.S. Supreme Court began to reconstitute the legal framework for relations between the races in America. Undoing the results of Reconstruction, the high court first declared the U.S. Civil Rights Act of 1875 unconstitutional with its rulings in a series of cases in 1883. The Supreme Court then laid the foundation for segregation in the twentieth century with its landmark 1896 decision, Plessy v. Ferguson, *which established the "separate but equal" doctrine in public facilities.*

In the mid-1880s, a majority of Ohio lawmakers desired to protect the rights of all citizens using public accommodations. To that end, the legislature passed the Ohio Civil Rights Act of 1884. As its preamble declares, the state law, strengthened in 1894, was intended to ban discrimination on the basis of "nativity, race, color, persuasion, religious or political," in all public facilities.[1]

WHEREAS, It is essential to just government that we recognize and protect all men as equal before the law, and that a democratic form of government should mete out equal and exact justice to all, of whatever nativity, race, color, persuasion, religious or political; and it being the appropriate object of legislation to enact great fundamental principles into law, therefore,

SECTION 1. *Be it enacted by the General Assembly of the State of Ohio,* That all persons within the jurisdiction of said state shall be entitled to the full and equal enjoyment of the accommodations, advantages, facilities and privilege of inns, public conveyances on land or water, theaters and other places of public amusement, subject only to the conditions and limitations established by law, and applicable alike to citizens of every race and color.

SEC. 2. That any person who shall violate any of the provisions of the foregoing section by denying to any citizen, except for reasons applicable alike to all citizens of every race and color, and regardless of color or race, the full enjoyment of any of the accommodations, advantages, facilities, or privileges in said section enumerated, or by aiding or inciting such denial, shall, for every such offense, forfeit and pay a sum not to exceed one hundred dollars to the person aggrieved thereby, to be recovered in any court of competent jurisdiction, in the county where said offense was committed; and shall also, for every such offense, be deemed guilty of a misdemeanor, and upon conviction thereof, shall be fined not to exceed one hundred dollars ($100), or shall be imprisoned not more than thirty days, or both; and provided, further, that a judgment in favor of the party aggrieved, or punishment upon an indictment, shall be a bar to either prosecution respectively.

SEC. 3. That no citizen of the state of Ohio, possessing all other qualifications which are or may be prescribed by law, shall be disqualified to serve as grand or petit juror in any court of said state, on account of race or color, and any officer or other person charged with any duty in the selection or summoning of jurors, who shall exclude or fail to summon any citizen for the cause aforesaid, shall on conviction thereof be deemed guilty of a misdemeanor, and be fined not more than one hundred dollars, or imprisoned not more than thirty days, or both.

1. State of Ohio, *General and Local Laws and Joint Resolutions* (Columbus: G. J. Brand & Co., 1884), 81:15–16; idem., *General and Local Acts Passed and Joint Resolutions Adopted* (Norwalk, Ohio: Laning Printing Co., 1894), 91:17–18.

X.4.　Race Relations and the Ohio Antilynching Law

Race relations deteriorated in Ohio, as it did in the nation, even with the passage of state civil rights legislation. Possibly the most disturbing manifestation of this condition was the increase in racially motivated violence, especially lynching, the most dramatic form of mob action occurring at century's end. Between 1889 and 1918 the National Association for the Advancement of Colored People calculated that 2,522 African Americans had been victims of lynch-mob violence across the nation. Although mob violence in the United States was not motivated solely by racial antagonisms, it did constitute over three-quarters of the lynchings conducted during this period. Although most incidents occurred in the South, where most of the African American population lived during this era, lynch mobs also acted in some northern states. In the southern and central counties of Ohio, transplanted Virginians and Kentuckians and their descendants coexisted with populations of African Americans.[1]

The General Assembly passed the 1896 legislation in response to the surge in lynch-mob actions in Ohio in the early 1890s. The mob action in southern and south-central Ohio occurred at a time when that violence reached its peak nationwide and sparked the efforts of numerous civil rights activists, especially those of Harry C. Smith, state legislator and editor of the Cleveland Gazette, *and reformer-writer Albion W. Tourgee, a prominent Radical Republican of the Reconstruction era. Smith and other Ohio African Americans began considering a legislative resolution to the issue of racial violence after the 1894 lynching of a black teenager accused of killing an aged couple on a farm in Adams County. The Smith Law (House Bill No. 123) was passed by the legislature on 10 April 1896.[2] Innovative and comprehensive, it embodied Tourgee's notion of community financial responsibility for damages caused by mob violence. Assuming that such violence could only occur with the consent of the community, the reformer believed that application of the principle of community liability would touch the "pocket nerve" of local men of property and standing, turning them into opponents of violence. The Smith Law quickly became a model for antilynching statutes in two southern states, South Carolina (1896) and Kentucky (1897), then West Virginia, as well as six northern and midwestern states after 1900.*[3]

SECTION 1. *Be it enacted by the General Assembly of the State of Ohio,* That any collection of individuals assembled for any unlawful purpose, intending to do damage or injury to any one or pretending to exercise correctional power over other persons by violence, and without authority of law, shall for the purpose of this act be regarded as a "mob," and any act of violence exercised by them upon the body of any person, shall constitute a "lynching."

SECTION 2. The term "serious injury," for the purposes of this act, shall include any such injury as shall permanently or temporarily disable the person receiving it from earning a livelihood by manual labor.

SECTION 3. Any person who shall be taken from the hands of the officers of justice in any county by a mob, and shall be assaulted by the same with whips, clubs, missiles, or in any other manner, shall be entitled to recover from the county in which such assault shall be made, the sum of one thousand dollars as damages, by action as hereinafter provided.

SECTION 4. Any person assaulted by a mob and suffering lynching at their hands, shall be entitled to recover of the county in which such assault is made, the sum of five hundred dollars; or if the injury received is serious, the sum of one thousand dollars; or if it result in permanent disability to earn a livelihood by manual labor, the sum of five thousand dollars.

SECTION 5. The legal representative of any person suffering death by lynching at the hands of a mob, in any county of this state, shall be entitled to recover of the county in which such lynching may occur, the sum of five thousand dollars damages for such unlawful killing. Said recovery shall be applied first to the maintenance of the family and education of the minor children of the person so lynched, if any be left surviving him, until such minor children shall become of legal age, and then distributed to the survivors, share and share alike, the widow receiving a child's share. If there be no wife or minor children left surviving such decedent, the said recovery shall be distributed among the next of kin according to the laws for the distribution of the personalty of the intestate. Such recovery shall not be regarded as part of the estate of the person lynched, nor be subject to any of his liabilities. Any person suffering death or injury at the hands of a mob engaged in an attempt to lynch another person, shall be deemed within the provisions of this act and he or his legal representatives shall have the same right of action thereunder.

1. David A. Gerber, "Lynching and Law and Order: Origin and Passage of the Ohio Anti-Lynching Law of 1896," *Ohio History* 83 (winter 1974): 33–34.

2. The State of Ohio, *General and Local Acts Passed and Joint Resolutions Adopted* (Columbus: J. L. Trauger, 1896), 92:136–37.

3. Gerber, "Lynching and Law and Order," 35–50.

X.5.   Law and the Shaping of Gender Relations: Legislators Define "The Rights and Liabilities of Husband and Wife"

The modern women's rights movement dates from the first national conference at Seneca Falls, New York, in 1848. The conferees' "Declaration of Sentiments" called for woman suffrage, greater educational and occupational opportunities, the passage of liberal marriage and divorce laws, and the extension of women's property rights. The "declaration" served as a platform for the women's rights activism of the 1850s and, indeed, for the remainder of the nineteenth century. Throughout the decade of the 1850s, women activists focused on political lobbying to obtain the passage of state laws liberalizing women's property and contract rights. Ohio's General Assembly enacted legislation in 1857 that secured the right of a married woman to control the earnings from her own property or joint holdings in case of the desertion of or incapacitation of her husband.[1]

Between 1874 and 1887, Ohio's legislature passed no fewer than fourteen statutes that expanded the rights of women to hold property, conduct business, and control the earnings of their enterprises. On 19 March 1887, the legislature enacted House Bill No. 31 that went beyond the enumeration of women's rights of property and contract to codify the economic rights and duties of husbands and wives in the marriage relationship.[2]

Section 1. *Be it enacted by the General Assembly of the State of Ohio, . . .*

CHAPTER 1.

HUSBAND AND WIFE

Sec. 3108. Husband and wife contract towards each other obligations of mutual respect, fidelity, and support.

Sec. 3109. The husband is the head of the family. He may choose any reasonable place or mode of living, and the wife must conform thereto.

Sec. 3110. The husband must support himself, his wife, and his minor children out of his property or by his labor. If he is unable to do so, the wife must assist him so far as she is able.

Sec. 3111. Neither husband nor wife has any interest in the property of the other, except as mentioned in sections 3110 and 4188, but neither can be excluded from the other's dwelling.

Sec. 3112. A husband or wife may enter into any engagement or transaction with the other, or with any other person, which either might if unmarried; subject, in transactions between themselves, to the general rules which control the actions of persons occupying confidential relations with each other.

Sec. 3113. A husband and wife cannot, by any contract with each other, alter their legal relations, except that they may agree to an immediate separation, and may make provision for the support of either of them and their children during the separation.

Sec. 3114. A married person may take, hold, and dispose of property, real or personal, the same as if unmarried.

Sec. 3115. Neither husband nor wife, as such, is answerable for the acts of the other.

Sec. 3116. If the husband neglects to make adequate provision for the support of his wife, any other person may, in good faith, supply her with the necessaries for her support, and recover the reasonable value thereof from the husband.

Sec. 3117. If the wife abandons the husband, he is not liable for her support until she offers to return, unless she was justified, by his misconduct, in abandoning him. . . .

CHAPTER 3

ESTATES IN DOWER

Sec. 4188. A widow or widower who has not relinquished or been barred of the same, shall be endowed of an estate for life in one-third of all the real property of which the deceased consort was seized as an estate of inheritance at any time during the marriage, and in one-third of all the real property of which the deceased consort, at decease, held the fee simple in reversion or remainder; and also in one-third of all the title or interest that the deceased consort had, at decease, in any real property held by article, bond, or other evidence of claim; and the widow or widower may remain in the mansion house of the deceased consort, free of charge, for one year, if dower is not sooner signed; but dower shall not be assigned to any widow or widower in any real property of which the deceased consort, at decease, held the fee simple in reversion or remainder, until the termination of the prior estate.

Sec. 4189. The conveyance of an estate or interest in real property, to a person in lieu of dower, to take effect on the death of the grantor, shall, if accepted by the grantee, bar the grantee's right of dower in the real property of the grantor; but if the conveyance was made when the grantee was within the age of minority, or during the marriage, the grantee may wave title to such real property and demand dower.

Sec. 4190. When a conveyance which is intended to be in lieu of dower, fails through any defect to be a legal bar thereto, and the widow or widower availing of such defect demands dower, the estate or interest conveyed to such widow or widower, with the intention to bar dower, shall thereupon cease.

Sec. 4191. A widow or widower lawfully evicted from real property conveyed in lieu of dower, or any part thereof, shall be endowed of so much of the residue of the real property of the deceased consort as will equal that from which such widow or widower is evicted.

Sec. 4192. A husband or wife who leaves the other and dwells in adultery, shall be barred of the right of dower in real property of the other, unless the offense is condoned by the injured consort.

Sec. 4193. If a husband or wife gives up any real property by collusion or fraud, or lose the same by default, the widow or widower may recover dower in the same. . . .

Section 4. The estate by the curtesy is abolished; but nothing contained in this act shall be construed as to effect vested rights; nor the provisions of any sections of the Revised Statutes, except such as are expressly amended or repealed by this act.

Section 5. In the interpretation of this act, unless the context shows that another sense was intended, the word "property" includes lands, tenements, and hereditaments, money, goods and chattels, rights and things in action, and evidences of debt; but this enumeration shall not be construed to require a strict construction of other words therein.

Section 6. All the provisions of law relating to the assignment of the dower of a wife, shall apply to the assignment of the dower of a husband as far as applicable.

1. Stacy A. Cordery, "Women in Industrializing America," in Charles W. Calhoun, ed., *The Gilded Age: Essays on the Origins of Modern America* (Wilmington, Del.: Scholarly Resources, 1996), 118; Sara M. Evans, *Born for Liberty: A History of Women in America* (New York: Free Press, 1989), 102–3; State of Ohio, *Acts of a General Nature and Local Laws and Joint Resolutions*, vol. 54 (Columbus: Richard Nevins, 1857), 219.

2. State of Ohio, *General and Local Acts Passed and Joint Resolutions Adopted*, vol. 84 (Columbus: Columbian Printing Co., 1887), 132–36.

X.6. Migration to Ohio in the Late Nineteenth Century: "The Girl Who Walked Home"

Historians of migration and immigration emphasize that not all new arrivals to a location have an enjoyable experience or stay at their new residence permanently. Whether moving from another state or from the country to the city, the migration experience at the turn of the last century could be harsh. In 1908 Harper's Bazaar *announced that it "will open its pages this year to a series of articles on 'The Girl Who Comes to the City,' written by those who have gone through the experience of coming to the city and either succeeding or failing there, during the last ten years." The magazine published the experiences of women between the ages of sixteen and thirty. The editors observed that: "An honest, accurate experience of one who has tried and failed is as necessary to a true presentation of whole subject as a story of a foothold won and kept." The following account, written by "A. B." from Boston, documents the ordeals of a young migrant to Columbus, Ohio, at the end of the nineteenth century.*[1]

It was a long time ago, but I feel sure conditions have not varied much in the years since I went from a suburb of Boston out to the city of Columbus, Ohio. I was nineteen years old. I had just lost a position, and although I could probably have obtained another in the same business—candy-making—I wanted to go West. I had a high-school education and visions of a position as school teacher in the country districts.

I had an uncle in Ohio who invited me to come out there. My parents objected. The expense of fitting me with clothing and paying my fare would all come at one time and they could ill afford it. Besides, the venture seemed to them foolish. But I was determined, and so one cold April day when snow was flying I left the station for my faraway destination, with joyful hopes.

I found that my uncle lived in a wild wooded district, far from neighbors, and where no work could be had for any one. My school idea failed, for I soon found that my desultory high-school education had not fitted me in the least for the hard examinations I would have to take to get a certificate to teach. I might have studied up, but my relatives were not rich. I could not remain a burden on their small income, and had brought a very small sum from home.

I decided to go to Columbus, the nearest city. A few miles out of the city my uncle had friends, and I was sent to them until I could find work. At that time—I don't know how it is now—the *Ohio State Journal* published advertisements for work free, and I took advantage of their kindness. But when the clerk asked me what I could do I was nonplussed. I could not do bookkeeping, though I had some knowledge of it. I could not write shorthand swiftly enough for any good. My smattering of French, German, and other studies did not qualify me for teaching pupils. So I stammered out that I hardly knew any honest work. The clerk nodded. Next day I found two letters awaiting me. Both wanted me to call to see about doing domestic work. I found the clerk had inserted an advertisement offering my services as a domestic. I had never done any housework, but I decided to try the places, for I considered that I had little choice. I took the first one, or, rather, the woman took me. I afterwards found out that she was rather ill tempered and worked a girl so hard that no one stayed there long. I was to receive $1.50 a week, and my mistress was to cook and to teach me. It was a hard place. I was soon so overworked that I used to fall asleep the moment I sat down anywhere, like Dickens's Fat Boy. At the end of seven weeks I knew I must leave, for I was utterly worn out. As I had spent little of my wages I thought I would take a room somewhere and try selling purses of a peculiar make with which an Eastern friend would supply me. I hired a neat little room for $2 a week, and fate must have been looking out for me, as I secured it with a widow who was very kind to me. I bought my meals. Having a good appetite, I found they cost me 55 cents a day—25 cents for a dinner and 15 cents each for the other meals. And I was always hungry at that. My laundry cost but 50 cents, as my hostess washed, and permitted me to iron at her fire. But $6 a week made big inroads on my little hoard, and I only sold three purses in two weeks. I foresaw that this state of affairs could not last, and I made a strenuous effort to get other occupation.

I tried to get clerking, but though one or two chances offered, the pay was too small. I began to be homesick, too. My dreams had not materialized and I longed unspeakably to see the old brown house, the big friendly elms, and the loved home faces. I cried myself to sleep every night, but I could not bring myself to tell my plight to my people.

When my last dollar was gone I sat down and faced the situation. Absolutely, so far as I could see, nothing remained but domestic service of the lowest kind and poorest paid, since I was a green hand. And I was so homesick. At school I had been famous for athletics, captain of our ball team and a member of a walking club.

I made up my mind to walk home and I did, barring many rides and helps which make another story. I sold some of my clothing and a small silver watch, and with the money bought overalls, blouse, and shoes. With my hair pinned up on top of my head, covered by a big broad rimmed hat, I made a very fair representation of a rather delicate sixteen or seventeen year old boy. I reserved a few pieces of my own clothing, which I carried in a bundle, and the rest I packed up to be sent later on when sent for. The account of my hardships and adventures in getting home do not belong here. I need only to say that I did, in time, arrive safely, and have never desired since then to try my fortune in any far-away strange city.

1. *Harper's Bazaar* 42 (June 1908): 591–92.

X.7.   Women on the Ohio Farm at Century's End: "What a Farmer's Wife Should Know"

Consider the following assessment of the life of a typical farmer's wife in late-nineteenth-century Ohio: "She bore large families, labored over cooking stoves, bent over preserving kettles, churned butter, packed cold meats, served harvest dinners, and washed, swept, and dusted. She did two days work in one and had to like it. . . . She had few pleasures, and they were simple and inexpensive."[1] But as the author of the previous quote knew, the rural life of a farmer's wife was not all work. There were diversions: magazines and catalogs in the mail, church socials in town, and the annual meeting of a county agricultural society. County associations held "Farmers' Institutes" where they discussed Ohio agricultural conditions and farm life. A portion of almost every society's agenda was given over to the consideration of the role of women on the farm. In 1891, Mrs. Hannah Longbon of Columbia Center, Ohio, offered her thoughts on "What a Farmer's Wife Should Know."[2]

There is more demanded of the farmer's wife than of any other woman that must earn her own living. She must have brain, heart and muscle.

The successful farmer's wife should be independent and trustful of her own ability. Self-reliance comes from a cultivated intellect, a well disciplined heart and a sound constitution. With these she is the happiest woman on earth.

Woman's real worth is in her home, and nowhere is practical wisdom better illustrated. Consequently she must first have a thorough knowledge of herself. She must know her power of endurance, her capabilities, her tastes and all her other endowments of nature, and those which she lacks she must cultivate and strengthen by practice.

After this the next most essential thing is an entire knowledge of domestic economy, for the physical and moral health of her household rests upon her to a great extent.

The properties of food and the best method of preparing it is a knowledge every woman should have. No one has mastered the art of cooking who does not know something of the chemistry of food and the purpose they serve in the system. It seems to me that the noblest lesson for womanhood is to know of the waste and supply of the human body and that which builds up the muscle, nerve and brain of her family. Therefore, she must know the chemistry of food. She should know that a person working in the open air, as a farmer, can not exist and work on the diet of a brain worker, but that he needs food of a nitrogenous or muscle-making element—such as vegetables, grain and lean meat—and that he can not do a day's work on the farm on novelties and delicacies, and that her children need a different diet than an adult. Good light-bread is the most essential food on the farm. Pharoah once hung his chief baker, and if the cause thereof was poor bread, I do not wonder at it. The old adage that "Bread is the staff of life," has sound sense in it, if it is good light-bread. But many a farmer's wife deals out stones instead of bread to her family.

She must know how to cook and bake as most conducive to the health of her family, for the first and greatest blessing God bestowed upon us is life; but life without health is almost a burden and a curse. She should understand the laws of hygiene, of the home and farm where they live.

She should be health inspector, if her husband is too busily engaged, or is not capable. In cities and towns one is provided for by the law, which prevents a great amount of sickness. She should understand the chemical analysis of water so as to be able to ascertain if it is pure or if the barnyard or other refuses are leached into the contents of "the old oaken bucket," which often overflows with poisonous germs.

She should know how to keep the back dooryard respectable, and not a receptacle for everything not in use or which has not found its proper place, for dirt is only matter out of place. The cellar, too, must be cared for by her, or at least inspected by her.

Why should farmers' families in the country, away from the bad vapors of the city, be so subject to malignant diseases? There is far more sickness among farmers than there ought to be. Bad conditioned cellars, small, close sleeping rooms, having the dooryard filled with too much shrubbery so as to obstruct sunlight and the free circulation of air, are some of the agents of disease that the farmer's wife has to battle with. Cleanliness is essential to health and is just as necessary in the country as in the city.

A farmer's wife should understand botany to some extent, also the medicinal qualities of herbs and plants within her reach, for with them she can shorten doctor bills—for many a person lies buried beneath the herb or weed that would have aided nature in restoring him to health and activity.

If she insists on regular eating, pure water, freedom of dress, with plenty of sunlight and pure air, which all farmers have the privilege of enjoying, she will secure for her family that health and happiness which by nature is or ought to be our inheritance.

Dress among the farmers is almost always a secondary matter, and there is too much neglect of personal appearance—and the largest part is among the women; she seems to think dress amounts to nothing, or that she has no time to waste on dress—but here she makes a serious mistake. I think that is one of the reasons that farmers have so many epithets applied to them, and that they must take a back seat on many occasions. In a farmer, possibly, genius might cause slovenly garments to be overlooked; but no genius can make a carelessly attired farmer's wife look respectable. I do not mean that because we can not buy the richest fabric, we must dress out of taste, for taste costs no money, only a little exercise of the brain. Not that she should be governed by fashion, by exposing one member of the body, and piling a heap of cloth on another member, but harmony of cloth and texture, in accordance with her means. She must be able to buy suitable dry goods for the family. Farmers need different clothing than city folks.

She must be a general seamstress and dress-maker; do the tailoring for the small boy, and *surely* know how to patch or mend; ought to know how to trim a hat for a girl, or possibly for herself; know how to raise poultry and calves once in a while, to be sure; know how to harness a horse, and care for one if necessary. I don't know if she should be concerned about the milking or not; if she does, it should only be in case of an emergency, for the house must go at the expense of the milking. Should know that "cleanliness is next to Godliness" in buttermaking, as well as in every thing else; and at what temperature cream rises best, how long it should stand before churning, and at what temperature to churn, and it will save her a great amount of labor. She should use her brain more at butter-making, and she will use her muscle less. She ought to know what crops are planted and reaped, and the amount of labor required in the operation. Should know the income and the expenditure of the farm, and what taxes are paid, that she may not ignorantly waste her husband's product, which means his labor. Ruskin, the English critic, says, "To waste the labor of any man, is to kill him." The policy that she is only his heir, is getting threadbare, for woman has proved that she is just as capable of carrying on business as a man only, he won't give her half a chance. She should understand political economy, and how to sell and buy farm products—in what shape they are most marketable; what products are in greatest demand, and where and when they will bring the highest price. Not that she should rule the farm, but, that she should be capable and understand their affairs. Duties never clash, for "united they stand, divided they fall." She must practice the motto of "early to bed, and early to rise," which gives her the satisfaction of knowing its divine service, by getting up and earning her breakfast before she eats it.

If there are signs of a farmer losing his farm, some of the first questions that will be asked are, did they rise early? Was his wife economical, or could she waste more with the teaspoon than her husband could earn with the shovel? Were their affairs well regulated? Did she help him in any way? Or did he have to wait on her half the forenoon, and come in early to help get supper in the evening?

A farmer's wife must be vigilant, for "eternal vigilance is the price of liberty" as much on the farm to-day, as it was in the days of Patrick Henry. You know that farmers as a class, are called penurious, stingy etc., and that their wives are stingier than they are.

As a class the farmers come nearer to eating bread in the sweat of their face than any other people. He must work hard in this day of commission men and adulteration, which has a tendency to get him in a rut, and often he does not look beyond. They should guard against this. To provide for others and our own comfort and independence is honorable and greatly to be commended; but that a farmer and his wife should work and slave in all sorts of weather, all their lives, even toward declining years, allowing themselves no pleasure or comfort, shows that they are narrow-souled and miserly. Money is a power with a farmer after a sort; but intelligence, free heartedness and moral virtue are nobler powers.

1. Philip D. Jordan, *Ohio Comes of Age, 1873-1900* (Columbus: Ohio State Archaeological and Historical Society, 1943), 102.

2. Hannah Longbon, "What a Farmer's Wife Should Know," in Ohio State Board of Agriculture, *Annual Report . . . for the Year 1891* (Columbus: Westbote Co., 1892), 501-3.

XI.   Agriculture and Industry in the Gilded Age

OHIO DEVELOPED WITHIN a midwestern regional economy that extended from the Pennsylvania border to central Minnesota. As it evolved throughout the nineteenth century, the Midwest's economy was firmly rooted in agriculture and the processing of natural resources. For the farmers of the region, it was a period of modernization. Ohio farmers constructed new, larger farmhouses and barns, purchased mass-produced appliances for the first time, and introduced newly invented planting and harvesting machinery. By the 1870s, most of the state's farmland had been cleared and cultivated. Indeed, some of the least productive land had already been abandoned by farmers under the pressure of declining prices and the costs of mechanization. In addition, the growth of Ohio cities began to create significant distinctions in land values and profits for farmers living near cities in contrast to ones tilling less productive land in isolated areas.

Midwest industry arose as one of three parts of the larger American manufacturing belt that spanned half the continent from New England to the Mississippi River. What was distinctive about the Midwest was its industry's close ties with agriculture and the processing of the region's abundant natural resources. That foundation can explain much about the causes of Midwest industrialization. The region's industry developed because of the modernization of agriculture and the requirements of companies extracting and processing natural resources, as well as the demands of new urban construction, and the needs of increasing numbers of consumer households.

The development of transportation facilities in the region had much to do with the geographic pattern of this industrialization. In 1860, the river cities of Cincinnati, St. Louis, and Louisville were the centers of midwestern manufacturing, a fact that demonstrated the importance of steamship and riverboat. By 1880, the successful development of the railroads altered the distribution of manufacturing. Chicago assumed the top spot in the ranking of industry towns, replacing Cincinnati, which slipped to second. For the remainder of the century, all the major industrial centers, with the exception of Minneapolis, would be major railroad hubs providing access to the region and the nation.

Where did Ohio fit in the overall development of the region? During this era, Ohio could claim two of the region's top five cities (Chicago, Cincinnati, Detroit, Cleveland, and Milwaukee) ranked in terms of overall industrial output. In 1880, eight of the region's twenty top industrial cities were in Ohio. After Cincinnati (distilling and brewing, carriage, and light manufacturing) and Cleveland (refining, heavy industry), came Toledo (refining and machinery), Columbus (printing, machinery), Dayton (appliances and machinery), Youngstown (basic steel), Akron (rubber products), and Springfield (agricultural implements).

The achievements of Ohio's successful industrial entrepreneurs would not have been possible without the infusion of new technical knowledge, an increasingly sophisticated web of transportation facilities, and the hard work of a diverse labor force. Consider, first, the inventors who created new knowledge and the innovators who successfully adapted it to the marketplace. The creations of Ohio inventors established entirely new industries or dramatically transformed others. Airplanes, air brakes, aluminum products, electric starters for automobiles, and steam boilers were the results of breakthroughs in scientific and technical knowledge achieved by Ohioans. The innovators who brought inventions to the marketplace were able to attract large amounts of investment capital from both inside and outside Ohio. For entrepreneurs without ready sources of funds or access to subsidies from the public treasuries, there existed a variety of established industrialists, or banks and brokerage houses, in New York or Chicago willing to provide the necessary assets.

The nineteenth-century transportation revolution facilitated Ohio's industrial transformation. Although the extensive antebellum canal system fell into disrepair after the Civil War, the state did little to modernize the "ditches." Only a few sections remained in service, with freight boats hauling the bulkiest of cargoes. It was the development of railroads and highways that paralleled the industrialization of the state. While providing the means for transporting freight and passengers to and from the urban, industrial centers, the railroads themselves were a source of economic stimulus to the state, as they hired thousands of workers for the construction, maintenance, and operation of a network of lines that totaled almost nine thousand miles by the turn of the century. By the 1890s, electric power opened up two new avenues of rail transportation: innovative electric traction "interurban" lines began to link cities across the state with fast, frequent service and electric trolley cars, as well as the less popular cable car lines, replaced horse-drawn passenger cars on the streets of Ohio's cities.[1]

The state's workforce grew rapidly in the three decades after Reconstruction. Ohio's urban industrial centers drew rural workers off the farm and attracted immigrants from central and eastern Europe. The influx of immigrants seeking to start over in the United States continued until 1914, when the outbreak of war in Europe abruptly halted the flow of unskilled labor to American industry.

The following selection of documents offers readers a general overview of the state's economic development and provides information on numerous aspects of industrialization. Several selections reveal the exploitative nature of the industrialization process, documenting the impact of deforestation on nineteenth-century Ohio and summarizing the employment of women and child labor in the state.

1. H. Roger Grant, *Ohio on the Move: Transportation in the Buckeye State,* a volume in the Ohio Bicentennial Series (Athens: Ohio University Press, 1999).

XI.1.   "The Recent Period" in Economic Development

If basic industry was the body of the midwestern regional economy during the Gilded Age, then the exploitation of its numerous natural resources was its lifeblood. A close look at Ohio's core industries—mining and manufacturing—reveals that they developed in three distinct but interconnected categories: first, the extraction and processing of natural resources; second, the production of basic iron and steel products, centered in cities like Youngstown and Cleveland; and, finally, the fabrication of metal into machinery and appliances, activities centered in such cities as Dayton and Columbus.

The document that follows is a short overview of Ohio's economic, especially manufacturing, development during the Gilded Age. It is from the State Centennial History of Ohio, *authored by Rowland H. Rerick.*[1]

The assessed value of the real estate of Ohio is 1,285 million dollars, four-fold the valuation of fifty years before. The farms of Ohio are yielding a hundred million bushels of corn annually, and forty million bushels of wheat. The coal product is 16,500,000 tons annually. . . .

The total product of Ohio oil up to 1876 was estimated at 200,000 barrels. Since then two hundred and forty million barrels have been taken from the Ohio fields, the greatest annual production being one-tenth of that total in 1896. Since 1894 Ohio has produced more than any other state. The total product from the State from 1876, it is estimated, would fill a row of 30,000-barrel tanks, that, set as closely as possible, would extend for one hundred and forty miles. The petroleum refineries of Ohio, mainly at Lima, Cleveland and Toledo, distill four million barrels of oil annually, for the manufacture of illuminating oil, gasoline, naphtha, lubricants and paraffin, of the total value of $8,000,000.

The railroad systems of the state have increased to about ten thousand miles of main line and four thousand miles of side tracks. Street railways have been extended to 1,560 miles of electric roads and nineteen of cable, and there were in the year 1900 sixty-eight electric railroads between cities, the beginning of a new era of transportation.

The total tonnage of sailing vessels, steamboats and water craft of all kinds owned in Ohio in 1900 was estimated at 461,286, the greatest of any state in the union except New York. The tonnage of steam vessels built at Cleveland in 1900 was 42,119, one-fourth of the total steamship building in the United States that year. The tonnage of the shipping of the Cuyahoga district in 1900 was 376,330, of the Sandusky district 49,000, of the Maumee district 19,000, the total closely approaching one-third of the aggregate tonnage of the shipping on the Great Lakes.

It is in manufacturing that the figures of the census of Ohio for the year 1900 are most impressive. The total value of the product of manufactories in 1850 was sixty-three millions. In 1900 it is eight hundred and thirty-two millions. The total wages paid increased in the same time from less than $14,000,000 and $154,000,000. The maximum number of wage earners at work in 1900 was 450,000. The main item in the great total of manufactures was steel and iron products, which had more than doubled and now had the enormous total valuation of $139,000,000. Foundry and machine shop products stood next with a total of $72,000,000, an increase of three-fourths. The total value of the flour and grist mill and grain foods products, is $44,000,000. The value of the annual product of lumber and timber and milling of that sort is over thirty millions, and the value of the product of liquors is almost exactly the same. Carriages and wagons and parts of vehicles are manufactured to the amount of $23,000,000 annually; clothing for men and women, $24,000,000, and boots and shoes, $18,000,000, the latter item being double what it was in 1890. The meat packing business shows a gain of twenty per cent, and a total product of twenty million dollars in value, half at Cincinnati, and three-fourths of the rest at Cleveland. Twenty millions a year also represents the product of each of the industries of printing and publishing and the manufacture of tobacco. The production of pottery, terra cotta and fire clay products, has doubled in ten years and has a total value of twelve millions. Among the industries that do not show such large products the most rapid increase is shown in the manufacture of electrical apparatus, which has increased ten fold in ten years and now has a total of nearly seven million dollars. The production of soap and candles, mostly subsidiary to the meat industry at Cincinnati, is worth eight millions a year. The grinding and roasting of coffee and spices, largely at Toledo, though not increasing, has a total product of $6,000,000.

Other considerable items in the total of Ohio's manufactures are agricultural implements, $14,000,000; railroad car shop products, $13,000,000; furniture, $4,500,000; paper and wood pulp, $6,500,000; rubber goods, $7,000,000, a five fold increase; leather, $5,000,000, and tin plate, a manufacture that grew from nothing in ten years to an annual product of $6,000,000.

The manufacture of iron and steel is mainly at Youngstown (the leading city of the State in that industry), Cleveland, Lorain, Bellaire, Mingo Junction, Niles, Steubenville and Canal Dover, which together produce about two-thirds of the total of the state. Columbus and Ironton are other important centers.

The production of pig iron in Ohio in 1900 was about two and [a] half million tons, second only to the product of Pennsylvania, and more than the entire product of the United States in 1875.

In 1900 there were forty-three blast furnaces and sixty-four rolling mills, in Ohio, the first producing a value of forty millions, and the second of nearly a hundred millions. So great is the development of this industry that the mines of the State do not produce much more than one per cent of the iron ore used, and the main dependence for coke is upon Pennsylvania and West Virginia. Since 1870 Ohio has occupied second place among the states in the production of iron and steel. She leads all the states in the manufacture of metal working machinery. She is third in flour and other grain products. Toledo, where the first grain warehouse was built in 1817, is sixth among the primary markets of America in grain receipts and fourth in corn receipts. . . .

One of the most interesting manufacturing cities of America is East Liverpool, where the making of yellow ware from Ohio clays was carried on from an early day. In

1872 the making of white ware was begun, and the industry has wonderfully developed in the last ten or twelve years, until four thousand wage earners are employed, and the annual product of white granite ware and semi-vitreous porcelain is nearly $3,000,000 worth a year, or nearly half the product of the entire United States. The art tiling of Zanesville and the art pottery of Cincinnati are also famous, as well as the sewer pipe of Akron and other places, and pressed brick, the manufacture of which was begun in Zanesville in 1861, and the paving brick that has made a great change in street improvements.

The greater manufacturing cities of the state may be grouped in classes according to the annual value of products, which is given here in round numbers. First are Cincinnati, with $158,000,000, and Cleveland, $140,000,000. In the next class are Columbus, $40,000,000; Toledo, $37,000,000; Dayton, $36,000,000; Youngstown, $35,000,000; Akron, $24,000,000. In the next, Springfield, Canton and Hamilton, ranging from $12,000,000 to $13,000,000. Other cities having a manufactured product exceeding $5,000,000 in value are Lorain, $9,500,000; Zanesville and Mingo Junction, each about $7,500,000; Mansfield, $7,000,000; Lima and Middleton, each over $6,500,000; with a product between $5,000,000 and $6,000,000, Piqua, Niles, Ironton, and East Liverpool. Bridgeport's product is nearly $5,000,000.

1. Rowland H. Rerick, *State Centennial History of Ohio* (Madison, Wis.: Northwestern Historical Association, 1902), 419–22.

XI.2.   The Exploitation of Natural Resources: "The Forestry Question in Ohio"

The degree of deforestation in heavily timbered states brought the increase in government supervision of that asset in the post–Civil War years. By 1887, five states—Ohio, New York, New Hampshire, Colorado, and California—and the national government had created administrative bureaus or commissions to assess the changing status of their forestland.[1] The legislature directed Ohio's new State Forestry Bureau "to thoroughly inquire into the character and extent of the forests of the state; to investigate the causes which are in operation to produce waste or decay; to suggest what legislation, if any, may be necessary for the rational system of forestry, adapted to the wants and conditions of this state." The bureau, established at the Ohio State University, was supervised by a three-man board of directors and charged with reporting annually to the governor.

Adolph Leue drafted "The Forestry Question in Ohio" for inclusion in the Forestry Bureau's second annual report in 1887.[2]

$\mathcal{A}$s to the rapid removal of our forests in almost all parts of the country, let us see what part we, the people of Ohio, have taken in this great work.

At the time of the first settlement by white people, Ohio was one of the most densely wooded States of the Union. With the exception of the wet prairies found on the great water-shed extending through the State in a northeasterly direction, and in the western portion, the whole State was one continuous tract of woodland, stocked with forest-trees of many different varieties, mostly of the deciduous kind.

From statistics we learn that in 1853 the woodlands of Ohio occupied 13,991, 426 acres, or 50.19 per cent. Of the superficial area of the State. The latest agricultural statistics show that there are only 4,258,767 acres of woodland in Ohio, or 16.69 per cent. of the entire area of the State. Thus, within the thirty-two years immediately following 1853, the woodland cleared in Ohio amounted to 9,732,659 acres, or 33.50 per cent. Of the superficial area of the State, or an annual decrease of more than one per cent.

In addition to this absolute clearing of thousands of acres annually, there is another, a sort of intermediate clearing, known in some parts of the State as "logging, by which many thousands of the best trees are removed from the remaining woodlands every year, so that, in many parts of our State, none but inferior trees of inferior varieties are met with. . . .

This growing scarcity of wood in Ohio and in the neighboring States necessitates the importation from greater distances, whereby the cost of transportation is added to the original price. The manufacturer, in order to balance his expense, raises the price of his manufactures, and the consumer of these articles is made to pay the penalty of the ruthless destruction of our home woodlands.

While all of these industries are more or less affected by this growing scarcity of timber, there are certain, and very important industries at that, which for want of material, indispensable to their existence, have been discontinued. As for example, several furnaces of Southern Ohio, at which formerly a very high grade of charcoal-iron was manufactured, have already been abandoned, and the abandonment of others is but a question of time.

Last year one of the largest tanneries of Cincinnati was discontinued because of the growing scarcity of tanbark. Kentucky, West Virginia, Indiana, and even Tennessee have, since Ohio ceased to furnish this valuable forest-product, supplied the Queen City of the West with tanbark, and so great has been the drain upon these States that they, too, are nearly stripped of their oak trees, especially along the railroads. The days of the tanning industry of Ohio, there can be no doubt, are numbered, unless by a wise foresight immediate action be taken to grow oak-coppices for the production of tanbark. Chattanooga now competes with our home tanneries in the Cincinnati market, and it is thought will ere long ruin some tanners there.

The decline of this industry will to some extent affect the cattle market; for, if the skins of animals bought and slaughtered in Cincinnati cannot be manufactured into leather in that city, but must be shipped to a southern or eastern place of manufacture, the price of animals furnishing these skins will depreciate, and the farmer, who raises and fattens cattle for the Cincinnati market, will receive for his product the full price, less the decline in the price of the skin, which will be the cost of transportation to the distant tanneries.

This destruction of our woodlands also prevents the development of new industries.

1. Dyan Zaslowsky and T. H. Watkins, *These American Lands* (Washington, D.C.: Island Press, 1994), esp. 64–65.

2. Adolph Leue, "The Forestry Question in Ohio," *Second Annual Report of the Forestry Bureau, 1886, Ohio Executive Documents* (Columbus, 1887), 6–15.

XI.3. Making the Farm Pay in Gilded Age Ohio: Avoiding "Mortgages, Misery and Sheriff's Sales"

By the last quarter of the nineteenth century Ohio farmers had begun to abandon unproductive farmland. Fields that had been under cultivation for three quarters of a century were allowed to revert to untamed thickets and wood lots. The state's southern counties, possessing some of the least productive farmland and located far from the new urban industrial centers, suffered from the worst declines in property values. Throughout the post–Civil War era, the problem of making the farm pay for itself was utmost on the minds of farmers whenever they congregated to discuss their common circumstances. Prescriptions offered by successful farmers and agricultural experts usually recommended scientific farming methods, including proper drainage, crop rotation, the use of manures or commercial fertilizers, and the proper maintenance of farm implements.[1]

The following paper, presented to an 1892 meeting of the Adams County Farmers' Institute by S. A. McClanahan of West Union, is representative of this advice.[2]

*I*n these days, when many farmers are complaining that farming doesn't pay, I thought it would be well enough to talk a little about how to make it pay.

Adams county farming lands are good, medium and bad, more of the bad, yet farming will pay in Adams county if properly managed, as I know from experience. Many of our farmers are going along in old ruts, raising some crop that is not paying them, often a crop not suited to their soil. In every neighborhood there are some farmers that are making farming pay. If it is not paying you, look and see how they are making it pay, maybe you can learn something from their methods. If the farm is not paying you, probably it is your fault. If you are raising wheat and only getting eight or ten bushels per acre, you had better quit and go at something else, for it don't pay. My idea is this. In order to make the farm pay do that which you and your lands are best adapted to. Make some line of cropping or stock raising a specialty, or money crop. For instance, if your farm is adapted to wheat, and you can raise paying crops of that grain, make it your special crop, and by manure and clover and better preparation of the soil, increase your yield. If it is adapted to corn, do the same thing. Whatever crop your land is best adapted to, give that crop special attention, and those portions of the farm that are not suited to cultivation, put down to grass and keep young, growing stock on them and use them to use up the by-products of the farm.

When the tillable land is not in crops, keep it in clover and grass. Make all the hay you can and feed it to young, growing stock. Keep all the stock on the farm it will carry, and keep the best you can get of the kind you are handling. Remember we are keeping stock for the profit there is in it, and it all depends on the kind and how it is kept whether it pays or not. Keep it under shelter and comfortable, feed liberally, but not wastefully, keep them growing all the while. Remember there is your profit. We keep young stock as machines to consume the by-products of the farm and convert them into beef, mutton and pork, and there is no money in letting the machine stop. Keep it going for profit, and convert the hay, fodder and surplus grain of the farm into flesh, milk, wool and manure; apply the latter to the crops and thereby get better crops and grass. I want to impress it on the mind of every farmer present that manure and grass are the only hope for Adams county farmers.

Too many of our farmers try to spread out too much and plow too many acres; undertake more than they can do. Don't do this. If you have been raising twenty or forty acres of corn and getting twenty or thirty bushels of inferior corn, it don't pay. Stop it, and put in ten or twenty acres and leave the other in grass. Put all the manure and fertilizer and labor on the ten or twenty acres that you would twenty or forty, and get fifty or sixty bushels of corn to the acre, of better quality and worth more per bushel to sell or feed. Apply the same rule to wheat. Don't be so particular about the acres as the bushels; bear in mind that the small yield of corn or wheat is generally of inferior quality, while the large yield is usually of superior quality.

If it costs the price of ten bushels of wheat or twenty bushels of corn per acre to pay for production, the man with twelve bushels of wheat and twenty-five bushels of corn hasn't much margin for profit. While with thirty of wheat and fifty or sixty of corn there is a good margin for profit, and it takes but little, if any, more labor to raise and harvest the large crop. The difference in quality will much more than bear the extra expense.

Too many farmers want to work six months and then rest six. That won't make the farm pay. What man with a trade, business or profession would make it pay at that rate? Not any. They find it necessary, in order to make it pay, to give all their time and attention to it. So if you would make the farm pay you must look after it and its interests twelve months of the year. The farm is your place of business, and in order to look after it, you must be there. Don't attempt to raise your crops around some grocery or saloon stove; they won't sell for cash. They only bring mortgages, misery and sheriff's sales.

And now fellow farmers if you wish to make the farm pay, keep your land covered up with clover and grass when not under cultivation. Pay as you go. Use all the manure you can get. Use industry and economy, seasoned with good judgment, and my word for it the farm will pay.

1. Philip D. Jordan, *Ohio Comes of Age, 1873–1900* (Columbus: Ohio State Archaeological and Historical Society, 1943), 100.

2. S. A. McClanahan, "How to Make the Farm Pay," in *Forty-Seventh Annual Report of the Ohio State Board of Agriculture* (Columbus, Ohio, 1892), 410-11.

XI.4. An Overview of a Core Industry: Andrew Roy's Report on Coal Mines and Mining

After a series of disasters in the coal fields, miners sent one of their leaders, Andrew Roy, a Scotsman, Civil War veteran, and survivor of Libby Prison, to lobby the state legislature for

*the passage of mine safety laws. The 1874 "Act to regulate Mines and Mining" authorized
the appointment of a mine inspector, specified his duties, and, more importantly, detailed the
responsibilities of mine operators in the state. Although it failed to specify enforcement measures in many critical areas, the law obligated employers to provide for safe exits, adequate
ventilation, effective communication, and reliable safety lamps for miners. In addition, it
imposed limitations on the employment of unqualified engineers and prohibited the use of
boys under the age of twelve in the mines.[1]*

*Governor William Allen appointed Roy as Ohio's first inspector of mines. The following
document is from the mining inspector's account of conditions in the state's coal fields published in the 1879 annual report of the Bureau of Labor Statistics.[2]*

The Ohio coal fields form part of the great Appalachian basin which extends
through portions of nine different States, to wit: Pennsylvania, Maryland, West
Virginia, Virginia, Kentucky, Ohio, Tennessee, Georgia and Alabama, and cover an
area variously estimated at from 50,000 to 55,000 square miles. The coal measures of
our State occupy from 10,000 to 12,000 square miles of this great coal field, or about
one-fourth of the area of the State. The western margin of the Ohio coal measures runs
through the counties of Trumbull, Geauga, Portage, Summit, Medina, Wayne, Holmes,
Jackson, Pike and Scioto. All the territory lying west and north of this line of outcrop
is occupied by the older formations—the sub-carboniferous Devonian and Sulurian
strata. All the territory east and south of the outcrop is occupied by coal bearing works.
The line of dip of the coal measures of the State is south 60° to 80° east, and from 25
to 30 feet to the mile. On the margin of the coal field in the counties named above, only
one bed of coal is due, the lower bed of the series, while along the Ohio river in the
counties of Harrison and Belmont, the measures are fully 1,500 to 1,600 feet thick, and
enclose no less than 40 to 50 different beds of coal, many of them too thin, however,
to be of any commercial value.

The seams of coal in course of development range in thickness from 28 inches to
11 feet; the thickest seam found in the State is 14 feet, the thinnest bed of any commercial value is reckoned at 1 foot in height, though midway beds are met as low as 2
to 6 inches, but no seam of one foot or less will ever be mined for centuries to come. The
maximum thickness of all the beds of coal would exceed a column of 80 feet in height,
were all the seams found in place where they are due, but owing to the numerous wants
and thinning down of every bed all over the coal area, 30 feet will be about the aggregate
thickness, and 9 feet the average thickness. After due allowance is made for slack and
waste in mining, there are no less than 60,900,000,000 tons of merchantable coal in the
State, which at the present rate of consumption would keep up the coal supply for
12,500 years. . . .

There are three hundred mines in the state which work more than ten men at
once, and nearly three hundred small mines which work from two to eight men during
winter and are mainly idle during summer. The largest establishments have an underground force employed of from 200 to 250 men and boys, 150 to 175 of whom, according to the varying conditions, will be engaged in digging and loading coal, 10 to 15

driving mules or horses, 4 to 6 laying track, and if the seam is less than four feet thick, 6 to 10 will be engaged blasting roof and taking up bottom to make hauling roads for mules; 2 to 6 are often required pumping and bailing water; 4 to 8 boys are employed tending trap doors. In the thick coals of the Hocking Valley, and where the mines are accessible by drift mining, not more than 12 per cent. of the miners are engaged in dead work, and most of this force is employed as drivers, hauling the coal from the working faces to the chutes outside.

There are 18,000 people employed in or about the coal mines of the State. The annual coal production or output is 5,225,000 tons, valued at the present selling price of coal at $8,000,000 at the pit's mouth. The first coal mined in Ohio was got by "stripping," near the village of Tallmadge, in Summit county, in the year 1810. In 1828 the first shipments were made to Cleveland from the mines of this county. The mines on the Ohio river at Pomeroy were opened in the year 1833. In 1840 the late Governor David Tod commenced shipping his famous Brier Hill coal to Cleveland. . . .

The number of men and boys employed in and around the coal mines of the State, as I have already stated, is 18,000, of whom 14,000 work underground. Since the passage of the mining law boys under twelve years of age are prohibited from working under ground. As, however, there is no penalty attached for any violation of this provision of the statute, it is optional with the miners whether they obey it or not. To their credit it must be stated, that they have very generally complied with the requirements of the act in this regard. The number of boys between the ages of 12 and 21 at work in the mines, is about 15 per cent. of the whole underground force of the State. . . .

The mining law of Ohio, which was enacted in 1874 after the burning of the Atwater slope in Portage county, is a bungling piece of legislation. Several of the most important sections of the law have no penalties attached for the due enforcement of their provisions.

The enactment of proper and necessary mining codes for the protection of the lives and safety of miners, and the appointment of properly qualified mining experts to see the laws enforced and obeyed, I regard as not only an act of justice and mercy to our fellow-citizens who daily imperil health, life, and limb in the gloomy chambers of the coal mine, but as tending to elevate the status of the miner and make conspiracy laws neither necessary nor desirable.

The miner is peculiarly surrounded. Deprivation of solar light, the awful gloom of the mine, the inhalation of an atmosphere contaminated by the noxious and poisonous gases of the mine, blanches the human face and impoverishes the human blood like vegetable products similarly deprived of solar light and a life-sustaining atmosphere. Moreover, the danger to life and limb, to which there is no parallel on earth, and which the miner often can not see to guard against, added to the awful hardness and gloom of the coal mine, affects the minds and emotions of our subterranean workmen, and not conspiracy laws are required to make them better citizens, but good, efficient laws for the proper protection of their lives, and health, and safety—laws made to be enforced and obeyed. . . .

There are other causes tending to produce discontent among miners, such as the irregularity of work and the manner in which the work of mining and loading the coal is done. Few of the mines run steady all year round. Most of the coal is shipped by rail, or river, or lake, to the coalless regions lying north and west of the coal field. During summer the river is too low for shipments, and in winter it is usually frozen up; in winter, also, lake navigation closes. The miner hews and loads the coal at the wall faces at so much per ton—usually fifty cents for coal four feet thick and upward. He is thus in a sense his own boss, and when cars are scarce and work slack during working hours, he spends his idle time with his fellows in the mine. At these social gatherings the question of wages and every possible grievance is discussed from one standpoint only, and he has become in consequence the best special pleader in the world. When he makes up his mind that he is entitled to an advance of wages, no power on earth can convince him to the contrary. Every person who fails to view the matter in the same light that he does, is regarded as an enemy of the workingmen—as a mere tool of the mine operator.

1. State of Ohio, *General and Local Laws and Joint Resolutions* (Columbus: G. J. Brand & Co., 1884), 21-26.

2. Andrew Roy, "Sketch of the Mines and Miners of the State," *Third Annual Report of the Bureau of Labor Statistics, 1879* (Columbus, Ohio: Nevins and Myers, 1880), 100-106.

XI.5. The Condition of Labor in Ohio: The Findings of the Bureau of Labor Statistics

From 1873 to 1877, Ohioans experienced the most severe economic recession in the state's history. The decline in trade in industry, occurring nationwide, triggered unemployment over 16 percent, as well as widespread wage cuts and underemployment of skilled workers. Industrial conflict, culminating in the Great Railroad Strike of 1877, paralyzed many of the industrial centers of the North.[1]

Legislators determined to come to grips with the declining fortunes of industry and the rising tide of conflict. Following a small group of eastern states, led by Massachusetts, Ohio created a bureau of labor statistics "to collect, assort, systematize, and present in annual reports . . . statistical details relating to all departments of labor in the State, especially in relation to the commercial, industrial, social, educational and sanitary condition of the laboring classes, and to the productive industries of the State." The 5 May 1877 act creating the bureau also provided for the appointment of a commissioner, hired at a salary of $2,000 and given a desk in the office of the State Board of Agriculture, to oversee the new agency's efforts.

The bureau's mandate was narrow. H. J. Walls, the first commissioner, after consulting with Ohio's attorney general, determined that "in fact the only power the Bureau had, was to ask questions, it being optional with those interrogated to answer or refuse to answer as to them seemed best."

To that end, Walls quickly developed two questionnaires. One questionnaire, the "Employers' General Blank," requested information on the nature of a firm's business. The bureau asked employers to provide information on such industrial relations matters as employment levels, wage rates, methods of wage payments, and success of apprenticeship pro-

grams. A second questionnaire, "Employes' Blank No. 1," asked workers to provide informa-
tion on a wide variety of subjects from family life to yearly earnings to work routines on the
shop floor. During its first year, the bureau sent 1,027 questionnaires to firms in the leading
industries in the state (coal mining, iron, and manufacturing concerns), receiving 405
responses. Simultaneously, it sent more than 700 questionnaires to workers (precise numbers
not reported). The bureau compiled its first annual report, to a large extent, from the data
drawn from the questionnaires; the following excerpt is Commissioner Wall's "Conclusions
and Recommendations."

From 1863 to 1873 was a decade of almost uninterrupted prosperity in the United States, and Ohio, as much as any other State, shared therein. While the population of the State between 1860 and 1870 increased only about 14 per cent., or from 2,339,511 in 1860, to 2,665,260 in 1870, the value of real and personal property increased 87 per cent., or from $1,193,398,422 to $2,235,130,300. The wealth per capita in 1860 was $510.32, and in 1870 it was $838.73.

In agriculture, the value of farms increased 55 per cent. between 1860 and 1870, and the value of farm machinery and implements increased 46 per cent. during the same period.

In manufactures, the number of establishments increased from 11,123 in 1860 to 22,773 in 1870, or over 100 per cent. The number of employés increased from 75,602 to 129,577, or over 71 per cent., and the value of products increased from $121,691,148 to $269,713,610, or over 100 per cent.

This vast increase in wealth and wealth-producing power, with the small relative increase in population, did not prevent our industries from becoming paralyzed, and workingmen by the hundreds and thousands denied the right to earn bread for themselves and families.

The wealth and wealth-producing power remain intact, the brains and muscle are eager for employment, and nothing prevents a new era of prosperity but the poverty of the masses. Their wants are unsupplied, and their inability to supply them is keeping the work-shops of the State closed, or nearly so. They must have work and wages before their wants can be supplied, but they can not, under existing conditions, commence production and increase consumption except at the will of others, who possess the wealth and machinery for production.

The system under which labor receives its reward—the wages system—is the main cause of labor's poverty. Wages are gauged, not by the value of services done, or the product of such labor, but by the present necessities of the laborer. The fact that wealth increased six times faster than population, and workingmen as a rule continued absolutely dependent on their daily employment for their daily bread, is evidence that wages do not bear a just proportion to product.

Coöperation for the production and distribution of wealth; a coöperation between capital and labor in which labor will be a recognized equal factor with capital, in which product and not wages will determine the reward of labor, must be the next step in labor's advancement from its present dependent condition.

As compared with the cost of the necessaries of life, the reduction of wages since 1872, in many branches of industry, has been excessive, and when to this is added the reduction in possible earnings caused by unsteady employment, the income of producers will show an average reduction of nearly 50 per cent. since 1872.

The prompt payment of wages is absolutely essential to any thing like independence or comfort on the part of wage laborers. Any system of payment such as "truck," "checks," "scrip," or store orders, in lieu of lawful money, or any system that compels the wage laborer to become a seeker for credit, should be absolutely prohibited by State laws which could be enforced.

From the facts elicited from the various organizations of workingmen, it is evident that nine-tenths of the disputes between employers and employés, resulting in strikes, could be avoided if the efforts of such organizations to establish the principle of arbitration were seconded by employers generally. As long as arbitration is offered by one party and refused by the other, the responsibility for strikes must rest with the party refusing.

Many of the grievances of workingmen are such as they themselves are responsible for, or which can only be remedied by enlightened public opinion. To remedy the evils and arouse public attention thereto, workingmen everywhere should organize social, educational, protective, and coöperative associations. First, that they may learn to know each other's wants and desires; second, that they may be able to penetrate the mysteries that are supposed to surround the labor question, especially the bearing of the various theories of finance, supply and demand, tariff, wages, etc., have upon the question; third, that they may be able to defend and protect each other, whenever such protection or defense may be necessary or essential; and, lastly, that they may eventually become the owners and controllers of the artificial productive forces of the country.

There are grievances, however, that legislation should remedy, and the following recommendations are made to the General Assembly:

1. That a law be passed, with proper penalties to secure its enforcement, that the wages of labor shall be paid in the legal tender money of the United States, and that in suits at law for wages, no payment other than in such legal tender money shall be allowed as a set-off against such claim.

2. That the contracting of the labor of prisoners in the penal and reformatory institutions of the State be prohibited from and after the expiration of present contracts.

3. That a law be passed authorizing the creation of coöperative associations for manufacturing and mining purposes.

4. That a penalty for violation be attached to the provisions of all mandatory laws, especially the laws bearing upon corporations, and the laws already on the statute books intended for the protection of the working classes.

5. That the law of appeals, "the stay law," be so amended that judgments given for wages of labor shall be paid within one week from date of judgment.

1. Eric Arnesen, "American Workers and the Labor Movement in the Late Nineteenth Century," in Charles W. Calhoun, ed., *The Gilded Age: Essays on the Origins of Modern America* (Wilmington, Del.: Scholarly Resources, 1996), 39–44.

XI.6. Female Labor in Industrializing Ohio: The Investigation of Working Women in Cincinnati

Throughout the last quarter of the nineteenth century, women working in industrial or domestic service jobs labored at a severe disadvantage. Women who responded to the Bureau of Labor Statistics questionnaires complained about the harshness of labor and the injustice of the rewards. "I do really think that our board is too high for the wages we get. My work is rather hard on my body; inspecting counting and keeping track of all the finished and unfinished work, brass, gold and steel screws, which bothers my head quite a little. It has made my eyes very weak," observed a watchmaker from Canton. Wages for working men were consistently higher than for working women, leading women to voice their complaints: "If a girls expenses are the same as a man's, and just as much depends upon them in most cases, why not pay her the same wages as a man gets, when she can do the work just as well, and give them a chance to earn an honest dollar without slaving in the kitchens for almost nothing." 1 But both men and women suffered. As the following document notes, wages for all workers fell during the Gilded Age. Prompted by chronic overproduction, prices and wages in industry tended to decline in the "long depression" of the late nineteenth century. Unemployment caused by recessions or seasonal layoffs reduced the annual earnings of workers.[2]

The home was often the workplace for women in industries such as the garment trades. Women took their work home, did specific tasks in the production process, and returned the finished product to the factory or shop to receive pay on a piecework basis.[3]

In 1889 the Bureau of Labor Statistics supplemented its usual informational questionnaires with the "personal visitation" of experts to develop a comprehensive picture of women's labor in the state. The commissioner of labor sent Mary L. Giffs of Cincinnati and Lizzie E. Milligan of Coshocton to investigate the "leading trades in which women are employed." The results of their inquiry, titled "The Trades Employing Women," followed three pages of comments made by working women on the questionnaires. Information was provided to the Cincinnati Enquirer for the story that ran on 13 April 1890.

*T*he Enquirer this morning presents some vitally interesting facts about working-women. The information is secured in advance from the annual report of the State Labor Commissioner. It relates particularly to the work of women in Cincinnati, and gives a gloomy picture of the condition right at home. The facts are official, the result of very careful investigation, and are therefore authentic. They present an exhibit that is startling, and should command the most earnest consideration. Here they are:

The Lines of Work. Principally investigated were tailoring, shoefitting, laundry work, housework, cloak and vest making, sewing of different kinds and restaurant work.

General conditions of women at work, and also home conditions, were particularly investigated; and, in many cases, most pitiable state of affairs was disclosed. It was no unusual thing to find families of from four to seven living in one small room, where light could seldom penetrate, and pure air never; where infancy and old age, sickness and health, all huddled together, were living on an income less than it takes to keep the average business man in cigars.

The destitution thus unearthed. Among the working people of Cincinnati, if caused by some sudden catastrophe such as swept over Louisville or Linn, would call forth the sympathy of the world, but, coming as it has, gradually, year by year, through the natural operation of business systems, it has been systematically ignored and its existence even denied.

Investigation has shown that the number of people in desperate circumstances was greater at the taking of statistics for 1889 than at any year previous, and that more people were out of employment, the number in Cincinnati alone being estimated at from 8,000 to 10,000.

Wages have been steadily on the decrease in some trades for twenty years.

Of the people who are the victims of these adverse circumstances, there are just two classes: those who have come down from better positions—a class which seems to be increasing—and those in the same condition in life into which they were born. But those to whom poverty has been a heritage do not feel its iron heel, as a rule, more keenly than do those of the other class, and thousands of both classes are at all times within a week of starvation. With both the battle of life is fierce and unremitting.

Children are crying for bread; old people, too old and infirm to work steadily are slowly starving to death, and hundreds of girls are being driven into the vortex of sin by the gaunt specter of want.

But, with all this, there is still a large element of good citizenship among them, and a degree of moral integrity that is surprising. Particularly is this true of the women, who choose lives of bitter privation rather than gilded paths of vice, and bravely live their chosen lives to the bitter end.

Among the many pitiful cases brought to light was one that may serve to illustrate the true condition of the homes of many unfortunate working people, and also to show under what terrible privations a woman must sometimes live and labor.

She was young, not more than 24 or 25. Her husband was an invalid and she had two children, a little boy of 3 or 4 years and an infant daughter. She was a tailoress, and was doing what is called shop tailoring—the cheapest work in the market. She went to the shop and got the work and took it home with her.

Her "home" was one small room about 12 by 14 on the ground floor of a queer, rambling old tenement house in the West End. The street in front gave no indication of a tenement house, and the only means of entrance was through an arched passage-way just large enough to admit a small wagon or dray, and through which undoubtedly the people moved their small belongings. This passage-way led back and opened into a sort of court-yard, around which the building rose four stories on every side. A row of windows and doors marked the entrance to perhaps twenty-five "homes" on (or in) the ground floor, while outside stairs led to the floors above, and a sort of outside corridor, somewhat on the plan of the Ohio Penitentiary, ran along the building just above the lower windows.

Her room was one of the first, and was even more cheerless within than it was prison-like without.

The bare floor, the blank and dingy walls, the few old wooden chairs, the unmade bed, the almost fireless stove around which the family were huddled, all spoke a mute language of privation and toil.

She ate by a bare wooden table near the one window, through which the struggling rays of the wintry day shone feebly from under the corridor without, and lighted up with a sort of chill and ghastly light the miserable home within.

By her side lay a pile of unfinished pants, and as her thin fingers moved deftly and swiftly over her work, making button-holes, sewing on buttons and doing all the numberless little things that go to make up "finishing," one foot was busily engaged rocking the little wooden chair upon which the baby daughter had her tiny bed.

A loaf of black rye bread, a little molasses in a bowl and a cup of water sat upon the table, and a little boy of some 3 or 4 years of age sat up in a high chair vainly striving to satisfy the craving hunger of childhood with this meager and doubtless oft-repeated diet. As though any thing had been lacking to prove to the investigator how great a luxury in that poor home were the things called common necessities in others, the little fellow lisped in a guileless baby way:

"Mamma, we's dot some suddar in de tubbard, ain't we, mamma?"

"Yes," answered the mother, flushing with embarrassment, and anxious to dismiss the subject.

"Mamma," continued the little one, not to be silenced upon a matter of such importance, "we has to teep that for baby, don't we, mamma? Mamma, some time when papa dits well we'll dit some more suddar, won't we, mamma, and den I tin have some too, tant I, mamma?"

The father, who sat by helpless with rheumatism, sighed deeply, but said not a word.

Here the little one woke from her uneasy slumbers with a frightened cry. The mother laid down her work and took up the babe, and as she nursed the child at her famished breast told the investigator something of her life.

For nearly two years her husband had been out of work, part of the time on account of sickness, but oftener because work could not be found. He used to be a teamster and owned his own team, but for a long time had been only a common laborer.

When misfortune first came she went into a tailor shop to work, thinking it would only be for a little while, but times grew harder and harder, until now they had nothing at all but her small earnings, which usually ranged from $1.50 to $2 per week. Before baby came she used to go to the shop, and then she made more money. Now she must work at home, and it was no unusual thing to put in eighteen, sometimes twenty, hours a day over her work.

But rent had to be paid, and though it was only $4 per month, yet it was sometimes hard to pay, with husband and baby both sick and needing food and medicine.

---

1. Excerpts from "Opinions of Working Women," appended to "The Trades Employing Women," in Bureau of Labor Statistics, *Annual Report . . . for the Year 1889* (Columbus: Westbote Co., 1890), 33.

2. Sara M. Evans, *Born for Liberty: A History of Women in America* (New York: Free Press, 1989), 132; Stacy A. Cordery, "Women in Industrializing America," in Charles W. Calhoun, ed., *The Gilded Age: Essays on the Origins of Modern America* (Wilmington, Del.: Scholarly Resources, 1996), 122.

3. Evans, *Born for Liberty,* 132.

XI.7. The Child Labor Problem in the Gilded Age: The Cincinnati Inquiry of 1894

The rapid postwar economic development drew large numbers of children into factories in a wide variety of traditional, labor-intensive trades and newly mechanized industries. Examining census data and other statistical evidence, Illinois reformer Florence Kelley estimated that there were 1,118,000 working children in the United States between the ages of ten and fifteen nationwide in 1880. Kelley found that these children often paid a very high price for the privilege of working in industry: gruesome deaths, maiming injuries, gradual deterioration of health, even exposure to adult vices.

Most state governments had done little to regulate employment practices for minors, and Ohio was no exception. Besides the 1852 legislation that specified a ten-hour workday for women and children under the age of eighteen, the only other regulation was the 1874 prohibition on the employment of children under the age of twelve in the mines.

Building on earlier investigations of working men and women, the Bureau of Labor Statistics began developing a comprehensive picture of child labor in the state. In 1894, the bureau conducted its first investigative study of "Child-Labor in Cincinnati."[1]

*T*he investigation of child-labor has long been desired by the working people of Cincinnati. At the beginning of this undertaking we were led to believe that it was to be a difficult task, as the first manager approached refused our application for admittance to his factory. This confirmed the belief that there was really something to be found out. Employers, as a rule, were opposed to the idea of letting any one into the works to get the information direct from the employee, as such a method of inquiry usually reveals an entirely different state of affairs from that of accepting statements given at the office. In one cigar factory, where the proprietor said he did not think that he had a person under 16 years of age, we found thirty who were below this age, and several were as young as 12. The subject of child-labor in Cincinnati has long been neglected. On account of this lack of attention children have been taken advantage of to a very great extent.

OCCUPATION

The occupation is seldom taken into consideration. If the child is able and willing to fill a position the employer endeavors to make room for the applicant. The child being unable to consider his or her physical or mental welfare, will accept almost any kind of employment that will yield one or two dollars a week. Boys in shoe factories [where men were formerly employed] are believed to work harder than the men did, and for about 30 or 40 per cent. of the latter's wages. It cannot be ambition or thrift that prompts the child to go to work so young, for the children of the merchant and the landlord can be found in the same unpleasant and unhealthy occupations as those of the laborer and the widow.

AGE

It was not in 1894, nor during the present industrial depression, that children began to work in Cincinnati, but it was when the first unsupported widow succeeded in finding employment for her oldest child, who was perhaps able to do nothing more than carry an ordinary bucket of water. This was a discovery for the neighbors and a certain class of employers—to find that children could be advantageously used at certain occupations. From that time on the volume of child labor has been increasing, until we have the present condition, when great numbers of children are employed in almost every line of industry. They are put to work at the earliest possible age that the law allows. Owing to the construction placed upon the statutes by some employers, this is found in some instances to be not more than 12 years. A great many children who are apparently not more than 12 will, when asked, give their age at 14. It seems that many parents from the day their children are born wait impatiently for the time to come when they will be able to bring home a dollar a week. In 40 establishments, embracing 15 industries, and employing 7,699 persons, there are 946 children under 16 years of age, of which 318 began to work before the age of 14. This year has been an exceptional one for children starting to work. On account of the industrial depression, there has been a large number of those who left school last year in order to go to work that have been unable to find places.

LEARNING TRADES

Ask a boy if he is learning a trade and he will almost invariably say no. In addition to the development of machinery, we have systems of management which are rapidly depriving the workingman of his skill and maturing a generation of unskilled men and women. Instead of following in the footsteps of their fathers in the promotion of industry and art, many of the boys of to-day are instilled with a desire to make a living regardless of method. Instead of being taught a trade the boy is trained up to a certain standard and frequently displaces his instructor at the first opportunity. This system is extensively carried on in the shoe industry. Employers are averse to hiring adult or skilled help and never do it while they have a boy who is able to fill the position vacated—perhaps by his father or older brother. When he becomes an expert and considers his compensation unfair, he is pushed out by his follower and the position pays another dollar less per week. This applies to the women's department, also.

HOURS PER DAY

Ten hours is the standard day in manufacturing industries. While the present dullness has created the vast army of unemployed, it has also reduced the working day to a respectable length. At present it is about eight hours, which is considered only temporary. Laundries, during busy seasons, work as high as fifteen hours per day, three days a week. This is evened up by short time on Saturday and Monday, making the week sixty hours. Small girls in retail stores work as high as fourteen hours a day and sixty-five hours per week.

PIECE WORK

Piece work is taken advantage of in nearly all lines of manufacture, especially in the cigar and shoe industries, where injustice prevails to an inhuman degree. In some factories there is a system which overcomes all youthful carelessness. After working for weeks for nothing, girls are given a certain amount of tobacco with which to make a specified number of cigars. One fourteen-year old girl, making cheroots for five cents per 100, made 1,100 in one week, but was docked 22 cents for using too much tobacco, thus leaving her 33 cents for a week's wages. In shoe factories girls are working piece work for as low as $1.00 per week and are charged with all material which they deface. This material is used by the manufacturer after it has been paid for by the employe.

EFFECT ON HEALTH

The natural effects of a number of occupations at which children are employed is a delicate constitution. Working among tobacco, inking at shoe factories, running sand paper machines in shoe factories, bronzing picture frames and performing certain kinds of working in lithographing establishments are injurious to health. The fumes and dust are inhaled with bad results, and child-labor in such instances is strongly condemned by the medical fraternity. As a rule the sanitary condition of factories visited was good, so far as ventilation and cleanliness were concerned.

DISPLACING ADULT LABOR

At the present rate, appearances are that the child will usurp the tools of the carpenter and the blacksmith and cast these workmen adrift on the sea of indolence. Fifteen-year-old girls were found in stone yards polishing marble, an occupation which required the muscular exertion of a man. In the concern referred to the men had a strike in 1893 and the girls displaced them. While the boys and girls are now on the heels of the adults, it is through subdivision of the work and the assistance of machinery that the adult is becoming a less desired employe. It is a deplorable fact that the boy of to-day, in some industries, is doing much more work than his father or older brother did eight years ago and receiving much smaller compensation, thus depriving some fathers of adequate means of fulfilling their duty in supplying the wants of their households and educating their children.

DANGERS TO LIFE AND LIMB

In our record we have 135 children working with machinery. Nearly all of these machines were formerly operated by adult labor. While there is apparently no great liability to accident, boys and girls often meet with accidents through what the employer calls carelessness, but he continues to use children at the same places, thus defying the laws of nature in trying to make them careful.

EDUCATION

Children are allowed to go to school until they are acceptable to the employer, at which time they have passed the age of 12 and have been advanced to about the fourth or fifth reader, with a slight knowledge of grammar, geography, United States history and arithmetic, in addition to reading and writing. They are taken out of school without even a desire for education and sent to work, regardless of their physical or mental abilities. A few have said that they are working only during vacation, but many of these continue to be employed after the opening of school.

MORAL DEPRAVITY

It may be the impression among some parents that their children are better off in the factory than on the streets. This is a grave mistake, for there is no place so vile as some of the factories to the mind of the uneducated youth. The moral tone of the shop is often very low. Frequently the boy is initiated into the shop as a beer boy, thus encouraging a habit which is seldom discarded. In cigar factories both sexes are indiscriminately associated together, and morality is at a discount. Obscene language is used profusely and it has been given out that practices of the most foul nature are engaged in in the presence of girls. If such things cannot be otherwise prevented the law should require the complete separation of the sexes.

NECESSITY FOR CHILD LABOR

After inquiring into the circumstances, we find that child-labor is more of a custom than a necessity. While compelled to sympathize with the youthful toiler and to regard with compassion the sorrows of the unsupported widow, only scorn and contempt is felt for the unmerciful father whose lofty ambition is to erect tenements or decorate the interior of the rum shop at the expense of the health and morals of his children. Out of our records of 946 children employed, we have only 29 orphans; 204 are of deceased fathers and 39 of invalid fathers. Of the latter many are mechanics who have recently become disabled. We find that the average number of persons to a family is six, and the average income per family per week $13.50. In many cases we would find at work a child 14 years of age, who was the youngest of eight children. The income of such a family would be over $30 per week. It is certainly unnecessary in such instances for the child to be at work. He should be at school.

1. "Child-Labor in Cincinnati," in Bureau of Labor Statistics, *Annual Report . . . for the Year 1894* (Columbus: Westbote Co., 1895), 103–7.

XII. Progressivism in Ohio

THE PROGRESSIVE ERA WAS A PERIOD of reform beginning at the turn of the nineteenth century and lasting until the First World War. By the late 1890s, it was apparent to many Ohioans that the state and the nation were pursuing a rapid and reckless path to modernity. Large, powerful business corporations, unsafe factory workplaces, privileged public utilities, crowded tenement houses, and unregulated food processing and distribution characterized the industrial transformation of the late nineteenth century. Reform-minded citizens began to unite to change these conditions.

Who were Ohio's reform-minded "progressives"? Rarely did reformers come from a single socioeconomic group or embrace a single, coherent ideology. Indeed, they could be found among the most prominent business leaders of the state, among the officers of Ohio's established trade unions, and among the clergy of most faiths. There is little doubt, however, that the largely white, Protestant, middle class dominated most Ohio reform movements. Of this sizable group, some came from the traditional middle class of the nineteenth century, a group comprised of ministers, lawyers, and physicians; others were from the ranks of the new university-based professions, especially engineers, social workers, and academically trained economists.

But social class, ethnic background, or party affiliation mattered less than shared ideas. The most controversial champions of municipal reform efforts in Cleveland and Toledo came from the very same ranks of big business that received the greatest criticism from most progressives. Although a majority of reformers affiliated themselves with the Democratic Party in the years before the First World War, both parties had "progressive" wings. Similarly, although probably more middle-class Protestants populated reform organizations, prewar crusades such as the settlement house movement attracted Catholics and Jews as well.

Over the past three decades, historians have recognized that the variety of reformism makes categorization difficult. Municipal reformers struggled to reestablish popular control over their cities by regulating privately owned utilities, by replacing big city political machines, and by making government agencies more efficient; settlement house workers sought to improve the lives of inner city residents while shaping societal mores; labor leaders and social reformers fought for safer and more democratic workplaces.

Certainly the most well-known Ohio reformers were Samuel "Golden Rule" Jones, Tom L. Johnson, and Rev. Washington Gladden. Jones and Johnson, the mayors of Toledo and Cleveland respectively, were both enormously successful businessmen who were intimately familiar with the corrupt practices of urban political machines and privately owned utility companies. Washington Gladden, one of the architects of the Social Gospel movement in American Protestantism, entered politics to serve one term as a city councilman in Columbus. Gladden criticized the emerging corporate capitalist economy, with its "wage-labor system" and increasing disparities in incomes and wealth, as socially irresponsible. All three men saw the dangers of concentrated economic power in a democratic society, the influence that corporations exerted over the political process, and the need for greater harmony between social groups.

So what distinguished reformers from conservatives at the turn of the century? Was it a belief that government should play a larger role in the supervision of the state's and the nation's development? For most progressives, yes. Yet some were skeptical of government intervention in the marketplace and in society and embraced private solutions rather than public ones. These progressives, often prominent in business and organized labor circles, proposed self-regulation by private groups, such as unions, trade associations, and farm bureaus, instead of government supervision.

We must look closer at the beliefs of progressives and conservatives to understand what separated them in this crucial era. It seems that reformers shared a belief in one or more of the following three "clusters of ideas" or intellectual traditions widely discussed at the turn of the century. The first set of ideas was the old antimonopoly tradition. Those reformers fearful of the power of big business revived and legitimized these ideas. By 1900, it was acceptable to debate the legitimacy of corporate power in Ohio and the nation, a proposition that had been labeled radical a decade or two earlier. Some progressives wanted self-regulation by organized groups of businessmen, but others desired to prohibit business practices that prevented potential competitors from entering the market; others wanted to go further, creating state agencies to regulate trade practices and approve mergers; still others, fearful of the power of large corporations, campaigned for the dissolution of all big firms.

A second set of ideas, a belief in the interdependence of social classes and groups in the emerging industrial society, was embraced by most Ohio progressives in this era. The belief in interdependency, in the existence of "social bonds" that tied Americans together, ran counter to the traditional nineteenth-century emphasis on individualism.

The third notion, a belief in promoting "social efficiency," was accepted by many, but not all, reformers at the turn of the century. Those who embraced "efficiency" ideas usually advocated the application of management techniques or social science knowledge, or both, to the problems of society. In this manner, engineers, labor relations experts, and social welfare experts made their contributions to reform. Few, if any, reformers embraced all three of these ideological traditions; coalitions formed, shifted, and dissolved as concerned individuals, accepting one or more of the propositions, came together to change conditions in society.

The Christian Socialist ideas of Washington Gladden and the democratic beliefs of Frederic C. Howe, the first two selections in this chapter, provide revealing glimpses of the progressive worldview. The debates of the 1912 Constitutional Convention, the subject of the next series of documents, provide fairly clear distinctions between conservative and progressive reform stances on such key issues as municipal home rule, initiative and referendum, and woman suffrage.

Some reformers, motivated by the popular "efficiency" ideas of scientific managers and social scientists, championed innovation in the workplace and in municipal government. A series of documents demonstrate the nature of business, government, and conservation reform in the Miami Valley. After the devastating 1913 flood, National Cash Register's pioneering managerial reforms spilled over into the structural reform of municipal government, all in the name of efficiency and expertise. The Dayton city manager-council plan, influenced by earlier experiments in Galveston and Pittsburgh, offers the best example of progressive government from Ohio history.

These selections, among others, document the era of progressive reform that had an enormous impact on Ohio government, economy, and society for the remainder of the century.

XII.1. The Christian Socialist as Progressive Reformer: Reverend Washington Gladden's "Social Gospel" Thought

The Social Gospel was a turn-of-the-century doctrine that asserted that organized religion, through its existing church organizations, was responsible for not only the alleviation but also the reformation of the social ills present in the industrial capitalism. Washington Gladden, minister at the First Congregational Church in Columbus, Ohio, was one of the principal architects of this new doctrine. Gladden and other Social Gospelers spread their message in Sunday morning sermons, speeches in a variety of public forums, and numerous written works.

Central to Gladden's version of the Social Gospel was the quest for social justice based on Christian ethics. He called for the application of biblical principles to the conduct between and among social groups in industrializing America. Gladden, who embraced a Christian Socialist viewpoint, argued for the public ownership and operation of all "natural monopolies," including railroads, telegraph facilities, mines, and all public utilities, and the establishment of harmonious relations between labor and management by ending the destructive "wage-system" of modern capitalism. He exhorted fellow Ohioans to end the discrimination against racial and religious minorities that divided late-nineteenth-century society. Gladden's Social Gospel ideals are evident in the stance he took during his two-year term on the Columbus City Council at the turn of the century. Espousing an activist role for government, he campaigned for public ownership of utilities and for the reduction of streetcar fares to make transportation costs less onerous for the workingman.[1]

Through their efforts to curb the excesses of big business, to strengthen the social bonds that knit industrial society together, and to improve the quality of life, Gladden and other Social Gospelers made an important contribution to Progressive Era reformism.

In the following excerpts from his 1896 book, Tools and the Man, *Gladden expresses his view of the role government should play in the development of a Christian society.[2]*

*I*n the most curt and comprehensive fashion, let me proceed to name a number of points at which, according to my conception of the Christian ethics, the functions of the state might well be extended beyond the boundaries laid down by the advocates of *laissez faire*. . . .

1. The Christian state may furnish a certain amount of public instruction, and require its citizens to avail themselves of it. . . .

2. The sanitary supervision by which pure air and water are secured for all the people is another of the functions of the Christian state. Professor Walker thinks that this is fairly included within the police functions; that it is simply a measure of necessary protection; Mr. Spencer would scarcely agree with him; nevertheless, whether it be old or new theory, it is good sense and good Christian morality. . . .

4. The Christian state will find itself enlisted in the suppression of the saloon. Under the theory which limits the power of the state to the suppression of crime and the preservation of liberty of the citizen, this might be logically admissible; under the theory which commits the state to the promotion of the general welfare it is easily justified. Whatever manifestly tends to the detriment of society at large may and must be suppressed. The liquor interest has become a gigantic, consolidated, unsocial force, directly and malignantly assailing the community, undermining its thrift, corrupting its political life, destroying its peace; and against it, not merely the teacher with his science, and the preacher with his Bible, and the philanthropist with his sympathy for the fallen, but "All-of-us," with all the power we possess, must arise and do battle. . . .

6. I have no doubt that the state will also be compelled to limit the hours of labor in some callings, if not in all. With respect to the wisdom of such restriction upon the labor of women and children there can be no question. The fact that the machinery now in use in the various manufacturing industries will produce vastly more than the people can possibly consume, if it is kept in operation through all the hours of the present working day, indicates the wisdom of reducing the number of those hours. The simplest method for the accomplishment of this purpose may be the direct interference of the state. When "All-of-us" see that it is best for "All-of-us," "All-of-us" can say so and have it so. It is very often said that all these matters will regulate themselves if they are let alone. But they do not regulate themselves; the tendency to the degradation of the weak is irresistible. . . .

8. The Christian state has a great service to perform in healing strife, in making and publishing peace. It ought to stand forth as the peacemaker in the quarrel between the employers and employed. When the employer is an individual or a private company, perhaps the best thing that the state can do is to tender its good offices to assist the parties in coming to an understanding. To this end it may wisely furnish models and suggestions in certain rules of permissive legislation for the arbitration of labor disputes.

1. Ray Ginger, *Age of Excess: The United States from 1877 to 1914* (New York: Macmillan, 1975), 292; Page Smith, *America Enters the World: A People's History of the Progressive Era and World War I* (New York: Penguin Books, 1985), 830–32.

2. Washington Gladden, *Tools and the Man* (Boston: Houghton Mifflin, 1896), 281–308.

XII.2. Democratic Thought in the Progressive Era: The Confessions of an Ohio Reformer

Frederic C. Howe was one of many reform-minded citizens who thought about reinvigorating American democracy during the first third of the twentieth century. For him, as for such thinkers as John Dewey, Mary Parker Follette, and Edward Ward, progressivism was not merely a fight against big business and political bosses, nor even a struggle to institutionalize mechanisms by which people could govern themselves; it was an effort to embody democracy, to create forums in which citizens could debate and deliberate on the issues of the day. Unlike muckrakers who sought to mobilize the citizenry by informing them, reformers like Howe wanted a participatory democracy in which citizens exchanged ideas, sought consensus, and then acted on the decisions made in their deliberations. Only then, could a truly "democratic public" exist.

Born in Meadville, Pennsylvania, Fred Howe represented a mid-nineteenth-century generation reared on traditional conservative values. Howe was the son of a Quaker mother and an iconoclastic Scotch-Irish Presbyterian father who embraced both the Methodist Church and the Republican Party. After a conventional education at public school and Allegheny College, Fred Howe pursued graduate study in political science at the Johns Hopkins University. Howe transferred his allegiance from church and party to a new authority, social science knowledge. His training at Johns Hopkins in the historical development of institutions altered his perspective on the American society and economy. Soon after beginning a career in the law in Cleveland, Howe ran for political office as a reformer in the fight against big corporations and their allies, the political bosses.

As a Cleveland city councilman and state legislator, Howe came under the influence of Mayor Tom L. Johnson, the controversial, independent Democrat. In "tent meeting" experiments in Cleveland and across the state, Johnson urged citizens to establish community forums to discuss political questions. Mayor Johnson sought to educate his constituents through community tent meetings at which he explained his reform agenda in understandable terms. In his unsuccessful run for governor, Johnson took his show on the road. As he had done in Cleveland, the mayor lectured audiences on the evils of monopolistic business practices and corrupt machine politicians while extolling the virtues of his administration's innovative municipal government.

Howe took Johnson's ideas a step further, advocating the establishment of people's forums where experts could air their views in public, exchange ideas with citizens in question-and-answer sessions, and advance the policy-making process. Like his mentor, Mayor Johnson, Howe believed it was possible to define a solitary "public interest" through democratic deliberation and, thus, act in name of "the people." In his struggle against the city's powerful Republican Party political machine and its allies in the state legislature, Howe refined his notions of self-government and decentralization. To achieve both, he recognized that it was necessary to change the state's constitution to allow people to possess political instruments such as municipal home rule, legislative initiative and referendum, and the recall of judges.

In the following selection from his Confessions of a Reformer, first published in 1925, Howe summarizes his progressive perspective on American urban democracy. Graduate study had replaced the old authorities of church and party with the new authority of social science theory. Experience in partisan politics and reform in Cleveland during the Johnson years, however, thoroughly altered the theoretical perspective of the young lawyer, revealing how democracy in America functioned.[1]

ℳy text-book government had to be discarded; my worship of the Constitution scrapped. The state that I had believed in with religious fervor was gone. Like the anthropomorphic God of my childhood, it had never existed. But crashing beliefs cleared the air. I saw that democracy had not failed; it had never been tried. We had created confusion and had called it democracy. Professors at the university and textbook writers had talked and written about something that did not exist. It could not exist. In politics we lived a continuous lie.

I set down for myself principles that would constitute democracy. I applied biological processes to it. From source or other I had come to believe that Nature was very wise, and that her rules, by which billions upon billions of creatures were able to live, must be a reasonably good guide for the organized state. I took the private corporation as a guide. Business had succeeded in America and it worked with very simple machinery. It was not bothered by a constitution; it was not balked by checks and balances; it was not compelled to wait for years to achieve what it wanted. Its acts were not supervised by a distant supreme court. The freedom of a private corporation was close to license; what its officials wanted done was done. Mayors, governors, legislatures, city councils had no such power. In many ways the corporation that disposed of the city's garbage had more freedom of action than had the municipality that employed it. Here was a suggestion of machinery that worked well, even if it did not work in the interest of the public.

Business men had been given one instrument, the people another. The one was simple, direct, and powerful; the other confused, indirect, and helpless. We had freed the individual but imprisoned the community. We had given power to the corporation but not to the state. The text-books talked of political sovereignty, but what we really had was business sovereignty. And because the business corporation had power while the political corporation had not, the business corporation had become the state.

Nor had we followed what nature had to teach. We violated the instincts of man. Politics offered no returns to the man of talent, who wanted to see the fruit of his efforts. If business had been organized like the state, it would have been palsied. Business would have gone bankrupt under the confusion, the complexity, the endless delays which were demanded by the political state.

Taking the private corporation as a model, I evolved three basic principles; they were: Government should be easily understood and easily worked; it should respond immediately to the decision of the majority; the people should always rule.

Elaborated into a program of constitutional change, these principles involved:

(1) The easy nomination of all candidates by petition. There should be no conventions. Direct primaries are the fountainhead of democracy.

(2) Candidates should print their platforms in a few lines on the election ballots. Voters would then know what the man stood for.

(3) The short ballot.

(4) The recall of all elective officials, including judges.

(5) The initiative and referendum on the Constitution, on laws, on city ordinances.

(6) Complete home rule for cities. The city should be a state by itself, with power to do anything of a local nature that the people wanted done. A free city would be like the cities of ancient Greece, like the medieval Italian republics, like the cities of Germany today. It would be inspire patriotism. Able men would be attracted to the task of administering it.

(7) The State Assembly should consist of but one body of not more than fifty members. It should be in continuous session for a four-year term, the governor sitting with it and responsible to it for the exercise of wide powers.

(8) The courts should have merely civil and criminal jurisdiction. They should have no power to interfere with legislation. Congress and the State legislatures should be the sole judges of the constitutionality of their acts. The British Parliament and legislative bodies of other countries are supreme. America alone has created a third assembly chamber that has an absolute veto of the popular will.

Such a government would be democracy. It would be simple and easily understood. There would be no confusion, no delays. In such a state the people would be free. And they would be sovereign. Under the existing system they were neither sovereign nor free. We had stripped the state of sovereignty; the first thing to do was to restore it. Under such a system we could have a boss if we wanted one. Certainly we should have leaders. But we could hold the leader to responsibility. Things would be done in the open. We should not be living the lie of the existing system, which was not democracy but economic oligarchy. . . .

1. Frederic C. Howe, *The Confessions of a Reformer* (New York: Charles Scribner's Sons, 1925; reprint, Kent, Ohio: Kent State University Press, 1988), chap. 18.

XII.3. Creating the "Free City": The 1912 Constitutional Convention and the Debate over "Home Rule"

The 1851 Ohio Constitution provided for conventions at twenty-year intervals to revise the state's governing charter. A variety of reform movements gained popular support across the state just as the first opportunity for constitutional revision in the new century approached. Although various groups advocating woman suffrage, judicial reform, municipal home rule, and workers' compensation urged revision of the Ohio Constitution, three organizations made the most effective appeals to the public: the Direct Legislation League, an association led by Herbert Bigelow that pushed for the enactment of initiative and referendum reforms; the Ohio State Board of Commerce, which had promoted tax reform; and the liquor industry, which wanted saloon licensing.[1]

The fourth Ohio Constitutional Convention assembled at the State Capitol Building in Columbus on 9 January 1912. Of the 119 delegates, there were 46 lawyers, 25 farmers, 14 from business and finance, 10 representatives of organized labor, 6 educators, 4 ministers, 4 physicians, and the remainder from various other professions. Although Democrats outnum-

bered Republicans among the elected delegates to the 1912 convention, party meant less than individual attitudes toward change and modernization. Progressive reformers held a decisive majority in the makeup of the convention.

Once convened, the delegates elected the controversial Bigelow, a minister from Cincinnati, as their president. Then they immediately entered into a vigorous debate over the organization of the convention and the procedures they would follow. The convention delegated authority to Bigelow and their rules committee to organize the work of the body. They created nineteen committees, each comprising from seventeen to twenty-two delegates, to deliberate on the major reform issues of the day. The most active committees were those entrusted with addressing municipal government, initiative and referendum, taxation, education, liquor traffic, equal suffrage and elective franchise, good roads, judiciary, and labor.

It had been Cleveland's reformers who had sparked the movement for municipal government reform in Ohio. The Municipal Association of Cleveland had established a committee to draft a home rule amendment as early as 1910. The committee, led by Augustus R. Hatton and Newton D. Baker, canvassed the state to assess the degree of support for a constitutional amendment. The committee issued a report as the Constitutional Convention assembled in January 1912, then called representatives of all Ohio municipalities together in Columbus in late January. Conferees from the state's municipalities considered two draft home-rule proposals. One, written by representatives from Cincinnati, allowed the legislature to maintain direct legislative control over municipalities; the other, drafted by Cleveland reformers, proposed greater autonomy for cities. After considerable debate, conferees accepted the Cleveland draft and presented it to the Constitutional Convention. Advocates of the Cleveland proposal, led by Baker, encountered stiff opposition in committee. The compromise amendment coming out of committee granted the General Assembly the authority to restrict the power of cities to tax and incur debts.

The result of the two-day debate over home rule on the convention floor in April was a draft amendment that failed to incorporate any modernization of the municipal tax law, but did permit cities to tax franchises and mineral rights, two key sources of business profits.

The arguments for both sides of the home-rule issue, by delegates George W. Knight of Franklin County and David Cunningham of Cadiz in Harrison County, have been selected from the record of the proceedings of the Constitutional Convention.[2] A text of the final version of the home rule amendment follows.[3]

THE ARGUMENT FOR HOME RULE
GEORGE W. KNIGHT

The proposal undertakes to accomplish three things not now possible under the present constitution:

First, to make it possible for different cities in the state of Ohio to have, if they so desire, different forms and types of municipal organizations.

Under the present constitution it seems that it is not competent for the lawmaking body to classify municipalities, save in the two classes mentioned in the present constitution, namely, cities and villages; and the further provision which requires uniformity of laws for corporations makes it necessary that the legislature in enacting laws shall provide for one general uniform type of government for all cities and another general uniform type of government for all villages. With cities in the state varying in population from five thousand to half a million, it is obvious that either the large city must get along with crude machinery inadequate for its needs, or the small cities must have all the machinery of government adequate to a city of half a million. In either case the awkwardness is apparent and the burden of expense upon the smaller community is needlessly large. Therefore, the first thing that this proposal undertakes to do is to provide that municipalities shall . . . have the right, if they so desire, to frame charters for themselves, to provide each for itself such type or form of organization for municipal business as it desires.

The second thing, and the main thing, which the proposal undertakes to do is to get away from what is now the fixed rule of law, seemingly also required by the constitution, that municipal corporations, like all other corporations, shall be held strictly within the limit of the powers granted by the legislature to the corporation, and that no corporation, municipal or otherwise, may lawfully undertake to do anything which it has not been given specifically the power to do by the constitution or the lawmaking body. It has often been found under our present system, and undoubtedly would be found also in the future, that many things necessary from the standpoint of city life, which the city may need or urgently desire to do, can not be done because the lack of power specifically conferred on the municipality itself. Therefore, this proposal undertakes pretty nearly to reverse that rule and to provide that municipalities shall have the power to do those things which are not prohibited, that is, those things with reference to local government, with reference to the affairs which concern the municipality, which are not forbidden by the lawmaking power of the state, or are not in conflict with the general laws of the state under the police power and the general state regulation. So the presumption would now become a presumption in favor of the lawfulness of the municipalities' act, and that presumption would only be overcome by showing that the power had been denied to the municipalities or that it was against the general laws of the state.

In the third place the proposal expressly undertakes to make clearer or make broader the power of municipalities to control, either by leasing, constructing or acquiring from corporations now owning or operating the public utilities within the corporation and serving the corporation, the water supply, the lighting and heating supply and the other things—without specifying—which come within the purview of municipal public utilities, thus removing once and for all, all legitimate questions as to the authority of municipalities to undertake and carry on essential municipal activities.

These three things are the fundamental things which are undertaken by the proposal, and these three things taken together certainly constitute what may be termed, and rightly termed, municipal home rule.

THE ARGUMENT AGAINST HOME RULE
DAVID CUNNINGHAM

Proposal No. 272 has received less real general consideration in open convention than any other important proposal before this body, and I believe should have received the most careful attention. It is true that we are assured by members of the committee on Municipal Government that they had sweat blood over its consideration; that not a syllable of any word or even a preposition had been overlooked; that it was the best thing of the kind that had ever been framed by mortal men up to this time; that it embraced on this subject the garnered wisdom of a thousand years. Some of us think that it falls short of what is claimed for it. In the first place, the amended title is misleading. The title has been changed by the committee on Phraseology to "Municipal Home Rule." We think that title does not describe it at all and that it will have the effect to mislead and deceive the people. The title to describe in short the object of this proposal should be changed to something like this: "To provide an easy way for universal municipal bankruptcy." If the people are not deceived as to the real scope of this measure it will never be adopted.

Let us examine it for a few moments. It provides for a deluge of these corporations. Under it more than two thousand different and distinct municipal corporations can be organized in the state. This looks to me to be home rule run mad. So far as I am personally concerned I am in favor of granting the right of any city to establish a commission form of government. A proposal of twenty-five lines is all that is needed to provide this constitutional right. . . .

This proposal gives every little village and city in the state the right to buy in, or to condemn if it cannot buy, any and all public utilities inside its limit and issue bonds to pay for the same. For example, they can buy or build street-car lines, electric-light plants, gas plants and any other public utility that can be thought of, and extend them out into the country beyond the corporate limits and operate them. We are to have "no pent-up Uticas" in this great state of Ohio, and if there shall be in ten years a single village or city in the state that will not be absolutely bankrupt it will be because it will not be able to sell the bonds.

If the committee who framed up this measure had set themselves deliberately to work to propose the worst and most vicious form of municipal government in the world they couldn't have succeeded better; and hence I insist that if this measure is to be submitted in its present form that the title at least should be changed so as not to deceive the people, but at least give them a gentle hint as to its true character.

When all the money in the state is invested in the bonds issued to buy all these public utilities we will then have a single tax without mistake. The bonds will be exempt and the utilities themselves will no longer pay any taxes. The millions now paid by them into the public treasury will be no longer available; consequently there will be but little left except real estate to pay taxes on. We are launching our municipal bank on an unknown sea without the rudder of common sense to guide it, and for one I protest.

ARTICLE XVIII
MUNICIPAL CORPORATIONS

Sec. 1. Municipal corporations are hereby classified into cities and villages. All such corporations having a population of five thousand or over shall be cities; all others shall be villages. The method of transition from one class to the other shall be regulated by law.

Sec. 2. General laws shall be passed to provide for the incorporation and government of cities and villages; and additional laws may also be passed for the government of municipalities adopting the same; but no such additional law shall become operative in any municipality until it shall have been submitted to the electors thereof, and affirmed by a majority of those voting thereon, under regulations to be established by law.

Sec. 3. Municipalities shall have authority to exercise all powers of local self-government and to adopt and enforce within their limits such local police, sanitary and other similar regulations, as are not in conflict with general laws.

Sec. 4. Any municipality may acquire, construct, own, lease and operate within or without its corporate limits, any public utility the product or service of which is or is to be supplied to the municipality or its inhabitants, and may contract with others for any such product or service. The acquisition of any such public utility may be by condemnation or otherwise, and a municipality may acquire thereby the use of, or full title to, the property and franchise of any company or person supplying to the municipality or its inhabitants the service or product of any such utility.

Sec. 5. Any municipality proceeding to acquire, construct, own, lease or operate a public utility, or to contract with any person or company therefor, shall act by ordinance and no such ordinance shall take effect until after thirty days from its passage. If within said thirty days a petition signed by ten per centum of the electors of the municipality shall be filed with the executive authority thereof demanding a referendum on such ordinance it shall not take effect until submitted to the electors and approved by a majority of those voting thereon. The submission of any such question shall be governed by all the provisions of section 8 of this article as to the submission of the question of choosing a charter commission.

Sec. 6. Any municipality, owning or operating a public utility for the purpose of supplying the service or product thereof to the municipality or its inhabitants, may also sell and deliver to others any transportation service of such utility in an amount not exceeding in either case fifty per centum of the total service or product supplied by such utility within the municipality.

Sec. 7. Any municipality may frame and adopt or amend a charter for its government and may, subject to the provisions of section 3 of this article, exercise thereunder all powers of local self-government.

Sec. 8. The legislative authority of any city or village may be a two-thirds vote of its members, and under petition of ten per centum of the electors shall forthwith, provide by ordinance for the submission to the electors, of the question, "Shall commission be chosen to frame a charter[?]." The ordinance providing for the submission of such question shall require that it be submitted to the electors at the next regular municipal election if one shall occur not less than sixty nor more than one hundred and twenty days after its passage; otherwise it shall provide for the submission of the question at a special election to be called and held within the time aforesaid. The ballot containing such question shall bear no party designation, and provision shall be made thereon for the election from the municipality at large of fifteen electors who shall constitute a commission to frame a charter; provided that a majority of the electors voting on such question shall have voted in the affirmative. Any charter so framed shall be submitted to the electors of the municipality at an election to be held at a time fixed by the charter commission and within one year from the date of its election, provision for which shall be made by the legislative authority of the municipality in so far as not prescribed by general law. Not less than thirty days prior to such election the clerk of the municipality shall mail a copy of the proposed charter to each elector whose name appears upon the poll or registration books of the last regular or general election held therein. If such proposed charter is approved by a majority of the electors voting thereon it shall become the charter of such municipality at the time fixed therein. . . .

Sec. 12. Any municipality which acquires, constructs or extends any public utility and desires to raise money for such purposes may issue mortgage bonds therefor beyond the general limit of bonded indebtedness prescribed by law; provided that such mortgage bonds issued beyond the general limit of bonded indebtedness prescribed by law shall not impose any liability upon such municipality but shall be secured only upon the property and revenues of such public utility, including a franchise stating the terms upon which, in case of foreclosure, the purchaser may operate the same, which franchise shall in no case extend for a longer period than twenty years from the date of the sale of such utility and franchise on foreclosure.

Sec. 13. Laws may be passed to limit the power of municipalities to levy taxes and incur debts for local purposes, and may require reports from municipalities as to their financial condition and transactions, in such form as may be provided by law, and may provide for examination of the vouchers, books and accounts of all municipal authorities, or of public undertakings conducted by such authorities.

1. The following discussion of the 1912 Constitutional Convention stems from a reading of H. Landon Warner, *Progressivism in Ohio, 1897–1917* (Columbus: Ohio State University Press, 1964), chaps. 11 and 12.

2. *Proceedings and Debates of the Constitutional Convention of the State of Ohio*, 2 vols. (Columbus: F. J. Heer, 1913), 1:1433, 1861–62.

3. *Constitution of the State of Ohio with Amendments Approved by the People September 3, 1912.*

XII.4. The Essence of Direct Democracy: The Debate over the Initiative and Referendum Amendment to the Constitution

Possibly the most controversial issue at the 1912 Constitutional Convention was the amendment providing for initiative and referendum at the state and local levels. Those advocates of greater democracy in local government believed that initiative, referendum, and judicial recall were necessary instruments in the quest for popular sovereignty. Throughout 1908 and 1909, Herbert Bigelow and the Direct Election League had lobbied unsuccessfully to enact an amendment by legislation. Over the next several years, Bigelow focused on educational efforts. Well financed by the Joseph Fels Fund and supported by "single-tax" advocates like Mayor Tom Johnson, who saw initiative and referendum as the only mechanism to secure an equitable taxation system, Bigelow succeeded in spreading his message throughout the state. In 1911, Bigelow, Brand Whitlock, and other like-minded reformers established the Progressive Constitutional League. The league's advocacy campaign focused on the passage of amendments authorizing municipal home rule, popular recall of judges, and initiative and referendum by petition. Although many business organizations stayed neutral or approved of initiative and referendum, the Ohio Board of Commerce became a driving force behind the opposition to these reforms. In spite of powerful opposition, Bigelow helped to elect a large block of delegates to the 1912 convention who were dedicated to or supportive of these constitutional reforms.[1]

The debate over initiative and referendum, which fills a large section of the published proceedings of the convention, even drew the attention of Ohio's most eloquent former chief executive. An excerpt from the address of John B. Foraker, the former governor and senator, is presented here to document the opposition's case; the rebuttal by delegate Okey follows.[2]

THE ARGUMENT AGAINST INITIATIVE AND REFERENDUM
ADDRESS BY J. B. FORAKER

. . . . We should bear in mind, therefore, that if it be the purpose of the initiative and the referendum to secure an expression of the voters with respect to local legislation, we have all the power and authority now necessary for that purpose without changing our constitution; and that, in the second place, we are likely to get the most satisfactory expressions, only when the numbers to vote are smallest and the questions submitted are simplest; particularly is all this true when the questions submitted do not involve sumptuary legislation or affect individual rights. When these features are involved there is, as a rule, a large vote.

But what we are now called upon to consider is not the initiative and referendum as applied to local subdivisions and to simple and distinct propositions of legislation, such as whether a community shall be wet or dry, the courthouse shall be located at one place or another, a particular bridge shall be built or not built; but whether or not we shall have general legislation affecting the whole state, to be submitted to all the electors of the whole state; and not only general legislation, but the most complicated as well as the simplest kind of general legislation; and be compelled to accept or reject without privilege or power to debate or amend.

For the proposal, as you have formulated it, is that on the petition of a small percentage of the voters any law enacted by the legislature having general operation throughout the whole, shall be submitted to the voters of the whole state for their approval before it shall be allowed to go into operation; and that on a like petition any bill that anybody may draft shall be submitted to the whole body of the voters of the state for approval and that securing a majority vote in its favor it shall become a law, even beyond the power of the governor to veto it.

All concede that this involves a radical change in legislative methods, but the advocates of these propositions tell us that they do not involve an abandonment of representative government or any experiment, that they have been put into operation in Oregon, California, and a number of other states, and that they have been found effective for good results; that the movement was conceived and inaugurated to cure conditions of political bossism and corruption; that the people had lost control of their own government, and in this way control has been restored to them, and that no one should oppose these propositions unless he is afraid to trust the people, and that as wholesome results have been secured elsewhere, so, too, can they be secured here in Ohio.

There are a number of objections that should be considered.

In the first place, it would increase the burden of elections; if not by increasing the number, at least, by increasing our duties and responsibilities.

With only a duty of choosing between candidate and platforms we have found elections such a disagreeable responsibility that we have wisely sought to minimize their number and simplify their character.

In this behalf only a few years ago we abolished our October elections and later consolidated elections of congressmen and state officials so as to have all occur in even-numbered years and municipal and other local elections so as to have them occur in odd-numbered years.

If now in addition to candidates and platforms we are to be compelled to consider and vote on all kinds of local and state legislation every time we go to the ballot box, we shall find election day the busiest and burdensome of all the year, since although the mere voting may be a small matter, yet the duty that will be placed upon us by this change will be onerous indeed. . . .

Another objection, applicable to the referendum, is that it has a tendency to induce legislators to evade their responsibility as to troublesome questions of legislation, a vote on which, either for or against, they desire, for any reason to avoid. . . .

It is fundamental that every public official should act with respect to every measure he is called upon to consider, according to his conscientious conviction of duty.

And if he does not act that way he ought not act at all. Somebody ought to recall him. And yet it is common knowledge that we do not always get this highest and best service when it is known that no matter what action may be taken, it is not final, but subject to review. . . .

Many other objections might be made, but I shall mention only one more, probably the most serious of all. . . .

We have a representative form of government; our fathers were of the opinion that in a country of such vast areas as we have, with a population of millions, soon to be multiplied to hundreds of millions, direct government by the people was impracticable and impossible. They, therefore, provided for a popular government to be conducted, not by the people directly acting in its conduct, but by representatives of the people so acting—representatives chosen by the people because of their supposed character and qualifications for such service—all sworn to sustain the constitution of the state and the nation and all the laws of the country.

When this form of government was adopted it was thought to be a long step forward in the science and progress of enlightened government. It was thought to solve the difficult problem of how the people could conduct a government of their own.

For more than a hundred years we apparently unanimously flattered ourselves that we had successfully solved that problem; that we had popular government; that the people did control the government. We believe with Lincoln that our government was of the people, by the people and for the people.

All American people not only have believed this—more than a century of national life and experience—that they have had such a government, but they have become attached to it, because of the wonderful success they have achieved under it. This should, at least, admonish us to not make radical changes lightly or inconsiderably, but only after careful examination and with an intelligent conception, if we can get it, of the consequences. . . .

If representative government had been a failure there might be a good excuse for what is proposed, for in such a contingency it would behoove us to make some kind of change; but representative government has not been a failure. . . . Is it not true that in spite of everything we have made greater progress than any country on the face of the earth? It has not been a failure. Instead of being a failure it has been a triumphant success.

THE ARGUMENT IN FAVOR OF INITIATIVE AND REFERENDUM
MR. OKEY

We have been told by those who do not agree with the principles involved in the proposal now before this body that we would destroy representative government if the initiative and referendum were adopted. I think if those persons who assert that—and so far as I have heard it has been mere assertion, and they have not told us or attempted to define to this body what representative government is—I believe if we would know truly the foundation stones upon which this government rests we ought to go back to the first great charter of human liberty in this country, namely the Declaration of Independence. If you will examine that document you will find it makes certain fundamental declarations. It declares that government is instituted among men in order that they may have liberty, that they may have life and that they may follow the pursuit of happiness. It goes on further and declares that the people, who have adopted government, have a right, if the government in any particular fails to respond to and carry out their purpose, to change that form of government. They have a right to modify that form of government to the end that it may carry out the purposes for which it is intended. Now we know, and we all know, that if this is a representative government it must represent, and the question arises if it does represent whom should it represent? Should it represent the classes or should it represent the masses? And I take it that all legislation under a republican form of government can only have one object in view, namely that every law that is enacted shall rest equally in its effect upon the high and the low.

I believe that no law should be enacted that would affect unequally in the least degree the humblest citizen under our flag, and I say that any legislation that deviates from that principle, under our present form of government, is not representative government, but you have misrepresentative government; and therefore the design of this proposal before us is that our government may become more responsive to the will of the governed, the will of the people, and that is what we are here tonight to discuss, and that is the proposal that is now before us. . . .

1. H. Landon Warner, *Progressivism in Ohio, 1897-1917* (Columbus: Ohio State University Press, 1964), 296-300, 307.

2. *Proceedings and Debates of the Constitutional Convention of the State of Ohio,* 2 vols. (Columbus: F. J. Heer, 1913), 1:719-22, 726-29.

XII.5. The Debate over a Woman's Suffrage Amendment

Many Ohio progressives wanted to extend the suffrage provisions of the 1851 constitution. The existing charter limited the vote to "white male citizens of the United States" who had passed their twenty-first birthday and had resided in Ohio for at least one year. Because the Fifteenth Amendment of the U.S. Constitution had nullified the limitation, Ohio delegates were ready to amend their state charter accordingly. A women's suffrage amendment, however, faced overwhelming opposition, as it did in most regions of the nation outside the Pacific Coast and Rocky Mountain states. Although the Ohio Woman Suffrage Association had expended considerable energy lobbying for an extension of suffrage provisions and the Ohio Grange, the Ohio Federation of Labor, and many notable male reform organizations supported the cause, the state had limited women's voting rights to local school elections.

The following excerpt from the remarks of an opponent of suffrage extension, Allen Marshall of Coshocton, drawn from the convention's proceedings, has been selected to provide the most traditional argument in the debate over woman suffrage at the Constitutional Convention. F. M. Marriot of Delaware provided the argument for women's suffrage.[1]

THE ARGUMENT AGAINST SUFFRAGE BY ALLEN M. MARSHALL

"And God saw everything that He had made; and behold, it was very good. And the evening and the morning were the sixth day."

We have but little comment to make on the sixth or last day of creation, more than this, that at its conclusion He pronounced it very good. Still carrying out His divine principle of giving to everything its opposite, especially His creation of man and man's opposite, woman.

Thus, we have recorded one of the most wonderful acts of surgical skill known or that will be known in the world's history. This rib, this woman, was the crowning work of God's creation, last but not least. He placed her on the highest pinnacle of the wonderful pedestal of His creation, almost in hand-shaking distance of the angelic host of heaven, and I want to say if John D. Rockefeller at this moment would step into the halls of this Convention and upon some member of this body bestow a billion dollars endowment, it would be as a grain of sand on the seashore compared with the endowment given to woman by the hand of the wise Creator when He bestowed on her the endowments of helpmate, wife and mother.

An undeniable fact which we find before we come to the close of the third chapter of the book of Genesis: No part or particle of all God's creation ever received exalted place or rich endowment that God gave to woman whom he endowed with (I was going to say with the immortal power, and I guess I will) the power of motherhood. Would to God that woman could see herself today as the queen star in the firmament of creation, as her Creator sees her. And why is it that a few women over the state of Ohio have become so masculine in their conceptions of their divine place and sphere in the divine economy of creation that they want to make a fatal leap from the highest pinnacle of the pedestal of creation down to its base, alighting in the seething cauldron of political corruption? And not satisfied with this descent on their own part, they want to take with them in this fatal leap your daughters and my daughters, beautiful daughters,

daughters clothed in their white robes of virgin purity, down with them, alighting in the whirlpool of political corruption, and thus immersing their white robes of purity in the indelible stench of the political world, which time can never erase.

And yet they come to me asking my assistance in this, their fatal leap.

Should I conclude to cast my vote in behalf of this fatal leap, at that moment I should feel that heaven's recording angel had dotted down against me the equal of the — if not the — unpardonable sin. And again I would feel that I had committed treason against God and the government of High Heaven by my revolt against divine and natural law. And again, I should fully realize that I was casting my vote to blot out three of the most sacred words known in the world's vocabulary of six thousand years, namely, mother, home and heaven.

THE ARGUMENT FOR SUFFRAGE BY F. M. MARRIOTT

Are the women of Ohio less intelligent, deserving, brave and true? Will we stand and let Wisconsin, Kansas, Oregon and Nevada also show us the way? I say no, a thousand times no!

For more than sixty years the women of Ohio, our mothers and our wives, have been knocking at the door of equal rights, asking only for simple justice, and the doors have not been opened to let them in.

I say this to the everlasting shame of the men of Ohio. Today that army of mothers and wives is joined by our sisters and our daughters, and they are now unitedly appealing to this Convention for simple justice, appealing to be emancipated from the slavery in which men have held them for all these years.

Will we longer close our ears to their appeal and refuse their prayer? I say emphatically no. . . .

A so-called popular government which deprives one-half of its citizens the privilege of citizenship is a false pretense and is not a popular government in fact but in name only, and every state which withholds from its women the right to have a voice in its government violates the spirit, if not the letter, of the federal constitution.

Women are citizens, so declared by the constitution of the United States, and the state constitution which deprives any portion of her citizens of equal privilege with all other citizens is conceived in unwisdom and born of injustice.

A constitution which fails to guard the integrity of American citizenship, and to give all its citizens equal protection of law and participation in government, is and always will be a failure, because it is lacking in inherent honesty.

A successful and permanent government must rest primarily on recognition of the right of its citizens and the absolute sovereignty of its people. Upon these principles is built the superstructure of our republic. Their maintenance and perpetuation measure the life of the republic. These principles stand for the rights and liberties of the people, and for the power and majesty of the government. A republic, therefore, which does not recognize justice and equal rights to all its citizens cannot and ought not longer endure.

The greatest boon of American citizenship is the right to participate in government. When one-half of the citizenship is deprived of this right our boasted claim of a government of the people, by the people and for the people is a false claim, and Lincoln might well have said that "ours is a government, only we are ruled by men and not by man."

1. *Proceedings and Debates of the Constitutional Convention of the State of Ohio*, 2 vols. (Columbus: F. J. Heer, 1913), 1:605–7, 616–18.

XII.6. Cleansing the Urban Landscape: "Collecting and Hauling City Wastes" in Ohio's Major Cities

Progressives across the state and the nation expressed great concern over health and social welfare issues during the two decades before the First World War. The industrial transformation of the previous century had greatly expanded the populations of Ohio's major urban centers. The half dozen largest Ohio cities had grown rapidly in the late nineteenth century as factories expanded, commercial and residential construction accelerated, and immigrant workers and their families settled in. Not surprisingly, sanitary conditions deteriorated just as rapidly. Fifty years before, in the old "walking cities" of the mid-nineteenth century, few residents or their local government officials cared about the systematic collection and disposal of industrial, commercial, and residential wastes. By the end of the century, the problem of "city waste" became a serious concern for municipal officials. The following selection from "Equipment and Methods of Collecting and Hauling City Wastes," part of a larger report on waste collection in Ohio cities, documents the solutions that Ohioans devised to deal with the by-products of modernization.[1]

GARBAGE.

For the collection of garbage, particularly in the large cities of the state, special equipment suitable for the purpose is provided. Two general types of wagons are used. In Cleveland, Columbus, Cincinnati, Dayton, Steubenville, and Zanesville, covered steel tank wagon bodies are employed, and in the other cities studied the wagons are built with two platforms upon which the cans from the householders are placed directly. The Cleveland and Columbus wagons are of the same type and are designed for dumping their contents without the removal of the wagon bodies. At Cincinnati and Dayton the wagon bodies are removed from the running gear and subsequently dumped after transportation to the point of disposal. The platform wagons used in connection with the so-called can system are somewhat less economical than the tank wagons but are entirely suited for small cities where quantities of garbage are not great.

Rules governing the collection of garbage are similar in each of the cities where the work is organized. These rules apply particularly to the provision of proper receptacles, their location to facilitate removal, and where reduction plants are used the exclusion of rubbish and ashes from the garbage. Owing to the difficulty of rigid enforcement of the rules, they are in all of the cities violated to a greater or lesser degree, depending largely upon the character of the people.

In the smaller cities of the state the material is transported directly in the collection wagons to the disposal plants, but in the larger cities where the question of length of haul becomes of great importance there have been established loading stations where the garbage may be dumped into specially constructed cars or left in the wagon bodies which are placed on flat cars and thus transported to the point of final disposal. This method is practiced in each of the large cities in Ohio.

RUBBISH—ASHES.

Although separate collection of rubbish and ashes is practiced in certain localities, it was found that in each of the Ohio cities in which this work is carried on these wastes are collected and disposed of together. In only three of the cities of the state are there organized collection systems for this class of material, and in each of the others private scavengers are depended on. Special types of wagons are used in Cincinnati and at Cleveland, while at Dayton a modification of the slat board type of wagon is employed. Local conditions are met at Cincinnati by the use of a back dump wagon manufactured by the city street cleaning department, and at Cleveland by the use of a bottom dump wagon of standard make. The type of wagon is not of vast importance but it seems to be the consensus of opinion that for the best economic results the wagon should have the capacity of from three to four cubic yards where combined collection of ashes and rubbish is made.

As is the case with garbage collection, rules have been adopted in each of the cities regulating the collection of rubbish and ashes. Such rules in general provide for the receptacles to be used, the preparation of the material to facilitate collection, and the exclusion of garbage and other offensive material from the ashes and rubbish. These rules are generally enforced, but the difficulty in accomplishing this permits of more or less violation.

Aside from the equipment for removal of rubbish and ashes from households, city departments maintain minor equipment consisting of waste paper boxes and baskets located in streets and parks. This development has taken place in each of the large cities of the state and does much toward promoting the cleanliness of those cities. Where no rubbish collection is made, the street cleaning department attends to the removal of the waste paper thus accumulated.

STREET CLEANINGS.

In each of the cities of Ohio in which studies were made, there are municipal street cleaning departments more or less efficiently equipped. In the smaller cities the equipments are less adequate and in a state of more incomplete development than in the larger ones, and for this reason the studies were confined to observations in Cincinnati, Cleveland, and Columbus. In each of these cities well equipped departments are maintained and efficient work is accomplished.

The equipment of the street cleaning departments in these cities in general consists of flushing machines, machine sweepers, sprinkling carts, white wing outfits for hand cleaning, and wagons for the removal of street and catch basin dirt. The kind of equipment in these three cities varies with the method of cleaning practiced, the relative proportion of flushers, machine sweepers, etc., being dependent upon the relative amounts of cleaning done by different methods.

There were found to be practiced three general methods of street cleaning;

namely, flushing, machine sweeping, and hand cleaning. Flushing is carried on by the use of flushing machines alone as at Cleveland and Columbus, or by the use of flushing machines supplemented by machine sweepers as at Cincinnati. Machine sweeping is usually accomplished by the use of sprinkling carts and the old type of machine sweepers with a revolving broom. The practice at Cincinnati modifies this to the extent of substituting the flushing machines for the sprinkling carts. The hand cleaning method consists of the removal of the material from the surface of the streets by hand labor; brooms, shovels, and scrapers being employed. The street may or may not be sprinkled previous to cleaning.

At Cleveland and Cincinnati the street cleaning departments are especially equipped to carry on cleaning by flushing. At Cleveland machine sweeping has been almost entirely discarded and is now used to only a very small extent. At Cincinnati, however, the old equipment of the department, consisting principally of machine sweepers, has been retained to be used in conjunction with the flushing machines. In both of these cities hand cleaning is also an important method in use, and records indicate a greater area cleaned by this means than by any other method. At Columbus the equipment of the street cleaning department allows a relatively small amount of the work to be carried on by flushing, and in that city the machine sweeping method is most important. . . .

Whatever method of street cleaning is employed, it is necessary to remove the material collected in the gutters by the use of carts or wagons. Where machine sweeping or hand cleaning is done, this is usually accomplished soon after the material has been removed from the surface. When flushing is used, it is necessary to allow a number of hours to elapse to permit drainage and partial drying of the material in order that it may be handled with facility. The wagons provided are of special type in each of the cities, equipped with dumping appliances to suit local conditions.

1. State of Ohio, State Board of Health, "Report of a Study of the Collection and Disposal of City Wastes in Ohio," *Supplement to the Twenty-Fifth Annual Report, 1910* (Columbus: F. J. Heer, 1911), 14–16.

XII.7. "Business Progressivism" in Ohio: The Case of John H. Patterson and National Cash Register

John H. Patterson's intense desire to have National Cash Register, the firm he founded and presided over for several decades, control the market for business machinery made him a target of antimonopoly reformers and Justice Department lawyers. But although Patterson devised many novel (and sometimes nasty) ways to undo competitors, he was no ordinary Gilded Age robber baron. Under his leadership, NCR became a pioneer in modern managerial, sales, and personnel practices. Its innovative "pyramid" corporate structure, with numerous levels of middle managers operating separate departments and accountable through separate sets of books, became a model for companies at a formative time in the state's and the nation's history. Its committee system, described in the following document, provided manager and worker input at several levels.

The firm also initiated systematic sales promotion programs, established mandatory sales training schools and sales manuals, developed a guaranteed territory system for its salesmen, held the first sales conventions, and made its representatives memorize "sales pitches." But it was in the realm of personnel relations that NCR made its mark. By 1900, Patterson and top managers at NCR had established the most comprehensive program of employee benefits in the United States. The firm pioneered in five different areas of corporate "welfare work," categories in which the firm improved its employees' working and living conditions. In the category of physical improvements, NCR staged a minor architectural revolution in the factory by using glass to better lighting conditions and improved health and sanitation conditions by providing medical care and installing showers for workers. It offered educational opportunities for employees so they could improve their intellects. Patterson supported special activities that would improve the moral fiber of his workers. Similarly, NCR sponsored clubs and associations to better social conditions. Finally, Patterson assisted his workers financially by paying good wages and, in 1917, by offering a profit-sharing program.

The following selection, from an article published in the 1897 Bureau of Labor Statistics Report,[1] offers an overview of these innovations at NCR and the "progressive" views of its controversial founder.

A Wonderful Factory System.

*T*he National Cash Register Company, of Dayton, although but thirteen years old, has invested one million and a half dollars, and occupies one of the most beautiful suburbs of Dayton, Ohio, its factories attract the attention of every visitor to the city, and no trip is complete without a visit to the immense "Cash" plant. One of the greatest steps towards establishing a permanent era of good feeling between employer and employee, was the invention of Mr. John H. Patterson, the president of the company, of the wonderful factory system, which is becoming widely known as the "Dayton Plan." This system has become especially known by its unusual methods and extraordinary departures from established rules of business. One of the first peculiarities of this system is the absence in the factory of a superintendent. The employees govern themselves. The organization may well be likened to our government of the United States.

At the head of the organization are the president, Mr. John H. Patterson, and his brother, Mr. Frank J. Patterson, vice president. They occupy the position of a court of final resort. Directly under them and controlling the general business of the company is the executive committee, composed of the eight remaining officers of the company. The organization is then divided into three great divisions:

First—The Selling division, presided over directly by the managing agent of the company, and by the managing director, who is also at the head of the training school for agents. Under their authority and attending to the minor details of the business of the Selling division, are the office managers and traveling auditors, and under them the state agents and salesmen.

Second—The Office division, under the authority of the assistant secretary, who is chairman of the office committee, is composed of the heads of all office departments. Under this committee are smaller committees, such as the advertising committee, systems committee, agents' committee, etc., to attend to business of a special nature.

Third — The Making division, — the details of the business are under the control of what is known as the factory committee, composed of five heads of important factory departments. This committee occupies the position of a superintendent. Under the factory committee are committees for each different principle of machine manufactured, and to them are referred all questions arising in the factory. Suppose, for instance, a man in one of the factory departments meets with a difficulty and desires to obtain a decision thereon. He would first carry his suggestion or difficulty to the assistant foreman of his department; if he were unable to decide the matter, the assistant foreman would refer it to the foreman. The foreman might in turn take it to the committee whose business it is to attend to work of that kind. This committee may in turn refer it to the factory committee. If the factory committee feel that they do not like to take the responsibility of making the decision, they take it to the executive committee, and it may finally be decided by the president himself. In this way every employee has a chance for a hearing, and a profitable market for his ideas and suggestions.

Located in all parts of the factory are autographic registers designated by placards which read, "Prizes given for complaints or suggestions for any improvements in the manufacture of registers." Every six months $250 in gold is awarded in prizes to the employees in the rank and file for these complaints and suggestions. The same amount of money is awarded every six months for the best suggestions for the improvement of the business. Both office and factory employees are eligible to contest for this latter prize. In the treatment of the women employees, the National Cash Register Company differs materially from nearly every other large corporation in the world. In fact, so many privileges are given to the young women that the company has been accused of being over-partial, but several years' use of this system has proven their method to be the best of business sense. In the first place, all the young women employed by the company come to work at eight o'clock in the morning, just one hour and a quarter later than the men. At ten o'clock each morning they are given fifteen minutes' recess, during a portion of which time calisthenic exercises are indulged in. At noon all the three hundred young women are furnished with a tastefully cooked lunch at the expense of the company. In the afternoon they are given another fifteen minutes' recess and calisthenic exercises. At night they are allowed to go home fifteen minutes earlier than the men, thus avoiding the inconvenience of crowded street cars. They are given one-half holiday each week, at the company's expense, also a full day each month to do their shopping or to rest, at the company's expense. They are furnished with clean white aprons and sleeves, laundered by the company.

Situated in convenient parts of the factory are small rooms furnished with cots, to which young women may go in case of illness. Speaking of these privileges, Mr. Patterson, the president, says that "Though we have decreased the young women's time considerably, they do the same amount of work as they did when they were working the ten full hours. They give us better and quicker work for our kindnesses, and it has been a source of great profit to us."

The factory itself is fitted up with a view to the convenience and to promote the health of the employees.

"Give a person good surroundings," says Mr. Patterson, "and you will receive good work in return." The new factory building has been conceded by experts to be without doubt the best heated, best lighted and best ventilated factory building in the world. It is furnished with the latest improved shower baths, and the workmen are encouraged to use them.

At a recent assembly of the thirteen hundred employees, Mr. Patterson announced that the hours of the men would be reduced to nine and three-quarters per day, they to receive pay for ten hours.

"We wish to give the men the same privileges," said Mr. Patterson, "we have given the women, and if we are met half way, we hope to reduce your hours gradually until, in a few years, we reach the eight hour a day basis."

One of the most interesting departures and one, in fact, which is the foundation of the whole system, is the assembling of employees each week for the purpose of discussing the affairs of the company. On Friday of each week the officers of the company and the heads and assistant heads of the office and factory departments meet together and discuss topics concerning the business. These meetings are conducted by Robert's Rules of Order, and a great deal of valuable information is derived from them. The members of these meetings compose what is known as the "Advance Club," and may be likened to our National House of Representatives, as every department in the factory is represented there.

Another assembly of hardly less importance is that of the Officers' Club, which meets each day for lunch at the noon hour. This club is composed of the officers of the company and some twenty heads of departments. The table is under the supervision of a competent chef and his assistants and provides fare of the best quality.

Once each year, the agents of the company located all over the world meet the office and factory forces in a week's convention at the factory. These conventions are very interesting indeed, and the pecuniary result to the company has proven to be valuable enough to cause them to meet in co[n]ventions sometimes twice a year, although these conventions cost a great deal of money. A visit through the factory of the National Cash Register Company, a glance at the contented faces of all the employees, and a knowledge of the phenomenal business of the company, will convince the most skeptical of the success of this system to both the employer and employee. Yet, they are a monopoly in the strictest sense of that term. They are backed by capitalists, who claim to grant their humane privileges from purely a business standpoint, and their success has been wonderful. Already over a hundred thousand of the little cash register bells are tinkling all over the world. They are, indeed, an example for the corporations who are losing money by strikes of their employees.

1. "A Wonderful Factory System," *Twentieth Annual Report of the Bureau of Labor Statistics* (Norwalk, Ohio: Laning Printing Co., 1897), 13–16.

XII.8. "Forever Floodproof": The 1913 Flood and the Establishment of the Miami Conservancy

The 1913 flood devastated the Miami Valley in southwestern Ohio. Five days of torrential rain resulted in the destruction that is documented by the following report of the chief engineer. The flood was a turning point for progressive reform in that part of the state. It revealed the inability of traditional municipal government to act swiftly after a disaster; demonstrated that efficient business management techniques could be applied to government; persuaded business, political, and professional leaders to apply new scientific and engineering methods to water resource management in the valley; and convinced local leaders to replace "politics as usual" with a responsive city government that operated according to new, efficient business principles.

Consider the following record of the 1913 flood. The first selection is the introductory section from "The Flood of March, 1913," in the Report of Chief Engineer.[1] Immediately following is a summary of the plan for the Miami Conservancy project—a pioneering Progressive Era water conservation effort designed to manage the water resources of an entire river valley.[2]

THE FLOOD OF MARCH, 1913

*B*etween March 23 and 27, 1913, a flood of unusual magnitude and destructiveness occurred in the Miami Valley. It was caused by very heavy rainfall, covering a period of five days, falling upon saturated ground.

All the cities and towns in the valley suffered much damage and the whole flood plain of the river valley was submerged to a depth of from 10 to 20 feet. Although the cities were protected by levees of sufficient height to withstand ordinary flood conditions, these levees were all overtopped several feet.

Nearly all highway and railroad bridges in the valley were put out of service for several days and many of them were completely destroyed. In the entire valley approximately 400 people lost their lives. The property damage exceeded $60,000,000, not including the depreciation of real estate, and has been estimated as high as $150,000,000. The cities sustaining the heaviest damage are Dayton, Hamilton, Piqua, Troy, Middletown, Franklin, and Miamisburg.

SYNOPSIS OF THE RECOMMENDED PLAN

BY CHIEF ENGINEER ARTHUR E. MORGAN

The recommended plan consists of a series of five retarding basins, . . . supplemented by channel improvements through the cities. The retarding basins will be formed by dams built across the valleys of the Miami, Mad, and Stillwater Rivers, and on Twin and Loramie Creeks. Each dam will have permanent openings through its base through which the ordinary flow of the river and the flow during ordinary fresh-ets will pass unimpeded. During large floods the water which cannot pass through the outlet conduits will be held back temporarily in the basins above the dams. The con-duits are proportioned so that no more water can pass through them than can be car-ried safely in the improved channels through the cities below. In this manner, the runoff of a flood like that of 1913, which lasted but two or three days, would be dis-tributed over a period of about two weeks and its height would be correspondingly reduced.

During the 1913 flood about 1,415,000 acre feet of water fell over the drainage areas above the proposed dams. (An acre foot is the amount of water required to cover an acre one foot deep, 43,560 cubic feet). The total capacity of the retarding basins to the spillway level is 840,000 acre feet, or 60 per cent of the total rainfall of the 1913 flood. During the beginning of a flood, and again during its ending, when the flow is large, but not more than the channels will carry, nearly all will pass through the open-ings in the dams, and little or none will be stored. This leaves nearly the whole of the storage capacity of the basins available for cutting off the excess of flow when the main part of the flood is passing down the valley. Assuming, for the moment, that during a flood like that of 1913 all the rainfall would run off the ground surface, and none would be stored in the soil to run off slowly, there would remain 575,000 acre feet, or 40 per cent of the rainfall, to pass through the conduits. The conduits are planned of such size, however, that a considerably larger part of the flood flow assumed above would pass through them during this interval, so that a smaller part would be stored in the reser-voirs, and the water consequently would not rise to the spillway level. As the river chan-nels will be filled approximately to their full capacity during the entire time of the flood, it is only the peak of the flood, the part that the rivers cannot carry, which must be held back temporarily in the retarding basins. By improving the river channels through the cities as much as is reasonably practicable, the rate at which the water can be allowed to pass through the conduits is increased, and the amount that must be held back in the basins is lessened. . . .

The local flood control works at the various cities will consist of widening and deepening channels, correcting sharp bends, raising and lengthening bridges, protect-ing the sides and bottoms of channels with concrete at critical points, and building levees. . . .

Construction can proceed on all of the channel improvements and on nearly all of the dam construction at one time. Three years of active construction work should be sufficient for the substantial completion of the project.

1. State of Ohio, Miami Conservancy District, *Report of the Chief Engineer,* 3 vols. (Day-ton, Ohio: n.p., 1916), 1:27.
    2. Ibid., 17–18.

XII.9. Business Principles and Municipal Reform in the Miami Valley: Dayton's Commission-Manager Form of Government

Home rule allowed Ohioans to depart significantly from the mayoral-council model of municipal government that dominated American cities before 1900 and experiment with innovative models of municipal governance employed by cities outside of the state. When the devastating hurricane of September 1900 demonstrated the ineffectiveness of the existing mayoral government of Galveston, Texas, local business leaders led a movement to replace it with an at-large city commission system. In the new plan, a small, nonpartisan group of citizens, elected at large from the community, carried out both the legislative and executive functions of municipal government. Thus, commission members served as heads of the city's various administrative departments, supervising the daily work of the public employees.

But while almost three hundred cities across the nation adopted the successful Galveston model, many Progressive Era municipal reformers expressed concerns about commission government. The dual (administrative and deliberative) responsibilities of commissioners posed many problems and opened the door for corruption. Influenced by scientific management ideas, some municipal reformers advocated professional management in city government. In 1908, Staunton, Virginia, became the first American city to hire a professional city manager. The city manager supervised daily operations and reported to city council, the policy-making body of the municipality. Soon after, Sumter, South Carolina, adopted a mix of manager and commission models, combining the efficiencies of both plans. It was this model that Dayton embraced in the wake of the devastating 1913 flood.

Long before the disastrous flood, National Cash Register's John H. Patterson and other business leaders had campaigned for a change in city government. By late 1912, Ohio had approved a home rule amendment, Dayton's Chamber of Commerce had selected Patterson and other reformers to study each option, and the city's reformers had organized a Citizens' Committee to press for innovative, nonpartisan municipal government. When the city scheduled an election to select a panel to rewrite the city's charter for May 1913, the Citizens' Committee advanced a slate pledged to a modified commission-manager form of government. The flood demonstrated the ineffectiveness of traditional mayoral government and guaranteed the Citizens' slate an overwhelming victory. Daytonians endorsed the new municipal government plan in August 1913 and hired Henry Waite, a Cincinnati engineer, as its first city manager.[1]

The following excerpts are from Burton J. Hendrick's assessment of the Dayton experiment, "Taking the American City Out of Politics," written five years after the adoption of the new system.[2]

*F*or years the enlightened people of Dayton had fussed over the ever-present problem, "How can we improve our city government?" They sent experts abroad to study the matter in all its phases, hoping to find elsewhere a scheme that would fit local conditions. They ran the whole gamut of single-chamber plans, borough plans, commission plans, initiative, referendum, recall, and what not. Yet all this time the answer to their queries apparently lay at their very feet. Dayton's great industries had clearly evolved a system of government that produced the most satisfactory results. The business of administering Dayton—building roads, sewers, water works, collecting garbage and ashes, managing schools, police and fire departments—was just as much a business as that of making cash-registers, automobiles, and other manufactured products. Why not take the system that had proved so successful in business and use it for the city government? Already certain far-seeing citizens had caught a glimmering of this truth; it took a great natural calamity, however, to make it as clear as daylight. In March, 1913, came the great convulsion that will always figure in Dayton history as the "high water." The melting snows of winter rushed down into the Miami Valley, overwhelmed Dayton, flooded her banks, factories, and schools and forced the citizens to take to rowboats, high buildings, and the roofs of floating houses. This was the greatest crisis in the city's history, and it called for quick action. Dayton's officials stood around and wrung their hands helplessly, not having the slightest idea how to meet the situation. Since their lives had been spent in winning elections, making speeches, cultivating popularity among voters, and distributing political jobs, their helplessness in the face of such a crisis is not surprising. The managers and sub-managers of Dayton's factories immediately assumed control, and in a few hours they had completely organized the business of rescuing citizens, providing them with food and shelter and clothing. By the time the water went down a new Dayton had been planned to take the place of the old. Not only had the people been saved from destruction; they had had an unparalleled example of efficiency in government. . . . Why not take over the administration ideas that had given Dayton precisely the organization which had displaced its feudal charter when real administration was needed? It seemed not improbable that the same business organization that produced cash-registers, automobiles, agricultural implements, turbines, railway cars, and sewing-machines, could also sweep the streets, construct highways, remove garbage, build water-supply, maintain parks, manage the police and fire departments; in fine, perform the numerous activities which we have usually regarded as the exclusive province of politicians. Already a few inconspicuous communities elsewhere had experimented with this idea, and Dayton's new Bureau of Municipal Research had given some attention to the plan.

Dayton's experiences with the flood gave the example and created the public sentiment that made possible the change. The secret of business success, as illustrated in Dayton's corporations, was concentration of authority and responsibility. The stockholders elected a board of directors who had general supervision over affairs. This board did not attempt to control the detail of the business; in most instances it selected a president, or vice-president, gave him complete authority, and demanded results. This manager appointed the heads of departments, giving them authority in turn and in turn exacting results. Thus those twin forces of efficiency, authority and responsibility, became the predominant factors in the whole system. Why not introduce them as the governing powers in the city administration? Fundamentally that is the idea that lies at the basis of the "City Manager" plan. The stockholders—the citizens—elect a board of directors, the five commissioners. These gentlemen have a free hand to engage a manager, to purchase him in an open American market, and to pay him such a salary as the circumstances may warrant. This manager has complete authority to run the business of the city, and, since he has this authority, he can be held completely responsible for its success. He selects the heads of his departments, and is not obliged to select them from the city of Dayton. The relation of these heads to the city manager is identically that of the department heads of a great corporation to the chief executive; the relation of the manager to the city commission is the same as that of the executive to the directorate; and the relation of the commission to the voters is the same as that of the directorate to the stockholders. . . .

Let us not forget that the ultimate responsibility to the voters resides, not in the manager, but in a commission of five men. There are no aldermen, no councilmen, no Board of Estimate, none of the useless lumber that usually makes city administration so cumbersome and intricate. But the duties of the commission are not entirely ornamental. One of them, the one who gets the most votes, has the title of Mayor; he presides over the weekly meetings, represents the city on ceremonial occasions, and gets $1,800 a year salary, whereas the other commissioners get $1,200. This commission is the local legislature, in the same sense that the directorate is the legislature of the corporation. It meets weekly and passes such ordinances as its wisdom prescribes, and its approval is needed to perform the greatest function of government — the adoption of a budget. Its most important direct responsibility, however, is the selection of the manager, and, after performing this duty, its main occupation is keeping a close eye upon this important employee, and assuring itself that he measures up to the job. It engages this gentleman for no specific term, for it can "fire" him summarily if convinced that he is not properly doing his work. Clearly, therefore, the position of commissioner is one of great dignity and responsibility, and the first commission elected was almost ideally representative, its members comprising a labor leader in the printing trade, an office manager for a large industrial corporation, a manufacturer, a brick contractor, and a merchant. . . .

1. Judith Sealander, *Grand Plans: Business Progressivism and Social Change in Ohio's Miami Valley, 1890–1929* (Lexington: University Press of Kentucky, 1988), 94–96.

2. Burton J. Hendrick, "Taking the American City Out of Politics," *Harper's Monthly Magazine* 137 (1918): 106–13.

XII.10. Battling the Brothel: Ohio's "White Slavery" Law

Moral reform was important to most progressives. No social ill caused more consternation than "the trafficking in young women"; it caused a sensation in the Progressive Era. Reformers, journalists, fiction writers, even movie producers turned their attention to the problem. Private agencies and governments conducted investigations.

In part, the investigations and resulting legislation were political responses to the vice crusades by the National Vigilance Society, the American Society of Sanitary and Moral Prophylaxis, and the Bureau of Social Hygiene. These organizations, many of which reorganized into the American Social Hygiene Association in 1913, as well as the public investigations of key urban centers, published lengthy, and often quite lurid, reports and books on prostitution and its impact on society.

The Mann Act, the statute that made the transportation of a woman across state lines for "immoral purposes" a federal offense, was the product of a major national campaign against vice. Beginning in New York City in 1902, numerous cities impaneled vice commissions to investigate the extent of prostitution. By the end of the decade almost every state had passed antisolicitation statutes and more than thirty had enacted abatement laws to facilitate the closure of brothels. The following is a text of the Ohio law.[1]

House Bill No. 159

Be it enacted by the General Assembly of the State of Ohio: . . .

Sec. 13031-1. Any person who either by threats, or intimidation or by force or violence, or by deception, device or scheme takes, places, or causes to be taken or placed any female into a house of ill-fame for the purposes of prostitution, or any person who by force, violence, threats, intimidation or deception, or menace or duress takes or detains a female unlawfully with the intent to compel her to marry him or marry any other person or to be defiled; or any person who, being parent, guardian or having legal charge of the person of a female, consents to her taking or detention by any person for the purpose of prostitution, shall be guilty of pandering, and upon conviction thereof shall be punished by imprisonment in the penitentiary for a term of not less than two, nor more than twelve years and by a fine not more than five thousand dollars ($5,000.00).

Sec. 13031-2. Any person who shall place any female in the charge or custody of any person or persons for immoral purposes or in a house of prostitution with the intent that she shall lead a life of prostitution, or any person who shall compel any female to reside with him or with any other person for immoral purposes, or for the purpose of prostitution, or compel her to live a life of prostitution, is guilty of pandering, and upon conviction thereof shall be punished by imprisonment in the penitentiary not less than one year nor more than ten years and by a fine not more than one thousand dollars.

Sec. 13031-3. Any person who shall receive any money or other valuable thing for, or on account of, procuring for, or placing in, a house of prostitution or elsewhere, any female for the purpose of causing her to cohabit with any male person or persons, shall be guilty of a felony and upon conviction thereof shall be imprisoned in the penitentiary not less than three years nor more than ten years and fined not more than one thousand dollars.

Sec. 13031-4. Any person who places or leaves, or procures any other person or persons to place or leave, his wife in a house of prostitution shall be guilty of a felony and upon conviction thereof shall be imprisoned in the penitentiary not less than three years nor more than ten years and fined not more than one thousand dollars. . . .

Sec. 13031-6. Any person who shall knowingly transport or cause to be transported, or aids or assists in obtaining transportation for, by any means of conveyance, through or across this state, any female with the intent or purpose to induce, entice, or compel such female to become a prostitute or to reside in a disorderly house for the purpose of prostitution, shall be guilty of a felony and upon conviction thereof be imprisoned in the penitentiary not less than three years nor more than ten years. Any persons who shall commit the crime in this section mentioned may be prosecuted, indicted, tried and convicted in any county into or through which he shall have so transported any female as aforesaid.

Sec. 13031-9. Any person who by force, fraud, intimidation or threats places, or leaves any female of previous chaste life and character in a house of prostitution or house of assignation, or to lead a life of prostitution, shall be guilty of a felony and upon conviction thereof shall be imprisoned in the penitentiary not less than one year nor more than ten years and fined not more than one thousand dollars.

1. State of Ohio, *Legislative Acts Passed and Joint Resolutions Adopted* (Springfield, Ohio: Springfield Publishing Co., 1913), 103:188–90.

XIII. Ohio in the Great War

DURING THE FIRST WORLD WAR, the citizens of Columbus, Ohio, could demonstrate publicly their patriotism in a carnival-like atmosphere. Civic leaders had erected enormous billboards displaying the portraits of the Kaiser, Crown Prince Friedrich Wilhelm, and Germany's most prominent soldier, Marshal Paul von Hindenburg. Citizens who contributed money to the war effort received baseballs to hurl at the "Wicked Hun": the ringing of a bell marked every hit on a target and proclaimed the pitcher's loyalty to all within earshot. This effort to dramatize patriotism provides just one example of the numerous efforts to sell American intervention and mobilize Ohio's home front while its soldiers served on the battlefield.

Even before Congress declared war in April 1917, Ohio's business, government, and academic leaders began to prepare the Buckeye State for the possibility of war. Preparedness would not be easy; the ethnic and cultural differences existing in the state since the mid-1800s and intensified by the immigration of large numbers of central and eastern Europeans in later decades led to bitter divisions over policy. Immigrant Americans, especially those of Irish, German, or eastern European descent, were often Catholic and voted Democrat; descendants of original Ohio Country settlers were usually Protestant and voted Republican.

Not surprisingly, military preparedness, the preparation of young men for military service, met with mixed results in Ohio. When civic leaders, with the support of the U.S. Army, began opening military training camps, Ohioans were encouraged to participate in large numbers. Cincinnati's German Americans, who never fully embraced imperial Germany's expansionist desires, refused to give the officer's training camp movement their complete support. Even when pressured by employers to participate, many refused to volunteer for the camps.

The 1916 presidential election exacerbated existing ethnic and cultural divisions in Ohio. Wilson received a ninety-thousand-vote plurality in Ohio by pledging to keep America out of the European war and branding Republican candidate Charles Evans Hughes a warmonger. German Americans and organized labor turned out for Democrats in large numbers, electing James M. Cox governor and sending Atlee Pomerene of Canton to the U.S. Senate.

President Wilson reversed his stance on American intervention once the military situation on the Western Front deteriorated dramatically in early 1917 and Germany resumed unrestricted submarine warfare. On 2 April 1917, Wilson appeared before both houses of Congress to ask for a declaration of war. In the following vote, fifty-six members opposed the war resolution. One of the most notable opponents of U.S. intervention was Representative Isaac Sherwood, Democrat from Toledo and a distinguished combat veteran of the Civil War. In a lengthy dissent, Sherwood reminded fellow congressmen of President Washington's admonitions against "entangling alliances" and criticized the Wilson administration for acceding to the wishes of the British government, international financiers, and American munitions companies.

Once Congress declared war Ohio began an extensive economic and social, as well as military, mobilization. The chief coordinating organization for this mobilization was the Ohio Branch of the Council of National Defense. The state's CND branch resembled the national council, which was composed of key cabinet members and advised by prominent business and labor leaders. Governor Cox appointed a state advisory board to assist the Ohio branch in the formulation of transportation, finance, labor, and food policy and to deal with public relations problems.

Under the direction of the state CND, the Ohio Industrial Commission, an agency created in 1913 to administer worker compensation law and factory safety rules, assumed a central role in economic mobilization. The Industrial Commission was charged with the organization of the state's workforce. Initially, it acted as a "clearing house," allocating workers according to their skills to the relevant industries. Eventually, the commission recruited workers, enticing workers from southern states to come to Ohio's urban centers. By early 1918, major problems arose in coal mining and agriculture, forcing the reallocation of workers. To help prevent food shortages, the CND Food Conservation Committee promoted war garden projects.

Further manpower shortages occurred as conscription expanded the military and reduced the state's workforce. The state's Women's Committee played an active role in recruiting young women for nursing and clerical positions. The state, like much of the nation, became dependent on women, uneducated immigrants, and African Americans to fill the job openings in the factories and on the farms.

The state created an Americanization Committee, directed by Professor Raymond Moley, in order to tap the potential of immigrant workers. Moley's committee coordinated a state program to teach immigrant alien workers to read and write and, eventually, to receive their citizenship papers. Moley also directed a publicity campaign to persuade businessmen to establish educational programs for immigrant workers. Businesses across the state, following the lead of such firms as White Motor Company and Timken Roller Bearing Company, established language instruction and civics lessons, as well as education in basic industrial skills.

A widespread campaign to abridge the civil liberties of many Ohioans accompanied this acculturation effort. In 1917 and 1918, Congress passed espionage and sedition statutes that limited First Amendment freedoms. In a less systematic way,

anti-German sentiment, to a large degree influenced by Governor Cox's pronounce-
ments and the Americanization Committee's censorship, led to a variety of actions
against dissenters of all stripes. After the war, an antiradical and antiunion hysteria
added a new dimension to the repression, with the state legislature enacting a major
antisyndicalist labor law.

The following documents have been selected to demonstrate both the fervor of
preparedness advocates and the anguish of their opponents, and to reveal the impact of
the wartime mobilization on the state's economy and society.

XIII.1. Patriotism and Preparedness: Cincinnati's "Hats Off to the Flag" Parade, 1916

*In a letter to his wife, who had escaped the summer's heat by traveling to the family compound
on Canada's Murray Bay, Robert A. Taft described how he dutifully marched in Cincinnati's
24 June 1916 Preparedness Parade. Taft, then only ending his third year of private practice,
joined the ranks of the town's lawyers, standing shoulder to shoulder with young men from the
numerous firms of the city. He observed that Lawrence Maxwell Jr., the eminent former
solicitor general of the United States and senior partner of Maxwell & Ramsey, the firm in
which Taft began his career, marched in front, leading the law guild. On that day, Taft
certified his patriotism, then returned to office to sweat over the insignificant paperwork
allotted to the most junior members of the firm.*

*It was important to certify Cincinnati's patriotism. The "Queen City" had the state's larg-
est German population and many immigrants from the Austrian empire. The training camps,
or "Plattsburgh Movement," was beginning, but without much enthusiasm in the "Over-the-
Rhine" neighborhoods. Although few Germans enthusiastically supported the militaristic aris-
tocracies of central Europe, they were reluctant to prepare for what would undoubtedly be a
war against other Germans. Similarly, the Irish population of Ohio had little desire to ally
themselves with the Englishmen fighting in the trenches of the Western Front.*

*The following Cincinnati Enquirer account of the planned parade, published that
morning, provides a look at the political organization of patriotic action during the summer
of 1916 while offering glimpses of a society that only such a cultural event reveals.*[1]

"Hats Off to the Flag" will be the slogan of 55,000 patriotic men and women of
Cincinnati and environs, who will march in the Greater Cincinnati Preparedness Parade to-day.

The same slogan which aroused such a wave of patriotism in Cincinnati in 1898
will furnish inspiration to the thousands who will express their sentiment in favor of adequate national preparedness by participating in the big demonstration.

Everywhere the American flag will be in evidence. A foretaste of today's scenes was
furnished yesterday. Business blocks and residences were dressed in the national colors.
Old Glory waved on automobiles and vehicles of every description. Men and women
wore the flag.

The effect will be heightened to-day when the thousands of marchers pass in review, each carrying an American flag. No other emblem will be permitted in the parade, save the banners designating the names of the organizations marching.

Flag Raising in Morning.

The day's celebration will start at 11 o'clock this morning, when the American flag, which will be the only object before which the marchers will pass in official review, will be raised on the reviewing stand erected in front of the Government Building. The ceremony will be performed in the presence of the Citizens' Preparedness Parade Committee with a color guard from the First Regiment, O. N. G., as official escort. As the flag is raised to the top of the staff a company of trumpeters from the First Regiment will sound the "colors." After the ceremony a special police guard will be stationed near the reviewing stand until after the parade is ended.

Hats will be doffed by the marchers as they pass the color stand. It promises to be the most impressive patriotic demonstration ever held in Cincinnati.

Final arrangements for the parade were made by the Citizens' Preparedness Parade Committee yesterday. Later Grand Marshal Paul M. Millikin and his staff of aides and Marshals held a conference, at which the final instructions were issued.

'Twill Start Promptly.

The parade will start promptly at 1 o'clock from the mobilization point of the First Division, Race and Liberty streets.

The procession will move for 22 blocks. It will require 40 minutes for a participant to complete the full line of march. It will take more than four hours for the entire parade to pass a given point.

It is expected that fully one third of the entire list of marchers will be in motion within a few moments after the command is given to march. The organizations assembled south of Liberty street will join the other divisions as they pass, and it is expected that every section of the parade will be in motion at 2:30 o'clock.

The only halt in the parade will be when the head of the column reaches the color stand on government square. As it approaches this column a bomb will be fired from the roof of the Provident Bank Building as a signal for the procession to halt. The various bands then will play the hymn, "America," marchers and spectators joining in singing the first verse. At the conclusion of the mighty chorus the parade again will get in motion and complete the line of march.

Largest Ever Held Here.

The roster of organizations and individuals in the parade shows it to be the largest and most representative demonstration of citizens ever held in Cincinnati. Marching in the ranks, elbow to elbow, will be representatives of society and the residents of the tenements. Manufacturers will have for their "side partners" laborers, and all class, creed, religion, and affiliation will be set aside. Every participant is to have in mind only the slogan of the Parade Committee, "March for America." . . .

More than 100 more recruits were reported yesterday in the women's section, which will be part of the Seventh Division, in command of R. A. Colter. They will assemble at Fourteenth and Race streets at 2 o'clock.

Captain W. M. Coffin, of the U. S. Grant Camp, Sons of Veterans, has issued an invitation to all sons of veterans of the Civil War, whether members of the organization or not, to march with the camp. Those desiring to accept are requested to meet at Memorial Hall, Elm and Grant streets, at 12:30 o'clock, when they will be assigned to places in line and presented with American flags.

The members of the Trustees of the Cincinnati Southern Railroad will participate as part of the railway division.

Cincinnati Elks have invited the members of Newport and Covington lodges to march with them. The members of these organizations are requested to meet at the Elks Temple, Elm street, at 12:30 o'clock.

Despite the fact that union bands will not participate, the committee announced yesterday that there would be more than 40 musical organizations in line.

Complaint was made yesterday to Mayor Puchta that a few of the bands coming from the outside had been threatened in unsigned telegrams received early in the day.

Orders Police Guard For Bands.

The Mayor issued an order for police guards at the railroad stations to protect the musicians.

Members of the Chamber of Commerce who will march as individuals and not as members of subsidiary organizations will form at Fourth and Vine streets at noon.

The Grain Exchange of the Chamber of Commerce voted yesterday to close the Exchange to-day in observance of Preparedness Day. Other departments of the Chamber will be open as usual until noon.

Members of the Lumberman's Club and of the Lumber Exchange of the Chamber will march as a lumbermen's section. The arrangements by which all the lumbermen will parade together were perfected by a joint committee of the club and of the Exchange.

Federal officials yesterday morning made final arrangements for the formation of a Federal Division. Marshal Clore gave instructions that all officials and employees assemble at the Government Building at 1 o'clock, and move in a body to Fifteenth and Race, where the Sixth Division of the parade, of which the Federal Division will be a part, will form.

Letter Carriers in Uniforms.

The letter carriers will appear in full uniform, and will head the Federal Division. Other marchers will wear civilian attire and carry American flags.

"The Spirit of 1776," historic painting of the Revolution—fifer, color bearer and drummer—will be reproduced in life by the Ohio Society, Sons of the Revolution, by three descendants of Revolutionary soldiers, who will appear in Continental uniform at the head of the society in the parade. . . .

1. "Hats Off," *Cincinnati Enquirer,* 24 June 1916.

XIII.2. Mobilizing the Agricultural Sector for War: The Preparedness Proclamation of Governor James M. Cox

In the final days before American intervention in the Great War, Ohio Governor James Cox identified a weakness in the state's program of economic mobilization. Cox knew that the state's financial, industrial, and commercial institutions, already primed by their efforts to assist the Allied nations overseas and the U.S. armed forces at home, were ready to enter the European war. But the state's agricultural sector was not prepared.

In order to fight this first global war, American political and business leaders recognized that the mobilization of agriculture meant an intensification of farm production coupled with consumer conservation on the home front. To supply the ever-increasing demands of the military and the nations of Europe, American farmers needed to modernize. In the following proclamation, the governor encouraged farmers to mechanize by purchasing tractors and other labor-saving equipment. At the same time, Cox recognized that to avoid diverting crucial farm commodities away from their overseas destinations, citizen consumers had to practice conservation measures at home. Ohioans had to raise their own vegetables in backyard or community gardens and they had to cut consumption in their daily lives.

The governor's proclamation appeared in the Cleveland Plain Dealer *on 28 March 1917.*

Governor Cox's Preparedness Proclamation

It is unnecessary to elaborate on the turbulent condition of the world. We are so closely related to them that any surrender to the free and easy idea that things will turn out all right would be plain incompetence.

We are mobilizing our men, conserving our finance, protecting our public works, and resorting to the means of defense which experience suggests, but there seems to be no thought as to the importance of intensifying the energy of the soil. In our vast domain of fertile fields there will be thousands of wasted acres, notwithstanding the prices in prospect should give spur to thrift and an understanding of the importance of the elements of food should stir our patriotic endeavor.

A movement should be inaugurated at once in every community, rural and city, in order that the facilities which nature has given us may be availed of to the utmost.

The banks are full of money; credit is easy. Farmers can buy tractors on easy terms. There is no excuse for wasted land. Every acre should count, and this spirit of conservation should take hold of the cities as well as the country. Food supplies can be grown on vacant lots, gardens can be turned to use, and those who cannot render defense service can be of distinct value by simple husbandry. In the same proportion that a family contributes to its own necessities, it will be serving the nation.

Tractors can be purchased for the price of three teams of horses or mules, and the output is considerably more. They can be operated by night and by day. We can, if we bestir ourselves now, in the planting season, give a good account of Ohio. She has always done her part in time of hazard, and it behooves this generation, moved by the simple suggestion of modern devices, to make it worthy of the fathers who gave us what we have.

I, therefore, by authority vested in me as governor of the state, call upon everyone in Ohio to prepare to do his part as here suggested.
James M. Cox,
Governor

XIII.3. "Keep Faith with My People": Isaac Sherwood's Opposition to American Entry into the First World War

Acceptance of America's entry into the Great War was not unanimous. Among the elected representatives of the nation there were six senators and fifty members of the House of Representatives voting against the war resolution. Opponents mustered three arguments. The first stance had its roots in the traditional isolationist principles embraced by Americans, dating at least from the time of George Washington. The second set of arguments advanced stemmed from a widely held perception by many Americans that the war would be conducted for the benefit of certain classes and interest groups in the nation. Opponents like Robert M. LaFollette charged that special interests would exploit the nation for their own financial advantage. Both military intervention and conscription received criticism on this basis. Finally, there were antiwar spokesmen who argued that no cause was sufficiently noble to justify the slaughter of the trenches on the Western Front.[1]

No representative of the people voiced these arguments more eloquently than Representative Isaac Sherwood of Toledo, a veteran of the Civil War. A decorated soldier and survivor of numerous lengthy campaigns, he testified at length about the horrors of war. Sherwood criticized the special interests as well as the diplomats who supported Great Britain, America's historic enemy. Selected portions of his remarks, which are published in full in the Congressional Record, *follow.[2]*

*M*r. Chairman, I can not keep faith with my people by voting for this war resolution in its present form. I will vote for it if the provision to authorize an army to be sent across the Atlantic to participate in this European conflict is stricken out. I will vote for a resolution to use the naval forces of the United States to protect American interests and safeguard our national honor on all the seas and oceans of the world. I agree with the distinguished and experienced gentleman from California that sending untrained and unseasoned soldiers into the terrible trench battles of the allies is wholesale murder.

We have said to Germany that we have an unrestricted right to send ships to English ports. The seas are free. We have said to England that we have an unrestricted right to send ships to German ports. The seas are free. We said to England that her blockade was "illegal, indefensible, and ineffective." Therefore we were not bound by it.

We attempted to send ships to German ports. They were halted by British cruisers, and because they were not armed and did not resist, they were not sunk but towed into Kirkwall and declared British prizes. All ships that attempted to go to Hamburg or Bremen were captured and millions of dollars worth of contraband goods were confiscated. A matter of $17,000,000 worth of meats was made the subject of peaceful settlement with the Chicago packers, so as to silence this influential element. But the ships of the American Trans-Atlantic Co., sailing in trade between our ports and South American ports were seized and have recently been declared lawful prizes. All our differences with Great Britain were made a subject of peaceful arbitration. In upward of two years we have not sent any American ships to German ports. . . .

While we are discussing the ruthless submarine warfare it is conceded that a mine is the most cowardly and destructive of all war's barbarities, much more so than the submarine, and yet England mined the North Sea, one of the great oceans of the world, and also mined the harbors of several neutral countries and notified the world to keep out of that zone, and we kept out. Including Austria-Hungary and the coasts blockaded by Great Britain, we lost the markets for our products for over 175,000,000 people, and yet we submitted without breaking off diplomatic relations.

Germany established a war zone not nearly so extensive as that of Great Britain, because it is only 20 miles from shore, and notified not only the United States but all the countries of the world that vessels entering that zone, consigned to ports of England, do so at their peril. This was not aimed at the United States alone or any other country, but strictly a measure of protection and notice to all the countries of the world, and yet these war-crazed enthusiasts, who talk about national honor, would make us believe that this submarine warfare is aimed at the United States.

Germany agreed to give up her submarine campaign provided England allowed ships to reach German ports from neutral countries, including the United States. This England refused to do. Germany thereupon intensified her U-boat campaign under the law of retaliation, because the neutral nations declined to protest the law of neutral shipping, and our Government refused to take part in a coalition of neutral powers to protect themselves against British aggression upon their rights. This is history, however. We then informed Germany that she must confine her submarine campaign to limits which we held to be dictated by laws of humanity and international usage, and Germany agreed on condition that we should compel Great Britain to return to the recognized principles for the safety of neutral shipping. This reasonable request Great Britain refused to grant.

Waiting in vain nearly a year for us to effect means to let neutral ships travel the seas unrestricted by British orders, Germany announced a certain date after which all ships would be sunk without notice if they attempted to invade the German war zone, but agreed voluntarily to provide for the safety of American ships through a defined passage in their journey to British ports. As a result of this, the President broke off diplomatic relations with Germany. And the President called upon all the neutral countries of the world to also sever diplomatic relations with Germany. But not one neutral nation responded. . . . At the distance of 3,500 miles the undesirable and dangerous Kaiser looks the same to me as the great grandson of George III; in fact, all kings look alike to me. I am not willing to vote to send the gallant young manhood of America across the Atlantic Ocean to fight for either. . . .

And now we are going to war as an ally of the one nation in Europe that has always been our enemy and against the nation that has always been our friend. This is the record we are making to-day. Posterity will judge our actions by this record. . . .

Those Members of Congress who vote for this war resolution today are taking an awful responsibility. If this resolution was to provide for the national defense against any threatened foreign aggression I would vote for it, but we all know it is not. The President, in the presence of both Houses of Congress and the Cabinet and the Supreme Court and the bespangled Diplomatic Corps, in a spectacular and elaborately staged event, read a message to Congress and the country, declaring his purpose to enter the European conflict in the interest of world-wide democracy. Hence every Member on this floor knows that Germany has at this moment declared officially that she desires peace and not war with the United States; that her war blockade of England and the allies' coasts is for self-protection. Her official warning was sent to the United States and all neutral countries of the world to keep out of this established war zone. In violation of all the most sacred traditions of the past century and in violation of the vital and sacred admonitions of George Washington, warning this nation to avoid the conflicts of European empires; in violation of the Monroe Doctrine, we are now about to plunge this great peaceful Nation into a kings' war in Europe. This, too, in violation of our most vital and sacred promises made to the American people less than six months ago to keep this Nation out of this criminal European conflict. We are going into a world-wide war, a war of kings and emperors and kaisers, in which the best manhood of Europe has already been ruthlessly slaughtered. In order to add to the horrid holocaust the stalwart young manhood of America are to be forced into the conflict, and we are going to rush them into this slaughterhouse against the best and highest ideals of this Republic — peace, progress, and prosperity, and a government of the people, by the people, and for the people. . . .

As I love my country, I would use every honorable means to keep the young manhood of America out of this horrid holocaust of European slaughter. My experience in the Civil War has saddened all my life. I had my soul rent with indescribable agony, as I stood in the presence of comrades who were maimed, mangled, and dying on 42 battle fields of this Republic. As I love my country, I feel it is my sacred duty to keep the stalwart young men of today out of a barbarous war 3,500 miles away, in which we have no vital interest. And I am earnestly inquiring what the harvest will be outside of a wholesale slaughter of the patriotic manhood of the Nation. As I love my country, if war is inevitable, then I will be found standing by the country as I did from '61 to '65, and I will go to the front if accepted as a soldier whenever or wherever duty calls.

1. David M. Kennedy, *Over Here: The First World War and American Society* (New York: Oxford University Press, 1980), 21–23.

2. *Congressional Record,* 65th Cong., spec. sess., 1st sess., 5 April 1917, vol. 55, 335–38.

XIII.4. "Godspeed You Boys": Governor Cox's Farewell to the Fourth Ohio, October 1917

Ohio furnished almost a quarter of a million men for the military mobilization. Of that group, sixty-five hundred died while in service. The Fourth Ohio Regiment, a National Guard

*unit ready for mobilization, was one of the first to make the trip to France. The Ohio unit,
which had a long history of service to the state and the nation, joined New York's illustrious
"Fighting Sixty-ninth," the Fourth Alabama, and the Third Iowa regiments to form the core
of the Forty-second ("Rainbow") Division. The division, one of the first four to board ships for
Europe, prepared at its camp in Mineola on Long Island, New York, for the trip. During the
first week of October 1917, Governor James Cox; Mrs. Cox; their daughter, Helen; and the
adjutant general of the state of Ohio traveled to Mineola to bid the troops a formal farewell.
The governor and his party were met in New York City by Major General William A. Mann,
the division's commanding general, and his staff. They escorted the governor to the camp, where
he met with the Ohio troops, recently designated as the 166th Regiment, and gave the following
address.*[1]

Governor Cox Bids Farewell To Soldiers

So soon as it was known that orders to sail had been received by the Rainbow Division, the state that you have the honor to represent, and which is glorified by your service, desired that there might be some evidence of the interest in your comfort, your happiness, and your safety that is felt by every household back home. I have come to the very edge of the ocean to speak what is in the heart of Ohio, and I wish I possessed the power of thought and the facility of speech to express the emotions of our people.

There have been famous regiments in the armies of the Republic — there may be many more but there has not been, nor will there be, a regiment more famous than your own. You are the first Ohio unit in all the history of our government to cross the ocean. It is a compliment to the officers and men of the Fourth Ohio to have the War Department make you a part of the Rainbow Division, and to be thrown now into the strength of the western front means that no organization is fitter than your own.

When the history of the Fourth Ohio is written, it will not only be made up of the glorious achievement of its officers and men, but it will stand out forever because of the conspicuous honors that a combination of circumstances has brought to it. It will be recorded that for the first time in all history, a vast army is crossing the seas possessed of no desire and no lust for land or domain. Beyond question you will be ordered to the shores of France and you will bear the proud distinction of being the first to pay the debt we owe the Republic that helped our fathers to achieve their freedom.

Of all the human emotions, none is more magnificent than gratitude. I like to recall a circumstance of Lafayette's visit in 1825 which impressively spoke the indissoluble tie between France and the United States. Jefferson had written the Declaration of Independence, and his genius had fired the soul of Virginia and the whole country. Lafayette had stirred the hearts of France into sympathetic action for the American colonists. As an old man, he came back to the land that he had helped to free. Every community that he visited proclaimed him the hero of the hour, and spoke its gratitude. In the course of his pilgrimage, he went to Monticello, and as he approached the threshold, Jefferson, with the unsteady tread of years, met him on the front lawn, and the sons of the two Republics fell into each other's arms, and mixed their tears of joy.

The sons of France came to us in time of stress, and now you go to them, when a military autocracy threatens to pillage their land and destroy their government. What a wonderful part you play in the most wonderful of all the world dramas—the most impressive service of gratitude that history will ever write.

You can be grateful to the Almighty that you have lived in times like these, with their boundless opportunity to render a great service to the world. You can be grateful to stand here as representatives of a great state that has never failed to perform its part when a crisis came.

If the achievements of Ohio were taken from the history of the Civil War, the student would hardly be interested in its context. If the leadership in that struggle meant anything then we can proudly reflect upon Ohio having supplied the three greatest generals of our armies. You have traditions to maintain on foreign soil. You not only are part of the great national army, but you are sons of Ohio, and in your veins courses the blood of rugged men who exalted our citizenship.

It is a singular coincidence that history repeats itself in military formation. You are brigaded again with the famous 69th New York regiment. In the Civil War, the Fourth Ohio, and the 69th New York were in the Second Army corps under the superb Hancock. Their soldiers fought and died on many famous fields, and at Gettysburg they helped make the result of that great contest. The 69th lost more men killed in battle than any other New York regiment during the Civil War, and has kept up a continuous service from that time until now. The Fourth Ohio has not had a continuous history although it took part in the Porto Rican campaign during the Spanish-American War, and as now constituted it represents every part of the state because men have been drawn into it from every company in the Ohio National Guard.

How happy it is to reflect upon the meaning of the scenes before us here. Side by side in this division stand the sons of men who opposed each other in sectional hate at Gettysburg, at Antietam and at Chickamauga. The new generation looks back with equal pride upon Northern bravery and Southern valor. We proudly claim as Americans the military genius of Grant and Lee, of Sherman and Johnson. What a happy day it is for the old heroes who now look down from beyond the skies, and see this Union of the states—a brotherhood that will last as long as time itself.

We, of the finite mind, know not what is before you. It is not necessary in proof of your patriotism, nor of your heroism, to overdraw what lies ahead, and there is no desire to minimize the possibilities. War has its grim realities. You know its meaning better than I. God alone knows what part you may have to play. We know, however, that any task imposed by your nation's order will be done with zeal and bravery. We have no fears about your conduct. We know that the bayonet of no Ohio soldier will be disgraced by the blood of a woman or of a child. We believe in your chivalry as well as your bravery. Your going makes us sad but proud. I will carry home to the hills and valleys of your fair state the picture of your resolute and happy faces as you turn toward the sea. We will pray for your safety and your comfort. We will ask that the warmth of sun temper the blasts of winter, and that the stars of night shine out to you as the vigilant sentinels of our love. Godspeed you boys, and when you come back as part of the world's great victorious army, whether in broken or solid ranks, some one from the state will be here to speak a welcome.

1. James K. Mercer, *Ohio Legislative History, 1913–1917* (Columbus, Ohio: F. J. Heer Printing Co., 1917), 280–81.

XIII.5. Mobilizing Ohio's Workforce for War: The Ohio Industrial Commission and the Extension of "Labor Exchanges"

Once war came, the Ohio Branch of the Council of National Defense played a central role in the coordination of the state's mobilization effort. In June 1917, Governor Cox appointed a board of advisors to assist the council in counseling state administrators on the most efficient ways to mobilize Ohio's economy. The council addressed a variety problems affecting the state's transportation system, labor relations in its factories, the financing of the war effort, and the implementation of food conservation policies.

As the federal government expanded its military establishment with the conscription of able-bodied men, one of the most pressing problems for state government was the reorganization of Ohio's workforce. The council, in conjunction with the Ohio Industrial Commission, the agency charged with the oversight of industrial safety and workers' compensation claims, tackled the problem of labor shortages in the key sectors of the state's economy. They expanded the state's "labor exchanges," a system of seven public employment offices in the major urban industrial centers. Recognizing that the private sector was incapable of allocating workers to firms that were experiencing shortages, the Industrial Commission established fourteen additional offices to administer the state's market for labor.

The following report summarizes the initial steps taken by the Ohio Industrial Commission and the Ohio Branch of the Council of National Defense to carry out the task of mobilizing the state's workforce for war.[1]

WORK OF THE FREE LABOR EXCHANGES OF OHIO FOR THE YEAR ENDING JUNE 30, 1917

Summary

A study of the work of the public employment offices of the State for the last fiscal year is particularly valuable and interesting because of the expansion of the system in the latter part of the period to take care of war-time conditions. The success attending this expansion very clearly indicates the soundness of the principles underlying the organization of these labor exchanges.

The cumulative value of the work and organization of the seven exchanges which have been operated for some time under the direction of the Industrial Commission placed Ohio far in the lead when the necessity of this extended organization to care for war labor needs became evident. The system in vogue needed no radical change but proved adequate with the addition of new forms and additional help to care for the new work.

During the fiscal year covered by this report, there has been a greatly increased industrial activity in the State, very largely due to war orders, and a corresponding shortage of available help. With the declaration of war with Germany, attended with thousands of enlistments, the shortage of labor became more acute.

The country faced the necessity of increasing food production, building ships, aeroplanes and manufacturing stupendous supplies of guns, munitions and other war necessities. The "man problem" became at once one of the most serious problems to be considered.

The ability of the employment offices to distribute labor with a minimum loss to both employers and workers has been so clearly demonstrated that the immediate expansion of the system was at once accepted as a solution of this problem, as undoubtedly the apparent shortage of labor lay largely in the lack of sufficient means of distribution. Without such a means of distribution, men are likely to be out of work at one point and badly in need at another. This may occur in the same city as well as in different places in the State. . . .

The placing of farm workers had formerly been a part of the work of the labor exchanges, but, with the demand for an increased food production, it became necessary to expand this feature of the work. Additional workers were placed in the older offices, new forms were designed, provisions were made for keeping the offices open evenings and Saturday afternoons, and particular attention was paid to farm needs.

The scarcity of available help is shown by the fact that there was no increase in the daily average number of applicants in the Free Labor Exchanges during the fiscal year. There was an increase of only fifty in the total number of applicants for the year, a total of 348,043 having applied for work during the year 1916–17 and 347,993 during the previous year. Approximately one-third of the daily average of 1,141 applicants were new registrations.

Employers requested through the Free Labor Exchanges an average of 832 persons per day. An average of 712 persons per day were referred to them and an average of 577 were reported placed.

The total figures indicating the work of the offices for the year ending June 30, 1917, are given below, showing a comparison with similar figures indicating the work for the previous fiscal year:

	Year 1915–16	Year 1916–17
New Registrations	110,749	113,776
Renewals	237,244	234,267
Total Applicants for work	347, 993	348,043
Number requested by employers	205,558	253,687
Number referred to positions	171,520	217,029
Number reported placed	141,253	175,029

The tremendous increase in the number requested by employers indicated in the report for the fiscal year ending June 30, 1916, continued during the last fiscal year.

1. Industrial Commission of Ohio, Department of Investigation and Statistics, *Work of the Free Labor Exchanges of Ohio for the Year Ending June 30, 1917* (Columbus: F. J. Heer, 1918), 5–6.

XIII.6. Mobilizing Ohio's Workforce for War: Americanization Programs in Industry

State and local governments established wartime Americanization Committees in order to acculturate the recent immigrants among Ohio's workforce. Western Reserve University Prof. Raymond Moley, who served as head of both the state and Cleveland committees, coordinated a public and private sector campaign to indoctrinate alien workers in American law and culture. Moley's committees focused on promoting the value of education. They encouraged localities and companies to offer literacy and citizenship lessons, assisting private firms that provided after-hours classes for workers.

Many employers across the state embraced Americanization, but offered (and expected) more than reading, writing, and civics lessons. Some Ohio firms, especially those that began worker education even before U.S. intervention in the war, attempted to shape the values and mores of their workforce, to adjust immigrants to their industry. The following selections from the published research of William M. Leiserson, a specialist on industrial relations who taught at Antioch College, highlight the wartime activities of several prominent Ohio industrial firms that took a more comprehensive approach to Americanization.[1]

*T*he non-English-speaking worker is particularly in need of some intelligent system of introduction to his workplace. His inability to understand instructions and get information is not only a constant discouragement to him and a serious interference with his efficiency, but it becomes an actual menace in increasing factory hazards to himself and to his fellow workers.

Some of the introduction methods already developed to overcome the immigrant's handicap in this respect include a "protégé" system, whereby the new immigrant worker is assigned to an English-speaking employee who knows the work and the shop, and who looks after the newcomer until he adjusts himself, in much the same way that seniors in college take freshmen under their wings at the beginning of the school year. Other plants have "Americanization Committees," consisting of a number of representatives of each racial group employed, and the immigrant is instructed to avail himself freely of the services of the members of the committee who speak his language for any information he may need, or on any matters he may desire to bring to the attention of the management.

*T*he employment managers' idea is not to bargain for the cheapest man, but to get the best man for the work and pay according to production. This policy assures to the immigrant wage earner the same rate of pay that the native-born worker gets for the same work; and puts into practice the suggestion that if we want immigrant workers to become Americans they should be treated as Americans. . . .

To let wages lag behind increasing living costs is considered bad labor policy, and some companies developed cost of living bonuses, which increased or dropped with the movement in the index of prices.

1. William M. Leiserson, *Adjusting Immigrant to Industry* (New York: Harper & Brothers, 1924; reprint ed., New York: Arno Press, 1969), 96-98, 131-32.

XIII.7. Passage of Prohibition: Ohio's Great Debate over the Drink Question

Ohioans had been debating the alcohol question since the Gilded Age. Before the 1890s, the key organization in the state was the Women's Christian Temperance Union, a force for moderation. In 1893 advocates of complete prohibition of alcohol established the Anti-Saloon League. The league, with its headquarters in Westerville, assumed national prominence in the fight to outlaw drink. But regardless of its nationwide success, the league was unable to turn Ohio into a "dry" state.

With the passage of the 1908 Rose Law, Ohioans had a choice. Local option was instituted with the county as the basic governmental unit. Soon fifty-eight of eighty-eight counties had outlawed alcohol. At the Constitutional Convention of 1912 prohibitionists reluctantly supported a saloon licensing amendment that cleared the way for the legislature to enact a new statewide system regulating the number of saloons. The progressive reforms of 1912–14 had a contradictory effect on the drink question. Although initiative and referendum laws and home rule made it possible for the Prohibitionist movement to put the question to a statewide ballot, they also made it possible for "wets" to undo the efforts of "drys" at the local level.

Over the next half decade, opponents of alcohol tried valiantly to enact a statewide constitutional ban. But when put to referenda in 1914, 1915, and 1917, prohibition lost; finally they were victorious in 1918, only to have the enforcement legislation reversed the following year. The Crabbe (Prohibition Enforcement) Act of 1919, passed by the legislature, was defeated by the very same referendum process in the fall 1919 election. A second Crabbe Act, however, was passed in 1920. Even the popular vote on the Eighteenth Amendment to the U.S. Constitution lost in Ohio. The legislature's approval was eventually ruled sufficient.

The legislative record demonstrates the balance between wet and dry forces within the state. The following remarks by U.S. Sen. Atlee Pomerene, made before he cast his vote in August 1917 on the congressional joint resolution on the Federal Prohibition Amendment, gives readers an informative history of the debate over drink in Ohio while it furnishes a concise statement of his own views on the controversial question.[1]

THE ARGUMENT AGAINST PROHIBITION

SENATOR ATLEE POMERENE

*M*r. President, before the final vote is taken I desire to express briefly my reasons for the vote that I am going to cast upon this joint resolution.

I yield to no man in the desire to promote genuine temperance in my State and in the Union. I have tried to, and I think I always have lived a temperate life. I believe in living and letting live. I have an intense admiration for the genius of our institutions. I do not believe that the fundamental principles of our people have changed. I believe in democracy. I believe the principles of democracy are best conserved when we deal with all subjects in a spirit of moderation rather than by following the extremist on either side of any question. I always try to have before me as my guide not the view of the extremist on any subject, But I am intensely interested in knowing what the average man in my State thinks, and I always try to keep before me a picture of the composite Ohioan as I see him. Now, the question is, What is my duty to my constituency as I am permitted to see it? That leads me to review for a moment the conditions as they prevail in Ohio, and I am going to beg the indulgence of the Senate for just a few minutes while I advert to them. . . .

Mr. President, at the present time in Ohio we have residential district local option, township local option, municipal local option, and there is now pending before the people of our State a prohibition amendment which will be voted upon this fall. Under the Ohio constitution our people have the right by petition to initiate an amendment which will be voted upon this fall. Under the Ohio constitution our people have the right by petition to initiate an amendment to the constitution or new laws on this subject. They have full power, therefore, at any time to adopt prohibition or new legislation when they see fit so to do.

In my judgment, I must either ignore what seems to be the voice of Ohio, as evidenced by the result of the elections I have just referred to by voting for this amendment, or I must vote in favor of what I believe is the judgment of the people of Ohio by voting against it. . . .

The State of Kansas claimed the right to vote as she saw fit, without let or hindrance by any State of the Union, when she decided this question for herself. The State of Texas claims that right. The State of Washington claims that right. The State of Michigan claims that right; and, sirs, if they had the right, it seems to me that the people of Ohio should have the right to determine the liquor question for themselves.

And now, if I may, in the few minutes allowed me, I want to call attention to another proposition.

In 1910 the 13 States of Nevada, Wyoming, Delaware, Arizona, Idaho, New Mexico, Vermont, Utah, Montana, New Hampshire, North Dakota, South Dakota, and Oregon had, all told, 4,657,052 people. The State of Ohio had 4,767,121. In other words, in the year 1910 Ohio had 110,069 more people than the 13 States I have named. Yet if this amendment is to be submitted to the States for their votes, these 13 States, with less population than the State of Ohio, will have thirteen times as much voice as the State of Ohio in determining whether or not this amendment shall be added to the Constitution.

Again, 18 States—Nevada, Wyoming, Delaware, Arizona, Idaho, New Mexico, Vermont, Utah, Montana, New Hampshire, Rhode Island, North Dakota, South Dakota, Oregon, Maine, Florida, Colorado, and Connecticut—had, in 1910, 8,608,432 people; but the State of New York in that year had 9,113,614 people, or 505,182 more people than the 18 States I have named. Let me ask those who believe in democratic institutions since when has it come to pass that upon a question of this kind the principles of American government would permit these 18 States to have eighteen times the voice that New York shall have in amending the Constitution, if this amendment is to be submitted?

Inasmuch as Ohio in 1914 voted against prohibition by a majority of 85,152, and again in 1915, when a less vote was cast, by a majority of 55,408, thereby declaring her sentiments on the subject, how can I, as one of her Senators, vote for this resolution and put up to the people of the country the prohibition question in such form that we in Ohio will have only one-thirteenth as much influence in the adoption or rejection of prohibition as a fewer number of people in the 13 States of the Union to which I referred a moment ago, or thereby give to New York only one-eighteenth as much influence in determining this question as a fewer number of people in the 18 States which I have named? Surely the majority of voters in Ohio have some rights to be considered. Surely as their representative in the Senate I ought to bear this fact in mind in casting my vote. . . .

In my judgment the result will be much more satisfactory if this question is left to the people of each individual State to determine the kind of legislation they want upon the subject. For these reasons, in brief, I feel compelled to vote against the joint resolution.

1. *Congressional Record,* 65th Cong., 1st sess., 1 August 1917, vol. 55, 5640–41.

XIII.8. The Wartime Extension of Suffrage: War, Reform, and Voting Rights for Ohio Women

Throughout the era of the Great War, Ohioans also debated the issue of suffrage for women. Ohio voters had rejected a suffrage amendment recommended by the 1912 Constitutional Convention, one of eight amendments rejected by the citizenry that year. While some communities in the state used home rule to extend voting rights to women, a move to allow women to cast their ballots in presidential elections was defeated in a 1917 referendum.

But suffrage advocates continued to press for the vote. It was the war that served, once again, as the "catalyst" for reform. As the following joint resolution argues,[1] the success of women in industry, in "relief work," and in nursing was a major argument for many Ohioans that it was time for the extension of voting rights. After Congress passed the suffrage amendment in 1919, Ohio moved quickly to ratify it. The Nineteenth Amendment to the U.S. Constitution took effect the following year.

[Senate Joint Resolution No. 22.]
JOINT RESOLUTION

Petitioning the United States senators from Ohio to support the federal amendment as to woman suffrage.

WHEREAS, The woman's suffrage amendment has long been pending before the United States senate; and

WHEREAS, This amendment has been passed by the house of representatives; and

WHEREAS, Many of the states of the union have already granted the right of suffrage to women and the Republican party in its state platform has endorsed the same; and

WHEREAS, The women of the United States have rendered the most devoted and patriotic service, not only during the period of the great world war, but also in all our great wars; and

WHEREAS, The governmental, industrial and social program for the people of this country is of as great concern and interest to the women of this country as well as to the men; therefore

Be it resolved, That the senate and house of representatives of the state of Ohio do hereby request the two United States senators from the state of Ohio to vote for and assist in the passage of a resolution now pending in the United States senate for the submission to the several states the federal amendment granting the right of suffrage to women, and that a copy of this resolution signed by the speaker of the house of representatives and the president of the senate, be forwarded to each of the two United States senators, Warren G. Harding and Atlee Pomerene.

Clarence J. Brown,
President of the Senate.
Carl R. Kimball,
Speaker of the House of Representatives.

Adopted February 6, 1919.

1. State of Ohio, *Legislative Acts Passed and Joint Resolutions Adopted,* vol. 58, pt. 2, 1919, 1348–49.

XIII.9. The Limits of Opportunity for Ohio Women

Demobilization of the armed forces meant a return of millions of young men to the American workforce in 1919. This return to a peacetime economy led to the reversal of many of the economic gains made by women and minorities. African American men lost many of the industrial jobs they assumed during the wartime era of labor shortages; African American women lost even more ground, often returning to the domestic servant work of the prewar era.

While the war had been a catalyst for reform, peace imposed an economic and social retrenchment. The statute reproduced below demonstrates the powerful mix of gendered notions of proper womanhood that influenced lawmakers as the postwar decade was about to dawn.[1] While the law mandates improvements in the workplace, it draws a rigid gender line across the spectrum of available jobs in industrializing America.

Be it enacted by the General Assembly of the State of Ohio:
SECTION 1. That section 1008 of the General Code be amended and supplemental section 1008–1 be enacted to read as follows:

Sec. 1008. Every person, partnership or corporation employing females in any factory, workshop, business office, telephone or telegraph office, restaurant, bakery, millinery or dressmaking establishment, mercantile or other establishment shall provide a suitable seat for the use of each female so employed and shall permit the use of such seats when such female employees are not necessarily engaged in active duties for which they are employed and when the use thereof will not actually and necessarily interfere with the proper discharge of the duties of such employees, such seat to be constructed, where practicable, with an automatic back support and so adjusted as to be a fixture but not obstruct employees in the performance of duty, and shall further provide a suitable lunch room, separate and apart from the work room, and in establishments where lunch rooms are provided, female employees shall be entitled to no less than thirty minutes for meal time, provided, that in any establishment aforesaid in which it is found impracticable to provide a suitable lunch room, as aforesaid, female employees shall be entitled to not less than one hour for meal time during which hour they shall be permitted to leave the establishment.

Females over eighteen years of age shall not be employed or permitted or suffered to work in connection with any factory, workshop, telephone or telegraph office, millinery or dressmaking establishment, restaurant or in the distributing or transmitting of messages, or in or on any interurban or street railway car, or as ticket sellers or elevator operators or in any mercantile establishment located in any city, more than nine hours in any one day, except Saturday, when the hours of labor in mercantile establishments may be ten hours, or more than six days, or more than fifty hours in any one week, but meal time shall not be included as a part of the work hours of the week or day, provided, however, that no restriction as to hours of labor shall apply to canneries or establishments engaged in preparing for use perishable goods, during the season they are engaged in canning their products.

Sec. 1008-1. The employment of females in the following occupations or capacities is hereby prohibited, to-wit: as crossing watchman, section hand, express driver, moulder, bell hop, taxi driver, jitney driver, gas or electric meter reader, ticket seller except between the hours of six o'clock a.m. and ten o'clock p.m., as workers in blast furnaces, smelters, mines, quarries except in the offices thereof, shoe shining parlors, bowling alleys, pool rooms, bar rooms and saloons or public drinking places which cater to male customers exclusively and in which substitutes for intoxicating liquors are sold or advertised for sale, in delivery service on wagons or automobiles, in operating freight or baggage elevators, in baggage handling, freight handling and trucking of any kind, or in employments requiring frequent or repeated lifting of weights over twenty-five pounds.

1. State of Ohio, *Legislative Acts Passed and Joint Resolutions Adopted*, vol. 108, pt. 1, 1919, 540–41.

XIII.10. The War against "Kultur": Anti-German Sentiment and the Ake Law of 1919

Governor James Cox eagerly assumed the leadership of the postwar movement to rid Ohio of the vestiges of "Germanism." Continuing to foster anti-German sentiment even after the armistice, the governor was especially agitated about the influence of German culture in the school curricula. When Republicans advocated a more moderate measure that exempted private schools from scrutiny, the governor expressed outrage. The Ake Law, named for its sponsor, embodied the wishes of Governor Cox and extended legal supervision over the curricula of all schools in Ohio.[1]

Be it enacted by the General Assembly of the State of Ohio: . . .

Sec. 7762-1. That all subjects and branches taught in the elementary schools of the state of Ohio below the eighth grade shall be taught in the English language only. The board of education, trustees, directors and such other officers as may be in control, shall cause to be taught in the elementary schools all the branches named. . . . Provided, that the German language shall not be taught below the eighth grade in any of the elementary schools of this state.

Sec. 7762-2. All private and parochial schools and all schools maintained in connection with benevolent and correctional institutions within this state which instruct pupils who have not completed a course of study equivalent to that prescribed for the first seven grades of the elementary schools of this state, shall be taught in the English language only, and the person or persons, trustees or officials in control shall cause to be taught in them such branches of learning as prescribed . . . ; provided that the German language shall not be taught below the eighth grade in any such schools within this state.

Sec. 7762-3. Any person or persons violating the provisions of this act shall be guilty of a misdemeanor and shall be fined in any sum not less than twenty-five dollars nor more than one hundred dollars, and each separate day in which such act shall be violated shall constitute a separate offense.

Sec. 7762-4. In case any section or sections of this act shall be held to be unconstitutional by the supreme court of Ohio such decision shall not affect the validity of the remaining sections.

1. State of Ohio, *Legislative Acts Passed and Joint Resolutions Adopted,* vol. 108, pt. 1, 1919, 614–15.

XIV. The Interwar Years

THE TWO DECADES BETWEEN THE WORLD WARS was a perplexing, often disturbing period of change for Americans. The era must be seen within the context of long-term historical change. During these decades, Ohio and the nation were undergoing a crucial transition—a transition in economic, social, and cultural terms. The period marked the culmination of an ongoing transition from a largely traditional and rural society to a modern, urban one. That change had been under way since the Civil War. But there was more to the great changes in progress. There was a transition from an economy centered on labor and the production process to one oriented toward spending and consumption.

On the face of it, the Roaring Twenties seem unrelated to the depression decade. The first was seemingly prosperous and progressive, although restrained somewhat by an ingrained conservatism. The second decade is remembered as catastrophic, with the economic system prostrate, millions unemployed, and society divided along class lines.

Actually both decades were thoroughly intertwined. By the end of World War I, the nature of consumer spending in the nation had changed as a result of a long-term increase in national income. But the prosperity of the 1920s was fragile and unstable. Higher national income led to changing patterns of spending, to more commercial uses of leisure time. Certain industries—appliances, chemicals, and processed food, to name a few—benefited greatly during the twenties, but were not sufficiently large to carry the economy; other industries—most notably textiles, iron and steel, and lumber—suffered from declining markets. The weakness of both groups explains much not only about the depth of the depression after the stock market crash but also the nagging persistence of economic depression throughout the thirties.

What hindered these new consumer industries? The conditions for supporting these industries had not developed. The distribution of incomes to different social classes was not broad enough to sustain consumer spending. Similarly, the institutions and practices of a modern consumer economy—installment plans, credit accounts, consumer loans—would not be in place until after the next war.

The economic transition led to social and cultural change also. Ohio's industrialization attracted a thoroughly diverse workforce. Immigrants from southern and eastern Europe, African Americans from the South, and whites from rural Ohio and Appalachia had transformed the population of the state by the 1920s. Many native-born, white, Anglo-Saxon, Protestant Ohioans felt threatened by these diverse populations and their cultures. At the same time, new technologies and new consumer goods—especially automobiles, radios, movies, and popular magazines—when coupled with a greater emphasis on leisure activities, challenged traditional values and assumptions about life and reshaped social life. New methods of producing, managing, and selling goods were necessary in a decade of mass production, increased consumption, and more leisure time.

The great changes of the 1920s enthused those who embraced modern life and troubled those who rejected it. Women's rights, parochial school education, and the secular teachings of science all threatened a traditional nineteenth-century "American" way of life. For Ohio's more fundamentalist Protestants, the establishment of parochial schools by the Catholic populations of the state's urban, industrial centers was a direct challenge to traditional ways. For the most fervent believers, the members of Ohio's Ku Klux Klan, this challenge of modernity was a threat to white, Christian, and male-dominated America.

When the economic collapse came, Ohio and the nation reacted slowly. The following chapter documents the state's gradual acceptance of a larger role in relief, reform, and recovery. The state unemployment commission's report on the extent of the economic dislocation reveals the persistence of old attitudes. "Helping the Unemployed Help Themselves" was the motto of numerous communities; only a few, like Dayton, experimented with more radical solutions.

Official responses to the problem of direct relief in the depression went through several stages and provide a good illustration of changing attitudes. Before the onset of the Great Depression, relief matters were handled by either private charitable institutions or local government. In 1932, continuing efforts to supply direct relief, relief in the form of payments to pensioners, the unemployed, and the poor, were administered by a state relief commission, with the assistance of local governments. With the inauguration of Franklin D. Roosevelt in 1933, a major change in the location of social responsibility occurred. The federal government assumed responsibility during the first years of the New Deal, creating sweeping programs and projects. For certain programs, the relief commission continued as the administrative agency; for others, supervision came from the various bureaucracies of the new Roosevelt administration. But by 1935, the president, ready to move on to other problems, reversed course on the matter of relief, handing responsibility back to the states.

But governments at all levels were beginning to recognize that a massive public investment was necessary to rejuvenate Ohio and the nation. One of the following selections documents the achievements of the Rural Electrification Administration's efforts in one congressional district of Ohio. Two other selections, the Mort Plan and the resulting School Foundation Program Law for the advancement of public education, demonstrate the recognition that modern public education is a necessity in an industrializing society.

XIV.1. Recreation for the Modern Society: The Cleveland Recreation Survey of 1920

Many Progressive Era reformers believed that urban public space should be utilized to improve the morals and civic pride of city residents. Reformers turned to parks, initially seen as the means to bring urban dwellers close to nature, in this quest for moral and civic improvement. At the turn of the century, city officials and planners examined how to design parks to develop civic pride, reflect specific social values, and celebrate American society.[1]

In the immediate post–World War I era, the advances in technology that led to greater leisure time and consumption made recreation an even more important factor in everyday lives. As historian George W. Knepper observed, "Cleveland was a national leader in trying to meet modern problems of poverty, illiteracy, disease, and family trauma."[2] The city's search for "progressive" solutions to societal ills led its leaders to establish the Community Fund in 1919 in an effort to support the indigent. Civic leaders also commissioned a major seven-part survey of local recreational opportunities and facilities. The survey was unprecedented in its comprehensiveness, examining the private, commercial side—the "cheap amusements"—of the postwar period, as well as the public side of recreation. The following article offers a summary of the findings of the Cleveland Survey.[3]

The Cleveland Recreation Survey

*W*orkers in the leisure time field will find many invaluable suggestions in the seven reports of the Cleveland Recreation Survey which have appeared under the titles Delinquency and Spare Time, School Work and Spare Time, Wholesome Citizens and Spare Time, The Sphere of Private Organizations, The Commercialization of Recreation, Public Provision for Recreation and A Community Recreation Program.

The comprehensiveness of the material brought together, the vast amount of general information which is condensed into these reports and the broad application possible from many of the conclusions drawn make them of universal interest. . . .

Some of the significant facts brought out in the last four volumes of the series are as follows:

The Sphere of Private Agencies There is a distinct need along recreational lines, it is pointed out in the introduction to this report, which cannot be met by commercial recreations, or by public recreation "which is limited by lack of funds and difficulty of administration to little more than caring for the wholesale, absolute necessary needs of children of school age, on the playground and on the street and of the grown folks in the parks." However much the advocates of municipal recreation may take issue with a statement which so limits the field of public recreation in its efforts to reach adults— and the experiences of Milwaukee and other cities in the use of schools as social centers make such a limitation of public recreation appear rather too severe—no one will challenge the statement that there is a very distinct and important place for private recreation operated either on a cooperative or philanthropic basis.

In its report on the sphere of private agencies, the Survey has shown very clearly the contributions which are being made to the recreational life of specialized groups by such agencies as the Young Men's Christian Association, the Young Women's Christian Association, the churches, the industries, the settlements, clubs and societies of various kinds and by the art museum. It further points out the limitations which attach themselves to these private agencies and suggests how these groups maybe made more positive forces in the city's leisure time life. Especially significant is the discussion on industrial recreation, particularly as it relates to the employee as a citizen of the community. "Outside of the factory, there is a more extensive problem of recreation for the industrial workers' off-time hours. Here the recreation problem of the industrial worker is very much the recreation problem of people who earn their living in other ways. He wishes group recreation and this grouping will be sometimes along the line of his work companions and sometimes along the line of his neighborhood or racial companions. Both are needed in developing industrial recreation from the work-shop out. So the wise employer will observe the co-operative principle of control and support of recreation facilities, cooperation both with the group of his own workers and the larger community groups of which his workers are a part."

One will go far to find as telling a statement as is made in the chapter on "Cooperative Recreation among the Foreign Born," of the contribution of the foreign born to American civilization or so sympathetic a presentation of the "genuine self-created pleasures" of the various races represented in a large city's population.

The Commercialization of Recreation One can but feel after reading this report that in the main Cleveland is unusually fortunate in the quantity and quality of its commercial recreation, which the Survey wisely and frankly recognizes as having a large and legitimate place in the sum of recreation agencies. The Survey does not as a result of its study attempt to initiate a crusade to transfer to governmental or philanthropic management the agencies now conducted for private profit, but believing that such agencies are meeting a distinct need, seeks only to determine the quantity and quality of such recreation, the forms of regulation adopted and the method of operation, and endeavors to discover what private and public recreation may learn from the experience of commercial recreation. Motion pictures, billiard rooms and bowling alleys, dance halls, coffee houses and saloons, commercial amusement parks, the baseball club, lake excursions and burlesque theatres are the forms of commercial recreation chosen for study and many interesting facts are presented regarding legal control, censorship, trade control and the conditions under which various forms of commercial recreation are carried on. Some may not agree that the enforcement of laws touching the regulation and control of motion picture theatres and some other forms of commercial amusement should be a function of the municipal recreation department, though one or two cities are successfully operating under such a plan; but that licensing power should be more carefully safe-guarded and administered and a definite unified policy of licensing and inspecting adopted, is a recommendation to which all public spirited citizens in all our cities will heartily subscribe. One is impressed with the broad mindedness with which the Survey views the entire field of commercial recreation with its problems of censorship and regulation and the constructiveness of its suggestions not only for eliminating existing evils through repression, regulation and the power of public opinion, but for making of still greater importance the really good features which commercial recreation has to offer.

1. Paul Boyer, *Urban Masses and Moral Order in America, 1820-1920* (Cambridge, Mass.: Harvard University Press, 1978), 240-41.

2. *Ohio and Its People* (Kent, Ohio: Kent State University Press, 1989), 360.

3. "The Cleveland Recreation Survey," *The Playground* 14 (December 1920): 550-53.

XIV.2. The Struggle to Preserve a White, Christian America: The Ohio Ku Klux Klan and the Niles Riot

Americans fought a cultural war in the Roaring Twenties. Those devoted to traditional, nine-teenth-century American life squared off against those who embraced the new century. In the growing urban, industrial cities of Ohio, White Anglo-Saxon Protestants expressed dissatisfaction with the rising populations of non-Protestants—immigrant Catholics and Jews, and blacks from the rural South. The most fervent pietists among these traditionalists especially feared the different moral codes of these non-Protestants. In Ohio cities, Catholics received the most criticism. Because of their failure to observe Sunday blue laws and vice ordinances, their desire to steer their children away from public schools, and their brash use of the power of urban political machines, Catholics were different.

The first selection is from an address by Klan Imperial Wizard D. W. Evans to the first state meeting held in Ohio, at Buckeye Lake, near Columbus, on 12 July 1923.[1] Following the statement of Klan doctrine is an account of the November 1924 riot between members of the Klan and Italian American Knights of the Flaming Circle at Niles.[2]

White Supremacy is Age Old

Now from the experience of centuries of mankind's history, the fact of white racial supremacy has been demonstrated in every age, under all conditions and everywhere upon the face of the earth.

Sixty centuries ago when all the races of the world took an even start in their journey from barbarism towards civilization and from darkness to light, the races were free and equal, not only in the sight of Almighty God as human beings, but alike free for action and alike capable of performance, but while the inferior races, which are all the races except the white race, were dallying with the primrose paths of pleasure, wasting part of their existence in idleness, sensuality and laziness, the men of the white race were moving steadily onward with ever increasing strides toward enlightenment and truth.

Thus from age to age, and from century to century, the distance between the races has ever been a widening distance.

Today, it is futile to attempt by legislative enactment or national aid to develop inferior races beyond their natural endowments and capacities. It will still be impossible to hold the dominant race from further lengthening the distance between them and the inferior races of the earth.

We must teach not alone the preservation of the purest and greatest racial blood strains the world has ever known, but we must teach the people of the dominant race to have a full and just appreciation of their duties under God and in the light of their past records and their consequent future responsibilities. For the people of a dominant race to be not only just and magnanimous, but kind and helpful to inferior peoples is a duty and responsibility of racial leadership. Thus, we must, through the enactment of just laws, just alike to all the people, be just to the people of less opportunity and consequently less ability. We must see that for every human being in this, our great country, the fullest opportunity for the enjoyment of liberty and the pursuit of happiness is afforded. This is a white man's burden, in a white man's country and I am bringing it to you as the greatest duty of the Knights of the Ku Klux Klan to correctly interpret and correctly perform it for God, for country, for family and for self.

I bring to you no doctrine of hatred, either of alien people or religious sect, but I want to leave with you a message of genuine responsibility for your own development and genuine responsibility for your own action as you act along these lines.

The Riot at Niles

Only prompt and effective action by the Ohio State militia prevented the riot which took place at the town of Niles on November 1 from resulting in something like a set battle between bodies of secret organizations—the Ku Klux Klan and the Knights of the Flaming Circle. As it was, the first reports stated that at least a dozen people had been injured and two probably fatally wounded, although we have not seen that either of the persons so seriously wounded has, in fact, died. An inquiry was at once set on foot by the civil authorities and order was restored, but reports of November 2 stated that the town was virtually an armed camp and that trouble was feared when the militia withdrew. Apparently the almost exclusive attention given by the papers in the following days to the election news has kept further reports and discussion of this affair at Niles out of view for the moment.

Major-General Hough, who at once began a military investigation of the affray, was formerly a Supreme Court Judge and is now a district attorney in one section of the State. He is quoted as making the remark, as to persons who might be indicted for rioting, "Whether they were Ku Klux Klansmen or anti-Klansmen—that makes no difference to us. To us they are all simply members of armed mobs."

Apparently behind this clash lies that same state of festering hatred which brought about the killing and wounding of a number of combatants not long ago at Herrin in Illinois. Wherever racial, religious, and industrial feelings have been wrought to a high pitch in such communities there is a danger of similar results. The current accounts state that a great gathering and parade of thousands of Ku Klux members had been planned to take place at Niles, but without masks, and that the parade was promptly abandoned when the trouble began. The local body of the Knights of the Flaming Circle called a meeting on the same day, and many hundreds assembled with the evident purpose of at least expressing antagonism to the Ku Klux Klan. It is alleged that the members of the Flaming Circle were urged to "avoid bringing women and children," and this, together with the fact that the meeting was called for the same day for which a permit to meet had been granted to the Klansmen, is cited by Klansmen as a strong reason for laying the primary responsibility on the Flaming Circle. It is also said by the Klan people that their opponents were patrolling the roads into Niles and interfering with the right of peaceful assembly on the part of the Klansmen. On the other hand, the "Circlers" assert that the first act of violence occurred when an automobile drove up to the meeting-place of the Flaming Circle and the occupants of the car "fired volley after volley into the crowd" and that this violence led to other firing on both sides and to the list of wounded persons. Each side claims that the other was armed with rifles and pistols, and the Klansmen say that the "Circlers" had bombs.

It makes no difference in public esteem, or in the eye of the law, what the political leanings or private differences of either of these two organizations are. So long as they comport themselves with due respect to law they are entitled the protection of the law against assault and violence. The incident is, however, an illustration of the fact that for a secret society to propagate political action or place one prejudice in combat with another is a dangerous and unAmerican proceeding.

1. Excerpt from "Imperial Wizard Outlines Klan Objectives before Immense Gathering in Ohio," *The Imperial Night-Hawk* (18 July 1923): 2-6.
2. "The Riot at Niles," *Outlook* 138 (12 November 1924): 396.

XIV.3. The Quest for Moral Order: The Enforcement of Prohibition in Ohio

State legislators established the office of the Prohibition commissioner to enforce Prohibition legislation enacted earlier. In late 1919, Congress passed the Volstead Act to enforce the Eighteenth Amendment to the U.S. Constitution. The federal government authorized the Bureau of Internal Revenue to conduct its day-to-day enforcement activities. Therefore, any offender faced the possibility of criminal charges on two levels, stemming from the condition of dual sovereignty that existed because of the American system of government.

In the following report, Commissioner B. F. McDonald describes the accomplishments of his state agency and explains its new focus on commercial profiteering.[1]

For the period from September 1st, 1924, to September 1st, 1925, the administration of this department reports the following:

Inspections	4,289
Arrests made	3,862
Convictions had	2,093
Fines assessed	$645,155.00
Total fines collected under Crabbe Act	2,202,764.64
Total fines paid into State Treasury	1,101,382.32
Samples Analyzed	131

During the fiscal year ending June 30ᵗʰ, 1925, this department expended on the work accomplished the sum of $105,702.02.

It will be noted that the number of inspections, arrests and convictions made through this department are but about half that of last year. This, due to the fact that during the past year we have had no card men working since the ruling of Attorney General Crabbe ruled out near one hundred such enforcement officers who were without expense to the State, being compensated through the local courts for the work they did. The results obtained, however, during the past year by regular inspectors has, in fact, exceeded that of any previous year.

During the past eight months under our direction more time and attention has been given to the apprehension of the chief violators such as transporters, operators of stills, and all those commercializing and dealing in illicit liquor in a large way. As a result of this action we have not apprehended so large a number of violators but we feel that our work has been, however, more effective in enforcing the prohibition law than formerly. I do not wish to convey the idea that we have not at any time molested the hip pocket bootlegger nor that such may feel that they will not be apprehended by men of this department in the future, but I do mean that the inspectors of this department have been directed to give their attention and have given their attention to the larger violators. We have since the first day of January, 1925, apprehended about 300 still operators, confiscated their stills and had the sentences thereon imposed, and since the first day of January, 1925, we have apprehended about 100 transporters, confiscated their cars, the same being sold and the proceeds thereof paid into the Treasury of the State and the treasuries of the various political subdivisions of the State and sentences imposed upon the violators. . . .

According to reports sent into this department out of the homes entered inspectors have found the law violated in four out of five entered, and in many cases where they found no specific violations they did find much evidence in the way of empty whiskey bottles, the odor of intoxicating liquors filling the house, and secret hiding places, trap doors, etc., evidently intended to conceal illicit liquors. The traffic in intoxicating liquors has been largely driven out of the public place of business and is to a great extent today carried on from residences, which, under the law, ceases to be a bona fide private dwelling when used for trafficking in intoxicating liquors. Unless curbed by the forces of the law the liquor traffic will continue to be carried on from the homes to an ever growing extent and we may fully expect propaganda against invasion of the home to be continued by the bootleggers and their sympathetic friends. You will note, too, that all those interested in this propaganda are opposed to the law and the constitution and are going their limit to break it down. I believe in protecting the sanctity of the home, but when a residence is used primarily as a distillery or a bootlegging joint under the guise of a private home, it must suffer the consequences.

1. B. F. McDonald, Prohibition Commissioner, *Fifth Annual Report of the Prohibition Commissioner* (Columbus: State of Ohio, 1925), 3-5.

XIV.4. The Impact of the Great Depression: "The Extent of Unemployment in Ohio," 1929–1932

Looking back at the 1920s, it is easy to see the contradictory nature of the decade's prosperity. The technological innovations responsible for such dramatic economic development—new open hearth steel furnaces, more powerful railroad locomotives, wondrous appliances for the home—were as destructive as they were beneficial. Industrial output and productivity soared; employment stayed flat. While many established firms dismissed workers after adopting new technologies, only a few firms in the mass-production industries added workers in any significant numbers. With stable or declining employment in the high-paying manufacturing jobs, consumption did not keep pace.

The question of "Who bears the risks?" becomes relevant once again. As the economy deteriorated, workers, not managers or stockholders, assumed the greatest risk. Factories shut down production lines but often continued to pay salaries and stock dividends out of accumulated surpluses.

In Ohio, the more advanced, urban industrial centers assumed the greatest risks. Once the depression hit, unemployment in the state's biggest cities—the ones that were often single-industry towns—was the highest: Toledo, Akron, and Youngstown were hit the hardest.

As the downward spiral of bank failures, plant closings, and layoffs began to paralyze the state, lawmakers established the Commission on Unemployment Insurance to assess the economy and make recommendations. The commission's report, most of which was drafted by William M. Leiserson, professor of economics at Antioch College, offered a thorough summary of the employment problem and offered state officials an innovative set of proposals for insurance. The following selection, section 3 of the report's first part, summarized the situation as of November 1932.[1]

III. Extent of Unemployment in Ohio

*I*n 1929 all of the industries in Ohio taken together furnished employment to a monthly average of 1,307,000 employees, and the combined wages of all of them for 1929 amounted to $1,925,600,000.

In December, 1930, payrolls carried 164,400 fewer workers than in December, 1929. The total earnings in 1930 were $323,600,000 less than in 1929. At close of 1931 there were 332,700 fewer employed than in December, 1929, and earnings for 1931 were $704,500,000 less than for 1929. During the first two years of the depression, therefore, the working people of the state lost in earnings and purchasing power something in excess of one billion dollars.

Largely on account of part-time work, wage and salary payments dropped more drastically than employment. Earnings were 36 per cent lower in 1931 than in 1929, while employment was 24 per cent lower; in 1930 the drop in employment was about 11 per cent, but wage and salary payments dropped 17 per cent.

THE PRESENT DEPRESSION

*T*his is a broad measure of unemployment since 1929 and of the losses it caused up to the beginning of the present year. The records for 1932 are not yet available. We know, however, that both employment and the amounts paid in wages and salaries have declined more drastically this year than they did in 1931.

On the basis of the indices of employment and earnings for manufacturing published by the United States Bureau of Labor Statistics, which correspond closely to the records for Ohio, we can estimate the losses in employment and earnings for the first part of the present year. From January to July, 1932, inclusive, on the basis of the manufacturing index, we estimate that the number of workers employed monthly in Ohio was 37 per cent less than in 1929. This means that there were about 484,000 fewer workers employed in 1932 than in 1929. Earnings for these seven months, on the basis of the manufacturing index, were about 44 per cent of what they were in 1929. This means that for the whole year of 1932 the loss in earnings will be about a billion dollars.

TABLE I. EMPLOYMENT, EARNINGS AND LOSSES, 1929-1932

Year	Average Monthly Number Employed	Decrease in Employment Since 1929	Per Cent Decrease Since 1920	Total Wage & Salary Payments	Losses Since 1929	Per Cent Loss Since 1929
1929	1,307,000	....	..	$1,925,600,000	....	..
1930	1,162,000	145,000	11	1,602,000,000	323,600,000	17
1931	991,000	316,000	24	1,221,200,000	704,400,000	36
1932*	823,000	484,000	37	847,300,000	1,078,300,000	56

*Estimated on basis of index numbers of U.S. Bureau of Labor Statistics for the first 7 months of 1932. The index is for manufacturing only, and therefore the unemployed and wage loss estimates may be too large. The other absolute figures are from the Division of Labor Statistics, Department of Industrial Relations.

According to the indices of the Bureau of Business Research, Ohio State University, it appears that Toledo is suffering more unemployment than any other city in the state. Employment in August, 1932, was 66 per cent below the peak of 1929; wage and salary payments must, therefore, have been reduced more than 70 per cent. Stark County had a loss of employment in the same period of about 60 per cent. Akron and Youngstown employment for August, 1932, was only about 50 per cent of the 1929 peak. Cincinnati and Columbus showed the smallest reduction in employment in the state, with 38 per cent less in August, 1932, than in the peak of 1929. Wage losses in all these cases, it is to be remembered, are always greater than the employment losses.

1. Ohio Commission on Unemployment Insurance, *Report of the Ohio Commission on Unemployment Insurance* (Columbus: State of Ohio, 1932), pt. 1, 23-24.

XIV.5. Ohio's Relief Efforts during the Depression Decade

In Ohio, as in other states, the provision of direct relief to families in need went through three phases during the depression decade of the 1930s. Before 1933 and President Franklin D. Roosevelt's "New Deal," the social burden of caring for needy families was borne first by private organizations and local governments, then by the state relief commission. With Roosevelt's inauguration, the federal government assumed responsibility for the provision of direct relief. Federal administrators, working through the apparatus established by the relief commission, supported local efforts with a generous injection of tax dollars. The third phase, beginning in 1935, saw a transfer of primary financial responsibility for direct relief back to local governments as the federal bureaucracy focused on public works.

The first document, "Relief = Subsistence," a section of part 2 of the Report of the Ohio Commission on Unemployment Insurance, completed in January 1933, provides a summary of the efforts in Ohio during that initial phase of the depression.[1] Then follows another section of the commission's report highlighting local programs to promote self-sufficiency among the unemployed families of the state.[2] The final document, part 2 of the state's 1935 monograph on relief activities, offers an overview of the federal relief efforts in the state by administrators of Roosevelt's First New Deal, conducted under the Federal Emergency Relief Act of 1933.[3]

RELIEF = SUBSISTENCE

*E*arly in 1932, Mr. Dykstra, City Manager of Cincinnati, reported that relief in Cincinnati was "at a minimum." Destitute families were being helped for a week and then pushed off for a week. Outdoor relief was between $7 and $8 a week per family, supplemented in case of dire distress from clothing, shoe and milk funds. By May, 1932, as testified before the Unemployment Insurance Commission hearings, relief was "less than $4 a week", although the minimum food budget for a family of 5 is estimated at $7.50 by the Associated Charities. All resources must be exhausted before this meager help is given. As for evictions—Cincinnati had 40 a day in April, 1932. Mr. Dykstra said:

> We are paying no rent at all. That of course is a very difficult problem because we are continually having evictions, and social workers, of both the city and the chest, are hard put to find places for people whose furniture has been put out on the street. Of course, there is a tremendous amount of just letting that ride. Landlords have been very patient, but they are getting to the place where they cannot pay taxes, and some of the landlords are on the relief agencies themselves for food.

The Columbus method of giving food only is well illustrated by the story of a family that lived across the street from the writer. The man of the family was an ex-minister who had gone into business and then lost his job. His wife and two small children and himself struggled along. A brother-in-law owning a small grocery supplied them with some food, but the gas was turned off, the lights went out, they had no heat in the house and winter was coming on. The children's clothes were too worn out to wear to school, so they stayed home. Finally the ex-minister went to the charities, and the charities offered him groceries. No heat, gas or light, but the only thing he could get elsewhere — food. His children cold and unclothed, the former minister turned to the small funds of a religious organization for which he was treasurer. At present he is in jail for embezzlement.

Not until the cupboard is bare, the gas shut off or the landlord at the door with eviction papers, can a family in Cleveland expect food, gas money or rent from the Associated Charities. Last spring Cleveland families were receiving from 40 to 60 per cent less than the minimum standard food budget — although that budget is "regarded by the national government and by our local health agencies as the absolute minimum below which we cannot go without jeopardizing the health of our families," says Mr. Edward D. Lynde, Director of the Associated Charities. For an average food expenditure in January of $3.48 per week, the day's menu included: Breakfast — oatmeal or cornmeal and cocoa for children, coffee for parents; Luncheon — bean soup, cabbage, bread; Dinner — macaroni with tomatoes plus milk for the children. "In 64 per cent of the cases no rent is paid by the Associated Charities," according to Mr. Lynde's report. In cases of 3-day eviction notices, the charities policy after March was to pay 25 per cent of a month's rent. "It is true that families are moved out after a landlord has kept them as long as he will, if a cheaper rent can be found. This undesirable policy is unlike A. C.'s normal rent policy but has been forced upon them by lack of funds." No gas bills are paid until a shut off card is received, and then not at all if coal stoves can be used for heating. Payment of any electric bills was discontinued in March, 1932. Even with such a reduced method of helping, "Only 5 out of every 10 families who apply each month receive relief," Mr. Lynde reported. As an editorial in the Plain Dealer says, "The record (in Mr. Lynde's report) . . . is a frank confession that our charity is now on the basis of little better than slow starvation."

CASE LOADS MOUNT

A further indication of the mass methods forced on the charities by a lack of relief funds and the enormous burden is in the size of case loads. Case workers in Dayton used to think that 125 families per worker per month was a heavy load. Now the average is between 300 and 400, and some carry as high as 450 families. All "rehabilitation work" is utterly precluded from the city charity program. In 1928, the average Toledo case worker carried 48 families a month. In 1931 that load had grown to 188 families, and in April, 1932, it had reached the unmanageable total of 250 families per case worker per month. (The standard average for efficient case worker is acknowledged to be about 40 families.) With relief being handed out wholesale, what have we but a dole, and what can we expect to result but pauperization?

HELPING THE UNEMPLOYED HELP THEMSELVES

*E*ver since the rain of "unemployment apples" in the streets of Ohio cities in 1930, citizens, social workers and others have been hatching schemes to assist the unemployed in providing for themselves. Many projects have been worked out in Ohio.

Gardening

Gardens for the unemployed have been among the most popular and apparently successful schemes (however hard on the farmers). At Youngstown, the thrift garden land is secured, the township prepares it, and the unemployed men are allowed to put in small gardens. Akron waxes enthusiastic over its "most elaborate, far-flung system of community-industrial gardening being undertaken in any American city in this third year of the depression." On 1,200 acres of land, over 2,000 unemployed men spend one day a week. In May, 1932, it was estimated that planting, cultivating, harvesting and canning would cost Akron less than $10,000. Mass production machinery and tools were used in the work. The original impetus came from Akron industries which had provided gardens for their employees. Firestone Tire and Rubber Company men have 140 acres of garden land. B. F. Goodrich Company men cultivate a 275-acre farm. Goodyear Tire and Rubber Company offers land to its employees to cultivate. It is said that even at the Akron Airport where the Zeppelins cast their shadows corn is being raised. In August, 1932, every Akron worker took home a week's supply of green beans, potatoes, sweet corn and assorted vegetables after his day's work. On their community farm, the entire operation and supervision is carried on by the unemployed. Nine hundred and ninety ex-factory workers produced 85 acres of potatoes, 50 of beans, 97 of corn, 30 of tomatoes, 5 of carrots, 11 of onions and 50 of other truck vegetables — at a cost of about $8,000 to the city of Akron.

Cleveland Associated Charities propose to use a 2,000-acre farm next year for the unemployed. Weeds growing in some of the individual garden plots assigned by charities to the unemployed roused consternation, and the agency threatened to cut off aid to those who neglected their gardens. On the whole, however, they were a valuable asset, for 7,500 applications have been received for next year's gardens. This year's area will be doubled in 1933, and 95 per cent of this year's gardeners will cultivate their plots again next spring. Dayton also had gardens for the unemployed. Even small towns like East Palestine provided a garden for each unemployed head of a family.

Work Relief

Regular work relief has not turned out so successfully, although it has been tried in almost every community in Ohio. It was expected to reduce the need for direct relief, but in a very few instances has this been true. The high expense entailed has prevented the schemes from lessening the burden of direct relief. In Cincinnati a program of work relief operated under the Division of Welfare and, supported by city funds through the winter of 1929–30, began again in December, 1930, and continued through the following summer.

Unemployed heads of families were assigned un-skilled work at $0.30 to $0.40 an hour, to prevent reduction of wages in general, and the number of hours per week reduced to 18. This kept the wage at $7.20 a week, plus car tickets and noon lunches. Clothing was distributed to the men's families without deducting from wages. The work done was in repair and improvement of public buildings, parks and highways. The city river-front was cleaned up. In other words, jobs were given which would not have been done otherwise. The cost in wages, lumber and such from December, 1929, through July, 1931, amounted to $315,471, or $73,971 more than was taken care of by the city and county appropriations. The excess was met partly by private donations but largely by the relief appropriations of the Division of Welfare. According to Mr. C. A. Dykstra their work relief continued into 1932 and cost the city in 1931, $432,000. In addition a Make-a-job Committee circularized and canvassed houses and offices for jobs. The Cincinnati Associated Charities also carried on work-relief in a few suburban towns.

Cleveland appropriated $1,111,960 for work relief to be performed through the Street, Park, Sewer and Bridge Departments of the city. At the first registration of applicants for work relief in October, 1930, 6,500 male heads of Cleveland families were registered. Each of these 6,500 was given some work before a second registration took place. At the second one, 11,200 men were registered, less than 1,000 names duplicating the first list. Work was given for 3 days a week, 8 hours a day at $0.60 an hour. No adjustment was made for fitness to work. Between October 13, 1930, and April 14, 1931, about 16,000 men averaged 12 days work, earning $57.60. The total amount spent for wages, materials and supervision (part being provided by city departments directing the work) came to $1,100,082. Little reduction in the direct relief demands resulted from this program, and the Associated Charities felt that the "psychological value of work was lost when men were unable to receive anywhere near steady employment." Since work relief proved more expensive than direct relief, the use of funds which would ordinarily go into direct relief for work relief came to be frowned upon in Cleveland.

An odd-job campaign located 5000 jobs in the winter of 1930–31, and another 2,500 in the spring. These ranged from half-day jobs to permanent ones. In November, 1932, unemployed men were put to work clearing a road, a project of the American Legion, under the auspices of the State Highway Department. Such projects are being conducted in many parts of the state.

The Dayton Family Welfare Association gave relief tickets in 1930 good in any Dayton grocery store for an 8-hour day's work. By January, 1931, 1000 cases a day piled up. The problem of cold weather, tools, transportation, noon meals and 1000 men a day swamped the project and little work was accomplished, according to Mr. F. O. Eichelberger, City Manager. In 1931 Dayton kept 100 men a day busy and gave the rest requisitions on the Dayton Commissary.

Trumbull County put men to work on township roads, paying $2.60 a day and giving each man applying 2 days' work. Smith Township "put in 37 miles of ditches along township highways and used the gasoline money that came to the township to give work relief to the unemployed in that township," said F. P. Agey at the Youngstown Hearing of the Commission. When the township was financially unable to continue, the county improved two county roads in Smith Township, giving each man 3 days work, or about $10 every 2 weeks. This kept 400 families in that community from starving last winter.

In Austin Township, trustees were supporting 150 families through work on the roads in the early months of 1932. In Mahoning County a "very small number of them (the destitute unemployed) are getting relief in employment," Mr. Agey testified.

Economical Idleness vs. Expensive Work

Toledo had a make-work program in 1930 and employed about 5,000 men from December to May, when it was discontinued because of the lack of money. It was more economical to support men in idleness, even though the men would have preferred jobs under a make-work program to charity.

The consensus of opinion about work relief seems to have been that it was too expensive in money for the results either from the relief standpoint or for the psychological effect on the unemployed. On December 8, 1932, Grand Rapids, Michigan, had to throw overboard its much bruited plan of work relief with scrip payments because it was too costly.

Not only is work relief costly, but as a device to sustain the morale of the unemployed, it fails. The unemployed men are not fooled into thinking themselves even semi-employed. They are putting in a few days work in return for relief which they would be given even if the work were not done.

DAYTON'S PRODUCTION UNITS

A Dayton group had the foresight to plan work for the unemployed on a practical local basis. As a result of this preparation by the Character Building Division of the Community Fund, Dayton has the Dayton Association of Cooperative Production Units in operation.

Because of this scheme some of the unemployed in Dayton are working, but not for wages. About 450 families are organized into 7 Production Units, varying in size from 50 to 110 families. The emphasis in these groups of unemployed is on production, although barter exists among the units and between individual units and outside individuals or groups. For instance, the East Dayton unit barters bread for groceries from the city Community store.

Besides producing bread, East Dayton mends shoes, builds furniture, makes dresses and shirts and can goods. The Home View Unit (negro), the first unit formed, also produces clothing. Its active members number 45, and the men among them make soap, cut wood and in the summer cultivate the unit's common garden. An old colored woman spins yarn on an old-fashioned wheel, and the women upstairs in the Home View Unit house use yarn to tie comforts. The Belmont Unit is building its own quarters out of brick from the city dump, and in the basement of this new building complete shoe machinery will be set up. The unit expects to swap shoes for soup with the Columbia Conserve Company.

RELIEF EFFORTS UNDER THE NEW DEAL

*T*he Federal Emergency Relief Act of 1933, signed by President Roosevelt on May 12 following the famous "100 days" of rapid Congressional action, acknowledged the need of states and other local political subdivisions for funds beyond those available to them through local taxes.

It appropriated $500,000,000 from the Reconstruction Finance Corporation, half of which was to be given outright to states unable to meet relief expenses, at the discretion of the Administrator, and the other half to be given on a matching basis to states still able to furnish a substantial part of the necessary funds.

On May 22 of that year, Harry L. Hopkins was named Federal Administrator for the new program, with full authority to establish rules and regulations for the expenditure of the funds under his control, and to determine the amount of state grants. Mr. Hopkins designated the State Relief Commission the administrative agent of the FERA in Ohio.

For the ensuing six months, then, Ohio drew heavily on the newly created funds, since already local methods for relief were proving inadequate to the emergency. In September, additional Section 3 Bond [utility excise tax] funds were made available in Ohio, but these still were not sufficient to support a program of work to take the place of direct relief; and it was becoming increasingly clear that some means of providing work for those capable and willing to do it was the necessary next step.

The answer to this need in Ohio and nationally, was the Civil Works Administration, established on November 15, 1933, under the direction of Harry L. Hopkins at Washington. Again, the State Relief Commission of Ohio was made administrative agent.

For four months there flourished in this state the most tremendous program of public work ever undertaken. About 100,000 men were removed from the relief rolls by December 1, and 10 days later an additional 100,000 from the borderline group, those who though unemployed were not yet reduced to applying for direct relief, were given their first paid work for many months.

From time to time additional quotas were allowed Ohio, chiefly through the representations of Adjutant General Henderson to the FERA at Washington, but partially, at least, because Ohio's program was so well planned and prepared that it was able to absorb immediately more than its original quota of 200,000 men. Other states, less well prepared, suffered quota cuts. The national goal was "4,000,000 men and women working by December 15."

After nearly $58,000,000 of CWA money had been loosed among Ohio consumers, with a consequent stimulation of retail sales, of a number of production goods industries, and with an immeasurably salutary effect on the morale of the state's unemployed, the Civil Works Administration closed its books on April 1, 1934, and gradually gave way to the FERA Works Division program.

The new program, and that which still is current, was more conservatively conceived, less expensive to administer. It was hoped that industry would begin to absorb those again thrown out of work by the new program, and that work relief employees, who now received not the stipulated minimum of $15 under CWA, but only enough to meet their barest physical needs, would drop off to accept private and more remunerative employment. . . .

In rural areas, relief is aimed at rehabilitation of farm families by assisting them to become self-supporting. Work projects are provided as a means of affording work in exchange, either for advances of food or other consumable items or for domestic livestock, poultry, tools, etc., furnished for self-subsistence purposes. The rural work projects will also provide opportunity for some cash income for those whose needs cannot be met in "kind," that is to say, by providing consumption and certain capital goods.

The relief of drought-stricken farm families is accomplished chiefly by providing work projects on which the heads of the families may earn relief in the form of wages with which to supply their own needs. The projects include food canning, dam and reservoir building, well digging, and other water-development and control work, as well as other permanent measures designed to alleviate drought conditions.

The relief per family is gauged to include feed for livestock on which the families depend for livelihood. . . .

Relief expenditures in Ohio during 1933 and 1934 included:

1933 Relief	44,399,312.22
1933 CWA	11,557,172.43
1934 Relief (estimated)	77,112,899.83
1934 CWA	46,428,783.43

Against these expenditures were peak relief loads as follows:

Single individuals	1933-	35,139
Families	1933-	219,041
Single individuals	1934-	59,692
Families	1934-	253,951

1. *Report of the Ohio Commission on Unemployment Insurance* (Columbus: State of Ohio, 1933), pt. 2, 142–43.

2. Ibid., 146–50.

3. *The State Relief Commission of Ohio and Its Activities* (Columbus: Publications Division, 1935), 34–35.

XIV.6. A Decade of Crisis on the Ohio Farm: Depression, "Agricultural Adjustment," and Soil Conservation Programs

Agriculture in Ohio, as in most parts of the nation, had suffered since the end of the First World War. The prolonged slump in prices throughout the 1920s, the precipitous downturn of the early 1930s, and continued agrarian protest had pressured the federal government into considering relief, recovery, and reform legislation for the nation's farms. The first major legislation of the 1920s, the McNary-Haugen plan would have created a two-tier price system, protecting American agriculture. The legislation, vetoed by President Calvin Coolidge in 1927 and 1928, would have allowed farmers to sell as much as possible in the U.S. market at a parity price, a price equal to those received for commodities in the prosperous pre–World War I years. Under McNary-Haugen, the federal government would have purchased all surpluses at the parity price and sold them abroad at lower world prices.

In 1929, Congress passed the Agricultural Marketing Act, legislation favored by the new Republican administration of President Herbert Hoover. The Marketing Act promoted the extension of producer-owned cooperatives in agriculture and established public-funded corporations to stabilize the price of farm commodities. The Federal Farm Board, funded with a $500 million appropriation, made loans to farm cooperatives over the next two years. By 1931, the board had taken possession of tons of unsold surpluses and had failed to stem the decline in agricultural prices.

In response to the severe conditions in rural America, the Roosevelt administration, advised by the nation's agricultural organizations, prominent journalists, and academic experts, devised a new approach to solving the farm problem. In May 1933, Congress passed the Agricultural Adjustment Act. The framers of the legislation intended to end the imbalance in the production and consumption of farm commodities by restoring prices to their prewar parity levels. The Agricultural Adjustment Administration (AAA) reorganized production and marketing across the nation. The AAA, working through the local Extension Service, coordinated the production of those farmers, organized in local producer associations, who signed up for the federal program. This attempt to contrive scarcity included limiting production, paying participating farmers benefits for not producing, setting prices charged by processors and distributors of farm products, and selling surpluses in foreign markets.

After the court declared key sections of the AAA unconstitutional, the Roosevelt administration pushed the Soil Conservation and Domestic Allotment Act through Congress to justify lower levels of agricultural output in the name of "soil conservation."

The first document is an excerpt from a state agricultural report by F. L. Morison on the overall farming situation.[1] The second article offers a specific assessment of the New Deal's efforts to stabilize the farm economy.[2]

OHIO'S FARM INCOME IN 1934

*T*he gross cash income of Ohio farmers from the sale of farm products in 1934, including rental and benefit payments made by the Agricultural Adjustment Administration, has been estimated at approximately 203 million dollars. This represents an increase of about 22 per cent over 1933 and is the best gross income farmers have had since 1930. Most of the improvement came in the last 6 months of 1934. Price increases resulting from the A. A. A. program and from the drouth began to work to the advantage of Ohio farmers in that period when most sales are normally made. Ohio suffered less from the drouth than areas west of the Mississippi.

TABLE 1. Estimated Gross Cash Income from the Sale of Products from Ohio Farms

(In thousands of dollars)

YEAR	Meat	Dairy	Grains	Poult.	Potato	Wool	Others	Total
1910–14	81,407	26,894	43,216	18,449	7,175	3,279	32,388	212,808
1930	92,953	65,757	29,717	40,739	7,029	3,539	41,286	281,020
1931	60,766	48,811	22,747	32,113	4,487	2,510	31,285	202,719
1932	44,925	35,106	19,021	23,038	3,019	1,429	24,102	150,640
1933	50,088	36,115	25,286	21,170	4,084	3,312	26,740	166,795
1934	60,824	44,179	32,964	26,371	3,310	3,968	31,168	202,784

The total income from meat animals, including benefit payments to hog producers cooperating in the A. A. A. program, was about 10 3/4 million dollars more in 1934 than in 1933, a 21 per cent increase. Marketings of livestock, particularly hogs, were considerably reduced, but this was more than offset by the increased prices received for hogs, veal calves, and lambs. Producers of dairy products received over 8 million dollars more than in 1933, an increase of 22 per cent. With increased prices for poultry and eggs, the income from sale of these products showed a 25 per cent increase. A comparison of recent years with the 1910 to 1914 average shows the increased relative importance of dairying and poultry raising in Ohio.

The potato crop gives an excellent example of what the farmer receives for a larger than normal crop. Although the potato crop of the nation was 20 per cent larger than that of last year and the Ohio crop was 40 per cent greater, the cash farm income from the sale of potatoes in Ohio was 19 per cent below that of 1933.

Considerable improvement is needed in consumer purchasing power before the farmer's income is restored to its 1910–1914 level, because prices paid by farmers are 26 per cent greater than during pre-war years.

The Farming Situation in Ohio, 1932–37

John McSweeney

. . . II. Agricultural Adjustment Programs the Basis

The production-adjustment programs of the A.A.A., with other recovery measures, were the basis for the marked agricultural change from 1933 to 1937.

Under these programs 236,988 crop-adjustment contracts from Ohio farmers were accepted by the A.A.A. Of these contracts 27,648 were tobacco, 110,200 corn-hog, 13,065 sugar beet, and 86,075 wheat.

Under the terms of these contracts Ohio farmers shifted many acres from the production of soil-depleting cash crops, in which price-depressing surpluses existed, to production of other crops which were soil conserving or soil improving in nature.

The agricultural adjustment programs, from their beginning in 1933, were concerned with good use of the land as well as with adjusting production to effective demand. It was recognized from the start that relieving a portion of the farm land from the soil-exhausting burden of surplus-crop production offered a chance to put this land to soil-conserving uses which farm specialists for many years had been advocating. . . .

The result of these A.A.A. programs and of the droughts of 1934 and 1936 was to reduce price-depressing surpluses of most major farm commodities to approximately normal carry-over levels. . . .

Under the adjustment programs through December 31, 1937, rental-benefit payments to producers of farm commodities were: Tobacco, $2,331,183.60; rye, $42.92; corn-hogs, $24,683,664.56; wheat, $6,262,922.72; and sugar beets, $1,409,174.02.

III. The Soil-Conservation Programs

The 1936 Agricultural Conservation Program. About 4,000,000 farmers in all parts of the Nation, members of about 2,700 county conservation associations, participated in the 1936 agricultural conservation program. Under this program two types of payments were offered to farmers for positive performance in conserving and improving their farm land. Soil-conserving payments were made for shifting acreage from soil-depleting to soil-conserving crops in 1936. Soil-building payments were made for 1936 seedings of soil-building crops, and for approved soil-building practices. . . .

In Ohio about 126,700 farmers organized into 88 county associations, participated in the 1936 program. Of the total Ohio cropland, about 63 percent, or 8,091,400 acres, was covered by applications for payments. The acreage diverted from soil-depleting crops (10,854 from tobacco and 448,737 from other crops) totaled 459,591 acres. Soil-building practices were put into effect on about 2,006,530 acres, as follows: New seedings of legumes and legume mixtures, perennial grasses for pasture, and green-manure crops, 1,859,114 acres; fertilizer and lime applications, 147,264 acres; and forest tree plantings, 152 acres.

For their positive soil-conserving and soil-building performances in this connection Ohio farmers participating in the 1936 program received $9,708,084 in conservation payments, including county association expenses.

1. Ohio Agricultural Experiment Station, *The Bimonthly Bulletin* 20 (March–April 1935): 99.

2. *Congressional Record,* 75th Cong., 3d sess., vol. 83, 1938, 2846-49.

XIV.7. Rural Electrification in Ohio

In 1933, the federal government established the Tennessee Valley Authority, the nation's first large-scale experiment with public power generation. The TVA, operating in a vast section of the nation's south-central region, impounded waterways, generated electricity, and distributed it to a variety of customers across the South. One of the TVA's early customers, the Alcorn County, Mississippi, rural electrical power cooperative, which purchased modern appliances and equipment with the financial assistance of the federal Electric Farm and Home Authority, achieved remarkable success in introducing electrical power to local farmers. The Alcorn cooperative's successful operations persuaded New Deal administrators to make a commitment to nationwide rural electrification. In May 1935, President Roosevelt, personally committed to this "power revolution" in America's farmlands, signed Executive Order 7037, creating the Rural Electrification Administration (REA). After private utility companies expressed their hostility to public power generation efforts, REA began to work through farmer-owned cooperatives. During its first thirteen months, the administration, which functioned as an agency within the WPA, allocated approximately $14 million in loans for electrification projects, with funds going mostly to cooperatives like Alcorn County.

REA's status changed dramatically in 1936. Administrators, hamstrung by relief program guidelines established for WPA operations, sought congressional help. Sympathetic legislators, led by Sen. George W. Norris of Nebraska, believed that REA's operations should be expanded and conducted by a permanent agency.

The next selection, "Rural Electrification in the Eleventh Congressional District of Ohio," is a text of the remarks of Rep. Harold K. Claypool made on the floor of the U.S. House of Representatives outlining the benefits of rural electrification.[1]

No utilization of the forces of Nature has brought so much comfort and happiness to the people of the world as has the adaptation of electricity to the necessary work of mankind. All credit must be given originally to the great inventive minds which made possible present uses of electricity and those who assembled the private capital to originate and promote its various uses. This Congress can claim credit for furthering this progress by the extension of electrification to the farmer to the extent that in Ohio alone $7,566,525 is authorized to be expended therein. I am pleased to say that more than one-seventh of this amount has gone to the Eleventh Ohio District, which I have the honor to represent. When this program was inaugurated, electricity was available to only a little more than 10 percent of the farms in my district. When we have completed the projects for which loans have already been approved, 50 percent of the farms in my district will be able to secure electric service; and, with pride in that achievement, I will not be content until the benefits of this boon to the human race has been extended to every farmhouse desiring it.

My district has been especially fortunate in securing loans of over $1,000,000 for rural electrification, despite large over-subscription of money available from the Government. I was pleased to actively support an additional appropriation in the independent offices appropriation bill for this purpose of $40,000,000, which will be available after July 1. Later, in the recovery bill, I assisted in asserting an item in that bill making $100,000,000 more available for rural electrification, so that a total of $140,000,000 will be available for this purpose for the year beginning July 1, 1938.

The two cooperatives in my district are the South Central Rural Electric Cooperative, Inc., with headquarters at Lancaster, and the Inter-County Rural Electric Cooperative, Inc., which serves Ross County. The first was organized by outstanding and progressive farmers in Fairfield, Perry, and Pickaway Counties, and a movement is now under way to bring the farmers of Hocking County into this organization, which I hope may be completed soon. It has been a pleasure as the representative in Congress of the Eleventh Ohio District, to present their applications for loans for the construction of rural electrification projects, which efforts have been very successful indeed. The South Central Cooperative has obtained a total of loans of $438,000, making available electricity to about 1,000 farms in Fairfield County, 300 in Pickaway County, and 350 in Perry County, a total of 1,650 in these 3 counties.

The Inter-County Rural electric Cooperative, Inc., has obtained loans which added to its pending application for $267,000 will make $645,200 available for this cooperative, making possible electricity for much over 1,000 farms in Ross County. Thus a total of 2,650 farms in the Eleventh Ohio District are extended the benefits of electricity.

American cities today and for many years past have enjoyed the light and power provided by this great industry of electricity with which the great names of Benjamin Franklin and Thomas Edison have been so closely connected and which industry has been promoted by the great industrial, financial, and political leaders of our country— and if this Congress can by pushing these benefits of light and power into the American farmhouses and thus lighten the burden of the producers of food for America it will, in my opinion, be entitled to a pardonable pride in this accomplishment.

1. *Congresional Record,* 75th Cong., 3d sess., vol. 83, 1938, 3173.

XIV.8. The Economic Crisis in Education: The Genesis of the First Ohio School Foundation Program Law

By March 1932, the state's school finances had deteriorated drastically. The depression had reduced revenues, and debt payments skimmed off a large portion of school budgets. The unprecedented school financial crisis of 1932 forced Governor George White to call for a thorough examination of the existing system by the director of education. Director B. O. Skinner organized the commission in May 1932. That body soon employed Professor Paul R. Mort, director of the School of Education, Teachers College, Columbia University, to direct the research staff assessing Ohio's educational system.

The Mort Plan was highly critical of the existing financial system. It asserted that the state relied excessively on property tax revenues to finance education and that local school board administrators possessed too much control. The first two of the three excerpts that follow are from Professor Mort's official report (1932).[1]

Although state legislators were not ready to adopt the Mort Plan, its recommendations influenced the new School Foundation Program enacted in 1935. The Foundation Program, from which the third excerpt is taken,[2] established a formula for subsidizing local schools that somewhat equalized the tax burden and allowed schools to operate efficiently.

George White to B. O. Skinner

March 8, 1932

Hon. B. O. Skinner,
Director of Education,
Columbus, Ohio.

My dear Director Skinner:

I am not unmindful of the financial situation that confronts many of our public schools. Personal observations, press dispatches, and reports from your office are convincing that many districts are facing a financial situation they have never been compelled to face before.

Delinquent taxes, caused by actual inability to pay, and the general depression through which our state, along with the country as a whole, is passing have all combined to reduce the expected revenues for the operation, in many places, of our schools.

It seems to me a comprehensive survey of the financial ability of the state as a whole, of the counties, and of the individual districts, so far as practical, might be made; may I suggest that you, as head of the educational interests of the state, take under consideration the advisability of appointing a commission which would head up such a survey. This survey, should in my judgment, be able to show how the schools may be conducted economically without loss of efficiency.

Ohio has an abundant supply of patriotic citizens who would be willing to sponsor such an undertaking. I have no doubt money could be found, and not from public funds, for such a work. There are many among our people who are deeply interested in public education and such people will help solve the problem of properly and adequately financing our schools in the future. I hope you will give the appointment of such a commission your serious attention.

Very sincerely yours,
George White, *Governor of Ohio*

INTRODUCTION

Need of Improving the Ohio System of School Support

Chapter I of this report outlines a democracy's fundamental duty in fulfilling its promise to provide equality of opportunity for its future citizens by means of an adequate system of public education. It outlines the growth of the realization of this responsibility in the State of Ohio from the first settlement of this territory to the present day. It shows that the state is responsible for setting up a minimum program of education below which no locality shall be allowed to go and that beyond this it is responsible for providing financing arrangements by which the burden of this minimum program shall be distributed equally among the people in all localities. It shows further that this responsibility demands proper provision for the financing of local initiative in the various school districts in the state in order that the school system may maintain and increase its efficiency. It points out that all the states in the Union are now faced with the necessity of rearranging their plans for financing education in such a way that the burden shall be better equalized not only with respect to the burdens carried in the various communities, but also with respect to the burdens carried by the various forms of taxation. It shows also that one of the reasons for the extreme difficulties in which many districts in Ohio now find themselves is the failure of Ohio to move as far along in bringing about these changes as a number of comparable states have been able to do.

It is of interest in this connection that information given in Chapter VI shows that the percentage of the total cost of education carried by state revenues in the five states with which Ohio is usually compared (New York, Michigan, California, Pennsylvania, and Massachusetts) varies from two to seven times the percentage carried by state revenues in Ohio. As compared with the practice in Ohio, Massachusetts state revenues carry double the percentage of the cost of education; in Pennsylvania state revenues carry four times as great a percentage; in California state revenues carry almost five times as great a percentage; in Michigan six times as great a percentage; and in New York seven times as great a percentage. Of all the states in the Union, only Kansas, Colorado, and Oregon provide a smaller percentage of the cost of education from state revenues than Ohio provides. . . .

The Proposed Plan

Chapter II describes the type of minimum program which Ohio should provide. Such a program would cost in the neighborhood of $60 per elementary pupil for all current expenditures. It would be difficult to reach this level immediately because of the large amount of expansion that would be required in many districts that are considerably below this $60 level in the type of educational program which they offer. A first step toward the correction of the present situation should be the equalization of the tax burden of a program costing $40 per elementary pupil in average daily attendance.

The proposed plan would operate as follows:

Equalization aid would be granted on the following basis: The total cost of a program amounting to $40 per elementary pupil and $68 per high school pupil would be computed.[3] To this would be added certain corrections for higher costs of living and the costs of transporting pupils. The result would be the cost of the minimum program, the burden of which the state is to equalize.

To determine the amount of equalization aid to be granted, the State would subtract from the above cost of a minimum program the following items:

1. An amount equal to a yield of tax of 0.35 mills on the valuation of property in the school district.

2. Funds received from the county 2,65 mills tax and from the distributable shares of the intangible tax.

3. Present state aid received except for vocational training and special classes.

The remainder, if any, would represent the amount of equalization aid that the state would grant to the district.

All but a comparatively few districts would obtain equalization aid, but it is proposed to guarantee to each district a minimum amount of $7 per elementary pupil in average daily attendance and $12 per high school pupil in average daily attendance. A provision is included also which would guarantee to districts receiving equalization aid in the school year 1932–1933 as much equalization aid per pupil as they received in that year. . . .

The annual amount of additional state aid which would be required to finance this program would be $20,000,000. It is proposed that this additional aid be obtained from taxes other than property taxes.

1935 SCHOOL FOUNDATION PROGRAM LAW

(House Bill No. 466)

Sec. 7595. There shall be a state public school fund in the state treasury, for the support and maintenance of the public school system and for the equalization of educational advantages throughout the state. To this fund shall be credited by the auditor of state any funds appropriated thereto by the general assembly and the proceeds of any taxes and fines which are by law to be applied to that fund and which are received by the treasurer of the state. The state public school fund shall be administered by the director of education, with the approval of the state controlling board and subject to the restrictions of law. . . .

Sec. 7595-Ib. If, in any school district which has a tax levy for current school operation of at least three mills, the revenue resources of any district are insufficient to enable the board of education thereof to conduct the schools in such district upon the minimum operating cost of a foundation program, as defined by or established pursuant to law, such district shall be entitled to receive additional aid, to be apportioned from the state public school fund by the director of education, . . .

The direction of education shall ascertain the amount required to supplement the revenue of such district to enable it to maintain the foundation program as hereinafter defined, and shall apportion the same to such district in the same manner and at the same time as other apportionments of the state public school fund are made to the school districts of the state, according to the provisions of this act.

All funds received from the state public school fund shall be used to pay current operating expenses only.

1. Paul R. Mort, *Equalizing Educational Opportunity in Ohio: A Preliminary Report of a Survey of State and Local Support of Public Schools in Ohio* (Columbus: Ohio School Survey Commission, 1932), foreword and 9–12.

2. *Legislative Acts Passed and Joint Resolutions Adopted,* vol. 116 (Columbus: F. J. Heer, 1935), 585–88.

3. Somewhat larger amounts in smaller schools because of the necessity of operating small classes.

XV. The World War II Era, 1939–1946

AMERICAN INVOLVEMENT IN the Second World War reinvigorated Ohio's and the nation's economy. After a decade of depression, the outbreak of war in Europe in 1939 led to the gradual awakening of America's military capacity and an attendant increase in industrial activity. Industrial output, employment, and workers' wages rose as the United States began to mobilize.

Ohio's agricultural sector prospered as the demand for foodstuffs came from overseas markets and from the rapidly increasing ranks of the American military. The skyrocketing demand for agricultural commodities sent prices, and, consequently, farm incomes soaring. For the first time in more than two decades, farmers enjoyed steadily improving real incomes as incoming revenues outpaced the increases in their cost of living. But regardless of the improving standard of living on Ohio farms, the nation's military mobilization led to fewer laborers on the state's farms and less acreage in cultivation.

The outflow of farmworkers, which began early in the war, brought a critical labor shortage on the state's farms. Initially, Ohioans attempted to replace the loss of farm labor by enlisting the women, children, and elderly members of farm families or hiring replacements from the rapidly shrinking pool of city and town labor. For many farms, especially those truck farms growing fruit, vegetables, and other produce through highly labor-intensive methods, family or nearby replacements proved insufficient. These operations turned to two outside sources of farm labor: migrant workers from Mexico and the Caribbean, and, by the second year of American involvement in the war, German and Italian prisoners lodged in camps around the state.

As in World War I, Ohioans faced the problem of feeding themselves while supplying the food needs of the U.S. armed forces as well as the Allied armies and nations overseas. To combat the shortage of foodstuffs at home, the state and federal governments encouraged individual citizens, local community organizations, and business establishments to promote a statewide "victory garden" movement. Ohioans cultivated more than 2.5 million gardens in the three growing seasons from spring 1943 to the end of the war.

Ohio contributed much to an industrial mobilization effort that by 1944 "was producing one ship a day and one aircraft every five minutes!"[1] The state, which had ranked in the top five in industrial output and employment before the war, had a workforce of approximately one million workers toiling in more than nine hundred different industries during the war years. Although Ohio's economy was dominated by agriculture and its core iron, steel, heavy machinery, and rubber products industries, the key contributions to the Allied war machine came from the state's aircraft, ordnance, and shipbuilding plants.

The four main urban industrial centers in Ohio took the lead in defense production. Cleveland ranked first in the state, producing in all three categories; Cincinnati ranked second, with an emphasis on aircraft; Akron, the center of rubber products production, came third; Dayton, with aircraft and machinery production firms, ranked fourth. Three other cities—Youngstown, Toledo, and Columbus—also made significant contributions to defense production.

In addition to urban-based private industry, important additions to the war effort came from federal arsenals at Ravenna, in Portage County, and Rossford, outside Toledo. Several federal ordnance plants and tank plants, scattered across the state, manufactured munitions and armored vehicles for the Allied armies.

The shortage of industrial labor that resulted from the expansion of manufacturing and the conscription of workers into the armed forces provided opportunities for women, African Americans, and white migrants from the upper South. Women filled job vacancies in almost every industry across the state. By 1944, women comprised almost a third of Ohio's workforce. The introduction of women on the shop floor often caused friction, especially during the early months of the war. Prevailing cultural attitudes, embraced by many individual men and by their union officers, made the integration of women difficult. A wage policy of paying women only a fraction of what men earned for the same work did not help to defuse the tension.

African Americans also took advantage of wartime job opportunities whenever possible in order to assume higher skilled, higher paying jobs in the state's industries. The war not only provided employment opportunities but contributed to an ongoing demographic shift in the nation. African Americans once again moved northward in large numbers from the South as they had done during the Great Migration period earlier in the century.

Employment often came only after a struggle. The federal government, after considerable pressure from African American leaders and sympathetic whites, instituted a policy of nondiscrimination in defense industry employment and gave blacks a chance to fight for their country. After President Roosevelt issued his June 1941 executive order prohibiting discriminatory employment policies in defense work, the federal government established the Fair Employment Practices Committee to enforce the new policy.

1. Paul Kennedy, *The Rise and Fall of the Great Powers: Economic Change and Military Conflict from 1500 to 2000* (New York: Random House, 1987), 355.

XV.1. Mobilizing Ohio's Farm Population for War

Ohioans responded once again to a war emergency in 1941. During the first twelve months of American involvement, as the United States expanded its armed forces and began to commit troops across the globe, young men began leaving Ohio farms in large numbers. Their departure, whether for military service or for high-paying urban, industrial jobs, left a void in the rural workforce. As the first of the following selections details,[1] in those early months three groups—older Ohioans, women, and children—carried the burden on the farms and filled that gap; by 1943, the labor shortage was so severe that it necessitated the importation of foreign workers. During the remainder of the war, numerous migrant workers and prisoners of war contributed to the effort on the farm. The second and third selections offer an overview of the mobilization and the record of one group of not-so-voluntary labor— German prisoners—on the farms and in the agricultural processing plants of the state around Defiance, Ohio.[2]

THE OHIO FARM LABOR SITUATION

F. L. Morison

A study of the Ohio farm labor situation was made during the months of October and November, 1942.[3] Part of this work was the study of 477 farms located in 16 typical communities in widely separated sections of the State.

This study revealed that there was approximately 8 per cent less manpower on these farms in 1942 than there had been in 1941. This reduction, amounting to an average of 1.8 months of man labor per farm for the year, does not take into account the longer days and the harder physical work which the operator and the members of his family put in during the past year. A large part of the reduction in manpower on Ohio farms was due to decreases in the numbers of regular hired men and male members of the operator's household between the ages of 18 and 45. These reductions were only partially offset by more work on the part of farm women, farm children of school age, and older men in the family, such as the operator's father.

In 1942, about one-half of the total labor on Ohio farms was performed by the operator, one-fourth by family labor, and one-fourth by hired labor, including both seasonal and regular help. Seasonal hired help was employed by nearly twice the number of farmers who kept a regular hired man on a monthly basis, although the latter kind of hired labor was more important in the aggregate.

An enumeration was made of all regular farm workers, including the operator, members of his family who were available for any farm work, and regular hired men. This enumeration showed that 6 per cent of the farms had more workers in October 1942 than a year ago; 70 per cent had the same number; and 24 per cent had fewer workers. On the entire 477 farms, there was a net loss of 99 workers, or about 1 less worker for every 5 farms. Most critical losses were the 23 per cent decline since October 1941 in the number of male family workers (other than the operator) between the ages of 18 and 45 and the 36 per cent decrease in the number of regular hired men.

The farm labor force is thus reduced not only in numbers, but also in experience. In October 1941, these 477 farms had a total of 214 regular hired men. During the 12-month period ending October 1942, 138 of these hired men left the farm, and only 60 new regular hired men were recruited. Of the latter number, only 38 had come from other farms. Nine had been working at industrial or other jobs, and 13 had been on WPA in 1941 or unemployed because they were ill or too old to work in industry. Only about half the farmers' sons who went to the armed services or to industry have been replaced. These replacements have often been by farm children not old enough to work in 1941. A number of farm women also helped with the milking or with field work for the first time in several years.

About seven farm workers went into the armed forces during the year for each six who left for industrial employment. To be sure, industry began to draw workers away from the farm long before the enactment of the Selective Service Act. There was some migration of industrial workers back to the farm, however, and in the past year, it would appear that the net loss of farm workers to industry has not been as large as the number who left the farm to enter the armed services.

[Summary of Wartime Mobilization of Ohio's Agricultural Sector]

*T*otal mobilization demanded a program for increased food production. The federal and state departments of agriculture organized to encourage the farmers toward greater efforts. The guarantee of a certain market and good prices also contributed to the increases. When Selective Service and industry drew men from the farms, labor assistants were set up in the offices of the County Agents to help provide farm workers. An emergency farm labor program brought Jamaicans, Mexicans, Barbadians, and other workers from the South into Ohio. By 1943, also, prisoners of war were being used. In 1944, 8140 farm laborers were imported, and during the past year 6936. Those workers were used mainly for work in connection with seasonal crops which called for hand labor, such as tomatoes, vegetables, fruits, and sugar beets. Thousands of townspeople and young people from the public schools of Ohio also took their turns in the fields.

As a result of the increased efforts on the farms, and in spite of declines in acreage under cultivation, agricultural production in Ohio between 1940 and 1945 experienced an overall increase of 30%. The production of wheat and corn each went up approximately 45%; soybeans, 127%; oats, 20%; eggs, 25%; and chickens, 15%. Hog numbers in 1944 had increased 35% above the 1939–41 average; milk cows increased 11% and other cattle, 16%. All grain-consuming animals increased by 1944 22% above the 1939–41 average. At the same time the production of truck crops increased by 9% in the five years of wartime. Vegetable production was increased by the Victory Garden campaign inaugurated in 1943. In the past three years there have been a total of 2,570,562 Victory Gardens in Ohio, which produced vegetable crops worth over $150,000,000.

It is interesting to consider the socio-economic result of this increase in farm production. By the end of the third year of the war, August 1942, agricultural income in Ohio had risen 88% from the income at the beginning of hostilities. By August 1945, as compared with August 1939, agricultural income was up 191%, or had almost tripled. Increased incomes were experienced especially on meat animals, dairy products, grains, poultry, and eggs. Ohio farm prices, as a whole, increased nearly 90% above the 1935-39 averages, while prices paid by farmers increased by about 50%. The social effect of this increased income to Ohio's rural population becomes even more significant when it is considered with the probable reduction of farm population through the draft and the migration of farm labor to industrial centers.

Prisoner of War Camp—Defiance

A preliminary survey of the possibilities of establishing a Prisoner of War Camp in Defiance County was made in July 1944 at the request of the Ohio War Manpower Commission. The proposed camp was to be a branch of the Prisoner of War Camp located at Camp Perry. From this survey it was determined that a definite need for prisoner of war labor existed in the Defiance area and that the former Civilian Conservation Corps camp located on East Second Street would be suitable for about six hundred prisoners.

Under the command of Captain Frank Bodenhorn one hundred and thirty German prisoners of war were sent from Camp Perry to Defiance on August 4, 1944. A tight guard was established around the area until the prisoners completed building a barbed wire fence eight feet high around the stockade site. Flood lights and guard towers were also placed around the entire compound. This work required three sixteen-hour work days.

The residents of Defiance made an immediate and lasting impression on the American personnel. The Defiance Chapter of the Red Cross, represented by Edward F. Wanley and Mrs. Helen Lawler, called on the Commanding Officer before the convoy had completed unloading and offered their services. Several local groups, the Red Cross, Rotary Club, Public Library, and many individuals jointly fitted up a day room for the guards before the camp had become fairly settled. The citizens of the community cooperated with the personnel of the camp throughout the period that the camp was activated.

After the camp was established it was necessary to erect three additional buildings, a barracks and a mess hall for the guards and a mess hall for the prisoners.

The camp was established to provide labor for the tomato fields and canning plants in the immediate vicinity. At first there was little demand for the labor, but after a few farmers had used some of the prisoners and found that they did good work and were not to be feared, the demand increased by leaps and bounds. The original plan was that not more than six hundred prisoners of war would be kept at Defiance for a period of three months. When, however, it was learned that their services could be used the year around, the camp was winterized. At the peak of activity in the fall of 1945, there were some eight hundred prisoners in the camp. Since the barracks were not adequate for this number, tents were erected between the hutments for about three hundred prisoners of war. The farmers in the Defiance area used the prisoners to pick tomatoes, to harvest wheat and corn, to fill silos, and to build fences. This labor was also used to increase industrial production in the community. One select group completely manned a large plant using only a few civilians as supervisors. Others worked in canning plants, tile mills, fertilizer factories, feed mills, furniture factories, trailer factories, and packing plants. During the period the prisoners worked in Defiance and the surrounding territory, they earned for the United States Treasury some five hundred thousand dollars.

No difficulties were experienced in handling the prisoners during the period of activation. One prisoner did become despondent and committed suicide by drowning in the Maumee River on August 20, 1944.

After the camp was closed on December 15, 1945, the Army turned over to the State of Ohio all buildings which had been erected, including a wash room complete with plumbing and water heaters, two mess halls complete with tables and ranges, some thirty space heaters, two large refrigerators, and considerable other equipment. It was felt that the cost of moving this property would exceed its value and the state officials were anxious to secure the material for use by state troops.

1. Ohio Agricultural Experiment Station, *Bimonthly Bulletin* 28 (January–February 1943): 3–4.

2. James H. Rodabaugh, "Ohio's War Record," *Communikay* 4 (April 1946): 2–6; and "Prisoner of War Camp—Defiance," *Communikay* 5 (September 1946): 4–5.

3. Mimeograph Bulletin No. 157, Department of Rural Economics and Rural Sociology, Ohio State University, Columbus. December 1942.

XV.2. The Mobilization of Ohio Industry for War

At the onset of war, Ohio ranked fourth among the various states in industrial production. As part of the large midwestern zone of heavy industry, Ohio developed around basic manufacturing: iron and steel production, heavy machinery, and automotive parts and rubber products. War contracts expanded and somewhat refocused that industrialism from 1940 to 1945. In Ohio, as in other industrial states, wartime investment capital flowed toward three key defense industries—aircraft, ordnance, and shipbuilding. With the allocation of dollars went the reallocation of labor, both skilled and unskilled, resulting in the expansion of many urban centers and the birth of many new communities. The establishment of large defense plants and publicly owned and operated arsenals and munitions factories had a considerable impact on the distribution of population in the state, constructing "new" communities like the residential housing for federal workers at Windham.

The following summary, taken from James H. Rodabaugh's "Ohio's War Record,"[1] provides an assessment of the nature and degree of the mobilization of the state's industrial plant and its factory workforce.

Ohio's great record of contribution to the war effort was made in industry. The manufacture of iron and steel and their products, vehicles, metal and metal products other than iron and steel, and rubber products experienced the largest increases during the war.

It was in the manufacture of iron and steel and their products that the Middle West was really the world heartland of this war. Iron ore came by boat from the great Mesabi Range through the Lakes to various ports. It was this carrying trade that lifted the Great Lakes tonnage to 184,155,384 net tons in 1944. This figure was 2 ¼ times greater than all the war cargoes carried that year by America's Atlantic-Pacific ocean-going merchant vessels. The number of Ohio's employees in the iron and steel industries jumped from 273,166 in June 1940 to 455,000 in June 1943, an increase of 63%; the number employed in the manufacture of vehicles increased from 45,536 to 244,210 — an increase of 436%; the number in the manufacture of metal products increased from 37,497 to 86,806 — or 131.5%; the number in rubber manufacturing increased 56% — from 46,626 to 72,643. In the three years 1940 to 1943, total employment in Ohio's major manufacturing industries increased 68% — from 754,886 to 1,268,685. All employment in Ohio increased 55% above the 1935-39 level by August 1943. From that time there was a steady decline of 31% by November 1945. . . .

The expanding labor market was accompanied by increasing wages. Between 1940 and 1943 Ohio manufacturing wage earners' average annual earnings increased 65% — from $1529 to $2524. By the beginning of 1945, these wage earners were averaging $53.00 for a 46 to 47-hour week. In general, however, wages declined 11% during 1945 from the 1944 level. By the end of the year the average was down to $44.76 for a 42-hour week. Between 1940 and 1943 clerical workers in manufacturing increased their annual earnings an average of 36% — from $1732 to $2354. At the same time salespeople (not traveling) increased but 32% — from $1859 to $2455. At the end of World War I there was still nearly a 24% differential between the wage earners and the salespeople. The point is that wage earners are receiving greater incomes as a result of the present war, and that clerical people and salespeople, whose incomes have not risen proportionately, have fallen — so far as their economic position is concerned — into the proletariat. Whether or not this will reflect upon their political and economic attitudes is an interesting question for the future.

The demand for labor opened the gates for white women and Negroes. In 1940 the Negro accounted for 2 1/2% of the total employment in war industries; in 1945 he accounted for 8.2% of the total. In the year previous to our entry into World War II, the United States Employment Service in Ohio placed only 3% of its Negro registrants in manufacturing industries; in 1944, when six times as many Negroes were placed in jobs by the U.S.E.S., 55% of them went into manufacturing. In 1940 the Negro supplied 2% of the skilled workers in Ohio industries; by 1945 he was furnishing 8%. Although Negroes received larger incomes than before the war, they were still, in general, in the lower income brackets. The result was that in the recent strikes the Negroes were the chief group to apply for relief. The Negro also made gains in participation in a number of labor unions, especially in the C.I.O. Thousands of women also went to work during the war period, being employed especially in aircraft industries, precision work, and sales and service industries. In Columbus the number of women workers reached a peak of 38% of total employment in July 1945. After V-J Day 70 to 80% of those applying for unemployment compensation were women. In July 1945 in Columbus women were drawing an average wage of 80 cents an hour in industry, 50 cents in service trades, and

5 to 6 dollars a day for household labor; by January 1946 these wages had reduced by approximately one third, except in the service trades. Office workers, too, who were demanding $125 to $150 a month had dropped to $100 to $150 a month average.

In Ohio by August 1943 total payrolls had increased 198% above the 1935–1939 level. This includes, of course, increased wages, 55% greater employment, and more manhours worked. Since that peak was reached there has been a reduction to 123% above the 1935–39 level by November 1945. During the war another economic revolution was in the making. In 1939 salaries and wages absorbed 66% of industrial income; by 1944 they absorbed 72%. At the same time proprietors' and property incomes reduced from 27% to 23%. Other income, i.e., from pensions, relief, and social security programs, reduced from 7% to 5%. The question is, of course, how far the middle incomes, i.e., the property and proprietors', may or can be reduced before the owners surrender their controls. The exigencies of war narrowed the owners' and investors' margin by more than 11% and extended the differential between incomes of salary and wages and property and proprietors' by nearly 26%. Thus, as far as income is concerned, the wage and salary earner is absorbing an increasingly larger share.

1. James H. Rodabaugh, "Ohio's War Record," *Communikay* 4 (April 1946): 2–6.

XV.3. Expanding the State's Transportation Infrastructure: Ohio's Wartime Highway System

The development of Ohio's highway system provides further evidence of the larger role played by government, whether federal or state, in the wartime activities of Ohioans. The Highway Department acted resolutely throughout the war era to assist farmers in crop planting and harvesting to provide adequate roads for the transportation of war materiel produced at defense plants within the state, and to move troops and their equipment to and from bases in the state.

Throughout the period of emergency, state highway administrators worked within guidelines set by federal agencies and the military that restricted the use of "critical materials" for construction purposes. Regardless of the restrictions, Ohio's Highway Department successfully extended the state's road network during the course of the war. From 1939 to 1943, the state contracted for 931 different projects totaling 2,425 miles at an expense of $86,419,829.[1] The following excerpt from the Report of the Ohio Department of Highways, *1939–1943 chronicles that agency's efforts to assist Ohioans in need, to cope (often in ingenious ways) with the numerous restraints on road construction and maintenance, and to help systematize the state's highways.*

WARTIME ACTIVITIES

HIGHWAY ORDNANCE COMPANY FOR ARMY

In 1942, the Ohio Department of Highways was requested by Charles Upham, Engineer-Director of the American Road Builders' Association, to secure personnel for new ordnance companies for the United States Army. Mr. Upham's request came at the direct behest of the Army, which was seeking to tap the road building industry's vast reservoir of skills essential for ordnance type of work.

The Department, through Director Sours, immediately publicized the intended formation of such a company in Ohio, and advertised for the necessary personnel, particularly urging the full cooperation and enlistment of its own qualified employees. Each of the twelve division offices of the Department became a recruiting center, accepting applications and seeking candidates for the Captain, three First Lieutenants and four Second Lieutenants who were to form the commissioned officers of the company.

In August, 1942, Paul E. Boyer of Anna, Chief Mechanic for the Department in Division Seven at Sidney, was selected by Army officers as Captain. During September, while the other officers reported to Camp Perry for training, Captain Boyer interviewed over 700 applicants for the company at various points in Ohio until 180 officers and men had been chosen.

Now known as the 528th Ordnance Company, these Ohioans spent the summer of 1943 on maneuvers under simulated combat conditions. Upon completion of the maneuvers, the company moved to Pine Camp, New York and in November an official card was received by the Department giving the new address of the unit as A.P.O. 4915, New York, New York.

SPECIAL ACTIVITIES

"Help The Farmer" Program

In the last week in May, 1943, the farmers of Ohio were confronted with an unusual condition. Incessant rains during the month of May had prevented the plowing and preparation of land for the planting of corn and soy beans and the time was fast approaching when these crops should be planted in order to mature before early frosts. This condition was particularly aggravated in the northwestern and central western portions of the State.

Coming at a time when every effort was being expended to help out in the war effort by increasing food production, this condition became a matter of serious concern. Officials of the Department of Agriculture, the Ohio State University Agriculture Extension Service and the Department of Highways formulated a plan to use Highway Department tractors in critical areas. This plan met the immediate support of Governor Bricker and was put in operation.

The Ohio State University Agriculture Extension Service was established as the operating agency for the placement of tractors on the farms and also set reasonable rates to charge for this service. Wheel-type tractors normally used for highway weed mowing and crawler tractors used for heavier work were assigned to the farm work. One, two, three, and five bottom plows were utilized with these tractors and as a result 4,119 acres were plowed, 8,614 acres were disced, 971 acres were cultipacked, dragged or harrowed and 175 acres were planted. One hundred and forty-four tractors worked on three eight-hour shifts in order to complete the work within the limited time available. This program received much favorable commendation as a real contribution to the home front effort. A similar crisis developed during the canning season and many Highway Department trucks were used to help get produce to the canneries. . . .

LOCATION, DESIGN AND PLANS
Many changes in design due to war scarcities

The impact of war resulted in a scarcity of steel, lumber, rubber, copper, bituminous material and many other construction materials. Changes in the design of pavement and drainage structures have been required to allow use of less critical materials. In view of the lowering of design standards coupled with the shortage of manpower and the increase in heavy truck traffic, it can be expected that the life of the war time constructed pavements will be somewhat lessened not only in Ohio but also throughout the nation.

The war restrictions have prevented the use of metal guard rail and castings for drainage structures.

Since guard rail metal could not be used, posts set to the proper interval for the metal rail were considered adequate to protect traffic under the reduced war time speeds. When metal becomes available it will be placed on the existing posts.

Manhole tops were re-designed to be constructed of concrete, materially reducing the amount of metal used as compared to the heavy castings normally used.

A catch basin grating was designed of wood while another was designed to use pre-cast concrete ribs. All of these temporary designs were made so that the permanent and durable standard designs could be used subsequent to the war.

The location of a highway improvement is of extreme importance. The factors determining locations are economy and safety. The costs of right of way and construction must be justified by savings to the motorist both in miles traveled and time saved. Considerable study has been given to this problem. Through the medium of aerial photographs the general path of a new or re-located highway has been determined, after which the necessary refinements have been established on the ground by the survey parties. Definite economies in time and money have resulted.

COORDINATION OF WAR PRIORITIES FOR HIGHWAYS

The road building industry, like all other industry, was brought under the priority system during the period of national defense activity prior to the actual declaration of war. It was determined that it was essential to expedite the construction of access roads to Army and Navy establishments, to war industries and to improve weak links of the strategic network of highways. This resulted in the establishment of a system of preference ratings for the various types of projects, with the highway projects most essential to the defense program receiving A-1 ratings and those least essential receiving A-10 ratings. These ratings were assigned so that the defense projects with the higher rating would receive priority in delivery of critical materials.

After Pearl Harbor the War Production Board issued Conservation Order No. L-41, deferring for the duration of the emergency all construction not essential to the war. Under this order it became necessary for the State to apply for authority to begin construction on projects requiring priority assistance to secure critical materials. Since

March 1943 it has been necessary for the State and other governmental units to request authority to begin construction on any project which costs one thousand dollars or more. This applies to all construction projects whether or not critical materials are required. This broader restriction on construction is necessary to conserve man power for war production.

Essential construction completed despite material shortages

Close co-operation between the Highway Department and the Public Roads Administration expedited acquisition of needed critical materials for essential road building with the result that this construction went forward without loss of time. In addition to the State highway projects numerous county and city projects were handled.

The use of asphalt and tar products for roads and highways was restricted and controlled from July 1, 1942 until September 1943. This restriction was placed in effect by Recommendation No. 45, issued by the Petroleum Co-ordinator for War. During this period the State Highway Department handled and transmitted to the Public Roads Administration requests for 2740 individual projects for the counties, cities, and State. The restrictions imposed by this order reduced the amount of bituminous material used on highways and driveways sufficiently to permit the pavement of military airports and roads used primarily for the transportation of war material.

1. State of Ohio, Department of Highways, *Report of the Ohio Department of Highways, 1939-1943* (Columbus: State of Ohio, 1944), 12.

XV.4. The "Toledo Plan" for Industrial Peace: The Postwar Experiment in Labor-Management Committees

Toledo's experiment in labor-management relations was part of a larger movement in industrial relations among industrial capitalist nations. In the immediate postwar period, Belgium and France established, and Canada continued, labor-management councils for the conciliation of industrial relations disputes. In the United States, Vermont created a statewide council and Louisville, Kentucky, established a similar board for its industries. One of the most publicized postwar labor relations experiments, however, was the eighteen-member committee established by the City of Toledo.

In the tradition of the nation's wartime labor boards, the Toledo experiment was tripartite, composed of "impartial" civic representatives, as well as labor and management representatives.[1]

The Toledo Plan

It was almost civil war. All afternoon and night, on Wednesday, May 23, strikers, strikebreakers, police, and company guards battled before the Electric Auto-Lite plant, in the occasional glare of a strikebreaker's burning automobile and amid clouds of choking tear gas and raining bricks. The National Guard was called out at midnight. On Thursday, when

the battle resumed, the soldiers used their bayonets. When a dozen of their own had been hos-
pitalized with cracked heads, they used their guns. When it was all over two men were dead,
200 had been injured, and the plant had suffered $150,000 damage.

That was in 1934. Toledo will long remember those bloody days. The strike was one of the worst in Ohio's history. It followed on three years of dry rot that began in 1931 when four of the city's banks had closed in one day. Thereafter, unemployment swelled. Toledo relief rolls led the nation. Businesses failed in waves. Labor violence gave the city a black eye. People moved away. The once prosperous News-Bee declined, was sold, and disappeared. The city that had produced a Brand Whitlock and a "Golden Rule" Jones could find no new leaders of courage and vision. Toledo felt, and looked, sick.

As the year 1946 ends Toledo has made an impressive comeback from those bitter times. The war, with its tonic effect on industry, gave the city the push it needed to find itself. From December 1941 to May 1945, Toledo war contracts averaged $1,000,000,000 a year—compared with a 1939 total of $361,000,000.

Willys-Overland sent jeeps around the world; Libby-Owens-Ford made 1,500,000 pieces of custom-built safety glass on aircraft war orders; a new Packard-operated aircraft-engine plant and a propeller plant were built; established manufacturers like Auto-Lite, National Supply, and Spicer (now the Dana Corp.) expanded; employment, in 1943, reached 173,000. It fell to 148,625 in September 1945 but has climbed back up to 158,000. And $110,000,000 of industrial expansion now on the books is expected to lift employment to the wartime peak by next October.

The Strike Doctors: More important, the city that watched the 1934 battle of the Auto-Lite plant, is trying to become a national leader in industrial peace. In April 1945, the City Council established a Labor-Management-Citizens Committee, the brain child of Vice Mayor Michael V. DiSalle. Composed of eighteen representatives—six from labor, six from management, and six from civic leaders—it serves as a voluntary mediation group. Its only power is the force of public opinion. But it has halved the rate of man-days lost in strikes. In only two cases were strikes called after the LMC had a chance to intervene—and those two lasted only two weeks. So far, 43 unions and 267 employers have asked for "certificates of participation," signifying their willingness to abide by the "Toledo Plan." Under the setup, when a strike impends, two members of the panel—one each from management and labor—talk to both sides and try to sell them the idea of getting together.

When a strike is actually called, the committee offers conciliation. If both sides accept, the chairman appoints three men to hear the case and make a recommendation. The keystone of the policy rests on the agreement of both sides that in any dispute the community's interest comes first.

The Toledo plan may soon get a try-out on a national scale. Recently its father, DiSalle, was called to the White House to explain it. Soon afterward, the United States Conciliation Service announced that a modified version of the plan would be tried out in its Philadelphia district. If successful, it would be extended to all the other districts.

1. *Newsweek,* 30 December 1946, 56–57.

XVI. Ohio in the Age of Affluence

Many Ohioans were able to enjoy the broad-based prosperity of the post–World War II period. Pent-up consumer demand, a dramatic surge in productivity, and the pump-priming effect of government spending fueled this prosperity. Although troubled somewhat by periodic recessions and a rising national debt, the national economic engine made the time period one of enormous economic abundance. More important, the standard of living for average Americans rose sharply; home, car, and television ownership became widespread in the decade of the fifties.

Ohio benefited as much as any state from the nation's postwar growth. The state's population jumped by 22 percent during the 1950s, reaching 9.7 million by the end of the decade. The flow of migrants from the South, both white and black, continued even after the war. By 1950, over one-half million African Americans resided in the state, making up 6.5 percent of the population.

The state's core industries thrived during this postwar period. The "Big Three" car makers added production and assembly capacity, solidifying Ohio's place as the second biggest auto-producing state behind Michigan. New industries such as aluminum moved into the Ohio River Valley to take advantage of the cheap river transportation and publicly subsidized power generation.

Government played a significant role in facilitating the state's economic growth. In addition to supporting power generation and water transport, all levels of government facilitated private industry, initially by building or updating the state's road network, then by investing in a wide variety of public services and infrastructure. During the administration of Gov. James A. Rhodes, the state inaugurated an unprecedented public investment campaign. Financed by an ultimately burdensome expansion of the state's debt, Ohio embarked on a massive capital building program in four areas: highways, higher education, parks and recreation, and industrial and commercial development. Rhodes deemed higher education of special importance, believing campuses should be so situated as to be accessible to every resident of the state no matter how far they resided from major urban centers. Therefore, Rhodes campaigned vigorously for the establishment of new state universities, the expansion of existing institutions, the construction of satellite "branch campuses" and community colleges, and the development of vocational and technical education centers around the state.

Although most Ohioans profited from the extensive postwar development and prosperity, not all groups enjoyed the benefits. Public education in some areas of the state was segregated by race in the early postwar period, as was residential housing. Industrial corporations, trade unions, and the apprenticeship programs they offered for new workers often excluded African Americans, a minority that composed about 8 percent of the state's population after the Second World War. Influenced by an increasingly national civil rights movement that gained momentum from the 1954 Supreme Court ruling in *Brown* v. *The Board of Education of Topeka, Kansas,* and fueled by the successful Montgomery, Alabama, bus boycott, Ohio lawmakers began to tackle the controversial questions of race relations and civil rights in the late 1950s.

In their effort to address long-standing inequities, the General Assembly enacted a landmark piece of civil rights legislation in 1959. Embracing the wartime spirit of economic opportunity for all able-bodied workers, Ohio lawmakers framed a set of fair employment practices to prohibit discrimination based on "race, color, religion, national origin, or ancestry."

To enforce this fight for equality under the law, the 1959 legislation mandated the establishment of a state civil rights commission. Lawmakers empowered the commissioners and their advisers with the authority to conduct investigations into discriminatory practices, hear the complaints of citizens, enact rulings or regulations to further the cause of civil rights, and, significantly, to direct an educational campaign in the public schools to alter cultural attitudes about race.

In a 1960 report, the civil rights commission outlined the extent of discrimination in various types of public facilities and accommodations across Ohio. The report confirmed the widely held view among experts that the old 1884 Public Accommodations Law lacked effectiveness. The commissioners reported that black Ohioans were unable to enjoy the economic, educational, medical, and recreational opportunities that the majority of the state's citizens benefited from on a daily basis. Throughout the decade of the sixties, the commission and the legislature set about rectifying those injustices.

Although the sixties witnessed massive economic growth, public investment, and legislative innovation, they also saw an increasing divisiveness in society resulting from the U.S. commitment to the conflict in Southeast Asia. The nation's deepening involvement in Vietnam after 1964 resulted in the growth of an increasingly militant antiwar movement. For five years that movement contested the federal government's military and foreign policy agenda. Antiwar protest around the nation culminated in demonstrations triggered by the 1 May 1970 invasion of Cambodia by U.S. and South Vietnamese troops. Kent State University student activists, participants in the nationwide student protest movement, reacted forcefully to the reality of a wider war in Asia. Kent activists torched the old ROTC building on the evening of 2 May and organized a protest rally for Monday, 4 May. Demonstrators and law enforcement officers confronted each other at the midday rally on the Kent commons. Unable to disperse the demonstrators, authorities committed guardsmen in an effort to quell the protest. In the tension-packed atmosphere, Ohio National Guard troops, frustrated by their inability to dislodge angry protestors from the high ground, began firing into the assembly. The gunfire ended the lives of four students.

In the immediate postwar years, the economic abundance and resulting higher living standards for the state's majority population led them to agree on a wide range of social and cultural, as well as political and economic, issues. By the late 1960s that consensus was crumbling. As a long era of growth and prosperity was drawing to a close, the ill effects of rapid growth began to appear. Environmental crises, a large, encumbering debt, racial strife, and student unrest were some of the problems that plagued Ohio and its people as the decade of the seventies unfolded.

XVI.1. Postwar Industrialization: The Basis for Prosperity and Growth in the State of Ohio

The United States enjoyed an unprecedented period of prosperity in the two decades following the Second World War. Ohio was both a cause and a beneficiary of that prosperity. The state benefited from the expansion of industrial plants and the payment of high wages in the private sector that went with the postwar wave of growth.

As the following selections demonstrate, Ohio continued to be a leading manufacturing state. But in the postwar years, several factors led to the extension of Ohio's industrialization beyond those traditional core industries to include such new industries as aluminum and electrical power generation. Raymond Moley emphasizes the pro-corporate, anti-CIO stance of the state's governing elite. From another perspective, it is obvious that inexpensive water transportation and a variety of governmental subsidies for industry made Ohio and the region an attractive place in the eyes of dozens of business site selection committees. The Ohio River Valley, in particular, expanded its manufacturing facilities to serve new atomic energy facilities and produce a variety of commodities for eastern markets.

The first selection offers readers a sample of Raymond Moley's unique perspective on the development and an excellent summary of the state's economy.[1] The second selection is an essay on the Ohio River Valley that furnishes a regional view of Ohio's success.[2]

Ohio, An Industrial Empire

*I*f you were to stand on the lake front in Cleveland one of these spring days, you would find a deep fascination in the endless succession of long ships, riding deep, moving toward Lake Erie ports. The cargoes of these ships are pouring into an industrial complex in which boundless optimism is the spirit of the moment. And great expectations are wholly justified by the economic and political facts.

Prosperity is no new experience for Ohio. In the 1860s and 1870s oil flowing from wells in Pennsylvania and eastern Ohio made Cleveland the chief refinery of the nation and brought a daring young man named Rockefeller the beginnings of a fabulous fortune. Cleveland and other harbors on the Great Lakes became the ports of entry for vast treasures of iron ore from the Mesabi and other fields near the upper lakes. This ore, with limestone from Michigan and coking coal from the Appalachians, created a broad industrial band which stretches from Buffalo to Pittsburgh and Wheeling, and to Gary and Chicago. That area became an industrial Ruhr, dwarfing its European counterpart.

In recent years any one of three ports in Ohio—Cleveland, Ashtabula, and Conneaut—have unloaded as much iron ore as the combined capacity of Germany, Japan, and Italy at the beginning of the second world war. Today the combined unloadings at these ports are greater than the capacity of Russia and all its satellites.

For a few years grave apprehensions lurked in the minds of businessmen in northern Ohio. Years of intensive mining to meet the needs of war had eaten away the Mesabi and other sources of high-grade ore. Then relief came with the opening of new sources in Labrador and the final approval of the St. Lawrence Seaway. Ohio stands to gain first and probably most from the new avenue.

Today Ohio ranks second to New York in manufacturing. The state turns out a large share of the nation's supply of iron and steel, rubber products, automotive parts, industrial machinery, machine tools, and construction and mining equipment. Its schools and colleges train great numbers of the technicians and managers required in industry.

Long ago there were indications that Ohio might be the center of the automobile industry. But Michigan, for a number of reasons, forged ahead. Now, however, there is evidence that the tide is returning. Cleveland boasts a new Ford foundry and engine assembly plant, the largest in the world, and immense General Motors plants. A Chrysler plant is building at Twinsburg. Since the outbreak of the second world war, Cincinnati has experienced an orderly expansion. Automotive, aircraft, and electrical plants have moved into Cincinnati to join the old, well-managed companies that made the city "solid." Akron thrives still as the "rubber capital of the world."

Aluminum manufacturing is building in the Ohio Valley, with plants by Kaiser and Olin Mathieson. A substantial chemical industry is growing along Lake Erie near Ashtabula where there is a fruitful combination of fresh, cold water, salt, and silica plus accessible limestone, electric power, and transportation facilities.

A very important political factor has encouraged expansion and drawn industry to Ohio, notably in the two decades in which the CIO has become a political force in other states. Most of Ohio's major industrial cities have had good and conservative government. Cincinnati has had not only good but reform government for several years. Cleveland has had excellent mayors for twenty years.

The state has had conservative governors since the election of John Bricker in 1938. Frank Lausche is serving his fifth term. Lausche has been plain evidence to all that there will be no capture of the state's government by the CIO such as has befallen the state of Michigan. There is no reason why industry will not flow to regions where there is some assurance of immunity from class government. This political climate will have its effect for years to come. All Ohioans will benefit—those who work and those who invest alike.

Big Boom Along the Ohio

William H. Hessler

From Pittsburgh, where the Allegheny and Monongahela sweep past the Golden Triangle to form the Ohio, it is 981 miles to Cairo, Illinois, where the high-banked, swiftly falling Ohio empties into the Mississippi. This 981-mile river is by all odds the busiest inland waterway in the United States, carrying more than twice the tonnage of its nearest competitor, the Gulf Intracoastal Waterway, and that passing through the Panama Canal.

The Ohio is the spinal artery of a rich and fast-growing industrial empire of steel, chemicals, aluminum, oil refining, atomic energy, electric power, and diversified manufacturing. The band of hilly country along the Ohio and its navigable tributaries is a super Ruhr. It produces more chemicals than the Ruhr Valley, three times as much steel, and many more than three times as much coal.

Since 1950, industrial expansion along the Ohio has been headlong. New or expanded plants represent fully $8 billion of investment in the seven years. And if one reaches up the tributaries—the Kanawha, Kentucky, Cumberland, Green, and Barren Rivers—to add in the new investment in plant in this greater area, the total since 1950 is more like $11 billion.

On the surface all this looks like a free-enterprise boom in the best American tradition, and in some part it is. But under a magnifying glass it has quite a different look. Two massive government investments have been important factors. One is in a complex of great atomic-energy installations that cost $1.6 billion—pump priming on a lordly scale—and the other is in river improvements, which over a span of 135 years have cost the government close to $200 million, or $300 million if maintenance and operating costs are counted in. It would be hard, perhaps impossible, to single out any major private investment in the Ohio River Valley in late years—certainly in heavy industry— that does not depend in some part for its validity on one of these two public investments.

The Erratic, Abundant Ohio

The economy of this region is a closely woven fabric. Coal, which remains our greatest source of energy, is lavishly spread through western Pennsylvania, West Virginia, southern Ohio, Kentucky, Tennessee, and the southern parts of Indiana and Illinois. These coal deposits, America's richest and largest, lie athwart the Ohio and its tributaries. Carried cheaply by river barge, this coal is not only vital in steelmaking but also makes possible the low-cost generation of electric power. This in turn fosters industries of every sort, but especially those which require enormous supplies of energy, such as the processing of aluminum and uranium.

The two basic sources of the spectacular growth of this industrial empire are the river itself and the coal fields—products of neither free enterprise nor government but gifts of Providence. Although erratic, the Ohio always provides abundant water. And water is singularly important. To make one ton of steel it takes seventy tons of water. To refine one barrel of oil it takes eighteen barrels of water. And for every ton of coal burned in a modern electric generating plant it takes one thousand tons of water to cool the condensers. For example, the new generating plant at Clifty Creek, Indiana, uses 1.4 billion gallons of water a day, more than New York City uses for all purposes.

The Ohio also provides amazingly low-cost transport for bulky commodities. There is the Ashland Oil and Refining Company, for instance, with headquarters and a refinery at Ashland, on the river at the northeast corner of Kentucky. Ashland has a fleet of modern diesel towboats and integrated steel barges that bring crude oil from the Gulf of Mexico up the Mississippi and the Ohio to Ashland, seventeen hundred miles, at a cost of one cent a gallon, less than it costs the same company to move gasoline ten miles by tank truck from the refinery into the nearby city of Ashland. . . .

The greatest gains from low-cost transport are in coal. The good coals of West Virginia and Kentucky can be brought by barge up or down the Ohio and delivered at riverbank for $1.25 to $1.40 a ton less than rail-borne coal. On this basis, electricity generated in steam plants on the banks of the Ohio is fully competitive with that of hydroelectric plants on the Tennessee River—and with allowance for better access to national markets, competitive with the cheapest hydro power in the West. It is this fact that has brought the aluminum industry into the valley and has led the Atomic Energy Commission to locate three giant installations in the valley since 1950—a gaseous-diffusion plant in Pike County, Ohio, north of Portsmouth; a similar plant near Paducah, Kentucky; and a feed-processing plant at Fernald, Ohio, on the outskirts of Cincinnati, to process ore concentrates—the simpler process preceding the gaseous-diffusion operation. Together the three installations represent an investment of $1.6 billion of public money.

An Economic Chain Reaction

In the interest of security against enemy attack, the AEC would have preferred greater dispersion, but so vast were its power requirements that the middle and lower reaches of the Ohio seemed a logical choice. The two gaseous-diffusion plants, Portsmouth and Paducah, each require two million kilowatts of firm power seven days a week, 365 days a year. If we add in the third gaseous-diffusion plant at Oak ridge, the total power consumption is more than fifty billion kilowatt-hours a year. That is twice the amount used by the highly industrialized state of Ohio, and about one-tenth of the total energy used in the United States. Surplus power in such quantities was not at hand, and so four of the largest generating plants in the world were built to serve the Portsmouth and Paducah facilities.

This is where AEC's $1.6-billion investment began to produce an economic chain reaction. First, of course, was the construction cost of the installation—a payroll of $2 million a month at Portsmouth-AEC, spread over four essentially rural counties of Ohio. Then came the power plants. One was built by TVA, the 1.5-million-kilowatt Shawnee station alongside the Paducah diffusion plant. The other three, nearly as large, were built with private investment funds by two combinations of Ohio Valley utility concerns.

The two built to serve Portsmouth-AEC, the Clifty Creek and Kyger Creek stations, were designed, erected, and operated by the Ohio Valley Electric Corporation, which is owned by fifteen utility companies in the region.

Located near Madison, Indiana, and Gallipolis, Ohio, almost three hundred miles apart, they are virtually identical, and are the last word in steam power generation. These plants feed current to Portsmouth-AEC at 330,000 volts—the highest voltage used in the United States for power transmission. They are efficiently planned, use low-priced river coal, and have only one customer, who uses power at a uniform rate, day and night, the year round. Consequently the AEC gets its power for less than four mills per kilowatt-hour. This is of interest to taxpayers, since these AEC plants spend nearly half their operating budgets for electric power. . . .

The Relevant Rule of Thumb
. . . The economic chain reaction of AEC investment reaches back into the coal fields of adjoining states, into the barge trade and railroads, but it also reaches out in other directions. There is, for example, a new super-highway in southern Ohio, a region not at all famous for good roads, linking the AEC-Goodyear plant with Portsmouth to the south and Columbus to the north. There is new housing for perhaps half of Goodyear's twenty-eight hundred employees there—the other half having been recruited from among natives of the four-county area. There are new supermarkets, new filling stations, new opportunities for professional men, new recreational facilities—a whole maze of service industries that have come in or expanded to serve a larger population and share in the spending of a new payroll—currently $1,350,000 a month at AEC-Goodyear.

There also has been purely private investment in industrial plant. Much the same factors that led the AEC to choose plant sites in Atom Valley have brought various large chemical enterprises into the river valleys of West Virginia, and steel production has been expanded at a dozen points along the Ohio. This flood of new investment in heavy industry is augmented by countless smaller outlays in a diversity of lines—from the manufacture of Geiger counters and guided-missile control systems to jet aircraft and machine tools.

General industry is attracted by economical electric power, and in turn, capacity has been soaring along this valley during and since the war. In round numbers during the past seven years privately owned power companies have invested half a billion dollars in generating facilities to serve AEC's massive needs, and $1.5 billion in other new and expanded plants to serve private industry and commercial and household consumers.

The most spectacular case of new free enterprise in the valley is the arrival of aluminum within the past three years—Kaiser, Alcoa, and Olin Mathieson, each with a plant in Ravenswood, West Virginia, will serve to illustrate. Kaiser had operated only on the West Coast with hydroelectric power, for aluminum is a fantastically power-hungry process. Kaiser has built and operates a finishing plant with nine hundred employees making sheet, plate, and foil aluminum. Kaiser also has seven thousand workers at present on construction of a primary-reduction plant at the same site, which by 1958 will be turning out 440 million pounds of ingots a year. Total investment now exceeds $200 million. A permanent work force of forty-five hundred to five thousand is anticipated that will stretch the seams of Ravenswood (1954 pop., 1,170).

Kaiser's shift from the West Coast hydroelectric country to the upper Ohio Valley is justified economically by three factors. One is nearness to markets. About seventy per cent of the nation's total market for aluminum products is within five hundred miles of Ravenswood—and two thousand miles or more from the Pacific Northwest. The second factor is economical power. Kaiser buys electricity—enough for all Chicago's needs—from the Ohio Power Company at about four mills per kilowatt-hour. To be sure, this is twice the cost of hydro power in the West, but Kaiser saves the cost of moving bauxite, or aluminum oxide, across the country and then bringing most of the finished products back. The third factor is water transportation. The bauxite comes from strip mines in Jamaica, is processed (or will be) at a mill on the Louisiana coast, and then reduced to metal and fabricated for consumers at the riverbank plant in West Virginia. The whole operation is tied together by water transportation, the cheapest there is. . . .

Let's Face It

The valley of the Tennessee and to a lesser degree those of the Missouri, the Columbia, and the Colorado have undergone immense and invigorating changes as a result of Federal investment. In the Ohio Valley there is no OVA, but there is an orderly program of development.

If the dramatic development of the Ohio Valley in late years poses a problem, it is not one of engineering or economics but of semantics. At any gathering of business clans along the Ohio, one may hear stout champions of private enterprise rising in their places after a hearty dinner to sound the praises of private investment, unfettered enterprise, and the wonders of the industrial technology achieved by American business. In the utmost sincerity, these devoted adherents to laissez faire will condemn government interference in business and subsidies to agriculture. Yet without any sense of inconsistency they will plead with equal fervor for the expenditure of new Federal millions for high-level dams along the Ohio and a twelve-foot channel. Needless to say that at the mention of tolls for the use of this canalized river these champions of private enterprise will scream with anguish.

How long will it be until there is an honest recognition that our economic system is a hybrid of public and private initiative, of public and private investment? There are many things that private enterprise can do better. But there are some things government can do better—among them the harnessing of rivers. In the fabulously rich valley of the Ohio, the government has done and is doing a first-rate job. And its work on the river is the foundation of the ebullient prosperity that swirls downstream from Pittsburgh to Cairo, Illinois—981 miles of unruly river, tamed by something akin to socialism for the uses of private enterprise.

1. Raymond Moley, "Ohio, An Industrial Empire," *Newsweek,* 30 April 1956, 112.
2. *The Reporter,* 19 September 1957, 22-25

XVI.2. Funding a Modern Educational System: The 1955 Ohio School Foundation Program

By 1955 lawmakers realized they had to restructure Ohio's educational system. The state's first foundation program law had been enacted in 1935 along with a 3 percent sales tax. Part of the revenues from the tax were allocated to the Public School Fund for distribution to the school districts according to the guidelines established by the school foundation program. The annual allocations of funds, however, only lasted four years, lapsing in 1939. From that year, the public schools received monies directly from the state general revenue fund. By the late 1940s, a new crisis had developed. State support had dwindled dramatically in relation to operating costs. Lawmakers recognized that for the state to halt, if not reverse, this dangerous trend, a revised foundation program had to be established. After a lengthy study, the General Assembly's Ohio School Survey Committee recommended changes that legislators accepted as the basis for a new foundation program in 1955. The following excerpt, from the 1969 "Report of the Committee to Study the School Foundation Program," provides a summary of the formula for public education in the state for the remainder of the era.[1]

The 1955 School Foundation Program

*T*he "new" school foundation program increased substantially the total amount of state support for Ohio's schools and provided financial incentives for the improvement of staffing and programs.

Under the 1955 school foundation program the basic payment to each district was calculated according to a formula which may be abbreviated as follows: Operating Expenses Allowance + Salary and Retirement Allowance + Transportation Allowance – Local Effort = Amount of State Aid.

This equation represents the core mathematical computation used to determine the state's share of total school operating costs. Further explanation of some of the formula's key terms is needed for an understanding of what the computation means.

Teacher Units. The operating expenses allowance, the salary allowance, and the retirement and sick leave allowance are based upon the "teacher unit." The number of teacher units for a district is composed of basic units and additional units. Basic units are computed by dividing the number of pupils in average daily membership (ADM) by 30 for grades one through twelve, and by dividing the number of pupils in kindergarten by 60. Other basic units include special classes for handicapped children and for vocational education . . . .

Additional units for supervision, administration, and special instruction are based upon the total number of basic units computed for the school district. For every 8 basic units, an additional unit is credited for administration and special instruction. One additional unit is allowed for supervision for the first 50 basic units, and one for each 100 basic units thereafter.

The method for calculating the number of teacher units has not been essentially changed since 1955 and remains one of the most fundamental provisions in the foundation formula for the determination of state support. . . .

Guaranteed Minimum Payment. This payment, based on the standard approved teacher unit calculation, assures that no district shall receive less than a set minimum payment per teacher unit from the foundation program. If the total amount of state support, determined by adding together the positive factors and subtracting from this sum the amount of the local effort, is less than the district would receive if the guaranteed minimum scale were used, then state support will be the amount determined by the minimum guarantee.

1. Ohio Legislative Service Commission, *Report of the Committee to Study the Ohio School Foundation Program* (Columbus: State of Ohio, 1969).

XVI.3. Constructing the Modern Transportation Infrastructure: Ohio and the Interstate Highway System

Regardless of wartime modernization efforts, Ohio's state highway system was woefully inadequate for the economic development and population growth of the postwar era. To their credit, Ohio lawmakers recognized the inadequacy of the state's transportation infrastructure and financed its extension through bond issues and a higher gasoline tax in the 1950s. Their most innovative step was the construction of the Ohio Turnpike and the creation of a commission to supervise it. The turnpike, built to link with similar roads in operation or planned for Pennsylvania and Indiana, was one of the state's big success stories, generating enormous revenues from east-west travel across the region.

It was the Interstate Highway System, conceived by the Eisenhower administration and funded mostly by federal tax dollars, that made the greatest impact on the state and the lives of its citizens. The 1956 Interstate Highway Act, the largest and most expensive public works project in the nation's history, provided for the construction of 41,000 miles of superhighways. To a greater degree than any of Eisenhower's defense and economic planners had foreseen, it revolutionized the transportation of goods and people over long distances. In Ohio, as in the rest of the nation, the great roads accelerated the growth of suburbs, increased America's dependency on automobiles, furthered the demise of the nation's rail system, and, initiating a dangerous trend, drove up gasoline consumption.

After a slow start, Ohio took the lead in utilizing federal funds to construct those roads planned for the state. By 1963, the Buckeye State was the leading contractor of interstate road construction in the nation. Although it took years to complete, the network connected the state's capital and its key urban, industrial centers while establishing links to adjacent states.

The following selection, a report that the Ohio Department of Highways prepared in December 1962, not long after the election of Gov. James A. Rhodes, details the early progress of interstate road builders in Ohio and exemplifies the "can-do" spirit of the times.[1]

Ohio's Interstate Highway System

*L*atest reports from the U.S. Bureau of Public Roads place Ohio once again out in front of all other states in the utilization of Interstate Highway funds. As of September 30, 1962, Ohio had amassed a lead of $107 million over the next highest State in total value of Interstate Highway projects completed, and had a lead of over $100 million in the amount of Federal funds allocated for Interstate projects.

These examples of continuing leadership show that Ohio, over the past four years, has gained the maximum advantage from available highway funds by converting revenues into finished highways as rapidly as sound planning and engineering will allow.

Between 1959 and 1963, the Ohio Department of Highways placed 349.6 miles of Interstate Highways under contract at a total cost of $676,118,822. Both of these figures represent an Interstate Highway program that has placed Ohio well ahead of the national schedule for completion of the 41,000 mile Interstate network.

More than half of this investment was for Urban Interstate Highways, serving the long-neglected traffic needs of Ohio's cities. An investment of $352.3 million in Urban Interstate freeways since 1959 has restored balance to a program that had seen only 16¼ miles of these highways placed under contract in 1957–58.

Upon completion of the Interstate system, Ohio will be served by eight Interstate Highways. Urban areas of the state will be further seven by eleven Interstate Spur and Loop Routes. These routes will link all of Ohio's major cities with one another and with the 41,000 mile National Interstate System that will serve 90 per cent of all continental U.S. cities with populations of 50,000 or more.

The $26.70 paid annually (for 15 years) by each Ohio motorist towards the completion of the Interstate System will eventually result in an annual savings of $94. This latter figure will continually increase with added Interstate use over the years.

It is estimated that the following annual benefits will be derived upon completion of Ohio's Interstate System: A saving of 240 lives; Elimination of 60,000 accidents; A saving of $33 million in vehicle operating costs; A saving of $51 million in accident costs; and, A saving of $57 million in reduced truck travel time.

1. Ohio Department of Highways, *4-Year Report to the Governor, 1959–1962* (Columbus: F. J. Heer, 1962), 38.

XVI.4. The Rise of the Modern Civil Rights Movement in Ohio: The 1959 Fair Employment Practices Act

As the Cotton South fell into agricultural decline at midcentury, a movement for the reform of race relations — a civil rights movement — arose in that region to secure equality under the law for those African Americans who remained in Dixie. Throughout the decade of the 1950s, this movement was able to accelerate the rate of change in racial relations. The movement received a boost from the 1954 U.S. Supreme Court decision in Brown v. Board of

Education of Topeka, Kansas, *that struck down legally enforced segregation in schooling. Two years later, Rev. Martin Luther King Jr. led African Americans in Montgomery, Alabama, in a successful boycott of the town's segregated bus transportation system. In 1957, President Dwight D. Eisenhower sent federal troops to enforce court-ordered school desegregation. That same year, Congress passed the first civil rights bill since the era of Reconstruction.*

In Ohio, lawmakers delayed and debated school desegregation. Education administrators argued over whether the state school board could withhold funds from school districts that disregarded the U.S. Supreme Court's 1954 mandate. The Hillsboro School System, the southern Ohio district most noted as a practitioner of segregation, was the target of Ohio civil rights advocates. Debate continued until Ohio Atty. Gen. C. William O'Neill rendered an opinion that the school board had the authority to withhold funds.[1] The pace of change in Ohio began to accelerate as well.

The legislature passed the first in a series of new civil rights laws in 1959.[2] New statutory authority was badly needed. Although the 1884 Public Accommodations Law banned discrimination in public facilities, it was rarely enforced. No state legislation applied directly to discrimination in employment practices according to race, color, religion, or national origin. The passage of the 1959 legislation furnished the state with a code of fair employment practices and a civil rights commission to enforce the law. The intent of lawmakers to make the Ohio Civil Rights Commission an agent of cultural change is evident in the authority it was granted for conducting sweeping educational campaigns in the public schools, as well as exercising broad enforcement powers.

(Amended Senate Bill No. 10)

AN ACT

Be it enacted by the General Assembly of the State of Ohio: . . .
Unlawful discriminatory practices.

Sec. 4112.02. It shall be an unlawful discriminatory practice:

(A) For any employer, because of the race, color, religion, national origin or ancestry of any person, to refuse to hire or otherwise to discriminate against him with respect to hire, tenure, terms, conditions or privileges of employment, or any matter directly or indirectly related to employment.

(B) For an employment agency, because of race, color, religion, national origin, or ancestry to:

(1) Refuse or fail to accept, register, classify properly, or refer for employment, or otherwise to discriminate against any person.

(2) Comply with a request from an employer for referral of applicants for employment if the request indicates directly or indirectly that the employer fails to comply with the provisions of sections 4112.01 to 4112.07, inclusive, of the Revised Code.

(C) For any labor organization to:

(1) Limit or classify its membership on the basis of race, color, religion, national origin or ancestry;

(2) Discriminate against any person or limit his employment opportunities, or otherwise adversely affect his status as an employee, or his wages, hours, or employment conditions, because of his race, color, religion, national origin or ancestry.

(D) For any employer, labor organization, or joint labor-management committee controlling apprentice training programs to discriminate against any person because of his race, color, religion, national origin, or ancestry in admission to, or employment in any program established to provide apprentice training.

(E) Except where based on a bona fide occupational qualification certified in advance by the commission, for any employer, employment agency or labor organization prior to employment or admission to membership, to:

(1) Elicit or attempt to elicit any information concerning the race, color, religion, national origin, or ancestry of an applicant for employment or membership;

(2) Make or keep a record of the race, color, religion, national origin, or ancestry of any applicant for employment or membership;

(3) Use any form of application for employment, or personnel or membership blank seeking information regarding race, color, religion, national origin, or ancestry;

(4) Print or publish or cause to be printed of published any notice or advertisement relating to employment or membership indicating any preference, limitation, specification, or discrimination, based upon race, color, religion, national origin, or ancestry;

(5) Announce or follow a policy of denying, or limiting, through a quota system or otherwise, employment or membership opportunities of any group because of race, color, religion, national origin, or ancestry of such group;

(6) Utilize in the recruitment or hiring of persons any employment agency, placement service, training school or center, labor organization, or any other employee-referring source known to discriminate against persons because of their race, color, religion, national origin, or ancestry.

(F) For any person seeking employment to publish or cause to be published any advertisement which specifies or in any manner indicates his race, color, religion, national origin, or ancestry, or expresses a limitation or preference as to the race, color, religion, national origin, or ancestry of any prospective employer. . . .

Ohio civil rights commission.

Sec. 4112.03. There is hereby created the Ohio civil rights commission to consist of five members, not more than three of whom shall be of the same political party, to be appointed by the governor, with the advice and consent of the senate, one of whom shall be designated by the governor as chairman. . . .

Powers and duties of the commission.

Sec. 4112.04 (A) The commission shall:

(1) Establish and maintain a principal office in the city of Columbus and such other offices within the state as it may deem necessary;

(2) Appoint an executive director who shall serve at the pleasure of the commission and be its principal administrative officer. . . .

(3) Appoint hearing examiners and other employees and agents as it may deem necessary. . . .

(4) Adopt, promulgate, amend and rescind rules and regulations. . . .

(5) Formulate policies to effectuate the purposes of sections 4112.01 to 4112.08. . . .

(6) Receive, investigate and pass upon written charges made under oath of practices prohibited by section 4112.02 of the Revised Code;

(7) Make periodic surveys of the existence and effect of discrimination because of race, color, religion, national origin, or ancestry on the enjoyment of civil rights by persons within the state;

(8) Report, from time to time, but not less than once a year, to the general assembly and the governor, describing in detail the investigations, proceedings and hearings it has conducted and their outcome, the decisions it has rendered and the other work performed by it, ...

1. *Opinions of the Attorney General of Ohio for the Period from January 1, 1956 to January 14, 1957* (Columbus: F. J. Heer, 1957), 514–21.

2. *Legislative Acts Passed and Joint Resolutions Adopted,* vol. 128 (Columbus: F. J. Heer, 1959), 12–16.

XVI.5. The State of Race Relations in Ohio: The 1960 Report of the Ohio Civil Rights Commission on Discrimination

Enforcement of the laws against discrimination in public accommodations and facilities had been a problem since the passage of the state's 1884 law. The 1959 civil rights legislation mandated the establishment, for the first time, of an enforcement agency within the state government. The Ohio Civil Rights Commission set about its work expeditiously. Because the effectiveness of the 1884 act had been questioned numerous times, commissioners decided to conduct a systematic study of the adequacy of that statute. The commission conducted the study within a context of increasing racial unrest: a large number of complaints had been filed with the commission during its first year and interracial tension had heightened during and after picketing of restaurants in Xenia, Lorain, and Cincinnati.[1]

The following excerpts of the findings and recommendations of the commission's investigation into discrimination in public accommodations reveal, in no uncertain terms, the breadth and depth of the problem in Ohio.[2]

DISCRIMINATION IN PUBLIC ACCOMMODATIONS IN OHIO

Summary of Findings and Conclusions

Discrimination in public accommodation and places of public service based on race, color, religion, national origin or ancestry exists in Ohio despite a law declaring such discrimination to be illegal. It exists in big cities and smaller communities and to a greater degree in communities of southern Ohio than in northern Ohio.

The principal recipients of discriminatory treatment are Negroes, dark-skin Puerto Ricans and Mexican-Americans. In few instances were persons of the Jewish faith, and even more rarely of the Catholic faith, discriminated against in public accommodation or services.

Experienced observers believe that discrimination in this field is more widespread than available data indicates because of unreported cases caused by either lack of knowledge of statutory prohibition or lack of confidence in the law.

The treatment accorded principally non-whites ranges from restrained or unfriendly acceptance to complete denial of service which may be accompanied by antagonistic rebuffs and upon occasion, physical assaults. . . .

Findings by Major Category

Conclusions on Effectiveness of Current Statute. The experience of citizens in securing relief against discrimination under Section 2901.35, commonly known as the Ohio Public Accommodation Statute, under the criminal or civil provisions of the Statute, varies by geography. The outcome of the cases often reflects a bias by juries and/or public prosecutors, as well as police officers in their role as witnesses, toward the concept of equal public accommodation for all Ohio citizens, regardless of the evidence of the discriminatory treatment.

The range of data collected indicates that there is a grave number of incidents of violations of the Civil Rights Statute. It is also reported that legal action is seldom taken. The current law is an unwieldy, uncertain provision for helping to assure citizens of their rights.

In small communities, it is reported that local police officers are especially reluctant to enforce the public accommodation law. Furthermore, "outside" attorneys are reluctant to accept cases due to the disproportionate time and effort involved. The law, therefore, is rendered meaningless for minority group persons so situated.

The law as presently constituted is virtually useless to travelers discriminated against while in Ohio en route to distant parts, due to the requirement of local court appearance. Further, the reluctance on the part of local authorities to prosecute cases under the law frequently renders a hardship on citizens when discriminated against because of their inability to pay attorney fees and court costs. The statute is clearly outmoded and ineffective in accommodating the rights to equality of access to public accommodations and services for all well-mannered and orderly persons regardless of race, religion and national origin.

The present statute has no provision against discriminatory practices where based on religion, national origin or ancestry. The freedom of movement enjoyed by persons of darker skin, though not Negro, who with increasing frequency are travelers in the United States, may not be deemed covered by any language of the law since it refers only to "color and race."

Recommendation

The Ohio Civil Rights Commission finds that the denial of full and equal use of public accommodations and services, because of a person's race, color, religion, national origin or ancestry is detrimental to and in conflict with the interests and welfare of the people and government of Ohio.

The Commission believes that problems involving the rights of citizens requires a search for solutions within law and is in keeping with the traditions of American democracy. The Commission recommends to the 104th General Assembly that it enact legislation with effective enforcement provisions and procedures to the end that full enjoyment of public accommodations and services shall be the right of all regardless of race, color, religion, national origin or ancestry.

1. Ohio Civil Rights Commission, *Discrimination in Public Accommodations in Ohio: A Report by the Ohio Civil Rights Commission* (Columbus: State of Ohio, 1960), 5-6.
2. Ibid., 8, 17-18.

XVI.6. A "New Look" for Higher Education: Governor James Rhodes and the Growth of the State University System

The decade of the 1960s was a time of economic growth and extensive public investment. During Governor James Rhodes's first two terms, private industry, especially the "Big Three" auto makers, expanded already sizable production and assembly facilities in the state. This expansion culminated in the construction of General Motors' massive Lordstown Plant in Mahoning County in 1966.

Rhodes personally presided over the most extensive "capital building" programs in the state's history. The governor attained voter approval for four bond issues totaling $1.8 billion for the development of highways, industrial sites, parks and recreations, and higher education.

The governor allocated a large portion of these new funds to higher education. His goal was plainly stated: construct some sort of higher educational facility within thirty miles of each Ohioan. To attain this goal, the state more than doubled the number of public universities, began the development of new medical schools, reached non-traditional students through the expansion of community colleges and university branch campuses, and supported vocational training around the state. The first document in the following selection outlines the investment program in higher education.[1]

Ohio's New Look in Public Higher Education

*B*efore 1963, more than fifty years had passed since Ohio last established a new state university campus. In the four years since 1963, new state universities have been founded at Cleveland and at Dayton; the Universities of Akron and Toledo, formerly sponsored by municipal governments, and privately-sponsored Youngstown University, have become state universities; the University of Cincinnati, long a municipal university, has become affiliated with the state university system; and a new state medical college has been established at Toledo.

Ohio's New Look in public Higher Education features thirteen senior universities and colleges rather than six of earlier years. Greatly expanded programs at all levels of instruction and research are possible within this new system of senior universities.

New to the Ohio scene is the comprehensive two-year Community College. Operating within a local taxing district but receiving state-aid as well, the Community College offers two years of traditional college instruction, two-year programs of Technical education designed to prepare young people for immediate employment, and special classes for working adults. New Community Colleges have been established at Cleveland, at Lorain, at Dayton, and at Mentor in Lake County.

Designed to specialize in preparing Ohio young people for employment through two-year programs of technical education, five new Technical Institutes have been established. At Columbus, at Springfield, at Steubenville, at Canton, and in a five-county district south of Toledo, these Institutes will grant Associate Degrees in Engineering, Business, Health, and Service Technologies. Graduates will be prepared for such paraprofessional positions as Engineering Assistant, Data Processing Analyst, Laboratory Technician and Mental Health Worker.

Technical education programs will be offered in Community Colleges and University Branches as well as in Technical Institutes, and constitute a major feature of the New Look in Ohio's system of public higher education. In addition, Community and Technical Colleges established by the Universities of Akron, Toledo, Cincinnati, and Youngstown University are strongly oriented toward two-year Technical education programs.

A third type of two-year campus adds to the new system of commuter centers developed throughout Ohio during the past four years. The University Branch is a two-year College Campus geographically removed from the central campus of a senior university, but operated as a integral part of the central university program. Eighteen new campuses for University Branches have been built or are under construction at various locations throughout Ohio. A student may receive the same courses of study during the first two years of college work at a branch campus as he would receive on the central campus of a state university. At the beginning of his third year, he may move onto the central campus to complete his program, being well prepared for advanced study as the student enrolling on the central campus as a freshman.

In addition to two years of traditional college courses, branches are also developing programs of Technical education for students desiring to seek employment after two years of study.

Considerable savings are available to Ohio students who can now live at home while attending a two-year commuter college.

At twelve locations in Ohio, students may enroll in evening programs of college-level study sponsored by the state universities. These programs are called Academic Centers and usually operate in high school plants made available by local school officials.

Expanded enrollment capacities and new facilities for upper levels of teaching and research have been provided on the campuses of Ohio's long-established senior university campuses. New emphasis on graduate levels of instruction and the strengthening of all teaching programs have greatly increased the abilities of these universities to serve as special centers of excellence, concentrating particularly upon services to junior and senior students and students pursuing graduate and professional courses of study.

New attention has been given as well to drawing these senior universities into closer relationships with Ohio's businesses and industries, so that the State's business community can benefit from university-based research and technical information.

Increasing numbers of our college students must seek formal education beyond the bachelor's degree if our needs for scientists and teachers and professional persons are to be met. Ohio has greatly increased its resources for educating its citizens in the higher levels of knowledge by urging more of its state universities to develop masters and doctoral-level programs. In addition to the comprehensive, doctoral-level offerings of the Ohio State University, Ohio is now encouraging and supporting carefully selected programs at Bowling Green State, Kent State, Miami and Ohio Universities, and the Universities of Akron and Toledo. In addition, state support is now provided for the expansion of graduate programs of the University of Cincinnati.

At the Masters degree level, new programs are being initiated for the first time at Cleveland State, Wright State, Central State, and Youngstown State Universities.

Impressive new capacities for graduate level instruction represent a major feature of Ohio's New Look in public higher education.

While reaching higher toward graduate-level programs at its senior universities, Ohio is also greatly broadening its offerings in the first two years of college work and expanding the geographical availability of higher education.

Two-year, occupationally oriented, Technical education is for the first time receiving a great deal of attention as Ohio seeks to help a larger proportion of its young people prepare for productive employment. A whole new level of education for employment is being developed by the Community Colleges, the Technical Institutes, and the University Branches, leading to award of the Associate Degree and closely attuned to specific occupational needs of young Ohioans.

Through its new system of nearly thirty two-year campuses of various types and its new urban universities, Ohio now offers higher education within commuting distance of almost every young person's home. Never before has opportunity for education beyond the high school been so accessible to all Ohio citizens.

1. Ohio Board of Regents, *Ohio's New Look in Public Higher Education: A Progress Report on Public Higher Education in Ohio* (Columbus: State of Ohio, 1968).

XVI.7. The Environmental Crisis: The Burning River Incident

By the late 1960s, it was clear that Ohio had one of the worst environmental records in the nation. Toxic waste dumps in several counties were so lethal that they qualified for clean-up funds from the federal government's controversial "superfund." Pollution in the Ohio River watershed became such a problem in the postwar period that the eight affected states established the Ohio River Valley Sanitary Commission (ORSANCO). But the factories of the steelmakers and the power generation plants of the utility companies in the newly developing

Ohio River Valley remained among the leading polluters of the atmosphere. These plants even affected the quality of the air over West Virginia, the western counties of Virginia, and the scenic Blue Ridge Parkway, although those states were, in part, polluted by their own numerous paper factories and power plants. To the north, Ohioans saw the gradual destruction of Lake Erie. Industrial and commercial waste products flooded into the southernmost of the Great Lakes, with large amounts borne by Ohio's rivers.

The Cuyahoga River had suffered from man-made pollution from the early days of settlement. At one point in the early years of statehood, it is said, residents could walk across the river by stepping on the logs, debris, and garbage that clogged the mouth of the Cuyahoga at Cleveland. By 1969, industrial, commercial, and residential wastes had choked the crooked river; when floating flammable materials caught fire, the river and the city became national jokes. But the incident was, for many, a turning in the region's environmental crisis. The burning river incident, described in the following document, dramatized the situation, leading to greater activism and regulatory efforts in the postindustrial era.[1]

A burning oil slick floating on Cuyahoga River caused $50,000 damage to key railroad trestles at the foot of Campbell Road Hill S.E. about noon yesterday, closing one to traffic.

Battalion 7 Fire Chief Bernard E. Campbell said the fire was reported at 11:56 a.m. and was under control by 12:20 p.m. The burning slick floated under the wooden bridges and set them on fire. Cause of the blaze was undetermined, said Campbell.

A fireboat battled the flames on the water while units from three battalions brought the fire on the trestles under control. Campbell said a bridge belonging to Norfolk & Western Railway Co. sustained $45,000 damage, closing both of its tracks.

The other, one-track trestle is open. The fire did $5,000 damage to the timbers of this Newburgh & South Shore Railroad Co. crossing.

Flames climbed as high as five stories, said Campbell.

Campbell pointed out a fireboat patrols the Cuyahoga River daily checking for oil slicks and clearing them away. He said waterfront industries are responsible, dumping oil wastes into the river rather than reclaiming them.

1. *Cleveland Plain Dealer,* 23 June 1969.

XVI.8. May 4th: The 1970 Shootings at Kent State University

Economic expansion in the private sector and sizable public investment in transportation, education, mental health, and recreational facilities marked the decade of the sixties in Ohio. The state university system was one of the beneficiaries of the governor's program of public investment. These centers of public higher education, like similar institutions in many states across the nation, expanded to meet the demands of the nation's post–World War II population explosion. The decade also witnessed a dramatic increase in the nation's commitment to fight communism on a global scale. After 1964, President Lyndon B. Johnson and his administration escalated the war in Vietnam, triggering an emotional, divisive debate over American military and foreign policy. Johnson's escalation of the war led to the rise of a national antiwar movement, centered on college campuses, that challenged American policies. For five years, college-based protestors conducted marches and teach-ins to garner support to end the war and the draft that helped fuel it.

Events at Kent State University in 1970, to a large degree, marked the culmination of that nationwide protest movement. By that year, Kent State was no longer a small, midwestern normal school whose primary mission was the education of Ohio teachers. The university, with its nine-hundred-acre Kent campus, had profited enormously from the Rhodes capital building and program development campaign. As it expanded in the late 1960s, Kent constructed new buildings, added new degree programs, and hired scores of freshly trained, research-oriented faculty.

Along with the greater expectations came greater activism. By 1970, few Kent students embraced the traditional values of the World War II generation; a sizable number of faculty and students maintained ties with antiwar and civil rights activists around the nation. When the invasion of Cambodia by U.S. and South Vietnamese troops triggered a new round of protest on the nation's campuses, Kent State was in the forefront. Protestors burned the old ROTC building on the night of 2 May. Ohio National Guard troops arrived soon afterward, bivouacked on the edge of campus, and began quieting the fears of townspeople. Two thousand students gathered on the commons for an anti-invasion rally at midday on Monday, 4 May. When demonstrators refused to obey police orders to leave, guardsmen moved into position and advanced. The Guard then conducted an unsuccessful twenty-five-minute effort to disperse the protestors.[1] Frustrated at their lack of success and forced to endure the taunts and rock-throwing of the most radical demonstrators (as others looked on), some guardsmen turned on the students and fired. They killed four, wounded nine.

The following documents are the statements from both parties to the subsequent litigation settlement, arrived at in January 1979.[2]

Statement by the Governor, the Generals, the Command Officers and the Guardsmen

In retrospect, the tragedy of May 4, 1970 should not have occurred. The students may have believed that they were right in continuing their mass protest in response to the Cambodian invasion, even though this protest followed the posting and reading by the University of an order to ban rallies and an order to disperse. These orders have since been determined by the Sixth Circuit Court of Appeals to have been lawful.

Some of the Guardsmen on Blanket Hill, fearful and anxious from prior events, may have believed in their own minds that their lives were in danger. Hindsight suggests that another method would have resolved the confrontation. Better ways must be found to deal with such confrontations.

We devoutly wish that a means had been found to avoid the May 4 events culminating in the Guard shootings and irreversible deaths and injuries. We deeply regret those events and are profoundly saddened by the deaths of four students and the wounding of nine others which resulted. We hope that the agreement to end this litigation will help to assuage the tragic memories regarding that sad day.

Statement by the Parents: January 4, 1979

A settlement of the Kent State civil suit has been reached out of court in an agreement mediated by Federal Judge William Thomas, and for this we are grateful.

The settlement provides for the payment of $675,000 in damages by the State of Ohio and for a signed statement of regret and intention by Governor James A. Rhodes, Generals Del Corso and Canterbury, and officers and men of the Ohio National Guard.

We, as families of the victims of the shooting by the Ohio National Guard at Kent State University, May 4, 1970, wish to interpret what we believe to be the significance of this settlement.

We accepted the settlement out of court, but negotiated by the court, because we determined that it accomplished to the greatest extent possible under present law, the objectives toward which we as families have struggled during the past eight years.

Those objectives have been as follows:

1. Insofar as possible, to hold the State of Ohio accountable for the actions of its officials and agents in the event of May 4, 1970.

2. To demonstrate that the excessive use of force by the agents of government would be met by a formidable citizen challenge.

3. To exhaustively utilize the judicial system in the United States and demonstrate to an understandably skeptical generation that the system can work when extraordinary pressure is applied to it, as in this case.

4. To assert that the human rights of American citizens, particularly those citizens in dissent of governmental policies, must be effected and protected.

5. To obtain sufficient financial support for Mr. Dean Kahler, one of the victims of the shooting, that he may have a modicum of security as he spends the rest of his life in a wheelchair.

The State of Ohio although protected by doctrine of sovereign immunity and consequently not legally responsible in a technical sense, has now recognized its responsibility by paying a substantial amount of money in damages for the injuries and deaths caused by the shooting.

State officials, national guard command officers, and guardsmen have signed a statement submitted to the families of the victims of the shootings which not only expresses regret and sorrow—eight years belatedly—but also recognizes that another method than the use of loaded combat rifles could have resolved the confrontation at Kent State University. The statement also asserts that better ways must be found for future confrontations which may take place.

The Scranton Commission which investigated campus disorders in the Summer of 1970 said that the Kent State shooting was, "unnecessary, unwarranted, and inexcusable."

The signed statement of the officials and the guardsmen at least now agrees that the shooting and killing was unnecessary, and now at last, the State of Ohio has assumed responsibility for the act.

We recognize that many others related to the May 4, 1970 event have also suffered
during the past eight years—including Kent State University students, faculty, and administrators, as well as Ohio National Guardsmen and their families. Indeed, we believe
that some of the guardsmen on Blanket Hill on that fateful day also became victims of
an Ohio National Guard policy which sent them into a potential citizen confrontation
with loaded combat rifles. We did not want those individual guardsmen to be personally liable for the actions of others and the policy of a government agency under whose
orders they served.

Yet, the doctrine of sovereign immunity which protects the State of Ohio from
being sued without its permission, made it necessary for us to take individuals to court.
Only then did the State respond—furnishing more than two million dollars for the legal costs of the defense of officials and guardsmen and finally being willing to pay costs
and damages of the victims of the shooting.

We want to thank those who have sustained us in our long struggle for an expression of justice. More than 35,000 individuals made contributions of money for our legal
costs. Students and faculty at many campuses, but particularly at Kent State University
have furnished us effective support. The American Civil Liberties Union and its volunteer attorneys—as well as many other lawyers—have skillfully and devotedly served us
throughout these years. The Board of Church and Society of the United Methodist
Church has faithfully supported us and coordinated our struggle from the beginning.
We are grateful to them.

Because of the experience that we have had during the past eight and one-half
years, there are other words which we are compelled to speak. We have become convinced that the issue of the excessive use of force—or the use of deadly force—by law
enforcement agencies or those acting with the authority of law enforcement agencies, is
a critical national issue to which the attention of the American people must be drawn.

President Carter, on December 6, 1978, in his speech on the Thirteenth Anniversary of the Universal Declaration of Human Rights, said, "Of all human rights, the
most basic is to be free of arbitrary violence . . ." He then noted that citizens should have
the right to be free of violence which comes from governments.

We deplore violence in every form for any cause and from every source. Yet, we
believe the average American is little aware of the official violence which has been used
across our land indiscriminately and unjustifiably. Twenty-eight students have been
killed on campuses in the past ten years. A long but unnumbered list of residents in minority communities have been killed by police unnecessarily.

We find it significant that just a few weeks ago the United States Commission on
Civil rights held a consultation in Washington, D.C. on, "Police Practices and the Preservation of Civil Rights" in preparation for the conducting of hearings on the use of
deadly force in selected cities. That is the issue with which we have had to be concerned.
It is an issue with which a growing number of citizens are becoming concerned.

Through our long legal and political struggle we have become convinced that the present federal law which protects citizens from the deprivation of their civil rights by law enforcement agencies or those acting with their authority, is weak and inadequate. It is a provision which is little used—but, when it is used, it has little use. A citizen can be killed by those acting under the color of the law almost with impunity. The families of the victims of those shootings or killings have little recourse and then only through an expensive and lengthy process.

We believe that citizens and law enforcement must, in the words of the signed statement of the settlement, find better ways. We appeal for those better ways to be used not only on campuses but in cities and communities across the land. We plead for a federal law which will compel the consideration and use of those better ways.

We are simply average citizens who have attempted to be loyal to our country and constructive and responsible in our actions, but we have not had an average experience. We have learned through a tragic event that loyalty to our nation and its principles sometimes requires resistance to our government and its policies—a lesson many young people, including the children of some of us, had learned earlier. That has been our struggle and for others this struggle goes on. We will try to support them.

For Allison, Sandra, Jeffrey, and William,

For Peace and Justice,

Mr. and Mrs. Arthur Krause

Mr. and Mrs. Louis Schroeder

Mr. and Mrs. Martin Scheuer

Mr. and Mrs. Arthur Holstein

1. Scott L. Bills, "The Sixties, Kent State, and Historical Memory," in *Kent and Jackson State, 1970-1990* (Silver Spring, Md.: Vietnam Generation, 1990), 166-69.

2. Documents published in Ibid., 48, 49-51.

XVII. The Postindustrial Age

Ohio's long run of prosperity ended in the decade of the 1970s, only to be followed by a second reversal of fortune in the late 1980s. As the seventies began, Ohio's core manufacturing industries began a steep decline. We called this trend "deindustrialization," because it removed the work of thousands of laborers, often without touching the buildings or even the machinery of the aging plants. No better example exists than the case of Youngstown Sheet and Tube Company, the case documented in the first selection of this chapter. Conglomerate financiers bought old Sheet and Tube, one of the top steelmakers in the nation and a centerpiece of the Mahoning Valley economy, systematically siphoned off its vast cash inflows, expanded nonsteel ventures, and failed to modernize the aging steel plant. When they determined it was no longer viable, top managers of the conglomerate shut down the plant.

But deindustrialization was part of a larger, more complex economic transition. Over Ohio and the nation during the past two decades, the economy has been transforming itself from one dominated by traditional, mass-production, assembly-line industries to one increasingly characterized by flexible-production, high-technology industries. By the end of the twentieth century, the most promising industries were those influenced by the new informational revolution or ones using the waves of new knowledge generated by experts in such disciplines as chemical physics.

With the decline of the old "rust belt" industries came an increased awareness of the environment. With every passing year, Ohioans became more aware of the great degree to which the established, core industries and the power generation plants of the Ohio River Valley polluted the environment. They have also become aware, recently, of the problems of suburbanization and the need to conserve historic and scenic tracts of land. Two of the selections in this chapter deal with environmental issues. In one case, the preservation of threatened and endangered plants across the state of Ohio is examined. In another case, the preservation of the scenic and historic lands of the Cuyahoga River Valley, achieved by granting the lands federal recreation area status, is assessed.

Throughout the late 1980s into the 1990s, Ohio made an economic "comeback."

The final two selections in this volume deal with that industrial rebirth. Business journals recognized the advantages that Ohio still possessed and the new incentives the state government was willing to extend in order to attract or expand business investment. Site selection experts from the business community rated Ohio first among individual states in the early 1990s. The state racked up an impressive number of business investments. Once again, as in the postwar decades, private sector industrial firms were investing in Ohio; but, as in the past, the public sector was providing some key incentives to attract manufacturing and commerce.

Part of the state's investment in industrial development was its generous investment in the research of applied scientists working at numerous public and private universities and notable research centers in the state. New government-business-academic partnerships seemed to be one path to high-tech success.

By the end of the 1990s, Ohio's economy and society were in the process of undergoing a significant transformation. The state was not without its problems, as in the case of the severe underfunding of education, but no more drastic dislocations, like those of the 1970s, seemed to threaten the future.

XVII.1. Deindustrialization in the Rust Belt: The Case of Youngstown Sheet and Tube Company

The phenomenon of deindustrialization was first noticed in the wake of the 1974–75 recession, when many plants in the manufacturing zones of the Northeast and Midwest failed to reopen once recovery commenced. A closer look at the phenomenon reveals a process that was rooted in the successes and excesses of the post–World War II period.

Before 1970 the core industries of Ohio and the nation—iron and steel, heavy machinery, vehicles, rubber products, coal mining—had little to fear from Europe and the Far East. But by the midpoint in the Vietnam War, new competitors, the beneficiaries of American-assisted "economic miracles," emerged to threaten U.S. industrial supremacy on the North American continent and across the globe. The aging manufacturing plants of Ohio, Pennsylvania, and other Rust Belt states often found themselves incapable of competing with their modern overseas rivals. The nation began to accumulate deficits. Their crippling effect on the economy was exacerbated by the high costs of the Vietnam War and Lyndon Johnson's Great Society social programs. In 1968 the nation was overwhelmed by the economic crisis that resulted from the mounting deficits. In the face of the crisis, the United States began massive devaluations of the American dollar and bankers raised interest rates to attract more money.

Conditions worsened in the 1970s. High interest rates allowed investors to shop around for high and quick returns. Corporate money managers, like the executives at Lykes Corp., LTV, and other conglomerates, quickly realized that there were quicker ways to make money than by modernizing outmoded industrial plants. Factories that sustained their profitability into the seventies were often targets of managers who skimmed cash from their treasuries to invest in nonmanufacturing ventures.

The following selections from The Deindustrialization of America *document the case of Youngstown Sheet and Tube in the decade of the 1970s.*[1]

*P*robably the most famous modern conglomerate-related plant closing in America was the 1977 shutdown of the Youngstown Sheet and Tube Company in Ohio. In 1969 Sheet and Tube, then the nation's eighth largest steelmaking firm, was purchased by a New Orleans–based conglomerate, the Lykes Corporation. The acquisition was financed mainly by a loan that Lykes promised to pay off out of Sheet and Tube's very substantial cash flow. During the next eight years, Lykes used Sheet and Tube's cash to amortize the debt and to expand its non-steel operations. . . . In the decade before the merger, investment in plant and equipment averaged $72 million a year and increased each year at an average rate of $9.3 million. After the acquisition by Lykes, the average fell to about $34 million per year and would have had a zero growth trend if not for a few investment projects begun in 1975 and then quickly abandoned. . . . In the years immediately following the acquisition, Lykes pursued a strategy of planned disinvestment in its recent acquisition. By the time changing market conditions had convinced Lykes that it might make sense to remain in Youngstown after all, there were no longer sufficient reserves to finance the necessary retooling.

It is also true that Lykes's bankers were redlining both the company and the town by this time — refusing to invest in either. Nevertheless, most financial analysts seem to agree that "Lykes must bear responsibility for a good deal of the failure at Youngstown Sheet and Tube." As Business Week said in its 3 October 1977 issue: "The conglomerator's steel acquisitions were seen as cash boxes for corporate growth in other areas."

In a rather absurd postscript to the closing — which . . . cost 4,100 Ohio workers their jobs — Lykes merged in 1978 with the conglomerate Ling-Temco-Vought (LTV), owner of the nation's next largest steelmaker. The argument used in court by Lykes and LTV to overcome antitrust objections to the merger was that their steel business was "failing" and could only be rescued by achieving financial scale economies through merger! The now-completed merger makes Lykes-LTV the nation's third largest producer of steel. Such is the history of how an industry "naturally" becomes more concentrated. . . .

In the wake of the Youngstown Sheet and Tube closing, Policy Management Associates concluded that in the first thirty-nine months following the shutdown, the communities around Youngstown would lose up to $8 million in taxes, the county government another $1 million, the state $8 million, and the federal treasury as much as $15 million — for a total tax loss that would approach $32 million. The managers of the Campbell Works themselves projected that the town of Campbell (situated on the edge of Youngstown) would suffer an annual loss of over half a million dollars in personal income taxes, and an additional $130,000 in yearly property taxes. They forecast that the school budget deficit would rise by $1 million.

The steel firm's managers were not altogether wrong, but they sorely underestimated the financial shock to the community. As a result of the Campbell closing, the townspeople were forced to increase their own property taxes by more than $11 million in one year — from $39.8 to $51 million. More than half the increase came when voters approved a $5.8 million increase in September 1979. A total of $3.5 million was added to the existing $10.8 million school levy so that the same number of dollars would be produced when valuations dropped. Even then, the Campbell schools had to obtain a

$750,000 loan from the state to keep classrooms open, and became the first in Ohio to apply for a second emergency loan from the state to avoid complete bankruptcy.

Moreover, these tax losses can have a hidden cost, to the extent that they impair a municipality's ability to float its bonds. Campbell itself had negotiated the sale of a bond issue just before the shutdown but was unable to complete it when — immediately after Sheet and Tube's demise — the buyer backed out. . . .

Disinvestment on large scale draws on the government treasury in two ways. First, it immediately reduces tax revenues. Then, gradually, it increases the need for additional public expenditures. In some instances, particularly in smaller towns and cities, or when an entire industry lays off a large portion of its work force, both occur simultaneously. Tax receipts fall precisely when the need for public expenditures rise.

Thus, when the Youngstown Sheet and Tube closing was removing $32 million from the public treasury, various relief programs — mainly Trade Readjustment Assistance (TRA) — were costing another $34 to $38 million. By this accounting, the public loss from the shutdown could have reached nearly $70 million in slightly over three years. This amounts to more than $17,000 per displaced worker, very little of which was paid for by Lykes, the conglomerate owners who closed the mill. . . .

. . . The response of the steelworkers, their families, advisors, and local elected officials was to organize in Ohio's Mahoning Valley a movement whose demands included several concrete proposals for worker ownership of the mill. Although the plans were ultimately blocked by ambivalent bureaucrats in the federal government, without whose assistance the scheme for worker control of steel making in Youngstown could not succeed, the story is instructive.

When the New Orleans–based conglomerate, the Lykes Corporation, first announced the Campbell shutdown in September 1977, instead of railing against Lykes, foreign imports, or government regulations, a group of local clergymen and trade unionists formed a new political organization, the Ecumenical Coalition to Save Mahoning Valley. From the beginning, their objective was a community takeover of the plant. After pledging their own savings to purchase stock in such an enterprise, they were able to convince the U.S. Department of Housing and Urban Development to grant them $300,000 to finance a detailed technical feasibility study. The contract was given to the National Center for Economic Alternatives (NCEA), whose interim findings were becoming clear by late spring 1978 (the final report itself was not released until September). The NCEA researchers, led by Gar Alperovitz and Jeff Faux, concluded that a profitable community takeover could work if the federal government would provide $15 million in front-end grants, and $394 million in federally guaranteed loans and procurement guarantees, and if the new enterprise could gain access to Sheet and Tube's old customer list.

Carter Administration officials, particularly White House advisor Jack Watson, had initially pledged support "in principle." But as the proposal became more concrete, the administration backed off. Then in June, against the advice of his own antitrust division, Attorney General Griffin Bell approved a merger between Lykes and LTV, whose steel-making subsidiary, Jones and Laughlin, thereby acquired Sheet and Tube's customer list. The merger meant that Lykes would still indirectly be in the steel business and so be unwilling to sell the Campbell works to the Coalition. In any case, later that summer, the U.S. Economic Development Administration and the White House rejected the grant and loan proposals, thus killing the plan for good. Without some short-term aid, embryonic worker—or community-owned enterprises are almost impossible to get off the ground, no matter how many jobs they might save.

The problem is at least partly a legal one, too. For in the absence of federal legislation, even appeals to the courts for assistance have no standing. When workers at U. S. Steel in Ohio went to court to try to get their plants reopened in early 1980, the trial judge, Thomas Lambros, found the workers' case compelling but ruled that he could provide no remedy until plant-closing legislation was passed.

> This court has spent many hours searching for a way to cut to the heart of this economic reality, that obsolescence and market forces demand the closing of the Mahoning Valley plant, and yet the lives of 3500 workers and their families and the supporting Youngstown community cannot be dismissed as inconsequential. United States Steel should not be permitted to leave the Youngstown area devastated after drawing from the life blood of the community for so many years.
>
> Unfortunately, the mechanism to reach this ideal settlement, to recognize this new property right, is not now in existence in the code of laws of our nation.

1. Barry Bluestone and Bennett Harrison, *The Deindustrialization of America: Plant Closings, Community Abandonment, and the Dismantling of Basic Industry* (New York: Basic Books, 1982), 73-75, 152-53, 252-54.

XVII.2. People in Need: The State Report on the Problem of Homelessness in Ohio

Cincinnati authorities first discussed the problem of homelessness during the recession of the mid-1870s. As historian Steven J. Ross discovered, the "tramp" element had become "a fixed institution" in the city by 1876.[1] The capitalist industrialization that transformed Ohio and the nation had little room for those who could not succeed in a market-based economy. One portion of those early Ohio tramps were habitually lazy, in the eyes of the city fathers; others, the "worthy and honest homeless," who sought work during the day, could always find shelter in the city's police stations from dusk till dawn.

Those who thrive in modern society still categorize and classify the "homeless." What follows is a critical assessment of the problem of homelessness by a team of medical and social scientific investigators in the employ of the Ohio Department of Mental Health. Their report was completed in February 1985. The research team, led by principal investigators Dee Roth and Jerry Bean, had received a grant from the National Institute of Mental Health to conduct the study of homeless men and women and determine to what extent the widely held myths about 1980s homelessness were accurate.[2]

SUMMARY OF RESULTS

*P*erhaps the most important findings of the research are that homelessness is a multi-faceted issue, that homeless people have a variety of problems, and that there are subtypes within the homeless population which need to be distinguished in order for the phenomenon of homelessness to be more fully understood.

The Homeless Person Survey

After hearing at length from nearly 1000 homeless people across Ohio, economic factors emerged as the primary theme. For half the group, economic reasons were the major cause of their homelessness, and nearly one quarter (21.3%) cited family conflict as the reason they were without a home.

Many of the stereotypes of homeless people in the popular literature were not supported by study findings. Our group was less mobile—most had stayed in two or fewer places in the past month—and less transient than might have been expected: 63.5 percent had either been born in the counties in which they were interviewed or had lived there longer than a year. Most (87.3%) had worked at some point in their lives, and a quarter had worked for pay in the past month. Nearly half of those who had been employed in the past but were not working now said they had looked for a job but had been unable to find one. Almost two-thirds (63.4%) had some source of income in the past month, primarily from welfare, earnings, or Social Security. The picture that emerges is one of a largely indigenous population made up of people who are not totally without funds but whose income is not sufficient to pay for permanent housing.

In addition to their lack of housing, jobs, and resources, homeless people have a variety of other problems. Only a third (36.0%) said they had relatives they could count on, and 41 percent said they had friends they could count on. This seems to indicate that not all homeless people are isolated from social support as has been portrayed in the popular literature. However, comparative data from a needs assessment in five rural Southern Ohio counties provides a more realistic contrast. In that study, 92.4 percent of the general population said they had relatives they count on and 94.9 percent said they had friends. A third of our sample (30.7%) had physical health problems, and almost an equal percentage (30.8%) had psychiatric problems. Thirty percent had had a psychiatric hospitalization. Well over half (64.2%) said they had been drinking some or a lot in the past month, and 26.6 percent indicated they had sought help for a drinking problems at some point in their lives.

Differences Between Urban and Non-Urban Homeless People

Differences were found between urban and non-urban (those from mixed and rural counties) homeless groups on some of the study variables but not on others. While nearly half of both groups cited economic reasons as the primary cause of their homelessness, family problems was a greater cause in non-urban areas (28.6%) than in urban areas (19.5%). Respondents in the urban counties (42.3%) were far more likely to report they were born in the county in which the interview took place than were respondents in non-urban counties (28.6%). Of those individuals who were not native to the county, non-urban homeless people (49.6%) were more likely to have migrated from elsewhere within Ohio. By contrast, non-native urban homeless people (65.2%) were more likely to have come from another state. Urban homeless people (22.1%) were more likely than non-urban people (8.1%) to have migrated seeking work, while non-urban people (43.7%) were more like[ly] than their urban counterparts (19.7%) to have moved to be near friends or relatives.

A high percentage of both urban and non-urban homeless people had held a job at some point in their lives, but non-urban respondents (32.8%) were more likely than urban respondents (22.2%) to have worked for pay in the past month. For those not now working, 61.8 percent of non-urban people and 43.9 percent of urban people said they had looked for work but were unable to find a job. Non-urban respondents (79.4%) were more likely than urban respondents (59.8%) to report having had income the past month, but welfare and earnings were the major sources for both groups.

There were substantial differences evidenced in social support networks. Non-urban homeless people were ten percent more likely to say they have relatives they can count on and twenty percent more likely to say they have friends they can count on for help. Nearly one quarter of urban homeless people said they had no relatives, in contrast to 9.5 percent of non-urban homeless people. Rates of physical health problems, psychiatric problems and psychiatric hospitalization did not differ substantially, but urban respondents were somewhat more likely to report problems with alcohol use.

Types of Homelessness

Three distinct sub-types of homeless people emerged out of the data analysis: Street People, who do not use shelters, Shelter People, and Resource People—individuals who do not use shelters and are to stay in hotels or with family and friends for short periods of time. Resource People were found to have been homeless for a shorter period of time (median of 35 days) than Street People (median of 60 days) or Shelter People (median of 90 days), but there were no substantial differences across groups in their reasons for homelessness. Street People and Resource People were slightly more likely to be native residents of their counties, but the differences were not large. . . .

Homelessness and Mental Health

. . . As indicated previously, 29.9 percent of our respondent group said that they had experienced at least one psychiatric hospitalization in any type of facility. Eighteen percent of the overall sample indicated that they had been in a state mental hospital, with a median number of hospitalizations of two. Most of the state-hospitalized respondents were last released in 1983 or 1984 (45.5%), but nearly one-fourth (23.9%) were last released in 1978 or earlier. Upon their last release from a state hospital, 60 percent of the respondents said that community living arrangements had been made for them, and most (88.0%) went to the place arranged.

The conclusion that most homeless people are "deinstitutionalized" simply does not emerge from these data. The numbers given above do not correspond to a widespread and systematic contribution to homelessness by Ohio's state hospitals and community mental health system. Only six percent of our total respondent group reported having been last hospitalized during the period 1960–1980 when the state hospital system census had a dramatic decline. Since 1980, there has been only a minimal decline in state hospital populations with an increased emphasis on community-based care. Compared to the pre-1980 time period, since 1980 only a slightly higher percentage of our total respondent group (10.7%) were found to have been last released from a state hospital. Also, in the survey of community mental health agencies, it was determined that approximately four percent of the patients discharged from state hospitals during FY 1982–1983 were found to be homeless.

1. Steven J. Ross, *Workers on the Edge: Work, Leisure, and Politics in Industrializing Cincinnati, 1788–1890* (New York: Columbia University Press, 1985), 243.

2. Dee Roth, Jerry Bean, Nancy Lust, Traian Saveanu, *Homelessness in Ohio: A Study of People in Need* (Columbus: Ohio Department of Mental Health, 1985), 134–36.

XVII.3. Balancing Recreation and Preservation in the Postindustrial Period

Northeast Ohio has attempted to preserve sections of the Cuyahoga since the First World War. In 1919, Cleveland combined several tracts of land into its metroparks system. Creating the "Emerald Necklace" was one of a series of steps taken by Clevelanders to preserve the scenic and historic lands surrounding the city and secure public space for recreational purposes. Akron followed with its own metroparks system several years later. Since the decade of the twenties, both cities have systematically added land to their metroparks system. As the following report observes, however, while the city and state had already set aside land, there existed no integrated park system to preserve the great expanse of river valley land between the two urban centers.

The following 3 December 1974 report of the Committee on Interior and Insular Affairs asserts that establishing a national recreation area would preserve the historic and scenic values of the Cuyahoga River Valley while allowing citizens to pursue a variety of recreational activities.[1] By the late 1990s, the CVNRA had become one of the most popular recreational sites in the state.

PROVIDING FOR THE ESTABLISHMENT OF THE CUYAHOGA VALLEY NATIONAL RECREATION AREA

REPORT

[To accompany H.R. 7077]

PURPOSE

H. R. 7077, as amended by the Committee on Interior and Insular Affairs, would provide for the establishment of the Cuyahoga Valley National Recreational Area in the State of Ohio. The proposed recreation area includes portions of the Cuyahoga River

Valley between Cleveland and Akron, Ohio, and protects numerous sites of historic significance, in addition to preserving this pastoral, relatively undeveloped valley as a setting for outdoor recreation.

BACKGROUND AND NEED FOR LEGISLATION

With headwaters rising not far from eastern Lake Erie, the upper Cuyahoga River flows southward as if to join the tributary streams of the Ohio River drainage. But in northeast Ohio, the river turns dramatically west along the Akron escarpment, and at last flows northward, eventually discharging in Lake Erie at Cleveland, Ohio.

The river valley was home to early Indian tribes, as documented by numerous archaeological sites dating back as far as 600 b.c. The valley, connecting what are now the urban centers of Cleveland and Akron, was of importance to the native cultures because of the route it offered to link the Great Lakes with the Ohio River. The short portage across the watershed divide led to the valley area being declared sacred ground so that it might remain open as a trading route.

With the arrival of European man in this area, the importance of the valley as a gateway to the unsettled western lands increased. Early in the nineteenth century, the construction of the Ohio Canal up the valley and across the divide opened a prosperous era as a major commercial route. With the construction of railroad systems, however, the waterway system and the valley faded from attention.

Now the Cuyahoga Valley remains little altered from its natural state. Although both Cleveland and Akron have grown into major urban centers, the valley which links them still retains its rural character. The river itself, although its waters are degraded by upstream pollution, still meanders through a floodplain backed by heavily wooded valley walls and ravines. The century-old canal system is still in place.

H.R. 7077 and similar bills introduced in this Congress recognize the importance of the Cuyahoga Valley not only for the historical values it contains, but also for its potential to serve the outdoor recreation needs of the nearly five million residents of the surrounding area.

The valley today, while retaining its rural character, is under increasing development pressure on all fronts. The suburbs of both cities are spreading inexorably toward the valley, and the entire area is becoming increasingly interlaced with roadway and utility corridors.

The immense value in retaining the valley as a source of recreation and outdoor enjoyment has already been widely recognized. The State of Ohio and the Metropolitan Park systems of both Akron and Cleveland have already acquired portions of the area for park purposes. An acquisition program in cooperation with the Bureau of Outdoor Recreation is already underway, with an eventual goal of placing some 14,500 acres in park status.

But the present acquisition program contemplates that the land base will take many years to secure. Establishment of a Federal area, on the other hand, is intended to permit rapid land acquisition which will both preclude adverse development and also minimize the increased costs of further delay in a time of rapidly increasing land values.

Beyond the land acquisition itself, the proposed legislation is intended to provide an area managed at the high standards of the National Park Service. By being placed under unified, professional management, the Cuyahoga Valley should grow in importance as the surrounding area becomes increasingly developed. It will serve in particular as a unit of the National Park System which will be readily accessible to this large urban population. H.R. 7077 affords the opportunity to secure this important resource now.

1. U.S. House, 1974, Committee on Interior and Insular Affairs, *Providing for the Establishment of the Cuyahoga National Recreation Area,* 93d Cong., 2d sess., H. Rept. 93-1511, 4-6.

XVII.4. Environmentalism in the Postindustrial Era: The Report on Endangered Plant Species in Ohio

The environmentalism of the 1970s dealt with such broad issues as air and water pollution, issues that affected every citizen. In contrast, the rhetoric of leading environmental movement spokesmen tended to focus on the distance between humans and the natural world around them. Despite the National Environmental Policy Act of 1969 and the efforts of the Environmental Protection Agency, the ideology of environmentalism has emphasized such "outdoor issues" as species preservation. This historic influence on environmental policy led to the passage of the Endangered Species Act of 1973. Philosophers and naturalists since James Fenimore Cooper have cautioned Americans against the destructive excesses of commercial society that led to the elimination of numerous species as Anglo-American settlement progresses on the North American continent.[1]

The 1973 federal act was the culmination of a process of developing protective legislation at the national level that began during the mid-1960s. The Ohio General Assembly had already moved in a similar direction with the passage of the 1970 Ohio Natural Areas Act (Ohio Revised Code, chapter 1517), which created a state nature preserve system. This system created a mechanism for the protection of habitat for rare plants and animals. Eight years later legislators passed an endangered plant species act in 1978 (Ohio Revised Code, chapter 1518). This state law authorized the Division of Natural Areas and Preserves to designate and protect endangered or threatened plants. The first list of such species, which appeared in 1980, contained 417 species; the second, revised list, dated 1982, reduced that number to 392; a third, the 1984 list drawn up the same year as the following document, had only 367.[2] *The following excerpt is from a publication that began development in 1977 as part of a project of the Ohio Natural Heritage Program, a joint venture of the Ohio Division of Natural Areas and Preserves and The Nature Conservancy.*[3]

Causes of Plant Rarity in Ohio

The presence of man has altered the Ohio landscape since the first Americans pushed north into the newly deglaciated land at the close of the Pleistocene. The change affected by Native Americans was minimal. Periodic fires and clearing of land for agriculture had only a minor impact on the natural environment. Possibly more significant was the unintentional introduction of new species along trade routes and the intentional introduction of cultivated species.

European settlement of the Northwest Territory, including the Ohio country, initiated habitat alteration and destruction on a massive scale and at an ever-accelerating pace. Forests were cleared, prairies plowed, and wetlands drained. Even the most extensive natural features were conquered by man's perseverance and industrial efficiency. The Black Swamp of northwest Ohio was logged, drained, and cultivated. The Ohio River was radically altered into a series of artificial lakes. Channelization and impoundment destroyed the natural characteristics of many of Ohio's rivers and streams. Great tracts of forest were turned into charcoal for iron furnaces which belched toxic fumes. The very hills themselves were gouged into craters by coal mines and re-shaped for human convenience. Sheep, cattle, and pigs grazed and rooted at will through woodlands and prairies. Herbicides and pesticides were applied indiscriminately. The air and water were poisoned and befouled in the name of progress and cultivation. Ohio's natural areas today are minute remnants of a beautiful past. The destruction still continues and these fragments of Ohio's past are in constant danger of annihilation.

An indirect, though significant, influence of man has been the spread of non-indigenous plant species, pests, and diseases. The introduction of these alien species usually has been inadvertent. Some, however, were intentionally introduced into North America. Multiflora rose (Rosa multiflora) and purple loosestrife (Lythrum salicaria) are examples, the first introduced for fencerows and to provide wildlife habitat and the second as a garden ornamental. Both today are noxious weeds, firmly established in disturbed habitats. Native species can not compete with these aggressive aliens in such situations, and thus are eliminated. Non-indigenous pests and diseases may attack native species which lack a natural resistance to them. Dutch elm disease and the chestnut blight have changed forever the aspect of Ohio's woodlands. Great tracts of eastern forests have been defoliated by the gypsy moth. This pest is yet infrequent in Ohio, but some pathologists believe a similar fate is likely here.

Many rare plant species are successional in nature, that is, they occur only during particular stages in the succession of plant communities. In this category are many species of prairies, forest openings, and river and lake shores. Such species never were common in Ohio, even prior to European settlement. The continued existence of these species is dependent upon constant change in the environment. Man has halted or controlled the natural processes necessary for the survival of successional species. Wildfire in prairies and forests provided new habitat for species of natural openings and also prevented the closing of these openings by the growth of woody species. Drainage ditches and channelized streams have so lowered seasonal water tables that woody plants now can grow successfully in areas where previously they would be suppressed by spring flooding. This results in a loss of wet, open habitats and of the species dependent on regular inundations. Many interesting successional species grew on mudflats and sandbars along the Ohio River and other large streams. Flood control projects now regulate the dynamic processes which provided habitat for these species. A significant proportion of Ohio's endangered and threatened plant species require environmental change for their survival.

1. Hal K. Rothman, *The Greening of a Nation: Environmentalism in the United States since 1945* (New York: Harcourt Brace, 1998), 126–27.

2. *Ohio Endangered and Threatened Vascular Plants: Abstracts of State-Listed Taxa* (Columbus: Division of Natural Areas and Preserves, 1984), ix, 3–6.

3. Ibid., 12–13.

XVII.5. The Rebirth of Ohio Industry: Capitalizing on Old Assets and Providing New Incentives

Ohio industry enjoyed a rebirth in the 1990s that surprised the economic experts. That should not be surprising. The state still possessed many of the crucial advantages that set it apart from other midwestern or industrializing states. A perfect crossroads location, a temperate climate, a wealth of natural resources, and a large, educated, and skilled workforce were all important factors in the first industrial transformation of Ohio. Business also had easy access to new technologies such as those developed by the Polymer Valley and Liquid Crystal Corridor academic centers and the NASA-Lewis Research Center.

A favorable political and social climate existed again. Under Gov. George Voinovich the state was as hospitable toward business and industry as any in the nation, and certainly as hospitable as the conditions observed by Raymond Moley in 1956.

The following article, taken from Site Selection, *provides the data that reveals exactly how favorably Ohio is seen by the business community.*[1]

Ohio Wins Landslide Victory in 1993 Facility-Location Race

*R*emember Reagan vs. Mondale in 1984? Or Nixon vs. McGovern in 1972? Those elections were classic *landslide* victories, with the outcome not even close.

In much the same way, the race among states to win the 1993 corporate facility-location title was equally close. Meaning, of course, it wasn't close at all.

The landslide winner? Ohio. In fact, the Buckeye State's facility-location performance last year was so impressive (689 new and expanded facilities) that it recorded upwards of 300 more facilities than its nearest competitor.

Perennial Sunbelt economic development powerhouses took the remaining spots among the top five. Texas landed 386 facilities to take second place, edging out North Carolina (376 facilities), followed by Florida (286) and California (198).

Taking a look at the bigger, nationwide picture, there's solid evidence that the economy is picking up a strong head of steam as it leaves the 1990–91 recession behind. *Site Selection* recorded a total of 4,161 new and expanded U.S. corporate facilities in 1993, an increase of almost 8 percent from 1992. . . .

NO CONTEST: OHIO EASILY WINS NO.1 SPOT FOR '93

Proving that successful economic development isn't just a Sunbelt phenomenon, Ohio landed 689 new and expanded corporate facilities in 1993 and left most other states in the dust. . . .

Obviously, both new and expanding companies are finding Ohio a fertile ground for conducting business.

"Ohio has created an inviting climate for business with job-creation incentives, worker's compensation reform and education improvements," says Ohio Gov. George V. Voinovich. "Our mission now is to build upon this momentum."

Ohio Dept. Of Development officials say these incentives, combined with aggressive marketing, have been a boon for the state.

"We have created incentives which build win-win relationships," Director Donald E. Jakeway says. "And we have been aggressive, but cost-effective in our marketing strategy for these programs."

John W. Damschroder, the agency's special projects director, says the state's improved incentives and business climate, plus aggressive marketing, have indeed generated renewed interest in Ohio as a business location. "Requests for information on business opportunities in Ohio have gone from 10 calls a month to 2,500 a month," he says.

Site-selection experts say there are good reasons for Ohio's recent facility-location success.

"Ohio has a lot of things going for it," says Bill Dorsey, director of siting and consulting services for corporate location consultant Fluor Daniel. "For example, Ohio has a geographic location that's second to none. It's close to major markets in the Mid-Atlantic states and Eastern states.

"Ohio also has professional, aggressive leadership in the development field at both the state and the regional and local levels. The state leaders are very dynamic and aggressive. The people there will find a way to make a deal work."

1. *Site Selection* 39 (February 1994): 12–14.

XVII.6. Building the Crystal Corridor: The Rise of a Modern, High-Technology Economy in Ohio

Deindustrialization partly masked the early stages of the current informational-technological revolution that is shaping this new industrial transformation of Ohio. The new industrial base is not (at least obviously) rooted in the wealth of natural resources possessed by the state. The newest industries have a much closer relationship to the state's educational infrastructure. With their need for new knowledge, firms developing liquid crystal displays and polymers are more closely wedded to, if not products of, the academic community of the state.

We see at the beginning of the twenty-first century creative business-government-academic partnerships for the development of these high-tech ventures. None is more creative than the Liquid Crystal Institute's role in facilitating the development of new generations of its constantly changing product. Like the Akron-Case Western polymer consortium, the LCI hopes that industry can capitalize on waves of knowledge created by specialists in a single "applied science" and facilitate the development of a surrounding enterprise zone devoted to utilizing that knowledge.[1]

BUILDING THE 'CRYSTAL CORRIDOR'

*W*hile computers are currently the most important application of flat-panel-display technology, there is far more to its potential, believes J. William Doane, recently retired professor of physics at Ohio's Kent State University and former director of the university's Liquid Crystal Institute. "Today's computer monitors and television screens are merely the most obvious commercial extensions of the old LCD technology, the one that was invented in 1967 by Kent State scientist James Fergason. Those applications are prominent today because they fit the characteristics and capabilities of today's TFT LCD technologies and because Pacific Rim countries have been willing to invest the $300 million to $1 billion to build individual plants for what has become an investment-intensive industry."

He believes that the future market for LCDs is far broader than defined by current commercial technologies. While he admires and applauds their success, Doane seeks to build a commercial enterprise around advanced display technologies such as the new cholesteric LCD technology developed at Kent State. Able to reflect light efficiently without the need for polarizing filters, cholesteric LCDs can be bright and legible in ambient light without the need for backlighting. The technology promises the high-resolution, low-power displays demanded by hand-held electronic devices.

Doane's vision is to work with local businesses in Northeast Ohio to establish a "crystal corridor" that emulates the synergistic relationship of Stanford University with the silicon valley industries it spawned. He characterizes the manufacturing methods for the cholesteric LCDs, of which he is the primary innovator, as low-cost, but with high-end characteristics.

Consider an LCD so efficient that battery life would be extended many-fold. Then visualize that energy efficiency coupled with high legibility—resulting in readability that rivals that of paper. Cap those dream specs with Doane's claim that the cost of a production facility to build millions of displays per year would be as low as $20 million—a fraction of the investment that would be required to establish a plant for the production of active matrix (TFT) LCDs.

Probably the technology's biggest advantage is that all of its benefits are possible without the active-matrix electronics—a transistor at each pixel—that conventional LCDs require to achieve high contrast and resolution.

Doane believes that low cost, legibility, and low energy consumption are the necessary prerequisites for new markets that will rival the significance and size of current applications for LCDs. His dream is for a "crystal corridor" to begin not with replacement markets, or exotic high-end explorations at the outer boundaries of consumer needs, but with the small, simple, highly readable displays that will be the ubiquitous interface between tomorrow's computer-embedded products and their users.

To support such a future the Liquid Crystal Institute will open its new $13.2 million facility in September. Although Doane is retiring from the university, he will continue to serve his vision as director of research and development for Kent Display Systems, a firm he cofounded. Its mission is to further innovation by moving new display technology to the market. As part of the crystal corridor, Kent Display Systems will be able to conveniently access the resources of the Institute, including a prototype manufacturing line—donated by Lucent Technologies—aimed at helping companies test new LCD products.

1. *Industry Week,* 19 August 1996, 98.

Credits

Index

Arnold, Benedict, 245
arsenals, federal, 376
Articles of Confederation, 45, 47, 53, 54, 61
Asbury, Francis, 180
Ashby, Benjamin, 41
Ashland, Ky., 392
Ashland Oil and Refining Co., 392
Ashtabula, Ohio, 390
Ashtabula County, Ohio, 155, 182, 205, 219,
    232, 236, 241, 242, 255
Ashtabula River, 93
Associated Charities, 360, 361, 363
atomic energy, 391–93
Atomic Energy Commission (AEC), 392–93
Athens, Ohio, 91, 179, 193
Athens County, Ohio, 250, 264
Athens Vigilance Committee, 210
"Atom Valley," 393
Atwater Slope (coal), 289
Auglaize County, Ohio, 168, 213, 214, 218, 220
Auglaize River, 81, 84, 89
Aurora, Ohio, 120, 121, 182
Austinburg, Ohio, 180–82
Austria, 216, 244, 332, 337

Backus, Elijah, 115
Bacon, John G., 229–30
Badger, Joseph, 177, 180–82; memoir, 181–82
Bagot, Charles, 137–38
Baker, Newton D., 307
Baker's Cabin, 22–23, 39
Baldwin, Michael, 108
Baldwin-Wallace College, 179
Ball, James V., 129
Baltimore & Ohio Railroad, 160
Baltimore Republican, 163
Baptist Church, 171, 173, 175, 179, 180
Barbee, Brigadier General, 83
Barclay, Robert H., 133, 135
Barker, Joseph, 63
Barnet, James, 238
Barren River, 391
Bates, Joshua L., 240
Battle of Antietam, 340
Battle of Appomattox, 233, 236, 259
Battle of Bull Run, 233–35, 237, 239
Battle of Chancellorsville, 233
Battle of Chicamauga, 340
Battle of Coshocton, 24, 41
Battle of Fallen Timbers, 71, 81–85, 88, 125, 135
Battle of Gettysburg, 242, 249, 340
Battle of Lake Erie, 133, 137

Battle of Olentangy, 41, 73
Battle of Piqua, 24, 41
Battle of Sandusky, 41, 73
Battle of the Thames River, 134–35, 163
Battle of Tippecanoe Creek, 124, 136, 163
Battle of Trafalgar, 133
Battle of Vicksburg, 244
Battle of Yorktown, 24
Baumeler (Bimeler), Joseph, 185
Bay of Fundy, 44
Bean, Jerry, 414
"Beautiful Ohio," 3
Beaver Wars (Wars of the Iroquois), 4, 5, 18, 47
Beckwith, George, 181–82
Beecher, Henry Ward, 226
Beecher, Lyman, 226
Belgium, 385
Bell, Griffin, 413
Bell, John (Gen.), 156
Bellaire, Ohio, 283
Bellefontaine, Ohio, 169, 268
Bellevue, Ohio, 161
Belmont County, Ohio, 146, 181, 206, 288
Beloit College, 202
Belpre, Ohio, 118–19
Ben Hur, A Tale of the Christ, 235
Berea, Ohio, 179
Bergholz, Ohio, 250
Bermuda, 243
Bethel Church, 171, 173, 175
B. F. Goodrich Co., 362
Big Bottom, Ohio, 76
Big Hannaona, Chief, 29
Bigelow, Herbert, 306, 307
Biggerstaff, Captain, 158
Billings, John S., 196
Birney, James G., 205, 208–12
Bishop, Professor, 197–98
Bishop, Robert H., 193
black codes, 111–13, 205
Black Hoof (Shawnee Chief), 20
Black Laws in the Old Northwest, 112, 113n. 1
Black Swamp, 108, 420
"Bleeding Kansas," 232
Blennerhassett, Harman, 115–18
Blennerhassett's Island, 119
"bloody shirt," 268–70
Blue Jacket (Shawnee Chief), 71, 82
"Blue Laws," 265, 354
Blue Ridge Mountains, 237
Bodenhorn, Frank, 379
Bonaparte, Napoleon, 115, 124, 245